AF505355

QUOTATIONS FOR THE FAST LANE

Quotations for the Fast Lane

Compiled by
RICHARD W. POUND

McGill-Queen's University Press
Montreal & Kingston • London • Ithaca

Legal deposit fourth quarter 2013
Bibliothèque nationale du Québec

Printed in Canada on acid-free paper that is 100% ancient forest free
(100% post-consumer recycled), processed chlorine free

McGill-Queen's University Press acknowledges the support of the Canada
Council for the Arts for our publishing program. We also acknowledge the
financial support of the Government of Canada through the Canada Book
Fund for our publishing activities.

Library and Archives Canada Cataloguing in Publication

Pound, Richard W., compiler
Quotations for the fast lane/compiled by Richard W. Pound.

Issued in print and electronic formats.
ISBN 978-0-7735-4298-3 (bound). – ISBN 978-0-7735-9019-9 (ePDF). –
ISBN 978-0-7735-9020-5 (ePUB).

1. Conduct of life – Quotations, maxims, etc. 2. Quotations, English. I. Title.

PN6084.C556P69 2013   082   C2013-904211-3
                                                                          C2013-904212-1

This book was typeset by Interscript in 10/13 Sabon.

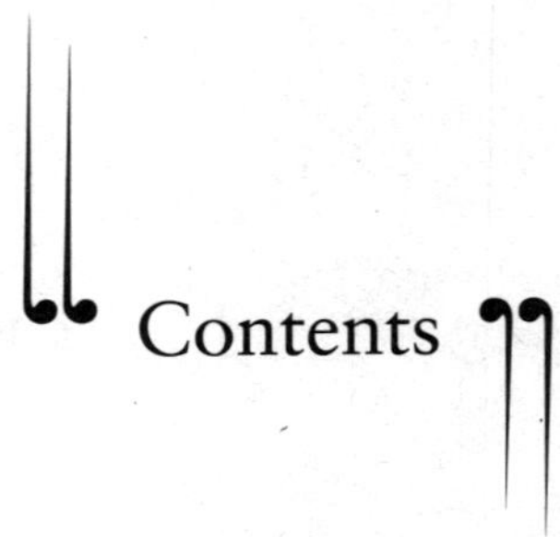# Contents

" Introduction "

Sometimes a theme can be present from the start of a course of conduct, while on other occasions, it may emerge only in retrospect. In this collection of quotations, the original purpose of keeping handy some quotations for use on the occasion of speaking engagements gradually evolved into a broader range of references relevant to identifiable audiences and some of the more general issues of life as they thrust themselves upon us. It was never my intention to produce a scholarly treatise, drawing on the classics, although I have nevertheless included some tidbits that seemed particularly appealing. Nor was it my intention to have lengthy documentary references to sources: it was the thought that mattered and the name of the person (where known) who uttered it. These quotations are designed to trigger further thoughts and ideas. Anyone who needs the full reference is free to follow up.

The theme, therefore, tends to be somewhat edgy and challenging. A friend, perusing the collection, observed that it looked like the sort of resource that a Type-A person might like to have on hand. I am delighted to develop that theme, but without being so obvious as to title the Work (notwithstanding a certain temptation to do so) something like "Useful Quotations for Type-A People."

On the other hand, it seemed to me that many people, whether genuine Type-As themselves, or just wannabes, might love to have such a handy collection. In addition, almost everyone knows Type-A people and often looks for birthday or holiday presents for them. That, I thought, would almost certainly appeal to a publisher. Plus, the collection is organic and lends itself to subsequent editions. The target audience is such that it simply cannot bear not being up to date, so there was a natural market and, of course, a steady stream of revenues for the publisher, not to mention pittances for the editor.

I gave earnest consideration to Mark Twain's advice that, since everyone to whom a book is dedicated invariably buys a copy, one should dedicate the work to the person with the most common name, like John Smith. My remarkable self-restraint in that respect puts to rest (if only partially) the crass commercial animus of this work. Keeping an academic publisher in a financial position to eat a better grade of cat food is, in itself, however, a worthy social undertaking for which, someday, it will undoubtedly receive its just reward, and I my just deserts.

More important in the eventual choice of title was my concern that readers might be a bit nervous when picking up the book with an overt reference to Type-A, and worry that someone may see them. Even with the more benign title, if you are reading this in the bookstore, you probably have your back to the crowd, so that no one can observe you toying with such an explosive work.

It is the lot of the Type-A person that those who lack, but nevertheless aspire to, the status constantly try to undermine the very objective they seek to achieve. It is obviously some variant of a zero sum calculation, the opposite of all boats rising on a higher tide. The lowest common denominator seems a status more appealing to society than the tall poppy syndrome that marks the Type-A. The challenge for the Type-A is not to allow doubts to creep in and to maintain the deserved pride of leadership inherent in the status. This, in an age of increasing media banality, fast food, and a vacuum in political leadership, can be easier said than done.

We must recognize that the world turns as a result of our desire to get things done, despite the apparent efforts of the Type-B personalities (if they can be dignified with this description) to prevent any meaningful or timely achievement. Everywhere you look, there is evidence of this subtle plot to put treacle in the wheels of progress. It is all wrapped up in apparent innocence and diffuse concerns – never effectively articulated – but we know better. Alert Type-A persons can spot these inhibiting life forms, whose conduct invariably gives them away. For beginners amongst us, here are but a few sample observations of the Type-B genus.

DRIVING

- They never seem to want to get anywhere, despite resolute occupation of the passing lane when they drive and an unwillingness to approach, let alone exceed, any posted speed limit.
- Their decisions to turn or exit come upon them by some revelation not comprehensible to any but themselves and are taken either at the last second or after immense deliberation that reduces them to an even

slower crawl while they decide whether Exit 37 may follow or precede Exit 36 and inch into the proper lane, leaving a wake of accidents and near accidents.

- On two-lane streets, they centre themselves directly over the lane divider.
- This seems to help them concentrate on their cellular phone conversation.
- When the light turns green, they never notice.
- When they approach intersections on a green light, they slow down until the light turns yellow, then bolt through as the light turns red, leaving you first in line at yet another interminable red light.
- Turn signals are only used after they have stopped in the intersection to decide which way to turn, only then to change their minds.
- The rear-view mirror is a device used only for checking personal appearance.
- Parallel parking in heavy traffic requires three or more attempts before they discover there is a fire hydrant, following which they drift back into the lane to begin a new search.
- When they double-park, they lock their keys in the car.
- If there is a snowflake within 100 km, their top speed drops to 10 kph.
- Passengers are far more worthy of their attention than the traffic.
- In the morning, they do not want to get to work on time.
- In the evening, they do not want to get home.

RESTAURANTS

- When confronted with a buffet table, they mill about, incapable of making a single decision, as the line behind them stretches farther and farther back.
- Menus in restaurants are impenetrable mysteries, as deep as life itself, that require minute and repeated explanation from exasperated waiters, long after everyone else has made their choices and wait, faint from hunger for them to make a series of agonized decisions, often repeatedly changed.
- In check-out lines, they use credit cards to pay for a $5 sandwich, after lengthy searches in purses or wallets for a card that may be honoured by the restaurant, and then cannot remember their PIN.
- In groups, they request a single bill and then divide it up, to the third decimal point, always ending up a few dollars short and have to start again, with each person taking more out of the pot than they put in, and each needing change.
- They all have the same colour coats and the same boots and have the coat checks mixed up.
- Everyone takes a doggie bag and they, too, get mixed up.

COMMERCIAL TRANSACTIONS
- When they see you coming, they always get to automated tellers just ahead of you and then proceed to conduct a lifetime of complicated business.
- Use of a credit card to get out of a parking lot is a morning's work.
- They try on every item in the store before deciding on what, if anything, to buy.
- It is only when they reach the cashier that they remember what it was that they really came to buy and leave to search for it while you wait.
- Somewhere in their purse, wallet, or pocket is an out-of-date discount coupon for every single item they wish to purchase and they insist on discussing with the store manager why it is not their fault that they did not use it on time.
- The only acceptable fruit or vegetable is hidden at the bottom of each pile.

AIRLINE TRAVEL
- At airport check-in, they have tickets that are not quite right and that have to be re-issued, after discussion of several variations of round-the-world itineraries, with many stopovers.
- They try to wangle upgrades that are not available, to their apparent great surprise, but on which they patiently persist, until the supervisor arrives, so that they can begin their explanations all over again.
- They have multiple pieces of baggage that are invariably over the allowable weight and for which complicated payment arrangements must be made while you wait.
- At the boarding gate, they have always misplaced their boarding pass, cannot find a photo ID, or have several awkward-sized packages that will not fit anywhere.
- On board, the numbering system of the seats is beyond their ken and they fill the aisles for minutes on end, trying to find their seats and then trying to fit the many packages into the overhead compartments, before returning to the front of the plane to rummage through the magazine collection, oblivious to the existence of other passengers.
- On arrival, they all have huge families waiting for them, who greet them at the door and hear the story of the full trip while everyone waits behind them.
- They have lost the ticket for the airport parking and require extensive negotiations with the attendant, their ally, who speaks no known language and has no authority to act.

- They forget to fill out customs declarations until they get to the customs officer, another ally, who explains every tariff item while they fill out the form.
- They sit at window seats and have small, but active, bladders, timed to require clumsy exit from the row the moment you begin to eat, work, or sleep.
- They know you will be fascinated by every detail about their family and their medical condition, with particular attention to lugubrious and intimate operations.
- If they sleep, they snore.
- If they do not sleep, they thrash about as if they were covered in itching powder.
- Their children all throw up.

Readers should be on continual lookout for more evidence of this viral tendency that threatens the Type-A status. Any observations that may help us spot future variations of this behaviour will be gratefully received and published in future editions of this work.

But then, I am back to commercial success … which is good.

I confidently expect that the next big breakthrough in medical research will be the identification of the Type-B personality as the principal cause of strokes, heart attacks, and high blood pressure in important people – far more than innocent bits of cholesterol.

We have a duty to educate them; it is, in fact, their fault that they are imperfect. They need to be made aware of their failings and the desirability of being more like us. It is idiotic to do only one thing at a time when there is so much to be done and to be forgiving of anything less than efficiency and perfection.

So, rejoice in being Type-A. Worry about any symptoms you spot in yourself that may suggest infection by the Type-B virus. It doesn't take a lifetime to smell the bloody roses. Five or six seconds ought to do it.

Oh, and by the way, be sure your blood type is A+, even if you have to get a transfusion.

Richard W. Pound, A+
Command Centre, 2013

QUOTATIONS FOR THE FAST LANE

ABILITY
Ability is a poor man's wealth.
Matthew Wren

Ability will never catch up with the demand for it.
Malcolm Forbes

People of great ability do not emerge, as a rule, from the happiest background. So far as my own observation goes, I would conclude that ability, although hereditary, is improved by an early measure of adversity and improved again by a later measure of success.
C. Northcote Parkinson

ABOMINATION
An abomination unto the Lord, but a very present help in time of trouble.
Anonymous

ABSENCE
Absence diminishes commonplace passions and increases great ones, as the wind extinguishes candles and kindles fire.
François, duc de La Rochefoucauld

I feel so miserable without you; it's almost like having you here.
Stephen Bishop

ABSENT
The absent are always in the wrong.
Philippe Néricault Destouches

ABSOLUTES
No absolute is going to make the lion lie down with the lamb: unless the lamb is inside.
D.H. Lawrence

ABSTINENCE
Abstainer, *n.* A weak person who yields to the temptation of denying himself a pleasure.
Ambrose Bierce

Taking the pledge will not make bad liquor good, but it will improve it.
Mark Twain

Abstinence signifies higher purpose, moral scruples, lack of opportunity, lack of satisfaction, fear of punishment, or incapacity.
Anonymous

Abstinence is a good thing, but it should always be practised in moderation.

Anonymous

ABSURD
The absurd man is he who never changes.

Auguste Barthélemy

Look for the absurd in everything and you will find it.

Jules Renard

ABSURDITY
Every absurdity has a champion to defend it.

Oliver Goldsmith

At any street corner the feeling of absurdity can strike any man in the face.

Albert Camus

Absurdity refutes itself.

Thomas Bartholin

The privilege of absurdity, to which no living creature is subject but man only.

Thomas Hobbes

ACCEPTANCE
The art of acceptance is the art of making someone who has just done you a small favour wish that he might have done you a greater one.

Russell Lynes

ACCIDENTS
Accidents will occur in the best-regulated families.

Charles Dickens

ACCOMMODATION
He who trims himself to suit everybody will soon whittle himself away.

Raymond Hull

ACCOMPLICE
He who holds the ladder is as bad as the thief.

German proverb

ACCOMPLISHMENTS
Knowledge may give weight, but accomplishments give lustre, and many more people see than weigh.

Lord Chesterfield

Small deeds done are better than great deeds planned.

Peter Marshall

The world which credits what is done/Is cold to all that might have been.

Alfred, Lord Tennyson

Those who have done nothing, fancy themselves capable of everything: while those who have exerted themselves to the utmost only feel the limitation of their powers.

William Hazlitt

I am looking for a lot of men who have an infinite capacity to not know what can't be done.

Henry Ford

In the end, you're measured not by how much you undertake, but by what you finally accomplish.

Donald Trump

If you have accomplished all that you have planned for yourself, you have not planned enough.

Edward Everett Hale

The less a person accomplishes in a day, the more he talks during meals.

Takayuki Ikkaku, Arisa Hosaka, and Toshihiro Kawabata

We do well only the things we like doing.

Colette

I long to accomplish a great and noble task, but it is my chief duty to accomplish small tasks as if they were great and noble.

Helen Keller

The sports page records people's accomplishments; the front page nothing but their failures.

Justice Earl Warren

Man is always more than he can know of himself; consequently, his accomplishments, time and time again, will come as a surprise to him.

Golo Mann

The history of what man has accomplished in this world, is at bottom the history of the great men who have worked there.

Thomas Carlyle

There are basically two types of people. People who accomplish things, and people who claim to have accomplished things. The first group is less crowded.

Mark Twain

The shortest way to do many things is to do only one thing at once.

Samuel Smiles

ACCOUNTABILITY
It is time to restore the American precept that each individual is accountable for his actions.

Ronald Reagan

It is not only what we do, but also what we do not do, for which we are accountable.

Molière

ACCOUNTANTS
The difference between an introverted and an extroverted accountant is that the extrovert looks at your shoes.

Anonymous

ACCUSATIONS
Even doubtful accusations leave a stain behind them.

Thomas Fuller, MD

When a man points a finger at someone else, he should remember that four of his fingers are pointing at himself.

Louis Nizer

ACHIEVEMENT
There is no limit to what a man can achieve as long as he doesn't care who gets the credit.

Bob Woodruff

It is amazing what you can accomplish if you do not care who gets the credit.

Harry S. Truman

There is no penalty for over-achievement.

George Miller

We can spend our whole lives underachieving.

Philip Crosby

Ours is a world where people don't know what they want and are willing to go through hell to get it.

Don Marquis

I believe you rarely achieve more than you expect.

Carol Grosse

I found Rome a city of bricks and left it a city of marble.

Caesar Augustus

From above, we can hear the crowd below, growling and grumbling and taking it easy.

Robert Dollar

The greatest pleasure in life is doing what people say you cannot do.

Walter Bagehot

In the long run men hit only what they aim at. Therefore, though they should fall immediately, they had better aim at something high.

Henry David Thoreau

What you have become is the price you paid to get what you used to want.

Mignon McLaughlin

It's not what you are; it's what you don't become that hurts.

Oscar Levant

You're not going to get anywhere if you think you're already there.

Anonymous

He who would do some great thing in this short life must apply himself to work with such a concentration of his forces as, to idle spectators who live only to amuse themselves, looks like insanity.

Francis Parkman

Having what you want is not nearly so interesting as getting what you want.

Sydney Tremayne

Well done is better than well said.

Benjamin Franklin

The secret of getting things done is to act!

Dante Alighieri

I've found that often, just when you think you've hit the wall, you experience a breakthrough that takes you to new heights of accomplishment.

Stedman Graham

High achievement always takes place in the framework of high expectation.

Jack Kinder

But, in history, practical usefulness never determines the moral value of an achievement.

Stefan Zweig

They can because they think they can.

Virgil

Seek not out the things that are too hard for thee, neither search the things that are above thy strength.

Ecclesiasticus 3:21

Achievement, *n.* The death of endeavour and the birth of disgust.

Ambrose Bierce

The achievements which society rewards are won at the cost of diminution of personality.

Benjamin Jowett

Great things are done when men and mountains meet;/This is not done by jostling in the street.

William Blake

ACQUAINTANCE

Acquaintance, *n.* A person whom we know well enough to borrow from, but not well enough to lend to.

Ambrose Bierce

The wisest man I have ever known once said to me: "Nine out of ten people improve on acquaintance" and I have found his words true.

Frank Swinnerton

ACTING

The most important thing in acting is honesty. If you can fake that, you've got it made.

George Burns

Acting is the art of being private in public.

William Hutt

Acting is standing up naked and turning around very slowly.

Rosalind Russell

If an actor acts it out, I hardly listen. I keep worrying about whether he's going to do something phoney every minute.

Holden Caulfield

If it's a good script I'll do it. And if it's a bad script, and they pay me enough, I'll do it.

George Burns

One of my chief regrets during my years in the theatre is that I couldn't sit in the audience and watch me.

John Barrymore

Just know your lines, and don't bump into the furniture.

Noel Coward

If at first you don't succeed, try, try, try again. Then use a stunt double.

Arnold Schwarzenegger

If you're doing the devil, look for the angel in him. If you're doing the angel, look for the devil in him.

Hume Cronyn

ACTION

Never mistake motion for action.

Ernest Hemingway

Never confuse motion with action.

Benjamin Franklin

All mankind is divided into three classes: those that are immovable, those that are movable, and those that move.

Benjamin Franklin

A good edge is good for nothing, if it has nothing to cut.

Thomas Fuller, MD

The ancestor of every action is a thought.

> *Ralph Waldo Emerson*

Word is a shadow of a deed.

> *Democritus*

The profit of a good action is to have done it.

> *Seneca*

One starts an action/Simply because one must do something.

> *T.S. Eliot*

You can't unscramble scrambled eggs.

> *American proverb*

Seize the day (*Carpe diem*): trust not to the morrow.

> *Horace*

Give me today, and take tomorrow.

> *Anonymous*

What may be done at any time will be done at no time.

> *Scottish proverb*

An idea not coupled with action will never get bigger than the brain cell it occupied.

> *Arnold Glasgow*

A thought that does not result in an action is nothing much, and an action that does not proceed from a thought is nothing at all.

> *Georges Bernanos*

When bad men combine, the good must associate; else they will fall one by one, an unpitied sacrifice in a contemptible struggle.

> *Edmund Burke*

Everywhere in life the true question is, not what we have gained, but what we do.

> *Thomas Carlyle*

Action cures fear, inaction creates terror.

> *Douglas Horton*

First ponder, then dare!

> *Helmuth von Moltke*

Action springs not from thought, but from a readiness for responsibility.

> *Dietrich Bonhoeffer*

The best way to avoid a bad action is by doing a good one for there is no difficulty in the world like that of trying to do nothing.

> *John Clare*

Action is thought tempered by illusion.

> *Elbert Hubbard*

To every action there is always opposed an equal reaction.

> *Sir Isaac Newton*

ACTIONS

Words without actions are assassins of idealism.

> *Herbert Hoover*

Do what you can, with what you have, where you are.

> *Unknown*

Rebellion against your handicaps gets you nowhere. Self-pity gets you nowhere. One must have the adventurous daring to accept oneself as a bundle of possibilities and undertake the most interesting game in the world – making the most of one's best.

Harry Emerson Fosdick

As I grow older, I pay less attention to what men say. I just watch what they do.

Andrew Carnegie

Don't stand shivering upon the bank; plunge in at once, and have it over.

Thomas Chandler Haliburton

Don't let what you cannot do interfere with what you can do.

Anonymous

It is no profit to have learned well, if you neglect to do well.

Publilius Syrus

A man's most open actions have a secret side to them.

Joseph Conrad

What you do speaks so loud I cannot hear what you say.

Ralph Waldo Emerson

We are all inclined to judge ourselves by our ideals, others by their acts.

Harold Nicolson

He who means well is useless unless he does well.

Plautus

Could everything be done twice, everything would be done better.

German proverb

A stone thrown at the right time is better than gold given at the wrong time.

Persian proverb

To do certain crazy things, one must behave like a coachman who has let go of the reins and fallen asleep.

Jules Renard

You cannot write in the chimney with charcoal.

Russian proverb

Actions lie louder than words.

Carolyn Wells

It is circumstances and proper timing that give an action its character and make it either good or bad.

Agesilaus

He who desires but acts not breeds pestilence.

William Blake

The actions of men are the best interpreters of their thoughts.

John Locke

You don't make sheep any fatter by weighing them.

Scottish proverb

Strong reasons make strong actions.

William Shakespeare

Men imagine that they communicate their virtue or vice only by overt actions, and do not see that virtue or vice emit a breath every moment.

Ralph Waldo Emerson

We become just by performing just actions, temperate by performing temperate actions, brave by performing brave actions.

Aristotle

The shortest answer is doing.

George Herbert

What we think, or what we know or what we believe in is, in the end, of little consequence. The only consequence is what we do.

John Ruskin

A superior man is modest in his speech, but exceeds in his actions.

Confucius

Think nothing done while anything remained to be done.

Lucan

Men must be decided on what they will not do, and then they are able to act with vigour in what they ought to do.

Mencius

We know what a person thinks not when he tells us what he thinks, but by his actions.

Isaac Bashevis Singer

ACTIVISM
Organize, agitate, educate, must be our war cry.

Susan B. Anthony

ACTIVITY
Furious activity is no substitute for understanding.

H.H. Williams

Creative activity could be described as a type of learning process where the teacher and pupil are located in the same individual.

Arthur Koestler

ACTORS
We used to have actresses trying to become stars; now we have stars trying to become actresses.

Laurence Olivier

In the theatre, the director is God – but unfortunately, the actors are atheists.

Žarko Petan

You'd throw tomatoes at bad actors and performers and it was much more intentionally vicious. A pie might be more of a corrective. … You don't hurt anybody when you plop a pie in their face.

Jack Nachbar

Shakespeare is so tiring. You never get a chance to sit down unless you're a king.

Josephine Hull

Actors must practise restraint, else think what might happen in a love scene.

Cedric Hardwicke

The question actors most often get asked is how they can bear saying the same things over and over again, night after night, but God knows the answer to that is, don't we all anyway; might as well get paid for it.

Richard Brinsley Sheridan

You can pick out actors by the glazed look that comes into their eyes when the conversation wanders away from themselves.

Michael Wilding

ADAPT
Adapt or perish, now as ever, is Nature's inexorable imperative.

H.G. Wells

ADDICTION
Addiction is a friendship without a friend.

Connie Palmen

Every form of addiction is bad, no matter whether the narcotic be alcohol or morphine or idealism.

Carl Jung

ADEQUACY
He had delusions of adequacy.

Walter Kerr

ADJOURN
A motion to adjourn is always in order.

Robert Heinlein

ADMIRATION
It is better in some respects to be admired by those with whom you live, than to be loved by them. And this is not on account of any gratification of vanity, but because admiration is so much more tolerant than love.

Sir Arthur Helps

Admiration, *n.* Our polite recognition of another's resemblance to ourselves.

Ambrose Bierce

We always like those who admire us, but not always those whom we admire.

François, duc de La Rochefoucauld

Not to admire is all the art I know.

Lord Byron

ADOLESCENCE
In later life, we look at things in a more practical way, in full conformity with the rest of society, but adolescence is the only period in which we learn anything.

Marcel Proust

If a society is to preserve its stability and a degree of continuity, it must know how to keep its adolescents from imposing their tastes, attitudes, values, and fantasies on everyday life.

Eric Hoffer

Adolescence is a kind of emotional seasickness. Both are funny, but only in retrospect.

Arthur Koestler

ADULATION
Adulation is all right if you don't inhale.

Adlai Stevenson

ADULTHOOD
Adulthood is the ever-shrinking period between childhood and old

age. It is the apparent aim of modern industrial societies to reduce this period to a minimum.

Thomas Szasz

ADVANTAGE

It's them as take advantage that get advantage in this world.

George Eliot

Move only if there is a real advantage to be gained.

Sun Tzu

ADVENTURE

Adventure is just bad planning.

Roald Amundsen

ADVENTURERS

It behooves all adventurers to treat their good luck with reverence, neither bothering nor upsetting it.

François Rabelais

ADVERSITY

Even after a bad harvest there must be sowing.

Seneca

By trying we can easily endure adversity. Another man's I mean.

Mark Twain

Prosperity tries the fortunate; adversity the great.

Pliny the Younger

Adversity reveals genius; prosperity conceals it.

Horace

You can't have more bedbugs than a blanketful.

Spanish proverb

Adversity is the first path to truth.

Lord Byron

A smooth sea never made a skillful mariner; neither do uninterrupted prosperity and success qualify men for usefulness and happiness. If adversity hath killed thousands, prosperity hath killed his ten thousands; therefore adversity is to be preferred. The one deceives, the other instructs; the one is miserably happy, the other happily miserable; and therefore many philosophers have voluntarily sought adversity and commended it in their precepts.

Richard E. Burton

You'll never find a better sparring partner than adversity.

Walt Schmidt

The good things which belong to prosperity are to be wished, but the good things that belong to adversity are to be admired.

Seneca

If we had no winter, the spring would not be so pleasant: if we did not sometimes taste of adversity, prosperity would not be so welcome.

Anne Bradstreet

Adversity does teach who your real friends are.

Lois McMaster Bujold

It's how you handle adversity, not how it affects you. The main thing is never quit, never quit, never quit.

Bill Clinton

Look at a man in the midst of doubt and danger, and you will learn in his hour of adversity what he really is. It is then that true utterances are wrung from the recesses of his breast. The mask is torn off; the reality remains.

Lucretius

ADVERTISEMENTS
You can tell the ideals of a nation by its advertisements.

Norman Douglas

Ads are the cave art of the twentieth century.

Marshall McLuhan

When the gods wish to punish us, they make us believe our own advertising.

Daniel Boorstin

You can fool all the people all the time if the advertising is right and the budget is big enough.

Joseph E. Levine

Advertising is the greatest art form of the twentieth century.

Marshall McLuhan

No one dares suggest that neon lights blinking the message that "Jesus Saves" may be false advertising.

R. Laurence Moore

Committees can criticize advertisements, but they should never be allowed to create them.

David Ogilvy

Advertising may be described as the science of arresting the human intelligence long enough to get money from it.

Stephen Leacock

Doing business without advertising is like winking at a girl in the dark: you know what you are doing, but nobody else does.

Edgar Watson Howe

Historians and archeologists will discover that the advertisements of our time are the richest and most faithful reflections that any society ever made of its entire range of activities.

Marshall McLuhan

I have always believed that writing advertisements is the second most profitable form of publishing. The first, of course, is ransom notes.

Philip Dusenberry

ADVICE
"Be Yourself" is the worst advice you can give to some people.

Tom Mason

It is always a silly thing to give advice, but to give good advice is fatal.

Oscar Wilde

When we ask for advice, we are usually looking for an accomplice.

Marquis de la Grange

We are apt to be very pert at censuring others, where we will not endure advice ourselves.

William Penn

I have yet to hear a man ask for advice on how to combine marriage and a career.

Gloria Steinem

No one wants advice, only corroboration.

John Steinbeck

Never trust the advice of a man in difficulties.

Aesop

Hear the words of the wise, and apply thine heart unto my knowledge.

Proverbs 22:17

Why should we ever go abroad, even across the way, to ask a neighbour's advice? There is a nearer neighbour within us incessantly telling us how we should behave. But we wait for the neighbour without to tell us of some false, easier way.

Henry David Thoreau

There are more old drunkards than old doctors.

Benjamin Franklin

There is some advice that is too good – the advice to love your enemies, for example.

Edgar Watson Howe

Advice is what we ask for when we already know the answer but wish we didn't.

Erica Jong

Free advice is worth the price.

Robert Half

I intended to give you some advice but now I remember how much is left over from last year unused.

George Harris (addressing students at the start of an academic year)

Advice is like snow;/the softer it falls, the longer it dwells upon,/and the deeper it sinks into the mind.

Samuel Taylor Coleridge

To accept good advice is but to increase one's own ability.

Johann Wolfgang von Goethe

Many people who give admirable advice are totally incapable of taking it.

Anonymous

If you can distinguish between good advice and bad advice, then you don't need advice.

Murphy's Law: Book Three

I always pass on good advice. It is the only thing to do with it. It is never any use to oneself.

Oscar Wilde

When a man seeks your advice he generally wants your praise.

Lord Chesterfield

Some people like my advice so much that they frame it upon the wall instead of using it.

Gordon R. Dickson

As time passes we all get better at blazing a trail through the thicket of advice.

Margot Bennett

Advice is seldom welcome; and those who want it the most always like it the least.

Lord Chesterfield

ADVOCACY

It is wholly legitimate, in the pursuit of advocacy, to turn to its fullest account a knowledge of the psychology of those you seek to persuade. That – indeed – is much of what the technique of persuasion is about.

Sir David Napley

Just as there should be a reason for every word, there should be a reason for every sentence in the composition of written advocacy.

Paul M. Perell

AFFECTATION

Affected simplicity is an elegant imposture.

François, duc de La Rochefoucauld

Any affectation whatsoever in dress implies ... a flaw in the understanding.

Lord Chesterfield

Careless is she with artful care,/ Affecting to seem unaffected.

William Congreve

No man is ridiculous for being what he really is, but for affecting to be what he is not.

Lord Chesterfield

AFFECTION

Affection is the mortal illness of lonely people.

Gary Indiana

All my life affection has been showered upon me, and every forward step I have made has been taken in spite of it.

George Bernard Shaw

AFFLICTION

When an affliction happens to you, you either let it defeat you, or you defeat it.

Rosalind Russell

AFFLUENT SOCIETY

In the affluent society no useful distinction can be made between luxuries and necessaries.

John Kenneth Galbraith

AFRICA

The darkest thing about Africa has always been our ignorance of it.

George Kimble

There is always something new out of Africa.

Pliny the Elder

AFTER-THE-FACT

It's but little good you'll do a-watering the last year's crops.

George Eliot

AFTERLIFE

I don't believe in an afterlife, although I am bringing a change of underwear.

Woody Allen

AGE

For the unlearned, old age is winter; for the learned, it is the season of the harvest.

Hasidic saying

My hope is to have everybody die young as late as possible.

Jean Mayer

I'll never make the mistake of being seventy again.

Casey Stengel

If you want to grow old gracefully, don't try new dances.

Texas Bix Bender

When one has reached eighty-one one likes to sit back and let the world turn by itself, without trying to push.

Sean O'Casey

Every age has a keyhole to which its eye is pasted.

Mary McCarthy

The man who views the world at fifty the same way he did at twenty has wasted thirty years of his life.

Muhammad Ali

One of the delights of age, and beyond the grasp of youth, is that of Not Going.

J.B. Priestley

Age is not important – unless you're a cheese.

Helen Hayes

Age improves wine, compound interest, and nothing else I can think of.

T. Harry Thompson

We grow old more through indolence than age.

Queen Christina of Sweden

Don't let Father Time kick sand in your face.

Heathcote Williams

One starts to get young at the age of sixty, and then it is too late.

Pablo Picasso

It takes about ten years to get used to how old you are.

Unknown

Old age is like a plane flying through a storm. Once you are aboard, there's nothing you can do.

Golda Meir

Some people reach the age of sixty before others.

Lord Hood

Growing old is like being increasingly penalized for a crime you never committed.

Anthony Powell

There is nothing more liberating than age.

Liz Carpenter

The worst thing that could happen to anyone is getting older. It's like drawing the ace of spades and everyone gets it. Though being very young isn't always great either.

Woody Allen

Ah, well, perhaps one has to be very old before one learns how to be amused rather than shocked.

Pearl S. Buck

You're never too old to learn something stupid.

Anonymous

As one gets older, one discovers everything is going to be exactly the same with different hats on.

Noel Coward

I must be getting absent-minded. Whenever I complain that things aren't what they used to be, I always forget to include myself.

George Burns

Every age confutes old errors and begets new.

Thomas Fuller, MD

Keep on raging – to stop the aging.

The Deltones

The older one grows, the more one likes indecency.

Virginia Woolf

I'm not interested in age. People who tell their ages are silly. You're as old as you feel.

Elizabeth Arden

Life's tragedy is that we get old too soon and wise too late.

Benjamin Franklin

On balance, I find the world an entertaining place but shall be well content to leave it, holding with Horace that it is unseemly in the old and feeble to linger at the banquet, where they merely spoil the pleasure of other people.

Simon Raven

I don't need you to remind me of my age; I have a bladder to do that for me.

Stephen Fry

Every man over forty is a scoundrel.

George Bernard Shaw

Old age is the most unexpected of all things that happen to a man.

Leon Trotsky

One can always tell when one is getting old and serious by the way that holidays seem to interfere with one's work.

Bob Edwards

To grow old is to pass from passion to compassion.

Albert Camus

It doesn't matter how bold you are when the dangerous age is past.

Noel Coward

It is nonsense for you to talk of old age so long as you outrun young men in the race for service and in the midst of anxious times fill rooms with your laughter and inspire youth with hope when they are on the brink of despair.

Mohandas Gandhi

Age only matters when one is aging. Now that I have arrived at a great age, I might just as well be twenty.

Pablo Picasso

When you're fifty you start thinking about things you haven't thought about before. I used to think getting old was about vanity – but actually it's about losing people you love. Getting wrinkles is trivial.

Joyce Carol Oates

Age merely shows what children we remain.

Johann Wolfgang von Goethe

I think age is a very high price to pay for maturity.

Tom Stoppard

You know you're growing old when almost everything hurts, and what doesn't hurt doesn't work.

Hy Gardner

I don't hang around with people my own age. They're too old.

Frank Palmer

So the years hang like old clothes, forgotten in the wardrobe of our minds. Did I wear that? Who was I then?

Brian Moore

There are people who, like houses, are beautiful in dilapidation.

Logan Pearsall Smith

We have a saying in the movement that we don't trust anybody over thirty.

Jack Weinberg

Of late I have searched diligently to discover the advantages of age, and there is, I have concluded, only one. It is that lovely women treat your approaches with understanding rather than with disdain.

John Kenneth Galbraith

Age doesn't always bring wisdom, but it certainly makes it easier to fake.

Matthew McLachlan

You know you are getting old when the candles cost more than the cake.

Bob Hope

The trouble with our age is that it is all signpost and no destination.

Louis Kronenberger

The aging process has you firmly in its grasp if you never get the urge to throw a snowball.

Doug Larson

The older you get, the stronger the wind gets – and it's always in your face.

Pablo Picasso

One should never trust a woman who tells one her real age. A woman who would tell one that, would tell one anything.

Oscar Wilde

Things and people not actively in use age twice as fast.

Arnold Bennett

Growing old is no more than a bad habit which a busy man has no time to form.

André Maurois

All of a sudden, I'm older than my parents were when I thought they were old.

Lois Wyse

Here I am at the end of the road and at the top of the heap.

Pope John XXIII

AGGRESSION

What sex was to the Victorians, aggression is to us. We deplore it, sermonize over it, criticize it publicly and practise it privately. We are in favour of peace and go to war at the drop of a hat. ... And we certainly talk about it and write books about it.

Hans Eysenck

AGITATE

Only the guy who isn't rowing has time to rock the boat.

Jean-Paul Sartre

AGREEMENT

Nobody agrees with anyone else anyhow, but adults conceal it and infants show it.

Ogden Nash

Too much agreement kills a chat.

Eldridge Cleaver

Agreement is brought about by changing people's minds – other people's.

S.I. Hayakawa

When men and women agree, it is only in their conclusions: their reasons are always different.

George Santayana

My sad conviction is that people can only agree about what they're not really interested in.

Bertrand Russell

The man who agrees with everybody is not worth having anybody to agree with him.

Lord Palmerston

AIM

It is not enough to aim – you must hit.

Italian proverb

We aim above the mark to hit the mark.

Ralph Waldo Emerson

AIMLESS

Vacant heart and hand and eye,/Easy live and quiet die.

Sir Walter Scott

AIRLINES

The saying "getting there is half the fun" became obsolete with the advent of commercial airlines.

Henry J. Tillman

My inclination to go by Air Express is confirmed by the crash they had yesterday, which will make them careful in the immediate future.

A.E. Housman

AIRPORTS

The Devil himself had probably redesigned Hell in the light of information he had gained from observing airport layouts.

Anthony Price

It is no coincidence that in no known language does the phrase "as pretty as an airport" appear.

Douglas Adams

ALCOHOL

Alcohol is a good preservative for everything but brains.

Mary Pettibone Poole

Alcohol ... enables Parliament to do things at 11 at night that no sane person would do at 11 in the morning.

George Bernard Shaw

The sway of alcohol over mankind is unquestionably due to its power to stimulate the mystical faculties of human nature, usually crushed to earth by the cold facts and dry criticisms of the sober hour.

William James

I like to keep a bottle of stimulant handy in case I see a snake, which I also keep handy.

W.C. Fields

ALCOHOLISM

The intermediate stage between socialism and capitalism is alcoholism.

Norman Brenner

If the headache would only precede the intoxication, alcoholism would be a virtue.

Samuel Butler

ALIENATION

And I feel like a stranger in the land where I was born.

Dino Valente

ALIMONY

Alimony: bounty after the mutiny.

Max Kauffmann

Alimony – the ransom that the happy pay to the devil.

H.L. Mencken

Alimony is like buying oats for a dead horse.

Arthur (Bugs) Baer

Alimony is a system by which, when two people make a mistake, one of them keeps paying for it.

Peggy Joyce

ALIVE

Ask not what the world needs. Ask what makes you come alive ... then go do it. Because what the world needs is people who have come alive.

Howard Thurman

ALLIANCES

We cannot enter into alliances until we are acquainted with the designs of our neighbours.

Sun Tzu

ALONE

To dare to live alone is the rarest courage; since there are many who had rather meet their bitterest enemy in the field, than their own hearts in their closet.

Charles Caleb Colton

When you get a thing the way you want it, leave it alone.

Winston Churchill

Our language has wisely sensed the two sides of being alone. It has created the word loneliness to express the pain of being alone. And it has created the word solitude to express the glory of being alone.

Paul Tillich

Sometimes I think we're alone. Sometimes I think we're not. In either case, the thought is staggering.

R. Buckminster Fuller

What a commentary on our civilization, when being alone is considered suspect; when one has to apologize for it, make excuses, hide the fact that one practises it – like some secret vice!

Anne Morrow Lindbergh

ALTERNATIVES

Who will not feed the cats, must feed the mice and rats.

German proverb

Alternatives, and particularly desirable alternatives, grow only on imaginary trees.

Saul Bellow

The more alternatives, the more difficult the choice.

Abbé d'Allainville

Before you take anything away, you must have something better to put in its place.

Arthur Schopenhauer

There are occasions when it is undoubtedly better to incur loss than to make gain.

Plautus

AMATEUR

Remember that Noah's ark was built by amateurs and the Titanic by professionals.

Sir Arthur Gold

AMBIGUITY

Give me ambiguity or give me something else.

Elaine Stauff

AMBITION

Ambition is in fact the avarice of power.

Charles Caleb Colton

All my life I wanted to be somebody. Now I realize I should have been more specific.

Lily Tomlin

Well it is known that ambition can creep as well as soar.

Edmund Burke

If you do not raise your eyes, you will think you are the highest point.

Antonio Porchia

A man's feet must be planted in his country, but his eyes should survey the world.

George Santayana

Ah, but a man's reach should exceed his grasp – or what's a heaven for?

Robert Browning

He who would climb the ladder must begin at the bottom.

English proverb

Women who seek to be equal with men lack ambition.

Timothy Leary

Keep away from people who try to belittle your ambitions. Small people always do that, but the really great make you feel that you, too, can become great.

Mark Twain

Where none will sweat but for promotion.

William Shakespeare

Always do one thing less than you think you can do.

Bernard Baruch

When I was a kid, I always knew I would sing on the radio.

Johnny Cash

The same ambition can destroy or save,/And makes a patriot as it makes a knave.

Alexander Pope

Most people would succeed in small things if they were not troubled with great ambitions.

Henry Wadsworth Longfellow

No bird soars too high, if he soars with his own wings.

William Blake

Choked with ambition of the meanest sort.

William Shakespeare

A man's ambition is exactly proportioned to his powers. The height of the pinnacle is determined by the breadth of the base.

Ralph Waldo Emerson

Intelligence without ambition is a bird without wings.

Salvador Dali

Ambition is the last refuge of the failure.

Oscar Wilde

Ambition is a lust that is never quenched, but grows more inflamed and madder by enjoyment.

Thomas Otway

Soar not too high to fall; but stoop to rise.

Philip Massinger

Sorrow knocked at my door, but I was afraid;/Ambition called to me, but I dreaded the chances.

Edgar Lee Masters

AMERICA

America is a mistake, a giant mistake.

Sigmund Freud

The United States themselves are essentially the greatest poem.

Walt Whitman

It is by the goodness of God that in our country we have those three unspeakably precious things: freedom of speech, freedom of conscience, and the prudence never to practise either of them.

Mark Twain

America is much more than a geographical fact. It is a political and moral fact – the first community in which men set out in principle to institutionalize freedom, responsible government, and human equality.

Adlai Stevenson

America is the best half-educated country in the world.
Nicholas Murray Butler

America is the land of opportunity if you're a businessman in Japan.
Laurence J. Peter

The things that will destroy America are prosperity-at-any-price, peace-at-any-price, safety-first instead of duty-first, the love of soft living, and the get-rich-quick theory of life.
Theodore Roosevelt

America is a large friendly dog in a small room. Every time it wags its tail, it knocks over a chair.
Arnold Toynbee

Being a great power is no longer much fun.
David Schoenbaum

It's an appropriate coincidence that the word "American" ends in "I can."
Alexander Animator

America is not made out of a single stock. Here we have a great melting pot.
Woodrow Wilson

AMERICAN CULTURE

We are being swallowed up by the popular culture of the United States, but then the Americans are being swallowed up by it, too. It's just as much a threat to American culture as it is to ours.
Northrop Frye

In America, it is sport that is the opiate of the masses.
Russell Baker

Very little is known about the War of 1812 because the Americans lost it.
Eric Nicol

In America any boy may become president and I suppose it's just one of the risks he takes.
Adlai Stevenson

America and its demons, Europe and its ghosts.
Le Monde

I loathe the expression "What makes him tick." It is the American mind, looking for [a] simple and singular solution, that uses the foolish expression. A person not only ticks, he also chimes and strikes the hour, falls and breaks and has to be put together again, and sometimes stops like an electric clock in a thunderstorm.
James Thurber

The constitution gives every American the inalienable right to make a damn fool of himself.
John Ciardi

For a working man or woman to vote Republican this year is the same as a chicken voting for Colonel Sanders.
Walter Mondale

The immense popularity of American movies abroad demonstrates that Europe is the unfinished negative of which America is the proof.
Mary McCarthy

Whither goest thou, America, in thy shiny car in the night?

Jack Kerouac

Americans have an abiding belief in their ability to control reality by purely material means. Airline insurance replaces the fear of death with the comforting prospect of cash.

Cecil Beaton

I can't believe we still have the Miss America pageant. This is America! Where we're not supposed to judge people based on how they look, we're supposed to judge people based on how much money they make.

Heidi Joyce

The Americans ... have invented so wide a range of pithy and hackneyed phrases that they can carry on an amusing and animated conversation without giving a moment's reflection to what they are saying and so leave their minds free to consider the more important matters of big business and fornication.

W. Somerset Maugham

He held, too, in his enlightened way, that Americans have a perfect right to exist. But he did often find himself wishing Mr Rhodes had not enabled them to exercise that right in Oxford.

Max Beerbohm

Americans like fat books and thin women.

Russell Baker

AMERICAN INDIAN
The American Indian will never again control the American continent, but he will forever haunt it.

D.H. Lawrence

AMERICAN LIFE
American life is a powerful solvent. It seems to neutralize every intellectual element, however tough and alien it may be, and to fuse it in the native goodwill, complacency, thoughtlessness, and optimism.

George Santayana

There are no second acts in American lives.

F. Scott Fitzgerald

Buying is much more American than thinking.

Andy Warhol

AMERICAN STATESMAN
You can always get the truth from an American statesman after he has turned seventy or given up hope of the Presidency.

Wendell Phillips

AMMUNITION
Praise the Lord and pass the ammunition.

Howell Forgy at Pearl Harbor

AMNESIA
Amnesia is not knowing who one is and wanting desperately to find out. Euphoria is not knowing who one is and not caring. Ecstasy is knowing exactly who one is – and still not caring.

Tom Robbins

AMUSEMENT
Amusement is the happiness of those who cannot think.
Alexander Pope

ANACHRONISMS
What the world needs is more anachronisms.
Anonymous

ANALOGY
Though analogy is often misleading, it is the least misleading thing we have.
Samuel Butler

ANALYSIS
Analysis kills spontaneity. The grain once ground into flour, springs and germinates no more.
Henri-Frédéric Amiel

The moment a little boy is concerned with which is a jay and which is a sparrow, he can no longer see the birds or hear them sing.
Eric Berne

ANARCHY
My political opinions lean more and more to anarchy. The most improper job of any man, even saints, is bossing other men.
J.R.R. Tolkien

We started off trying to set up a small anarchist community, but people wouldn't obey the rules.
Alan Bennett

ANCESTORS
I am very grateful for the indiscriminate behaviour of my ancestors. I was conceived in St Petersburg, but born in London – Swiss Cottage, of course.
Peter Ustinov

It is indeed desirable to be well descended, but the glory belongs to our ancestors.
Plutarch

Ancestor worship must be an appealing idea to those who are about to become ancestors.
Steven Pinker

They who depend on the merits of ancestors, search in the roots of the tree for the fruits which the branches ought to produce.
Isaac Barrow

ANCIENT TIMES
Let others praise ancient times; I am glad I was born in these.
Ovid

ANECDOTES
Anecdotes and maxims are rich treasures to the man of the world, for he knows how to introduce the former at fit places in conversation, and to recollect the latter on proper occasions.
Johann Wolfgang von Goethe

ANGELS
Angels can fly because they take themselves lightly.
G.K. Chesterton

I keep myself supplied with my own angels and demons.

Ingmar Bergman

There is no reason why good cannot triumph as often as evil. The triumph of anything is a matter of organization. If there are such things as angels, I hope they are organized along the lines of the Mafia.

Kurt Vonnegut

ANGER

When a man angers you, he conquers you.

Tom Morrison

Speak when you're angry – and you'll make the best speech you'll ever regret.

Laurence J. Peter

Anger is never sudden. It is born of a long, prior irritation that has ulcerated the spirit and built up an accumulation of force that results in an explosion. It follows that a fine outburst of rage is by no means a sign of a direct, frank nature.

Cesare Pavese

Anger can be an expensive luxury.

Italian proverb

Be careful to do nothing while you are in anger: why put to sea in the violence of a storm?

Dandemis

Anger blows out the lamp of the mind.

Robert G. Ingersoll

Our anger and annoyance are more detrimental to us than the things themselves which anger or annoy us.

Marcus Aurelius

When angry, count ten before you speak; if very angry, count a hundred.

Thomas Jefferson

When angry, count four; when very angry, swear.

Mark Twain

It's so hard to write out of anger. I can't summon it. I can in daily life, which I do a lot. But when I'm at the page, it's just not helpful … it's not out of that place that serious thought comes.

Toni Morrison

Be careful of anger, it is only one letter away from danger.

Anonymous

Anger is a bad counsellor.

French proverb

Anger is never without an argument, but seldom with a good one.

George Savile, Marquess of Halifax

It is easy to fly into a passion – anybody can do that – but to be angry with the right person and to the right extent and at the right time and with the right object and in the right way – that is not easy, and it is not everyone who can do it.

Aristotle

If anger proceeds from a great cause, it turns to fury; if from a small cause, it is peevishness; and so it is always either terrible or ridiculous.

Jeremy Taylor

Holding on to anger is like grasping a hot coal with the intent of throwing it at someone else; you are the one who gets burned.

Buddha

ANGUISH

In struggling against anguish, one never produces serenity; the struggle against anguish only produces new forms of anguish.

Simone Weil

ANIMALS

There are two things for which animals are to be envied: they know nothing of future evils, or of what people say about them.

Voltaire

I'm all for killing animals and turning them into handbags. I just don't want to have to eat them.

Victoria Wood

To wear the arctic fox, you have to kill it.

Marianne Moore

Animals used to provide a low-life way to kill and get away with it, as they do still, but, more intriguingly, for some people they are an aperture through which wounds drain. The scapegoat of olden times, driven off for the bystanders' sins, has become a tender thing, a running injury. There, running away … is me: hurt it and you are hurting me.

Edward Hoagland

I am not over-fond of animals. I am merely astounded by them.

David Attenborough

My favourite animal is steak.

Fran Lebowitz

Animals have these advantages over man: They never hear the clock strike, they die without any idea of death, they have no theologians to instruct them, their last moments are not disturbed by unwelcome and unpleasant ceremonies, their funerals cost them nothing, and no one starts lawsuits over their wills.

Voltaire

If man was what he ought to be, he would be adored by the animals.

Henri-Frédéric Amiel

The greatness of a nation and its moral progress can be judged by the way its animals are treated.

Mohandas Gandhi

It is much easier to show compassion to animals. They are never wicked.

Haile Selassie

ANSWERS

Bromide as it may sound, some questions don't have answers, which is a terribly difficult lesson to learn.

Katharine Graham

It is not every question that deserves an answer.

Publilius Syrus

Questions show the mind's range; answers, its subtlety.

Joseph Joubert

Anybody who says, "This is the answer," is an idiot. There are going to be a multitude of answers. That's the point. It's all about diversity [of thoughts and approaches].

Bill McDonough

For every complex question there is an answer that is clear, simple, and wrong.

H.L. Mencken

An answer is always a form of death.

John Fowles

For many years now, you and I have been shushed like children and told there are no simple answers to the complex problems that are beyond our comprehension. Well, the truth is there are simple answers. They are just not easy ones.

Ronald Reagan

Ask me no more: what answer should I give?

Alfred, Lord Tennyson

Many people today don't want honest answers insofar as honest means unpleasant or disturbing. They want a soft answer that turneth away anxiety. They want answers that are, in effect, escapes.

Louis Kronenberger

ANTICIPATION

Sell not the bear's skin before you have caught him.

Thomas Fuller, MD

The best part of our lives we pass in counting on what is to come.

William Hazlitt

Prospect is often better than possession.

Thomas Fuller, MD

If pleasures are greatest in anticipation, just remember that this is also true of trouble.

Elbert Hubbard

They sicken of the calm, who know the storm.

Dorothy Parker

Do not climb the hill until you get to it.

English proverb

The arrow seen before cometh less rudely.

Dante Alighieri

Skate to where the puck is going, not to where it has been.

Walter Gretzky

We cannot make it rain, but we can see to it that the rain falls on prepared soil.

Henri Nouwen

Don't count your boobies until they are hatched.

James Thurber

The day is for mistake and error, sequence of time for success and

carrying it out. The one who antic-
ipates is master of the day.

Johann Wolfgang von Goethe

An intense anticipation itself transforms possibility into reality.

Samuel Smiles

What we anticipate seldom occurs;
what we least expected generally
happens.

Benjamin Disraeli

ANTS
Ants don't go to picnics; people
take picnics to them.

The Globe and Mail

Ants are so much like human
beings as to be an embarrassment.
They farm fungi, raise aphids as
livestock, launch armies into war,
use chemical sprays to alarm and
confuse enemies, capture slaves,
engage in child labour, exchange
information ceaselessly. They do
everything but watch television.

Lewis Thomas

ANXIETY
Nothing in the affairs of men is
worthy of great anxiety.

Plato

ANYWHERE
Anywhere is the centre of the
world.

Black Elk

APATHY
Science may have found a cure for
most evils; but it has found no
remedy for the worst of them all –
the apathy of human beings.

Helen Keller

APHORISMS
Someone who can write aphorisms
should not fritter away his time
writing essays.

Karl Kraus

APOCALYPTIC GROUPS
I am more worried about after
2000 than about 2000 itself ... The
real problem is that in the immediate period after disappointment –
the first decade of the next century
– one of the tendencies of disappointed apocalyptic groups is to
get nasty. They look for scapegoats.

Richard Landes

APOLOGY
A stiff apology is a second insult.

G.K. Chesterton

Apology is only egotism wrong
side out.

Oliver Wendell Holmes

Apologies only account for that
which they do not alter.

Benjamin Disraeli

APPEARANCE
God has given you one face, and
you make yourself another.

William Shakespeare

There is no one so bound to his
own face that he does not cherish
the hope of presenting another to
the world.

Antonio Machado

A clean glove often hides a dirty hand.

English proverb

It's not an optical illusion; it just looks that way.

Anonymous

Things are seldom what they seem,/ Skim milk masquerades as cream.

W.S. Gilbert

Take nothing on its looks; take everything on evidence. There's no better rule.

Charles Dickens

Have an open face, but conceal your thoughts.

Italian proverb

I was much farther out than you thought, and not waving but drowning.

Stevie Smith

Nothing succeeds like the appearance of success.

Christopher Lasch

If you would be powerful, pretend to be powerful.

John Horne Tooke

The big drum beats fast, but does not realize its hollowness.

Malay proverb

In great affairs men show themselves as they wish to be seen, in small things they show themselves as they are.

Chamfort

Nothing is so good as it seems beforehand.

George Eliot

The cowl does not make a monk.

Latin proverb

A good man often appears gauche simply because he does not take advantage of the myriad mean little chances of making himself look stylish. Preferring truth to form, he is not constantly at work upon the facade of his appearance.

Iris Murdoch

All is not golde that outward shineth bright.

John Lydgate

Things are not what they seem; or, to be more accurate, they are not only what they seem, but very much else besides.

Aldous Huxley

The person portrayed and the portrait are two entirely different things.

José Ortega y Gasset

Don't think there are no crocodiles because the water is calm.

Malay proverb

What I have to say is far more important than the length of my eyelashes.

Alanis Morissette

APPEASEMENT

Appeasers believe that if you keep on throwing steaks to a tiger, the tiger will become a vegetarian.

Heywood Broun

But we've proved it again and again,/That if once you have paid him the Dane-geld/You never get rid of the Dane.

Rudyard Kipling

An appeaser is one who feeds a crocodile – hoping it will eat him last.

Winston Churchill

APPETITES
Other people's appetites easily appear excessive when one doesn't share them.

André Gide

APPLAUSE
The applause of a single human being is of great consequence.

Samuel Johnson

Applause is the spur of noble minds, the end and aim of weak ones.

Charles Caleb Colton

APPRECIATION
People generally do not appreciate what they do not suffer for. A thing is held to be cheap if it did not cost dearly. Honour is lightly worn if it was easily obtained. Inherited liberty is too often carelessly used until it is repossessed through sacrifices.

Fred Robert Tiffany

Appreciation is a wonderful thing: It makes what is excellent in others belong to us as well.

Voltaire

APPROVAL
A unanimous chorus of approval is not an assurance of survival; authors who please everyone at once are quickly exhausted.

André Gide

Nothing's so apt to undermine your confidence in a product as knowing that the commercial selling it has been approved by the company that makes it.

Franklin P. Jones

APPROXIMATE
It is better to be approximately right than precisely wrong.

Warren Buffett

APRIL
It was a bright, cold day in April and the clocks were striking thirteen.

George Orwell

April comes like an idiot, babbling and strewing flowers.

Edna St Vincent Millay

ARCHER
The archer strikes the target partly by pulling, partly by letting go.

Bits & Pieces

ARCHITECT
A doctor can bury his mistakes, but an architect can only advise his clients to plant vines.

Frank Lloyd Wright

The great thing about being an architect is you can walk into your dreams.

Harold E. Wagoner

Each man is the architect of his own fate.

Sallust

ARCHITECTURE
All architecture is great architecture after sunset; perhaps architecture is really a nocturnal art, like the art of fireworks.

G.K. Chesterton

Architecture is the art of how to waste space.

Philip Johnson

Architecture in general is frozen music.

Friedrich von Schelling

Architecture is a visual art, and the buildings speak for themselves.

Julia Morgan

ARCHIVES
Of all national assets, archives are the most precious; they are the gift of one generation to another and the extent of our care of them marks the extent of our civilization.

Arthur Doughty

ARGUE
It is not necessary to understand things in order to argue about them.

Pierre-Augustin Caron de Beaumarchais

Be calm in arguing. Calmness is a great advantage.

George Herbert

ARGUMENT
Arguments derived from probabilities are idle.

Plato

Argument seldom convinces anyone contrary to his inclinations.

Thomas Fuller, MD

If ever there could be a proper time for mere catch arguments, that time is surely not now. In times like the present, men should utter nothing for which they would not willingly be held responsible through time and eternity.

Abraham Lincoln

Don't take the wrong side of an argument just because your opponent has taken the right side.

Baltasar Gracian

Gratuitous violence in argument betrays a conscious weakness of the cause, and is usually a sign of despair.

Junius

Silence is argument carried on by other means.

Che Guevara

There is no such thing as a convincing argument, although every man thinks he has one.

Edgar Watson Howe

The aim of argument, or of discussion, should not be victory, but progress.

Joseph Joubert

The best way I know of to win an argument is to start by being in the right.

Lord Hailsham

An idle reason lessens the weight of the good ones you gave before.

Jonathan Swift

Use soft words and hard arguments.

English proverb

People's minds are changed through observation and not through argument.

Will Rogers

The difficult part in an argument is not to defend one's opinion, but rather to know it.

André Maurois

I never make the mistake of arguing with people for whose opinion I have no respect.

Edward Gibbon

ARISTOCRACY
An aristocracy in a republic is like a chicken whose head has been cut off; it may run about in a lively way, but in fact it is dead.

Nancy Freeman-Mitford

ARITHMETIC
"Reeling and Writhing, of course, to begin with," the Mock Turtle replied, "And the different branches of arithmetic – Ambition, Distraction, Uglification and Derision."

Lewis Carroll

What would life be without arithmetic, but a scene of horrors?

Sydney Smith

ARMAGEDDON
Jonathan Miller: "When will it be, this end of which you have spoken?" Peter Cook: "In about 30 seconds time, according to the ancient pyramidic scrolls and my Ingersoll watch. ..." (Half a minute later): "Well, it's not quite the conflagration I'd been banking on. Never mind, lads, same time tomorrow – we must get a winner one day."

ARMED
Among other evils which being unarmed brings you, it causes you to be despised.

Niccolò Machiavelli

ARMIES
When armies are mobilized and issues joined, the man who is sorry over the fact will win.

Lao-Tse

Where great armies pass are calamitous years.

Lao-Tse

And here is the lesson I learned in the army. If you want to do a thing badly, you have to work at it as though you want to do it well.

Peter Ustinov

ARMOUR
The best armour is to keep out of range.

Italian proverb

ARROGANCE

Arrogance is still the occupational disease of rulers.

Walter Elliott

ART

Art is made by the alone for the alone.

Luis Barragán

Art for art's sake makes no more sense than gin for gin's sake.

W. Somerset Maugham

Interpretation is the revenge of the intellect upon art.

Susan Sontag

Art is the lie that enables us to realize the truth.

Pablo Picasso

There is nothing new in art except talent.

Anton Chekhov

Art is a revolt against fate.

André Malraux

A work of art is above all an adventure of the mind.

Eugène Ionesco

Bad art is a great deal worse than no art at all.

Oscar Wilde

If people only knew as much about painting as I do, they would never buy my pictures.

Edwin Landseer

Art is long and life is short; let us at least do something before we die.

William Morris

Half of art is knowing when to stop.

Arthur William Radford

Art is like a border of flowers along the course of civilization.

Lincoln Steffens

Art is either plagiarism or revolution.

Paul Gauguin

Without art, the crudeness of reality would make the world unbearable.

George Bernard Shaw

Art is on the side of the oppressed. ... For, if art is freedom of the spirit, how can it exist within the oppressors?

Nadine Gordimer

Art happens – no hovel is safe from it, no prince may depend upon it, the vastest intelligence cannot bring it about.

James McNeill Whistler

Art is the only work open to people who can't get along with others and still want to be special.

Alasdair Gray

What I detest most of all in the arts, what sets me on edge, is the ingenious, the clever. That is not at all the same as bad taste, which is good quality gone astray.

Gustave Flaubert

Art is I, Science is we.

Claude Bernard

Great is the art of beginning, but greater the art is of ending.
Henry Wadsworth Longfellow

Art is making something out of nothing and selling it.
Frank Zappa

Art is vice. You don't marry it legitimately, you rape it.
Edgar Dégas

Art does not reproduce the visible; rather it makes visible.
Paul Klee

Art advances between two chasms, which are frivolity and propaganda.
Albert Camus

Art is not a special sauce applied to ordinary cooking; it is the cooking itself if it is good.
W.R. Lethaby

Popular art is normally decried as vulgar by the cultivated people of its time; then it loses favour with its original audience as a new generation grows up; then it begins to merge into the softer lighting of "quaint," and cultivated people become interested in it, and finally it begins to take on the archaic dignity of the primitive.
Northrop Frye

Art is the terms of an armistice signed with fate.
Bernard DeVoto

Art is too serious to be taken seriously.
Ad Reinhardt

Through art we express our conception of what nature is not.
Pablo Picasso

Art washes away from the soul the dust of everyday life.
Pablo Picasso

In art and dream may you proceed with abandon. In life may you proceed with balance and stealth.
Patti Smith

Art has two constant, unending concerns: It always meditates on death and thus always creates life.
Boris Pasternak

Art is the tree of life. Science is the tree of death.
William Blake

I am curious to know what would happen if art were suddenly seen for what it is, namely, exact information on how to rearrange one's psyche in order to anticipate the next blow from our extended faculties.
Marshall McLuhan

In the end, art is small beer. The really serious things in life are earning one's living so as not to be a parasite and loving one's neighbour.
W.H. Auden

Art is not a handicraft; it is the transmission of feeling the artist has experienced.
Leo Tolstoy

One must not always think that feeling is everything. Art is nothing without form.

Gustave Flaubert

In art the best is good enough.

Johann Wolfgang von Goethe

Art is the only way to run away without leaving home.

Twyla Tharp

One's art goes as far and as deep as one's love goes.

Andrew Wyeth

Art is science made clear.

Jean Cocteau

In the vaunted works of Art/The master-stroke is Nature's part.

Ralph Waldo Emerson

Art comes to you proposing frankly to give nothing but the highest quality to your moments as they pass.

Walter Pater

ARTIFICE

Customary use of artifice is the sign of a small mind, and it almost always happens that he who uses it to cover one spot uncovers himself in another.

François, duc de La Rochefoucauld

ARTIFICIAL

The first duty in life is to be as artificial as possible. What the second duty is no one has yet discovered.

Oscar Wilde

ARTISTIC TEMPERAMENT

The artistic temperament is a disease that affects amateurs.

G.K. Chesterton

ARTISTS

Bad artists always admire each other's work.

Oscar Wilde

An artist must be a reactionary. He has to stand out against the tenor of the age and not go flopping along.

Evelyn Waugh

The ordinary man puts up a struggle against all that is not himself, whereas it is against himself, in a limited but all-essential field, that the artist has to battle.

André Malraux

Suffering is the main component of the artistic experience.

Samuel Beckett

No artist wants to be "understood." If he's "understood," he feels superficial. What an artist wants is not to be misunderstood.

Ned Rorem

An artist doesn't necessarily have deeper feelings than other people, but he can express these feelings.

Ned Rorem

An artist should be fit for the best society and keep out of it.

John Ruskin

The artist is a receptacle for emotions that come from all over the place: from the sky, from the earth, from a scrap of paper, from a passing shape, from a spider's web.

Pablo Picasso

The musician, the painter, the poet are, in a larger sense, no greater artists than the man of commerce.

W.S. Maverick

An artist is someone who produces things that people don't need to have but that he (for some reason) thinks it would be a good idea to give them.

Andy Warhol

The painter who is content with the praise of the world for what does not satisfy himself, is not an artist, but an artisan.

Washington Allston

The artist's egoism is outrageous. It must be: he is by nature a solipsist and the world exists only for him to exercise upon it his powers of creation.

W. Somerset Maugham

Too many of the artists of Wales spend too much time about the position of the artists of Wales. There is only one position for an artist anywhere: and that is upright.

Dylan Thomas

Every artist writes his own autobiography.

Havelock Ellis

An intellectual is a man who says a simple thing in a difficult way; an artist is a man who says a difficult thing in a simple way.

Charles Bukowski

Good artists exist simply in what they make, and consequently are perfectly uninteresting in what they are.

Oscar Wilde

Never trust the artist. Trust the tale.

D.H. Lawrence

No artist has ethical sympathies.

Oscar Wilde

An artist is his own fault.

John O'Hara

A good artist should be isolated. If he isn't isolated, something is wrong.

Orson Welles

The difference between a bad artist and a good artist is, that the bad artist seems to copy a great deal, the good one *does* copy a great deal.

William Blake

It seems likely that many of the young who don't wait for others to call them artists, but simply announce that they are, don't have the patience to make art.

Pauline Kael

I am not an adventurer by choice, but by fate.

Vincent van Gogh

An artist is a person who thinks more than there is to think, feels more than there is to feel, and sees more than there is to see.

John Oliver Hobbes

The torpid artist seeks inspiration at any cost, by virtue or by vice, by friend or fiend, by prayer or by wine.
Ralph Waldo Emerson

Every artist dips his brush in his own soul, and paints his own nature into his pictures.
Henry Ward Beecher

Only a born artist can endure the labour of becoming one.
Comtesse Diane

To admire an artist, you should not know him personally.
Jacinto Benavente

The little dissatisfaction which every artist feels at the completion of a work forms the germ of a new work.
Berthold Auerbach

ASK

Ask a lot, but take what's offered.
Russian proverb

We never reflect how pleasant it is to ask for nothing
Seneca

If there is something to gain and nothing to lose by asking, by all means ask!
W. Clement Stone

Oh, Jerry, don't let's ask for the stars – we have the moon.
Casey Robinson

Better ask twice than lose your way once.
Danish proverb

ASPIRATIONS

You aspire to great things? Begin with little ones.
St. Augustine

Normal is not something to aspire to, it's something to get away from.
Jodie Foster

Most of us who aspire to be tops in our fields don't really consider the amount of work required to stay tops.
Althea Gibson

Ultimately, the only power to which man should aspire is that which he exercises over himself.
Elie Wiesel

ASS

With the help of a surgeon, he might yet recover, and prove an ass.
William Shakespeare

ASSESSMENT

Look not every man on his own things, but every man also on the things of others.
Philippians 2:4

ASSISTANCE

In 1784 Benjamin Franklin wrote the following letter to a man named Benjamin Webb:

Dear Sir: Your situation grieves me and I send you herewith a banknote for ten louis d'or. I do not pretend to give such a sum; I only lend it to you. When you shall return to your country, you cannot fail of getting into some business that will in time enable you to pay all your debts.

In that case, when you meet with another honest man in similar distress, you must pay me by lending the sum to him, enjoining him to discharge the debt by a like operation when he shall be able and shall meet with such another opportunity.

I hope it may thus go through many hands before it meets with a knave that will stop its progress. This is a trick of mine for doing a deal of good with a little money. I am not rich enough to afford much in good works, and so am obliged to be cunning and make the most of a little.

With best wishes for your future prosperity, I am, dear sir, your most obedient servant.

B. Franklin

ASSISTANT
You're no good unless you are a good assistant – and if you are, you're too good to be an assistant.

Martin H. Fischer

ASSOCIATION
He that lies with dogs rises with fleas.

Proverb

ASSUMPTIONS
Assumptions are the termites of relationships.

Henry Winkler

Most human beings have an almost infinite capacity for taking things for granted.

Aldous Huxley

We must never assume that which is incapable of proof.

George Henry Lewes

What a man believes may be ascertained, not from his creed, but from the assumptions on which he habitually acts.

George Bernard Shaw

That life is worth living is the most necessary of assumptions, and were it not assumed, the most impossible of conclusions.

George Santayana

ASSURANCE
It generally happens that assurance keeps an even pace with ability.

Samuel Johnson

ASTROLOGY
Astrology proves just one scientific fact: there's one born every minute.

Patrick Moore

ASTRONOMY
Astronomy teaches us the correct use of the sun and the planets.

Stephen Leacock

To expect us to feel "humble" in the presence of astronomical dimensions merely because they are big, is a kind of cosmic snobbery ... what is significant is mind.

Herbert Samuel

ATHEISM
Atheism is a non-prophet organization.

George Carlin

ATHEIST
An atheist is a man who has no
invisible means of support.

John Buchan

To you, I'm an atheist; to God, I'm
the Loyal Opposition.

Woody Allen

I once wanted to become an atheist, but I gave up – they have no
holidays.

Henny Youngman

Whoever considers the study of
anatomy can never be an atheist.

Lord Herbert

ATMOSPHERE
You may be able to fool the voters,
but not the atmosphere.

Donella Meadows

ATOMS
Nations that split hairs shouldn't
split atoms.

John A. Lincoln

ATROCITIES
Those who can make you believe
absurdities can make you commit
atrocities.

Voltaire

ATTACK
The silent dog is the first to bite.

German proverb

I fear all I have done is awaken a
sleeping giant.

Admiral Isoroku Yamamoto

When a dog runs at you, whistle
for him.

Henry David Thoreau

ATTENTION
We despise no source that can pay
us a pleasing attention.

Mark Twain

ATTENTION SPAN
He has the attention span of a
lightning bolt.

Robert Redford

ATTITUDE
He's a man who, when he smells
flowers, looks around for coffins.

John le Carré

Is your cucumber bitter? Throw
it away. Are there briars in your
path? Turn aside. That is enough.
Do not go on to say, "Why were
things of this sort ever brought
into the world?"

Marcus Aurelius

Nothing in life is so exhilarating as
to be shot at without result.

Winston Churchill

Give me the ready hand rather
than the ready tongue.

Giuseppe Garibaldi

You can't teach an old dogma new
tricks.

Dorothy Parker

Man's attitude toward great qualities in others is often the same as toward high mountains – he admires them, but prefers to walk around them.

Moritz Saphir

Each day the world is born anew, for him who takes it rightly.

James Russell Lowell

About one-fifth of the people are against everything, all the time.

Robert F. Kennedy

Sour grapes can ne'er make sweet wine.

Thomas Fuller, MD

There are no menial jobs, only menial attitudes.

William Bennett

If you can't change your fate, change your attitude.

Chinese proverb

Attitudes are contagious. Are yours worth catching?

Anonymous

Haughty, silent faces should not deceive us: these are the timid ones.

Jules Renard

And remember, no matter where you go, there you are.

Buckaroo Banzai

You've got to take the bitter with the sour.

Samuel Goldwyn

Two men look through the same bars; one sees mud and one sees the stars.

Frederick Langbridge

Only the game fish swims upstream. But the sensible fish swims down.

Ogden Nash

You've got to accentuate the positive, eliminate the negative.

Johnny Mercer

Nothing seems really to matter; that's the charm of it.

Kenneth Grahame

Always look on the bright side of life. Always look on the light side of life.

Eric Idle

It's not what they take away from you that counts. It's what you do with what you have left.

Hubert H. Humphrey

There are two types of people: those who come into a room and say "Well, here I am," and those who come and say "Ah, there you are."

Frederick Collins

I try to avoid looking backward and keep looking forward.

Charlotte Brontë

The greatest discovery of any generation is that a human being can alter his life by altering his attitude.

William James

ATTRACTION
If people don't want to come, nothing will stop them.

Sol Hurok

AUDIENCES
If all the world's a stage, and all the men and women merely players, where do all the audiences come from?

Denis Norden

To have great poets, there must be great audiences too.

Walt Whitman

AUDITOR
An auditor is the guy who comes in after the battle to bayonet the wounded.

Anonymous

AUTHORS
What I like in a good author is not what he says, but what he whispers.

Logan Pearsall Smith

What no wife of an author can understand is that he's working when he's staring out of the window.

Burton Rascoe

AUTOBIOGRAPHIES
Autobiographies ought to begin with chapter two.

Ellery Sedgwick

AUTOCRAT
I shall be an autocrat, that's my trade; and the good Lord will forgive me, that's his.

Catherine the Great

AUTOMOBILE
The automobile changed our dress, manners, social customs, vacation habits, the shape of our cities, consumer purchasing patterns, common tastes, and positions in intercourse.

John Keats
(The Insolent Chariots, 1958)

AUTUMN
The leaves fall early this autumn, in wind.

Ezra Pound

A moral character is attached to autumnal scenes. The flowers fading like our hopes, the leaves falling like our years, the clouds fleeting like our illusions, the light diminishing like our intelligence, the sun growing colder like our affections, the rivers becoming frozen like our lives – all bear secret relations to our destinies.

François-René de Chateaubriand

AVAILABILITY
When something is too easily available … we often don't want it. Who likes to eat in an empty restaurant?

Robert Levine

AVARICE
When all other sins are old, avarice is still young.

French proverb

Avarice, the spur of industry.

David Hume

Poverty is in want of much, but avarice is in want of everything.

Publilius Syrus

AVERAGE
Never try to walk across a river because it has an average depth of four feet.

Martin Friedman

The overwhelming majority of people have more than the average (mean) number of legs.

E. Grebenik

I abhor averages. I like the individual case. A man may have six meals one day and none the next, making an average of three meals per day, but that is not a good way to live.

Louis D. Brandeis

AVOIDANCE
He can best avoid a snare who knows how to set one.

Publilius Syrus

It is easier to stay out than get out.

Mark Twain

Three things it is best to avoid: a strange dog, a flood, and a man who thinks he is wise.

Welsh saying

AWAKE
Better to get up late and be wide awake then, than to get up early and be asleep all day.

Matthew Henry

The average, healthy, well-adjusted adult gets up at seven-thirty in the morning feeling just plain terrible.

Jean Kerr

AWARDS
My career must be slipping. This is the first time I've been available to pick up an award.

Michael Caine

Awards are like piles. Sooner or later every bum gets one.

Maureen Lipman

AWARENESS
Only that day dawns to which we are awake.

Henry David Thoreau

Let us not look back in anger or forward in fear, but around in awareness.

James Thurber

If you don't know the score, you can be pretty certain that you're behind.

Francis O'Walsh

AWAY
Nothing ever goes away.

Barry Commoner

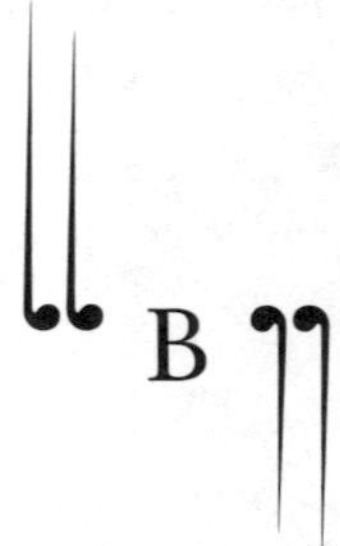

BABIES
Babies are such a nice way to start people.

Don Herold

A baby is born with the need to be loved and never outgrows it.

Frank A. Clark

How pleasant it is to see a human countenance which cannot be insincere!

Sophia Hawthorne

Babies are always more trouble than you thought – and more wonderful.

Charles Osgood

It is the nature of babies to be in bliss.

Deepak Chopra

BACHELORS
Bachelors know more about women than married men; if they didn't, they'd be married too.

H.L. Mencken

BACK DOOR
We often get in quicker by the back door than by the front.

Napoleon Bonaparte

BACKWARDS
A step backwards is a step in the right direction if you are facing the wrong way to begin with.

Jamie Smith

BAD APPLES
Nineteen fresh apples do not make a single rotten apple fresh.

Gunnar Myrdal

BAD CAUSES
He that hath the worst cause makes the most noise.

Thomas Fuller, MD

BAD COMPANY
Bad company ruins good morals.

I Corinthians 15:33

BAD DAYS
Bad is never good until something worse happens.

Danish proverb

Some mornings, it's just not worth chewing through the leather straps.
Emo Phillips

There are days when it takes all you've got just to keep up with the losers.

Robert Orben

BAD GUYS
The thing about bad guys is that they have the biggest bosomed blondes, they have great clothes and cars, and get great death scenes.

Eric Roberts

BAD HABITS
Ill habits gather by unseen degrees,/ As brooks make rivers, rivers run into seas.

John Dryden

BAD LANGUAGE
Among the middle class, especially among its more intellectually inclined members, impurity of language is taken as a symbol of purity of political and social sentiment. It is democratic to swear, and the more one does it, the more democratic one is. The frequent use of bad language demonstrates that one does not aim to set oneself apart from what is assumed to be the great mass of oppressed and suffering humanity. The use of bad language is thus – by implication – an act of compassion and solidarity.
Dr Theodore Dalrymple

BAD LAW
The best way to get a bad law repealed is to enforce it strictly.
Abraham Lincoln

BAD MEN
When bad men combine, the good must associate; else they will fall one by one, an unpitied sacrifice in a contemptible struggle.
Edmund Burke

BAD NEWS
Bad news travels fast and far.
Plutarch

BAFFLEGAB
Gay marriage is something that should be between a man and a woman.
Arnold Schwarzenegger

Having committed political suicide the [British] Conservative Party is now living to regret it.
Chris Patten

Reports that say that something hasn't happened are always interesting to me, because as we know, there are known knowns; there are things we know we know. We also know there are known unknowns; that is to say we know there are some things we do not know. But there are are also unknown unknowns – the ones we don't know we don't know.
Donald Rumsfeld

BALANCE
There are many in this old world of ours who hold that things break about even for all of us. I have observed, for example, that we all get the same amount of ice. The rich get it in the summertime and the poor get it in the winter.

Bat Masterson

BALDNESS
Baldness may indicate masculinity, but it diminishes one's opportunity to find out.

Cedric Hardwicke

BALL
The real business of a ball is to look out for a wife, to look after a wife, or to look after somebody else's wife.

R.S. Surtees

BALONEY
No matter how thin you slice it, it's still baloney.

Alfred E. Smith

BANALITY
Today, thanks to technical progress, the radio and television, to which we devote so many of the leisure hours once spent listening to parlour chatter and parlour music, have succeeded in lifting the manufacture of banality out of the sphere of handicraft and placed it in that of a major industry.

Nathalie Sarraute

Banality in the mouth of a failed businessman or an unpublished novelist sounds banal; in the mouth of David Rockefeller or Philip Roth the same words acquire the weight of oracle.

Lewis Lapham

BANISHMENT
Go, and never darken my towels again.

Groucho Marx

BARBARIANS
What will become of us without the barbarians? Those people were a kind of solution.

Constantine Cavafy

BARBER
The average barber now makes more money per word than the average writer.

Lane Olinghouse

A prating barber asked Archelaus how he would be trimmed. He answered, "In silence."

Plutarch

BARGAINS
A bargain is anything a customer thinks a store is losing money on.

Kin Hubbard

The bargain that yields mutual satisfaction is the only one that is apt to be repeated.

B.C. Forbes

Bargain: something you can't use at a price you can't resist.

Franklin P. Jones

BARTENDER

By the time a bartender knows what drink a man will have before he orders, there is little else about him worth knowing.

Don Marquis

BASEBALL

Baseball is 90 per cent mental. The other half is physical.

Yogi Berra

People ask me what I do in winter when there's no baseball. I'll tell you what I do. I stare out the window and wait for spring.

Rogers Hornsby

Baseball is religion without the mischief.

Thomas Boswell

Baseball is like church. Many attend, few understand.

Leo Durocher

BATTERIES

I bought some batteries, but they weren't included.

Steven Wright

BATTLES

You may have to fight a battle more than once to win it.

Margaret Thatcher

BEAUTY

Variety of uniformities makes complete beauty.

Sir Christopher Wren

The perception of beauty is a moral test.

Henry David Thoreau

The Sun would gain nothing in beauty by appearing but once a year.

Tom MacInnes

The test of Beauty is whether it can survive close knowledge.

Marjorie Kinnan Rawlings

Beauty can pierce one like a pain.

Thomas Mann

What is beautiful is moral, that is all there is to it.

Gustave Flaubert

The beauty of the world has two edges, one of laughter, one of anguish, cutting the heart asunder.

Virginia Woolf

At some point in life, the world's beauty becomes enough. You don't need to photograph, paint or even remember it. It is enough.

Toni Morrison

"Beauty is truth, truth beauty," that is all/Ye know on earth, and all ye need to know.

John Keats

Love built on beauty, soon as beauty, dies.

John Donne

Beauty is often worse than wine; intoxicating both the holder and the beholder.

Johann Zimmermann

The problem with beauty is that it's like being born rich and getting poorer.

Joan Collins

There is no excellent beauty that hath not some strangeness in the proportion.

Francis Bacon

That which is striking and beautiful is not always good; but that which is good is always beautiful.

Ninon de l'Enclos

Everything has beauty, though not everyone sees it.

Confucius

No woman can be a beauty without a fortune.

George Farquhar

BED
No matter how big or soft or warm your bed is, you still have to get out of it.

Grace Slick

I rise from bed the first thing in the morning not because I am dissatisfied with it, but because I cannot carry it with me during the day.

Bill Nye

BEEF
The beef industry has contributed to more American deaths than all the wars of this century, all natural disasters, and all automobile accidents combined.

Dr Neal Barnard

BEER
Beer is living proof that God loves us and wants us to be happy.

Benjamin Franklin

24 hours in a day, 24 beers in a case. Coincidence? I think not.

Steven Wright

To some, it's a six-pack, to me it's a Support Group. Salvation in a can!

Dave Howell

Without question, the greatest invention in the history of mankind is beer. Oh, I grant you that the wheel was also a fine invention, but the wheel does not go nearly as well with pizza.

Dave Barry

BEETHOVEN
If anybody has conducted a Beethoven performance, and doesn't have to go to an osteopath, then there's something wrong.

Simon Rattle

BEETLES
The Creator, if he exists, has a special preference for beetles.

J.B.S. Haldane

BEGGARS
There are people who can never forgive a beggar for their not having given him anything.

Karl Kraus

BEGINNING
The beginning is the most important part of any work, especially in the case of a young and tender

thing: for that is the time at which the character is being formed and the desired impression is more readily taken.

Plato

A good beginning makes a good ending.

Anonymous

You begin well in nothing except you end well.

Thomas Fuller, MD

I start where the last man left off.
Thomas Edison

Thus out of small beginnings greater things have been produced.
William Bradford

A hard beginning maketh a good ending.

John Heywood

Everything has been said before, but because nobody listens we have to keep going back and beginning all over again.

André Gide

Now this is not the end. It is not even the beginning of the end. But it is, perhaps, the end of the beginning.

Winston Churchill

Begin at the beginning … and go on til you come to the end: then stop.

Lewis Carroll

What we call the beginning is often the end/And to make an end is to make a beginning/The end is where we start from.

T.S. Eliot

BEHAVIOUR
Never descend to the ways of those above you.

George Mallaby

Do not do unto others as you would that they should do unto you. Their tastes may not be the same.

George Bernard Shaw

Men and nations behave wisely once they have exhausted all other alternatives.

Abba Eban

If you scatter thorns, don't go barefoot.

Italian proverb

With so many roosters crowing, the sun never comes up.

Italian proverb

When one is on one's best behaviour, one isn't always at one's best.
Alan Bennett

Everyone would like to behave like a pagan, with everyone else behaving like a Christian.

Albert Camus

Perfect behaviour is born of complete indifference.

Cesare Pavese

Very often the only way to get a quality in reality is to start behaving as if you had it already.

C.S. Lewis

There's no map to human behaviour.

Björk

BEINGS
It should not be believed that all things exist for the sake of man. On the contrary, all the other beings too have been intended for their own sake and not for the sake of someone else.

Moses Maimonides

BELIEF
One person with a belief is equal to a force of ninety-nine who have only interests.

John Stuart Mill

I can believe anything, provided it is incredible.

Oscar Wilde

Man can believe the impossible but man can never believe the improbable.

Oscar Wilde

We are inclined to believe those we do not know, because they have never deceived us.

Samuel Johnson

The brute necessity of believing something so long as life lasts does not justify anything in particular.

George Santayana

There is a great deal of difference in believing something still, and believing it again.

W.H. Auden

I would never die for my beliefs because I might be wrong.

Bertrand Russell

They can conquer who believe they can.

Virgil

Man is what he believes.

Anton Chekhov

Some things have to be believed to be seen.

Ralph Hodgson

To accomplish great things, we must not only act, but also dream; not only plan, but also believe.

Anatole France

So we have the strange phenomenon, as Kant assures us, of a mind believing with all its strength in the real presence of a set of things of no one of which it can form any notion whatsoever.

William James

Everyone believes easily whatever they fear or desire.

Jean de La Fontaine

People seldom do what they believe in. They do what is convenient, then repent.

Bob Dylan

You have to believe that the universe will provide.

Steve Crosby

Unless you believe, you will not understand.

St Augustine

BELIEF (UNWARRANTED)
Nothing is so firmly believed as that which we least know.

Michel de Montaigne

If there were a verb meaning "to believe falsely," it would not have any significant first person, present indicative.

Ludwig Wittgenstein

If you believe everything you read, better not read.

Japanese proverb

Everything one does enough of eventually generates its own interest and one then begins to believe in it.

Alan Dunn

Men are nearly always willing to believe what they wish.

Julius Caesar

People everywhere enjoy believing things that they know are not true. It spares them the ordeal of thinking for themselves and taking responsibility for what they know.

Brooks Atkinson

You spend your whole life believing that you're on the right track, only to discover that you're on the wrong train.

Anonymous

It is undesirable to believe a proposition when there is no ground whatsoever for supposing it to be true.

Bertrand Russell

We are all captives of the picture in our head – our belief that the world we have experienced is the world that really exists.

Walter Lippmann

BELLY

The belly is ungrateful – it always forgets we already gave it something.

Russian proverb

BEQUESTS

There are two lasting bequests we can give our children. One is roots. The other is wings.

Hodding Carter, Jr

BEST

There is always a best way of doing everything, if it be to boil an egg.

Ralph Waldo Emerson

The best is the enemy of the good.

Voltaire

You have got to do the best you can with what you've got.

C. Walden and C. McCarty

I am easily satisfied with the very best.

Winston Churchill

The best is the best, though a hundred judges have declared it so.

Sir Arthur Quiller-Couch

He who has done his best for his own time has lived for all times.

Friedrich von Schiller

BETRAYAL

Everyone has his own way of being betrayed.

Marcel Proust

Is it possible to succeed without any act of betrayal?

Jean Renoir

When you betray somebody else, you also betray yourself.

Isaac Bashevis Singer

BETTER
Any time things appear to be going better, you have overlooked something.

Anonymous

BETTING
Betting and such sports are only the stunted and twisted shapes of the original instinct of man for adventure and romance.

G.K. Chesterton

The race may not always be to the swift nor the victory to the strong, but that's how you bet.

Damon Runyon

BIBLE
The Bible tells us to love our neighbours, and also to love our enemies; probably because they are generally the same people.

G.K. Chesterton

BIBLICAL TABLOID HEADLINES (from "The Challenge" *Globe and Mail* 21 August and 4 September, 1993)

Job Outlook Dismal

Man Smites Og: Bashan King Dies in Battle with Israelites

Mole Suspected in Apostle Supper Club

Salt Futures Dive on News of Lot's Wife

Shortage of Galilean Fishermen Blamed on Itinerant Preacher

Pork Futures Soar in Wake of Gadarene Calamity

Dieticians Claim Loaves and Fishes Not a Balanced Meal

Social Contract Talks in 35th Day; Eight of Ten Points Agreed, but Adultery and Sabbath Shopping Could Be Deal Breakers, Says Source Close to Moses

Red Sea Parted, Bridge Plans on Hold

God Confirms Change to Six-day Work Week

More Troubles at Tower, Management Says Union "Doesn't Speak our Language"

Pharaoh Sets up Insect Task Force After Worst Locust Plague This Century

Innovative Rib Surgery Ensures Gender Balance

Pharaoh Slams Deity's "Pro-Israeli bias" as Threat to Mideast Peace Process

Man Brought Back to Life Sues Village Healer: "I Was Better Off Dead."

Galilean Council Initiates Pollution Probe After Man Walks on Water

Rescued Sheep Protests, "I Wasn't Lost!"

Get Haircut or Go: Delilah Issues Ultimatum

Methuselah Dead at 969; Sprightly Patriarch Attributed Longevity to Regular Begetting

Depletion of Fish Stocks Feared as Record Catch on Galilee Swamps Boats

God Creates Heavens; Earth Still Awaiting Permit

Solomon Renders Split Decision in Custody Battle

Four Horsemen Heading for Showdown, Psychic Predicts

Grieving Family Urges Ban on Slings for Minor

See page 4 for Revised Red Sea Tide Tables

One-quarter of World's Population Wiped out in Senseless Killing of Brother

Jonah Swears off Seafood; The Inside Story

Miracle at Wedding; Wine Merchants Protest

Thomas Casts Doubt on Reincarnation Theory

Correction: Lazarus Obituary

Social Services Questions Abraham: Was Sacrifice Threat Emotional Child Abuse?

David 1, Giants 0

Wine Was Watery, Say Canaan Wedding Guests

Witness Claims Lazarus Was Only Holding His Breath

Ark Offers Family Mystery Cruises

Burning Bush; Arson Suspected

Ezekiel Held for Psychiatric Examination

Salome Unveiling Causes Heads to Roll

Pests Found in Apple Trees Again, Garden Closed Until Further Notice

Three Wise Men to Pay Customs Duty on Imports

Angry Captive Destroys Philistine Temple; Samson "Fit to be Tied" Witnesses Say

Rains to Stop Soon, says Government Meteorologist; Noah's Prediction "Pure Hokum"

King Nebuchadnezzar Sues Furnace-Makers After Three Survive

Absalom Not Wearing Protective Headgear at Time of Riding Accident

No Plants Registered for Voyage; Noah Confronts Green Party

David–Bathsheba Love Talk Taped by Mossad

Lazarus Says Tomb Now Surplus

Unusual Same-Sex Stalking Charges Laid by Naomi Against Ruth

Local Prophet Before Human Rights Tribunal, Hires Male Disciples Only

Animal-rights Activists Demand End to Testing of Demons on Pigs

Gadarene Pig Farmer Sues Jesus for Loss of Herd

Proposed Environmental Assessment Delays Moses's Sea Crossing

Good-time Girl was Enemy Agent, Jericho Survivor Charges

OPEC Nations Debate Ramifications of "Miracle" Eight-day Oil

Mess of Pottage Scam Uncovered

Camel Stuck in Eye of Needle in Bizarre Religious Ritual

Ten New Laws Written in Stone; No Amending Formula, Says Moses

Fish Lands Man

Philistines Demand David be Tested for Steroids

Money-changers Demand Better Security

Judge Orders Ban on Publication of Evidence in Case of Susannah v. Elders

"Let There Be light" Decree Boosts Sun-block Stocks

Who Turned On the Lights? Creation Enters Second Day

Carpenter Won't Fix Tables Damaged by Errant Son

Noah Still Dubious; Plans Ark II

Gabriel Courier Co. Delivers News of Miracle Baby to Childless Couple

Eden Apple Co. Opens "Pick Your Own" Orchard

Police Not Releasing Name of Young Offender in "Goliath" Slaying

Sodom, Gomorrah See Record Temperatures

Canadian Plows to Aid Cleanup of Record Fall of Manna from Heaven

BICYCLE

Get a bicycle. You will not regret it. If you live.

Mark Twain

The bicycle, the bicycle surely, should always be the vehicle of novelists and poets.

Christopher Morley

Every time I see an adult on a bicycle, I no longer despair for the future of the human race.

H.G. Wells

BIGAMY

Bigamy is having one wife/husband too many. Monogamy is the same.

Oscar Wilde

BIGOTS

How it infuriates a bigot when he is forced to drag out his dark convictions!

Logan Pearsall Smith

We call a man a bigot or a slave of dogma because he is a thinker who has thought thoroughly and to a definite end.

G.K. Chesterton

BIOGRAPHER

Then there is my noble and biographical friend who has added a new terror to death.

Sir Charles Wetherell
(said of Lord Campbell)

BIOGRAPHY

Biography is higher gossip.

Robert Winder

Biography lends to death a new terror.

Oscar Wilde

There is properly no history, only biography.

Ralph Waldo Emerson

Biography is a very definite religion bounded on the north by history, on the south by fiction, on the east by obituary, and on the west by tedium.

Philip Guedalla

BIRDS

Sir, we are a nest of singing birds.

Samuel Johnson

I hope you love birds, too. It is economical. It saves going to heaven.

Emily Dickinson

BIRTH

There is no cure for birth and death save to enjoy the interval.

George Santayana

I was born below par to the extent of two whiskies.

Charles Edward Montague

Man's main task in life is to give birth to himself.

Erich Fromm

Birth was the death of him.

Samuel Beckett

BIRTH CONTROL

Birth control is avoiding the issue.

Graffito

BIRTHDAY PRESENTS

If one doesn't get birthday presents, it can remobilize very painfully the persecutory anxiety which usually follows birth.

Henry Reed

BIRTHPLACE

The land where you were born lies lighter to your bones.

Emily G. Murphy

BISEXUALITY

Bisexuality doubles your chance of getting a date for Saturday night.

Woody Allen

BITE

The man recover'd of the bite;/The dog it was that died.

Oliver Goldsmith

BLACKMAIL

There is nothing more disgusting than blackmail, except giving in to blackmail.

Jean-Paul Desbiens

BLAME
Blame someone else and get on with your life.

Alan Woods

Blame is most readily averted by being so much like everybody else that one passes unnoticed.

John Dewey

BLASPHEMY
There is only one blasphemy, and that is the refusal to experience joy.

Paul Rudnick

BLIND
A blind man who sees is better than a seeing man who is blind.

Persian proverb

I have only one eye – I have a right to be blind sometimes: … I really do not see the signal.

Horatio, Lord Nelson

When the blind lead the blind, they will both fall into the water.

Chinese proverb

In the country of the blind, the one-eyed man is lucky to escape with his life.

Celia Green

BLUNDERS
The pain others give passes away in their later kindness, but that of our own blunders, especially when they hurt our vanity, never passes away.

William Butler Yeats

BLUSH
Man is the only animal that blushes – or has reason to.

Mark Twain

BOAST
If I seem to boast more than is becoming, my excuse is that I brag for humanity rather than for myself.

Henry David Thoreau

BODY
Controversial U.S. dancer Isadora Duncan (1878–1927): "Imagine a child with my body and your brain." Outspoken Irish playwright George Bernard Shaw (1856–1950): "Yes, but suppose it had my body and your brain."

A man possesses nothing certainly save a brief loan of his own body, yet the body of man is capable of much curious pleasure.

James Branch Cabell

We should conduct ourselves not as if we ought to live for the body, but as if we could not live without it.

Seneca

Your body is not the real you. It's just the meat you live in. I like that: It means that the real me doesn't really have a humongous butt.

Jessica Zafra

BOLDNESS
Boldness, and again boldness, and always boldness!

Georges Danton

BOMB

Then Russia got the bomb, but that's OK/'Cause the balance of power's maintained that way.

Tom Lehrer

The greatest danger of bombs is in the explosion of stupidity that they provoke.

Octave Mirbeau

BOOKS

There can hardly be a stranger commodity in the world than books. Printed by people who don't understand them; sold by people who don't understand them; bound, criticized and read by people who don't understand them; and now even written by people who don't understand them.

Georg Christoph Lichtenberg

The failure to read good books both enfeebles the vision and strengthens our most fatal tendency – the belief that the here and now is all there is.

Allan Bloom

Books are the carriers of civilization. Without books, history is silent, literature dumb, science crippled, thought and speculation at a standstill.

Barbara Tuchman

Read the best books first, or you may not have a chance to read them all.

Henry David Thoreau

It was books that taught me that the things that tormented me the most were the very things that connected me with all the people who were alive, or who had ever been alive.

James Baldwin

My books are life-affirming; that's why they don't attract the real satanists. It's all in the spirit of romance.

Anne Rice

The reason why so few good books are written is that so few people who can write know anything.

Walter Bagehot

The biggest seller is cookbooks and the second is diet books – how not to eat what you've just learned how to cook.

Andy Rooney

Wherever they burn books they will also, in the end, burn human beings.

Heinrich Heine

"What is the use of a book," thought Alice, "without pictures or conversations?"

Lewis Carroll

The books that help you the most are those that make you think the most. The hardest way of learning is that of easy reading: but a great book that comes from a great thinker is a ship of thought, deep freighted with truth and beauty.

Theodore Parker

Never judge a book by its movie.
J.W. Eagan

Thank you so much for your book.
I shall lose no time in reading it.
Benjamin Disraeli

Wear the old coat and buy the new
book.
Austin Phelps

Long books, when read, are usually over-praised, because the
reader wishes to convince others
and himself that he has not wasted
his time.
E.M. Forster

A book is the greatest interactive
medium of all time. You can under-
line it, write in the margins, fold
down a page, skip ahead. And you
can take it anywhere.
Michael Lynton

To produce a mighty book, you
must choose a mighty theme. No
great and enduring volume can
ever be written on the flea, though
many there be who have tried it.
Herman Melville

Books have the same enemies as
man: fire, moisture, animals, the
weather – and what's inside them.
Paul Valéry

A book full of brilliance imparts
some of it even to its opponents.
Friedrich Nietzsche

A book may be amusing with
numerous errors, or it may be very
dull without a single absurdity.
Oliver Goldsmith

A book is like a garden carried in
the pocket.
Chinese proverb

To have many books and never to
use them is like a child that will
have a candle burning by him all
the while he is asleep.
Henry Peacham

The world of books is the most
remarkable creation of man.
Nothing else that he builds ever
lasts.
Clarence Day

No book is so bad but some good
might be got out of it.
Pliny the Elder

Some books are to be tasted, others
to be swallowed, and some few to
be chewed and digested.
Francis Bacon

Books are like a mirror. If an ass
looks in, you can't expect an angel
to look out.
Arthur Schopenhauer

A book is only excusable so far as
it teaches something.
Voltaire

A book that is shut is but a block.
Proverb

The reason why borrowed books
are so seldom returned to their
owners is that it is much easier to
retain the books than what is in
them.
Michel de Montaigne

Books will speak plain when coun-
sellors blanch.

Francis Bacon

BOOKSTORE
A bookstore is one of the only
pieces of evidence we have that
people are still thinking.

Jerry Seinfeld

BORDERS
Borders are not visible, or religions,
or nationality. This is a great
advantage to mankind.

Yuri Gagarin

BORE
Take your choice: talk about others and be a gossip or talk about
yourself and be a bore.

Laurence J. Peter

It is a sad truth that everyone is a
bore to someone.

Llewellyn Miller

Bores bore each other too; but it
never seems to teach them anything.

Don Marquis

The secret of boring people lies in
telling them everything.

Voltaire

BOREDOM
The man who lets himself be bored
is even more contemptible than the
bore.

Samuel Butler

The effect of boredom on a large
scale in history is underestimated.

It is a main cause of revolutions,
and would soon bring an end to all
the static utopias and the farmyard
civilization of the Fabians.

Dean Inge

It is well-known that evils are alle-
viated by the fact that we bear
them in common. People seem to
regard boredom as one of these
and therefore get together in order
to be bored in common.

Arthur Schopenhauer

Man is the only animal that can be
bored.

Erich Fromm

Perhaps the world's second worst
crime is boredom. The first is being
a bore.

Jean Baudrillard

Ennui has made more gamblers
than avarice, more drunkards than
thirst, and perhaps as many sui-
cides as despair.

Charles Caleb Colton

BORING
Men are boring to women, because
there are only about twelve types
of us, and they know all the keys. I
only know this because I'm the
type they talk to.

Jack Nicholson

BORROWER
A borrower is a man who tries to
live within your means.

Dr O.A. Battista

... The old woman who triumphantly announced that she had borrowed money enough to pay all her debts.

P.L. Lord

BOUNDARY

Boundary, *n*. In political geography, an imaginary line between two nations, separating the imaginary rights of one from the imaginary rights of another.

Ambrose Bierce

BOURGEOIS

"Bourgeois," I observed, "is an epithet which the riff-raff apply to what is respectable, and the aristocracy to what is decent."

Anthony Hope

BOXING

He can run. But he can't hide.

Joe Louis

BOYS

Boys will be boys, and so will a lot of middle-aged men.

Kin Hubbard

BRAGGING

A man has the right to toot his own horn to his heart's content, so long as he stays in his own home, keeps the windows closed and does not make himself obnoxious to his neighbours.

Tiorio

Trumpet in a herd of elephants; crow in the company of cocks; bleat in a flock of goats.

Malay proverb

For God hates utterly / The bray of bragging tongues.

Sophocles

BRAIN

The brain thinks not by adding two and two to make four, but like a sheet of wet paper on which drops of watercolour paints are being splashed, merging into unforeseen configurations.

Guy Claxton

The brain is a wonderful organ. It starts working the moment you get up in the morning, and does not stop until you get into the office.

Robert Frost

The brain never stops thinking. If it has nothing else to do, it thinks of something to think about. Perhaps the question we have to ask is not why we have to dream, but why we have to think all the time.

Anthony Clare

I used to think the brain was the most important organ in the body, until I realized who was telling me that.

Emo Phillips

Brain, *n*. An apparatus with which we think we think.

Ambrose Bierce

The limit on human intelligence up to now has been set by the size of the brain that will pass through the birth canal … but within the next 100 years, I expect we will be able to grow babies outside the human body, so this limitation will be removed. Ultimately, however, increases in the size of the human brain through genetic engineering will come up against the problem that the body's chemical messengers responsible for our mental activity are relatively slow-moving. This means that further increases in the complexity of the brain will be at the expense of speed. We can be quick-witted or very intelligent, but not both.

Stephen Hawking

Only the man who finds everything wrong and expects it to get worse is thought to have a clear brain.

John Kenneth Galbraith

If the human brain were so simple that we could understand it, we would be so simple that we couldn't.

Emerson M. Pugh

No diet will remove all the fat from your body because the brain is entirely fat. Without a brain, you might look good, but all you could do is run for public office.

George Bernard Shaw

Every human brain is born not as a blank tablet (a tabula rasa) waiting to be filled by experience but as an exposed negative waiting to be slipped into developer fluid.

Edward O. Wilson

BRAINS

A good man can be stupid and still be good. But a bad man must have brains – absolutely.

Maxim Gorky

You can grow corn or potatoes, but you cannot grow brains. Brains come hard and they come high.

Sir William Osler

Brains function on a need-to-know basis, and the need-to-know in order to survive on the African plains as hunter-gatherers. It's pure bonus if we manage to understand a bit about relativity and quantum theory as well. I think it's a tremendous privilege that we can understand as much as we can.

Richard Dawkins

We, my Lords, may thank heaven that we have something better than our brains to depend upon.

Lord Chesterfield

The more you use your brain, the more brain you will have to use.

George A. Dorsey

Men can live without air for minutes, without water for weeks, without food for months, and without brains for years.

Unknown

Our brains have evolved to get us out of the rain, find where the berries are and keep us from getting killed. Our brains did not evolve to help us grasp really large numbers or to look at things in a hundred thousand dimensions.

Ronald L. Graham

BRAVERY
It is easy to be brave from a safe distance.

Aesop

True bravery is shown by performing without witnesses what one might be capable of doing before all the world.

François, duc de La Rochefoucauld

But the bravest are surely those who have the clearest vision of what is before them, glory and danger alike, and yet, notwithstanding, go out to meet it.

Thucydides

If you are brave too often, people will come to expect it of you.

Mignon McLaughlin

BRAWN
In the scale of the destinies, brawn will never weigh as much as brain.

James Russell Lowell

BREAKDOWN
One of the symptoms of an approaching nervous breakdown is the belief that one's work is terribly important.

Bertrand Russell

BREAK-OUT
Everybody's always talking about people breaking into houses, but there are more people in the world who want to break out of houses.

Thornton Wilder

BREATH
It's not going to matter how many breaths you took, but how many moments took your breath away.

Xiong Sheng

BREVITY
The fewer the words, the better the prayer.

Martin Luther

A multitude of words is no proof of a prudent mind.

Thales

Say all you have to say in the fewest possible words, or your reader will be sure to skip them; and in the plainest possible words, or he will certainly misunderstand them.

John Ruskin

BRIBES
They wouldn't be sufficiently degraded in their own estimation unless they were insulted by a very considerable bribe.

W.S. Gilbert

Never underestimate the effectiveness of a straight cash bribe.

Claud Cockburn

BRIDGE
One peek is worth two finesses.

Anonymous

More crimes are committed in the play of the trump suit in one session than are recorded in one day in the average city of under 50,000 population.

Alfred Sheinwold

Anyone can become a decent bidder. Most people can become decent players. When a person defends well, that person is deemed "a bridge player."

Matthew Granovetter

It's not the handling of difficult hands that makes the winning player. There aren't enough of them. It is the ability to avoid messing up the easy ones.

S.J. Simon

Regardless of what sadistic impulses we may harbour, winning bridge means helping your partner avoid mistakes.

Frank Stewart

BRIDGES
Don't cross your bridges until you get to them. We spend our lives defeating ourselves crossing bridges we never get to.

Bob Bales

BRILLIANCE
It's easy to be brilliant if you are not bothered about being right.

Hector McNeil

BRITAIN
When Britain wins a battle, she shouts, "God save the Queen"; when she loses, she votes down the prime minister.

Winston Churchill

The British have gained a reputation for being slow to anger because they stand in disciplined lines, but the more likely explanation is that they are so easily angered that they need the protection of queues.

Peter Collett

BROTHERHOOD
Human brotherhood may be a myth, and a weak one at that, but it is the only myth that has yet to murder someone in its cause.

Michael Ignatieff

Be my brother, or I will kill you.

Chamfort

The brotherhood of man is not a mere poet's dream: it is a most depressing and humiliating reality.

Oscar Wilde

That all men should be brothers is the dream of people who have no brothers.

Charles Chincolle

You can't spell "brothers" without at the same time spelling "others."

Baptist Standard

BUDGET
Balancing the budget is like going to heaven. Everybody wants to do it but nobody wants to do what you have to do to get there.

Phil Gramm

We didn't actually overspend our budget. The health commission allocation simply fell short of our expenditure.

Frank A. Clark

Budget: a mathematical confirmation of your suspicions.

A.A. Latimer

More and more these days I find myself pondering on how to reconcile my net income with my gross habits.

John Kirk Nelson

BUGS

Bugs are not going to inherit the Earth, they own it now. So we might as well make peace with the landlord.

Thomas Eisner

BULLETS

No matter how big you are, five bullets in you are bound to do something.

Becky Barron

BUMPER STICKERS

There's a difference between a philosophy and a bumper sticker.

Charles M. Schultz

If Barbie is so popular, why do you have to buy her friends?

Everyone has a photographic memory. Some don't have film.

I owe, I owe. It's off to work I go.

If you don't believe in abortions, don't have one.

Don't like my driving? Call 1-800-BUZZ-OFF.

Hang up and drive.

So many idiots, so few comets.

Attention: driver only carries $20 in ammunition.

If evolution is outlawed, only biologists will evolve.

Circumcision is a phallusy.

They're not hot flashes, they're power surges.

Christ is coming soon. Look busy.

Born-again pagan.

Love your mother (with a picture of the Earth)

I love pygmy owls – they taste like chicken.

Drive carefully, we need every taxpayer we can get.

Ultimately, it will be up to God to decide the guilt or innocence of Osama bin Laden. It is our job to arrange the meeting.

US Marines

BURDEN

A burden in the bush is worth two on your hands.

James Thurber

If he has no other burden, he'll take up a load of stones.

Malay proverb

BUREAUCRACY
I do not rule Russia; ten thousand clerks do.

Czar Nicholas I

Every revolution evaporates, leaving behind only the slime of a new bureaucracy.

Franz Kafka

The inner spirit of bureaucracy lies in the exciting interplay of non-ideas and the effervescent sparkling of human personalities engaged in nondirective pursuits.

James H. Boren

A memorandum is written not to inform the reader but to protect the writer.

Dean Acheson

There is only one giant machine operated by pygmies, and that is bureaucracy.

Honoré de Balzac

Any sufficiently advanced bureaucracy is indistinguishable from molasses.

Anonymous

BUREAUCRAT
Hell hath no fury like a bureaucrat scorned.

Milton Friedman

A bureaucrat is a Democrat who holds some office that a Republican wants.

Alben W. Barkley

Bureaucrats are the only people in the world who can say absolutely nothing and mean it.

Hugh Sidey

Guidelines for bureaucrats: When in charge, ponder. When in trouble, delegate. When in doubt, mumble.

James H. Boren

The perfect bureaucrat everywhere is the man who manages to make no decisions and escape all responsibilities.

Brooks Atkinson

BURGLARS
I am laughing to think what risks you take, to try to find money in a desk by night, where the legal owner can never find any by day.

Honoré de Balzac, on awakening to find a burglar in his room

BUSH
Do the Bushies and their minions wish to create a theocratic plutocracy or a plutocratic theocracy?

Geoffrey Ryan

BUSINESS
Business is the combination of sport and war.

André Maurois

My rule always was to do the business of the day in the day.

The Duke of Wellington

The only true battlefield of business is the mind of your constituents: the people you serve directly; your superiors and personal clients; and those you serve indirectly through your organization's products and services.

Donald G. Krause

If people ask, "How's business?" you must tell the truth, but you must be excited. Say: "Unbelievable!" because that'll cover it either way.

Tom Hopkins

All the business of war, and indeed, all the business of life, is to find out what you do not know by what you do.

The Duke of Wellington

Drive thy business or it shall drive thee.

Benjamin Franklin

Know your business and keep knowing your business.

Warren Buffett

The secret of business is to know something that no one else knows.

Aristotle Onassis

The purpose of a business is to get and keep a customer.

Theodore Levitt

Rise early, work late, strike oil.

J. Paul Getty

Your most unhappy customers are your greatest source of learning.

Bill Gates

The business of business is business.

Alfred P. Sloan

Business is like riding a bicycle. Either you keep moving or you fall down.

Frank Lloyd Wright

Exercise caution in your business affairs, for the world is full of trickery. But let this not blind you to what virtue there is; many persons strive for high ideals, and everywhere life is full of heroism.

Max Ehrmann

The incentive of business is to make a profit. But the objective of business is not to make a profit but to serve a need.

James F. Lincoln

It is difficult, but not impossible, to conduct strictly honest business.

Mohandas Gandhi

BUSINESS (MINDING ONE'S OWN)

We cannot be wrong in leaving other people's business alone.

Franco Sacchetti

BUSINESS (AND PLEASURE)

Business and pleasure, rightly understood, mutually assist each other, instead of being enemies, as silly or dull people often think them. No man tastes pleasures truly who does not earn them by previous business; and few people do business well who do nothing else.

Lord Chesterfield

BUSINESS TRIP
No one travelling on a business trip would be missed if he failed to arrive.

Thorstein Veblen

BUSY
If you want work well done, select a busy man: the other kind has no time.

Elbert Hubbard

The bee isn't really that busy – it just can't buzz any slower.

Elbert Hubbard

It is easier to be busy than to try to look busy.

Richard W. Pound

BUSYNESS
Extreme busyness, whether at school, or college, kirk or market, is a symptom of deficient vitality; and a faculty for idleness implies a catholic appetite and a strong sense of personal identity.

Robert Louis Stevenson

Nowadays, people don't ask how you are, they say, "Are you busy?," meaning, "Are you well?" If someone actually does ask how you are, the most cheerful answer, of course, is a robust "Busy!" to which the person will reply, "Good!" "Busy" used to be a negative sort of word. It meant having no time for yourself, no leisure. "No, I can't come out this weekend, I'm too busy." Sorry about that, you poor stiff.

Now, though, busyness is bullish. Conspicuous industriousness is the rule.

Richard Stengel

BUTLERS
Ice formed on the butler's upper slopes.

P.G. Wodehouse

BUTTERFLY EFFECT
Tiny differences in input could quickly become overwhelming differences in output. In weather, this (is) known as the Butterfly Effect – the notion that a butterfly stirring the air today in Peking can transform storm systems next month in New York.

James Gleick

CADS

All men fall into two main divisions: those who value human relationships, and those who value social or financial advancement. The first division are gentlemen; the second division are cads.

Norman Douglas

CALAMITY

Every calamity is a spur and a valuable hint.

Ralph Waldo Emerson

When any calamity has been suffered, the first thing to be remembered, is, how much has escaped.

Samuel Johnson

He who sees the calamity of other people finds his own calamity light.

Arabian proverb

Nine-tenths of the calamities which have befallen the human race had no other origin than the union of high intelligence with low desires.

Thomas Babington Macaulay

CALLING

It is a wild call and a clear call that may not be denied.

John Masefield

CALM

Be like a duck – keep calm and unruffled on the surface but paddle like the devil underneath.

Anonymous

If you can keep your head when all about you are losing theirs, it's just possible you haven't grasped the situation.

Jean Kerr

CANADA

You know what you need in Canada? You need a dozen or so educated Englishmen to come and teach you how to write.

J.B. Priestley

The planet is full of collective apparitions, like Canada, Brazil, the Swiss Congo, and the Common Market.

Jorge Luis Borges

What we do should have a Canadian character. Nobody looks his best in somebody else's clothes.

Vincent Massey

Canadians look down on the United States and consider it Hell. They are right to do so.

Irving Layton

I learned nothing about Canada in school. Canada was to the north; Mexico was to the south. The dumb kids got it wrong.

Larry King

Canadians do not even share myths – those imagined truths that find acceptance because they illuminate the soul and galvanize the national will.

Laurier LaPierre

Canada is one of the most fortunate of countries in that she has not had a battle on home ground for more than a century.

Mary Beacock Fryer

If I were asked by some stranger to North American culture to show him the most important religious building in Canada, I would take him to Toronto's Maple Leaf Gardens.

William Kilbourn

Geographically speaking, the average Canadian, according to a weighted centre of gravity for the population, lives in Alpena, Michigan, two hundred miles north of Detroit.

William Kilbourn

When I stand on a street in a Canadian city and look across the street, it couldn't be anywhere else but Canada, but how can I prove it?

Margaret Mead

The force of Canadian niceness, like the force of Canadian ennui, can be disconcerting to the foreigner.

Jan Morris

Canada has no cultural unity, no linguistic unity, no religious unity, no economic unity, no geographic unity. All it has is unity.

Kenneth Boulding

Canada is the only country in the world where being a nationalist automatically disqualifies someone – in media eyes – as a serious person.

Michael Valpy

Now I don't want you behaving like normal restrained Canadians.

Mick Jagger

When I first came to Canada, I had to say my backup boys were from Nashville or Memphis or somewhere – instead of Canadians, which is what they were ... This country's got everything but confidence.

Rompin' Ronnie Hawkins

Canada is a country so square, even the female impersonators are women.

Richard Benner

I don't even know what street Canada is on.

Al Capone

When they said Canada, I thought it would be up in the mountains somewhere.

Marilyn Monroe

Canada is an interesting place – the rest of the world thinks so, even if Canadians don't.

Terence Green

As Bytown [Ottawa] is not over-run with Americans it may probably turn out a moral, well-behaved town, and afford a lesson to its neighbours.

John MacTaggart

There is no authentic report of wolves ever having killed a human being in the Canadian North; although there must have been times when the temptation was well-nigh irresistible.

Farley Mowat

Canadians are generally indistinguishable from Americans and the surest way of telling the two apart is to make this observation to a Canadian.

Richard Starnes

No matter how the nation's books are finally audited, one asset outweighs all the liabilities – Canadian society is as free as any ever known in the record of an always tormented world.

Bruce Hutchison

A Canadian is someone who knows how to make love in a canoe.

Pierre Berton

I have to say here that Canadian literature, coast to coast, is literally squirming with fish. I could have done a whole anthology of fish stories alone. Seems they're as important in the minds of writers as they are in those of government negotiators, a rare overlap.

Margaret Atwood

Americans are benevolently ignorant about Canada, while Canadians are malevolently well-informed about the United States.

J. Bartlett Brebner

This is the only country in the world where, in thousands of gardens, tomato plants are held up with broken hockey sticks. This is a unique Canadian happening.

Robert Harney

Yet this is also Canada, my friend, yours to absolve of ruin, or make an end.

Malcolm Lowry

In the Conservative view, you have ten premiers and the prime minister as a kind of headwaiter to take the orders.

Pierre Elliott Trudeau

Canada, I assert, is wretchedly under-monstered.

Robertson Davies

I fear that I have not got much to say about Canada, not having seen much; what I got by going to Canada was a cold.

Henry David Thoreau

Canada is a country whose main exports are hockey players and cold fronts. Our main imports are baseball players and acid rain.

Pierre Elliott Trudeau

A Canadian is a fellow who has become a North American without becoming an American.

Arthur L. Phelps

Canada must be the only country in the world where a policeman is used as a national symbol.

Margaret Atwood

Mulroney will be in power a long time. Already, no one can remember anything he's said.

Barry Callaghan

Among the mainstays of my faith is the notion that it is essential to preserve the relatively gentle society on this side of the 49th parallel.

Peter C. Newman

The Divinity could be invoked as well in the English language as in the French.

Wilfrid Laurier

Geography has made America and Canada neighbors. History has made us friends. Economics has made us partners. And necessity has made us allies.

John F. Kennedy

Canada is like an old cow. The West feeds it. Ontario and Quebec milk it. And you can well imagine what it's doing in the Maritimes.

Tommy Douglas

Canadians love to sit in the dark trembling with fear at the weather forecasts.

Robert Morley

I don't have a moral plan. I'm a Canadian.

David Cronenberg

John Kenneth Galbraith and Marshal McLuhan are the two greatest Canadians that the United States has produced.

Anthony Burgess

Canada has never been a melting-pot; more like a tossed salad.

Arnold Edinborough

I didn't know that there were two languages in Canada. I just thought that there was one way to speak to my father and another to talk to my mother.

Louis St Laurent

CANCER
Cancer is not a death sentence, but rather it is a life sentence; it pushes one to live.

Marcia Smith

CANDLE
A candle loses nothing by lighting another candle.

Unknown

All the darkness in the world cannot extinguish the light of a single candle.

St Francis of Assisi

It is better to light a candle than curse the darkness.

Chinese proverb

CANDOUR
Candour and generosity, unless tempered by due moderation, lead to ruin.

Tacitus

CANNIBALISM
I believe in compulsory cannibalism. If people were forced to eat what they killed, there would be no more wars.

Abbie Hoffman

CAPABILITY
Capable persons are never liked.

George Bernard Shaw

CAPITAL MARKET
The capital market has the memory of an elephant, the legs of a hare, and the heart of a deer.

Luigi Einaudi

If the market falls several hundred points, the experts speak of a correction, but nobody ever calls a hundred point rise an error.

Walter Goodman

CAPITAL PUNISHMENT
Rich people do not go to death row. The saying in America is that with capital punishment, it is those without capital who get the punishment.

Michael Radelet

CAPITALISM
What kind of society isn't structured on greed? The problem of social organization is how to set up an arrangement under which greed will do the least harm; capitalism is that kind of a system.

Milton Friedman

War is capitalism with the gloves off.

Tom Stoppard

The inherent vice of capitalism is the unequal sharing of the blessings. The inherent blessing of socialism is the equal sharing of misery.

Winston Churchill

There is a serious tendency toward capitalism among the well-to-do peasants.

Mao Zedong

CAR
The car has become a secular sanctuary for the individual, his shrine to the self, his mobile Walden Pond.

Edward McDonagh

Is fuel efficiency really what we need most desperately? I say what we really need is a car that can be shot when it breaks down.

Russell Baker

A car for every purse and purpose.

Alfred P. Sloan

Everything in life is somewhere else, and you get there in a car.

E.B. White

CARDS

A man's idea in a card game is war, cruel, devastating, and pitiless. A lady's idea of it is a combination of larceny, embezzlement, and burglary.

Finley Peter Dunne

But cards are war, in disguise of a sport.

Charles Lamb

When your opponent's sittin' there holding all the aces, there's only one thing to do: kick over the table.

Dean Martin

Never play cards with any man named "Doc."

Nelson Algren

CARE

If you think nobody cares, miss a couple of payments.

Anonymous

If you make a slip in handling us, you die.

Rudyard Kipling

Want of Care does us much more Damage than want of Knowledge.

Thomas Fuller, MD

No loss should hit us which can be avoided with constant care.

A.P. Moller

CAREERS

Do not keep company with people who speak of careers. Not only are such people uninteresting in themselves; they also have no interest in anything interesting. ... Keep company with people who are interested in the world outside themselves. The one who never asks you what you are working on; who never inquires as to the success of your latest project; who never uses the word career as a noun – he is your friend.

Roger Rosenblatt

I thought I wanted a career. Turns out I just wanted a paycheque.

poster in a Los Angeles office

To do nothing and get something formed a boy's ideal of a manly career.

Benjamin Disraeli

On Career Day in high school, you don't walk around looking for the cartoon guy.

Gary Larson

CASES

He who knows only his own side of the case, knows little of that.

John Stuart Mill

CASTLES

Castles in the air – they are so easy to take refuge in. And so easy to build, too.

Henrik Ibsen

CATASTROPHE

The extent of the catastrophe that threatens gives the measure of the transformation that will be necessary in order to master it.

Lewis Mumford

CATEGORIZATION

Some of the most wonderful people are the ones who don't fit into boxes.

Tori Amos

CATHOLICS

Catholics and Communists have committed great crimes, but at least they have not stood aside, like an established society, and been indifferent. I would rather have blood on my hands than water like Pilate. … If you have abandoned one faith, do not abandon all faith. There is always an alternative to the faith we lose. Or is it the same faith under another name?

Graham Greene

CATS

Dogs come when they are called; cats take a message and get back to you.

Missy Dizick and Mary Bly

But the wildest of all the wild animals was the Cat. He walked by himself, and all places were alike to him.

Rudyard Kipling

I think one reason we admire cats, those of us who do, is their proficiency in one-upmanship. They always seem to come out on top, no matter what they are doing – or pretend they do. Rarely do you see a cat discomfited. They have no conscience, and they never regret. Maybe we secretly envy them.

Barbara Webster

When I play with my cat, who knows whether I do not make her more sport than she makes me? We mutually divert one another with our monkey-tricks.

Michel de Montaigne

Cruel, but composed and bland,/ Dumb, inscrutable and grand,/So Tiberius might have sat,/Had Tiberius been a cat.

Matthew Arnold

Cats are inquisitive, but hate to admit it.

Mason Cooley

You can't look at a sleeping cat and be tense.

Jane Pauley

Cats are smarter than dogs. You can't get eight cats to pull a sled through snow.

Jeff Valdez

If cats could talk, they wouldn't.

Nan Porter

When a man loves cats, I am his friend and comrade without further introduction.

Mark Twain

In ancient times cats were worshipped as gods; they have not forgotten this.

Terry Pratchett

CAUSE

I would rather discover one true cause than gain the kingdom of Persia.

Democritus

I would rather fail in a cause that will ultimately succeed than succeed in a cause that will ultimately fail.

Abraham Lincoln

No cause is inevitable in itself, and man can shape his world if he does not resign himself to ignorance.

Pearl S. Buck

What we call little things are merely the causes of great things; they are the beginning, the embryo, and it is the point of departure which, generally speaking, decides the whole future of an existence.

Henri-Frédéric Amiel

CAUTION

If thou canst not see the bottom, wade not.

English proverb

He that handles a nettle tenderly is soonest stung.

Thomas Fuller, MD

The most beaten paths are certainly the surest; but do not hope to scare up much game on them.

André Gide

Better one safe way than a hundred on which you cannot reckon.

Aesop

Fear to let a drop fall and you will spill a lot.

Malay proverb

In waking a tiger, use a long stick.

Mao Zedong

Wait until it is night before saying that it has been a fine day.

French proverb

I will walk on eggs.

Thomas Heywood

One should not wear earmuffs in the land of the rattlesnake.

Warner Winter

I regret the unhappiness of princes who are slaves to forms and fettered by caution.

Elizabeth I

Of all forms of caution, caution in love is perhaps the most fatal to true happiness.

Bertrand Russell

Look before you leap.

Aesop

Caution is the daughter of circumspection, but she tends to outgrow her mother.

Franz Grillparzer

He that will not sail til all dangers are over must never put to sea.

Thomas Fuller, MD

Have a care … where there is more sail than ballast.

William Penn

CAUTIOUS

The cautious seldom err.

Confucius

I would rather worry without need than live without heed.

Pierre-Augustin Caron de Beaumarchais

The policy of being too cautious is the greatest risk of all.
Jawaharlal Nehru

He was cautious, but he was careful not to show it.
Frederic Raphael

If one is forever cautious, can one remain a human being?
Alexandr Solzhenitsyn

CELEBRITIES
By seeming to anoint new celebrities and banish many of the old from the media spotlight, the public not only feels knowing, it gets the exhilaration of seeming to exercise power over the culture. The public giveth and the public taketh away. It is the only way we can redress the imbalance between the famous and ourselves.
Neal Gabler

CELEBRITY
Celebrity is a mask that eats into the face.
John Updike

Being a celebrity is probably the closest to being a beautiful woman that you can get.
Kevin Costner

A celebrity is a person who works hard all his life to become well known, then wears dark glasses to avoid being recognized.
Fred Allen

CEMETERIES
When you live next to the cemetery, you cannot weep for everyone.
Russian proverb

CENSORS
Censors tend to do what only psychotics do: they confuse reality with illusion.
David Cronenberg

Books won't stay banned. They won't burn. Ideas won't go to jail. In the long run of history, the censor and the inquisitor have always lost. The only sure weapon against bad ideas is better ideas. The source of better ideas is wisdom. The surest path to wisdom is a liberal education.
Alfred Whitney Griswold

CENSORSHIP
Censorship is the height of vanity.
Martha Graham

I believe in censorship. I made a fortune out of it.
Mae West

CENSURE
They have a right to censure that have a heart to help.
William Penn

CEREMONY
Ceremony is the invention of wise men to keep fools at a distance; as good breeding is an expedient to make fools and wise men equals.
Sir Richard Steele

CERTAINTY

I have lived in this world just long enough to look carefully the second time into things that I am the most certain of the first time.

Josh Billings

To be uncertain is to be uncomfortable, but to be certain is to be ridiculous.

Chinese proverb

Certainty generally is illusion, and repose is not the destiny of man.

Oliver Wendell Holmes, Jr

There is only one thing about which I am certain, and this is that there is very little about which one can be certain.

W. Somerset Maugham

He is no wise man who will quit a certainty for an uncertainty.

Samuel Johnson

Certainties are arrived at only on foot.

Antonio Porchia

In these matters, the only certainty is that nothing is certain.

Pliny the Elder

There is one thing certain, namely, that we can have nothing certain; therefore it is not certain that we can have nothing certain.

Samuel Butler

Nothing is settled. Everything can still be altered.

Claude Lévi-Strauss

It is not certain that everything is uncertain.

Blaise Pascal

An acre in Middlesex is better than a principality in Utopia.

Thomas Babington Macaulay

What men really want is not knowledge, but certainty.

Bertrand Russell

There are only three things in life that are certain: death, taxes, and computer upgrades.

Garth Wallbridge

Doubt is not a pleasant condition, but certainty is an absurd one.

Voltaire

The modern world lacks not only hiding places, but certainties.

Salman Rushdie

Chesterton taught me this: The only way to be sure of catching a train is to miss the one before it.

Pierre Daninos

Don't join a queue unless you know what is at the end of it.

Gerald Challis

CHALLENGE

What's too hard for a man must be worth looking into.

Kenyan proverb

We never know how high we are/ Till we are called to rise.

Emily Dickinson

Challenges are gifts that force us to search for a new centre of gravity. Don't fight them. Just find a different way to stand.

Oprah Winfrey

CHANCE

How can you say luck and chance are the same thing? Chance is the first step you take, luck is what comes afterwards.

Amy Tan

Our wisdom and deliberation for the most part follow the lead of chance.

Michel de Montaigne

There is a 50/50 chance of anything, because either it will or it won't.

Hank Phillippi

We do not what we ought;/What we ought not, we do;/And lean upon the thought/That chance will bring us through.

Matthew Arnold

He has two chances, slim and none, and slim just left the building.

Chick Hearn

The chances are your chances are awfully good.

Robert Allen

It's strange but true. Fat chance and slim chance mean the same thing.

Anonymous

I've never quite believed that one chance is all I get.

Anne Tyler

If there is anything that a man can do well, I say let him do it. Give him a chance.

Abraham Lincoln

A second chance does not always mean a happy ending.

Unknown

A throw of the dice will never eliminate chance.

Stéphane Mallarmé

CHANGE

If you want to make enemies, try to change something.

Woodrow Wilson

If we don't change, we don't grow. If we don't grow, we aren't really living.

Gail Sheehy

Things do not change; we change.

Henry David Thoreau

Things don't change but by and by our wishes change.

Marcel Proust

Change is one thing, progress is another. "Change" is scientific, "progress" is ethical; change is indisputable, whereas progress is a matter of controversy.

Bertrand Russell

Taking a new step, uttering a new word is what people fear most.

Fyodor Dostoyevsky

It is easier for us to erect monuments and rename expressways and light eternal flames than it is for us to change.

Stephen Rose

One of the greatest pains to human nature is the pain of a new idea.

Walter Bagehot

There is rarely any way to make people like change. You can only make them feel less threatened by it.
Unknown

The main dangers in this life are the people who want to change everything – or nothing.
Nancy Astor

When you can't change the direction of the wind – adjust your sails.
Anonymous

We cannot adjust the wind but we can adjust the set of the sails.
Jim Rohn

The only sense that is common in the long run, is the sense of change – and we all instinctively avoid it.
E.B. White

There is nothing more difficult to carry out, nor more doubtful of success, nor more dangerous to handle, than to institute a new order of things.
Niccolò Machiavelli

Learn to love change. Feel comfortable with your own creative intuition. Make compassion, care, harmony, and trust the foundation stones of business. Fall in love with new ideas.
Anita Roddick

Change is good, but dollars are better.
Anonymous

When you're through changing, you're through.
Bruce Barton

You must be the change you wish to see in the world. We must become the change we want to see.
Mohandas Gandhi

You cannot step twice into the same river, for other waters are continually flowing in.
Heraclitus

Old ways will always remain unless someone invents a new way and then lives or dies for it.
Elbert Hubbard

I wish to say what I think and feel today, with the proviso that tomorrow perhaps I shall contradict it all.
Ralph Waldo Emerson

No great improvements in the lot of mankind are possible, until a great change takes place in the fundamental constitution of their modes of thought.
John Stuart Mill

If we want things to stay as they are, things will have to change.
Giuseppe di Lampedusa

Change is not without inconvenience, even from worse to better.
Samuel Johnson

It rarely happens that Saul becomes Paul.
Max Planck

The old order changeth, yielding place to new.
Alfred, Lord Tennyson

It's a sign of the times /And a year ago I never could have seen it.
Tony Hatch

One never knows what will happen if things are suddenly changed. But do we know what will happen if they are not changed?
Elias Canetti

All changes, even the most longed for, have their melancholy; for what we leave behind is a part of ourselves; we must die to one life before we can enter into another.
Anatole France

Everyone thinks of changing the world, but no one thinks of changing himself.
Leo Tolstoy

The fastest way to change is to laugh at your folly – then you can let go and quickly move on.
Spencer Johnson

Because things are the way they are, things will not stay the way they are.
Bertolt Brecht

Inside yourself or outside, you never have to change what you see, only the way you see it.
Thaddeus Golas

Never believe that a few caring people can't change the world. For, indeed, that's all who ever have.
Margaret Mead

If you don't change today, your tomorrows will be like your yesterdays.
Anonymous

Never change a winning game; always change a losing one.
Bill Tilden

There is in the worst of fortune the best chances for a happy change.
Euripides

The world hates change; yet it is the only thing that has brought progress.
Charles F. Kettering

I cannot say whether things will get better if we change; what I can say is they must change if they are to get better.
Georg Christoph Lichtenberg

The more things change, the more they are the same.
Alphonse Karr

Change is not always progress. ... A fever of newness has been everywhere confused with the spirit of progress.
Henry Ford

In this world of change naught which comes stays and naught which goes is lost.
Anne Sophie Swetchine

The wheel of change moves on. Those who were down go up and those who were up go down.
Jawaharlal Nehru

When the music changes, so does the dance.

African proverb

To change one's life: 1. Start immediately. 2. Do it flamboyantly. 3. No exceptions.

William James

Control over change would seem to consist in moving not with it but ahead of it.

Marshall McLuhan

CHAOS
Chaos often breeds life, when order breeds habit.

Henry Adams

CHARACTER
A nation's character is the sum of its deeds; they constitute one common patrimony, the nation's inheritance.

Henry Clay

Character is what you are in the dark.

Dwight Moody

Little things affect little minds.

Benjamin Disraeli

You can tell a lot about a fellow's character by the way he eats jelly beans.

Ronald Reagan

Character is much easier kept than recovered.

Thomas Paine

A man never discloses his own character so clearly as when he describes another's.

Jean Paul

As we are, so we do; and as we do, so it is done to us; we are the builders of our fortunes.

Ralph Waldo Emerson

Judge of your natural character by what you do in your dreams.

Ralph Waldo Emerson

The ultimate measure of a man is not where he stands in moments of comfort and convenience, but where he stands at times of challenge and controversy.

Martin Luther King, Jr

A man is not good or bad for one action.

Thomas Fuller, MD

If you stand straight, do not fear a crooked shadow.

Chinese proverb

Character is simply habit long continued.

Plutarch

Nothing characterizes an individual more clearly than what he finds pleasurable – and nothing is better suited to show up his lack of character.

Hans Keller

Fortunate people seldom mend their ways, for when good luck crowns their misdeeds with success they think it is because they are right.

François, duc de La Rochefoucauld

During my eighty-seven years, I have witnessed a whole succession of technological revolutions. But none of them has done away with the need for character in the individual or the ability to think.

Bernard Baruch

When the character of a man is not clear to you, look at his friends.

Haitian proverb

Reputation is what you are in the limelight; character what you are in the dark. Many a man's reputation and character would not recognize each other if they met.

His Honour J. Tudor Rees

You cannot dream yourself into a character; you must hammer and forge yourself one.

James A. Froude

Tell me what company thou keepest, and I'll tell thee what thou art.

Miguel de Cervantes

Character is like a tree and reputation like its shadow. The shadow is what we think of it; the tree is the real thing.

Abraham Lincoln

Fear for one's daily bread destroys one's character.

Franz Kafka

The fate of a people depends much more on their character than on their intelligence.

Gustave Le Bon

People seem not to see that their opinion of the world is also a confession of their character.

Ralph Waldo Emerson

Talent develops in quiet places, character in the full current of human life.

Johann Wolfgang von Goethe

People with courage and character always seem sinister to the rest.

Hermann Hesse

The objection to conforming to usages that have become dead to you is that it scatters your force, loses your time, blears the impression of your character. ... Do your thing and I shall know you.

Ralph Waldo Emerson

Character cannot be developed in ease and quiet. Only through experiences of trial and suffering can the soul be strengthened, vision cleared, ambition inspired, and success achieved.

Helen Keller

CHARITY

No one would remember the Good Samaritan if he'd only had good intentions. He had money as well.

Margaret Thatcher

Charity downgrades those who receive it and hardens those who dispense it. All that is not a true change will disappear in the future society.

George Sand

One hand opened in charity is worth two closed in prayer.

Anonymous

Charity begins at home, but should not end there.

Thomas Fuller, MD

If those who owe us nothing gave us nothing, how poor we would be.
Antonio Porchia

Charity deals with symptoms instead of causes.
Lord Samuel

I do not pity the unfortunate poor who are in need of charity. I can help them. My heart goes out to the presumably fortunate rich who are not charitable. Nobody can help them.
Salem N. Baskin

CHARMER
A beauty is a woman you notice; a charmer is one who notices you.
Adlai Stevenson

CHARLATAN
Surely nobody would be a charlatan who could afford to be sincere.
Ralph Waldo Emerson

CHAUVINISM
Remember, my boy, that you are an Englishman and have consequently won first prize in the lottery of life.
Cecil Rhodes

CHEATING
I used to play golf with a guy who cheated so badly that he once had a hole in one and wrote down zero on the scorecard.
Bob Bruce

Better be cheated in the price than in the quality of [the] goods.
Baltasar Gracian

A thing worth having is a thing worth cheating for.
W.C. Fields

The world is like a game in which there are honest and dishonest players, so that a prince who plays in this game must learn how to cheat, not in order to do it, but in order not to be the dupe of others.
Frederick the Great

Thou shalt not steal; an empty feat,/ When it's so lucrative to cheat.
Arthur Hugh Clough

My dear old grandfather Litcock said, just before they sprung the trap, you can't cheat an honest man. Never give a sucker an even break or smarten up a chump.
George Marshall and Eddie Cline

I was thrown out of NYU my freshman year … for cheating on my metaphysics final. You know, I looked within the soul of the boy sitting next to me.
Woody Allen

Every man cheats in his own way, and he is only honest who is not discovered.
Susanna Centlivre

CHEER
The best way to cheer yourself is to cheer someone else up.
Mark Twain

CHEERFULNESS
Early morning cheerfulness can be extremely obnoxious.
William Feather

Cheerfulness is a quiet condition; glee, on the other hand, is only desperation on a good day.

Aidan Mathews

CHEESE

Gorbachev, lunching with Margaret Thatcher, recalls Charles de Gaulle's comment about it being very difficult to preside over a country that manufactures 120 kinds of cheese. "Imagine," Gorbachev says, "how much harder it is to run a country with over 120 different nationalities?" "Yes," interjects his deputy prime minister, Leonid Abalkin, "Especially if there is no cheese."

Anecdote in At the Highest Levels,
by Michael R. Beschloss and
Strobe Talbott

What happens to the hole when the cheese is gone?

Bertolt Brecht

How can anyone govern a nation that has 240 different kinds of cheese?

Charles de Gaulle

CHEOPS' LAW

No project was ever completed on time and within budget.

CHESS

Chess is as elaborate a waste of human intelligence as you can find outside an advertising agency.

Raymond Chandler

It is impossible to win gracefully at chess. No man has ever said "Mate" in a voice which failed to

sound to his opponent bitter, boastful, and malicious.

A.A. Milne

CHICAGO

I think that's how Chicago got started. A bunch of people in New York said, "Gee, I'm enjoying the crime and the poverty, but it just isn't cold enough. Let's go west."

Richard Jeni

CHICKEN OR EGG

The chicken must have come first – can you imagine God sitting on an egg?

Unknown

CHILD

A child, after all, knows most of the game – it is only an attitude to it that he lacks.

Graham Greene

The child is curious. He wants to make sense out of things, find out how things work, gain competence and control over himself and his environment, and do what he can see other people doing. He is open, perceptive, and experimental.

John Holt

At the birth of a child, if a mother could ask a fairy godmother to endow it with the most useful gift, that gift should be curiosity.

Eleanor Roosevelt

Any child with sense knew that you didn't involve yourself with the adult world if you weren't absolutely forced to. We lived on our side of the great divide and we crossed it at our peril.

Jill Tweedie

It now costs more to amuse a child than it once did to educate his father.

Vaughan Monroe

The child had every toy his father wanted.

Robert E. Whitten

CHILD'S PLAY
The understanding of atomic physics is child's play compared with the understanding of child's play.

David Kresh

CHILDHOOD
It's not a bad thing that children should occasionally, and politely, put parents in their place.

Colette

A happy childhood is poor preparation for human contacts.

Colette

I have a big house – and I hide a lot.

*Mary Ure on coping
with children*

Childhood – a period of waiting for the moment when I could send everyone and everything connected with it to hell.

Igor Stravinsky

A child becomes an adult when he realizes he has a right not only to be right but also to be wrong.

Thomas Szasz

Childhood is the kingdom where nobody dies. Nobody that matters.

Edna St Vincent Millay

There is always one moment in childhood when the door opens and lets the future in.

Graham Greene

A happy childhood is one of the best gifts that parents have it in their power to bestow.

Mary Cholmondeley

CHILDREN
Children have never been very good at listening to their elders, but they have never failed to imitate them.

James Baldwin

We do our best for our children, and hope they return the favour.

Anonymous

Children may close ears to advice, but open their eyes to example.

Anonymous

Children need models more than they need critics.

Joseph Joubert

Never lend your car to anyone to whom you have given birth.

Erma Bombeck

If you have a lot of tension and you get a headache, do what it says on the Aspirin bottle: "Take two tablets" and "Keep away from children."

Unknown

My husband and I are either going to buy a dog or have a child. We can't decide whether to ruin our carpet or ruin our lives.
Rita Rudner

Children are all foreigners.
Ralph Waldo Emerson

I love my kids, but I wouldn't want them for friends.
Janet Sorensen

Give a little love to a child and you get a great deal back.
John Ruskin

We want our children to fit in and to stand out. We rarely address the conflict between these goals.
Ellen Goodman

It is the securely attached child who is the most able to leave the mother's side in order to explore the environment and investigate the objects which it contains.
Anthony Storr

Nothing you do for children is ever wasted. They seem not to notice us, hovering, averting our eyes, and they seldom offer thanks, but what we do for them is never wasted.
Garrison Keillor

There is no such thing as other people's children.
Hillary Rodham Clinton

If men do not keep on speaking terms with children, they cease to be men, and become merely machines for eating and for earning money.
John Updike

I guess the real reason that my wife and I had children is the same reason that Napoleon had for invading Russia: it seemed like a good idea at the time.
Bill Cosby

It was no wonder that people were so horrible when they started life as children.
Kingsley Amis

We may prepare food for our children, chauffer them around, take them to the movies, buy them toys and ice cream, but nothing registers as deeply as a simple squeeze.
Stephanie Martson

I do not dislike extreme vivacity in children, but would see enough of it to make an animated character, when the violence of animal spirits shall subside in time. It is easier to restrain excess than to quicken stupidity.
Lydia Sigourney

Never fear spoiling children by making them too happy. Happiness is the atmosphere in which all good affections grow.
Ann Elizabeth Bray

Children ... after a certain age do not welcome parental advice. Perhaps people should switch children with their neighbours and friends for a while in the teen years.
Marian Wright Edelman

Remember that children, marriages, and flower gardens reflect the kind of care they get.

H. Jackson Brown, Jr

Men are generally more careful of the breed of their horses and dogs than of their children.

William Penn

You know your children are growing up when they start asking questions that have answers.

John J. Plomp

Never worry about the size of your Christmas tree. In the eyes of children, they are all thirty feet tall.

Larry Wilde

My mother says that when you have kids, you have to give up things … like your will to live.

Wendy Liebman

As a child I thought I hated everybody, but when I grew up I realized it was just children I didn't like.

Philip Larkin

The natural term of the affection of the human animal for its offspring is six years.

George Bernard Shaw

Nothing has a stronger influence on their children than the unlived lives of their parents.

Carl Jung

If you want to see what children can do, you must stop giving them things.

Norman Douglas

Your children are not your children. They are the sons and daughters of life's longing for itself.

Kahlil Gibran

If you want your children to turn out well, spend twice as much time with them as you think you should and half the amount of money.

Esther Selsdon

Children are not things to be molded, but are people to be unfolded.

Jess Lair

I have found that the best way to give advice to your children is to find out what they want and then advise them to do it.

Harry S. Truman

It's frightening to think that you mark your children merely by being yourself.

Simone de Beauvoir

What gift has Providence bestowed on man that is so dear to him as his children?

Cicero

It is true that children are expensive, time-consuming, patience-taxing additions to the family, but the sacrifices they demand are trivial to what they give.

Chad Walsh

Children are a great comfort in your old age – and they help you reach it faster, too.

Lionel M. Kaufman

If children make deductions for you, you must make allowances for them.

Raymond Duncan

If children did not ask questions, they would never learn how little adults know.

Raymond Duncan

Before I got married I had six theories about bringing up children; now I have six children and no theories.

Lord Rochester

It is easier to build strong children than to repair broken men.

Frederick Douglass

CHILDREN'S FANCY
It is, in some ways, but a pedestrian fancy that the child exhibits. It is the grown people who make the nursery stories; all the children do is jealously preserve the text.

Robert Louis Stevenson

CHINESE
Nothing and no one can destroy the Chinese people. They are relentless survivors. They are the oldest civilized people on Earth. Their civilization passes through phases but its basic characteristics remain the same. They yield, they bend to the wind, but they never break.

Pearl S. Buck

CHOCOLATE
As with most fine things, chocolate has its season ... Any month whose name contains the letter A, E or U is the proper time for chocolate.

Sandra Boynton

CHOICE
You have a choice of two things in life; remembering and hoping.

Paul Villeneuve

He who does anything because it is the custom, makes no choice.

John Stuart Mill

There's small choice in rotten apples.

William Shakespeare

Nobody can honestly think of himself as a strong character because, however successful he may be in overcoming them, he is necessarily aware of the doubts and temptations that accompany every important choice.

W.H. Auden

If we were not provided with the knack of being wrong, we could never get anything useful done. We think our way along by choosing between right and wrong alternatives, and the wrong choices have to be made as frequently as the wrong ones.

Lewis Thomas

Two roads diverged in a wood, and I – I took the one less travelled by, And that has made all the difference.

Robert Frost

If you come to a fork in the road, take it.

Yogi Berra

I see the better things, and approve; I follow the worse.

Ovid

The Other Line moves faster.

Barbara Ettore

The longer it takes you to select a cantaloupe the worse it is.

Kin Hubbard

If thou must choose/Between the chances, choose the odd:/Read The New Yorker, trust in God;/And take short views.

W.H. Auden

(When it comes to health care) Americans crave choice, and many of them choose to have no health care at all.

John Wing

CHRISTIAN
Scratch the Christian and you find the pagan – spoiled.

Israel Zangwill

CHRISTIANITY
We now begin to see that what we call Christianity – and what we identify as Christian tradition – actually represents only a small selection of specific sources, chosen from among dozens of others. Who made that selection, and for what reasons? Why were these other writings excluded and banned as "heresy"? What made them so dangerous?

Elaine Pagels

The greatest need today is not for more Christian people, but for more people who are Christian.

Rev. C.B. Wittstruck

CHRISTMAS
Christmas will soon be at our throats.

P.G. Wodehouse

A Merry Christmas to all my friends except two.

W.C. Fields

To perceive Christmas through its wrappings becomes more difficult with every year.

E.B. White

Christmas usually begins around the first of December with an office party and ends when you finally realize what you spent, around April 15th of the next year.

P.J. O'Rourke

The first rule in buying Christmas presents is to select something shiny. If the chosen object is of leather, the leather must look as if it had been well-greased; if of silver, it must gleam with the light that was never on sea or land. That is because the wariest person will often mistake shininess for expensiveness.

P.G. Wodehouse

A lovely thing about Christmas is that it's compulsory, like a thunderstorm, and we all go through it together.

Garrison Keillor

Christmas is a time when kids tell Santa what they want and adults pay for it. Deficits are when adults tell the government what they want – and their kids pay for it.

Richard Lamm

Christmas gifts are divided into two classes – those you don't like and those you don't get.

Frances Rodman

What I like about Christmas is that you can make people forget the past with the present.

Don Marquis

CHURCH
The church must be reminded that it is not the master or the servant of the state, but rather the conscience of the state.

Martin Luther King, Jr

The Church Militant and the Church Triumphant have become the Church Social and the Church Bizarre.

Robert Benson

CIGARETTE
The cigarette does the smoking – you're just the sucker.

Unknown

Cigarettes are very like weasels. Perfectly harmless until you put one in your mouth and try to set fire to it.

Boothby Graffoe

CIRCLES
We all of us live too much in circles.

Benjamin Disraeli

CIRCUMSTANCES
Circumstances alter cases.

Sam Slick

The people who get on in this world are the people who get up and look for the circumstances they want, and, if they can't find them, make them.

George Bernard Shaw

CIRCUMSTANTIAL EVIDENCE
Some circumstantial evidence is very strong, as when you find a trout in the milk.

Henry David Thoreau

"Circumstantial evidence is a very tricky thing," answered Holmes thoughtfully. "It may seem to point very straight to one thing, but if you shift your own point of view a little, you may find it pointing in an equally uncompromising manner to something entirely different."

Arthur Conan Doyle

CITIZEN
The job of a citizen is to keep his mouth open.

Günter Grass

CITY

The city is not a concrete jungle, it is a human zoo.

Desmond Morris

CIVILITY

Civility costs nothing and buys everything.

Lady Mary Wortley Montagu

CIVILIZATION

When people ask me to compare the twentieth century to older civilizations, I always say the same thing: "The situation is normal."

Will Durant

The end of the human race will be that it will eventually die of civilization.

Ralph Waldo Emerson

Civilization is nothing more than the effort to reduce the use of force to the last resort.

José Ortega y Gasset

To be able to fill leisure intelligently is the last product of civilization.

Bertrand Russell

The civilized are those who get more out of life than the uncivilized, and for this the uncivilized have not forgiven them.

Cyril Connolly

Civilizations die from philosophical calm, irony, and the sense of fair play quite as surely as they die of debauchery.

Joseph Wood Krutch

A decent provision for the poor is the true test of civilization.

Samuel Johnson

The path of civilization is paved with tin cans.

Elbert Hubbard

A high civilization is a pyramid: it can stand only on a broad base; its primary prerequisite is a strong and soundly consolidated mediocrity.

Friedrich Nietzsche

Civilizations in decline are consistently characterized by a tendency towards standardization and uniformity.

Arnold Toynbee

The first human who hurled an insult instead of a stone was the founder of civilization.

Sigmund Freud

Civilization is a method of living, an attitude of equal respect for all men.

Jane Addams

The true test of civilization is not the census, nor the size of the cities, nor the crops – no, but the kind of man the country turns out.

Ralph Waldo Emerson

The major advances in civilization are processes that all but wreck the societies in which they occur.

Alfred North Whitehead

Civilizations break down and go to pieces if and when a challenge confronts them which they fail to meet.
Arnold Toynbee

Civilization is the art of living in towns of such size that everyone does not know everyone else.
Julian James

The real index of civilization is when people are kinder than they need to be.
Louis de Bernières

CLARITY
I see but one rule: to be clear. If I am not clear, all my world crumbles to nothing.
Stendhal

Clearness is so eminently one of the characteristics of truth that often it even passes for truth itself.
Joseph Joubert

CLASS
I'll go through life either first class or third, but never in second.
Noel Coward

At the bottom, people tend to believe that class is defined by the amount of money you have. In the middle, people grant that money has something to do with it, but think education and the kind of work you do almost equally important. Nearer the top, people perceive that taste, values, ideas, style, and behaviour are indispensable criteria of class, regardless of money or occupation or education.
Paul Fussell

Class is an aura of confidence that is being sure without being cocky. Class has nothing to do with money. Class never runs scared. It is self-discipline and self-knowledge. It's the surefootedness that comes with having proved you can meet life.
Ann Landers

There are only two classes in society: those who get more than they earn, and those who earn more than they get.
Holbrook Jackson

CLASSIC
A classic is something that everybody wants to have read and nobody wants to read.
Mark Twain

A classic is classic not because it conforms to certain structural rules, or fits certain definitions ... It is classic because of a certain eternal and irrepressible freshness.
Ezra Pound

CLEANLINESS
Man's partial good resolutions that always succumb to ingrained habit are like the cleaning, scrubbing, and adorning that we practice on Sundays and feast days. We always get dirty again, to be sure, but such a partial cleaning process has the advantage of upholding the principle of cleanliness.
Johann Wolfgang von Goethe

CLEAR SIGHT
Hundreds of people can talk for one who can think, but thousands

can think for one who can see. To see clearly is poetry, prophecy, and religion – all in one.

John Ruskin

CLEVER

Here is a good rule of thumb:/Too clever is dumb.

Ogden Nash

All clever men are birds of prey.

English proverb

The height of cleverness is being able to conceal it.

François, duc de La Rochefoucauld

Cleverness is serviceable for everything, sufficient for nothing.

Henri-Frédéric Amiel

It is no use trying to be clever – we are all clever here; just try to be kind – a little kind.

Dr F.J. Foakes Jackson

CLICHÉS

Let's have some new clichés.

Samuel Goldwyn

The cliché organizes life; it expropriates people's identity; it becomes ruler, defence lawyer, judge, and the law.

Vaclav Havel

If you want to use a cliché, you must take full responsibility for it yourself and not try to fob it off on anon., or on society.

Lewis Thomas

CLIMATE

I believe we should all behave quite differently if we lived in a warm, sunny climate all the time.

Noel Coward

Climate is what you expect, weather is what you get.

Robert Heinlein

CLOCKS

What time would it be if all the clocks were stopped?

Zen saying

CLOTHES

We should distrust any enterprise that requires new clothes.

Henry David Thoreau

Somebody did complain to me that my clothes were so loud they couldn't hear me sing.

Cyndi Lauper

CLUBS

It is easier for a man to be loyal to his club than to his planet; the by-laws are shorter, and he is personally acquainted with the other members.

E.B. White

A right rule for a club would be "Admit no man whose presence excludes any one topic."

Ralph Waldo Emerson

COACHES

Coaches who can outline plays on a blackboard are a dime a dozen. The ones who win get inside their players and motivate.

Vince Lombardi

COCOON

There is at bottom only one problem in the world. ... How does one break through? How does one get into the open? How does one burst the cocoon and become a butterfly?

Thomas Mann

COCKTAIL HOUR

The pause between the errors and trials of the day and the hopes of the night.

Herbert Hoover

COFFEE

Wake up and smell the coffee.

Anonymous

If I can't have my little demitasse of coffee three times a day, I'm just a dried-up piece of roast goat.

Johann Sebastian Bach

Never drink black coffee at lunch; it will keep you awake all afternoon.

Jilly Cooper

COLD

'Tis bitter cold and I am sick at heart.

William Shakespeare

COLLABORATION

I wanted to collaborate because, you know, I get lonely.

Woody Allen

Every sin is the result of a collaboration.

Stephen Crane

COLLEGE

If you have a college degree, you can be sure of one thing ... you have a college degree.

Donna Blaurock

Colleges hate geniuses, just as convents hate saints.

Ralph Waldo Emerson

A college education shows a man how little other people know.

Thomas Chandler Haliburton

College is a refuge from hasty judgment.

Robert Frost

COLOUR

You can buy a Ford in any colour so long as it's black.

Henry Ford

COMEDIAN

The test of a real comedian is whether you laugh at him before he opens his mouth.

George Jean Nathan

COMEDY

What's the secret of great com...? Timing.

Richard Curtis and Rowan Atkinson

The only rules comedy can tolerate are those of taste, and the only limitations those of libel.

James Thurber

Comedy is simply a funny way of being serious.

Peter Ustinov

COMFORT
When the stomach is full, it is easy to talk of fasting.

St Jerome

The desire of acquiring the comforts of the world haunts the imagination of the poor, and the dread of losing them that of the rich.

Alexis de Tocqueville

COMMANDMENT
The first and great commandment is, don't let them scare you.

Elmer Davis

COMMENT
Comment is free but facts are on expenses.

Tom Stoppard

COMMITMENT
If you dip your arm into the pickle-pot, let it be up to the elbow.

Malay proverb

Commitment is never an act of moderation.

Kenneth G. Mills

COMMITTEES
A committee saves minutes and wastes hours.

Anonymous

A committee is a cul-de-sac down which ideas are lured, and quietly strangled.

Barnett Cocks

No monument is dedicated to a committee.

Lester J. Pourciau

What is a committee? A group of the unwilling, picked from the unfit, to do the unnecessary.

Richard Harkness

A group of the unfit appointed by the unwilling to do the unnecessary.

Carl C. Byers

A committee of one gets things done.

Joe Ryan

A camel is a horse designed by a committee.

Alec Issigonis

The committee was divided between the theorists, who had done all their thinking long ago, or had had it done for them, and the pragmatists, who hoped to discover what it was they thought in the process of saying it.

Ian McEwan

Committees of twenty deliberate plenty,/Committees of ten act now and then,/But most jobs are done by committees of one.

Old rhyme

Nothing is impossible until it is sent to a committee.

James H. Boren

There is a tendency for the person in the most powerful position in an organization to spend all of his time serving on committees and signing letters.

Sir William Osler

If a committee is allowed to discuss a bad idea long enough, it will inevitably vote to implement the idea simply because so much work has already been done on it.

Ken Cruickshank

Any committee that is the slightest use is composed of people who are too busy to want to sit on it for a second longer than they have to.

Katharine Whitehorn

The most efficient part of any organization is a standing committee. The minute you give them chairs, the meetings last forever.

Robert Orben

Muddle is the extra unknown personality in any committee.

Anthony Sampson

Committees are consumers and sometimes sterilizers of ideas, rarely creators of them.

Henry Kissinger

If Moses had been a committee, the Israelites would still be in Egypt.

J.B. Hughes

Nothing is ever accomplished by a committee unless it consists of three members, one of whom happens to be sick and the other absent.

Hendrik Van Loon

COMMON LINKS

Our most basic common link is that we all inhabit this planet.

John F. Kennedy

COMMON SENSE

Everybody gets so much information all day long that they lose their common sense.

Gertrude Stein

It is a thousand times better to have common sense without education than to have education without common sense.

Robert G. Ingersoll

Nothing astonishes men so much as common sense and plain dealing.

Ralph Waldo Emerson

Good intentions are useless in the absence of common sense.

Jami

Pedantry prides herself on being wrong by rules, while common sense is contented to be right without them.

Charles Caleb Colton

Logic is one thing and common sense another.

Elbert Hubbard

There are forty kinds of lunacy, but only one kind of common sense.

Anonymous

Common sense is not so common.

Voltaire

Common sense is the knack of seeing things as they are, and doing things as they ought to be done.

Harriet Beecher Stowe

Common sense is genius dressed in its working clothes.

Ralph Waldo Emerson

COMMUNICATION

To effectively communicate, we must realize that we are all different in the way we perceive the world and use this understanding as a guide to our communication with others.

Anthony Robbins

Think like a wise man but communicate in the language of the people.

William Butler Yeats

What we've got here is failure to communicate.

Frank R. Pierson

After all, when you come right down to it, how many people speak the same language even when they speak the same language?

Russell Hoban

Evil communications corrupt good manners.

I Corinthians:15:33

The single biggest problem in communication is the illusion that it has taken place.

George Bernard Shaw

COMMUNIST

A communist is one who has nothing and wishes to share it with the world.

Anonymous

The Communist Party USA today announced the transfer of its financial portfolio from Merrill Lynch, effective immediately.

Party press release

Every year, humanity takes a step towards communism. Maybe not you, but at all events your grandson will surely be a communist.

Nikita Khrushchev

Communism is like one big phone company.

Lenny Bruce

COMMUNITY

We didn't all come over on the same ship, but we're all in the same boat.

Bernard Baruch

COMPANY

Man loves company – even if it is only that of a small, burning candle.

Georg Christoph Lichtenberg

COMPARISON

Comparison, more than reality, makes men happy or wretched.

Thomas Fuller, MD

Nothing is good or bad but by comparison.

Thomas Fuller, MD

COMPASSION

Compassion is the chief law of human existence.

Fyodor Dostoyevsky

If you want others to be happy, practise compassion. If you want to be happy, practise compassion.

Dalai Lama

Compassion is a two-way street.

Frank Capra

COMPETITION

Know ye not that they which run in a race run all, but one receiveth the prize?

I Corinthians 9:24

Competition brings out the best in products and the worst in people.

David Sarnoff

If you think squash is competitive, try flower arranging.

Alan Bennett

A horse never runs so fast as when he has other horses to catch up and outpace.

Ovid

Man is a gaming animal. He must always be trying to get the better in something or other.

Charles Lamb

If you can't lick 'em in the alley, you can't lick 'em on the ice.

Conn Smythe

A competitor will find a way to win. Competitors take bad breaks and use them to drive themselves just that much harder. Quitters take bad breaks and use them as reasons to give up.

Nancy Lopez

Everything now being done is going to be done differently; it's going to be done better, and if you don't do it, your competitor will.

Anonymous

The only competition worthy of a wise man is with himself.

Anna Jameson

COMPETITOR'S CREED

Every morning when the sun comes up, the gazelle wakes. He knows that he must outrun the fastest lion or he will be eaten. When the sun comes up, the lion also wakes. He knows that he must outrun the slowest gazelle or he will starve. In the end, it doesn't really matter whether you are a lion or a gazelle. When the sun comes up, you'd better be running.

Management proverb (quoted by Joe Martin, Deloitte & Touche, published in The Globe & Mail, 7 July 1992)

COMPLAINING

I can't complain, but sometimes I still do.

Joe Walsh

The world is so dreadfully managed, one hardly knows to whom to complain.

Ronald Firbank

Behold I was without shoes and complained until I met a man who had no feet.

Arabic saying

Complaint is the sincerest part of our devotion.

Jonathan Swift

It will generally be found that men who are constantly lamenting their ill luck are only reaping the consequences of their own neglect, mismanagement, and improvidence, or want of application.

Samuel Smiles

Sir, Saturday morning, although recurring at regular and well-foreseen intervals, always seems to take this railway by surprise.

W.S. Gilbert

Why, since we are always complaining of our ills, are we constantly employed in redoubling them?

Voltaire

The worst wheel of the cart makes the most noise.

Benjamin Franklin

It is a general error to suppose the loudest complainers for the public to be the most anxious for its welfare.

Edmund Burke

COMPLEXES

A man should not strive to eliminate his complexes, but to get into accord with them: they are legitimately what directs his conduct in the world.

Sigmund Freud

COMPLICATIONS

There's no limit to how complicated things can get, on account of one thing always leading to another.

E.B. White

COMPLIMENTS

Never let a day go by without giving at least three people a compliment.

Anonymous

When you cannot get a compliment in any other way, pay yourself one.

Mark Twain

To say a compliment well is a high art, and few possess it.

Mark Twain

Compliments cost nothing, yet many pay dear for them.

German proverb

The paying of compliments is a middle-class convention, for this class needs the assurance compliments provide. In the upper class, there's never any doubt of one's value, and it all goes without saying.

Paul Fussell

The best thing you can do behind a person's back is pat it.

Franklin P. Jones

COMPOSERS
(SPEAKING OF EACH OTHER)

I played over the music of that scoundrel Brahms. What a giftless bastard!

Peter Tchaikovsky

[Bruckner's symphonies are] symphonic boa-constrictors.

Johannes Brahms

Berlioz composes by splashing his pen over the manuscript and leaving the issue to chance.

Frederick Chopin

Wagner is evidently mad.

Hector Berlioz

Rossini would have been a great composer if his teacher had spanked him enough on the backside.

Ludwig von Beethoven

[Arnold Schonberg would] be better off shovelling snow.

Richard Strauss

COMPREHENSION

Grasp the subject, the words will follow.

Cato the Elder

COMPROMISE

Don't compromise yourself. You're all you've got.

Janis Joplin

You might as well fall flat on your face as lean over too far backward.

James Thurber

A compromise is the art of dividing a cake in such a way that everyone believes he has the biggest piece.

Ludwig Erhard

Better bend than break.

Scottish proverb

The English spirit of compromise tempts us to believe that injustice, when it is halved, becomes justice.

Lord Samuel

When the final result is expected to be a compromise, it is often prudent to start from an extreme position.

John Maynard Keynes

COMPUTERS

The real danger is not that computers will begin to think like men, but that men will begin to think like computers.

Sydney J. Harris

Not even computers will replace computers, because committees buy computers.

Edward Shepherd Mead

Electronic aids, particularly domestic computers, will help the inner migration, the opting out of reality.

J.G. Ballard

Electronic computers are just a cheap imitation of the original, which is the brain. And as we develop the technology of biology, I think we'll have to start thinking of our own bodies as machines. That's because we'll be able to understand how they work, replace broken parts, and fix malfunctioning systems. At the same time, it will be possible to build machines out of the same components our bodies are built out of ... I'm as fond of my body as anyone else, but if I can be 200 with a body of silicon, I'll take it.

Dr W. Daniel Hillis

You can't fail to get along with a computer; it will never turn on you, it will never insist on talking about what it wants to talk about or doing what it wants to do. It will never find you boring, never forget to call, never ask for a favor.

Greg Easterbrook

Computers are useless. They can only give you answers.

Pablo Picasso

What do people mean when they say the computer went down on them?

Marilyn Pittman

Computers can figure out all kinds of problems, except the things in the world that just don't add up.

James F. Magary

In a few seconds a computer can make a mistake so great that it would take many men many months to equal it.

Merle M. Meacham

The computer is no better than its program.

Elting Elmore Morison

Part of the inhumanity of the computer is that, once it is completely programmed and working smoothly, it is completely honest.

Isaac Asimov

I do not fear computers. I fear the lack of them.

Isaac Asimov

The question of whether computers can think is just like the question of whether submarines can swim.

Edsger Dijkstra

CONCEIT
The conceited man relates only to his own great deeds, and only the evil ones of others.

Baruch Spinoza

Try not to despise yourself too much – it's only conceit.

P.J. Kavanagh

What renders us so bitter against those who trick us is that they believe themselves to be more clever than we are.

François, duc de La Rochefoucauld

CONCENTRATION
To do two things at once is to do neither.

Publilius Syrus

Depend on it, sir, when a man knows he is to be hanged in a fortnight, it concentrates his mind wonderfully.

Samuel Johnson

The principles of war, not merely one principle, can be condensed into a single word – "concentration." But for truth this needs to be amplified as the "concentration of strength against weakness …"

B.H. Liddell Hart

CONCEPT (FUZZY)
There is nothing worse than a sharp image of a fuzzy concept.

Ansel Adams

CONCESSIONS
The concessions of the weak are the concessions of fear.

Edmund Burke

CONCILIATION
The one sure way to conciliate a tiger is to allow oneself to be devoured.

Konrad Adenauer

CONCLUSION
A conclusion is the place where you got tired thinking.

Martin H. Fischer

As long as a study is cultivated by narrow minds, they will draw from it narrow conclusions.

John Stuart Mill

The open mind never acts: when we have done our utmost to arrive at a reasonable conclusion, we still … must close our minds for the moment with a snap, and act dogmatically on our conclusions.

George Bernard Shaw

CONDEMNATION
I wonder how anyone can have the face to condemn others when he reflects upon his own thoughts.

W. Somerset Maugham

If it is the devil that tempts the young to enjoy themselves, is it not, perhaps, the same personage that persuades the old to condemn their enjoyment? And is not condemnation perhaps merely the form of excitement appropriate to old age?

Bertrand Russell

CONDUCT
Conduct is more convincing than language.

John Woolman

Wrong is wrong, even if everybody is doing it, and right is right even if nobody is doing it.

Bishop Fulton J. Sheen

It seems to me that if you or I must choose between two courses of action, we should remember our dying and try so to live that our death brings no pleasure to the world.

John Steinbeck

But indeed Conviction, were it never so excellent, is worthless til it convert itself into Conduct.

Thomas Carlyle

Do not choose to be wrong for the sake of being different.

Herbert Samuel

CONDUCTOR
Show me an orchestra that likes its conductor and I'll show you a lousy conductor.

Goddard Lieberson

CONFESS
To confess a fault freely is the next thing to being innocent.

Publilius Syrus

CONFIDE
It is very true that we seldom confide in those who are better than ourselves.

Albert Camus

CONFIDENCE
As is our confidence, so is our capacity.

William Hazlitt

Confidence that one is of value and significance as a unique individual is one of the most precious possessions which anyone can have.

Anthony Storr

Confidence comes out of a combination of confidence and hunger.

Arnold Palmer

Confidence is a thing not to be produced by compulsion. Men cannot be forced to trust.

Daniel Webster

Without rebuilding the confidence between parties, you will never succeed.

Harri Holkeri

CONFIDENTIALITY
The ship of state is the only one that leaks from the top.

John F. Kennedy

The ship of state is the only known vessel that leaks from the top.

James Reston

CONFLICT
What sets us against one another is not our aims – they all come to the same thing – but our methods, which are the fruit of our varied reasoning.

Antoine de Saint-Exupéry

When there are two conflicting versions of a story, the wise course is to believe the one in which people appear at their worst.

H. Allen Smith

Whoever seeks to set one race against another seeks to enslave all races.

Franklin D. Roosevelt

In the Middle East, the conflict today is a matter of generations and not of cultures.

Shimon Peres

CONFORMITY
The faces of men, while sheep in credulity, are wolves for conformity.

Carl Van Doren

Never forget that only dead fish swim with the stream.

Malcolm Muggeridge

I dance to the tune that is played.

Spanish proverb

I think the reward for conformity is that everyone likes you except yourself.

Rita Mae Brown

We are half-ruined by conformity, but we should be wholly ruined without it.

Charles Dudley Warner

Avoid the reeking herd; Shun the polluted flock.

Elinor Wylie

Where all think alike, no one thinks very much.

Walter Lippmann

If they give you ruled paper, write the other way.

Juan Ramon Jimenez

Allow me to furnish the interior of my head as I please, and I will put up with a hat like everybody else's.
Henri Bergson

When a race of plants is pretty well established, the seed-raisers do not pick out the best plants, but merely go over their seed-beds, and pull up the "rogues," as they call the plants that deviate from the proper standard.
Charles Darwin

CONFUSION
A confused army leads to another's victory.
Sun Tzu

If you're not confused, you're not paying attention.
Anonymous

I'm not confused. I'm just well mixed.
Robert Frost

In the theatre of confusion, knowing the location of the exits is what counts.
Mason Cooley

CONGRESS
Suppose you were an idiot. ... And suppose you were a member of Congress. ... But I repeat myself.
Mark Twain

There is no distinctly American criminal class save Congress.
Mark Twain

Talk is cheap – except when Congress does it. The government is like a baby's alimentary canal, with a happy appetite at one end and no responsibility at the other.
Ronald Reagan

If we are to preserve freedom and keep constitutional government alive in America, it cannot be left to a President and his agents alone to decide what must be kept secret. Congress, if it is to check the abuse of executive power, must retain its right to inquiry and independent judgment.
Frank Church

CONQUER
Conquer but don't triumph.
Marie von Ebner-Eschenbach

You must either conquer and rule or serve and lose, suffer or triumph, be the anvil or the hammer.
Johann Wolfgang von Goethe

CONSCIENCE
Conscience is a mother-in-law whose visit never ends.
H.L. Mencken

The difficulty is to know conscience from self-interest.
W.D. Howells

A guilty conscience is the mother of invention.
Carolyn Wells

Conscience is that inner voice that warns us someone may be looking.
H.L. Mencken

Conscience gets a lot of the credit that belongs to cold feet.
Anonymous

A lot of people mistake a short memory for a clear conscience.

Doug Larson

Conscience is the perfect interpreter of life.

Karl Barth

Labour to keep alive in your breast that little spark of celestial fire called conscience.

George Washington

The one thing that doesn't abide by majority rule is a person's conscience.

Harper Lee

Conscience: self-esteem with a halo.

Irving Layton

The conscience is … a brake, not a guide; a fence, not a way. It raises its voice after a wrong deed has been committed, but often fails to give us direction in advance of our actions.

Abraham Joshua Heschel

The safest course is to do nothing against one's conscience. With this secret, we can enjoy life and have no fear from death.

Voltaire

Good friends, good books, and a sleepy conscience: this is the ideal life.

Mark Twain

There is no pillow so soft as a clear conscience.

French proverb

Trust that man in nothing who has not a conscience in everything.

Laurence Sterne

CONSCIOUSNESS

My consciousness is fine – it's my pay that needs raising.

Phyllis Diller

Consciousness is defined as that annoying time between naps.

Anonymous

CONSEQUENCES

He that will keep a monkey should pay for the glass that he breaks.

John Selden

In nature there are neither rewards nor punishments – there are consequences.

Robert G. Ingersoll

A great flame follows a little spark.

Dante Alighieri

I wear the chain I forged in life.
Charles Dickens (Jacob Marley in A Christmas Carol)

He who sows the wind harvests the storm.

Arab proverb

Consequences, shmonsequences! So long as I'm rich!

Daffy Duck

Nothing is worth doing unless the consequences may be serious.

George Bernard Shaw

CONSERVATIONIST

A true conservationist is a man who knows that the world is not given by his fathers but borrowed from his children.

John James Audubon

CONSERVATIVE

A conservative is a man who is too cowardly to fight and too fat to run.

Elbert Hubbard

I am not even sure what it means when one says he is a conservative in fiscal affairs and a liberal in human affairs. I assume it means that you will strongly recommend the building of a great many schools to accommodate the needs of our children, but not provide the money.

Adlai Stevenson

A conservative is a worshiper of dead radicals.

Anonymous

When a nation's young men are conservative, its funeral bell is already rung.

Henry Ward Beecher

The highest function of conservatism is to keep what progressiveness has accomplished.

R.H. Fulton

The modern conservative is engaged in one of man's oldest exercises in moral philosophy ... the search for a superior moral justification for selfishness.

John Kenneth Galbraith

CONSISTENCY

Consistency is contrary to nature, contrary to life. The only completely consistent people are the dead.

Aldous Huxley

Consistency is the last refuge of the unimaginative.

Oscar Wilde

We cannot remain consistent with the world save by growing inconsistent with our past selves.

Havelock Ellis

Consistency requires you to be as ignorant today as you were a year ago.

Bernard Berenson

It is easier to say things that are new than to reconcile things that have been said already.

Marquis de Vauvenargues

I'd rather be right than consistent.

Al Davis

CONSOLE

Anything that consoles is fake.

Iris Murdoch

CONSPIRACY

The wronger a conspiracy is, the better it is.

Mark Twain

CONSPIRACY THEORIES

We who are mere dots used to believe it was God's plan when a dot that was a precious child or spouse ceased moving, and we found some relief from pain in that. We couldn't know the plan, but our faith told us there was a plan. Now we've subtracted God from the plan, but the plan remains, and lacking clear evidence to the contrary, we take some pleasure from ascribing our misfortune and our tragedy to dark agencies. Thinking of them makes it much easier to abide the dot lifestyle.

Stephen Hunter

CONSTITUTION
Our Constitution was not written in the sands to be washed away by each wave of new judges blown in by each successive political wave.

Hugo L. Black

We are never conscious of our constitutions until they are out of order.

W.H. Mallock

A rigid Constitution necessarily represents the past, not the present.

Lord Bryce

CONSULTANTS
The proper and ethical task of a strategic planning consultant is to build client independence, not dependence on the consultant.

Clark Crouch

CONSUMERISM
To some degree, the triumph of consumerism is the triumph of the popular will. You may not like what is manufactured, advertised, packaged, branded, and broadcast, but it is far closer to what most people want most of the time than at any other period of modern history.

James B. Twitchell

The issue [of consumerism] is deeper than greed and selfishness.

Material consumption – buying and possessing things – has become the primary way of belonging in America and around the world. If we can't buy, if we can't consume, we simply can't belong.

Jim Wallis

CONTACT
There are four ways, and only four ways, in which we have contact with the world. We are evaluated and classified by these four contacts: what we do, how we look, what we say, and how we say it.

Dale Carnegie

CONTEMPLATION
The contemplative life is often miserable. You should do more, think less, and not watch yourself living.

Chamfort

The national distrust of the contemplative temperament arises less from an innate Philistinism than from a suspicion of anything that cannot be counted, stuffed, framed, or mounted over the fireplace in the den.

Lewis Lapham

CONTENT
Content is disillusioning to behold: what is there to be content about?

Virginia Woolf

CONTENTION
Better little with content than much with contention.

Benjamin Franklin

CONTENTMENT

To be content with little is difficult;
to be content with much, impossible.

Marie von Ebner-Eschenbach

Too many people miss the silver
lining because they're expecting
gold.

Maurice Seitter

How is it, Maecenas, that no one
lives contented with his lot,
whether he has planned it for himself or fate has flung him into it,
but yet he praises those who follow
different paths?

Horace

CONTINGENCIES

O to be self-balanced for contingencies.

Walt Whitman

Consider the little mouse, how
sagacious an animal it is which
never entrusts its life to one hole
only.

Plautus

CONTINUITY

Continuity does not rule out fresh
approaches to fresh situations.

Dean Rusk

Continuity in everything is unpleasant. Cold is agreeable, that we may
get warm.

Blaise Pascal

CONTRADICT

Do I contradict myself? Very well
then I contradict myself (I am large,
I contain multitudes).

Walt Whitman

CONTRADICTION

In formal logic, a contradiction is a
signal of defeat: but in the evolution of real knowledge it marks the
first step in progress toward a victory.

Alfred North Whitehead

CONTRIBUTIONS

If you want to live a long life, focus
on making contributions.

Hans Selye

CONTROL

If everything seems under control,
you're just not going fast enough.

Mario Andretti

The ship that will not obey the
helm will have to obey the rocks.

English proverb

CONTROVERSY

I am continually fascinated at the
difficulty intelligent people have in
distinguishing between what is
controversial from what is merely
offensive.

Nora Ephron

CONVALESCENCE

I enjoy convalescence. It is the part
that makes the illness worthwhile.

George Bernard Shaw

CONVENT

Convent, *n.* A place of retirement
for women who wish for leisure to
meditate upon the sin of idleness.

Ambrose Bierce

CONVERSATION

If other people are going to talk, conversation is simply impossible.

James McNeill Whistler

For good or ill, your conversation is your advertisement. For every time you open your mouth, you let men look into your mind.

Bruce Barton

A subtle conversation, that is the Garden of Eden.

Caliph Ali Ben Ali

There are only two things in ordinary conversation which ordinary people dislike – information and wit.

Stephen Leacock

A gossip is one who talks to you about others; a bore is one who talks to you about himself; and a brilliant conversationalist is one who talks to you about yourself.

Lisa Kirk

In a conversation, keep in mind that you're more interested in what you have to say than anyone else is.

Andy Rooney

A good conversationalist is not one who remembers what was said, but says what someone wants to remember.

John Mason Brown

The value of the average conversation could be enormously improved by the constant use of four simple words: "I do not know."

André Maurois

Conversation should touch everything, but should concentrate itself on nothing.

Oscar Wilde

It's all right to hold a conversation, but you should let go of it now and then.

Richard Armour

No animal should ever jump up on the dining-room furniture unless absolutely certain that he can hold his own in the conversation.

Fran Lebowitz

CONVERSION

You have not converted a man because you have silenced him.

John Morley

CONVICTION

Some men are just as firmly convinced of what they think as others of what they know.

Aristotle

The strength or weakness of our conviction depends more on our courage than on our intelligence.

Marquis de Vauvenargues

At eighteen, our convictions are hills from which we look; at forty-five, they are caves in which we hide.

F. Scott Fitzgerald

I hate to see a thing done by halves; if it be right, do it boldly; if it be wrong, leave it undone.

Bernard Gilpin

CONVINCE
If you cannot convince them, confuse them.

Harry S. Truman

In theory it is easy to convince an ignorant person; in actual life, men not only object to offer themselves to be convinced, but hate the man who has convinced them.

Epictetus

COOKING
Cooking is like love. It should be entered into with abandon or not at all.

Harriet Van Horne

COOKS
Woe to the cook whose sauce has no sting.

Geoffrey Chaucer

Heaven sends us good meat, but the devil sends us cooks.

David Garrick

COOL
Uncool people never hurt anybody – all they do is collect stamps, read science-fiction books, and stand on the end of railway platforms staring at trains.

Ben Elton

CO-OPERATION
Great discoveries and improvements invariably involve the co-operation of many minds.

Alexander Graham Bell

Co-operation, like other difficult things, can be learned only by practice: and to be capable of it in great things, a people must be gradually trained to it in small. Now, the whole course of advancing civilization is a series of such training.

John Stuart Mill

Once we discover Martian space ships hovering over Earth's air space, we will all come together.

Lester B. Pearson

When spider webs unite, they can tie up a lion.

Ethiopian proverb

It is difficult for men of different nations to work shoulder to shoulder when they carry a chip on one and a gun on the other.

Adrian Anderson

COPY
Fie on clients who cannot leave copy alone and fie on copywriters who can.

Harry Pesin

CORRUPTION
All things may corrupt when minds are prone to evil.

Ovid

Cynics regarded everybody as equally corrupt. ... Idealists regarded everybody as equally corrupt, except themselves.

Robert Anton Wilson

The accomplice to the crime of corruption is frequently our own indifference.

Bess Myerson

Corruption is nature's way of restoring our faith in democracy.

Peter Ustinov

Corruption is authority plus monopoly minus transparency.

Unknown

COST
Nothing costs so much as what is given us.

Thomas Fuller, MD

Costs merely register competing attractions.

Frank H. Knight

Those things are dearest to us that have cost us most.

Michel de Montaigne

COST OF LIVING
The high cost of living hasn't affected its popularity.

Anonymous

In spite of the cost of living, it's still popular.

Laurence J. Peter

What some people mistake for the high cost of living is really the cost of high living.

Doug Larson

COUNSEL
For by wise counsel thou shall make thy war.

Proverbs 24:6

COUNT
One has to be able to count if only so that at fifty one doesn't marry a girl of twenty.

Maxim Gorky

COUNTING
Counting is the religion of this generation; it is its hope and its salvation.

Gertrude Stein

COUNTRY
God made the country, and man made the town.

William Cowper

It is my belief, Watson, founded upon my experience, that the lowest and vilest alleys of London do not present a more dreadful record of sin than does the smiling and beautiful countryside.

Arthur Conan Doyle

Anybody can be good in the country.

Oscar Wilde

I'd rather wake up in the middle of nowhere than in any city on Earth.

Steve McQueen

There is virtue in country houses, in gardens and orchards, in fields, streams and groves, in rustic recreations and plain manners, that neither cities nor universities enjoy.

Amos Bronson Alcott

A simple way to take measure of a country is to look at how many want in … and how many want out.

Tony Blair

Who saves his country, saves himself, saves all things, and all things saved do bless him! Who lets his country die, lets all things die, dies himself ignobly, and all things dying curse him!

Benjamin Hill

COUPLES

All couples fight. I bet if Mother Teresa had married Gandhi, they'd have fought over who ate less.

Richard Helzer

COURAGE

He who loses wealth loses much; he who loses a friend loses more; but he who loses courage loses all.

Miguel de Cervantes

There is plenty of courage among us for the abstract but not for the concrete.

Helen Keller

This is courage in a man: to bear unflinchingly what heaven sends.

Euripides

The secret of happiness is freedom; the secret of freedom, courage.

Thucydides

Any danger spot is tenable if men – brave men – will make it so.

John F. Kennedy

Two-thirds of help is to give courage.

Irish proverb

Sometimes, even to live is an act of courage.

Seneca

Courage is the ladder on which all other virtues mount.

Clare Boothe Luce

Life shrinks or expands in proportion to one's courage.

Anaïs Nin

Courage is being scared to death but saddling up anyway.

John Wayne

Courage is the price that life exacts for granting peace.

Amelia Earhart

To persevere, trusting in what hopes he has is courage in a man. The coward despairs.

Euripides

Until the day of his death, no man can be sure of his courage.

Jean Anouilh

Courage is not the absence of fear, but rather the judgment that something else is more important than fear.

Ambrose Redmoon

Faced with what is right, to leave undone shows a lack of courage.

Confucius

Courage is the power to let go of the familiar.

Raymond Lindquist

A stout heart breaks bad luck.

Miguel de Cervantes

The essence of courage is not that your heart should not quake, but that nobody else shall know that it does.

E.F. Benson

Courage is almost a contradiction in terms. It means a strong desire to live taking the form of readiness to die.

G.K. Chesterton

Courage: a special kind of knowledge; the knowledge of how to fear what ought to be feared, and not to fear what ought not to be feared.

Plato

It is curious – curious that physical courage should be so common in the world, and moral courage so rare.

Mark Twain

I beg you to take courage; the brave soul can mend even disaster.

Catherine the Great

COURT
When you go into court you are putting your fate into the hands of twelve people who weren't smart enough to get out of jury duty.

Norm Crosby

The probation service have found out that there are two types of person appearing before the courts – those who have problems and those who are problems.

Simon Cohen

There is a higher court than courts of justice and that is the court of conscience. It supersedes all other courts.

Mohandas Gandhi

COURTESY
Knowledge, ability, experience, are of little avail in reaching high success if courtesy be lacking. Courtesy

is the one passport that will be accepted without question in every land, in every office, in every home, in every heart in the world. For nothing commends itself so well as kindness; and courtesy is kindness.

George D. Powers

Courtesy is the shortest distance between two people.

Anonymous

COW
The cow is of the bovine ilk;/One end is moo, the other, milk.

Ogden Nash

Who was the guy who first looked at a cow and said, "I think I'll drink whatever comes out of these things when I squeeze 'em!"?

Bill Watterson

COWARD
The coward calls the brave man rash; the rash man calls him a coward.

Aristotle

All men would be cowards if they durst.

John Wilmot, Earl of Rochester

Everyone considered him the coward of the county.

Kenny Rogers

Many would be cowards if they had courage enough.

Thomas Fuller, MD

Thou art essentially a natural coward without instinct.

William Shakespeare

Cowards do not count in battle; they are there, but not in it.

Euripides

CRADLE
The hand that rocks the cradle is the hand that rules the world.

William Ross Wallace

CRANK LETTERS (REPLY)
Dear Sir:
This is to inform you that some crackpot is using your name and has recently written to me over your signature putting forth views so eccentric in nature and so much at variance with your usual logical style that the letter could not possibly be from you. I felt I owed it to you to bring this to your attention.

John Diefenbaker

CREATION
Every successful creative person creates with an audience of one in mind.

Kurt Vonnegut

I don't think anybody in our business is creative. What we do is copy something better than the next person.

Henry Siegel

CREATIVE THINKING
Creative thinking may mean simply the realization that there's not particular virtue in doing things the way they've always been done.

Rudolph Flesch

Think before you speak is criticism's motto; speak before you think, creation's.

E.M. Forster

We live at a time when man believes himself fabulously capable of creation, but he does not know what to create. Lord of all things, he is not lord of himself. He feels lost amid his own abundance. With more means at its disposal, more knowledge, more techniques than ever, it turns out that the world today goes the same way as the worst of the worlds that have been: it simply drifts.

José Ortega y Gasset

CREATIVITY
Creativity … is mankind's ultimate capital asset, and the only one with which man has been endowed.

Arnold Toynbee

Creativity is the ability to see relationships where none exist.

Thomas Disch

Another word for creativity is courage.

George Prince

Creativity is the power to connect the seemingly unconnected.

William Plomer

Creativity is piercing the mundane to find the marvelous.

Bill Moyers

When Alexander the Great visited Diogenes and asked whether he could do anything for the famed teacher, Diogenes replied, "Only stand out of my light." Perhaps one day we shall know how to heighten creativity. Until then, one of the best things we can do for creative men and women is to stand out of their light.

John W. Gardner

The secret to creativity is knowing how to hide your sources.

Albert Einstein

Creativity is allowing yourself to make mistakes. Art is knowing which ones to keep.

Scott Adams

Our salvation lies not in knowing, but in creating.

Friedrich Nietzsche

The greatest real thrill that life offers is to create, to construct, to develop something useful. Too often we fail to recognize and pay tribute to the creative spirit. It is that spirit that creates our jobs.

Alfred P. Sloan

CREDIT

The world is divided into people who do things and people who get the credit.

Dwight Morrow

An American credit card ... is just as good in Europe as American gold used to be.

Edward Bellamy

CREDITORS

Creditors have better memories than debtors.

Benjamin Franklin

CREDO

You were born knowing all you need to know, and don't you forget it. Avoid getting any education that smacks of the ordinary and the mundane. You're not ordinary ... It's vital that you know that your uniqueness will get you through every crisis. You'll get by just by being you. Training is for the masses, not for classy folk like yourself. You're fated to be rich and famous, and you don't have to do one more thing to get it other than what you've already done. Just sit back and be your own uniquely great and lovable self.

Ben Stein

CREDULITY

The most positive men are the most credulous.

Alexander Pope

Credulity is the man's weakness, but the child's strength.

Charles Lamb

CRIME

The study of crime begins with the knowledge of oneself.

Henry Miller

It is worse than a crime: it is a blunder.

Joseph Fouché

Really premeditated crimes are those that are not committed.

Leonardo Sciascia

Obviously, crime pays, or there'd be no crime.

G. Gordon Liddy

A first impulse was never a crime.
Pierre Corneille

No man was ever more than about nine meals away from crime or suicide.
Eric Sevareid

Our crime against criminals is that we treat them as villains.
Friedrich Nietzsche

Crime, like virtue, has its degrees.
Jean Racine

Stripped of ethical rationalizations and philosophical pretentions, a crime is anything that a group in power chooses to prohibit.
Freda Adler

There is no den in the wide world to hide a rogue. Commit a crime and the earth is made of glass.
Ralph Waldo Emerson

Heaven takes care that no man secures happiness by crime.
Vittorio Alfieri

Once in the racket, you're always in it.
Al Capone

Crime is naught but misdirected energy.
Emma Goldman

The greatest crimes are caused by surfeit, not by want.
Aristotle

It's strange that men should take up crime when there are so many legal ways to be dishonest.
Anonymous

It is the talk, and not the intrigue, that's the crime.
George Granville

I haven't committed a crime. What I did was fail to comply with the law.
David Dinkins

If you share your friend's crime, you make it your own.
Latin proverb

Society prepares the crime; the criminal commits it.
Vittorio Alfieri

All men have crimes, and most of them are hidden.
Maxwell Anderson

CRISIS
In time of crisis, we must all decide again and again whom we love.
Frank O'Hara

Great emergencies and crises show us how much greater our vital resources are than we had supposed.
William James

The Chinese use two brush strokes to write the word "crisis." One brush stroke stands for danger; the other for opportunity. In a crisis, be aware of the danger – but recognize the opportunity.
Richard M. Nixon

In crisis is cleverness born.
Chinese proverb

Any idiot can face a crisis – it's day to day living that wears you out.
Anton Chekhov

CRITICISM

A fly, Sir, may sting a stately horse and make him wince; but one is still an insect, and the other is a horse still.

Samuel Johnson

The fight against Communism diminished us. That's why we were unable to rejoice at our victory. It left us in a false and corrosive orthodoxy. It licensed our excesses, and we didn't like ourselves the better for them. It dulled our love of dissent and our sense of life's adventure.

In my country, and perhaps in yours, the service industries of criticism have almost drowned the magic of creation. Our intellectuals hate too much: our press revels in public executions. We are poisoning ourselves with malice. Yet we take no risks. We are not brave. Our orthodoxy still gives us no way out.

Yet we have never been so free. We no longer need to clip the wings of our humanity. It's time we flew again.

John le Carré

Criticism should not be querulous and wasting, all knife and root-puller, but guiding, instructive, inspiring – a south wind, not an east wind.

Ralph Waldo Emerson

If you hear someone is speaking ill of you, instead of trying to defend yourself you should say: "He obviously does not know me very well, since there are so many other faults he could have mentioned."

Epictetus

To avoid criticism – do nothing, say nothing, be nothing.

Elbert Hubbard

Honest criticism is hard to take, particularly from a relative, a friend, an acquaintance, or a stranger.

Franklin P. Jones

It is much easier to be critical than to be correct.

Benjamin Disraeli

Doubt is an element of criticism, and the tendency of criticism is necessarily skeptical.

Benjamin Disraeli

People ask you for criticism, but they only want praise.

W. Somerset Maugham

I do not resent criticism, even when, for the sake of emphasis, it parts for the time with reality.

Winston Churchill

I have never found, in a long experience of politics, that criticism is ever inhibited by ignorance.

Harold Macmillan

Criticism is prejudice made plausible.

H.L. Mencken

Criticism often takes from the tree caterpillars and blossoms together.

Jean Paul

A better mousetrap, or a better automobile, or a better concept of freedom, may seem to occur as inspiration; but no such "inspiration" is possible unless the inspired mind has first perceived the existing mousetrap, automobile, or concept to be inadequate. Criticism, that is to say, and the doubt out of which it arises, are the prior conditions to progress of any sort.

Philip Wylie

Criticism is easy; art is difficult.

Philippe Néricault Destouches

Criticism prevents art from forgetting, prevents it from sinking into conformity.

Richard Ellmann

Long experience has taught me that to be criticized is not always to be wrong.

Anthony Eden

No matter: I will live so that none shall believe him.

Plato

Few persons have the wisdom to prefer censure, which is useful to them, to praise, which deceives them.

François, duc de La Rochefoucauld

When you sling mud, you lose ground.

Adlai Stevenson

CRITICS

Asking a working writer what he feels about critics is like asking a lamppost what it feels about dogs.

John Osborne

It is not the critic who counts, not the man who points out how the strong man stumbled or where the doer of deeds could have done better.

The credit belongs to the man who is actually in the arena; whose face is marred by dust and sweat and blood; who strives valiantly; who errs and comes short again and again; who knows the great enthusiasms, the great devotions, and spends himself in a worthy cause; who, at the best, knows in the end the triumph of high achievement; and who, at the worst, if he fails, at least fails while daring greatly, so that his place shall never be with those cold and timid souls who know neither victory nor defeat.

Theodore Roosevelt

A critic is a man who prefers the indolence of opinion to the trials of action.

John Mason Brown

Insects sting, not from malice, but because they want to live. It is the same with critics – they desire our blood, not our pain.

Friedrich Nietzsche

The critics are right nine times out of ten.

H.L. Mencken

No degree of dullness can safeguard a work against the determination of critics to find it fascinating.

Harold Rosenberg

A drama critic is a man who leaves no turn unstoned.

George Bernard Shaw

Critics search for ages for the wrong word which, to give them credit, they eventually find.

Peter Ustinov

A critic is a man created to praise greater men than himself, but he is never able to find them.

Richard Le Gallienne

A critic is a man who knows the way but can't drive the car.

Kenneth Tynan

If you think it is so easy to be a critic, so difficult to be a poet or a painter or film experimenter, may I suggest you try both? You may discover why there are so few critics, so many poets.

Pauline Kael

While the critic caused me a somewhat uneasy breakfast, I contented myself with the knowledge that I had given him a perfectly ghastly evening.

Jeremy Sinden

He has a right to criticize who has a heart to help.

Abraham Lincoln

CROWD
Every crowd has a silver lining.

P.T. Barnum

The crowd gives the leader new strength.

Evenius

To be a member of a crowd is an experience closely akin to alcoholic intoxication. Most human beings feel a craving to escape from the cramping limitations of their ego, to take periodical holidays from their all too familiar, all too squalid little selves.

Aldous Huxley

CROWN
A crown is merely a hat that lets the rain in.

Frederick the Great

Uneasy lies the head that wears the crown.

William Shakespeare

CROWS
Most people dislike crows because they are just like we are. They hang around in groups and make a lot of noise. They're troublemakers who like to take the easy way out.

Dr Carolee Caffrey

CRY
Why begin, then cry for something that might have been?/No, I'd rather have nothing at all.

Jack Lawrence and Arthur Altman

CRYSTAL BALL
There's an old Newfoundland saying: he who lives by the crystal ball must learn to eat ground glass.

Michael Walker

CULT
A cult is a religion with no political power.

Tom Wolfe

CULTURE

One of the fatalities of our culture is that it has idealized immaturity.
H.A. Overstreet

The only culture you want to preserve is bacterial. Real culture is something you strive to attain, not something you keep in a pickle jar.
Louis Dudek

A culture is no better than its woods.
W.H. Auden

A culture is in its finest flower before it starts to analyze itself.
Alfred North Whitehead

Culture is smitten with counting and measuring; it feels out of place and uncomfortable with the innumerable.
Jean Dubuffet

Culture is to know the best that has been thought and said in the world.
Matthew Arnold

Whenever I hear the word "culture" ... I release the safety catch on my pistol.
Hanns Johst

CUNNING

A man has made great progress in cunning when he does not seem too clever to others.
Jean de La Bruyère

The weak in courage is strong in cunning.
William Blake

Cunning is neither the consequence of sense, nor does it give sense. A proof that it is not sense is that cunning people never imagine that others can see through them.
Horace Walpole

Nothing doth more hurt in a state than that cunning men pass for wise.
Francis Bacon

Cunning ... is the sense of our weakness, and an attempt to effect by concealment what we cannot do openly and by force.
William Hazlitt

CURE

I see the cure is not worth the pain.
Caius Marius

CURIOSITY

Curiosity will conquer fear even more than bravery will.
James Stephens

The cure for boredom is curiosity. There is no cure for curiosity.
Ellen Parr

Curiosity is one of the permanent and certain characteristics of a vigorous mind.
Samuel Johnson

Curiosity being one of the forms of self-revelation, a systematically incurious person remains always partly mysterious.
Joseph Conrad

Curiosity is one of the lowest of the human faculties. You will have noticed that in daily life when people are inquisitive they nearly always have bad memories and are usually stupid at bottom.

E.M. Forster

Why is it that beautiful women never seem to have any curiosity? Is it because they know they're classical? With classical things, the Lord finished the job. Ordinary ugly people know they're deficient and they go on looking for the pieces.

Penelope Gilliatt

Curiosity has its own reason for existing. One cannot help but be in awe when he contemplates the mysteries of eternity, of life, of the marvelous structure of reality.

Albert Einstein

Curiosity is as much the parent of attention, as attention is of memory.

Richard Whately

Curiosity may be pictured as being made up of chains of small questions extending outwards, sometimes over huge distances, from a central hub composed of a few blunt, large questions.

Alain de Botton

When curiosity is alive, we are attracted to many things; we discover many worlds.

Eric Booth

The first and simplest emotion which we discover in the human mind, is curiosity.

Edmund Burke

My father has spanked me, and my mother has spanked me; all my aunts and uncles have spanked me for my insatiable curiosity; and I still want to know what the Crocodile has for dinner!

Rudyard Kipling

There always comes a time when curiosity becomes a sin.

Anatole France

CURRENT
When a thing is current, it creates currency.

Marshall McLuhan

CURSES
Curses are like young chickens – they always come home to roost.

Robert Southey

CUSTOM
Custom may lead a man to many errors, but it justifies none.

Henry Fielding

Customs are made for customary circumstances, and customary characters.

John Stuart Mill

He who does anything because it is the custom, makes no choice.

John Stuart Mill

How many things, both just and unjust, are sanctioned by custom!

Terence

There is no conceivable human action which custom has not at one time justified and at another condemned.

Joseph Wood Krutch

An old custom is so sacred when it is bad!

Hector Berlioz

A custom without truth is but an old error.

Thomas Fuller, MD

The perpetual obstacle to all human advancement is custom.

John Stuart Mill

CUT
Never cut what you can untie.

Joseph Joubert

CYNICISM
If I'm realistic at all, people translate that into cynicism.

Woody Allen

The opposite of creativity is cynicism.

Esa Saarinen

The power of accurate observation is commonly called cynicism by those who have not got it.

George Bernard Shaw

Cynicism is an unpleasant way of saying the truth.

Lillian Hellman

Cynicism is cheap – you can buy it at any Monoprix store – it's built into all poor-quality goods.

Graham Greene

Cynicism is intellectual dandyism.

George Meredith

CYNICS
The cynic never grows up, but commits intellectual suicide.

Charles Reynolds Brown

It takes a clever man to turn cynic and a wise man to be clever enough not to.

Fannie Hurst

What is a cynic? A man who knows the price of everything and the value of nothing.

Oscar Wilde

A cynic is not merely one who reads bitter lessons from the past; he is one who is prematurely disappointed in the future.

Sydney J. Harris

A cynic is a man who, when he smells flowers, looks around for a coffin.

H.L. Mencken

DAILY LIFE
In daily life what distinguishes the master is the using those materials he has, instead of looking about for what are more renowned, or what others have used well.
Ralph Waldo Emerson

DANCE
The man who can't dance thinks the band is no good.
Polish proverb

For children and youth, dancing in the parlour or on the green may be a very pleasant and healthful amusement, but when we see older people dancing we are ready to ask with the Chinese: "Why don't you have your servants do it for you?"
Sir Joshua Reynolds

Lighter than a cork/I danced on the waves.
Arthur Rimbaud

The trouble with nude dancing is that not everything stops when the music stops.
Robert Helpmann

Dancing is wonderful training for girls, it's the first way you learn to guess what a man is going to do before he does it.
Christopher Morley

Get up and dance, get up and smile, get up and drink to the days that are gone in the shortest while.
Simon Fowler

DANDELIONS
If dandelions were hard to grow, they would be most welcome on any lawn.
Andrew V. Mason

DANGER
Don't think there are no crocodiles just because the water is calm.
Malay proverb

Our safety is not in blindness, but in facing our dangers.
Friedrich von Schiller

Those who will play with cats must expect to be scratched.
Miguel de Cervantes

Dangers, by being despised, grow great.

Edmund Burke

Water can be good and bad, useful and dangerous. To the danger, however, a remedy has been found: learning to swim.

Democritus

Danger and delight grow on one stalk.

English proverb

DARING

All serious daring starts from within.

Eudora Welty

Enter these enchanted woods,/You who dare.

George Meredith

Against the bold, daring is unsafe.

Ovid

DARK

At one stride comes the dark.

Samuel Taylor Coleridge

DARK AGES

In the future the so-called Dark Ages will perhaps be lengthened to include our own.

Georg Christoph Lichtenberg

DARK SIDE

Everyone is a moon, and has a dark side which he never shows to anybody.

Mark Twain

DARLING

Darling: the popular form of address used in speaking to a person of the opposite sex whose name you cannot at the moment recall.

Oliver Herford

DATA

Data data everywhere but not a thought to think.

Theodore Roszak

The plural of anecdote is not data.

Roger Brinner

The more the data banks record about each one of us, the less we exist.

Marshall McLuhan

DATES

I was on a date recently, and the guy took me horseback riding. That was kind of fun, until we ran out of quarters.

Susie Loucks

I've been on so many blind dates, I should get a free dog.

Wendy Liebman

DAUGHTERS

To a father waxing old, nothing is dearer than a daughter. Sons have spirits of higher pitch, but less inclined to sweet, enduring fondness.

Euripides

I have a daughter who can spin straw into gold.

Rumpelstiltskin, Grimm's Fairy Tales

DAWN

Not knowing when the dawn will come I open every door.

Emily Dickinson

DAYS

Why are our days numbered and not, say, lettered?

Woody Allen

We should count each day a separate life.

Seneca

I think I could enjoy the day more if it didn't start so early.

Tom Wilson

There's no such thing in anyone's life as an unimportant day.

Alexander Woolcott

Only that day dawns to which we are awake.

Henry David Thoreau

Nothing is worth more than this day.

Johann Wolfgang von Goethe

DEAD

The dead don't die. They look on and help.

D.H. Lawrence

We owe respect to the living; to the dead we owe only truth.

Voltaire

There are more dead people than living. And their numbers are increasing. The living are getting rarer.

Eugène Ionesco

DEADLINE

A deadline is negative inspiration. Still, it's better than no inspiration at all.

Rita Mae Brown

DEATH

One dies only once, and it's for such a long time!

Molière

When I die, I want to die like my grandfather, peacefully, in my sleep and with a smile on my face, not terrified and screaming, like the passengers in his car.

Unknown

Death does determine life ... Once life is finished it acquires a sense; up to that point it has not got a sense; its sense is suspended and therefore ambiguous.

Pier Paolo Pasolini

He who lives more lives than one/ More deaths than one must die.

Oscar Wilde

Death is not the greatest loss in life. The greatest loss is what dies inside us while we live.

Norman Cousins

A useless life is an early death.

Johann Wolfgang von Goethe

True, you can't take it with you, but then, that's not the place where it comes in handy.

Brendan Francis

It's not that I'm afraid to die. I just don't want to be there when it happens.

Woody Allen

If Mr Selwyn calls again, show him up; if I am alive I shall be delighted to see him; and if I am dead he would like to see me.

Lord Holland

After your death you will be what you were before your birth.

Arthur Schopenhauer

No, it is better not. She would only ask me to take a message to Albert.

Benjamin Disraeli

Once you're dead, you're made for life.

Jimi Hendrix

In the long run, we are all dead.

John Maynard Keynes

Those who welcome death have only tried it from the ears up.

Wilson Mizner

It is a good thing to escape from death.

Sophocles

If there wasn't death, I think you couldn't go on.

Stevie Smith

The moment you're born you're done for!

Arnold Bennett

After the first death, there is no other.

Dylan Thomas

Death is the mother of beauty.

Wallace Stevens

Death asks no entrance fee to let you in.

Allen Tate

The timing of death, like the ending of a story, gives a changed meaning to what preceded it.

Mary Catherine Bateson

I am one of those unfortunates to whom death is less hideous than explanations.

D.B. Wyndham Lewis

You've never seen death? Look in the mirror every day and you will see it like bees working in a glass hive.

Jean Cocteau

So softly death succeeded life in her,/She did but dream of heaven, and she was there.

John Dryden

Death is one moment, and life is so many of them.

Tennessee Williams

Do not seek death. Death will find you. But seek the road which makes death a fulfilment.

Dag Hammarskjold

Even very young children need to be informed about dying. Explain the concept of death very carefully to your child. This will make threatening him with it much more effective.

P.J. O'Rourke

Death is softer by far than tyranny.

Aeschylus

Peace, Peace! He is not dead, he doth not sleep – He hath awakened from the dream of life.

Percy Bysshe Shelley

Death is the sound of distant thunder at a picnic.

W.H. Auden

As for death, one gets used to it – even if it's only other people's death you get used to.

Enid Bagnold

Let no man fear to die, we love to sleep all, and death is but the sounder sleep.

Francis Beaumont

Neither the sun nor death can be looked at with a steady eye.

François, duc de La Rochefoucauld

Death will be a great relief. No more interviews.

Katharine Hepburn

Death is a commingling of eternity with time; in the death of a good man, eternity is seen looking through time.

Johann Wolfgang von Goethe

Death is nothing to us, since when we are, death has not come, and when death has come, we are not.

Epicurus

If we don't know life, how can we know death?

Confucius

Death never takes the wise man by surprise; he is always ready to go.

Jean de La Fontaine

Death is more universal than life; everyone dies but not everyone lives.

Alan Sachs

No one knows whether death, which people fear to be the greatest evil, may not be the greatest good.

Plato

The aims of life are the best defence against death.

Primo Levi

Death means a lot of money, honey. Death can really make you look like a star.

Andy Warhol

Death must be distinguished from dying with which it is often confused.

Sydney Smith

If death did not exist today, it would be necessary to invent it.

Voltaire

To himself everyone is an immortal; he may know that he is going to die, but he can never know that he is dead.

Samuel Butler

DEATH BEAM
They called me crazy in 1896 when I announced the discovery of cosmic rays. Again and again they jeered me when I discovered something new. Years later, they would admit that I was right. I suppose it will be the same old story now when I say that I have discovered a hitherto unknown source of energy – the Death Beam.

Nicola Tesla

DEBATE
It is better to debate a question without settling it, than to settle it without debate.

Joseph Joubert

Debate is the death of conversation.

Emil Ludwig

DEBAUCHERY
Debauchery is liberating because it creates no obligations. In it you possess only yourself; hence it remains the favourite pastime of the great lovers of their own person.

Albert Camus

DEBT
In the midst of life we are in debt.

Ethel Watts Mumford

How will living each day for the rest of your life in debt make you happier?

Jeff Yeager

We can only pay our debt to the past by putting the future in debt to us.

John Buchan

A small debt produces a debtor; a large one, an enemy.

Publilius Syrus

We pay the debts of the last generation by issuing bonds payable by the next generation.

Laurence J. Peter

My father taught me never to owe anyone anything, not even a kindness.

Hetty Green

DECADENCE
Decadence can find agents only when it wears the mask of progress.

George Bernard Shaw

DECAY
All things are subject to decay and when fate summons, monarchs must obey.

John Dryden

DECEIT
Our distrust justifies the deceit in others.

François, duc de La Rochefoucauld

Everything that deceives may be said to enchant.

Plato

One deceit needs many others, and so the whole house is built in the air and must soon come to the ground.

Baltasar Gracian

DECEIVERS
There are three kinds of deceivers: fools, those who deceive themselves but not others; knaves, those who deceive others but not themselves, and philosophers, those who deceive both themselves and others.

Anonymous

It is a double pleasure to deceive the deceiver.

Jean de La Fontaine

There are many people who have grave scruples about deceiving others but think it as nothing to deceive themselves.

Eric Hoffer

He that once deceives is ever suspected.

Proverb

DECEPTION

We are never so easily deceived as when we imagine we are deceiving others.

François, duc de La Rochefoucauld

We are never deceived; we deceive ourselves.

Johann Wolfgang von Goethe

Who will not be deceived must have as many eyes as hairs on his head.

German proverb

People always overdo the matter when they attempt deception

Charles Dudley Warner

It is more tolerable to be refused than deceived.

Publilius Syrus

Fool me once, shame on you. Fool me twice, shame on me.

Anonymous

DECIDE

Decide, v.i., To succumb to the preponderance of one set of influences over another set.

Ambrose Bierce

The first step to getting the things you want out of life is this: Decide what you want.

Ben Stein

Nothing is more difficult, and therefore more precious, than to be able to decide.

Napoleon Bonaparte

DECISIONS

It is vain to hope to please all alike. Let a man stand with his face in what direction he will, he must necessarily turn his back on one half of the world.

George Dennison Prentice

The man who is denied the opportunity of taking decisions of importance begins to regard as important the decisions he is allowed to take. He becomes fussy about filing, keen on seeing that pencils are sharpened, eager to ensure that windows are open (or shut) and apt to use two or three different-coloured inks.

C. Northcote Parkinson

Be willing to make decisions. Don't fall victim to what I call the "ready-aim-aim-aim syndrome." You must be willing to fire.

T. Boone Pickens

Give your decisions, never your reasons; your decisions may be right, your reasons are sure to be wrong.

Earl of Mansfield

When it is not necessary to make a decision, it is necessary not to make a decision.

Lord Falkland

Don't be afraid to take a big step if one is indicated; you can't cross a chasm in two small jumps.

David Lloyd George

Every decision is liberating, even if it leads to disaster. Otherwise, why do so many people walk upright and with open eyes into their misfortune?

Elias Canetti

The hardest thing in life is to know which bridge to cross and which to burn.

David Russell

If we could first know where we are and whither we were tending, we could better judge what to do and how to do it.

Abraham Lincoln

A good decision is based on knowledge and not on numbers.

Plato

All our final decisions are made in a state of mind that is not going to last.

Marcel Proust

There is no stigma attached to recognizing a bad decision in time to install a better one.

Laurence J. Peter

The quality of decision is like the well-timed swoop of a falcon which enables it to strike and destroy its victim.

Sun Tzu

Ever notice that "what the hell" is always the right decision?

Marilyn Monroe

DECISIVENESS

Tender-handed stroke a nettle,/ And it stings you for your pains;/ Grasp it like a man of mettle,/And soft as silk it remains.

Aaron Hill

We know what happens to people who stay in the middle of the road. They get run down.

Aneurin Bevan

The man who insists upon seeing with perfect clearness before he decides, never decides.

Henri-Frédéric Amiel

DECLINE

The downhill path is easy, but there's no turning back.

Christina Rossetti

DEEDS

Our deeds determine us, as much as we determine our deeds.

George Eliot

When all is said and done, more is said than done.

Unknown

Even though men flatter themselves on their great deeds, they are not often the results of great designs, but simply the results of chance.

François, duc de La Rochefoucauld

Thinking well is wise; planning well, wiser; but doing well is the wisest and best of all.

Persian proverb

DEFEAT
Victory has a hundred fathers, but defeat is an orphan.

Count Galeazzo Ciano

Like snatching defeat from the jaws of victory.

Abraham Lincoln

We are not interested in the possibilities of defeat; they do not exist.

Queen Victoria

DEFENCE
Isn't the best defence always a good attack?

Ovid

DEFICIT
The deficit is big enough to take care of itself.

Ronald Reagan

DEGRADATION
Gurowski asked, "Where is this bog? I wish to earn some money. I wish to dig peat." "O no, indeed, sir, you cannot do this kind of degrading work." "I cannot be degraded. I am Gurowski."

Ralph Waldo Emerson

DÉJÀ VU
This is like déjà vu all over again.

Yogi Berra

DELAY
One of these days is none of these days.

English proverb

Delay is preferable to error.

Thomas Jefferson

Never do today what you can do as well tomorrow; because something may occur to make you regret your premature action.

Aaron Burr

Delay always breeds danger; and to protract a great design is often to ruin it.

Miguel de Cervantes

Delay is the deadliest form of denial.

C. Northcote Parkinson

DELEGATION
That man is great who can use the brains of others to carry out his work.

Donn Platt

DELIBERATION
Deliberation, *n.* The act of examining one's bread to determine which side it is buttered on.

Ambrose Bierce

Deliberating is not delaying.

Unknown

DELUSIONS
He had delusions of adequacy.

Walter Kerr

No man is happy without a delusion of some kind. Delusions are as necessary to our happiness as realities.

Christian Nestell Bovee

The house of delusions is cheap to build but draughty to live in.

A.E. Housman

DEMAGOGUES

In every age, the vilest specimens of human nature are to be found among demagogues.

Thomas Babington Macaulay

It is an easy and vulgar thing to please the mob, and not a very arduous task to astonish them; but to benefit and improve them is a work fraught with difficulty and teeming with danger.

Charles Caleb Colton

DEMANDS

Walking into a noisy classroom, the instructor slapped a hand on the desk and ordered sharply: "I demand pandemonium!" The class quieted down immediately.

"It isn't what you demand," explained the instructor, "but the way you demand it."

Unknown

DEMOCRACY

Democracy means government by the uneducated, while aristocracy means government by the badly educated.

G.K. Chesterton

You don't have a democracy. It's a photocracy.

Robert G. Menzies

Democracy means the bludgeoning of the people by the people for the people.

Oscar Wilde

Democracy is also a form of religion; it is the worship of jackals by jackasses.

H.L. Mencken

Democracy is the art of running the circus from the monkey cage.

H.L. Mencken

Democracy is a process by which people choose who will get the blame.

Bertrand Russell

Democracy is only an experiment in government and it has the obvious disadvantage of counting votes instead of weighing them.

Dean Inge

It's not the voting that's democracy, it's the counting.

Tom Stoppard

People who want to understand democracy should spend less time in the library with Aristotle and more time on the buses and in the subway.

Simeon Strunsky

Democracy is measured not by its leaders doing extraordinary things, but by its citizens doing ordinary things extraordinarily well.

John Gardner

Democracy is the recurrent suspicion that more than half of the people are right more than half of the time.

E.B. White

Democracy must be something more than two wolves and a sheep voting on what to have for dinner.

James Bovard

Democracy passes into despotism.

Plato

All the ills of democracy can be cured by more democracy.

Alfred E. Smith

Democracy is the theory that the common people know what they want, and deserve to get it good and hard.

H.L. Mencken

Under a democracy, one party always devotes its chief energies to trying to prove that the other party is unfit to rule – and both commonly succeed, and are right.

H.L. Mencken

Democracy is the only system that persists in asking the powers that be whether they are the powers that ought to be.

Sydney J. Harris

To acquire immunity to eloquence is of the utmost importance to the citizens of a democracy.

Bertrand Russell

The constant danger to democracy lies in the tendency of the individual to hide himself in the crowd – to defend his own failure to act

forthrightly according to conviction under the false excuse that the effort of one in one hundred forty million has no significance.

Dwight D. Eisenhower

Democracy is good. I say this because other systems are worse.

Jawaharlal Nehru

Man's capacity for justice makes democracy possible, but man's inclination to injustice makes democracy necessary.

Reinhold Niebuhr

The thing about democracy, beloveds, is that it is not neat, orderly, or quiet. It requires a relish for confusion.

Molly Ivins

We have put our faith in the hands of The People, the same folks who by and large (1) find politics boring and (2) are ignorant and irrational about public affairs.

Rick Shenkman

In the nineteenth century, philosophers believed that the human being was infinitely perfectible and therefore worthy of democracy. On the basis of the twentieth century, I believe that the human being is infinitely corruptible and therefore in need of democracy.

Alan Borovoy

I hate democracy as a political system. It stops you getting things done.

Bernie Ecclestone

False democracy shouts, "Every man down to the level of the average." True democracy cries, "All men up to the height of their fullest capacity for service and achievement."

Nicholas Murray Butler

Democracy is threatened by the inertia of good people, by the selfishness of most people, and by the evil designs of a few people.

Stanley King

The chief support of an autocracy is a standing army. The chief support of a democracy is an educated people.

Lotus D. Coffman

A modern democracy is a tyranny whose borders are undefined.

Norman Mailer

The test of democracy is freedom of criticism.

David Ben-Gurion

DENIAL
To deny all is to confess all.

Spanish proverb

Never believe anything until it has been officially denied.

Claud Cockburn

I really didn't say everything I said.

Yogi Berra

DENTOPEDALOGY
Dentopedalogy is the science of opening your mouth and putting

your foot in it. I've been practising it for years.

Prince Philip,
Duke of Edinburgh

DEPENDENCE
Dependence entails vulnerability. The relationship between the hunter and the hunted, therefore, has a certain equality. Ultimately, no one can be superior to that upon which he depends.

Hugh Brody

DEPRAVITY
No one ever suddenly became depraved.

Juvenal

DEPRESSION
But cloud instead, and ever-during dark / Surrounds me, from the cheerful ways of men / Cut off …

John Milton

Depression is the inability to construct a future.

Rollo May

DEPRIVATION
Once in the wilds of Afghanistan, I lost my corkscrew, and we were forced to live on nothing but food and water for days.

W.C. Fields

DESIGN
Never design anything the plant is not already equipped to build.

Raymond Hull

Design is not just what it looks like and feels like. Design is how it works.

Steve Jobs

DESIRE
There is nothing like desire for preventing the thing one says from bearing any resemblance to what one has in mind.

Marcel Proust

If your desires be endless, your cares and fears will be so too.

Thomas Fuller, MD

Where there is no desire, there will be no industry.

John Locke

The desire for imaginary benefits often involves the loss of present blessings.

Aesop

Having the fewest wants, I am nearest to the gods.

Socrates

Remember that not getting what you want is sometimes a wonderful stroke of luck.

Dalai Lama

No one can have all he wants, but a man can refrain from wanting what he has not, and cheerfully make the best of a bird in the hand.

Seneca

Great desire obtains little.

Burmese proverb

Modern man lives under the illusion that he knows what he wants, while he actually wants what he is supposed to want.

Erich Fromm

DESK
A desk is a dangerous place from which to watch the world.

John le Carré

DESPAIR
Despair, in short, seeks its own environment as surely as water finds its own level.

A. Alvarez

Despair is the conclusion of fools.

Benjamin Disraeli

To tell men that they cannot help themselves is to fling them into recklessness and despair.

James A. Froude

DESPERATION
Desperation is sometimes as powerful an inspirer as genius.

Benjamin Disraeli

When we are flat on our backs there is no way to look but up.

Roger W. Babson

DESPISE
It is easy to despise what you cannot get.

Aesop

We often despise what is most useful to us.

Aesop

DESPOTS

A despot easily forgives his subjects for not loving him, provided they do not love each other.

Alexis de Tocqueville

DESTINY

There are born victims, born to have their throats cut, as the cutthroats are born to be hanged.

Aldous Huxley

We are not permitted to choose the frame of our destiny. But what we put into it is ours.

Dag Hammarskjold

Destiny has two ways of crushing us – by refusing our wishes and by fulfilling them.

Henri-Frédéric Amiel

Destiny waits alike for the free man as well as him enslaved by another's might.

Aeschylus

DESTRUCTION

To build may have to be the slow and laborious task of years. To destroy can be the thoughtless act of a single day.

Winston Churchill

The modern world seems to have no notion of preserving different things side by side, of allowing its proper and proportionate place to each, of saving the whole varied heritage of culture. It has no notion except that of simplifying something by destroying nearly everything.

G.K. Chesterton

What is this world of ours? A complex entity subject to sudden changes which all indicate a tendency to destruction.

Denis Diderot

Do not men die fast enough without being destroyed by one another?

François de Salignac

DETAILS

It has long been an axiom of mine that the little things are infinitely the most important.

Arthur Conan Doyle

Our life is frittered away by detail. Simplify, simplify, simplify.

Henry David Thoreau

The world can never be learned by learning all its details.

Ralph Waldo Emerson

DETECTION

Detection is, or ought to be, an exact science, and should be treated in the same cold and unemotional manner.

Arthur Conan Doyle

DETERMINATION

Let us not be content to wait and see what will happen, but give us the determination to make the right things happen.

Peter Marshall

The difference between the impossible and the possible lies in a person's determination.

Tommy Lasorda

He who is firm and resolute in will molds the world to himself.

Johann Wolfgang von Goethe

DETERRENCE
One sword keeps another in the sheath.

George Herbert

Men are not hanged for stealing horses, but that horses may not be stolen.

George Savile, Marquess of Halifax

DETRACTORS
Next to the joy of the egotist is the joy of the detractor.

Agnes Repplier

DEVELOPMENT
I am convinced that nothing we do is more important than hiring and developing people. At the end of the day you bet on people, not on strategies.

Lawrence Bossidy

DEVELOPMENT (NEW)
The "silly" question is the first intimation of some totally new development.

Alfred North Whitehead

DEVIL
The devil's most devilish when respectable.

Elizabeth Barrett Browning

The proof that the Devil exists, acts, and succeeds is precisely that we no longer believe in him.

Denis de Rougemont

DIAMONDS
No pressure, no diamonds.

Mary Case

Diamonds are a girl's best friend.

Leo Robin

Kissing your hand may make you feel very good, but a diamond and sapphire bracelet lasts forever.

Anita Loos

DIAPER
Diaper backwards spells repaid. Think about it.

Marshall McLuhan

DICTATORS
Dictators ride to and fro upon tigers, which they dare not dismount.

Winston Churchill

DICTIONARY
He has never been known to use a word that might send a reader to a dictionary.

William Faulkner (about Ernest Hemingway)

DIE
The idea is to die young as late as possible.

Ashley Montagu

But you do not die of being sick, you die of being alive.

Michel de Montaigne

All say, "How hard it is to die" – a strange complaint to come from the mouths of people who have had to live.

Mark Twain

Die, v.: To stop sinning suddenly.

Elbert Hubbard

DIETS

Diets are for those who are thick and tired of it.

Anonymous

The second day of a diet is easier than the first. By the second day, you're off it.

Jackie Gleason

Some people eat too much; some people eat too little. Nothing else about diet really matters.

Kary Mullis

DIFFERENCES

It were not best that we should all think alike; it is difference of opinion that makes horse races.

Mark Twain

Resemblances are the shadows of differences. Different people see different similarities and similar differences.

Vladimir Nabokov

The shoe that fits one person pinches another.

Carl Jung

One man's poison ivy is another man's spinach.

George Ade

It's easy to make a buck. It's a lot tougher to make a difference.

Tom Brokaw

Share our similarities, celebrate our differences.

M. Scott Peck

It is so easy to exchange meaning; it is so easy to see the difference.

Gertrude Stein

You don't have to be disabled to be different, everybody's different.

Daniel Tammet

DIFFICULTIES

In youth we run into difficulties; in old age, difficulties run into us.

Josh Billings

He who accounts all things easy will have many difficulties.

Lao-Tse

All things are difficult before they are easy.

Thomas Fuller, MD

By heaven methinks it were an easy leap.

William Shakespeare

The Queen had only one way of settling all difficulties, great or small. "Off with his head!" she said, without even looking round.

Lewis Carroll

Difficulty is the excuse history never accepts.

Edward R. Murrow

A man's worst difficulties begin when he is able to do as he likes.

Thomas Henry Huxley

There is such a choice of difficulties that I am myself at a loss how to determine.

James Wolfe

Because a thing seems difficult for you, do not think it impossible for anyone to accomplish.

Marcus Aurelius

DIGESTION
I am convinced digestion is the great secret of life.

Sydney Smith

DIGITAL
The days of the digital watch are numbered.

Tom Stoppard

DIGNITY
Dignity does not consist in possessing honours, but deserving them.

Anonymous

Where is there dignity unless there is honesty?

Cicero

The only kind of dignity which is genuine is that which is not diminished by the indifference of others.

Dag Hammarskjold

Remember this – that there is a proper dignity and proportion to be observed in the performance of every act of life.

Marcus Aurelius

A sense of one's own dignity is as admirable when kept to oneself as it is ridiculous when displayed to others.

François, duc de La Rochefoucauld

There is no dignity quite so impressive, and no independence quite so important, as living within your means.

Calvin Coolidge

Where boasting ends, there dignity begins.

Edward Young

Where dignity is consciously striven for, pompousness inevitably turns up.

Gerald Bullett

DILEMMA
Believe me, there exists no such dilemma as that in which a gentleman is placed when he is forced to reply to a blackguard.

Edgar Allan Poe

You will, therefore, permit me to concede your entire argument, and yet contrive means to escape your dilemma.

Johann Wolfgang von Goethe

DILIGENCE
Few things are impossible to diligence and skill.

Samuel Johnson

Diligence is the mother of good fortune.

Miguel de Cervantes

DINING
One cannot think well, love well, sleep well, if one has not dined well.

Virginia Woolf

DINING ROOM

A dining room table with children's eager, hungry faces around it, ceases to be a mere dining room table, and becomes an altar.

Simeon Strunsky

DINNER

Everything ends this way in France. Weddings, christenings, duels, burials, affairs of state – everything is a pretext for a good dinner.

Jean Anouilh

A man seldom thinks with more earnestness of anything than he does of his dinner.

Samuel Johnson

Music with dinner is an insult both to the cook and the violinist.

G.K. Chesterton

DIPLOMACY

Diplomacy is to do and say the nastiest thing in the nicest way.

Isaac Goldberg

To say nothing, especially when speaking, is half the art of diplomacy.

Will Durant

All diplomacy is the continuation of war by other means.

Zhou Enlai

Take the diplomacy out of war and the thing would fall flat in a week.

Will Rogers

DIPLOMATS

A diplomat is a man who thinks twice before he says nothing.

Anonymous

An ambassador is an honest man sent to lie abroad for the commonwealth.

Sir Henry Wotton

DIRECTION

It is no longer clear which way is up, even if one wants to rise.

David Riesman

What is the use of running when we are not on the right road?

German proverb

Rowing harder doesn't help if the boat is headed in the wrong direction.

Kenichi Ohmae

When you don't know where you're going, any road will take you there.

Lewis Carroll

We must ask where we are and whither we are tending.

Abraham Lincoln

If you board the wrong train, it is no use running along the corridor in the other direction.

Dietrich Bonhoeffer

I find the great thing in this world is not so much where we stand as in what direction we are moving.

Oliver Wendell Holmes

We live in an age disturbed, confused, bewildered, afraid of its own forces, in search not merely of its road, but even of its direction.

Woodrow Wilson

DIRT

Dirt is not dirt, but only something in the wrong place.

Lord Palmerston

It is almost impossible to throw a little dirt on someone without getting a little on yourself.

Abigail Van Buren

Martin, if dirts was trumps, what hands you would hold!

Charles Lamb

DISAPPOINTMENT

Disappointments should be cremated, not embalmed.

Henry S. Haskins

Disappointments are to the soul what the thunderstorm is to the air.

Friedrich von Schiller

As for disappointing them, I should not so much mind; but I can't abide to disappoint myself.

Oliver Goldsmith

An old man once said, "When I was young, I was poor; when old, I became rich; but in each condition I found disappointment. When I had the faculties for enjoyment, I had not the means; when the means came, the faculties were gone."

Madame de Gasparin

DISARMAMENT

The Venus de Milo is the Goddess of Disarmament.

Al Boliska

DISASTER

The man does better who runs from disaster than he who is caught by it.

Homer

Even if it is to be, what end do you serve by running to meet distress?

Seneca

If the sky fall, hold up your hands.

Spanish proverb

The sky was too delicate a blue, the sea too green, the breeze too gentle.

Paul Verlaine

DISBELIEF

As a rule we disbelieve all the facts and theories for which we have no use.

William James

DISCIPLINE

Reasonable orders are easy enough to obey; it is capricious, bureaucratic, or plain idiotic demands that form the habit of discipline.

Barbara Tuchman

She has the head. But I never own to it before her; Discipline must be maintained.

Charles Dickens

A stern discipline pervades all nature, which is a little cruel that it may be very kind.

Edmund Spenser

No steam or gas ever drives anything until it is confined. No Niagara is ever turned into light and power until it is tunneled. No life ever grows until it is focused, dedicated, disciplined.

Harry Emerson Fosdick

DISCO DANCING

Disco dancing is … just the steady thump of a giant moron knocking in an endless nail.

Clive James

DISCONTENTMENT

There is no greater guilt than discontentment.

Lao-Tse

DISCOVERY

Discovery consists of looking at the same thing as everyone else and thinking something different.

Albert Szent-Györgyi

Man cannot discover new oceans unless he has the courage to lose sight of the shore.

André Gide

We often discover what *will* do, by finding out what will not do; and probably he who never made a mistake never made a discovery.

Samuel Smiles

The greatest obstacle to discovery is not ignorance – it is the illusion of knowledge.

Daniel Boorstin

People who read a great deal rarely make great discoveries. I do not say this in excuse of laziness, but because invention presupposes an extensive independent contemplation of things.

Georg Christoph Lichtenberg

The real voyage of discovery consists not in seeking new landscapes, but in having new eyes.

Marcel Proust

The more original a discovery, the more obvious it seems afterwards.

Arthur Koestler

The world will freely offer itself to you to be unmasked, it has no choice, it will roll in ecstasy at your feet.

Franz Kafka

The most exciting phrase to hear in science, the one that heralds new discoveries, is not "Eureka!" but "That's funny …"

Isaac Asimov

First doubt, then inquire, then discover. This has been the process with all our great thinkers.

H.T. Buckle

DISCRETION

A dram of discretion is worth a pound of wisdom.

German proverb

Judgment is not upon all occasions required, but discretion always is.

Lord Chesterfield

The better part of valour is discretion.

William Shakespeare

Not only to say the right thing in the right place, but, far more difficult still, to leave unsaid the wrong thing at the tempting moment.

George A. Sala

Discretion in speech is more than eloquence.

Francis Bacon

DISCUSSION (FREE)
Men are never so likely to settle a question rightly as when they discuss it freely.

Thomas Babington Macaulay

We believe it is better to discuss a question even without settling it than to settle a question without discussing it.

Adlai Stevenson

If we had more time for discussion we should probably have made a great many more mistakes.

Leon Trotsky

DISEASE
Is not disease the rule of existence?

Henry David Thoreau

Disease generally begins that equality which death completes.

Samuel Johnson

He who conceals his disease cannot expect to be cured.

Ethiopian proverb

If a lot of cures are suggested for a disease, it means the disease is incurable.

Anton Chekhov

DISGRUNTLED
He spoke with a certain what-is-it in his voice, and I could see that, if not actually disgruntled, he was far from being gruntled.

P.G. Wodehouse

DISGUISE
There is no disguise that can hide love for long where it exists, or simulate it where it does not.

François, duc de La Rochefoucauld

DISHONESTY
I have known a vast quantity of nonsense talked about bad men not looking you in the face. Don't trust that idea. Dishonesty will stare honesty out of countenance any day in the week, if there is anything to be got from it.

Charles Dickens

DISMISSAL
You have good leave to leave us; when we need/Your use and counsel we shall send for you.

William Shakespeare

DISPUTANTS
True disputants are like true sportsmen: their whole delight is in the pursuit.

Alexander Pope

DISPUTE
In a philosophical dispute, he gains most who is defeated, since he learns most.

Epicurus

DISSENT

I personally am inclined to approach [housework] the way governments treat dissent: Ignore it until it revolts.

Barbara Kingsolver

DISTANCE

If a man makes me keep my distance, the comfort is, he keeps his at the same time.

Jonathan Swift

Distance doesn't matter. It is only the first step that is difficult.

Marquise du Deffand

DISTRACTION

Do not let what you cannot do interfere with what you can do.

John Wooden

DISTRUST

Distrust all in whom the impulse to punish is powerful.

Friedrich Nietzsche

DIVERSION

Only two things does (the modern citizen) anxiously wish for – bread and the big game.

Juvenal

DIVORCE

No one ever filed for divorce on a full stomach.

Mama Leone

Ah, yes, divorce … from the Latin word meaning to rip out a man's genitals through his wallet.

Robin Williams

The happiest time of anyone's life is just after the first divorce.

John Kenneth Galbraith

A divorce is like an amputation; you survive, but there's less of you.

Margaret Atwood

DOCTORS

There are more old drunkards than old physicians.

François Rabelais

The reason doctors are so dangerous is that they believe in what they are doing.

Robert Mendelsohn

Medicines cure diseases, but doctors cure patients.

Carl Jung

If the doctor told me I had six minutes to live, I'd type a little faster.

Isaac Asimov

The best doctor in the world is the veterinarian. He can't ask his patients what is the matter – he's got to just know.

Will Rogers

DOCTRINE

To be effective a doctrine must not be understood, but has to be believed in. We can be absolutely certain only about things we do not understand. A doctrine that is understood is shorn of its strength.

Eric Hoffer

DOGMA

Every dogma has its day, but ideals are eternal.

Israel Zangwill

Truths turn into dogmas the moment they are disputed.

G.K. Chesterton

The dogmas of the quiet past are inadequate to the stormy present. The occasion is piled high with difficulty, and we must rise to the occasion. As our case is new, so we must think anew and act anew. We must disenthrall ourselves, and then we shall save our country.

Abraham Lincoln

You can't teach an old dogma new tricks.

Unknown

DOGMATISM

There are two kinds of people in the world: the conscious dogmatists and the unconscious dogmatists. I have always found myself that the unconscious dogmatists were by far the most dogmatic.

G.K. Chesterton

The greater the ignorance, the greater the dogmatism.

Sir William Osler

DOGS

I wonder if other dogs think poodles are members of a weird religious cult.

Rita Rudner

A boy can learn a lot from a dog: obedience, loyalty, and the importance of turning around three times before lying down.

Robert Benchley

They say the dog is man's best friend. I don't believe that. How many of your friends have you neutered.

Larry Reeb

I loathe people who keep dogs. They are cowards who haven't got the guts to bite people themselves.

August Strindberg

You can say any foolish thing to a dog, and the dog will give you a look that says. "My God, you're right! I never would have thought of that!"

Dave Barry

Nothing in the world is friendlier than a wet dog.

Dan Bennett

If you pick up a starving dog and make him prosperous, he will not bite you. This is the principal difference between a dog and a man.

Mark Twain

If dogs could talk, perhaps we would find it as hard to get along with them as we do with people.

Josef Čapek

Never buy a dog to do your own barking.

Humphrey Bourne

The reason a dog has so many friends is that he wags his tail instead of his tongue.

Don Hetland

Don't accept your dog's admiration as conclusive evidence that you are wonderful.

Ann Landers

If there are no dogs in Heaven, then when I die I want to go where they went.

Will Rogers

There is no psychiatrist in the world like a puppy licking your face.

Bern Williams

A dog is the only thing on earth that loves you more than he loves himself.

Josh Billings

The average dog is a nicer person than the average person.

Andy Rooney

We give dogs time we can spare, space we can spare, and love we can spare. And in return, dogs give us their all. It's the best deal man has ever made.

M. Acklam

Dogs love their friends and bite their enemies, quite unlike people, who are incapable of pure love and always have to mix love and hate.

Sigmund Freud

Dogs need to sniff the ground; it's how they keep abreast of current events. The ground is a giant dog newspaper, containing all kinds of late-breaking dog news items, which, if they are especially urgent, are often continued in the next yard.

Dave Barry

Anybody who doesn't know what soap tastes like never washed a dog.

Franklin P. Jones

If I have any beliefs about immortality, it is that certain dogs I have known will go to heaven, and very, very few persons.

James Thurber

If your dog is fat, you aren't getting enough exercise.

Unknown

My dog is worried about the economy because Alpo is up to $3.00 a can. That's almost $21.00 in dog money.

Joe Weinstein

Ever consider what our dogs must think of us? I mean, here we come back from a grocery store with the most amazing haul – chicken, pork, half a cow. They must think we're the greatest hunters on earth!

Anne Tyler

Women and cats will do as they please, and men and dogs should relax and get used to the idea.

Robert Heinlein

Dogs are not our whole life, but they make our lives whole.

Roger Caras

If you think dogs can't count, try putting three dog biscuits in your pocket and then giving Fido only two of them.

Phil Pastoret

I've seen a look in dogs' eyes, a quickly vanishing look of amazed contempt, and I am convinced that basically dogs think humans are nuts.

John Steinbeck

No one appreciates the very special genius of your conversation as the dog does.

Christopher Morley

The dog ... commends himself to our favour by affording play to our propensity for mastery.

Thorstein Veblen

DOING BADLY
If a thing is worth doing, it is worth doing badly.

G.K. Chesterton

DOING GOOD
Do not wait for extraordinary circumstances to do good; try to use ordinary situations.

Jean-Paul Richter

One has to do good for it to exist in the world.

Marie von Ebner-Eschenbach

DOING WELL
If a thing is not worth doing, it is not worth doing well.

Donald O. Hebb

DOLLAR
I believe in the dollar. Everything I earn, I spend.

Joan Crawford

DOOR
A door is what a dog is perpetually on the wrong side of.

Ogden Nash

DOORMAN
Doorman – a genius who can open the door of your car with one hand, help you in with the other, and still have one left for the tip.

Dorothy Kilgallen

DOUBLETHINK
Doublethink is the power of simultaneously holding two contradictory beliefs in one's mind, and accepting both of them.

George Orwell

DOUBTS
His doubts are better than most people's certainties.

Philip Yorke, Earl of Hardwicke

Ten thousand difficulties do not make one doubt.

John Henry Newman

You are never dedicated to something you have complete confidence in. No one is fanatically shouting that the sun is going to rise tomorrow. They know it's going to rise tomorrow. When people are fanatically dedicated to political or religious faiths or any other kind of dogmas or goals, it's always because these dogmas or goals are in doubt.

Robert Pirsig

I respect faith, but doubt is what gets you an education.

Wilson Mizner

Doubts are more cruel than the worst of truths.

Molière

If a man will be content to begin with doubts, he shall end in certainty.

Francis Bacon

When there is doubt, supplant it with action.

Thomas Carlyle

To give a reason for anything is to breed a doubt.

William Hazlitt

DOVE

How come the dove gets to be the peace symbol? How about the pillow? It has more feathers than the dove, and it doesn't have that dangerous beak.

Jack Handey

DRAMA

Drama is life with the dull bits cut out.

Alfred Hitchcock

DREAMERS

Like all dreamers I confuse disenchantment with truth.

Mark Twain

There are some people who live in a dream world, and there are some who face reality; and then there are those who turn one into the other.

Douglas Everett

DREAMS

Dreams are true while they last, and do we not live in dreams?

Alfred, Lord Tennyson

His life was a sort of dream, as are most lives with the mainspring left out.

F. Scott Fitzgerald

People who remember dreams in the morning are probably having very disturbed sleep at night.

James Horne

You see things: and you say "Why?"/But I dream things that never were:/and say "Why not?"

George Bernard Shaw

If you can dream it, you can do it.

Walt Disney

If you can build castles in the air, your work need not be lost; that is where they should be. Now put the foundations under them.

Henry David Thoreau

The best way to make your dreams come true is to wake up.

J.M. Power

You don't need anyone's permission to pursue your dreams. Don't let anyone tell you it can't be done. Learn to pilot your life.

Ron Hall

If there were dreams to sell, what would you buy?

Thomas Lovell Beddoes

Can any of the tribe [of metaphysicians] inform us why all the operations of the mind are carried on with undiminished strength and activity in dreams, except the judgment, which alone is suspended and dormant?

Charles Caleb Colton

No, there's nothing half so sweet in life/As love's young dream.

Thomas Moore

I stand for freedom of expression, doing what you believe in, and going after your dreams.
Madonna

No person has the right to rain on your dreams.
Marian Wright Edelman

It takes a lot of courage to show your dreams to someone else.
Erma Bombeck

Dreams in life may seem impossible. They are not. Impossible dreams are achieved one goal at a time.
Herman Cain

Take, if you must, this little bag of dreams,/Unloose the cord, and they will wrap you round.
William Butler Yeats

If a little dreaming is dangerous, the cure for it is not to dream less but to dream more, to dream all the time.
Marcel Proust

Those who have compared our life to a dream were right … We sleeping wake, and waking sleep.
Michel de Montaigne

All of us may be surrealists in our dreams, but in our worries we are incorrigibly bourgeois.
Adam Phillips

Those who dream by day are cognizant of many things that escape those who dream only by night.
Edgar Allan Poe

Hold fast to dreams, for if dreams die, life is a broken winged bird that cannot fly.
Langston Hughes

The more you can dream, the more you can do.
Michael Korda

Be careful what you water your dreams with. Water them with worry and fear and you will produce weeds that choke the life from your dream.
Lao-Tse

DRESS
Those who make their dress a principal part of themselves will, in general, become of no more value than their dress.
William Hazlitt

A woman's dress should be like a barbed wire fence: serving its purpose without obstructing the view.
Sophia Loren

Once you can accept the universe as being something expanding into an infinite nothing which is something, wearing stripes with plaid is easy.
Albert Einstein

DRINKING
I feel sorry for people who don't drink. When they wake up in the morning, that's as good as they are going to feel all day.
Frank Sinatra

An intelligent man is sometimes forced to be drunk to spend time with his fools.

Ernest Hemingway

When I read about the evils of drinking, I gave up reading.

Henny Youngman

Drinking makes such fools of people, and people are such fools to begin with, that it's compounding a felony.

Robert Benchley

DRIVING
Drive slowly and enjoy the scenery – drive fast and join the scenery.

Douglas Horton

If you drink, don't drive. Don't even putt.

Dean Martin

The problem with the designated driver program, it's not a desirable job, but if you ever get sucked into doing it, have fun with it. At the end of the night, drop them off at the wrong house.

Jeff Foxworthy

People don't come here to learn to drive. They come here to get a driver's licence.

Jacques Rabio

(A driver) is a king on a vinyl bucket-seat throne, changing direction with the turn of a wheel, changing the climate with a flick of the button, changing the music with the switch of a dial.

Andrew H. Malcolm

Nothing improves a person's driving like a police car right in back of him.

Dr O.A. Battista

If soldiers were asked to do in battle what the average motorist does on weekends for fun, the officer in charge would be court-martialled for brutality.

Malcolm Muggeridge

DROPOUT
If one defines "dropout" to mean a person who has given up serious effort to meet his responsibilities, then every business office, government agency, golf club, and university faculty would yield its quota.

John W. Gardner

DRUGS
I hate to advocate drugs, alcohol, violence or insanity to anyone, but they've always worked for me.

Hunter S. Thompson

DRUNK
Thought when sober, said when drunk.

Saying

DRUNKENNESS
Sobriety diminishes, discriminates, and says no; drunkenness expands, unites, and says yes. Not through mere perversity do men run after it.

William James

DUCK
If it looks like a duck, and quacks like a duck, we have at least to

consider the possibility that we have a small aquatic bird of the family anatidae on our hands.

Douglas Adams

DULL

It is to be noted that when any part of this paper appears dull, there is a design in it.

Sir Richard Steele

Mr Zola is determined to show us that, if he has not got genius, he can at least be dull.

Oscar Wilde

He is not only dull himself, he is the cause of dullness in others.

Samuel Johnson

DULLNESS

The commonplace needs no defence,/ Dullness is in the critic's eye,/Without a licence life evolves/From some dim phase its own surprise.

William Plomer

DUMB BLONDES

I'm not offended by all the dumb blonde jokes because I know I'm not dumb ... and I also know that I'm not blonde.

Dolly Parton

I am a marvelous housekeeper. Every time I leave a man I keep his house.

Zsa Zsa Gabor

DUPLICATION

We must avoid duplication of effort, because that is being done by others.

Arthur Mitchell

DUTY

A sense of duty is moral glue, constantly subject to stress.

William Safire

When I'm not thanked at all, I'm thanked enough;/I've done my duty, and I've done no more.

Henry Fielding

I ought, therefore I can.

Immanuel Kant

It is easier to do one's duty to others than to one's self. If you do your duty to others, you are considered reliable. If you do your duty to yourself, you are considered selfish.

Thomas Szasz

If we believe a thing to be bad, ... it is our duty to try to prevent it and to darn the consequences.

Lord Milner

Make it a point to do something every day that you don't want to do. This is the golden rule for acquiring the habit of doing your duty without pain.

Mark Twain

We know of only one duty, and that is to love.

Albert Camus

One has two duties – to be worried and not to be worried.

E.M. Forster

My duty is to obey orders.

Stonewall Jackson

What I must do is all that concerns me, not what people think.

Ralph Waldo Emerson

Do your duty and a little more, and the future will take care of itself.

Andrew Carnegie

In doing what we ought we deserve no praise.

St Augustine

The only prize which is infallibly gained by performing one duty well is the power of performing another.

F.H.W. Myers

DWARFS

We are like dwarfs standing upon the shoulders of giants and so able to see farther than the ancients.

Bernard of Chartres

DYING

A man's dying is more of the survivors' affair than his own.

Thomas Mann

DYNAMICS

There is a science of dynamics in man's fortune and nature, as well as of mechanics.

Thomas Carlyle

DYSLEXIA

DAM = Mothers Against Dyslexia

Then there was the dyslexic agnostic who lay awake at night pondering the existence of Dog.

The dyslexic cop who spent Saturday nights handing out IUDs.

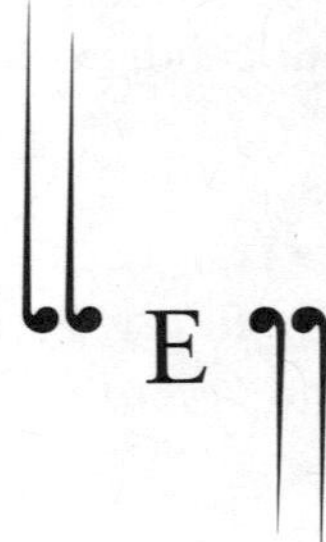

E-MAIL
Yes, your company reads your e-mail.

Time magazine

The e-mail of the species is deadlier than the mail.

Stephen Fry

EARLY
Early to rise and early to bed makes a male healthy and wealthy and dead.

James Thurber

EARNESTNESS
Earnest people are often people who habitually look on the serious side of things that have no serious side.

Van Wyck Brooks

EARTH
Viewed from the distance of the Moon, the astonishing thing about the Earth...is that it is alive. ... Aloft, floating free beneath the moist, gleaming membrane of bright blue sky, is the rising earth, the only exuberant thing in this part of the cosmos. ... It has the organized, self-contained look of a live creature, full of information, marvellously skilled in handling the Sun.

Lewis Thomas

The whole Earth is the tomb of famous men.

Pericles

There are no passengers on space-ship earth. We are all crew.

Marshall McLuhan

We could have saved the Earth but we were too damned cheap.

Kurt Vonnegut

There is no reason whatever to believe that the order of nature has any greater bias in favour of man than it had in favour of the ich-thyosaur or the pterodactyl.

H.G. Wells

The Earth is just too small and fragile a basket for the human race to keep all its eggs in.

Robert Heinlein

We do not inherit the Earth from our ancestors; we borrow it from our children.
Chief Seattle

EAST
Oh, East is East, and West is West, and never the twain shall meet.
Rudyard Kipling

EASY
Take the world nice and easy and the world will take you the same.
Irish proverb

Things that would have made the fame of a less clever man seemed tricks in his hands. It is a mistake to do things too easily.
H.G. Wells

EAT
There's nothing on Earth to do here but look at the view and eat. You can imagine the result since I do not like to look at views.
Zelda Fitzgerald

Tell me what you eat, and I will tell you what you are.
Anthelme Brillat-Savarin

World only has two things: Things you can eat and things you can not eat.
Hironobu Sakaguchi

ECCENTRIC
We might define an eccentric as a man who is a law unto himself, and a crank as one who having determined what the law is, insists on laying it down to others.
Louis Kronenberger

Eccentricity has always abounded when and where strength of character has abounded; and the amount of eccentricity has generally been proportional to the amount of genius, mental vigour and moral courage it contained. That so few dare to be eccentric marks the chief danger of the time.
John Stuart Mill

Eccentricity is not, as dull people would have us believe, a form of madness. It is often a kind of innocent pride, and the man of genius and the aristocrat are frequently regarded as eccentrics because genius and aristocrat are entirely unafraid of and uninfluenced by the opinions and vagaries of the crowd.
Dame Edith Sitwell

ECONOMIC OUTLOOK
Put all your eggs in one basket and watch that basket.
Mark Twain

ECONOMICS
He who will not economize will have to agonize.
Confucius

I learned more about economics from one South Dakota dust storm than I did in all my years in college.
Hubert H. Humphrey

The stoical scheme of supplying our wants, by lopping off our desires, is like cutting off our feet when we want shoes.
Jonathan Swift

Avarice and usury and precaution must be our gods for a little longer still.

John Maynard Keynes

ECONOMISTS

We have two classes of forecasters: Those who don't know – and those who don't know they don't know.

John Kenneth Galbraith

If all the economists were laid end to end, they would not reach a conclusion.

George Bernard Shaw

If the masses are confused by their ignorance, the economists seem to be equally confused by their learning.

Fraser Robertson

If economists could manage to get themselves thought of as humble, competent people, on a level with dentists, that would be splendid!

John Maynard Keynes

Once economists were asked: "If you're so smart, why ain't you rich?" Today they're asked: "Now you've proved you ain't so smart, how come you got so rich?"

Edgar Fiedler

An economist is an expert who will know tomorrow why the things he predicted yesterday didn't happen today.

Laurence J. Peter

No real English gentleman, in his secret soul, was ever sorry for the death of a political economist.

Walter Bagehot

ECONOMY

Mere parsimony is not economy ... Expense, and great expense, may be an essential part of true economy.

Edmund Burke

Economy is a distributive virtue, and consists not in saving but selection. Parsimony requires no providence, no sagacity, no powers of combination, no comparison, no judgment.

Edmund Burke

Economy is going without something you do want in case you should, some day, want something you probably won't want.

Anthony Hope

There is no economy in going to bed early to save candles if the result is twins.

Chinese proverb

EDGE

The Edge ... there is no honest way to explain it because the only people who really know where it is are the ones who have gone over.

Hunter S. Thompson

EDITORS

Some editors are failed writers, but so are most writers.

T.S. Eliot

An editor is a person who knows more about writing than writers do but who has escaped the terrible desire to write.

E.B. White

EDUCATION

Education is what you must acquire without any interference from your schooling.

Mark Twain

We must reject that most dismal and fatuous notion that education is a preparation for life.

Northrop Frye

Human history becomes more and more a race between education and catastrophe.

H.G. Wells

Should we force science down the throats of those that have no taste for it? Is it our duty to drag them kicking and screaming into the twenty-first century? I am afraid that it is.

George Porter

Only the educated are free.

Epictetus

To repeat what others have said, requires education; to challenge it, requires brains.

Mary Pettibone Poole

One of the chief objects of education should be to widen the windows through which we view the world.

Arnold Glasgow

Creative minds always have been known to survive any kind of bad training.

Anna Freud

Between the semi-educated, who offer simplistic answers to complex questions, and the overeducated, who offer complicated answers to simple questions, it is a wonder that any questions get satisfactorily settled at all.

Sydney J. Harris

Soap and education are not so sudden as a massacre, but they are more deadly in the long run.

Mark Twain

Education consists mainly in what we have unlearned.

Mark Twain

No pleasure, no learning. No learning, no pleasure.

Wang Ken

When you don't have an education, you've got to use your brains.

Anonymous

Education is a wonderful thing. If you couldn't sign your name you'd have to pay cash.

Rita Mae Brown

Education is what survives when what has been learned has been forgotten.

B.F. Skinner

We receive three educations, one from our parents, one from our schoolmasters, and one from the world. The third contradicts all that the first two teach us.

Montesquieu

Nothing will kill the movies except education.

Will Rogers

The well-meaning people who talk about education as if it were a substance distributed by coupon in large or small quantities never exhibit any understanding of the truth that you cannot teach anybody anything that he does not want to learn.

George Sampson

And if the student finds that this [school subject] is not to his taste, well, that is regrettable. Most regrettable. His taste should not be consulted; it is being formed.

Flannery O'Connor

The aim of education is the knowledge not of fact but of values.

Dean Inge

Education does not mean teaching people to know what they do not know; it means teaching them to behave as they do not behave.

John Ruskin

In one century, we went from teaching Latin and Greek in high school to offering remedial English in college.

Joseph Sobran

Education is the ability to listen to almost anything without losing your temper or your self-confidence.

Robert Frost

Education is a progressive discovery of our own ignorance.

Will Durant

I have never let my schooling interfere with my education.

Mark Twain

Sit at the feet of the master long enough, and they'll start to smell.

John Sauget

Lack of education is an extraordinary handicap when one is being offensive.

Josephine Tey

At present we educate people only up to the point where they can earn a living and marry; then education ceases altogether, as though a complete mental outfit had been acquired. ... Vast numbers of men and women thus spend their entire lives in complete ignorance of the most important things.

Carl Jung

The highest result of education is tolerance.

Helen Keller

The advantage of a classical education is that it enables you to despise the wealth which it prevents you from achieving.

Russell Green

Rewards and punishments are the lowest form of education.

Chuang Tzu

Cauliflower is nothing but cabbage with a college education.

Mark Twain

It is the mark of an educated mind to be able to entertain a thought without accepting it.

Aristotle

Education is learning what you didn't even know you didn't know.

Daniel Boorstin

Education is a better safeguard of liberty than a standing army.

Edward Everett

Education is a companion which no misfortune can depress, no crime destroy, no enemy alienate, no despotism enslave. At home, a friend; abroad, an introduction; in solitude, a solace; and in society, an ornament. Without it, what is man? A splendid slave, a reasoning savage.

Charles Varle

A man who has never gone to school may steal from a freight car; but if he has a university education, he may steal the whole railroad.

Theodore Roosevelt

His lack of education is more than compensated for by his keenly developed moral bankruptcy.

Woody Allen

Education: the path from cocky ignorance to miserable uncertainty.

Mark Twain

Nothing that you will learn in the course of your studies will be of the slightest use to you in after life – save only this – that if you work hard and intelligently, you should be able to detect when a man is talking rot, and that, in my view, is the main, if not the sole, purpose of education.

J.A. Smith

Education is an admirable thing, but it is well to remember from time to time that nothing that is worth knowing can be taught.

Oscar Wilde

Sam will not enjoy his childhood. ... Sam is being educated not so as to enjoy himself, but so other people will enjoy him.

Roger Scruton

The three great stumbling blocks in a girl's education ... homard à l'Americaine, a boiled egg, and asparagus.

Colette

The great difficulty in education is to get experience out of ideas.

George Santayana

Anyone who tries to make a distinction between education and entertainment doesn't know the first thing about either.

Marshall McLuhan

The direction in which education starts a man will determine his future in life.

Plato

Education is not the filling of a bucket, but the lighting of a fire.

William Butler Yeats

My education was interrupted only by my schooling.

Winston Churchill

A lesson that is never learned can never be too often taught.

Seneca

When you educate a man you educate an individual; when you

educate a woman you educate a whole family.

Robert MacIver

Educating the mind without educating the heart is no education at all.

Aristotle

EFFICIENCY
Efficiency is intelligent laziness.

David Dunham

To be effective is to do the right thing. To be efficient is to do it the right way.

Anonymous

Efficiency is concerned with doing things right. Effectiveness is doing the right things.

Peter Drucker

EFFORTS
I have always tried to hide my efforts and wished my works to have the light joyousness of spring-time which never lets anyone suspect the labours it has cost me.

Henri Matisse

The bitter and the sweet come from the outside, the hard from within, from one's own efforts.

Albert Einstein

You can't always get what you want, but if you try, sometimes you just might find you get what you need.

Mick Jagger and Keith Richards

There are no traffic jams when you go the extra mile.

Anonymous

It is the feeling of exerting effort that exhilarates us, as a grasshopper is exhilarated by jumping. A hard job, full of impediments, is thus more satisfying than an easy job.

H.L. Mencken

EGO
There's a world of difference between a strong ego which is essential and a large ego – which can be destructive. The guy with a strong ego knows his own strength. He is confident … But the guy with a large ego is always looking for recognition. He constantly needs to be patted on the back.

Lee Iacocca

EGOTISM
Egotism is the anesthetic that dulls the pain of stupidity.

Frank Leahy

Egotism is the anesthetic given by a kindly nature to relieve the pain of being a damned fool.

Bellamy Brooks

Take egotism out, and you would castrate the benefactor.

Ralph Waldo Emerson

There are two kinds of egotists: those who admit it, and the rest of us.

Laurence J. Peter

To speak highly of one with whom we are intimate is a species of egotism.

William Hazlitt

If egotism means a terrific interest in one's self, egotism is absolutely essential to efficient living.
Arnold Bennett

EGOTISTS
One nice thing about egotists – they don't talk about other people.
Lucille Harper

An egotist is a man who thinks that if he hadn't been born, people would have wondered why.
Dan Post

EGYPT
Egypt: Where the Israelites would still be if Moses had been a bureaucrat.
Laurence J. Peter

ELECTIONS
Do you ever get the feeling that the only reason we have elections is to find out if the polls were right?
Robert Orben

An elected official is one who gets fifty-one per cent of the vote cast by forty per cent of the sixty per cent of voters who registered.
Dan Bennett

Our elections are free, it's in the results where eventually we pay.
Bill Stern

An election is coming. Universal peace is declared and the foxes have a sincere interest in prolonging the lives of the poultry.
T.S. Eliot

It is enough that the people know there was an election. The people who cast the votes decide nothing. The people who count the votes decide everything.
Joseph Stalin

Win or lose, we go shopping after the election.
Imelda Marcos

I have given the matter the fullest consideration and, having examined the problem from all of its angles, reached the conclusion that it [his defeat in an election] was because I didn't get enough votes.
Howard Green

ELECTRICITY

All power corrupts but we need the electricity.
Anonymous

Never hire an electrician whose eyebrows are scorched.
Mason Wilder

Ben Franklin may have discovered electricity – but it is the man who invented the meter who made the money.
Earl Warren

ELEGANCE
Elegance is refusal.
Coco Chanel

Elegance is good taste plus a dash of daring.
Carmel Snow

ELEMENT
Cold dark deep and absolutely clear, element bearable to no mortal.
Elizabeth Bishop

ELITIST
There are no elitist people, there are only elitist ideas.
Jonathan Miller

ELOQUENCE
Eloquence is vehement simplicity.
Richard Cecil

Eloquence may set fire to reason.
Oliver Wendell Holmes

Of all eloquence a nickname is the most concise; of all arguments, the most unanswerable.
William Hazlitt

True eloquence consists in saying all that is necessary, and nothing but what is necessary.
François, duc de La Rochefoucauld

The prime purpose of eloquence is to keep other people from talking.
Louis Vermeil

Discretion in speech is more than eloquence.
Francis Bacon

ELVIS
If life were fair, Elvis would be alive and all the impersonators would be dead.
Johnny Carson

EMBARRASSMENT
To my embarrassment I was born in bed with a lady.
Wilson Mizner

EMOTION
Anyone who says he is not emotional is not getting what he should out of life.
Ezer Weizman

In the stifling of the emotions beware of the suffocation of the soul.
Thomas Shaw

Nothing vivifies, and nothing kills, like the emotions.
Joseph Roux

I don't think life would be worth living if one were not constantly the prey of one's emotions.
Sir John Betjeman

Poor Faulkner. Does he really think big emotions come from big words?
*Ernest Hemingway
(about William Faulkner)*

EMPIRES
The empires of the future are empires of the mind.
Winston Churchill

EMPLOYMENT
A corporation prefers to offer a job to a man who already has one … To obtain entry into paradise, in terms of employment, you should be in a full state of grace.
Alan Harrington

ENCOURAGEMENT

A good horse should be seldom spurred.

Thomas Fuller, MD

ENCYCLOPEDIA

I am not going to buy my kids an encyclopedia. Let them walk to school like I did.

Yogi Berra

ENDING

Great is the art of beginning, but greater the art is of ending.

Henry Wadsworth Longfellow

Men perish because they cannot join the beginning with the end.

Alcmaeon

Better is the end of a thing than the beginning thereof.

Ecclesiastes 7:8

To make an end is to make a beginning.

T.S. Eliot

The happy ending is our national belief.

Mary McCarthy

If I see an ending, I can work backward.

Arthur Miller

ENDURANCE

He who limps is still walking.

Stanislaw J. Lec

Some days are for living. Others are for getting through.

Malcolm Forbes

ENEMIES

Speak well of your enemies - remember you made them.

Anonymous

A man cannot be too careful in the choice of his enemies.

Oscar Wilde

It is your enemies who keep you straight. For real use, one active, sneering enemy is worth two ordinary friends.

Edgar Watson Howe

This is no time for making new enemies.

Voltaire, on his deathbed, being asked to renounce the devil

We often give our enemies the means for our own destruction.

Aesop

An enemy's gift is ruinous and no gift.

Sophocles

A man's worst enemy can't wish him what he thinks up for himself.

Yiddish proverb

We have found the enemy and he is us!

Pogo

Do not swallow a bait offered by the enemy.

Sun Tzu

The wise learn many things from their enemies.

Aristophanes

Our worst enemies here are not the ignorant and the simple, however

cruel; our worst enemies are the intelligent and corrupt.
Graham Greene

I'm lonesome; they are all dying; I have hardly a warm personal enemy left.
James McNeill Whistler

It's an old axiom of mine: marry your enemies and behead your friends.
Robert N. Lee

Never interrupt your enemy when he is making a mistake.
Napoleon Bonaparte

Would that mine enemy had written a book.
Job 31:35

He who has a thousand friends has not a friend to spare, And he who has one enemy will meet him everywhere.
Ali ibn Abi Talib

You can discover what your enemy fears most by observing the means he uses to frighten you.
Eric Hoffer

I ask you to judge me by the enemies I have made.
Franklin D. Roosevelt

He hasn't an enemy in the world — but all his friends hate him.
Eddie Cantor

Enemies are made, not born.
Unknown

If we could read the secret history of our enemies, we should find in each man's life sorrow and suffering enough to disarm all hostility.
Henry Wadsworth Longfellow

Use your enemy's hand to catch a snake.
Persian proverb

He who cannot agree with his enemies is controlled by them.
Chinese proverb

Arthur Murray and Groucho Marx were discussing a certain actress. "She's her own worst enemy," Murray observed. "Not while I'm alive, she isn't," retorted Groucho icily.
Andrew B. Hecht

Friend is sometimes a word devoid of meaning; enemy never.
Victor Hugo

When the enemy has failed in all other artifices, he will propose friendship; that under its appearance he may effect what he could not compass as an open adversary.
Sa'di

He who has not forgiven an enemy has not yet tasted one of the most sublime enjoyments of life.
Johann Kaspar Lavater

ENERGY
Energy rightly applied and directed will accomplish anything.
The maxim of Nellie Bly

The world belongs to the energetic.
Ralph Waldo Emerson

The longer I live, the more I am certain that the great difference between the feeble and the powerful, between the great and the insignificant is energy – invincible determination – a purpose once fixed, and then death or victory. This quality will do anything that can be done in this world.

Sir Thomas Buxton

ENGINEERING TERMINOLOGY

"Customer satisfaction is assured." (We are so far behind schedule that the customer is happy to receive it.)

"All new." (Parts not interchangeable with the previous design.)

"Rugged." (Too damn heavy to lift.)

"Low maintenance." (Impossible to fix if broken.)

compiled by Oliver Capio

ENGLAND

England has forty-two religions and only two sauces.

Voltaire

England and America are two countries separated by a common language.

George Bernard Shaw

ENGLISH

I don't think the English take anybody particularly seriously if they can help it. The English have tried to colonize humour.

Peter Ustinov

The English nation is never so great as in adversity.

Benjamin Disraeli

Of all the nations in the world at present, the English are the stupidest in speech, the wisest in action.

Thomas Carlyle

ENGLISH GENTLEMAN

The English country gentleman galloping after a fox – the unspeakable in full pursuit of the uneatable.

Oscar Wilde

One of the characteristics of the English people is a certain complacent candour about their most obvious defects.

Lady Violet Bonham Carter

ENGLISH LANGUAGE

If you can describe clearly without a diagram the proper way of making this or that knot, then you are a master of the English language.

Hilaire Belloc

If the English language made any sense, a catastrophe would be an apostrophe with fur.

Doug Larson

ENJOYMENT

If you are going to do something wrong, at least enjoy it.

Leo Rosten

For most men, an ignorant enjoyment is better than an informed one; it is better to conceive the sky as a blue dome than a dark cavity:

and the cloud as a golden throne than a sleety mist.

John Ruskin

Enjoy to the full the resources that are within thy reach.

Pindar

It is a curious thing that people only ask you if you are enjoying yourself when you aren't.

Edith Nesbit

People seem to enjoy things more when they know a lot of other people have been left out of the pleasure.

Russell Baker

ENLIGHTENMENT
Before enlightenment: Chopping wood, Carrying water.

After enlightenment: Chopping wood, Carrying water.

Zen proverb

ENOUGH
Enough is as good as a feast.

John Heywood

Nothing is enough to the man for whom enough is too little.

Epicurus

You never know what is enough unless you know what is more than enough.

William Blake

ENTERTAINMENT MEDIUM
There's a standard formula for success in the entertainment medium and that is: Beat it to death if it succeeds.

Ernie Kovacs

ENTHUSIASM
Enthusiasm is a virtue seldom met with in seasons of calm and unruffled prosperity.

Thomas Chalmers

Nothing is so contagious as enthusiasm.

Edward Bulwer-Lytton

I prefer the errors of enthusiasm to the indifference of wisdom.

Anatole France

If you are not fired with enthusiasm, you'll be fired with enthusiasm.

Vince Lombardi

Every production of genius must be the product of enthusiasm.

Benjamin Disraeli

Enthusiasm, *n.* A distemper of youth, curable by small doses of repentance in connection with outward applications of experience.

Ambrose Bierce

If you can give your son or daughter only one gift, let it be enthusiasm.

Bruce Barton

Years wrinkle the skin, but to give up enthusiasm wrinkles the soul.

Samuel Ullman

If we're not enthusiastic, we can't get things done. If we're over-enthusiastic, we run into the danger of being fanatical.

Woodrow Wyatt

Manufacture enthusiasm as you go and grow.

Maggie Kuhn

Enthusiasm is one of the most powerful engines of success. When you do a thing, do it with your might. Put your whole soul into it. Stamp it with your own personality. Be active, be energetic, be enthusiastic and faithful, and you will accomplish your object. Nothing great was ever achieved without enthusiasm.

Ralph Waldo Emerson

The worst bankruptcy in the world is the person who has lost his enthusiasm.

H.W. Arnold

Enthusiasm for a cause sometimes warps judgment.

William Howard Taft

ENTHUSIASTS
It is unfortunate, considering that enthusiasm moves the world, that so few enthusiasts can be trusted to speak the truth.

Arthur Balfour

ENTREPRENEUR
You don't deserve to be called an entrepreneur unless you've mortgaged your house to the business.

Ted Rogers

ENVIRONMENT
The emergence of intelligence, I am convinced, tends to unbalance the ecology. In other words, intelligence is the great polluter. It is not until a creature begins to manage its environment that nature is thrown into disorder.

Clifford Simak

All men and women, even those whose lives appear on the surface to be thoroughly conventional, invent themselves to a very great extent. Man is unique in the ways that he does not come to terms with his environment. Every other species adapts by passively responding to its environment, the place where it happens to have been born. In contrast, man is what he chooses to be. Eccentrics take that basic human prerogative of free choice and force it to the limit.

Dr David Weeks
and Jamie James

The environment is everything that isn't me.

Albert Einstein

In our confusion, we've concentrated on money, to the neglect of those things that actually sustain life.

David Korten

Make your holistic goal one hundred per cent of what you want and zero per cent how it is going to be achieved.

Alan Savory

I am certain of only thing: business as we know it is destroying the Earth, including all cultures and living systems. Never before has there been a system so ubiquitous, so destructive, and so well managed. It is our creation.

Paul Hawken

The magnificence of mountains, the serenity of nature – nothing is safe from the idiot marks of man's passing.

Loudon Wainwright

Complete adaptation to environment means death. The essential point in all response is the desire to control environment.

John Dewey

ENVY

As rust corrupts iron, so envy corrupts men.

Antisthenes

The torment of envy is like a grain of sand in the eye.

Chinese proverb

If envy were a disease, everyone would be sick.

Proverb

How much better a thing it is to be envied than to be pitied.

Herodotus

The dullard's envy of brilliant men is always assuaged by the suspicion that they will come to a bad end.

Max Beerbohm

Love looks through a telescope; envy through a microscope.

Josh Billings

EPIGRAMS

If true that notion, which but few contest,/That in the way of wit short things are best,/Then in good epigrams two virtues meet,/For 'tis their glory to be short and sweet.

Anonymous

The day of the jewelled epigram is passed and, whether one likes it or not, one is moving into the stern puritanical era of the four-letter word.

Noel Annan

An epigram is striking a verbal match on the seat of your intellectual pants.

John A. Lincoln

An epigram often flashes light into regions where reason shines but dimly.

E.P. Whipple

EQUAL OPPORTUNITY

Equal opportunity means everyone will have a fair chance at becoming incompetent.

Laurence J. Peter

EQUALITY

Equality may perhaps be a right, but no power on Earth can ever turn it into a fact.

Honoré de Balzac

Before God we are all equally wise – and equally foolish.

Albert Einstein

It is better that some should be unhappy than that none should be happy, which would be the case in a general state of equality.

Samuel Johnson

All animals are equal, but some animals are more equal than others.

George Orwell

The cry of equality pulls everyone down.

Iris Murdoch

Idiots are always in favour of inequality of income (their only chance of eminence), and the really great are in favour of equality.

George Bernard Shaw

When I speak of The Case for Equality, I mean human equality; and that, of course, can only mean one thing: it means equality of income.

George Bernard Shaw

EQUALS

The trouble with treating people as equals is that the first thing you know they may be doing the same thing to you.

Peter De Vries

What makes equality such a difficult business is that we only want it with our superiors.

Henry Becque

All men are born equal, but quite a few eventually get over it.

Lord Mancroft

ERA

An era can be said to have ended when its basic illusions are exhausted.

Arthur Miller

ERR

To err is human, to blame the next guy even more so.

Unknown

To err is dysfunctional, to forgive codependent.

Berton Averre

To err is human, but when the eraser wears out ahead of the pencil, you're overdoing it.

Josh Jenkins

To err is human, not to, animal.

Robert Frost

ERROR

Every absurdity has a champion to defend it, for error is always talkative.

Oliver Goldsmith

All human error is impatience, a premature renunciation of method, a delusive pinning down of a delusion.

Franz Kafka

Things could be worse. Suppose your errors were counted and published every day, like those of a baseball player.

Anonymous

"It is destiny!" – dark apology for every error.

Edward Bulwer-Lytton

The world always makes the assumption that the exposure of an error is identical with the discovery of the truth – that error and truth are simply opposite. They are nothing of the sort. What the world turns to, when it has been cured of one error, is usually simply another error, and maybe one worse than the first one.

H.L. Mencken

All erroneous ideas would perish of their own accord if expressed clearly.

Marquis de Vauvenargues

The man who can own up to his error is greater than he who merely knows how to avoid making it.

Cardinal de Retz

No doubt about it: Error is the rule; truth is the accident of error.

Georges Duhamel

The progress of rivers to the ocean is not so rapid as that of man to error.

Voltaire

Love truth but pardon error.

Voltaire

Admitting Error clears the Score,/ And proves you Wiser than before.

Arthur Guiterman

It is one thing to show a man that he is in error and another to put him in possession of the truth.

John Locke

One's opponent must be weaned from error by patience and sympathy.

Mohandas Gandhi

Life is only error, and death is knowledge.

Friedrich von Schiller

If you shut the door to all error, truth will be shut out.

Rabindranath Tagore

Every error under the sun seems to arise from thinking that you are right yourself because you are yourself, and other people are wrong because they are not you.

Thomas Hardy

All men are liable to error.

John Locke

Errors, like straws, upon the surface flow;/He who would search for pearls must dive below.

John Dryden

A subtle thought that is in error may yet give rise to fruitful inquiry that can establish truths of great value.

Isaac Asimov

Error is to truth as sleep is to waking. I have observed that one turns, as if refreshed, from error back to truth.

Johann Wolfgang von Goethe

Error is always in haste.

Thomas Fuller, MD

Therefore, acknowledge your error and be attentive.

Christopher Marlowe

Nothing bolsters a man's disposition like having enough courage to admit he was wrong.

Dr O.A. Battista

An error gracefully acknowledged is a victory won.

Caroline Gascoigne

Give me a fruitful error any time, full of seeds, bursting with its own corrections. You can keep your sterile truth for yourself.

Vilfredo Pareto

ERUDITION

Erudition can produce foliage without bearing fruit. There are a great many shallow heads who are astonishingly knowledgeable. What we have to discover for ourselves leaves behind in our mind a pathway that can also be used on another occasion.

Georg Christoph Lichtenberg

ESCAPE

When the mouse laughs at the cat, there is a hole nearby.

Nigerian proverb

Of all escape mechanisms, death is the most efficient.

H.L. Mencken

Of all the thirty-six alternatives, running away is the best.

Chinese proverb

ESTABLISHMENT

If you attack the establishment long enough and hard enough, they will make you a member of it.

Art Buchwald

ETERNITY

All things from eternity are of like forms and come round in a circle.

Marcus Aurelius

We feel and know by experience that we are eternal.

Baruch Spinoza

As if you could kill time without injuring eternity.

Henry David Thoreau

There are men I could spend eternity with, but not this life.

Kathleen Thompson Norris

Eternity's a terrible thought. I mean, where's it all going to end?

Tom Stoppard

Eternity is boring, particularly towards the end.

Woody Allen

Eternity is not something that begins after you are dead. It is going on all the time. We are in it now.

Charlotte P. Gilman

ETHICAL

An ethical man is a Christian holding four aces.

Mark Twain

ETHICISTS

Over the past couple of decades, the ethics industry has kicked into high gear. We now have a growing number of professional ethicists. … Ethics missionaries are driven by the assumption that improving our moral lives is a matter of developing our conceptual understanding and analytical acumen. The fantasy seems to be that if up-and-coming accountants just knew a little more about ethics, then they would know better than to falsify their reports so as to drive up the value of company stock. But sheer ignorance is seldom the moral problem. More knowledge is not what is needed. Take it from Kierkegaard: The moral challenge is simply to abide by the knowledge that we already have.

Gordon Marino

ETHICS
Ethics is nothing else than reverence for life.

Albert Schweitzer

EUROPE
Europe is the unfinished negative of which America is the proof.

Mary McCarthy

A very large group says, I am for Europe but not so large and not so fast.

Maurice de Hond

EVENING
I've had a perfectly wonderful evening. But this wasn't it.

Groucho Marx

EVENTS
When I can't handle events, I let them handle themselves.

Henry Ford

Events play cat-and-mouse with our ideas. They belong to a quite different species and even when seeming to bear out our preconceptions are never quite as we expected. Foresight is a dream from which the event wakes us.

Paul Valéry

I claim not to have controlled events, but confess plainly that events have controlled me.

Abraham Lincoln

It is one thing to be moved by events; it is another thing to be mastered by them.

Ralph W. Stockman

People to whom nothing has ever happened cannot understand the unimportance of events.

T.S. Eliot

EVIDENCE
Take nothing on its looks; take everything on evidence. There's no better rule.

Charles Dickens

EVIL
If evil be said of thee, and it is true, correct it: if it be a lie, laugh at it.

Epictetus

It is a sin to believe in the evil of others – but it is seldom a mistake.

H.L. Mencken

Few men are sufficiently discerning to appreciate all the evil they do.

François, duc de La Rochefoucauld

There aren't very many really evil people. But there are an awful lot of selfish ones.

Walter Cronkite

When choosing between two evils, I always like to try the one I've never tried before.

Mae West

May the forces of evil become confused on the way to your house.

George Carlin

The wise man avoids evil by anticipating it.

Publilius Syrus

We are no more responsible for the evil thoughts which pass through our minds than a scarecrow [is] for the birds which fly over the seed-plot he has to guard; the sole responsibility in each case is to prevent them from settling.

Churton Collins

Evil draws men together.

Aristotle

I have discovered that all human evil comes from this, man's being unable to sit still in a room.

Blaise Pascal

Yield not to evils, but attack all the more boldly.

Virgil

A resolution to avoid an evil is seldom framed til the evil is so far advanced as to make avoidance impossible.

Thomas Hardy

Evil is obvious only in retrospect.

Gloria Steinem

I and the public know/What all schoolchildren learn,/Those to whom evil is done/Do evil in return.

W.H. Auden

Evil is unspectacular and always human, and shares our bed and eats at our own table.

W.H. Auden

Nothing is easier than to denounce the evildoer; nothing is more difficult than to understand him.

Fyodor Dostoyevsky

No man chooses evil because it is evil; he only mistakes it for happiness, the good he seeks.

Mary Shelley

Most of the greatest evils that man has inflicted upon man have come through people feeling quite certain about something which, in fact, was false.

Bertrand Russell

There are a thousand hacking at the branches of evil to one who is striking at the root.

Henry David Thoreau

He who does not punish evil commands it to be done.

Leonardo da Vinci

EVOLUTION

My theory of evolution is that Darwin was adopted.

Steven Wright

There are no shortcuts in evolution.

Louis D. Brandeis

Everything is what it is because it got that way.

D'Arcy Thompson

We will now discuss in a little more detail the struggle for existence.

Charles Darwin

EXACT
It is better to be lucky. But I would rather be exact. Then when luck comes, you are ready.
Ernest Hemingway

EXAGGERATION
An exaggeration is a truth that has lost its temper.
Kahlil Gibran

To exaggerate is to weaken.
Jean-François de La Harpe

EXAMINATIONS
Examinations are formidable, even to the best-prepared, for the greatest fool may ask more than the wisest man can answer.
Charles Caleb Colton

EXAMPLE
You can preach a better sermon with your life than with your lips.
Oliver Goldsmith

Do not seek to follow in the footsteps of the men of old; seek what they sought.
Matsuo Basho

Even a useless person can serve as a bad example.
Unknown

Nothing is so contagious as example, and our every really good or bad action inspires a similar one.
François, duc de La Rochefoucauld

It is no use walking anywhere to preach unless our walking is our preaching.
St Francis of Assisi

Preach not to others what they should eat, but eat as becomes you, and be silent.
Epictetus

A good example is the best sermon.
Proverb

EXASPERATION
The mass of men lead lives of quiet exasperation.
Phyllis McGinley

EXCELLENCE
There are no speed limits on the road to excellence.
David W. Johnson

We measure the excellency of other men by some excellency we conceive to be in ourselves.
John Selden

To fight and conquer in all your battles is not supreme excellence; supreme excellence consists in breaking the enemy's resistance without fighting.
Sun Tzu

We are what we repeatedly do. Excellence, then, is not an act, but a habit.
Aristotle

EXCEPTIONS
The mark of an exceptional company is how it treats its exceptions.
Joe DeGeorge, Federal Express

Exceptions prove the rule – and wreck the budget.
Olin Miller

EXCESS

Excess on occasion is exhilarating. It prevents moderation from acquiring the deadening effect of habit.

W. Somerset Maugham

Stretch a bow to the very full, / And you will wish you had stopped in time.

Lao-Tse

The road of excess leads to the palace of wisdom.

William Blake

When water covers the head, a hundred fathoms are as one.

Persian proverb

If I can't have too many truffles, I'll do without truffles.

Colette

They are as sick that surfeit with too much as they that starve with nothing.

William Shakespeare

Moderation is a fatal thing; nothing succeeds like excess.

Oscar Wilde

The archer who overshoots misses as well as he that falls short.

Proverb

The best things carried to excess are wrong.

Charles Churchill

Do not remove a fly from your friend's forehead with a hatchet.

Chinese proverb

EXCUSES

He who excuses himself accuses himself.

Gabriel Meurier

The longer the excuse, the less likely it's true.

Robert Half

Several excuses are always less convincing than one.

Aldous Huxley

It is better to offer no excuse than a bad one.

George Washington

Excuses are the nails used to build a house of failure.

Don Wilder

A man who wants to do something will find a way; a man who doesn't will find an excuse.

Stephen Dolley, Jr

The boy who is good at excuses is generally good for nothing else.

Samuel Foote

EXECUTIVE

A good executive is one who makes people contentedly settle for less than they meant to get, in return for more than they meant to give.

Mignon McLaughlin

Three characteristics of top executives are: slow speech, impressive appearance, and a complete lack of sense of humour.

Johnson O'Connor

EXERCISE
The need for exercise is a modern superstition, invented by people who ate too much and had nothing to think about. Athletics don't make anybody either long-lived or useful.

George Santayana

I've given up exercise. No pain, no pain.

Anonymous

It is exercise alone that supports the spirits, and keeps the mind in vigour.

Cicero

Those who think they have not time for bodily exercise will sooner or later have to find time for illness.

Edward Stanley

EXHILARATION
Exhilaration is that feeling you get just after a great idea hits you and just before you realize what's wrong with it. ·

Anonymous

EXISTENCE
Call a thing immoral or ugly, soul-destroying or a degradation of man, a peril to the peace of the world or to the well-being of future generations: As long as you have not shown it to be "uneconomic" you have not really questioned its right to exist, grow, and prosper.

E.F. Schumacher

Existence precedes and rules essence.

Jean-Paul Sartre

The more unintelligent a man is, the less mysterious existence seems to him.

Arthur Schopenhauer

Let us be moral. Let us contemplate existence.

Charles Dickens

EXPANSION
Executive behaviour is based on the managerial myth that future organizational expansion will resolve past institutional incompetence.

Doug Moseley

EXPECTATION
Nothing is so good as it seems beforehand.

George Eliot

If you cannot catch a bird of paradise, better take a wet hen.

Nikita Khrushchev

Blessed is he who expects nothing, for he shall never be disappointed.

Alexander Pope

It's just as unpleasant to get more than you bargain for as to get less.

George Bernard Shaw

For people who live on expectations, to face up to their realization is something of an ordeal.

Elizabeth Bowen

Expect nothing. Live frugally on surprise.

Alice Walker

Stretch your legs according to your quilt. (Cut your coat according to your cloth.)

Syrian proverb

If things do not turn out as we wish, we should wish for them as they turn out.

Aristotle

There is nothing in a caterpillar that tells you it's going to be a butterfly.

R. Buckminster Fuller

EXPEDIENCY
No man is justified in doing evil on the grounds of expediency.

Theodore Roosevelt

EXPENSES
It's not hard to meet expenses, they're everywhere.

Will Rogers

Beware of little expense; a small leak will sink a great ship.

Benjamin Franklin

EXPERIENCE
Experience is not what happens to you; it is what you do with what happens to you.

Aldous Huxley

Experience teaches you that the man who looks you straight in the eye, particularly if he adds a firm handshake, is hiding something.

Clifton Fadiman

Experience is that marvellous thing that enables you to recognize a mistake when you make it again.

Franklin P. Jones

Experience is what you get from being inexperienced.

Franklin P. Jones

Experience is a comb, which nature gives to men when they are bald.

Proverb

Too high an appreciation of our talents is the chief cause why experience preaches to us all in vain.

Charles Caleb Colton

We learn from experience. A man never wakes up his second baby just to see it smile.

Grace Williams

Experience is a good teacher, but her fees are very high.

Dean Inge

The school of hard knocks is an accelerated curriculum.

Menander

You cannot create experience. You must undergo it.

Albert Camus

I was thinking that we all learn by experience, but some of us have to go to summer school.

Peter De Vries

Only the wearer knows where the shoe pinches.

English proverb

We should be careful to get out of an experience only the wisdom that is in it – and stop there; lest we be like the cat that sits down on a hot stove-lid. She will not sit down on a hot stove-lid again – and that is well; but also she will not sit down on a cold one anymore.

Mark Twain

Experience teaches us only one thing at a time – and hardly that in my case.

Mark Twain

Human beings, who are almost unique in having the ability to learn from the experience of others, are also remarkable for their apparent disinclination to do so.

Douglas Adams

Experience has two things to teach: The first is that we must correct a great deal; the second, that we must not correct too much.

Eugène Delacroix

Information's pretty thin stuff, unless mixed with experience.

Clarence Day

Experience dulls the edges of all our dogmas.

Gilbert Murray

Experience is only half of experience.

Johann Wolfgang von Goethe

All experience is an arch to build up.

Henry Adams

He who neglects to drink of the spring of experience is likely to die of thirst in the desert of ignorance.

Ling Po

Experience is a good school, but the fees are high.

Heinrich Heine

A farmer learns more from a bad harvest than a good one.

Anonymous

Experience is one thing you can't get for nothing.

Oscar Wilde

Experience is simply the name we give our mistakes.

Oscar Wilde

The years teach much which the days never know.

Ralph Waldo Emerson

When a person with money meets a person with experience, the person with the experience winds up with the money and the person with the money winds up with the experience.

Harvey Mackay

Men are wise in proportion, not to their experience, but to their capacity for experience.

George Bernard Shaw

Experience is a hard teacher because she gives the test first, the lesson afterward.

Vernon Law

A smooth sea never made a skillful mariner.

English proverb

No one is ever old enough to know better.

Holbrook Jackson

A new broom sweeps clean but an old one knows the corners.

English saying

You've got to know when to hold 'em,/Know when to fold 'em,/ Know when to walk away.

Don Schlitz

In the business world, everyone is paid in two coins: cash and experience. Take the experience first; the cash will come later.

Harold Geneen

Experience isn't interesting til it begins to repeat itself – in fact, til it does that, it hardly is experience.

Elizabeth Bowen

If men could learn from history, what lessons might it teach us! But passion and party blind our eyes, and the light that experience gives is a lantern on the stern, which shines only on the waves behind us.

Samuel Taylor Coleridge

Education is when you read the fine print; experience is what you get when you don't.

Pete Seeger

We had the experience but missed the meaning.

T.S. Eliot

Experience is a dim lamp, which only lights the one who bears it.

Louis-Ferdinand Céline

Without trials and tribulations, no one can become a Buddha.

Chinese proverb

Careful. We don't want to learn from this.

Bill Watterson

Experience is what you get when you don't get what you want.

Unknown

Experience is the child of Thought, and Thought is the child of Action. We cannot learn men from books.

Benjamin Disraeli

In my experience, by the time they find out you know nothing about it, you know something about it.

George Melly

Even brute beasts and wandering birds do not fall into the same traps or nets twice.

St Jerome

I like to think of my behaviour in the Sixties as a "learning experience." Then again, I like to think of anything stupid I've done as a "learning experience." It makes me feel less stupid.

P.J. O'Rourke

I have but one lamp by which my feet are guided, and that is the lamp of experience.

Patrick Henry

EXPERIMENTS

There is no such thing as a failed experiment, only experiments with unexpected outcomes.

R. Buckminster Fuller

All life is an experiment. The more experiments you make the better. What if they are a little coarse, and you may get your coat soiled or torn? What if you do fail, and get fairly rolled in the dirt once or

twice? Up again, you shall never be so afraid of a tumble.
Ralph Waldo Emerson

A fool ... is a man who has never tried an experiment in his life.
Erasmus Darwin

EXPERTS
An expert is a person who avoids the small errors as he sweeps on to the grand fallacy.
Benjamin Stolberg

When facts are few, experts are many.
Donald R. Gannon

Make three correct guesses consecutively and you will establish a reputation as an expert.
Laurence J. Peter

An expert is a man who has stopped thinking. Why should he think? He is an expert.
Frank Lloyd Wright

No lesson seems to be so deeply inculcated by the experience of life as that you should never trust experts. If you believe the doctors, nothing is wholesome; if you believe the theologians, nothing is innocent; if you believe the soldiers, nothing is safe. They all require to have their strong wine diluted by a very large admixture of insipid common sense.
Lord Salisbury

Experts are never right or wrong; they win or lose. Right and wrong are decided by proof; winning and losing are decided by who is doing the talking or talks the loudest, has the last, latest or only word, and is quoted by reporters.
M.A. Zeidner

An expert is one who knows more and more about less and less.
Nicholas Murray Butler

An expert is a man who tells you a simple thing in a confused way in such a fashion as to make you think the confusion is your own fault.
William B. Castle

An expert is a person who has made all the mistakes that can be made in a very narrow field.
Niels Bohr

The real secret of the expert is to make logic seem like flair.
Hugh Kelsey

EXPLANATIONS
There is no waste of time in life like that of making explanations.
Benjamin Disraeli

Never explain. Your friends do not need it and your enemies will not believe you anyway.
Elbert Hubbard

"Shut up," he explained.
Ring Lardner

EXPRESSING ONESELF
Think like a wise man but express yourself like the common people.
William Butler Yeats

EXPRESSION
Expression is the dress of thought.
Alexander Pope

EXTINCTION
Millennarian fervour, it is true, tends to get edged to the margins of society, because you have to be poor, dumb, defeated, exploited, or otherwise down on your luck to want the world to end. But mild millennarianism ... is compatible with a rational reading of the evidence. Every known species has become extinct or shown signs of potential extinctions; so humankind is unlikely to be exempt. Nothing has ever had immunity from destruction, so why should we?
Felipe Fernández-Armesto

EXTRAORDINARY
There are no extraordinary men ... just extraordinary circumstances that ordinary men are forced to deal with.
Admiral William Halsey

EXTREMISTS
Extremists think "communication" means agreeing with them.
Leo Rosten

EYE
The ear tends to be lazy, craves the familiar, and is shocked by the unexpected; the eye, on the other hand, tends to be impatient, craves the novel, and is bored by repetition.
W.H. Auden

What you don't see with your eyes, don't invent with your mouth.
Jewish proverb

Eyes are more accurate witnesses than ears.
Heraclitus

Truly it has been said, that to a clear eye the smallest fact is a window through which the Infinite may be seen.
Thomas Henry Huxley

The eye sees only what the mind is prepared to comprehend.
Henri Bergson

Sometimes when you look into his eyes you get the feeling that someone else is driving.
David Letterman

EYEBROWS
If you're counting my eyebrows, I can help you. There are two.
*Billy Wilder
and Charles Brackett*

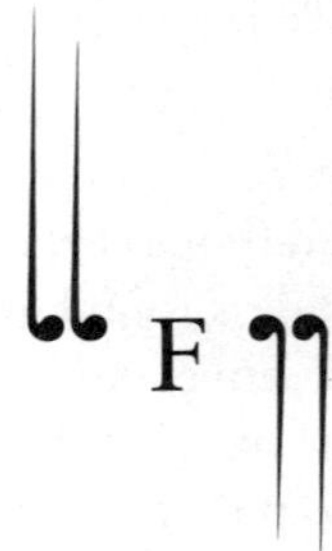

FACE
Be it ever so homely, there's no face like one's own.

Anonymous

The best way to save face is to keep the lower half of it shut.

Unknown

There's no art to find the mind's construction in the face.

William Shakespeare

The serial number of a human specimen is the face, that accidental and unrepeatable combination of features. It reflects neither character nor soul, nor what we call the self. The face is only the serial number of a specimen.

Milan Kundera

I never forget a face, but in your case I'll be glad to make an exception.

Groucho Marx

The face is the most important and mysterious surface we deal with.

Daniel McNeill

At fifty, everyone has the face he deserves.

George Orwell

FACILITATORS
To be an effective facilitator, you need to enable participants to lead the group in the direction you know they need to go.

Clark Crouch

FACTS
The facts will eventually test all our theories, and they form, after all, the only impartial jury to which we can appeal.

Louis Agassiz

Facts do not cease to exist because they are ignored.

Aldous Huxley

In all of this world, there is nothing more dismal than a fact.

Jim Moran

To treat your facts with imagination is one thing, but to imagine your facts is another.

John Burroughs

The facts are always less than what really happened.

Nadine Gordimer

A fact is a simple statement that everyone believes. It is innocent, unless found guilty. A hypothesis is a novel suggestion that no one wants to believe. It is guilty, until found effective.

Edward Teller

Facts are stupid things.

Ronald Reagan

An ounce of fact is worth a ton of conjecture.

Anonymous

If facts do not conform to the theory, they must be disposed of.

N.R.F. Maier

If facts conflict with a theory, either the theory must be changed or the facts.

Baruch Spinoza

Facts, or what a man believes to be the facts, are delightful. Get your facts first, and then you can distort them as much as you please.

Mark Twain

Every story has three sides, yours, mine, and the facts.

René Fumoleau

A wise man recognizes the convenience of a general statement, but he bows to the authority of a particular fact.

Oliver Wendell Holmes

Creatures whose mainspring is curiosity enjoy the accumulating of facts far more than the pausing at times to reflect on those facts.

Clarence Day

Facts are ventriloquists' dummies. Sitting on a wise man's knee they may be made to utter words of wisdom; elsewhere, they say nothing, or talk nonsense, or indulge in sheer diabolism.

Aldous Huxley

There are no facts, only interpretations.

Friedrich Nietzsche

Here, as elsewhere, the search for causes must follow the collection of facts.

Hippolyte Taine

FAILURE

Not failure, but low aim, is crime.

James Russell Lowell

People aren't failures until they begin to blame somebody else.

Unknown

Failure is more frequently from want of energy than want of capital.

Daniel Webster

Show me a thoroughly satisfied man – and I will show you a failure.

Thomas Edison

Half the failures in life arise from pulling in one's horse as it is leaping.

Julius Hare

Generally, it is our failures that civilize us. Triumph confirms us in our habits.

Clive James

The only people who never fail are those who never try.

Ilka Chase

There is much to be said for failure. It is more interesting than success.

Max Beerbohm

O human race! Born to ascend on wings,/Why do you fall at such a little wind?

Dante Alighieri

The line between failure and success is so fine that we scarcely know when we pass it; so fine that we are often on the line and do not know it.

Elbert Hubbard

If we don't succeed, we run the risk of failure.

Dan Quayle

Flops are a part of life's menu, and I've never been a girl to miss out on any of the courses.

Rosalind Russell

Whoever is aware of his own failing will not find fault with the failings of other men.

Sa'di

A person of twelve professions and thirteen failures.

Dutch proverb

Every great improvement has come after repeated failure. Virtually nothing comes out right the first time. Failures, repeated failures, are posts on the road to achievement.

Charles F. Kettering

A fool often fails because he thinks what is difficult is easy, and a wise man because he thinks what is easy is difficult.

Churton Collins

Failure is the opportunity to begin again more intelligently.

Unknown

Failure is success if we learn from it.

Malcolm Forbes

Failure is the condiment that gives success its flavour.

Truman Capote

We are all failures – at least, all the best of us are.

J.M. Barrie

There are only two kinds of people who fail: Those who listen to nobody, and … those who listen to everybody.

Thomas M. Beshere, Jr

I would rather fail in a cause that will ultimately succeed than succeed in a cause that will ultimately fail.

Woodrow Wilson

We all have a few failures under our belt. It's what makes us ready for the successes.

Randy K. Milholland

Defeat is not the worst of failures. Not to have tried is the true failure.

George Edward Woodberry

FAIR

He never wants anything but what's right and fair; only when you come to settle what's right and fair, it's everything that he wants and nothing that you want.

Thomas Hughes

FAIR PLAY

The hard, half-apathetic expression of one who deems anything possible at the hands of Time and Chance, except, perhaps, fair play.

Thomas Hardy

Lloyd George could not see a belt without hitting below it.

Margot Asquith

One should always play fairly when one has the winning cards.

Oscar Wilde

FAIRY TALES

Fairy tales are loved by the child not because the imagery he finds within them conforms to what goes on within him, but because ... these stories always result in a happy outcome, which the child cannot imagine on his own.

Bruno Bettelheim

FAITH

Faith may be defined briefly as an illogical belief in the occurrence of the improbable.

H.L. Mencken

We walk by faith, not by sight.

II Corinthians: 5:7

Faith is the substance of things hoped for, the evidence of things not seen.

Hebrews 11:1

It is at night that faith in light is admirable.

Edmond Rostand

There are similarities between absolute power and absolute faith: a demand for absolute obedience, a readiness to attempt the impossible, a bias for simple solutions – to cut the knot rather than unravel it, the viewing of compromise as surrender. Both absolute power and absolute faith are instruments of dehumanization. Hence, absolute faith corrupts as absolutely as absolute power.

Eric Hoffer

Faith is much better than belief. Belief is when someone else does the thinking.

R. Buckminster Fuller

In faith there is enough light for those who want to believe and enough shadows to blind those who don't.

Blaise Pascal

It was the schoolboy who said, "Faith is believing what you know ain't so."

Mark Twain

We must have infinite faith in each other. If we have not, we must never let it leak out that we have not.

Henry David Thoreau

Faith moves mountains, but you have to keep pushing while you are praying.
Mason Cooley

It was, of course, a grand and impressive thing to do, to mistrust the obvious and to pin one's faith in things which could not be seen.
Galen

If you have any faith, give me a share of it. Your doubts you may keep to yourself, for I have plenty of my own.
Johann Wolfgang von Goethe

FAITHLESS
It is the faithless who know love's tragedies.
Oscar Wilde

FAKE
Fake it until you make it.
Alcoholics Anonymous

FALLACIES
Fallacies do not cease to be fallacies because they become fashions.
G.K. Chesterton

FALLIBILITY
Anyone who idolizes you is going to hate you when he discovers that you are fallible. He never forgives. He has deceived himself, and he blames you for it.
Elbert Hubbard

FALSE FRIENDS
A false friend and a shadow attend only when the sun shines.
Benjamin Franklin

FALSE KNOWLEDGE
Beware of false knowledge; it is more dangerous than ignorance.
George Bernard Shaw

FALSE PRETENSES
I do not approve of guys using false pretenses on dolls, except, of course, when nothing else will do.
Damon Runyaon

FALSEHOODS
Falsehoods not only quarrel with truth, but usually quarrel among themselves.
Daniel Webster

False in one thing, false in everything.
Legal maxim

Whatever is only almost true is quite false, and among the most dangerous of errors, because being so near the truth, it is the more likely to lead astray.
Henry Ward Beecher

Truth is blinding, like light. Falsehood, on the contrary, is a beautiful twilight that enhances every object.
Albert Camus

FAME
The fame of great men ought always to be estimated by the means used to acquire it.
François, duc de La Rochefoucauld

A special fame is reserved for the beautiful and the damned, whose money, talent, and fame can be forgiven because it never made them happy. These are our true folk heroes, for when a democracy bestows vast rewards on a very few, it is natural that those less blessed would seek to equalize this imbalance by choosing to admire people [such as Elvis, James Dean, and Marilyn Monroe] they can also pity.

Elizabeth Kaye

Fame is proof that the people are gullible.

Ralph Waldo Emerson

One of the drawbacks of fame is that one can never escape from it.

Dame Nellie Melba

Now when I bore people at a party, they think it's their fault.

Henry Kissinger

"I am world famous," Dr Parks said, "all over Canada."

Mordecai Richler

He's very, very well known. I'd say he's world famous in Melbourne.

Dame Edna Everage
(Barry Humphries)

Fame is different from popularity. It is less demanding for a start and has more to do with talent than virtue. But not even much to do with talent.

Jim Crace

The cool thing about being famous is travelling. I have always wanted to travel across seas, like to Canada and stuff.

Britney Spears

I was the toast of two continents: Greenland and Australia.

Dorothy Parker

The charm of fame is so great that we like every object to which it is attached, even death.

Blaise Pascal

A test of whether you have achieved true fame is when a deranged person believes himself to be you.

Anonymous

Some people fear gaining fame the way pigs fear gaining weight.

Chinese proverb

All fame is dangerous; good bringeth envy, bad shame.

Proverb

It's better to be famous than not famous because you get unfairly pampered.

Woody Allen

FAMILIARITY

Familiarity breeds attempt.

Goodman Ace

The aspects of things that are most important for us are hidden because of their simplicity and familiarity.

Ludwig Wittgenstein

Familiarity breeds.

Graffito

In the human world, it seems to me that the feeling of living among growing millions of others has produced alterations in the way we address one another. More nicknames, fewer honorifics, unwarranted endearments. To try to salvage a sense of human intimacy in a quick-contact world, a certain overfamiliarity is setting in.

Deirdre McNamer

The human tendency prefers familiar horrors to unknown delights.

Fred Woodworth

Familiarity breeds contempt – and children.

Mark Twain

FAMILIES

All happy families resemble one another, but each unhappy family is unhappy in its own way.

Leo Tolstoy

A happy family is but an earlier heaven.

Sir John Bowring

Many men can make a fortune, but very few can build a family.

J.S. Bryan

Call it a clan, call it a network, call it a tribe, call it a family. Whatever you call it, whoever you are, you need one.

Jane Howard

Other things may change us, but we start and end with the family.

Anthony Brandt

A family is a unit composed not only of children but of men, women, an occasional animal, and the common cold.

Ogden Nash

Where does the family start? It starts with a young man falling in love with a girl – no superior alternative has yet been found.

Winston Churchill

Q. What would have made combining a family and career easier for you? A. Being born a man.

Unknown

FAMOUS LAST WORDS

The cinema is little more than a fad. It's canned drama. What audiences really want to see is flesh and blood on the stage.

Movies are a fad. Audiences really want to see live actors on a stage.

Charlie Chaplin

Machines are good at chess but hopeless at recognizing patterns, learning, and fibbing – things a three-year-old child does every day.

John Naughton

Who the hell wants to hear actors talk?

Harry M. Warner

There is no likelihood that man can ever tap the power of the atom.

Robert Millikan

There is not the slightest indication that nuclear energy will ever be obtainable.

Albert Einstein

Heavier than air flying machines are impossible.

Lord Kelvin

Newspapers will ultimately engross all literature – there will be nothing else published but newspapers.
> *Alphonse de Lamartine*

X-rays are a hoax.
> *Lord Kelvin*

Radio has no future.
> *Lord Kelvin*

Television won't matter in your lifetime or mine.
> *R.S. Lambert*

I think there is a world market for maybe five computers.
> *Thomas Watson, Sr*

There is no reason for any individual to have a computer in his home.
> *Ken Olsen*

Computers in the future may weigh only 1.5 tons.
> *Popular Mechanics*

The horse is here to stay, but the automobile is only a novelty, a fad.
> *The president of The Michigan Savings Bank, advising Horace Rackman, lawyer to Henry Ford, not to invest in The Ford Motor Co. (Rackman ignored the advice. In 1903 he bought $5,000 worth of the stock, later unloading it for $12.5 million.)*

Airplanes are interesting toys, but of no military value.
> *Marshal Ferdinand Foch*

Stocks have reached what looks like a permanently high plateau.
> *Irving Fisher, professor of economics, Yale University, 17 October 1929*

We don't like their sound, and guitar music is on the way out.
> *Decca Records executive, rejecting a Beatles demo tape, 1962*

Everything that can be invented has been invented.
> *Charles Duell, US Commissioner of Patents, 1899*

640K ought to be enough for anybody.
> *Bill Gates*

Sensible and responsible women do not want to vote.
> *Grover Cleveland*

FANATICISM
Fanaticism consists in redoubling your effort when you have forgotten your aim.
> *George Santayana*

FARM
A farm is an irregular patch of nettles bounded by short-term notes, containing a fool and his wife who didn't know enough to stay in the city.
> *S.J. Perelman*

FARMERS
When tillage begins, other arts follow. The farmers, therefore, are the founders of human civilization.
> *Daniel Webster*

City people envy the farmer – but not to such an extent that they take advantage of the continuous opportunities to be one.

Bob Edwards, Calgary Eye Opener (1912)

It brings up happy old days when I was only a farmer and not an agriculturist.

O. Henry

FARMING

Italians come to ruin most generally in three ways – women, gambling, and farming. My family chose the slowest one.

Pope John XXIII

It is thus with farming, if you do one thing late, you will be late in all your work.

Cato the Elder

Let the farmer forevermore be honoured in his calling, for they who labour in the earth are the chosen people of God.

Thomas Jefferson

FASCINATING

There are only two kinds of people who are really fascinating – people who know absolutely everything, and people who know absolutely nothing.

Oscar Wilde

FASHION

Fashion is something that goes in one year and out the other.

Unknown

It is fashion's business to manipulate our memories. Fashion is in ceaseless pursuit of things that are about to look familiar and in uneasy flight from things that have just become a bore. Pretending frenziedly to market enthusiasm for novelty, in fact it sells disgust for previous modes.

Kennedy Fraser

I base most of my fashion taste on what doesn't itch.

Gilda Radner

If high heels were so wonderful, men would be wearing them.

Sue Grafton

Every generation laughs at the old fashions but religiously follows the new.

Henry David Thoreau

Fashion is something barbarous, for it produces innovation without reason and imitation without benefit.

George Santayana

Does fashion matter? Only if you're out of it.

Kim Campbell

Fashion, though in a strange way, represents all manly virtue. It is virtue gone to seed.

Ralph Waldo Emerson

Fashion is made to become unfashionable.

Coco Chanel

A fashion is nothing but an induced epidemic.

George Bernard Shaw

Never be the first or the last in the fashion.

> *Lord Chesterfield*

What would we say if men changed the length of their trousers every year?

> *Nancy Astor*

Fashion is gentility running away from vulgarity, and afraid of being overtaken.

> *William Hazlitt*

Fashion matters considerably more than horoscopes, rather more than dog shows and slightly more than hockey.

> *Roy Blount, Jr*

FASHIONABLE

You cannot be both fashionable and first-rate.

> *Logan Pearsall Smith*

FAST TALKING

The trouble with talking too fast is you may say something you haven't thought of yet.

> *Ann Landers*

FATE

We may become the makers of our fate when we have ceased to pose as its prophets.

> *Sir Karl Popper*

If fate means you lose, give him a good fight anyhow.

> *William McFee*

Fate leads the willing and drags along the reluctant.

> *Seneca*

Granting our wish one of Fate's saddest jokes is!

> *James Russell Lowell*

Fate is not an eagle; it creeps like a rat.

> *Elizabeth Bowen*

I am the master of my fate: /I am the captain of my soul.

> *W.E. Henley*

I do not believe in a fate that falls on men however they act, but I do believe in a fate that falls on them unless they act.

> *G.K. Chesterton*

Men at some time are master of their fates: /The fault, dear Brutus, is not in our stars, /But in ourselves, that we are underlings.

> *William Shakespeare*

The glories of our blood and state are shadows, not substantial things; there is no armour against fate. Death lays his icy hand on kings.

> *James Shirley*

There is no fate that cannot be surmounted by scorn.

> *Albert Camus*

Human reason needs only to will more strongly than fate, and she IS fate!

> *Thomas Mann*

Fate gave, what Chance shall not control, /His sad lucidity of soul.

> *Matthew Arnold*

There is no return game between a man and his stars.

> *Samuel Beckett*

Fate is unalterable only in the sense that given a cause, a certain result must follow, but no cause is inevitable in itself, and man can shape his world if he does not resign himself to ignorance.

Pearl S. Buck

We may become the makers of our fate when we have ceased to pose as its prophets.

Sir Karl Popper

They who see the Flying Dutchman never, never reach the shore.

John O'Reilly

FATHERS
That is the thankless position of the father in the family – the provider for all, and the enemy of all.

August Strindberg

If a man lives without being a father, he will die without having been a human being.

Russian proverb

The most important thing a father can do for his children is to love their mother.

Theodore Hesburgh

Mothers are a biological necessity; fathers are a social invention.

Margaret Mead

My heart belongs to Daddy.

Cole Porter

It is easy to become a father, but very difficult to be a father.

Wilhelm Busch

Today, while the titular head of the family may still be the father, everyone knows that he is little more than chairman, at most, of the entertainment committee.

Ashley Montagu

FATIGUE
Fatigue is often caused not by work but by worry, frustration, and resentment. We rarely get tired when we are doing something interesting and exciting.

Dale Carnegie

We are tired by the work we do not do, not by what we do.

Florence C. Brillhart

FAULTS
The greatest of faults, I should say, is to be conscious of none.

Thomas Carlyle

When you have faults, do not fear to abandon them.

Confucius

If we had no faults of our own, we would not take so much pleasure in noticing them in others.

François, duc de La Rochefoucauld

A man does not mind being blamed for his faults, and being punished for them, and he patiently suffers much for them; but he becomes impatient if he is required to give them up.

Johann Wolfgang von Goethe

He is lifeless that is faultless.

English proverb

Deal with the faults of others as gently as you deal with your own.
Chinese proverb

We confess to little faults only to persuade ourselves that we have no great ones.
François, duc de La Rochefoucauld

It had only one fault. It was kind of lousy.
James Thurber

Teach me to feel another's woe, to hide the fault I see.
Alexander Pope

Misfortunes one can endure – they come from outside, they are accidents. But to suffer for one's own faults – ah! – there is the sting of life.
Oscar Wilde

Always acknowledge a fault. This will throw those in authority off their guard and give you an opportunity to commit more.
Mark Twain

If you wish to be loved, show more of your faults than your virtues.
Edward Bulwer-Lytton

The real fault is to have faults and not amend them.
Confucius

People who have no faults are terrible; there is no way to take advantage of them.
Anatole France

We try to make virtues out of the faults we have no wish to correct.
François, duc de La Rochefoucauld

Forget others' faults by remembering your own.
Proverb

FAVOUR
The man who confers a favour would rather not be repaid in the same coin.
Aristotle

Most people return small favours, acknowledge middling ones, and repay great ones with ingratitude.
Benjamin Franklin

FEAR
There are few monsters who warrant the fear we have of them.
André Gide

Of all the passions, fear weakens judgment most.
Cardinal de Retz

He who is too much afraid of being duped has lost the power of being magnanimous.
Henri-Frédéric Amiel

He who fears he shall suffer, already suffers what he fears.
Michel de Montaigne

To fear the worst oft cures the worse.
William Shakespeare

Present fears are less than horrible imaginings.
William Shakespeare

Fear makes the wolf bigger than he is.

German proverb

No passion so effectually robs the mind of all its powers of acting and reasoning as fear.

Edmund Burke

We are all dangerous til our fears grow thoughtful.

John Ciardi

Fear and hope are alike underneath.

Richard Ford

Fear is implanted in us as a preservative from evil; but its duty, like that of other passions, is not to overbear reason but to assist it.

Samuel Johnson

Who is more foolish, the child afraid of the dark or the man afraid of the light?

Maurice Freehill

O! How vain and vile a passion is this fear!/What base uncomely things it makes men do.

Ben Jonson

No greater hell than to be a slave to fear.

Ben Jonson

Excessive fear is always powerless.

Aeschylus

It takes up too much time, being afraid.

Pierre Elliott Trudeau

When men are ruled by fear, they strive to prevent the very changes that will abate it.

Alan Paton

Men are not afraid of things, but of how they view them.

Epictetus

Just as courage imperils life, fear protects it.

Leonardo da Vinci

The first and greatest commandment is don't let them scare you.

Elmer Davis

All fear is painful, and when conduces not to safety, is painful without use. Every consideration, therefore, by which groundless terrors may be removed, adds something to human happiness.

Samuel Johnson

There were all kinds of things of which I was afraid at first, from grizzly bears to "mean" horses and gunfighters, but by acting as if I was not afraid I gradually ceased to be afraid.

Theodore Roosevelt

Fear has the largest eyes of all.

Boris Pasternak

To him who is in fear everything rustles.

Sophocles

Love is what we were born with. Fear is what we learned here.

Marianne Williamson

The most destructive element in the human mind is fear. Fear creates aggressiveness.

Dorothy Thompson

Only when we are no longer afraid do we begin to live.

Dorothy Thompson

Deep into that darkness peering, long I stood there wondering, fearing.

Edgar Allan Poe

Fear always springs from ignorance.

Ralph Waldo Emerson

Of all the liars in the world, sometimes the worst are your own fears.
Rudyard Kipling

I am never afraid of what I know.
Anna Sewell

He has not learned the first lesson of life who does not every day surmount a fear.

John Dryden

FEELINGS
Better to be without logic than without feeling.

Charlotte Brontë

All great discoveries are made by people whose feelings run ahead of their thinking.

C.H. Oakhurst

You cannot make yourself feel something you do not feel, but you can make yourself do right in spite of your feelings.

Pearl S. Buck

FEET
Why isn't there a special name for the tops of your feet?

Lily Tomlin

FEMALE
The she-bear thus accosted rends the peasant tooth and nail / For the female of the species is more deadly than the male.

Rudyard Kipling

FEMINISTS
Some of us are becoming the men we wanted to marry.

Gloria Steinem

Our struggle today is not to have a female Einstein get appointed as an assistant professor. It is for a woman schlemiel to get as quickly promoted as a male schlemiel.

Bella Abzug

FEROCITY
Ferocity and cunning ... are useful to the individual only because there is so large a proportion of the same traits actively present in the human environment to which he is exposed. Any individual who enters the competitive struggle without the due endowment of these traits is at a disadvantage, somewhat as a hornless steer would find himself at a disadvantage in a drove of horned cattle.

Thorstein Veblen

FICTION
Reporting the extreme things as if they were the average things will start you on the art of fiction.

F. Scott Fitzgerald

The trouble with fiction is that it makes too much sense, whereas reality never makes sense.

Aldous Huxley

Literature is a luxury; fiction is a necessity.

G.K. Chesterton

The truer the facts, the better the fiction.

Virginia Woolf

Fiction gives us a second chance that life denies us.

Paul Theroux

FIDELITY

Fidelity, *n.* A virtue peculiar to those who are about to be betrayed.

Ambrose Bierce

FIFTH ACE

He said it was not always the timid fellow with four conventional aces in his hand who won the highest honors. "It is often," he said, "the fifth ace that makes all the difference between success and failure."

J.B. Morton

FIGHTING

It is a perplexing and unpleasant truth that when men already feel they have "something worth fighting for," they do not feel like fighting.

Eric Hoffer

He will win who knows when to fight and when not to fight.

Sun Tzu

He who fights too long against dragons becomes a dragon.

Friedrich Nietzsche

If the row comes, remember the Maine, and show the world how American sailors can fight.

Clifford Berryman

FIGURE

One figure can sometimes add up to a lot.

Wesley Ruggles

FILM

Film is more than the twentieth-century art. It's another part of the twentieth-century mind. It's the world seen from inside.

Don DeLillo

A good film is when the price of the dinner, the theatre admission, and the babysitter were worth it.

Alfred Hitchcock

Shoot a few scenes out of focus. I want to win the foreign film award.

Billy Wilder

Good films get smaller audiences, but more of the viewer.

Jean-Luc Godard

Does art reflect life? In movies, yes. Because more than any other art form, films have been a mirror held up to society's porous face.

Marjorie Rosen

The making of a picture ... is an endless contention of tawdry egos, some of them powerful, almost all of them vociferous, and almost none of them capable of anything much more creative than credit-stealing and self-promotion.

Raymond Chandler

I went into films for the most shallow reasons: to meet women and not have an arduous life of drudgery.

Woody Allen

FINE PRINT
The big print giveth and the fine print taketh away.

Fulton J. Sheen

FINGERS
On the other hand, you have different fingers.

Steven Wright

FISH STORIES
Do not tell fish stories where the people know you; but particularly, don't tell them where they know the fish.

Mark Twain

Fishing: a delusion entirely surrounded by liars in old clothes.

Don Marquis

FISHING POLES
If people concentrated on the really important things in life, there'd be a shortage of fishing poles.

Doug Larson

FITTING IN
You had better be a round peg in a square hole than a square peg in a round hole. The latter is in for life, while the first is only an indeterminate sentence.

Elbert Hubbard

FLAME
I recognize the signals of the ancient flame.

Dante Alighieri

FLATTERY
It is flattering some men to endure them.

John Morley

What really flatters a man is that you think him worth flattering.

George Bernard Shaw

Flattery is all right, so long as you don't inhale.

Adlai Stevenson

We despise no source that can pay us pleasing attention.

Mark Twain

Flattery sits in the parlour when plain dealing is kicked out of doors.

Thomas Fuller, MD

Beware of one who flatters unduly; he will also censure unjustly.

Arab proverb

Flatterers look like friends, as wolves like dogs.

George Chapman

FLAWS
I myself am made entirely of flaws, stitched together with good intentions.

Augusten Burroughs

FLEAS
Great fleas have little fleas upon their backs to bite 'em,/And little

fleas have lesser fleas, and so ad infinitum.

Augustus De Morgan

FLEXIBILITY

There is more than one path through the palms to the beach.

Hawaiian proverb

The great thing in this world is not so much where we stand, as in what direction we are moving ... we must sail sometimes with the wind and sometimes against it.

Oliver Wendell Holmes

Better is to bow than break.

John Heywood

FLIRT

In order to avoid being called a flirt, she always yielded easily.

Charles-Maurice de Talleyrand

FLOODS

The only thing that stops God from sending another flood is that the first one was useless.

Chamfort

FLORIDA

My parents didn't want to move to Florida, but they turned sixty, and that's the law.

Jerry Seinfeld

FLOWERS

If you want to say it with flowers, a single rose says: "I'm cheap."

Delta Burke

Our national flower is the concrete cloverleaf.

Lewis Mumford

Flowers are words even a baby can understand.

Quentin Crisp

In the language of flowers, the yellow rose means friendship, the red rose means love – and the orchid usually means business.

D.O. Flynn

FLY

God in his wisdom made the fly / And then forgot to tell us why.

Ogden Nash

FLYING

This new sport is comparable to no other. It is, in my opinion, one of the most intoxicating forms of sport, and will, I am sure, become one of the most popular. Many of us will perish before then, but that prospect will not dismay the braver spirits. ... It is so delicious to fly like a bird!

Marie Marvingt

If God had really intended men to fly, he'd make it easier to get to the airport.

George Winters

You define a good flight by negatives: You didn't get hijacked, you didn't crash, you didn't throw up, you weren't late, you weren't nauseated by the food. So you are grateful.

Paul Theroux

FOG
The fog comes on little cat feet.
Carl Sandburg

FOGIES
The world is burdened with young fogies. Old men with ossified minds are easily dealt with. But men who look young, act young, and everlastingly harp on the fact that they are young, but who nevertheless think and act with a degree of caution that would be excessive in their grandfathers, are the curse of the world. Their very conservatism is secondhand, and they don't know what they are conserving.
Robertson Davies

FOLK SAYINGS (CANADIAN)
Hard to tell from its looks how far a frog will jump.

He's got more tongue than a Mountie's boot.

I'll tow that alongside awhile, before I bring it aboard.

Heavier than a dead minister.

He's got his solar panels on the north side.
Bill Casselman

FOLLY
The folly which we might have ourselves committed is the one which we are least ready to pardon in another.
Joseph Roux

The chief characteristic of folly is that it mistakes itself for wisdom.
Fray Luis de León

One man's folly is another man's wife.
Helen Rowland

Folly is often more cruel in the consequence than malice can be in the intent.
George Savile, Marquess of Halifax

If to talk to oneself when alone is folly, it must be doubly unwise to listen to oneself in the presence of others.
Baltasar Gracian

FOOD
Food is an important part of a balanced diet.
Fran Lebowitz

A food is not necessarily essential just because your child hates it.
Katharine Whitehorn

Food is the most primitive form of comfort.
Sheila Graham

What makes food such a tyranny for women? A man, after all, may in times of crisis, hit the bottle (or another person), but he rarely hits the fridge.
Joanna Trollope

We may find in the long run that tinned food is a deadlier weapon than the machine gun.
George Orwell

I no longer prepare food or drink with more than one ingredient.
Cyra McFadden

There ain't no such thing as wrong food.
Sean Stewart

Italy will always have the best food.
Diane von Furstenberg

FOOLED
We don't get fooled again.
The Who

Being fooled, by foolery thrive;/ There's place and means for every man alive.
William Shakespeare

It is true that you may fool all the people some of the time; you can even fool some of the people all the time; but you cannot fool all of the people all the time.
Abraham Lincoln

It may be true that you can't fool all the people all the time, but you can fool enough of them to rule a large country.
Will Durant

You can fool too many of the people too much of the time.
James Thurber

FOOLISH
If fifty million people say a foolish thing, it is still a foolish thing.
Bertrand Russell

Mix a little foolishness with your serious plans: It's lovely to be silly at the right moment.
Horace

FOOLS
The ultimate effect of shielding men from the effects of folly is to fill the world with fools.
Herbert Spencer

Learned fools are the greatest fools.
Proverb

Every man is a damn fool for at least five minutes every day; wisdom consists of not exceeding the limit.
Elbert Hubbard

Let us be thankful for the fools. But for them the rest of us could not succeed.
Mark Twain

If you can't spot the sucker in the game in the first ten minutes, then it must be you.
Poker saying

He who despairs of the human condition is a coward, but he who has hope for it is a fool.
Albert Camus

A fool in a hurry drinks tea with a fork.
Norma Gleason

There are two kinds of fools: one says "This is old, therefore it is good"; the other says, "This is new, therefore it is better."
Dean Inge

It's only damned fools who argue! Never Contradict. Never Explain. Never Apologize. Those are the secrets of a happy life.

British Admiral Jackie Fisher

Suffer fools gladly. They may be right.

Holbrook Jackson

Everybody loves a fool, but nobody wants him for a son.

Malinke (West African) proverb

The haste of a fool is the slowest thing in the world.

Thomas Shadwell

A fool and his money are soon invited everywhere.

Elsie, Lady Mendl

Fools give you reasons, wise men never try.

Oscar Hammerstein

The greatest lesson in life is to know that fools are right some-times.

Winston Churchill

Fools act on imagination without knowledge, pedants act on knowl-edge without imagination.

Alfred North Whitehead

Foolproof implies a finite number of fools.

Anonymous

There are more fools in the world than there are people.

Heinrich Heine

The fool doth think he is wise, but the wise man knows himself to be a fool.

William Shakespeare

If the fools do not control the world, it isn't because they are not in the majority.

Edgar Watson Howe

The best way to convince a fool that he is wrong is to let him have his own way.

Josh Billings

There is no need to fasten a bell to a fool.

Danish proverb

Little is needed to make a wise man happy, but nothing can content a fool.

François, duc de La Rochefoucauld

A fool sees not the same tree that a wise man sees.

William Blake

A knowledgeable fool is a greater fool than an ignorant one.

Molière

A fellow who is always declaring he is no fool usually has his suspi-cions.

Wilson Mizner

Anyone who feels at ease in the world today is a fool.

Robert Hitchens

Fools out of favour grudge at knaves in place.

Daniel Defoe

A fool and his money are soon parted. What I want to know is how they got together in the first place.

Cyril Fletcher

Young men think old men are fools; but old men know young men are fools.

George Chapman

I'm all in favour of keeping dangerous weapons out of the hands of fools. Let's start with typewriters.

Frank Lloyd Wright

But there comes a moment in everybody's life when he must decide whether he'll live among human beings or not – a fool among fools, or a fool alone.

Thornton Wilder

Ninety-nine percent of the people in the world are fools, and the rest are in great danger of contagion.

Thornton Wilder

The wise man does at once what the fool does finally.

Baltasar Gracian

When we play the fool, how wide the theatre expands!

Walter Savage Landor

After the event, even a fool is wise.

Homer

There is a fool born every minute.

P.T. Barnum

No woman really makes a fool out of a man – she merely gives him the opportunity to develop his natural capacities.

Warren Hammer

FOOTBALL
Don't worry about it. It's just a bunch of guys with an odd-shaped ball.

Bill Parcels

It was an ideal day for football – too cold for the spectators and too cold for the players.

Red Smith

All I know most surely about morality and obligations, I owe to football.

Albert Camus

Whoever invented football should be worshipped as a God.

Hugo Sanchez

Football is the opera of the people.
Stafford Heginbotham

Football combines the two worst things about America: It is violence punctuated by committee meetings.
George F. Will

FOOTBALL FANS
The natural state of the football fan is bitter disappointment, no matter what the score.

Nick Hornby

Anyone who watches three games of football in a row should be declared legally dead.

Erma Bombeck

FORBEARANCE
There is, however, a limit at which forbearance ceases to be a virtue.

Edmund Burke

FORBIDDEN
Things forbidden have a secret charm.

Tacitus

FORCE
Are you going to come quietly, or do I have to use earplugs?

Spike Milligan

Brute force without wisdom falls by its own weight.

Horace

When force is necessary, there it must be applied boldly, decisively, and completely. But one must know the limitations of force; one must know when to blend force with a maneuver, a blow with an agreement.

Leon Trotsky

The direct use of force is such a poor solution to any problem, it is generally employed only by small children and large nations.

David Friedman

Force is all-conquering, but its victories are short-lived.

Abraham Lincoln

FORCE FIELD
Remember – you can't beam through a force field. So, don't try it.

William Shatner

FORECASTING
Forecasting is very difficult – especially if it's about the future.

Edgar Fiedler

We have two classes of forecasters: those who don't know – and those who don't know they don't know.

John Kenneth Galbraith

Never mistake a clear view for a short distance.

Paul Saffo

FOREIGN AID
Foreign aid might be defined as a transfer from poor people in rich countries to rich people in poor countries.

Douglas Casey

FOREIGN SECRETARY
A Foreign Secretary ... is always faced with this cruel dilemma. Nothing he can say can do very much good, and almost anything he may say may do a great deal of harm.

Harold MacMillan

FOREIGNER
We cannot bring ourselves to believe it possible that a foreigner should in any respect be wiser than ourselves.

Anthony Trollope

FORESIGHT
In action, be primitive; in foresight, a strategist.

René Char

No one thinks of the winter when the grass is green.

Rudyard Kipling

FOREWARNING
A forewarned man is worth two.
Spanish proverb

O that a man might know/The end
of this day's business ere it come!
William Shakespeare

FORGET
If you wish to forget anything on
the spot, make a note that this
thing is to be remembered.
Edgar Allan Poe

Till you forget, we shall not twice
have died.
John E. Nixon

We have all forgot more than we
remember.
Thomas Fuller, MD

We learn so little and forget so
much.
Sir John Davies

Better by far that you should forget
and smile than remember and be
sad.
Christina Rossetti

To forgive is human, to forget
divine.
James Grand

Good to forgive;/Better to forget.
Robert Browning

The remedy for wrongs is to forget
them.
Publilius Syrus

FORGIVE
The stupid neither forgive nor forget; the naive forgive and forget;
the wise forgive but do not forget.
Thomas Szasz

Those who cannot forgive others
break the bridge over which they
themselves must pass.
Confucius

There are many circumstances in
life where it is possible to effect by
forgiveness every object which you
propose to effect by resentment.
Sydney Smith

It is easier to forgive an enemy than
to forgive a friend.
William Blake

Nobuddy ever fergits where he
buried a hatchet.
Abe Martin

One of the secrets of a long and
fruitful life is to forgive everybody
everything every night before you
go to bed.
Ann Landers

If I've done anything I'm sorry for,
I'm willing to be forgiven.
Edward Noyes Westcott

Forgive your enemies. Never forget
their names.
John F. Kennedy

He who forgives readily only
invites offence.
Cinna

FORGIVENESS
Life is an adventure in forgiveness.
Norman Cousins

Forgiveness is better than revenge,
for forgiveness is the sign of a gentle nature, but revenge is the sign of
a savage nature.
Epictetus

The weak can never forgive. Forgiveness is the attribute of the strong.

Mohandas Gandhi

FORM

When one starts from a portrait and seeks by successive eliminations to find pure form ... one inevitably ends up with an egg.

Pablo Picasso

FORMS

Forms are for mediocrity, and it is fortunate that mediocrity can act only according to routine. Ability takes its form unhindered.

Napoleon Bonaparte

FORTUNE

It is we that are blind, not Fortune.

Sir Thomas Browne

He who asks fortune-tellers the future unwittingly forfeits an inner intimation of coming events that is a thousand times more exact than anything they may say.

Walter Benjamin

How fortune brings to earth the oversure!

Petrarch

Want to make a small fortune? Start with a large fortune – and then hire an advertising agency.

Herbert Kelleher

Fortune pays you sometimes for the intensity of her favours by the shortness of their duration. She soon tires of carrying anyone long on her shoulders.

Baltasar Gracian

When Fortune comes, seize her in front with a sure hand, because behind she is bald.

Leonardo da Vinci

We must master our good fortune, or it will master us.

Publilius Syrus

Let everyone witness how many different cards fortune has up her sleeve when she wants to ruin a man.

Benvenuto Cellini

Fortune does not change men, it unmasks them.

Suzanne Necker

Fortune sides with him who dares.

Virgil

Fortune never appears so blind as to those whom she does no good.

François, duc de La Rochefoucauld

Fortune brings in some boats that are not steered.

William Shakespeare

Here is a rule to remember in future, when anything tempts you to be bitter: not "This is a misfortune," but "To bear this worthily is good fortune."

Marcus Aurelius

Fortune does not arrive in pairs, and troubles do not come singly.

Chinese proverb

There is in the worst of fortune the best of chances for a happy change.

Euripides

Don't wait for your ship to come in, swim out to it.

Anonymous

No man is crushed by hostile Fortune who is not first deceived by her smiles.

Seneca

A man is never so on trial as in the moment of excessive good fortune.

Lew Wallace

The good effect of fortune may be short-lived. To build on it is to build on sand.

Seigneur de Racan

Fortunes ... come tumbling into some men's laps.

Francis Bacon

FOUNDATIONS
The loftiest edifices need the deepest foundations.

George Santayana

FRANCE
What kind of country puts up more resistance to Disney than they did to the Nazis?

Conan O'Brien

France is a place where the money falls apart in your hands but you can't tear the toilet paper.

Billy Wilder

FRAUD
There are some frauds so well conducted that it would be stupidity not to be deceived by them.

Charles Caleb Colton

FRECKLES
Four be the things I'd better been without: love, curiosity, freckles, and doubt.

Dorothy Parker

FREE AGENT
We are no more free agents than the queen of clubs when she victoriously takes prisoner the knave of hearts.

Lady Mary Wortley Montagu

FREE GIFTS
You pay a great deal too dear for what's given freely.

William Shakespeare

FREE MARKET
The advantage of a free market is that it allows millions of decision-makers to respond individually to freely determined prices, allocating resources – labor, capital and human ingenuity – in a manner that can't be mimicked by a central plan, however brilliant the central planner.

Friedrich von Hayek

FREE SOCIETY
My definition of a free society is a society where it is safe to be unpopular.

Adlai Stevenson

FREE SPEECH
Everyone is in favour of free speech. Hardly a day passes without it being extolled, but some people's idea of it is that they are free

to say what they like, but if anyone says anything back, that is an outrage.

Winston Churchill

The right to be heard does not automatically include the right to be taken seriously.

Hubert H. Humphrey

A people which is able to say everything becomes able to do everything.

Napoleon Bonaparte

FREE THOUGHT
If there is any principle of the Constitution that more imperatively calls for attachment than any other, it is the principle of free thought – not free thought for those who agree with us but freedom for the thought that we hate.

Oliver Wendell Holmes, Jr

FREE TRADE
Free trade, one of the greatest blessings which a government can confer upon a people, is in almost every country unpopular.

Thomas Babington Macaulay

FREE WILL
We have to believe in free will. We've got no choice.

Isaac Bashevis Singer

We ride through life on the beast within us. Beat the animal, but you can't make it think.

Luigi Pirandello

FREEDOM
Freedom is a habit that must be kept alive by use.

F.R. Scott

If we don't believe in freedom of expression for people we despise, we don't believe in it at all.

Noam Chomsky

This is a free country. Folks have a right to send me letters, and I have a right not to read them.

William Faulkner

Freedom is what you do with what's been done to you.

Jean-Paul Sartre

Who dares not speak his free thoughts is a slave.

Euripides

Never wear your best trousers when you go out to fight for freedom and truth.

Henrik Ibsen

Those who deny freedom to others deserve it not for themselves.

Abraham Lincoln

The freedom of the individual is tied thoroughly and completely with the sanctity of private property.

Stephen Roman

Aren't people absurd! They never use the freedoms they do have but demand those they don't have; they have freedom of thought, they demand freedom of speech.

Søren Kierkegaard

Freedom is the right to be wrong, not the right to do wrong.
>*Bits & Pieces*

Is something a blow against your freedom just because it can seriously damage your wealth?
Jonathan Lynn and Sir Antony Jay

On the mountains there is freedom!/The world is perfect everywhere,/Save where man comes with his torment.
>*Friedrich von Schiller*

Freedom is just chaos with better lighting.
>*Alan Dean Foster*

I know but one freedom, and that is the freedom of the mind.
>*Antoine de Saint-Exupéry*

Freedom is always and exclusively freedom for the one who thinks differently.
>*Rosa Luxemburg*

To win true freedom, you must be a slave to philosophy.
>*Epicurus*

When people are free to do as they please, they usually imitate each other.
>*Eric Hoffer*

As a nation of freemen we must live through all time, or die by suicide.
>*Abraham Lincoln*

Freedom is something people take, and people are as free as they want to be.
>*James Baldwin*

It is often safer to be in chains than to be free.
>*Franz Kafka*

The basic test of freedom is perhaps less in what we are free to do than in what we are free not to do. It is the freedom to refrain, withdraw and abstain which makes a totalitarian regime impossible.
>*Eric Hoffer*

Better to die standing than to live on your knees.
>*Che Guevara*

Like a bird on the wire, like a drunk in a midnight choir I have tried in my way to be free.
>*Leonard Cohen*

In giving freedom to the slave, we assure freedom to the free – honorable alike in what we give and what we preserve.
>*Abraham Lincoln*

The more obligations we accept that are self-imposed, the freer we are.
>*John W. Schroeder*

Freedom is a precious thing today. Those who have it cherish it; those who fear it want to destroy it; and those who don't have it, will still fight for it.
>*Harvey C. Jacobs*

He is free ... whose impulses are unimpeded, whose desires attain their purpose, who falls not into what he would avoid.
>*Epictetus*

FRENCH
The French are a logical people, which is one reason the English dislike them so intensely. The other is that they own France, a country which we have always judged to be much too good for them.
Robert Morley

The French are wiser than they seem, and the Spaniards seem wiser than they are.

Francis Bacon

FREUDIAN SLIP
A Freudian slip is when you say one thing but mean your mother.
Unknown

FRIEND
The friend who understands you, creates you.

Romain Rolland

If you would win a man to your cause, first convince him that you are his sincere friend.

Abraham Lincoln

He that would lose a friend for jest deserves to die a beggar by the bargain.

Sir Thomas Fuller

God save me from my friends, I can protect myself from my enemies.

Marshal Villars

It's the friends that you can call up at 4 a.m. that matter.

Marlene Dietrich

We need two kinds of acquaintances: one to complain to, while we boast to the other.
Logan Pearsall Smith

I hate it in friends when they come too late to help.

Euripides

"Stay" is a charming word in a friend's vocabulary.
Louisa May Alcott

Hold a true friend with both hands.
Nigerian proverb

A friend is a present which you give yourself.
Robert Louis Stevenson

A friend's eye is a good mirror.
Irish proverb

The best mirror is an old friend.
George Herbert

A true friend is the most precious of all possessions and the one we take least thought about acquiring.
François, duc de La Rochefoucauld

I was the kid next door's imaginary friend.

Emo Phillips

Some men are better served by their bitter-tongued enemies than by their sweet-smiling friends; because the former often tell the truth, the latter, never.
Cato the Younger

It is in the thirties that we want friends. In the forties, we know they won't save us any more than love did.

F. Scott Fitzgerald

You can always tell a real friend: When you've made a fool of yourself he doesn't feel you've done a permanent job.

Laurence J. Peter

A true friend is someone who knows you better than you know yourself.

Matthew Cheng

He makes no friend who has never made a foe.

Alfred, Lord Tennyson

A friend in power is a friend lost.

Henry Adams

You cannot be friends upon any other terms than upon the terms of equality.

Woodrow Wilson

The friend who holds your hand and says the wrong thing is made of dearer stuff than the one who stays away.

Barbara Kingsolver

I awoke this morning with devout thanksgiving for my friends, the old and the new.

Ralph Waldo Emerson

One loyal friend is worth ten thousand relatives.

Euripides

It was his peculiar happiness that he scarcely ever found a stranger whom he did not leave a friend;

but it must likewise be added, that he had not often a friend long without obliging him to become a stranger.

Samuel Johnson

One's friends are that part of the human race with which one can be human.

George Santayana

A four-legged friend, a four-legged friend, He'll never let you down.

Jack Brook

Show me somebody who can't tell his friends from his enemies, and I'll show you somebody who's going to end up with no friends.

Jim Lehrer

One can't complain. I have my friends. Someone spoke to me only yesterday.

A.A. Milne

When one is trying to do something beyond his known powers it is useless to seek the approval of friends. Friends are at their best in moments of defeat.

Henry Miller

Treat your friends as you do your pictures, and place them in their best light.

Jennie Jerome Churchill

I step over to his table and give him a medium hello, and he looks up and gives me a medium hello right back, for, to tell the truth, Maury and I are never bosom friends.

Damon Runyon

We want all our friends to tell us of our bad qualities; it is only the particular ass that does so that we can't tolerate.

William Jones

If anything lucky happens to you, don't fail to go and tell it to your friends in order to annoy them.

Casimir, Comte de Montrond

If you have no enemies, you are apt to be in the same predicament in regard to friends.

Elbert Hubbard

A friend will see you through when others see that you are through.

Louis Sobol

A courageous foe is better than a cowardly friend.

Proverb

A friend in power is a friend lost.

Henry Adams

True friends visit us in prosperity only when invited, but in adversity they come without invitation.

Theophrastus

Our worst enemies are often the friends we once talked to as only a friend should.

Adrian Anderson

It is one of the blessings of old friends that you can afford to be stupid with them.

Ralph Waldo Emerson

A true friend is someone who likes you despite your achievements.

Arnold Bennett

FRIENDSHIP

That friendship will not continue to the end which is begun for an end.

Francis Quarles

You cannot shake hands with a clenched fist.

Anonymous

Friendship is love minus sex and plus reason. Love is friendship plus sex and minus reason.

Mason Cooley

True friendship comes when silence between two people is comfortable.

Dave Tyson Gentry

Friendship is a strong and habitual inclination in two persons to promote the good and happiness of one another.

Eustace Budgell

Do not let a little dispute injure a great friendship.

Dalai Lama

A man of active and resilient mind outwears his friendships just as certainly as he outwears his love affairs, his politics, and his epistemology.

H.L. Mencken

I always felt that the great high privilege, relief, and comfort of friendship was that one had to explain nothing.

Katherine Mansfield

If you want long friendships, develop a short memory.

Anonymous

Friendship is like money, easier made than kept.

Samuel Butler

It is wise to apply the oil of refined politeness to the mechanisms of friendship.

Colette

Agreement in likes and dislikes – this, and this only, is what constitutes true friendship.

Catiline

Friendships last when each friend thinks he has a slight superiority over the other.

Honoré de Balzac

FRUGALITY

Take care of the pence and the pounds will take care of themselves.

William Lowndes

He who is frugal is the richest of men, and the miser is the poorest.

Chamfort

Without frugality none can be rich, and with it very few would be poor.

Samuel Johnson

FUGITIVE

I feel like a fugitive from the law of averages.

William Mauldin

FULFILLMENT

We have what we seek, it is there all the time, and if we give it time, it will make itself known to us.

Thomas Merton

FUN

Most of the time I don't have much fun. The rest of the time I don't have any fun at all.

Woody Allen

Every time I hear that word, I cringe. Fun! I think it's disgusting; it's just running around. It's not my idea of pleasure.

Vivienne Westwood

Great lords have their pleasures, but the people have fun.

Montesquieu

No, you never get any fun out of the things you haven't done.

Ogden Nash

People must not do things for fun. We are not here for fun. There is no reference to fun in any Act of Parliament.

A.P. Herbert

FUNERALS

Why is it that we rejoice at a birth and grieve at a funeral? Is it because we are not the person involved?

Mark Twain

I didn't attend the funeral, but I sent a nice letter saying I approved of it.

Mark Twain

FUNNY

Everything is funny as long as it is happening to somebody else.

Will Rogers

When a thing is funny, search it carefully for a hidden truth.

George Bernard Shaw

Only man has dignity; only man, therefore, can be funny.

Ronald Knox

It's hard to be funny when you have to be clean.

Mae West

There's nothing funnier than the human animal.

Walt Disney

FURY

Great fury, like great whiskey, requires long fermentation.

Truman Capote

FUTILITY

Conspicuous futility is something only for the young. One cannot go on "despairing of life" into a ripe old age.

George Orwell

FUTURE

The best preparation for tomorrow is to do today's work supremely well.

Sir William Osler

The future is no more uncertain than the present.

Walt Whitman

The wise man guards against the future as if it were the present.

Publilius Syrus

In the future everyone will be world famous for fifteen minutes.

Andy Warhol

The danger of the past was that men became slaves. The danger of the future is that men may become robots.

Erich Fromm

The best prophet of the future is the past.

John Sherman

It is horrible to see everything that one detested in the past coming back wearing the colours of the future.

Jean Rostand

I have seen the Future – and it was being repaired.

Mel Calman

The future is like heaven – everyone exalts it, but no one wants to go there now.

James Baldwin

Still round the corner there may wait, a new road, or a secret gate.

J.R.R. Tolkien

And all your future lies beneath your hat.

John Oldham

I never think of the future. It comes soon enough.

Albert Einstein

In a hundred years? All new people.

Anne Lamott

The only reason people want to be masters of the future is to change the past.

Milan Kundera

All of us are looking at the future with yesterday's eyes.

Dan Burns

No one can walk backwards into the future.

Joseph Hergesheimer

If you do not think about the future, you cannot have one.

John Galsworthy

You can never plan the future by the past.

Edmund Burke

The future has a way of arriving unannounced.

George F. Will

Future, *n.* That period of time in which our affairs prosper, our friends are true and our happiness is assured.

Ambrose Bierce

The future will be better tomorrow.

Dan Quayle

One should never place one's trust in the future. It doesn't deserve it.

André Chamson

The best way to predict the future is to invent it.

Alan Kay

The future is hidden even from the men who make it.

Anatole France

Let us attend to the present, and as to the future we shall know how to manage when the occasion arrives.

Pierre Corneille

The future lies ahead.

Mort Sahl

What happens when the future has come and gone?

Robert Half

To know the road ahead, ask those coming back.

Chinese proverb

The past cannot be changed, the future is still in your power.

Hugh White

We already have the statistics for the future: the growth percentages of population, overpopulation, desertification. The future is already in place.

Günter Grass

The enemies of the future are always the very nicest people.

Christopher Morley

Upper classes are a nation's past; the middle-class is its future.

Ayn Rand

Normal people think of the past, clever people think of the present, only stupid people think of the future.

Vietnamese saying

The future is only the past again. Only the cynic knows the future because he has seen it all before.

Adam Phillips

Only a signal shown and a distant voice in the darkness.
Henry Wadsworth Longfellow

One thing is clear: We don't have the option of turning away from the future. No one gets to vote on whether technology is going to change our lives.
Bill Gates

To pin all your hopes upon the future is to consign those hopes to a hypothesis, which is to say, a nothingness. Here and now is what we must contend with.
Angela Carter

My interest is in the future because I am going to spend the rest of my life there.
Charles F. Kettering

The future influences the present just as much as the past.
Friedrich Nietzsche

Real generosity toward the future consists in giving all to what is present.
Albert Camus

The trouble with our times is that the future is not what it used to be.
Paul Valéry

The future will one day be the present and will seem as unimportant as the present does now.
W. Somerset Maugham

It is being afraid of the future that makes the future fearful.
Jan Smuts

I hold that man is in the right who is most closely in league with the future.
Henrik Ibsen

When all else is lost, the future still remains.
Christian Nestell Bovee

I don't know where I'm going from here, but I promise it won't be boring.
David Bowie

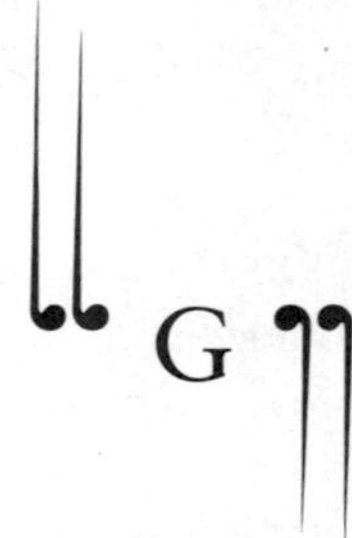

GAFFE

A gaffe is when a politician tells the truth.

Michael Kinsley

GAG

In the end, everything is a gag.

Charlie Chaplin

GAMBLING

The best throw of the dice is to throw them away.

English proverb

Gambling: The sure way of getting nothing for something.

Wilson Mizner

A man is beat when he goes for broke and wagers the sum of his resources on a single number.

John Clellon Holmes

I never hear the rattling of dice that it does not sound to me like the funeral bell of the whole family.

Douglas Jerrold

An old adage has it that gambling is a tax for people who can't do math.

Utne Reader

GAME SHOWS

Game shows are designed to make us feel better about the random, useless facts that are all we have left of our education.

Chuck Palahniuk

GAMES

No human being is innocent, but there is a class of innocent human actions called Games.

W.H. Auden

Most games are lost, not won.

Casey Stengel

GARDENERS

Like a gardener, I believe that what goes down must come up.

Lynwood L. Giacómini

What a man needs in gardening is a cast-iron back, with a hinge in it.

Charles Dudley Warner

GARDENING

Gardening is an active participation in the deepest mysteries of the universe.

Thomas Berry

GARDENS
I have a rock garden. Last week, three of them died.
Richard Diran

GAZE
To gaze is to think.
Salvador Dali

GENE POOL
The problem with the gene pool is, that there is no lifeguard.
Steven Wright

GENERALIZATIONS
All generalizations are dangerous, even this one.
Alexandre Dumas

Generalizations are generally wrong.
Lady Mary Wortley Montagu

To generalize is to be an idiot. To particularize is the lone distinction of merit – general knowledges are those knowledges that idiots possess.
William Blake

GENERALS
It is not the job of the general to be winning. It is his job to win.
Nancy Banks-Smith

GENERATIONS
We think of generations as a twenty-year unit, which is about as long as it takes one batch of humans to create its successors. But to adolescents, a generation lasts about three years, as long as it takes a group of them to take over a school and start laying down the stylistic rules. ... Style is how adolescent generations mark out their territory. *This is who we are. This is who we aren't.* ... "They're all the same kid," my older son said, after glimpsing the eighth-graders during their sidewalk procession. "He's right," my younger son said. "But they're not the kid he thinks they are."
John Powers

The most aggravating thing about the younger generation is that I no longer belong to it.
John Dryden

Our parents' age (worse than our grandparents') has produced us, more worthless still, who will soon give rise to a yet more vicious generation.
Horace

GENEROSITY
We'd all like a reputation for generosity and we'd all like to buy it cheap.
Mignon McLaughlin

There is as much greatness of mind in acknowledging a good turn, as in doing it.
Seneca

Generosity gives assistance rather than advice.
Marquis de Vauvenargues

Real generosity is doing something nice for someone who will never find out.
Frank Howard Clark

Generosity is giving more than you can, and pride is taking less than you need.

Kahlil Gibran

GENIUS
Genius does what it must; talent does what it can.

Unknown

Genius is nothing but a greater aptitude for patience.

George-Louis Leclerc de Buffon

Talent is what you possess; genius is what possesses you.

Malcolm Cowley

Sometimes men come by the name of genius in the same way that certain insects come by the name of centipede – not because they have a hundred feet, but because most people can't count above fourteen.

Georg Christoph Lichtenberg

Attention makes the genius. All learning, fancy, science, and skill depend upon it. Newton traced his great discoveries to it. It builds bridges, opens new worlds, heals disease, carries on the business of the world. Without it, taste is useless and the beauties of literature unobserved.

Robert Willmott

There was never a genius without a tincture of madness.

Aristotle

Talent is that which is in a man's power; genius is that in whose power a man is.

James Russell Lowell

Genius ... means little more than the faculty of perceiving in an unhabitual way.

William James

Every family should have at least three children. Then, if one is a genius, the other two can support him.

George Coote

Talent is a very common family trait; genius belongs rather to individuals – just as you find one giant or one dwarf in a family, but rarely a full brood of either. Talent is often to be envied, and genius very commonly to be pitied. It stands twice the chance of the other of dying in a hospital, in jail, in debt, in bad repute. It is a perpetual insult to mediocrity; its every word is a trespass against somebody's vested ideas.

Oliver Wendell Holmes

Genius is the ability to act wisely without precedent – the power to do the right things for the first time.

Elbert Hubbard

I can't tell you if genius is hereditary because heaven has granted me no offspring.

James McNeill Whistler

In every work of genius we recognize our rejected thoughts.

Ralph Waldo Emerson

Genius is one per cent inspiration, ninety-nine per cent perspiration.

Thomas Edison

The principal mark of genius is not perfection but originality, the opening of new frontiers.

Arthur Koestler

When a true genius appears in the world, you may know him by this sign, that the dunces are all in confederacy against him.

Jonathan Swift

Geniuses are the luckiest of mortals because what they must do is the same as what they most wanted to do.

W.H. Auden

Everyone is a genius at least once a year. The real geniuses simply have their bright ideas closer together.

Georg Christoph Lichtenberg

Talent hits a target no one else can hit; genius hits a target no one else can see.

Arthur Schopenhauer

A man of genius makes no mistakes; his errors are volitional and are the portals of discovery.

James Joyce

Doing easily what others find difficult is talent; doing what is impossible for talent is genius.

Henri-Frédéric Amiel

Genius is much greater than knowledge, but it can seldom be a substitute for it.

John Bailey

One good guess doesn't make a man a genius any more than a hole in one makes him a good golfer.

Dr O.A. Battista

With the stones we cast at them, geniuses build new roads for us.

Paul Eldridge

Men of genius do not excel in any profession because they labour in it, but they labour in it because they excel.

William Hazlitt

It's a pity one can't imagine what one can't compare to anything. Genius is an African who dreams up snow.

Vladimir Nabokov

GENTLEMAN

A gentleman takes as much trouble to discover what is right as the lesser men take to discover what will pay.

Confucius

This is the final test of a gentleman: his respect for those who can be of no possible service to him.

William Lyon Phelps

A gentleman is a man who can play the accordion but doesn't.

Unknown

My experience has been that the time to test a true gentleman is to observe him when he is in contact with individuals of a race that is less fortunate than his own.

Booker T. Washington

GENTLENESS

There is nothing stronger in the world than gentleness.

Han Suyin

GETTING THERE
You have to be going to a pretty awful place if getting there is half the fun.

Miss Piggy

GETTING UP
It was such a lovely day I thought it was a pity to get up.

W. Somerset Maugham

GHOSTS
you want to know/whether i believe in ghosts/of course i do not believe in them/if you had known as many of them as i have/you would not believe in them either.

Don Marquis

GIANTS
If I have seen further, it is because I have stood on the shoulders of giants.

Sir Isaac Newton

GIFTS
Rich gifts wax poor when givers prove unkind.

William Shakespeare

Some people have a knack of putting upon you gifts of no real value, to engage you to substantial gratitude. We thank them for nothing.

Charles Lamb

There is no benefit in the gifts of a bad man.

Euripides

When a woman keeps score, no matter how big or small a gift of love is, it scores one point; each gift has equal value … A man, however, thinks he scores one point for one small gift and thirty points for a big gift.

John Gray

Enemies' gifts are no gifts and do no good.

Sophocles

A gift long expected is sold, not given.

Italian proverb

GIRLS
Girls just want to have funds.

Adrienne E. Gusoff

GIVING
Blessed are those who can give without remembering, and take without forgetting.

Elizabeth Bibesco

The manner of giving is worth more than the gift.

Pierre Corneille

It is one of the most beautiful compensations of life that no man can sincerely try to help another without helping himself.

John P. Webster

We like to give but hate to lose.

Eric Hoffer

There is sublime thieving in all giving. Someone gives us all he has and we are his.

Eric Hoffer

... and in the end it was said of him in the balance of life and in the sum of small and all things, he gave more than he took.

William Milton

One can know nothing of giving aught that is worthy to give unless he also knows how to take.

Havelock Ellis

Nothing that I am able to give to you do I find worthy of you, and only in this way do I discover that I am a poor man. And so I give to you the only thing that I possess – myself.

Aeschines

One must be poor to know the luxury of giving.

George Eliot

A hundred times every day I remind myself that my inner and outer life depend on the labours of other men, living and dead, and that I must exert myself in order to give in the same measure as I have received.

Albert Einstein

If you have much, give of your wealth; if you have little, give of your heart.

Arab proverb

The miser and the pig are of no use til death.

François, duc de La Rochefoucauld

The only wealth which you will keep forever is the wealth which you have given away.

Martial

GLORY

Glory is fleeting, but obscurity is forever.

Napoleon Bonaparte

Our greatest glory is not in never failing, but rising every time we fall.

Confucius

Glory seldom comes to those who dream of it, to fewer still who don't.

Anonymous

No more hope, no more glory, not for the nation, not for the world I dare say, no more parades.

Ford Madox Ford

The deed is everything, the glory nothing.

Johann Wolfgang von Goethe

It is a worthier thing to deserve honour than to possess it.

Proverb

Glory is largely a theatrical concept. There is no striving for glory without a vivid awareness of an audience – the knowledge that our mighty deeds will come to the ears of our contemporaries or "of those who are to be."

Eric Hoffer

GLUTTONY

Gluttony is not a secret vice.

Orson Welles

I'm not a glutton, I'm an explorer of food.

Erma Bombeck

Gluttony kills more than the sword.
George Herbert

I think it's important to encourage gluttony in all its formats.
Lydia Lunch

GOALS

People are not lazy. They simply have impotent goals – goals that do not inspire them.
Anthony Robbins

The soul that has no established aim loses itself.
Michel de Montaigne

It is not enough to take steps which may some day lead to a goal; each step must itself be a goal and a step likewise.
Johann Wolfgang von Goethe

No matter how many bad breaks along the way, I must keep my sights on the final goal, to win, win, win.

Billie Jean King

Goals are dreams with deadlines.
Diana Scharf-Hunt

Goals are SMART ... Specific, Measurable, Achievable, Realistic, and Timely.

Anonymous

Setting a goal is not the main thing. It is deciding how you will go about achieving it and staying with that plan.

Tom Landry

A good system shortens the road to the goal.

Orison Swett Marden

Their starting point is different, and their courses are not the same.
Alexis de Tocqueville

It is an age frequented by violence as desperate men seek ill-defined goals.
Speech from the Throne, Canada

If you don't know where you are going, any road will take you there.
Lewis Carroll

Think little goals and expect little achievements. Think big goals and win big success.

Dr David Schwartz

If you aspire to the highest place it is no disgrace to stop at the second, or even the third.

Cicero

Well-being and happiness never appeared to me as an absolute aim. I am even inclined to compare such moral aims to the ambitions of a pig.

Albert Einstein

To live only for some future goal is shallow. It is the sides of the mountain that sustain life, not the top.
Robert Pirsig

GOD

In the nineteenth century the problem was that God is dead; in the twentieth century the problem is that man is dead.

Erich Fromm

God helps those who get up early.
Spanish proverb

God gives the nuts, but He does not crack them.
Proverb

God is on the side not of the heavy battalions, but of the best shots.
Voltaire

God is a comedian playing to an audience too afraid to laugh.
Voltaire

If God did not exist, it would be necessary for us to invent Him.
Voltaire

It isn't just that I don't believe in God and naturally, hope there is no God! I don't want there to be a God; I don't want the universe to be like that.
Thomas Nagel

God heard the embattled nations sing and shout/"Gott strafe England!" and "God save the King!"/ God this God that and God the other thing/"Good God," said God, "I've got my work cut out."
J.C. Squire

God will pardon me. It's his business.
Heinrich Heine

Many people believe that they are attracted by God or nature, when they are only repelled by man.
Dean Inge

You can't imagine the extra work I had when I was a god.
Emperor Hirohito of Japan

If triangles had a God, He'd have three sides.
Yiddish proverb

When I told the people of Northern Ireland that I was an atheist, a woman in the audience stood up and said, "Yes, but is it the God of the Catholics or the God of the Protestants in whom you don't believe?"
Quentin Crisp

If God wanted us to fly, He would have given us tickets.
Mel Brooks

If you talk to God, you are praying; if God talks to you, you have schizophrenia.
Thomas Szasz

The problem is that God gives men a brain and a penis, and only enough blood to run one at a time.
Robin Williams

God is subtle but he is not malicious.
Albert Einstein

God looks at the clean hands, not the full ones.
Publilius Syrus

God is love, but get it in writing.
Gypsy Rose Lee

God is so great that the greatness precludes existence.
Raimundo Panikkar

God hath chosen the foolish things of the world to confound the wise.
I Corinthians 1:27

If God lived on Earth, people would break his windows.
Jewish proverb

People see God every day, they just don't recognize him.
Pearl Bailey

If you want to know what God thinks of money, just look at the people he gave it to.
Dorothy Parker

The world is proof that God is a committee.
Bob Stokes

It is the final proof of God's omnipotence that he need not exist in order to save us.
Peter De Vries

We are no more than God's curiosity about himself.
Thomas Mann

What if God is a woman? Not only am I going to hell, but I'll never know why.
Adam Ferrara

God does not play dice.
Albert Einstein

God is really only another artist. He made the elephant, the giraffe, and cat. He has no real style but keeps trying new ideas.
Pablo Picasso

I think God honours the fact that I want to believe in him, whether I feel sure or not.
Anonymous

An act of God was defined as something which no reasonable man could have expected.
A.P. Herbert

If a clock proves the existence of a clockmaker and the world does not prove the existence of a supreme architect, then I consent to be called a fool.
Voltaire

It is as impossible for man to demonstrate the existence of God as it would be for Sherlock Holmes to demonstrate the existence of Arthur Conan Doyle.
Frederick Buechner

GODS
Ask the gods nothing excessive.
Aeschylus

The gods delight in an odd number.
Pliny the Elder

Our fearsome gods have only changed their names: they now rhyme with "-ism."
Carl Jung

The gods have their own rules.
Ovid

GOING
If you don't know where you're going, you will wind up somewhere else.
Yogi Berra

You got to be careful if you don't know where you're going, because you might not get there.
Yogi Berra

GOLD
All that glisters is not gold.
William Shakespeare

GOLDEN AGE
There are two golden ages: the mythical one in the past and the mythical one in the future. While it is naive to believe in the former, it is now a sign of sophistication to believe in the latter.
Anthony Daniels

GOLDEN RULE
The golden rule is that there are no golden rules.
George Bernard Shaw

GOLF
Man blames fate for other accidents, but feels personally responsible when he makes a hole-in-one.
Bishop Fulton J. Sheen

If you watch a game, it's fun. If you play it, it's recreation. If you work at it, it's golf.
Bob Hope

The least thing upset him on the links. He missed short putts because of the uproar of the butterflies in the adjoining meadows.
P.G. Wodehouse

The main idea in golf as in life, I suppose, is to learn to accept what cannot be altered, and to keep on doing one's own reasoned and resolute best whether the prospect be bleak or rosy.
Bobby Jones

I know I'm getting better at golf because I'm hitting fewer spectators.
Gerald Ford

… unlike marriage, golf is a war from the start.
John Updike

There are three ways of learning golf: by study, which is most wearisome; by imitation, which is the most fallacious; and by experience, which is most bitter.
Robert Browning

You don't hit anything with your backswing. So don't rush it.
Doug Ford

If profanity had any influence on the flight of the ball, the game would be played far better than it is.
Horace G. Hutchinson

The only time my prayers are never answered is on the golf course.
Billy Graham

Golf appeals to the idiot in us and the child. Just how childlike golf players become is proven by their frequent inability to count past five.
John Updike

They say golf is like life, but don't believe them. Golf is more complicated than that.
Gardner Dickinson

Golf is a day spent in a round of strenuous idleness.
William Wordsworth

Eighteen holes of match play will teach you more about your foe than eighteen years of dealing with him across a desk.

Grantland Rice

It is good sportsmanship not to pick up lost golf balls while they are still rolling.

Mark Twain

Golf and sex are the only things you can enjoy without being good at either of them.

Jimmy Demaret

May thy ball lie in green pastures, and not in still waters.

Ben Hogan

Golf is a game invented by the same people who think music comes out of a bagpipe.

Lee Trevino

The difference between golf and government is that in golf you can't improve your lie.

George Deukmejian

Don't play too much golf. Two rounds a day are plenty.

Harry Vardon

I don't say my golf game is bad, but if I grew tomatoes, they'd come up sliced.

Arnold Palmer

If you are going to throw a club, it is important to throw it ahead of you, down the fairway, so you don't have to waste energy going back to pick it up.

Tommy Bolt

If profanity had any influence on the flight of the ball, the game of golf would be played far better than it is.

Horace G. Hutchinson

If you think it's hard to meet new people, try picking up the wrong golf ball.

Jack Lemmon

I'm hitting the woods just great, but having a terrible time getting out of them.

Buddy Hackett

My handicap? Woods and irons.

Chris Codiroli

Golf has probably kept more people sane than psychiatrists have.

Harvey Penick

Give me my golf clubs, fresh air and a beautiful partner, and you can keep my golf clubs and the fresh air.

Jack Benny

It took me seventeen years to get three thousand hits in baseball. I did it in one afternoon on the golf course.

Hank Aaron

The reason the pro tells you to keep your head down is so you can't see him laughing.

Phyllis Diller

GOOD
Have I done the world good, or have I added a menace?

Guglielmo Marconi

It is absurd to divide people into good and bad. People are charming or tedious.

Oscar Wilde

Confidence in the goodness of another is proof of one's goodness.
Michel de Montaigne

If merely "feeling good" could decide, drunkenness would be the supremely valid human experience.
William James

Good is not good where better is expected.

Thomas Fuller, MD

On the whole, human beings want to be good – but not too good and not quite all the time.

George Orwell

The meaning of good and bad, of better and worse, is simply helping or hurting.

Ralph Waldo Emerson

Do good by stealth, and blush to find it fame.

Alexander Pope

It used to be a good hotel, but that proves nothing – I used to be a good boy.

Mark Twain

Every man is guilty of all the good he did not do.

Voltaire

Do you wish people to believe good of you? Don't speak.

Blaise Pascal

To be good is noble, but to teach others how to be good is nobler – and less trouble.

Mark Twain

There is an idea abroad among moral people that they should make their neighbours good. One person I have to make good: myself.

Robert Louis Stevenson

My only policy is to profess evil and do good.

George Bernard Shaw

He who wishes to secure the good of others has already secured his own.

Confucius

Terrible is the temptation to be good.

Bertolt Brecht

The good die young – because they see it's no use living if you've got to be good.

John Barrymore

It is not enough to do good; one must do it in a good way.

Marquis de Condorcet

He who is too busy doing good finds no time to be good.

Rabindranath Tagore

Everyone asks if a man is rich, no one if he is good.

Euripides

When we are happy we are always good, but when we are good we are not always happy.

Oscar Wilde

You can fake being cool, but you can't fake being good.
Chuck Klosterman

It is so much easier to do good than to be good.
B.C. Forbes

It is not enough to do good; one must do it in a good way.
Marquis de Condorcet

GOOD COMPANY

Nine-tenths of the people were created so you would want to be with the other tenth.
Horace Walpole

GOOD DEED

One good deed is better than three days of fasting at a shrine.
Japanese saying

No good deed ever goes unpunished.
Brooks Thomas

Neither fire nor wind, birth nor death can erase our good deeds.
Buddha

How far that little candle throws his beams!/So shines a good deed in a naughty world.
William Shakespeare

Good words make us laugh; good deeds make us silent.
French proverb

GOOD EXAMPLE

Really, if the lower orders don't set us a good example, what on earth is the use of them?
Oscar Wilde

Doing a good turn will not make you dizzy.
Anonymous

Few things are harder to put up with than the annoyance of a good example.
Mark Twain

GOOD FORTUNE

Good or bad fortune usually comes to those who have more of the one than the other.
François, duc de La Rochefoucauld

I make the most of all that comes,/ And the least of all that goes.
Sara Teasdale

It is permitted me to take good fortune where I find it.
Molière

A man is never so on trial as in the moment of excessive good fortune.
Lew Wallace

GOOD IDEAS

The best way to have a good idea is to have lots of ideas.
Linus Pauling

Ours is the only country deliberately founded on a good idea.
John Gunther

GOOD IMPRESSION

You can create a good impression on yourself by being right ... but for creating a good impression on others there is nothing to beat being totally and catastrophically wrong.
Michael Frayn

GOOD INTENTIONS
The road of good intentions is paved with hell.

Spencer Ante

If I knew for a certainty that a man was coming to my house with the conscious design of doing me good, I should run for my life.

Henry David Thoreau

GOOD LIFE
The good life, as I conceive it, is a happy life. I do not mean that if you are good you will be happy – I mean that if you are happy you will be good.

Bertrand Russell

GOOD LISTENER
A good listener is a good talker with a sore throat.

Katharine Whitehorn

GOOD LOOKS
She got her looks from her father. He's a plastic surgeon.

Groucho Marx

GOOD MEN
Good men need no recommendation and bad men it wouldn't help.

Jewish proverb

A good man does good merely by living.

Edward Bulwer-Lytton

GOOD OLD DAYS
In every age, "the good old days" were a myth. No one ever thought they were good at the time. For every age has consisted of crises that seemed intolerable to the people who lived through them.

Brooks Atkinson

GOOD PEOPLE
The good people sleep much better at night than the bad people. Of course, the bad people enjoy the waking hours much more.

Woody Allen

GOOD SOCIETY
Mostly, we are good when it makes sense. A good society is one that makes sense of being good.

Ian McEwan

GOOD TASTE
Good taste is the worst vice ever invented.

Dame Edith Sitwell

It is a common error to think of bad taste as sterile. Rather, it is good taste, and good taste alone, that possesses the power to sterilize and is always the first handicap to any creative functioning. One has only to consider the good taste of the French: It has encouraged them not to do anything.

Salvador Dali

GOOD THOUGHTS
We are all capable of evil thoughts, but only very rarely of evil deeds. We can all do good deeds, but very few can think good thoughts.

Cesare Pavese

GOOD TURN
One good turn gets most of the blanket.

Anonymous

GOODNESS

Goodness makes greatness truly valuable, and greatness makes goodness much more serviceable.
Matthew Henry

Goodness is the only investment that never fails.
Henry David Thoreau

GOSSIP

Who gossips to you will gossip of you.

Turkish proverb

Whoever gossips to you will gossip about you.

Spanish proverb

No one gossips about other people's secret vices.

Bertrand Russell

Wolfgang Pauli, the quantum physics pioneer, once said of a colleague's appallingly off-base theory: "It's not even wrong." That's the time zone we're in here.
Phil Bronstein

What Paul says about Peter tells us more about Paul than about Peter.
Baruch Spinoza

Not all women are guilty of repeating gossip. One of them has to start it.

Ellis C. Galt

Gossip is when you hear something you like about someone you don't.
Earl Wilson

She always tells stories in the present vindictive.

Tom Peace

Gossip needn't be false to be evil – there's a lot of truth that shouldn't be passed around.
Frank A. Clark

Gossip is the opiate of the oppressed.
Erica Jong

GOURMET

A gourmet can tell from the flavour whether a woodcock's leg is the one on which the bird was accustomed to roost.
Lucius Beebe

GOVERN

To govern mankind, one must not overrate them.
Lord Chesterfield

To govern is always to choose among disadvantages.
Charles de Gaulle

Let the people think they govern, and they will be governed.
William Penn

GOVERNMENT

I don't make jokes. I just watch the government and report the facts.
Will Rogers

No man's life, liberty, or property are safe while the legislature is in session.

Mark Twain

It is dangerous to be right when the government is wrong.
Voltaire

In general, the art of government consists in taking as much money as possible from one party of citizens to give to the other.

Voltaire

Government is the great fiction, through which everybody endeavours to live at the expense of everybody else.

Frédéric Bastiat

Passion and prejudice govern the world; only under the name of reason.

John Wesley

It's getting harder and harder to support the government in the manner to which it has become accustomed.

Unknown

Government's view of the economy could be summed up in a few short phrases: If it moves, tax it. If it keeps moving, regulate it. And if it stops moving, subsidize it.

Ronald Reagan

If you want government to intervene domestically, you're a liberal. If you want government to intervene overseas, you're a conservative. If you want government to intervene everywhere, you're a moderate. If you don't want government to intervene anywhere, you're an extremist.

Joseph Sobran

It is every citizen's duty to support his government – but not necessarily in the style to which it has become accustomed.

Canadian Tax Highlights

That government is the strongest in which every man feels himself a part.

Thomas Jefferson

Government by the people is possible, but highly improbable.

J. William Fulbright

Governments last as long as the under-taxed can defend themselves against the over-taxed.

Bernard Berenson

Those that think must govern those that toil.

Oliver Goldsmith

All government – indeed every human benefit and enjoyment, every virtue and every prudent act – is founded on compromise and barter.

Edmund Burke

An event has happened, upon which it is difficult to speak, and impossible to remain silent.

Edmund Burke

Government is a contrivance of human wisdom to provide for human wants. Men have a right that these wants should be provided for by this wisdom.

Edmund Burke

Government must be responsive to the needs and dreams of its people.

Mary Ellen Withrow

Whenever you have an efficient government, you have a dictatorship.

Harry S. Truman

Every country has the government it deserves.

Joseph-Marie Maistre

A government which robs Peter to pay Paul can always depend on the support of Paul.

George Bernard Shaw

Giving money and power to government is like giving whiskey and car keys to teenage boys.

P.J. O'Rourke

The government must be the trustee for the little man, because no one else will be. The powerful can usually help themselves – and frequently do.

Adlai Stevenson

Since the beginning of time, governments have been mainly engaged in kicking people around. The astonishing achievement of modern times in the Western world is that the citizens should do the kicking.

Adlai Stevenson

Government cannot be stronger or more tough-minded than its people. It cannot be more inflexibly committed to the task than they. It cannot be wiser than the people.

Adlai Stevenson

Government is too big and too important to be left to the politicians.

Chester Bowles

Thought control is a copyright of totalitarianism, and we have no claim to it. It is not the function of our government to keep the citizen from falling into error, it is the function of the citizen to keep the government from falling into error.

Robert H. Jackson

A difficulty for every solution.

Herbert Samuel

Momentary loss or even the shock of moral sensibilities is perhaps a passing thing, but the breaking down of the faith of the people in honesty of their government and in the integrity of their institutions, the lowering of respect for the standards of honor which prevail in high places, are crimes for which punishments can never atone.

Herbert Hoover

Government, like dress, is the badge of lost innocence; the palaces of kings are built upon the ruins of the bowers of paradise.

Thomas Paine

A successful administration is one that addresses foreign and domestic issues as problems to be solved, not as political ground to be gained.

William Milton

A popular government without popular information or the means of acquiring it is but a prologue to a farce or a tragedy or perhaps both.

James Madison

Government is not reason; it is not eloquence; it is force! It is a dangerous servant and a terrible master.

George Washington

What the government gives you the government can take away, and once it starts taking away, it can take more than it gave.

Samuel Gompers

If people behaved like governments, you'd call the cops.

Kelvin Throop

A strong government always wars on the superior man. Its regimenting of the inferior goes on, too, but it is harmless; they can't be made worse.

H.L. Mencken

All governments are like wheelbarrows – useful instruments, but they need to be pushed.

Bishop of Sheffield

A community that allows officials to tyrannize over it abdicates its right to live.

Wickham Steed

Though the people support the government the government should not support the people.

Grover Cleveland

Our system of government is like an hourglass; when one side's quite run out, we turn up the other and go on again.

Douglas Jerrold

Liberty and order are the most precious possessions of man, and the essence of the problem of government is reconciliation of the two.

George Sutherland

The government that shakes its fist first and its finger afterwards falls into contempt.

Elihu Root

Government is a trust, and the officers of government are trustees; and both the trust and the trustees are created for the benefit of the people.

Henry Clay

The ship of state is one vessel that seems to move best in a fog.

Unknown

You can fool too many of the people too much of the time.

James Thurber

The Government are carrying an immense weight. Untold treasures are in their hands. They are doing the very best they can. Don't badger them.

Abraham Lincoln

Dear Government … I'm going to have a serious talk with you if I ever find anyone to talk to.

Stieg Larsson

GRAND OLD MAN
A "Grand Old Man." That means on our continent any one with snow-white hair who has kept out of jail til eighty.

Stephen Leacock

GRANDPARENTS
The reason grandparents and grandchildren get along so well is that they have a common enemy.

Sam Levenson

GRATITUDE
Gratitude is the heart's memory.
French proverb

Blessed is he who expects no gratitude, for he will not be disappointed.
W.C. Bennett

Gratitude appears to be a state of mind. It is linked in part to a state of wonder, something that we often associate with childhood. And wonder is about looking beyond what is right in front of us. That's what we do when we teach kids to say "please" and "thank you." We want them to develop a sense of empathy and begin to think, "What was involved in what that person did for me? " or "What will that person actually have to do to carry out what I just asked for? "
Maurice Elias

Gratitude is merely the secret hope of further favours.
François, duc de La Rochefoucauld

Gratitude is something of which none of us can give too much. For on the smiles, the thanks we give, our little gestures of appreciation, our neighbours build up their philosophy of life.
A.J. Cronin

I defended almost 140 people for murder in this country and I think in all of the cases I received just one Christmas card from all of these defendants.
Samuel Leibowitz

Gratitude, like love, is never a dependable international emotion.
Joseph Alsop

GRAVE
The only difference between a rut and a grave is the depth.
Old saying

We each day dig our graves with our teeth.
Samuel Smiles

GREAT
To do great things is difficult, but to command great things is more difficult.
Friedrich Nietzsche

All great deeds and all great thoughts have a ridiculous beginning.
Albert Camus

They're only truly great who are truly good.
George Chapman

The really great person is the person who makes every person feel great.
G.K. Chesterton

GREAT MEN
Few great men could pass Personnel.
Paul Goodman

He only is a great man who can neglect the applause of the multitude and enjoy himself independent of its favour.
Joseph Addison

The defects of great men are the consolation of dunces.

Isaac Disraeli

Great men are not always idiots.

Karen Elizabeth Gordon

GREAT MINDS
Great minds have purposes; little minds have wishes. Little minds are subdued by misfortunes; great minds rise above them.

Washington Irving

GREAT ORGANIZATIONS
It is the willingness of people to give of themselves over and above the demands of the job that distinguishes the great from the merely adequate organization.

Peter Drucker

I have never found that pay and pay alone would either bring together or hold good people. I think it was the game itself.

Harvey C. Firestone

GREATNESS
It is the nature of all greatness not to be exact.

Edmund Burke

We feel that we are greater than we know.

William Wordsworth

Ready to jump through any hoop/ To be the great man of a little group?

Edmond Rostand

Not a day passes over this earth, but men and women of no note do great deeds, speak great words, and suffer noble sorrows.

Charles Reed

In reaffirming the greatness of our nation, we understand that greatness is never a given. It must be earned.

Barack Obama

GREED
We are all born brave, trusting, and greedy, and most of us remain greedy.

Mignon McLaughlin

Like the greedy merchants of bazaars, if we get out of life what we ask for, we are unhappy for not having asked for more.

Paul Eldridge

I am not hungry; but thank goodness, I am greedy.

Punch

The covetous man is ever in want.

Horace

GREEKS
I fear Greeks, even when they bring gifts.

Virgil

GRIEF
All things grow with time, except grief.

Yiddish proverb

Happiness is beneficial for the body, but it is grief that develops the powers of the mind.

Marcel Proust

Memory nourishes the heart, and grief abates.

Marcel Proust

Grief shared is half grief; joy shared is double joy.

Honduran proverb

GROSS NATIONAL PRODUCT
The gross national product does not allow for the health of our children, the quality of their education, or the joy of their play. It does not include the beauty of our poetry or the strength of our marriages, the intelligence of our public debate, or the integrity of our public officials. It measures neither our wit nor our courage, neither our wisdom nor our learning, neither our compassion nor our devotion to our country. It measures everything, in short, except that which makes life worthwhile.

Robert F. Kennedy

GROUNDHOG DAY
This is pitiful. A thousand people freezing their butts off waiting to worship a rat.

Bill Murray

GROW
Why stay we on the earth unless to grow?

Robert Browning

GROWING UP
You grow up the day you have your first laugh – at yourself.

Ethel Barrymore

By the time I'd grown up, I naturally supposed that I'd be grown up.

Eva Babitz

GROWTH
Growth for the sake of growth is the ideology of the cancer cell.

Edward Abbey

GUARDS
But who is to guard the guards themselves?

Juvenal

GUESS
Guess if you can and choose if you dare.

Pierre Corneille

GUIDANCE
Only human beings guide their behaviour by a knowledge of what happened before they were born and a preconception of what may happen after they are dead; thus only humans find their way by a light that illuminates more than the patch of ground they stand on.

Peter and Jean Medawar

Guide us in the right path.

Koran

You gotta have a swine to show you where the truffles are.

Edward Albee

GUILT
In former days, everyone found the assumption of innocence so easy; today we find fatally easy the assumption of guilt.

Amanda Cross

It is only too easy to compel a sensitive human being to feel guilty about anything.

Morton Irving Seiden

It is criminal to steal a purse, daring to steal a fortune, a mark of greatness to steal a crown. The blame diminishes as the guilt increases.

Friedrich von Schiller

It is quite gratifying to feel guilty if you haven't done anything wrong: how noble! Whereas it is rather hard and certainly depressing to admit guilt and to repent.

Hannah Arendt

GUILTY
The guilty think all talk is of themselves.

Geoffrey Chaucer

Every man is guilty of all the good he didn't do.

Voltaire

There may be responsible persons, but there are no guilty ones.

Albert Camus

A guilty conscience needs no accuser.

Proverb

GUNS
You can get much farther with a kind word and a gun than you can with a kind word alone.

Al Capone

Guns don't kill people, people kill people, (and monkeys do too if they have a gun).

Eddie Izzard

If guns don't kill people, but people kill people, why do we give people guns when they go to war? Why not just send the people?

Ozzy Osbourne

There's no evidence that I'm aware of that guns protect liberty.

Alan Dershowitz

GUTS
The guts uphold the heart.

Thomas Fuller, MD

GYM MEMBERSHIP
Business has always been about trust. For this reason, the conduct of business has always needed a mechanism by which to estimate the trustworthiness of a prospective employee, partner or client. ... [Business has achieved it] by enforcing the rules of physical fitness. Gym membership today fills the same role as church membership more than a century ago. It is a testament of character.

Ronald Dworkin

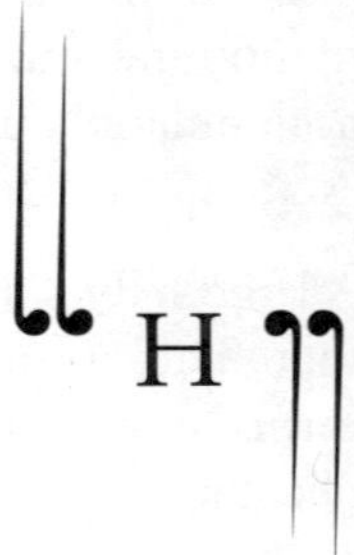

HABIT

A nail is driven out by another nail; habit is overcome by habit.

Erasmus

Habit is stronger than reason.

George Santayana

Infinite toil would not enable you to sweep away a mist; but by ascending a little, you may often overlook it altogether. So it is with our moral improvement; we wrestle fiercely with a vicious habit, which would have no hold on us if we ascended into a higher moral atmosphere.

Sir Arthur Helps

A man's habit clings/And he will wear tomorrow what today he wears.

Edna St Vincent Millay

Nothing so needs reforming as other people's habits.

Mark Twain

Man like every other animal is by nature indolent. If nothing spurs him on, then he will hardly think, and will behave from habit like an automaton.

Albert Einstein

Habit, *n.* A shackle for the free.

Ambrose Bierce

The chains of habit are too weak to be felt until they are too strong to be broken.

Samuel Johnson

To fall into a habit is to begin to cease to be.

Miguel de Unamuno

Habit will reconcile us to everything but change.

Charles Caleb Colton

Unless we extensively program our behaviour, we waste tremendous amounts of information-processing capacity on trivia. Watch a committee break for lunch and then return to the same room: almost invariably its members seek out the same seats they occupied earlier. ... Choosing the same seat spares us the need to survey and evaluate other possibilities.

Alvin Toffler

It seems, in fact, as though the second half of a man's life is made up of nothing but the habits he has accumulated during the first half.

Fyodor Dostoyevsky

All the habits and rules of his life that had seemed so firm, had turned out suddenly false and inapplicable.

Leo Tolstoy

We love our habits more than our income, often more than our life.

Bertrand Russell

HAIRCUTS
Some of the worst mistakes of my life have been haircuts.

Jim Morrison

HALLOWE'EN
[Hallowe'en] is a fine American tradition of teaching our children to beg door-to-door dressed as mass murderers and co-dependent women. The planning takes weeks, but it's worth it just to see how lively a four-year-old can get after mainstreaming Milk Duds for three hours.

Cathy Crimmons

HALLUCINATIONS
We live amid hallucinations; and this especial trap is laid to trip our feet with, and all are tripped up first and last.

Ralph Waldo Emerson

HANG
Gentlemen, we must all hang together, or we shall most assuredly all hang separately.

Benjamin Franklin, at the signing of the Declaration of Independence

Never saw off the branch you are on, unless you are being hanged from it.

Stanisław J. Lec

It is the loose ends with which men hang themselves.

Zelda Fitzgerald

HANGOVER
You pay for the liquor, the hangover is free.

Graffito

A hangover is the wrath of grapes.

Anonymous

A real hangover is nothing to try out family remedies on. The only cure for a real hangover is death.

Robert Benchley

He resolved, having done it once, never to move his eyeballs again ... His mouth had been used as a latrine by some small creature of the night, and then as its mausoleum.

Kingsley Amis

HAPPEN
Nothing, like something, happens anywhere.

Philip Larkin

Things do not happen. They are made to happen.

John F. Kennedy

HAPPINESS
All happiness depends on a leisurely breakfast.

John Gunther

We act as though comfort and luxury were the chief requirements of life, when all that we need to make us really happy is something to be enthusiastic about.

Charles Kingsley

When I was young, I used to think that wealth and power would bring me happiness. I was right.

Gahan Wilson

There is only one way to achieve happiness on this terrestrial ball/ And that is either to have a clear conscience or none at all.

Ogden Nash

Happy is the man to whom God gives with sparing hand what is sufficient for his needs.

Horace

Before we set our hearts too much upon anything, let us examine how happy they are, who already possess it.

François, duc de La Rochefoucauld

If we only wanted to be happy, it would be easy; but we want to be happier than other people, and that is always difficult, since we think them happier than they are.

Montesquieu

Knowledge of what is possible is the beginning of happiness.

George Santayana

One is never either as happy or as unhappy as one imagines.

François, duc de La Rochefoucauld

In vain do they talk of happiness who never subdued an impulse in obedience to a principle. ... He who never sacrificed a present to a future good, or a personal to a general one, can speak of happiness only as the blind speak of colour.

Horace Mann

If happiness in self-content is placed. The wise are wretched, and fools only blessed.

William Congreve

Happiness is composed of misfortunes avoided.

Alphonse Karr

The really happy person is one who can enjoy the scenery when on a detour.

Unknown

Happiness is not a station you arrive at, but a manner of travelling.

Margaret Lee Runbeck

There is only one way to happiness and that is to cease worrying about things which are beyond the power of our will.

Epictetus

This planet has – or rather had – a problem, which was this: most of the people living on it were unhappy for pretty much of the time. Many solutions were suggested for this problem, but most of these were largely concerned with the movement of small green pieces of paper, which is odd because on the whole it wasn't the small green pieces of paper that were unhappy.

Douglas Adams

Philosophical happiness is to want little; civil or vulgar happiness is to want much and enjoy much.

Edmund Burke

To marvel at nothing is just about the one and only thing, Numicius, that can make a man happy and keep him that way.

Horace

There is in all of us an impediment to perfect happiness, namely, weariness of what we possess and a desire for what we have not.

Madame de Rieux

Every time I talk to a savant I feel quite sure that happiness is no longer a possibility. Yet when I talk with my gardener, I'm convinced of the opposite.

Bertrand Russell

One of the keys to happiness is a bad memory.

Rita Mae Brown

Happiness does not reside in strength or money; it lies in rightness and many-sidedness.

Democritus

Happiness is a wine of rarest vintage, and seems insipid to a vulgar taste.

Logan Pearsall Smith

Happiness, *n.* An agreeable sensation arising from contemplating the misery of another.

Ambrose Bierce

Pleasure comes with the fulfillment of desire – getting what you want and wanting what you get. Happiness comes with the fulfillment of the person. And much of our moral confusion comes from the fact that we no longer know what happiness is, nor how to obtain it.

Roger Scruton

Happiness is no laughing matter.

Richard Whately

Ask yourself whether you are happy, and you will cease to be so.

John Stuart Mill

Happiness is not good for work.

Charles Darwin

Success is getting what you want, and happiness is wanting what you get.

Dave Gardner

Success is getting what you want. Happiness is wanting what you get.

Dale Carnegie

Shall I give you my recipe for happiness? I find everything useful and nothing indispensable. I find everything wonderful and nothing miraculous. I reverence the body. I avoid first causes like the plague.

Norman Douglas

I don't need my happiness, my well-being, to be based on winning and losing.

Chris Evert

Happiness makes up in height for what it lacks in length.

Robert Frost

Three grand essentials to happiness in this life are something to do, something to love, and something to hope for.

Joseph Addison

People do belong to each other, because that's the only chance anybody's got for real happiness.

George Axelrod

There can be no happiness if the things we believe are different from the things we do.

Freya Stark

The pursuit of happiness is a most ridiculous phrase: if you pursue happiness you'll never find it.

C.P. Snow

Happiness isn't something you experience; it's something you remember.

Oscar Levant

If I could drop dead right now, I'd be the happiest man alive.

Samuel Goldwyn

I believe four ingredients are necessary for happiness: health, warm personal relationships, sufficient means to keep you from want, and successful work.

Bertrand Russell

Happiness is a way station between too little and too much.

Channing Pollock

Give a man health and a course to steer, and he'll never stop to trouble about whether he's happy or not.

George Bernard Shaw

If what Proust says is true, that happiness is the absence of fever, then I will never know happiness. For I am possessed by a fever for knowledge, experience, and creation.

Anaïs Nin

Some cause happiness wherever they go; others whenever they go.

Oscar Wilde

Most of us believe in trying to make other people happy only if they can be happy in ways which we approve.

Robert S. Lynd

The supreme happiness of life is the conviction that we are loved; loved for ourselves – say rather, loved in spite of ourselves.

Victor Hugo

Happiness is nothing more than good health and a bad memory.

Albert Schweitzer

The happiest is the person who suffers the least pain; the most miserable who enjoys the least pleasure.

Jean-Jacques Rousseau

A great obstacle to happiness is the expectation of too great a happiness.

Bernard de Fontenelle

Nobody really cares if you're miserable so you might as well be happy.

Cynthia Helms

True happiness, we are told, consists in getting out of one's self. But the point is not only to get out — you must stay out. And to stay out, you must have some absorbing errand.

Henry James

Happiness is having a large, loving, caring, close-knit family in another city.

George Burns

The object of living is work, experience, happiness. There is joy in work. All that money can do is buy someone else's work in exchange for our own. There is no happiness except in the realization that we have accomplished something.

Henry Ford

True happiness consists in making happy.

Kiraturjunija of Bharavi

It is not easy to find happiness in ourselves, and it is not possible to find it elsewhere.

Agnes Repplier

I have learned to seek my happiness by limiting my desires, rather than in attempting to satisfy them.

John Stuart Mill

The man who would be truly happy should not study to enlarge his estate, but to contract his desires.

Plato

The secret of happiness is curiosity.

Norman Douglas

Do not envy the appearance of happiness in any man, for you do not know his secret griefs.

Dandemis

Happiness is a butterfly which, when pursued, is always beyond our grasp, but which, if you will sit down quietly, may alight upon you.

Nathaniel Hawthorne

HARD-HEARTED
What makes people hard-hearted is this, that each man has, or fancies he has, as much as he can bear in his own troubles.

Arthur Schopenhauer

HARD WORK
When a man tells you he got rich through hard work, ask him, "Whose?"

Don Marquis

HARDSHIP
Maybe one day we will be glad to remember even these hardships.

Virgil

HARES
In real life, of course, it is the hare who wins. Every time. Look around you. And in any case it is my contention that Aesop was writing for

the tortoise market. ... Hares have no time to read. They are too busy winning the game.

Anita Brookner

HARM

No people do such harm as those who go about doing good.

Bishop Mandell Creighton

It is often better to have a great deal of harm happen to one than a little. A great deal may rouse you to remove what a little will only accustom you to endure.

Fulke Greville

No one can harm the man who does himself no wrong.

Saint John Chrysostom

HARMLESSNESS

Let harmlessness be the keynote of your life.

Alice Bailey

HARMONY

The hidden harmony is better than the obvious one.

Heraclitus

HARVARD

I would rather be governed by the first three hundred names in the Boston telephone book than by the Faculty of Harvard University.

William F. Buckley, Jr

HASTE

One of the most pernicious effects of haste is obscurity.

Samuel Johnson

One of the great disadvantages of hurry is that it takes such a long time.

G.K. Chesterton

Too swift arrives as tardy as too slow.

William Shakespeare

Whatever is produced in haste goes hastily to waste.

Sa'di

Haste in every business brings failures.

Herodotus

What is done hastily cannot be done prudently.

Publilius Syrus

Whoever is in a hurry, shows that the thing he is about to do is too big for him.

Lord Chesterfield

Do not be hasty to praise or blame; speak always as though you were giving testimony before the judgment seat of the gods.

Seneca

HAT

(when asked by a scoffer) Do you call that thing on your head a hat? the reply was, Do you call that thing under your hat a head?

Baron Ludwig Holberg

He can't think without his hat.

Samuel Beckett

HATE

Hate is not the opposite of love, apathy is.

Rollo May

Take care that no one hates you justly.

Publilius Syrus

The love of wicked men converts to fear,/That fear to hate, and hate turns one or both/To worthy danger and deserved death.

William Shakespeare

If you hate a person, you hate something in him that is part of yourself. What isn't part of ourselves doesn't disturb us.

Hermann Hesse

Hating people is like burning down your own house to get rid of a rat.

Harry Emerson Fosdick

HATRED

Hatred, which could destroy so much, never failed to destroy the man who hated, and this was an immutable law.

James Baldwin

Now hatred is by far the longest pleasure;/Men love in haste, but they detest at leisure.

Lord Byron

HEADLINES

Some people make headlines while others make history.

Philip Elmer-DeWitt

HEALING

Healing is a matter of time, but it is sometimes also a matter of opportunity.

Hippocrates

HEALTH

Only do always in health what you have often promised to do when you are sick.

Sigismund, Holy Roman Emperor

A cloudy day or a little sunshine have as great an influence on many constitutions as the most real blessings or misfortunes.

Joseph Addison

Quit worrying about your health. It will go away.

Robert Orben

Preserving health by too severe a rule is a worrisome malady.

François, duc de La Rochefoucauld

What use is a good head if the legs won't carry it?

Yiddish proverb

Health consists of having the same diseases as one's neighbours.

Quentin Crisp

Having good health is very different from only being not sick.

Pliny the Younger

Good health and good sense are two of life's greatest blessings.

Publilius Syrus

Restore a man to his health, his purse lies open to thee.

Robert Burton

HEALTH CARE

If you think health care is expensive now, wait until you see what it costs when it's free.

P.J. O'Rourke

HEALTH NUTS

Health nuts are going to feel stupid some day, lying in hospitals dying of nothing.

Redd Foxx

HEAR

People don't hear what you say, but interpret what you say.

Graham McNally

HEART

Measure men around the heart.

English proverb

The thing that eats the heart is mostly heart.

Stanley Kunitz

Don't worry about your heart, it will last you all of your life.

Dr Albert Bach

There are places in the heart that do not yet exist; suffering has to enter in for them to come to be.

Leon Bloy

It is not flesh and blood but the heart which makes us fathers and sons.

Friedrich von Schiller

Some people wear their heart upon their sleeve. I wear mine underneath my right pant leg, strapped to my boot.

Ani DiFranco

My heart is a lonely hunter that hunts on a lonely hill.

Fiona McLeod

The head never rules the heart, but just becomes its partner in crime.

Mignon McLaughlin

HEARTTHROBS

Heartthrobs are a dime a dozen.

Brad Pitt

HEAT WAVE

If you saw a heat wave, would you wave back?

Steven Wright

HEAVEN / HELL

I don't like to commit myself about heaven and hell – you see, I have friends in both places.

Mark Twain

Heaven is the place the donkey at last catches up with the carrot.

Anonymous

Maybe this world is another planet's Hell.

Aldous Huxley

Hell has three gates: lust, anger, and greed.

Bhagavad Gita

Where am I going and why am I in this handbasket?

Bumper Sticker

To different minds, the same world is a hell, and a heaven.

Ralph Waldo Emerson

In heaven, all the interesting people are missing.

Friedrich Nietzsche

Hell is full of musical amateurs

George Bernard Shaw

Heaven never seals off all exits.

Chinese proverb

The safest road to Hell is the gradual one – the gentle slope, soft

underfoot, without sudden turnings, without milestones, without signposts.
C.S. Lewis

If there is, in fact, a Heaven and a Hell, all we know for sure is that Hell will be a viciously overcrowded version of Phoenix.
Hunter S. Thompson

The wind of heaven is that which blows between a horse's ears.
Arabian proverb

Death and love are the two wings that bear the good man to heaven.
Michelangelo

Bricks and mortar won't make a staircase to heaven.
Arthur Conan Doyle

There is not a fiercer hell than the failure in a great object.
John Keats

I'm not concerned about all hell breaking loose, but that a part of hell will break loose … it'll be much harder to detect.
George Carlin

It's true Heaven forbids some pleasures, but a compromise can usually be found.
Molière

HELP
You may help a lame dog over a stile, but he is still a lame dog on the other side.
Ernest Newman

On reflecting that he had done nothing to help anybody all day, Emperor Titus uttered these memorable and praiseworthy words: "Friends, I have lost a day."
Gaius Suetonius

HELPFULNESS
It was as helpful as throwing a drowning man both ends of the rope.
Arthur (Bugs) Baer

It is hideous and coarse to assume that we can do something for others – and it is vile not to endeavour to do it.
Edward Dahlberg

It is one of the beautiful compensations of this life that no one can sincerely try to help another without helping himself.
Charles Dudley Warner

HELPING HAND
We are here on Earth to do good to others. What the others are here for, I don't know.
W.H. Auden

See me safe up, and for my coming down, let me shift for myself.
Thomas More, on ascending the scaffold

HERD
One is born into a herd of buffaloes and must be glad if one is not trampled underfoot before one's time.
Albert Einstein

HERETIC

A heretic ... is a fellow who disagrees with you regarding something neither of you knows anything about.

William Cowper Brann

HERO

To become a hero, one must give an order to oneself.

Simone Weil

Heroes are very human, most of them; very easily touched by praise.

Max Beerbohm

A hero is a man who does what he can.

Romain Rolland

The greatest obstacle to being heroic is the doubt whether one may not be going to prove one's self a fool. The truest heroism is to resist the doubt.

Nathaniel Hawthorne

Everyone is necessarily the hero of his own life story.

John Barth

Every hero becomes a bore at last.

Ralph Waldo Emerson

Being a hero is about the shortest-lived profession on earth.

Will Rogers

Everybody has a need for heroes, I think, to mold themselves after, people they want to be like. You have to be able to dream, but those dreams should be about real people who have actually done things.

David Thomas

We can't all be heroes because somebody has to sit on the curb and clap as they go by.

Will Rogers

How important it is for us to recognize and celebrate our heroes and she-roes.

Maya Angelou

The real hero is always a hero by mistake; he dreams of being an honest coward like everybody else.

Umberto Eco

Part of the magic of heroes and heroines has always been their ability to embody a vision of life that at the moment is not yet developed enough. ... Heroes are not always just reflections of what has already happened but are also harbingers of what is to come.

Todd Brennan

The legacy of heroes is the memory of a great name and the inheritance of a great example.

Benjamin Disraeli

A hero is someone we can admire without apology.

Kitty Kelley

There are heroes in evil as well as in good.

François, duc de La Rochefoucauld

The crowd worships its heroes fanatically while they are in fashion, but it likes to turn about and roll them in the mud of satire in order to teach them who made them and how easily it can unmake them.

William Graham Sumner

HESITATION
He who hesitates is sometimes saved.

James Thurber

He who hesitates is probably right.
Graffito

We often wait too long to do what must be done today, in a world that gives us only one day at a time, without any assurance of tomorrow.

Mahzor

It's all right to hesitate if you then go ahead.

Bertolt Brecht

He who hesitates is a damn fool.
Mae West

Never put off doing something useful for fear of evil that may never arrive.

James Watson

Hesitation increases in relation to risk in equal portion to age.
Ernest Hemingway

HIDDEN
There it was, hidden in alphabetical order.

Rita Holt

HIERARCHY
The probability of, and resulting cost of, incompetence increases in direct proportion to the size of the hierarchy.

Chris Gundlach

The inevitable result of improved and enlarged communication between different levels in a hierarchy is a vastly increased area of misunderstanding.

Thomas L. Martin, Jr

HIGHWAY
Thanks to the Interstate Highway System, it is now possible to travel from coast to coast without seeing anything.

Charles Kuralt

HINDSIGHT
After the ship has sunk everyone knows how she might have been saved.

Italian proverb

Hindsight is an exact science.
Anonymous

HISTORIANS
Historians have been drug dealers to the addicts of national self-affirmation.

E.J. Hobsbawm

Historians may lie but history cannot.

George Saintsbury

A historian is a prophet in reverse.
Friedrich von Schlegel

It has been said that though God cannot alter the past, historians can; it is perhaps because they can be useful to Him in this respect that He tolerates their existence.

Samuel Butler

History repeats itself. Historians repeat each other.

Philip Guedalla

HISTORY

If history repeats itself, and the unexpected always happens, how incapable must Man be of learning from experience!

George Bernard Shaw

History would be an excellent thing if only it were true.

Leo Tolstoy

History is a collection of agreed upon lies.

Voltaire

Human blunders usually do more to shape human history than human wickedness.

A.J.P. Taylor

It is not history that makes judgments, but judgments that make history.

Gaëtan Picon

Our ignorance of history makes us libel our own times. People have always been like this.

Gustave Flaubert

There is properly no history, only biography.

Ralph Waldo Emerson

All history is the record of man's signal failure to thwart his destiny …

Henry Miller

Universal history is the history of a few metaphors.

Jorge Luis Borges

History says, if it pleases, Excuse me, I beg your pardon, it will never happen again if I can help it.

Carl Sandburg

The only lesson history has taught us is that man has not yet learned anything from history.

Unknown

Like most of those who study history, [Napoleon III] learned from the mistakes of the past how to make new ones.

A.J.P. Taylor

A generation which ignores history has no past and no future.

Robert Heinlein

History is indeed little more than the register of the crimes, follies, and misfortunes of mankind.

Edward Gibbon

News is the first rough draft of history

Benjamin Bradlee

History will be kind to me for I intend to write it.

Winston Churchill

One of the lessons of history is that nothing is often a good thing to do and always a clever thing to say.

Will Durant

We learn from history that we do not learn from history.

G.W.F. Hegel

History is a vast early warning system.

Norman Cousins

History is more or less bunk.

Henry Ford

History is the essence of innumerable biographies.

Thomas Carlyle

Anybody can make history. Only a great man can write it.

Oscar Wilde

A wise man does not try to hurry history.

Adlai Stevenson

The world's history is the world's judgment.

Friedrich von Schiller

History gets thicker as it approaches recent times.

A.J.P. Taylor

Happy the people whose annals are blank in history books.

Montesquieu

The history of every country begins in the heart of a man or a woman.

Willa Cather

The unhistorical are usually, without knowing it, enslaved to a fairly recent past.

C.S. Lewis

History is the short trudge from Adam to atom.

Leonard Louis Levinson

History not used is nothing, for an intellectual life is action, like practical life, and if you don't use the stuff – well, it might as well be dead.

Arnold Toynbee

The farther back you can look, the farther forward you are likely to see.

Winston Churchill

There are only two great currents in the history of mankind: the baseness which makes conservatives and the envy which makes revolutionaries.

Jules de Goncourt

History is past politics, and politics is present history.

E.A. Freeman

Sure, history will judge him right, but you know what a crock history is!

Mal Hancock

History teaches us the mistakes we are going to make.

Laurence J. Peter

In history as in human life, regret does not bring back a lost moment and a thousand years will not recover something lost in a single hour.

Stefan Zweig

More history is made by secret handshakes than by battles, bills, and proclamations.

John Barth

History balances the frustration of "how far we have to go" with the satisfaction of "how far we have come." It teaches us tolerance for the human shortcomings and imperfections which are not uniquely of our generation, but of all time.

Lewis F. Powell, Jr.

Hegel says that all great events and personalities in world history reappear in one fashion or another. He forgot to add: the first time as tragedy, the second as farce.

Karl Marx

Most history is guessing, and the rest is prejudice.

Will and Ariel Durant

The very ink with which all history is written is merely fluid prejudice.

Mark Twain

In history an additional result is commonly produced by human actions beyond that which they aim at and obtain – that which they immediately recognize and desire.

G.W.F. Hegel

History is the sum total of the things that could have been avoided.

Konrad Adenauer

Men make history and not the other way 'round. In periods where there is no leadership, society stands still. Progress occurs when courageous, skillful leaders seize the opportunity to change things for the better.

Harry S. Truman

History never looks like history when you are living through it.

John W. Gardner

A people without the knowledge of their past history, origin, and culture is like a tree without roots.

Marcus Garvey

HOCKEY

How would you like a job where every time you make a mistake, a big red light goes on and 18,000 people boo?

Jacques Plante

They always try to play with our minds. But that won't work with our club. We've got twenty guys without brains.

Bobby Clarke

They are just grown-up kids who have learned on the frozen creek or flooded corner lot that hockey is the greatest thrill of all.

Lester Patrick

When hell freezes over, I'll play hockey there, too.

Unknown

You miss 100 per cent of the shots you never take.

Wayne Gretzky

Hockey players wear numbers because you can't always identify the body with dental records.

Unknown

The three important elements of hockey are: forecheck, backcheck, and pay cheque.

Gilbert Perreault

Play every game as if it is your last one.

Guy Lafleur

We take the shortest route to the puck and arrive in ill humour.
Bobby Clarke

HOG

One disadvantage of being a hog is that at any moment some blundering fool may try to make a silk purse out of your wife's ear.
J.B. Morton

HOLIDAY

A perpetual holiday is a good working definition of hell.
George Bernard Shaw

Holidays are an expensive trial of strength. The only satisfaction comes from survival.
Jonathan Miller

HOLLYWOOD

You can take all the sincerity in Hollywood, place it in the navel of a fruit fly and have room left over for three caraway seeds and a producer's heart.

Fred Allen

However flawed and occasionally inaccurate Hollywood's history of the world may have been, there is this to be said for it, that it was certainly better fun than the real thing.
George MacDonald Fraser

Hollywood is a great place if you're an orange.

Fred Allen

Strip away the phony tinsel of Hollywood and you find the real tinsel underneath.
Oscar Levant

What I like about Hollywood is that one can get along by knowing two words of English – swell and lousy.

Vicki Baum

Hollywood's like Egypt, full of crumbled pyramids. It'll never come back. It'll just keep on crumbling until finally the wind blows the last studio prop across the sands.

David O. Selznick

Half the people in Hollywood are dying to be discovered and the other half are afraid they will be.
Lionel Barrymore

HOME

A house is a home when it shelters the body and comforts the soul.
Phillip Moffitt

Home is not where you live but where they understand you.
Christian Morgenstern

It is the personality of the mistress that the home expresses. Men are forever guests in our homes, no matter how much happiness they may find there.
Elsie de Wolfe, Lady Mendl

To be happy at home is the ultimate aim of all ambition; the end to which every enterprise and labour tends, and of which every desire prompts the prosecution.
Samuel Johnson

It is a most miserable thing to feel ashamed of home.

Charles Dickens

A man's home may seem to be his castle on the outside; inside, it is more often his nursery.

Clare Boothe Luce

HONESTY
Honesty is something you can't wear out.

Waylon Jennings

There's one way to find out if a man is honest – ask him. If he says, "Yes," you know he is a crook.

Groucho Marx

Honesty is the best image.

Tom Wilson

Honesty is the best policy; but he who is governed by that maxim is not an honest man.

Richard Whately

Solitaire is the only thing in life that demands absolute honesty.

Hugh Wheeler

No legacy is so rich as honesty.

William Shakespeare

Everybody's honest in one way or another. The trouble is, there's only one official way.

Jean Anouilh

Take note, take note, O world!/To be direct and honest is not safe.

William Shakespeare

Honesty may be the best policy, but it's important to remember that apparently, by elimination, dishonesty is the second-best policy.

George Carlin

People who are brutally honest get more satisfaction out of the brutality than out of the honesty.

Richard J. Needham

Honesty is a good thing but it is not profitable to its possessor unless it is kept under control.

Don Marquis

Honesty is like an icicle; if once it melts, that is the end.

American proverb

If honesty did not exist, we ought to invent it as the best means of getting rich.

Comte de Mirabeau

He that loseth his honesty hath nothing else to lose.

John Lyly

Honesty is the first chapter in the book of wisdom.

Thomas Jefferson

HONEYMOON
People take shorter honeymoons nowadays, but they take them more often.

Sally Poplin

Centuries ago it was the custom for newlyweds to serve honey to all guests in their home for a month after marriage and from that custom we get the term honeymoon.

Edward L. Friedman

HONOUR
Show me the man you honour and I will know what kind of man you are, for it shows me what your

ideal of manhood is, and what kind of man you long to be.
Thomas Carlyle

What is honored in a country will prosper there.
Plato

Many shall be restored that are now fallen and many

Shall fall that now are in honour.
Horace

But if it be a sin to covet honour,/ I am the most offending soul alive.
William Shakespeare

There could be no honour in a sure success, but much might be wrested from a sure defeat.
T.E. Lawrence

The louder he talked of his honour, the faster we counted our spoons.
Ralph Waldo Emerson

Honour is something we don't think about much anymore; and this neglect explains the otherwise baffling fact that so many of us are quick to blame traditional institutions nowadays, and to insist that our own failings should really be attributed to the failings of whatever institution we have fallen out of the habit of honouring.
Lee Harris

Honour isn't about making the right choices. It's about dealing with the consequences.
Midori Koto

HOPE

Not to hope for things to last forever, is what the year teaches and even the hour which snatches a nice day away.
Horace

Hope is a good breakfast, but it is a bad supper.
Francis Bacon

It's good to hope; it's the waiting that spoils it.
Yiddish proverb

Hope deceives more men than cunning.
Marquis de Vauvenargues

Never give out while there is hope; but hope not beyond reason, for that shows more desire than judgment.
William Penn

If you do not hope, you will not find what is beyond your hopes.
St Clement of Alexandria

He that lives in hope danceth without music.
George Herbert

Hope is the feeling you have that the feeling you have isn't permanent.
Jean Kerr

We must rediscover the distinction between hope and expectation.
Ivan Illich

Hope is definitely not the same as optimism. It is not the conviction that something will turn out well, but the certainty that something makes sense, regardless of how it turns out.

Vaclav Havel

For hope is but the dream of those that wake.

Matthew Prior

Hope is the thing with feathers that perches in the soul – and sings the tunes without the words – and never stops at all.

Emily Dickinson

Even in a time of elephantine vanity and greed, one never has to look far to see the campfires of gentle people.

Garrison Keillor

It is the around-the-corner brand of hope that prompts people into action, while the distant hope acts as an opiate.

Eric Hoffer

I strongly wish for what I faintly hope.

John Dryden

HOPELESS
There are no hopeless situations – only people who are hopeless about them.

Dinah Shore

HORSE SENSE
Horse sense is the thing a horse has which keeps it from betting on people.

W.C. Fields

HOSPITAL
A hospital bed is a parked taxi with the meter running.

Groucho Marx

HOSPITALITY
Never mistake endurance for hospitality.

Anonymous

HOTEL
This is an elegant hotel! Room service has an unlisted number.

Henny Youngman

HOUSE
A house is a machine for loving in.

Craig McGregor

The ornament of a house is the friends who frequent it.

Ralph Waldo Emerson

HOUSEKEEPING
Keeping house is as unpleasant and filthy as coal mining, and the pay's a lot worse.

P.J. O'Rourke

Housework can't kill you, but why take a chance?

Phyllis Diller

I personally am inclined to approach [housework] the way governments treat dissent: ignore it until it revolts.

Barbara Kingsolver

HUMAN
The human race has improved everything except the human race.

Adlai Stevenson

The essence of being human is that one does not seek perfection.

George Orwell

We are human because, at a very early stage in the history of the species, our ancestors discovered a way of preserving and disseminating the results of experience.

Aldous Huxley

Human beings were invented by water as a device for transporting itself from one place to another.

Tom Robbins

The human condition is such that pain and effort are not just symptoms which can be removed without changing life itself; they are the modes in which life itself, together with the necessity to which it is bound, makes itself felt. For mortals, the "easy life of the gods" would be a useless life.

Hannah Arendt

. HUMAN NATURE .

Human nature is not of itself vicious.

Thomas Paine

Most human beings have an almost infinite capacity for taking things for granted.

Aldous Huxley

The human race, to which so many of my readers belong, has been playing at children's games from the beginning, and will probably do it until the end, which is a nuisance for the few people who grow up.

G.K. Chesterton

It is part of human nature to hate the man you have hurt.

Tacitus

Civilized ages inherit the human nature which was victorious in barbarous ages, and that nature is, in many respects, not at all suited to civilized circumstances.

Walter Bagehot

The sun, the moon, and the stars would have disappeared long ago had they happened to be within the reach of predatory human hands.

Havelock Ellis

Human action can be modified to some extent, but human nature cannot be changed.

Abraham Lincoln

Whoever sets himself to base his political thinking on a re-examination of the working of human nature, must begin by trying to overcome his own tendency to exaggerate the intellectuality of mankind.

Graham Wallas

HUMAN RIGHTS

There is only one basic human right, the right to do as you damn well please. And with it comes the only basic human duty, the duty to take the consequences.

P.J. O'Rourke

America did not invent human rights. In a very real sense, it is the other way around. Human rights invented America.

Jimmy Carter

HUMANITY

Humanity is just a work in progress.

Tennessee Williams

We must all learn to be guests of each other.

George Steiner

Humanity only begins for man with self-surrender.

Henri-Frédéric Amiel

You must not lose faith in humanity. Humanity is an ocean; if a few drops of the ocean are dirty, the ocean does not become dirty.

Mohandas Gandhi

We are each of us angels with only one wing; and we can fly only by embracing one another.

Luciano de Crescenzo

So long as we live among men, let us cherish humanity.

André Gide

This manifold restless motion [of humanity] is produced and kept up by the agency of two simple impulses – hunger and the sexual instinct; aided a little, perhaps, by the influence of boredom, but by nothing else.

Arthur Schopenhauer

HUMILIATION

We all have these places where shy humiliations gambol on sunny afternoons.

W.H. Auden

It has always been a mystery to me how men can feel themselves honored by the humiliation of their fellow beings.

Mohandas Gandhi

HUMILITY

Become humble as the market goes your way.

Bernard Baruch

It ain't the heat; it's the humility.

Yogi Berra

The best way to be right or wrong is humbly.

Dr O.A. Battista

The higher we are placed, the more humbly should we walk.

Cicero

It isn't well to have too much humility. The man who gets into the habit of refusing to take credit for good work he does is quite apt to be surprised when he discovers that people accept his denials as the truth.

B.C. Forbes

What the world needs is more geniuses with humility. There are so few of us left.

Oscar Levant

Humility is the mother of giants. One sees great things from the valley; only small things from the peak.

G.K. Chesterton

HUMOUR

Nothing in man is more serious than his sense of humour; it is the sign that he wants all the truth.

Mark Van Doren

All my humour is based upon destruction and despair. If the whole world were tranquil, without disease and violence, I'd be standing in the breadline right in back of J. Edgar Hoover.

Lenny Bruce

The wit makes fun of other persons; the satirist makes fun of the world; the humorist makes fun of himself, but in so doing, he identifies himself with people.

James Thurber

I'm learning the difference between humour and comedy, between the laugh that lasts and the one that evaporates as soon as it hits air. Humour is giving, and comedy is taking away. Humour is companionable, comedy cold. Humour is character, comedy personality.

Roger Rosenblatt

Nowadays if you're funny at anyone's expense they run to the UN and say, "I must have an ombudsman to protect me."

Robertson Davies

Every survival kit should include a sense of humour.

Frank Baer

Humour is the best way of dealing with complete and utter nonsense ... Because we are mad, we are prone to making absurd conclusions regardless of the evidence. The only true wisdom in life is [coping with] complete and utter confusion.

John Lydon (Johnny Rotten)

One doesn't have a sense of humour. It has you.

Larry Gelbart

A good half of the humour of the late Mark Twain consisted of admitting frankly the possession of vices and weaknesses that all of us have and few of us care to acknowledge. Practically all the sagacity of George Bernard Shaw consists of bellowing vociferously what everyone knows.

H.L. Mencken

When humor goes, there goes civilization.

Erma Bombeck

Humour is always based on a modicum of truth. Have you ever heard a joke about a father-in-law?

Dick Clark

HUMOUR BOOKS

Relax: You May Have Only a Few Minutes Left, by Loretta LaRoche
Stressed is Desserts Spelled Backwards, by Brian Seaward
I'm Alive and the Doctor's Dead, by Sue Buchanan
301 Ways to Have Fun at Work, by Dave Hemsath and Leslie Yerkes

Fun? But We're Married, by Lois and Joel Davitz

HUNCH
A hunch is creativity trying to tell you something.
Frank Capra

HUNGER
The belly overreaches the head.
French proverb

Hunger is the best sauce in the world.
Miguel de Cervantes

When the stomach speaks wisdom is silent.
Arab proverb

Being unwanted, unloved, uncared for, forgotten by everybody, I think that is a much greater poverty than the person who has nothing to eat. We must find each other.
Mother Teresa

Hungry people cannot be good at learning or producing anything, except perhaps violence.
Pearl Bailey

A hungry man is not a free man.
Adlai Stevenson

You better cut the pizza in four pieces, because I'm not hungry enough to eat six.
Yogi Berra

HUNTING
It is very strange, and very melancholy, that the paucity of human pleasures should persuade us ever to call hunting one of them.
Samuel Johnson

HURRY
We can outrun the wind and the storm, but we cannot outrun the demon of Hurry.
John Burroughs

Whoever is in a hurry shows that the thing he is about to do is too big for him.
Lord Chesterfield

Hurry, hurry has no blessing.
Swahili proverb

We shall sooner overtake the dawn by remaining here than by hurrying over the hills of the west.
Henry David Thoreau

Hurry! I never hurry. I have no time to hurry.
Igor Stravinsky (responding to publisher's request that he hurry completion of a composition)

HUSBANDS
American women expect to find in their husbands a perfection that English women only hope to find in their butlers.
W. Somerset Maugham

An archaeologist is the best husband any woman can have: the older she gets, the more interested he is in her.
Agatha Christie

The husband who decides to surprise his wife is often very much surprised himself.

Voltaire

HYPOCHONDRIA
The best cure for hypochondria is to forget about your own body and get interested in someone else's.

Goodman Ace

HYPOCRISY
Hypocrisy is the necessary burden of villainy.

Albert Camus

No man is a hypocrite in his pleasures.

Samuel Johnson

Self-deception is nature; hypocrisy is art.

Mason Cooley

Hypocrisy can afford to be magnificent in its promises; for never intending to go beyond promises, it costs nothing.

Edmund Burke

Hypocrisy is the most difficult and nerve-racking vice that any man can pursue; it needs an unceasing vigilance and a rare detachment of spirit. It cannot, like adultery or gluttony, be practised at spare moments; it is a wholetime job.

W. Somerset Maugham

HYSTERIA
My quiet exterior used to be a mask for hysteria. After seven years of analysis, it just became a habit.

Gene Wilder

ICE
Everybody in life gets the same amount of ice. The rich get it in the summer and the poor in the winter.
Bat Masterson

If we're skating on thin ice, then we might as well dance.
Jesse Winchester

ICONOCLAST
In the whole range of human occupations, is it possible to imagine a poorer thing to be than an iconoclast? It is the lowest of all the unskilled trades.
G.K. Chesterton

IDEALISM
Idealism increases in direct proportion to one's distance from the problem.
John Galsworthy

Idealism is the noble toga that political gentlemen drape over their will to power.
Aldous Huxley

The idealist walks on his toes, the materialist on his talons.
Malcolm de Chazal

IDEALISTS
An idealist is one who, on noticing that a rose smells better than a cabbage, concludes that it will also make better soup.
H.L. Mencken

An idealist is a person who helps others be prosperous.
Henry Ford

Idealist: a cynic in the making.
Irving Layton

IDEALS
Ideals are very often formed in the effort to escape from the hard task of dealing with facts.
William Graham Sumner

I keep my ideals, because in spite of everything I still believe that people are really good at heart.
Anne Frank

The power of ideals is incalculable. We see no power in a drop of water. But let it get into a crack in a rock and be turned to ice, and it splits the rock; turned into steam, it drives the pistons of the most powerful engines. Something has happened to it that makes active and effective the power that is latent in it.

Albert Schweitzer

IDEAS
Serious people have few ideas. People with ideas are seldom serious.

Paul Valéry

She never lets ideas interrupt the easy flow of her conversation.

Jean Webster

A powerful idea communicates some of its strength to him who challenges it.

Marcel Proust

A fixed idea ends in madness or heroism.

Victor Hugo

Not to engage in the pursuit of ideas is to live like ants instead of men.

Mortimer J. Adler

Let us remind ourselves that last year's fresh idea is today's cliché.

Austen Briggs

An idea isn't responsible for the people who believe in it.

Don Marquis

A man with a new idea is a crank until the idea succeeds.

Mark Twain

If at first the idea is not absurd, there is no hope for it.

Albert Einstein

Between the idea and the reality falls the shadow.

T.S. Eliot

Launching a breakthrough idea is like shooting skeet. People's needs change, so you must aim well ahead of the target to hit it.

Ray Kurzweil

Nothing is more dangerous than an idea, when it's the only one we have.

Alain

Man's mind, stretched to a new idea, never goes back to its original dimensions.

Oliver Wendell Holmes

Lack of money is no obstacle. Lack of ideas is an obstacle.

Ken Hakuta

The stock of ideas which mankind has to work with is very limited, like the alphabet, and can at best have an air of freshness given it by new arrangements and combinations, or by application to new times and circumstances.

James Russell Lowell

Our ideas are only intellectual instruments which we use to break into phenomena; we must change them when they have served their purpose, as we change a blunt lancet we have used long enough.

Claude Bernard

Men become susceptible to ideas, not by discussion and argument, but by seeing them personified and by loving the person who so embodies them.

Lewis Mumford

No idea is so antiquated that it was not once modern. No idea is so modern that it will not someday be antiquated.

Ellen Glasgow

An invasion of armies can be resisted, but not an idea whose time has come.

Victor Hugo

To die for an idea is to set a rather high price on conjecture.

Anatole France

I pressed down on the mental accelerator. The old lemon throbbed fiercely. I got an idea.

P.G. Wodehouse

Many ideas grow better when transplanted into another mind than in the one where they sprang up.

Oliver Wendell Holmes

Everything you see and touch was once an invisible idea until someone chose to bring it into being. Any powerful idea is absolutely fascinating and absolutely useless until we choose to use it.

Richard Bach

In our society, the simplest person is involved with ideas. Every person we meet in the course of our daily life, no matter how unlettered he may be, is groping with sentences toward a sense of his life and his position in it; and he has what almost always goes with an

impulse to ideology, a good deal of animus and anger.

Lionel Trilling

When ideas fail, words come in very handy.

Johann Wolfgang von Goethe

Every time a man puts a new idea across, he finds ten men who thought of it before he did – but they only thought of it.

Anonymous

There are infinitely more ideas impressed on our mind than we can possibly attend to or perceive.

John Norris

Great ideas often receive violent opposition from mediocre minds.

Albert Einstein

An idea is salvation by imagination.

Frank Lloyd Wright

I can't understand why people are frightened of new ideas. I'm frightened of the old ones.

John Cage

When I have an idea, I turn down the flame, as if it were a little alcohol stove, as low as it will go. Then it explodes and that is my idea.

Ernest Hemingway

Nothing is more important to the future of an idea than the first step you take to try it out.

Dr O.A. Battista

One of the greatest pains to human nature is the pain of a new idea.

Walter Bagehot

It's very good for an idea to be commonplace. The important thing is that a new idea should develop out of what is already there so that it soon becomes an old acquaintance. Old acquaintances aren't by any means always welcome, but at least one can't be mistaken as to who or what they are.

Penelope Fitzgerald

If an idea is important enough it is worth laughing at.

Alan Plater

It is better to entertain an idea than to take it home to live with you for the rest of your life.

Randall Jarrell

Ideas, like fleas, jump from person to person, but they don't bite everyone.

Unknown

Any man who afflicts the human race with ideas must be prepared to see them misunderstood.

H.L. Mencken

The air of ideas is the only air worth breathing.

Edith Wharton

Don't worry about people stealing your ideas. If your ideas are any good, you'll have to ram them down people's throats.

Howard Aiken

Man is ready to die for an idea, provided that idea is not quite clear to him.

Paul Eldridge

Every revolutionary idea – in science, politics, art, or whatever – seems to evoke three stages of reaction. They may be summed up by the phrases: (1) "It's completely impossible – don't waste my time"; (2) "It's possible, but it's not worth doing"; (3) "I said it was a good idea all along."

Arthur C. Clarke

IDENTITY

How can we know the dancer from the dance?

William Butler Yeats

IDIOTS

Idiots have always been exploited, and that is only right. The day they cease to be, they will triumph, and the world will be lost.

Alfred Capus

The portrait of a blinking idiot.

William Shakespeare

IDLENESS

Too much idleness, I have observed, fills up a man's time much more completely, and leaves him less his own master, than any sort of employment whatsoever.

Edmund Burke

Do not allow idleness to deceive you; for while you give him today he steals tomorrow from you.

Alfred Crowquill (Alfred Forrester)

Any fool can be fussy and rid himself of energy all over the place, but a man has to have something in him before he can settle down to do nothing.

J.B. Priestley

Nothing is so intolerable to a man as being fully at rest, without passion, without business, without entertainment, without care. It is then that he recognizes that he is empty, insufficient, dependent, ineffectual.

Blaise Pascal

It is impossible to enjoy idling thoroughly unless one has plenty of work to do. There is no fun in doing nothing when you have nothing to do.

Jerome K. Jerome

We would all be idle if we could.

Samuel Johnson

Idleness is the stupidity of the body, and stupidity is the idleness of the mind.

Johann Gottfried Seume

IDOLS
Idols need not be smashed; they crumble of themselves.

Anonymous

IGNORANCE
He that knows little often repeats it.

Thomas Fuller, MD

If ignorance is bliss, 'Tis folly to be wise.

Thomas Gray

A man is never astonished that he doesn't know what another does, but he is surprised at the gross ignorance of the other in not knowing what he does.

Thomas Chandler Haliburton

Ignorance alone makes monsters and bugbears; our actual acquaintances are very commonplace people.

William Hazlitt

There is nothing more frightening than active ignorance.

There is nothing more frightful than ignorance in action.

Johann Wolfgang von Goethe

The ignorant man always adores what he cannot understand.

Cesare Lombroso

Most ignorance is vincible ignorance. We don't know because we don't want to know.

Aldous Huxley

I know of no disease of the soul but ignorance.

Ben Jonson

If ignorance is bliss, why aren't more people happy?

Leonard Rossiter

Better to be ignorant of a matter than half know it.

Publilius Syrus

When ignorance gets started, it knows no bounds.

Will Rogers

Everybody is ignorant, only on different subjects.

Will Rogers

The trouble ain't that people are ignorant; it's that they know so much that ain't so.

Josh Billings

I do not approve of anything that tampers with natural ignorance. Ignorance is like a delicate exotic fruit. Touch it and the bloom is gone.

Oscar Wilde

I am not ashamed to admit that I am ignorant of what I do not know.

Cicero

Genuine ignorance is … profitable because it is likely to be accompanied by humility, curiosity, and open-mindedness; whereas ability to repeat catch-phrases, cant terms, familiar propositions, gives the conceit of learning and coats the mind with varnish waterproof to new ideas.

John Dewey

To be ignorant of one's ignorance is the malady of the ignorant.

Amos Bronson Alcott

You can't fool me; I'm too ignorant.

Anonymous

Our knowledge can only be finite, while our ignorance must necessarily be infinite.

Sir Karl Popper

It is bad enough that people are dying of AIDS, but no one should die of ignorance.

Elizabeth Taylor

Ignorance is not innocence but sin.

Robert Browning

Not ignorance, but ignorance of ignorance is the death of knowledge.

Alfred North Whitehead

If knowledge creates problems, it is not through ignorance that we can solve them.

Isaac Asimov

I … hold there is no sin but ignorance.

Christopher Marlowe

I do not believe in the collective wisdom of individual ignorance.

Thomas Carlyle

ILLITERACY

There is that indescribable freshness and unconsciousness about an illiterate person that humbles and mocks the power of the noblest expressive genius.

Walt Whitman

According to the United Nations' latest count, of the approximately 3,000 languages spoken in the world today, only some 78 have a literature. Of those 78, a scant five or six enjoy a truly international audience. Literates make up a very small minority of the world's population, but they make their force felt out of all proportion to their number.

Barry Sanders

The illiterate of the twenty-first century will not be those who cannot read and write, but those who cannot learn, unlearn, and relearn.

Alvin Toffler

ILLNESS
She was dangerously ill, now she's dangerously well.

Anonymous

If a man thinks about his physical or moral state, he usually discovers that he is ill.

Johann Wolfgang von Goethe

Illness is the night-side of life, a more onerous citizenship.

Susan Sontag

Illness is the most heeded of doctors: To kindness and wisdom we make promises only; pain we obey.

Marcel Proust

It's no fun being sick when you don't feel well.

Olga Shoaff

Illness is not something a person has, it's another way of being.

Jonathan Miller

I've just learned about his illness. Let's hope it is nothing trivial.

Irvin S. Cobb

ILLUSION
Illusion is the first of all pleasures.

Oscar Wilde

The most dangerous of our calculations are those we call illusions.

Georges Bernanos

It is respectable to have no illusions, and safe and profitable and dull.

Joseph Conrad

Illusions are art, for the felling person, and it is by art that you live, if you do.

Elizabeth Bowen

IMAGE-MAKERS
The image-makers encourage the individual to fashion himself into a smooth coin, negotiable in any market.

John W. Gardner

IMAGINATION
Imagination is the beginning of creation. You imagine what you desire, you will what you imagine, and at last you create what you will.

George Bernard Shaw

Imagination and fiction make up more than three-quarters of our real life.

Simone Weil

Imagination is one of the last remaining legal means you have to gain an unfair advantage over your competition.

Pat Fallon

Where there is no imagination there is no horror.

Arthur Conan Doyle

Castles in the air – they're so easy to take refuge in. So easy to build, too.

Henrik Ibsen

Imagination is more important than knowledge. Knowledge is limited. Imagination circles the world

Albert Einstein

Imagination is the highest kite one can fly.

Lauren Bacall

Imagination grows by exercise and contrary to common belief is more powerful in the mature than in the young.

W. Somerset Maugham

There are no days in life so memorable as those which vibrated to some stroke of the imagination.

Ralph Waldo Emerson

The most imaginative people are the most credulous, for to them everything is possible.

Alexander Chase

Fantasies are more than substitutes for unpleasant realities, they are also dress rehearsals. All acts performed in the world begin in the imagination.

Barbara Grizzuti Harrison

Imagination is the mad boarder.

Nicolas Malebranche

I have imagination, and nothing that is real is alien to me.

George Santayana

Everything you can imagine is real.

Pablo Picasso

Imagination is the one weapon in the war against reality.

Jules de Gaultier

It is the spirit of the age to believe that any fact, no matter how suspect, is superior to any imaginative exercise, no matter how true.

Gore Vidal

Imagination, *n.* A warehouse of facts, with poet and liar in joint ownership.

Ambrose Bierce

The hardest thing to imagine is yourself.

David Wevill

I like to have a thing suggested rather than told in full. When every detail is given, the mind rests satisfied and the imagination loses the desire to use its own wings.

Thomas Bailey Aldrich

Imagination is man's power over nature.

Wallace Stevens

Fortunately, somewhere between chance and mystery lies imagination, the only thing that protects our freedom, despite the fact that people keep trying to reduce it or kill it off altogether.

Luis Buñuel

You can't depend on your eyes when your imagination is out of focus.

Mark Twain

Imagination lit every lamp in this country, built every church, performed every act of kindness and progress, created more and better things for more people. It is the priceless ingredient for a better day.

Henry J. Taylor

Were it not for imagination, Sir, a man would be as happy in the arms of a chambermaid as of a Duchess.

Samuel Johnson

The imagination may be compared to Adam's dream – he awoke and found it truth.

John Keats

IMBECILES
When a finger points to the moon the imbecile looks at the finger.

Chinese proverb

IMITATION
We are, in truth, more than half what we are by imitation. The great point is, to choose good models and to study them with care.

Lord Chesterfield

Always imitate the behaviour of winners when you lose.

George Meredith

IMMATURITY
The mark of the immature man is that he wants to die nobly for a cause, while the mark of the mature man is that he wants to live humbly for one.

Wilhelm Stekel

You can only be young once. But you can always be immature.

Dave Barry

IMMORALITY
There is no greater immorality than to occupy a place you cannot fill.

Napoleon Bonaparte

IMMORTALITY
Millions long for immortality who do not know what to do with themselves on a rainy Sunday afternoon.

Susan Ertz

If all else fails, immortality can always be assured by spectacular error.

John Kenneth Galbraith

The only thing wrong with immortality is that it tends to go on forever.

Herb Caen

The nearest approach to immortality on earth is a government bureau.

James Byrnes

It is a good thing when a man is different from your image of him. It shows he isn't a type. If he were, it would be the end of him as a man. But if you can't place him in a category, it means that at least part of him is what a human being ought to be. He has risen above himself, he has a grain of immortality.

Boris Pasternak

I don't want to achieve immortality through my work. I want to achieve it through not dying.

Woody Allen

The first condition of immortality is death.

Stanislaw J. Lec

It may make a difference to all eternity whether we do right or wrong today.

James Freeman Clarke

IMPARTIALITY
There are only two ways to be quite unprejudiced and impartial. One is to be completely ignorant.

The other is to be completely indifferent. Bias and prejudice are attitudes to be kept in mind, not attitudes to be avoided.

Charles P. Curtis

IMPATIENCE

Successful salespeople, authors, executives, and workers of every sort need patience. The great liability of youth is not inexperience but impatience.

William Feather

Impatient people always arrive too late.

Jean Dutourd

IMPERFECTION

A good garden may have some weeds.

Thomas Fuller, MD

We're all somewhat courageous and we're all considerably cowardly. We're all imperfect and life is simply a perpetual, unending struggle against those imperfections.

Sidney Poitier

Some beautiful things are more impressive when left imperfect than when too highly finished.

François, duc de La Rochefoucauld

IMPORTANCE

It is well to remember that the entire population of the universe, with one trifling exception, is composed of others.

John Andrew Holmes

It is completely unimportant. That is why it is so interesting.

At any given time there are more important people in the world than important jobs to contain them.

Bunk Carter

It's almost impossible to overestimate the unimportance of most things.

John Logue

IMPOSSIBLE

Few things are of themselves impossible, and we lack the application to make them a success rather than the means.

François, duc de La Rochefoucauld

If an elderly but distinguished scientist says that something is possible he is almost certainly right, but if he says that it is impossible he is very probably wrong.

Arthur C. Clarke

It's kind of fun to do the impossible.

Walt Disney

Probable impossibilities are to be preferred to improbable possibilities.

Aristotle

There's no getting blood out of a turnip.

Marryat Frederick

Only he who can see the invisible can do the impossible.

Frank Gaines

IMPRESSIONS
The world is for thousands a freak show; the images flicker past and vanish; the impressions remain flat and unconnected in the soul.
Johann Wolfgang von Goethe

IMPROBABLE
Man can believe the impossible, but man can never believe the improbable.
Oscar Wilde

It is nearly always the most improbable things that really come to pass.
E.T.A. Hoffman

IMPROVEMENT
There's only one corner of the universe you can be certain of improving and that's your own self.
Aldous Huxley

None will improve your lot/If you yourselves do not.
Bertolt Brecht

If a way to the Better there be, it exacts a full look at the worst.
Thomas Hardy

If the only new thing we have to offer is an improved version of the past, then today can only be inferior to yesterday. Hypnotized by images of the past, we risk losing all capacity for creative change.
Robert Hewison

I know of no more encouraging fact than the unquestionable ability of man to elevate his life by conscious endeavour.
Henry David Thoreau

He is one of the people who would be enormously improved by death.
Saki

It was tough to get better when you had so many telling you that you were better than you really were.
Jim Craig

Men will not be content to manufacture life: they will want to improve on it.
J.D. Bernal

IMPROVISE
In the long history of humankind (and animalkind, too) those who learned to collaborate and improvise most effectively have prevailed.
Charles Darwin

IMPULSE
Have no truck with first impulses for they are always generous ones.
Casimir, Comte de Montrond

Great things are not done by impulse, but by a series of small things brought together.
Vincent van Gogh

INACCURACY
A little inaccuracy sometimes saves tons of explanations.
Saki

INANIMATE OBJECTS
The goal of all inanimate objects is to resist man and ultimately defeat him.
Russell Baker

INAUDIBLE
We listen to it and do not hear it;
Its name is The Inaudible.

Lao-Tse

INCLUSIVE
It is only human supremacy, which
is as unacceptable as racism and
sexism, that makes us afraid of
being more inclusive.

Ingrid Newkirk

INCOME
If your outgo exceeds your income,
your upkeep will be your downfall.

Anonymous

Idiots are always in favour of
inequality of income (their only
chance of eminence), and the really
great in favour of equality.

George Bernard Shaw

INCOME TAX
The hardest thing in the world to
understand is income tax.

Albert Einstein

The only thing that hurts more
than paying an income tax is not
having to pay an income tax.

Lord Thomas Dewar

Income tax has made more liars
out of the American people than
golf has.

Will Rogers

In filling out an income tax return,
let an accountant instead of your
conscience be your guide.

Will Rogers

The income tax people are very
nice. They're letting me keep my
own mother.

Henny Youngman

Taxes, after all, are the dues that
we pay for the privileges of membership in an organized society.

Franklin D. Roosevelt

I believe we should all pay our tax
bill with a smile. I tried – but they
wanted cash.

Unknown

INCOMMUNICABLE
I distrust the incommunicable: it is
the source of all violence.

Jean-Paul Sartre

INCOMPATABILITY
It was towards the end of June that
incompatibility became established
between them like a new season of
the year.

Colette

INCONSTANCY
Nothing that is not a real crime
makes a man appear so contemptible and little in the eyes of the
world as inconstancy, especially
when it regards religion or party.

Joseph Addison

INCONVENIENCE
People put up with a lot of inconvenience in order to be in the place
where they want to be.

Carter Burwell

INDECENCY
I don't see how an article of clothing can be indecent. A person, yes.
Robert Heinlein

Indecency is self-annihilating.
Louis L. Mann

INDECISION
Nothing is so exhausting as indecision, and nothing is so futile.
Bertrand Russell

INDEPENDENCE
Let all your views in life be directed to a solid, however moderate, independence; without it, no man can be happy, nor even honest.
Junius

There is often as much independence in not being led, as in not being driven.
Tryon Edwards

Nothing grows well in the shade of a big tree.
Constantin Brancusi

A great step toward independence is a good-humoured stomach, one that is willing to endure rough treatment.
Seneca

INDIFFERENCE
The worst sin toward our fellow creatures is not to hate them, but to be indifferent to them; that's the essence of inhumanity.
George Bernard Shaw

INDIGNATION (MORAL)
Moral indignation is jealousy with a halo.
H.G. Wells

A good indignation makes an excellent speech.
Ralph Waldo Emerson

INDISCIPLINE
Blind and unwavering indiscipline at all times constitutes the real strength of all free men.
Alfred Jarry

INDIVIDUALISM
Individualism is rather like innocence; there must be something unconscious about it.
Louis Kronenberger

Individualism, with its rapacious and exploitative attitude toward the world, is the antithesis of that individuality which is the authentic self realized within a genuine community.
Page Smith

INDIVIDUALITY
Individuality or unity? I say there's room for both.
Brian Celio

INDOLENCE
Though you may have known clever men who were indolent, you never knew a great man who was so; and when I hear a young man spoken of as giving promise of great genius, the first question I ask about him always is: Does he work?
John Ruskin

INDUSTRIOUS
It is not enough to be industrious, so are the ants. What are you industrious about?

Henry David Thoreau

INDUSTRY
Life without industry is guilt, and industry without art is brutality.

John Ruskin

Industry is a better horse to ride than genius.

Walter Lippmann

INEQUALITY
The worst form of inequality is to try to make unequal things equal.

Aristotle

Without inequality there is no joy.

Samuel Johnson

INEVITABILITY
There is no good in arguing with the inevitable. The only good argument available with an east wind is to put on your overcoat.

James Russell Lowell

Science fiction writers foresee the inevitable, and although problems and catastrophes may be inevitable, solutions are not.

Isaac Asimov

INFERIORITY
Nobody can make you feel inferior without your consent.

Eleanor Roosevelt

Everyone … has a feeling of inferiority. But the feeling of inferiority is not a disease; it is rather a stimulant to health, normal striving and development. It becomes a pathological condition only when the sense of inadequacy overcomes the individual and, far from stimulating him to useful activity, makes him depressed and incapable of development.

Alfred Adler

It is fit I should commit offence to my inferiors.

William Shakespeare

INFIDELITY
It is necessary to the happiness of man that he be mentally faithful to himself. Infidelity does not consist in believing, or disbelieving, it consists in professing to believe what one does not believe.

Thomas Paine

INFINITIVE
Word has somehow got around that the split infinitive is always wrong. That is a piece with the outworn notion that it is always wrong to strike a lady.

James Thurber

INFINITUDE
All finite things reveal infinitude.

Theodore Roethke

If you wish to advance into the infinite, explore the finite in all directions.

Johann Wolfgang von Goethe

INFLATION
It's kind of like duck hunting. You aim ahead of the duck, not at the

duck. The same is true of inflation. You have to act in advance.

Sung Won Sohn

One of the benefits of inflation is that kids can no longer get sick on a nickel's worth of candy.

Journeyman Barber *magazine*

Inflation: a state of affairs when you never had it so good or parted with it so fast.

Changing Times magazine

INFLUENCE
Influence is like a savings account. The less you use it, the more you've got.

Andrew Young

INFORMATION
Information is the currency of democracy.

Ralph Nader

We all get heavier as we get older because there is more information in our heads.

Vlade Divac

It is a very sad thing that nowadays there is so little useless information.

Oscar Wilde

Information is the oxygen of the modern age. It seeps through the walls topped by barbed wire; it wafts across the electrified borders.

Ronald Reagan

INFORMED
It is better to be un-informed than ill-informed.

Keith Duckworth

INGRATITUDE
People who bite the hand that feeds them usually lick the boot that kicks them.

Eric Hoffer

Do you know what is harder to bear than the reverses of fortune? It is the baseness, the hideous ingratitude of man.

Napoleon Bonaparte

A man is very apt to complain of the ingratitude of those who have risen far above him.

Samuel Johnson

INHERIT
We should know how to inherit, because inheriting is culture.

Thomas Mann

INHERITANCE
Say not you know another entirely, til you have divided an inheritance with him.

Johann Kaspar Lavater

Sometimes the poorest man leaves his children the richest inheritances.

Ruth E. Renkel

The tears of an heir are laughter under a mask.

Publilius Syrus

INHUMANITY
In the nineteenth century, inhumanity meant cruelty; in the twentieth century it means schizoid self-alienation. The danger of the past was that men became slaves.

The danger of the future is that men may become robots.

Erich Fromm

INITIATIVE
It is much easier to ask for forgiveness than for permission.

Unknown

Everything comes to him who hustles while he waits.

Thomas Edison

We often get in quicker by the back door than by the front.

Napoleon Bonaparte

Get them before they get you.

Anonymous

Don't wait for your ship to come in – swim out to it.

Anonymous

INNOCENCE
It's innocence when it charms us, ignorance when it doesn't.

Mignon McLaughlin

The truly innocent are those who not only are guiltless themselves, but who think others are.

Josh Billings

What is our innocence, what is our guilt? All are naked, none is safe.

Marianne Moore

INNOCENT
You can't blame the innocent; they are always guiltless. All you can do is control them or eliminate them.

Graham Greene

INNOVATION
Innovation is the central issue in economic prosperity.

Michael Porter

Just as energy is the basis of life itself, and ideas the source of innovation, so is innovation the vital spark of all human change, improvement and progress.

Theodore Levitt

Instead of pouring knowledge into people's heads, we need to help them grind a new set of eyeglasses so that we can see the world in a new way.

J.S. Brown

INQUIRY
Do not block the way of inquiry.

Charles Sanders Peirce

INSANITY
Insanity is hereditary; you can get it from your children.

Sam Levenson

In individuals, insanity is rare, but in groups, parties, nations, and epochs it is the rule.

Friedrich Nietzsche

When dealing with the insane, the best method is to pretend to be sane.

Hermann Hesse

INSECTS
We hope that, when the insects take over the world, they will remember with gratitude how we took them along on all our picnics.

Bill Vaughan

INSIGHT
Nothing is more terrible than activity without insight.
Thomas Carlyle

A moment's insight is sometimes worth a life's experience.
Oliver Wendell Holmes, Jr

INSISTENCE
One who is too insistent on his own views finds few to agree with him.
Lao-Tse

INSOMNIA
The best cure for insomnia is to get a lot of sleep.
W.C. Fields

The last refuge of the insomniac is a sense of superiority to the sleeping world.
Leonard Cohen

Insomnia: a contagious disease often transmitted from babies to parents.
Shannon Fife

INSPIRATION
Keep your fears to yourself but share your inspiration.
Robert Louis Stevenson

So-called "inspiration" is no more than an extreme example of a process which constantly goes on in the minds of all of us.
Anthony Storr

Inspiration descends only in flashes, to clothe circumstances; it is not stored up in a barrel, like salt herrings, to be doled out.
Patrick White

Inspiration may be a form of super-consciousness, or perhaps of sub-consciousness – I wouldn't know. But I am sure it is the antithesis of self-consciousness.
Aaron Copland

INSTANT GRATIFICATION
Instant gratification takes too long.
Carrie Fisher

INSTINCTS
A few strong instincts, and a few plain rules.
William Wordsworth

Be a good animal, true to your instincts.
D.H. Lawrence

Everything good is instinct – and, as a result, easy, necessary, free.
Friedrich Nietzsche

INSTRUCTIONS
When all else fails, read instructions.
Graffito

INSULT
The only gracious way to accept an insult is to ignore it; if you can't ignore it, top it; if you can't top it, laugh at it; if you can't laugh at it, it's probably deserved.
Russell Lynes

An injury is much sooner forgotten than an insult.
Lord Chesterfield

There are two insults people won't endure: the assertion that they have no sense of humour and the doubly impertinent assertion that they have never known trouble.

Sinclair Lewis

INSURANCE
What can't be cured, must be insured.

Oliver Herford

INTEGRITY
Some persons are likeable in spite of their unswerving integrity.

Don Marquis

Integrity is the lifeblood of democracy. Deceit is a poison in its veins.

Edward Kennedy

There can be no friendship without confidence; and no confidence, without integrity.

Proverb

INTELLECT
The highest intellects, like the tops of mountains, are the first to catch and to reflect the dawn.

Thomas Babington Macaulay

Intellect is invisible to the man who has none.

Arthur Schopenhauer

INTELLECTUAL
Definition of an intellectual: someone who can listen to Rossini's "William Tell" Overture without thinking of the Lone Ranger.

Unknown

An intellectual is not only a person for whom books are essential but one for whom an idea, however elementary, absorbs and orders his life.

André Malraux

An intellectual is "a man who writes his own speeches."

C. Wright Mills

The terrifying thing about modern intellectuals everywhere is that they are always changing idols.

Charles Simic

An intellectual is a man who takes more words than necessary to tell more than he knows.

Dwight D. Eisenhower

An intellectual is a man who does not know how to park a bike.

Spiro T. Agnew

An intellectual is someone whose mind watches itself.

Albert Camus

As Marshall McLuhan [put it]: "Moral indignation is a technique used to endow the idiot with dignity." Precisely which intellectuals of the twentieth century were or were not idiots is a debatable point, but it is hard to argue with the definition I once heard a French diplomat offer at a dinner party: "An intellectual is a person knowledgeable in one field who speaks out only in others."

Tom Wolfe

Intellectual passion dries out sensuality.

Leonardo da Vinci

There is a Northwest passage to the intellectual World.
Laurence Sterne

[Intellectuals are] ingenious fools too clever to be wise, though brilliant at inventing the most ingenious reasons for their fatuous beliefs. But, tiresome as intellectuals can be, even they are probably much less menacing and pernicious to the world than anti-intellectuals.
F.L. Lucas

The learned are seldom pretty fellows, and in many cases their appearance tends to discourage a love of study in the young.
H.L. Mencken

INTELLIGENCE
Respond intelligently even to unintelligent treatment.
Lao-Tse

He who knows much about others may be learned, but he who understands himself is more intelligent. He who controls others may be powerful, but he who has mastered himself is mightier still.
Lao-Tse

One can live in the shadow of an idea without grasping it.
Elizabeth Bowen

A man is not necessarily intelligent because he has plenty of ideas, any more than he is a good general because he has plenty of soldiers.
Chamfort

No man is smart, except by comparison with others who know less; the smartest man who ever lived has reason to be ashamed of himself.
Edgar Watson Howe

Intelligence is what you use when you don't know what to do.
Jean Piaget

What a distressing contrast there is between the radiant intelligence of the child and the feeble mentality of the average adult.
Sigmund Freud

Intelligence is not all that important in the exercise of power and is often, in point of fact, useless. Just as a leader doesn't need intelligence, a man in my job doesn't need too much of it either.
Henry Kissinger

Intelligence is almost useless to someone who has no other quality.
Alexis Carrel

Artificial intelligence is no match for artificial stupidity.
Unknown

Intelligence is not to make no mistakes/But quickly to see how to make them good.
Bertolt Brecht

It has yet to be proven that intelligence has any survival value.
Arthur C. Clarke

Nothing so gives the illusion of intelligence as personal association with large sums of money.
John Kenneth Galbraith

Intelligence is quickness to apprehend, as distinct from ability, which is capacity to act wisely on the thing apprehended.
Alfred North Whitehead

There is no such thing as an underestimate of average intelligence.
Henry Adams

Military intelligence is a contradiction in terms.
Groucho Marx

There is … more [intelligence] requisite to be an honest man than there is to be a knave.
George Savile,
Marquess of Halifax

The more intelligence one has the more people one finds original. Commonplace people see no difference between men.
Blaise Pascal

The test of a first-rate intelligence is the ability to hold two opposed ideas in the mind at the same time, and still retain the ability to function. One should, for example, be able to see that things are hopeless and yet be determined to make them otherwise.
F. Scott Fitzgerald

Thus the best human intelligence is still decidedly barbarous; it fights in heavy armour and keeps a fool at court.
George Santayana

There are some men who are so intelligent that you wonder whether anything can still interest them.
Maurice Martin du Gard

INTENTION
I may not have gone where I intended to go, but I think I have ended up where I intended to be.
Douglas Adams

A truth that's told with bad intent/ Beats all the lies you can invent.
William Blake

INTERDEPENDENCE
All men are caught in an inescapable network of mutuality.
Martin Luther King, Jr

It takes two men to make one brother.
Israel Zangwill

INTEREST
Interest makes some people blind, and others quick-sighted.
Francis Beaumont

INTERESTING
Nothing is interesting if you're not interested.
Anne Morrow Lindbergh

INTERESTS
We have no eternal allies; we have no perpetual enemies. Our interests are eternal and perpetual, and those interests it is our duty to follow.
Lord Palmerston

INTERNAL WORLD

We contain an internal world which is just as active and complicated as the one we live in. It is an interior of which we are largely unaware, and one to which we have no personal access. We cannot be tourists in our own insides.

Dr Jonathan Miller

INTERNATIONAL

How horrible, fantastic, incredible it is that we should be digging trenches and trying on gas masks here because of a quarrel in a faraway country between people of whom we know nothing.

Neville Chamberlain

INTERNET

There's a danger of the Internet just becoming loud, ugly, and boring with a thousand voices screaming for attention.

Matt Drudge

Praise Allah for the Internet. With the Web making self-censorship irrelevant – someone else is bound to say what you won't – it became a place where intellectual risk-takers finally exhaled.

Irshad Manji

INTERPRETATION

Interpretation is the revenge of the intellect upon art.

Susan Sontag

INTERVIEWS

Interviews are funny things because I keep having to improvise what I think I think I think. In fact I never give it a thought.

Tom Stoppard

INTOLERANCE

Intolerance itself is a form of egoism, and to condemn egoism intolerantly is to share it.

George Santayana

Intolerance betrays want of faith in one's cause.

Mohandas Gandhi

INTRIGUE

There are masked words abroad, I say, which nobody understands.

John Ruskin

INTUITION

Often you just have to rely on your intuition.

Bill Gates

The intuitive mind is a sacred gift, and the rational mind is a faithful servant. We have created a society that honours the servant and has forgotten the gift.

Albert Einstein

Intuition is not infallible; it only seems to be the truth. It is a message which we may interpret wrongly.

Christina Stead

INVENT

To invent, you need a good imagination and a pile of junk.

Thomas Edison

INVENTIONS

I just invent, then wait until man comes around to needing what I've invented.

R. Buckminster Fuller

There ought to be a monument to the man who invented neon lights … There's a boy who really made something out of nothing.

Raymond Chandler

Getting caught is the mother of invention.

Robert Byrne

If you took away everything in the world that had to be invented, there'd be nothing left except a lot of people getting rained on.

Tom Stoppard

Invention, strictly speaking, is little more than a new combination of those images which have previously been gathered and deposited in the memory. Nothing can be made of nothing; he who has laid up no materials can produce no combinations.

Sir Joshua Reynolds

When man wanted to make a machine that would walk he created the wheel, which does not resemble a leg.

Guillaume Apollinaire

INVENTORS

Only an inventor knows how to borrow.

Ralph Waldo Emerson

We owe a lot to Thomas Edison — if it wasn't for him, we'd be watching television by candlelight.

Milton Berle

INVEST

Never invest money in anything that eats or needs repainting.

Billy Rose

He has spent all his life letting down empty buckets into empty well; and he is frittering away his age in trying to draw them up again.

Sydney Smith

You must lose a fly to catch a trout.

George Herbert

Sometimes your best investments are the ones you don't make.

Donald Trump

IRISH

We in coming days may be still the indomitable Irishry.

William Butler Yeats

I am troubled; I'm dissatisfied, I'm Irish.

Marianne Moore

The Irish do not want anyone to wish them well; they want everyone to wish their enemies ill.

Harold Nicolson

I never met anyone in Ireland who understood the Irish question, except one Englishman who had only been there a week.

Major Sir Keith Fraser

IRONY
Irony may be a universal device but it is also a divisive and unstable one.

Alexander Star

IRREPLACEABLE
To be irreplaceable, one must always be different.

Coco Chanel

IRRESISTIBLE
Only that which does not teach, which does not cry out, which does not condescend, which does not explain, is irresistible.

William Butler Yeats

IRRESPONSIBILITY
Perhaps it is better to be irresponsible and right than responsible and wrong.

Winston Churchill

"JACKETSPEAK"

Provocative and enlightening = querulous and crabby

Compelling = no big words

Breathtaking and compelling = hackneyed and no big words

Definitive = beware: footnotes

Sprawling = unedited

Controversial = inadequately researched

Monumental = see "sprawling"

A groundbreaking achievement = deserves to be interred

Daring = smutty

A daring breakthrough = smutty and degenerate

Engaging = aimed at Barbie Doll collectors

Enchanting = warning: may induce insulin shock

*The Globe and Mail
(Charles Macli)*

JAIL

I know not whether Laws be right,/ Or whether Laws be wrong;/All that we know who lie in gaol/Is that the wall is strong.

Oscar Wilde

JANUARY

January, month of empty pockets! … Let us endure this evil month, anxious as a theatrical producer's forehead.

Colette

JAUNDICE

All looks yellow to a jaundiced eye.

Alexander Pope

JEALOUSY

Jealousy is an awkward homage which inferiority renders to merit.

Madeleine de Puisieux

Jealousy is the mark of an embittered man.

William Butler Yeats

In jealousy there is more self-love than love.

*François, duc de La
Rochefoucauld*

Jealousy is a terrible thing. It resembles love, only it is love's contrary. Instead of wishing for the welfare of the object loved, it desires the dependence of that object upon itself, and its own triumph.

Henri-Frédéric Amiel

JEST
A jest often decides matters of importance more effectually and happily than seriousness.

Horace

JESTER
There is no better role to play among the great than that of jester.

Denis Diderot

JEWELRY
Never wear artistic jewelry; it ruins a woman's reputation.

Colette

JOB
A job is death without the dignity.

Brendan Behan

Look for a tough wedge for a tough log.

Publilius Syrus

All paid jobs absorb and degrade the mind.

Aristotle

Oh, you hate your job? Why didn't you say so? There's a support group for that. It's called EVERYBODY and they meet at the bar.

Drew Carey

In an undeveloped country, when you are absent, your job is taken away from you; in a developed country, a new one is piled on you.

Charles Issawi

If you have a job without aggravations, you don't have a job.

Malcolm Forbes

It's strange how unimportant your job is when you ask for a raise, and how important it is when you want a day off.

Howie Lasseter

The most rewarding way to change jobs is to change yourself.

J. Sig Paulson

JOGGING
The only reason I would take up jogging is so I could hear heavy breathing again.

Erma Bombeck

JOKES
Behind every joke there is a deep cultural grievance. You cannot have a joke without a grievance.

Marshall McLuhan

A difference of taste in jokes is a great strain on the affections.

George Eliot

Many a folly, which all the serious preaching in the world could not cure, has been driven from the stage of living realities by a joke.

William Fleet

At bottom, the world isn't a joke. We only joke about it to avoid an issue with someone, to let someone know that we know he's there with his questions; to disarm him by seeming to have heard and done justice to his side of the standing argument.

Robert Frost

Forgive, O Lord, my little jokes on Thee,/And I'll forgive Thy great big one on me.

Robert Frost

The problem with political jokes is they get elected.

Henry Cate VII

The gods, too, are fond of a joke.

Aristotle

A thing is funny when – in some way that is not actually offensive or frightening – it upsets the established order. Every joke is a tiny revolution ... Whatever destroys dignity and brings down the mighty from their seats, preferably with a bump, is funny.

George Orwell

One nice thing about telling a clean joke is there's a good chance no one's heard it before.

Doug Larson

JOSTLING
No man lives without jostling and being jostled; in all ways he has to elbow his way through the world, giving and receiving offence.

Thomas Carlyle

JOURNALISM
There is much to be said in favour of modern journalism. By giving us the opinions of the uneducated, it keeps us in touch with the ignorance of the community.

Oscar Wilde

Journalism is the only thinkable alternative to working.

Jeffrey Bernard

Journalism largely consists in saying "Lord Jones Dead" to people who never knew Lord Jones was alive.

G.K. Chesterton

Journalism – a profession whose business it is to explain to others what it personally does not understand.

Lord Northcliffe

People may expect too much from journalism. Not only do they expect it to be entertaining, they expect it to be true.

Lewis Lapham

JOURNALISTS
Most journalists are restless voyeurs who see the warts on the world, the imperfections in people and places ... gloom is their game, the spectacle their passion, normality their nemesis.

Gay Talese

A journalist is a grumbler, a censurer, a giver of advice, a regent of sovereigns, a tutor of nations. Four hostile newspapers are more to be feared than a thousand bayonets.

Napoleon Bonaparte

We journalists tell the public which way the cat is jumping. The public will take care of the cat.

Arthur Hays Sulzberger

JOURNEYS
An involuntary return to the point of departure is, without doubt, the most disturbing of all journeys.
Ian Sinclair

JOYS
Great joys, like griefs, are silent.
Shackerley Marmion

Grief can take care of itself, but to get the full value of joy you must have somebody to divide it with.
Mark Twain

Joy is not in things; it is in us.
Richard Wagner

JUDGE
Judge: a law student who marks his own papers.
H.L. Mencken

I'm glad to meet an honest judge.
last words of Fiorello H. La Guardia

As, for the safety of society, we commit honest maniacs to Bedlam, so judges should be withdrawn from their bench, whose erroneous biases are leading us to dissolution.
Thomas Jefferson

A good judge conceives quickly, judges slowly.
Proverb

JUDGING
It is well, when judging a friend, to remember that he is judging you with the same godlike and superior impartiality.
Arnold Bennett

The number of those who undergo the fatigue of judging for themselves is very small indeed.
Richard Brinsley Sheridan

JUDGMENT
We should not fear the strategies of our enemies – only the possible mistakes in our own judgment.
Unknown

Judge a man by his questions rather than by his answers.
Voltaire

Snap judgments often snap back.
Anonymous

You can't depend on your judgment when your imagination is out of focus.
Mark Twain

Good judgment comes from experience, and experience comes from bad judgment.
Barry LePatner

Judgment comes from experience, and great judgment comes from bad experience.
Saying

Obviously, a man's judgment cannot be better than the information on which he has based it.
Arthur Hays Sulzberger

Sir Roger told them, with the air of a man who would not give his judgement rashly, that much might be said on both sides.
Joseph Addison

Don't judge a man until you have walked two moons in his moccasins.
Native American proverb

Every man ought to be a judge of pictures, and every man is so who has not been connoisseured out of his senses.
William Blake

Knowledge is the treasure, but judgment the treasurer of a wise man.
William Penn

If you are pained by external things, it is not they that disturb you, but your own judgment of them. And it is in your power to wipe out that judgment now.
Marcus Aurelius

Rightness of judgment is bitterness to the heart.
Euripides

Most people have ears, but few have judgment.
Lord Chesterfield

At twenty years of age, the will reigns; at thirty, the wit; and at forty, the judgment.
Benjamin Franklin

Everyone complains of his memory, but no one complains of his judgment.
François, duc de La Rochefoucauld

A Daniel come to judgment!
William Shakespeare

One of the most serious mistakes we can make is to confuse the thing we call "intelligence" with another thing called "judgment." The two do not always, or necessarily, go together; many persons of high intelligence have notoriously poor judgment.
Sydney J. Harris

We judge ourselves by what we feel capable of doing, while others judge us by what we have already done.
Henry Wadsworth Longfellow

God himself, sir, does not propose to judge a man until the end of his days.
Samuel Johnson

JUDGMENT (BAD)
Men of ill-judgment oft ignore the good that lies within their hands, til they have lost it.
Sophocles

JUDGMENT (LAST)
I shall tell you a great secret, my friend. Do not wait for the last judgment; it takes place every day.
Albert Camus

JUDGMENT (RUSH TO)
But now all these and all things else hear the trumpet, and must rush to judgment.
Ralph Waldo Emerson

JUSTICE
Justice is too good for some people and not good enough for the rest.
Norman Douglas

Injustice all around is justice.
Persian proverb

I have a secret passion for mercy … but justice is what keeps happening to people.

Ross Macdonald

Justice is the insurance we have on our lives and property, and obedience is the premium we pay for it.

William Penn

Wrong must not win by technicalities.

Aeschylus

The price of justice is eternal publicity.

Arnold Bennett

Let justice be done, though the world perish.

Emperor Ferdinand I

Never pray for justice, because you might get some.

Margaret Atwood

It is easy to do justice – very hard to do right. Unfortunately, while the appeal of justice is intellectual, the appeal of right appears for some odd reason to induce tears in the court.

Terence Rattigan

Justice is like a train that is nearly always late.

Yevgeny Yevtushenko

Everything secret degenerates, even the administration of justice.

Lord Acton

The first reward of justice is the consciousness that we are acting justly.

Jean-Jacques Rousseau

Justice is simply the advantage of the stronger.

Thrasymachus

Justice denied anywhere diminishes justice everywhere.

Martin Luther King, Jr

Injustice is relatively easy to bear; it is justice that hurts.

H.L. Mencken

JUSTIFICATION
The end cannot justify the means, for the simple and obvious reason that the means employed determine the nature of the ends produced.

Aldous Huxley

KAFKA

You don't actually have to be intelligent if you can just create the impression. This can usually be accomplished by a reference to Kafka. Even if you never read any of his – or her – works.

Bob Newhart

KARATE

Karate is a form of martial arts in which people who have had years and years of training can, using only their hands and feet, make some of the worst movies in the history of the world.

Dave Barry

KIDNAPPING

When I was kidnapped, my parents snapped into action. They rented out my room.

Woody Allen

KILLING

How many times do I have to kill before I get a name in the paper or some national attention?

Kansas serial killer, complaining by letter to police

There are many things worth living for, a few things worth dying for, and nothing worth killing for.

Tom Robbins

KINDNESS

Forget injuries, never forget kindnesses.

Chinese proverb

Be kind to unkind people – they need it the most.

Anonymous

In this world, you must be a bit too kind in order to be kind.

Pierre Marivaux

Always be a little kinder than necessary.

J.M. Barrie

A fellow-feeling makes one wondrous kind.

David Garrick

Kindness is the golden chain by which society is bound together.

Johann Wolfgang von Goethe

The older you get, the more you realize that kindness is synonymous with happiness.

Lionel Barrymore

Kindness – a language which the dumb can speak, and the deaf can understand.

Christian Nestell Bovee

KING

Who draws his sword against the king, must throw away the scabbard.

English proverb

Is the king dead? the empire unpossess'd?

William Shakespeare

KINSHIP

Kinship is healing; we are physicians to each other.

Oliver Sacks

KISSES

People who throw kisses are mighty near hopelessly lazy.

Bob Hope

A kiss is a lovely trick designed by nature to stop speech when it has become superfluous.

Ingrid Bergman

KITCHEN

Show me a man who lives alone and has a perpetually clean kitchen, and eight times out of nine I'll show you a man with detestable spiritual qualities.

Charles Bukowski

KNAVE

What cannot a neat knave with a smooth tale / Make a woman believe?

John Webster

He who says there is no such thing as an honest man, you may be sure is himself a knave.

George Berkley

KNOW-NOTHINGS

The know-nothings are less of a problem than the feel-nothings.

Anonymous

KNOWLEDGE

A wise question is half of knowledge.

Francis Bacon

The mind is the man, and knowledge mind; the man is but what he knoweth.

Francis Bacon

Nobody knows anything until he is fifty.

F.H. Underhill

Nobody knows enough, but many know too much.

Marie von Ebner-Eschenbach

The knowledge that you can have is inexhaustible, and what is inexhaustible is benevolent. The knowledge that you cannot have is of the riddles of birth and death, of our future destiny and the purposes of God. Here there is no knowledge, but illusions that restrict freedom and limit hope. Accept the mystery behind knowledge: It is not darkness, but shadow.

Northrop Frye

The more I read, the more I meditate; and the more I acquire, the more I am able to affirm that I know nothing.

Voltaire

Knowledge is said to be power; and it is power in the same sense that wood is fuel. Wood on fire is fuel. Knowledge on fire is power.

Henry MacKenzie

We know accurately only when we know little; with knowledge doubt increases.

Johann Wolfgang von Goethe

Be avaricious of time; do not give any moment without receiving it in value; only allow the hours to go from you with as much regret as you give your gold; do not allow a single day to pass without increasing the treasure of your knowledge and virtue.

Nicholas Le Tourneux

I do not know which makes a man more conservative – to know nothing but the present or nothing but the past.

John Maynard Keynes

In order that knowledge be properly digested, it must have been swallowed with a good appetite.

Anatole France

I prefer tongue-tied knowledge to ignorant loquacity.

Cicero

Knowledge is power, if you know it about the right person.

Ethel Watts Mumford

In expanding the field of knowledge, we but increase the horizon of ignorance.

Henry Miller

What can give us surer knowledge than our senses? With what else can we better distinguish the true from the false?

Lucretius

Some drink deeply from the river of knowledge. Others only gargle.

Woody Allen

Every step by which men add to their knowledge and skills is a step also by which they can control other men.

Max Lerner

I hold myself indebted to any one from whose enlightened understanding another ray of knowledge communicates to mine. Really, to inform the mind is to correct and enlarge the heart.

Junius

What one knows is, in youth, of little moment; they know enough who know how to learn.

Henry Adams

Knowledge is of two kinds: we know a subject ourselves, or we know where we can find information on it.

Samuel Johnson

Knowledge is the true organ of sight, not the eyes.

Panchatantra

It is better to know nothing than to know everything by halves.

Friedrich Nietzsche

We owe almost all our knowledge not to those who have agreed, but to those who have differed.

Charles Caleb Colton

If a little knowledge is dangerous, where is the man who has so much as to be out of danger?

Thomas Henry Huxley

Since we cannot be universal and know all that is to be known of everything, we ought to know a little about everything.

Blaise Pascal

Know thyself.

Oracle, Delphi

'Tis not knowing much, but what is useful, that makes a wise man.

Thomas Fuller, MD

As we acquire more knowledge, things do not become more comprehensible, but more mysterious.

Albert Schweitzer

It is better to know nothing than to know what ain't so.

Josh Billings

The more you know the less the better.

Billy Connolly

The fox knows many things – the hedgehog one big one.

Archilochus

Knowledge – that is, education in its true sense – is our best protection against unreasoning prejudice and panic-making fear, whether engendered by special interest, illiberal minorities, or panic-stricken leaders.

Franklin D. Roosevelt

Every increase in knowledge may possibly render depravity more depraved, as well as it may increase the strength of virtue. It is in itself only power; and its value depends on its application.

Sydney Smith

The only good is knowledge and the only evil is ignorance.

Socrates

If you have knowledge, let others light their candles at it.

Margaret Fuller

Real knowledge, like everything else of value, is not to be obtained easily. It must be worked for, studied for, thought for, and, more than all, must be prayed for.

Thomas Arnold

We are drowning in information but starved for knowledge.

John Naisbitt

To the small part of ignorance that we arrange and classify we give the name knowledge.

Ambrose Bierce

There was never an age in which useless knowledge was more important than our own.

C.E.M. Joad

Apart from the known and unknown, what else is there?

Harold Pinter

Knowing is false understanding. Not knowing is blind ignorance.
Nan Ch'uan

When a man's knowledge is not in order, the more knowledge he has, the greater will be his confusion.
Herbert Spencer

Knowledge leads either to reverence or arrogance.
Anonymous

To really know someone is to have loved and hated him in turn.
Marcel Jouhandeau

We must know, if only in order to learn not to know. The supreme lesson of human consciousness is to learn how not to know. That is, how not to interfere.
D.H. Lawrence

A smattering of everything and a knowledge of nothing.
Charles Dickens

Knowledge is invariably a matter of degree: you cannot put your finger upon even the simplest datum and say "this we know."
T.S. Eliot

Knowledge is indivisible. When people grow wise in one direction, they are sure to make it easier for themselves to grow wise in other directions as well.
Isaac Asimov

What each man does is based not on direct and certain knowledge, but on pictures made by himself or given to him.
Walter Lippmann

Knowledge is the most democratic source of power.
Alvin Toffler

They never open their mouths without subtracting from the sum of human knowledge.
Thomas Brackett Reed

One must not try to know the unknowable, though one was quite powerless to ignore it.
Henry Adams

It is safer to know too little than too much.
Samuel Butler

When you know a thing to hold that you know it, and when you do not know a thing to know that you do not, this is knowledge.
Confucius

The best part of our knowledge is that which teaches us where knowledge leaves off and ignorance begins.
Oliver Wendell Holmes

Experience indicates that knowledge cannot be imparted. It can only be acquired.
Norman G. Shidle

We are here and it is now. Further than that, all human knowledge is moonshine.
H.L. Mencken

Everything has been said, yet few have taken advantage of it. Since all our knowledge is essentially banal, it can only be of value to minds that are not.
Raoul Vaneigem

The only fence against the world is a thorough knowledge of it.

John Locke

Knowledge does not keep any better than fish.

Alfred North Whitehead

Knowledge is a comfortable and necessary retreat and shelter for us in advanced age, and if we do not plant it while young, it will give us no shade when we grow old.

Lord Chesterfield

If I had read as much as other men, I should have known no more than they.

Thomas Hobbes

LABELS

One of the unpardonable sins, in the eyes of most people, is for a man to go about unlabelled. The world regards such a person as the police do an unmuzzled dog, not under proper control.

Thomas Henry Huxley

LABORATORY

I used to be a laboratory myself once.

Keith Richards

LABOUR

I pity the man who wants a coat so cheap that the man or woman who produces the cloth shall starve in the process.

Benjamin Harrison

Labour is the superior of capital and deserves much the higher consideration.

Abraham Lincoln

Physical labour not only does not exclude the possibility of mental activity, but improves and stimulates it.

Leo Tolstoy

The reward of labour is life. Is that not enough?

William Morris

LABOUR UNIONS

It is one of the characteristics of a free and democratic nation that it have free and independent labour unions.

Franklin D. Roosevelt

LADY

The attributes of a great lady may still be found in the four S's: Sincerity, Simplicity, Sympathy, Serenity.

Emily Post

LANDSCAPE

It was a soft, reposeful summer landscape, as lovely as a dream, and as lonesome as Sunday.

Mark Twain

LANGUAGE

If language is not correct, then what is said is not what is meant; if what is said is not what is meant, then what ought to be done remains undone.

Confucius

Language, particularly language in public, is very serious business because the way people talk is an indication of the way they are, how they feel, where they put the limits, where their culture is. If measuring offensive language in American culture tells us anything, it is that something elemental has changed since mid-century, leaving us awash in a four-letter-word frenzy.

Charles Madigan

Language most shews a man: Speak, that I may see thee.

Ben Jonson

Language is the amber in which a thousand precious thoughts have been safely embedded and pre-served.

Richard Trench

I wonder what language truck drivers are using, now that every-one is using theirs?

Beryl Pfizer

Man invented language to satisfy his deep need to complain.

Lily Tomlin

Since the concepts people live by are derived only from perceptions and from language and since the perceptions are received and inter-preted only in light of earlier con-cepts, man comes pretty close to living in a house that language built.

Russell R.W. Smith

As the Latin languages are not composed of two diverse elements, as English is of Latin and German, so the Latin mind does not have two spheres of sentiment, one vulgar and the other sublime. All changes are variations on a single key, which is the key of intelligence.

George Santayana

Language exerts a hidden power, like a moon on the tides.

Rita Mae Brown

In language, the ignorant have pre-scribed laws to the learned.

Richard Duppa

The limits of my language mean the limits of my world.

Ludwig Wittgenstein

Language is a part of our organism and no less complicated than it.

Ludwig Wittgenstein

Language is a cracked kettle on which we beat out tunes for bears to dance to, while all the time we long to move the stars to pity.

Gustave Flaubert

A different language is a different vision of life.

Federico Fellini

Language is the most imperfect and expensive means yet discov-ered for communicating thought.

William James

Those who know nothing of for-eign languages know nothing of their own.

Johann Wolfgang von Goethe

The difference between the right word and the almost right word is the difference between lightning and the lightning bug.

Mark Twain

There are hundreds of languages in the world, but a smile speaks them all.

Unknown

No one has a finer command of language than the person who keeps his mouth shut.

Sam Rayburn

Language is a city to the building of which every human being brought a stone.

Ralph Waldo Emerson

LATENESS

I have noticed that the people who are late are often so much jollier than the people who have to wait for them.

E.V. Lucas

LAUGHTER

Strange, when you come to think of it, that of all the countless folk who have lived before our time on this planet, not one is known in history or in legend as having died of laughter.

Max Beerbohm

Among those whom I like, I can find no common denominator, but among those whom I love, I can; all of them make me laugh.

W.H. Auden

There are some things that are so serious you have to laugh at them.

Niels Bohr

The world should laugh more. But after having eaten.

Cantinflas

Laugh when you can. Everything has its time.

Voltaire

He who laughs last has not heard the bad news.

Bertolt Brecht

Laughter is the shortest distance between two people.

Victor Borge

In this life, he laughs longest who laughs last.

John Masefield

The most wasted of all days is one without laughter.

E.E. Cummings

It's an odd job, making decent people laugh.

Molière

I am irrevocably betrothed to laughter, the sound of which has always seemed to me the most civilized music in the world.

Peter Ustinov

There is a kind of laughter people laugh at public events, as if a joke were a charity auction and they want to be seen to be bidding.

William McIlvanney

Mick Jagger told me that the lines on his face were laughter lines, but nothing is that funny.

George Melly

When people are laughing, they're generally not killing each other.
Alan Alda

If you were God, would you have invented laughter?
Christopher Fry

It better befits a man to laugh at life than to lament it.
Seneca

No one is more profoundly sad than he who laughs too much.
Jean-Paul Richter

Laughter is an instant Vacation.
Milton Berle

What soap is to the body, laughter is to the soul.
Yiddish proverb

A good laugh and a long sleep are the best cures in the doctor's book.
Irish proverb

A hearty laugh gives one a dry cleaning, while a good cry is a wet wash.
Puzant Kevork Thomajan

I've always thought that a big laugh is really a loud noise from the soul saying, "Ain't that the truth."
Quincy Jones

Maturity is a bitter disappointment for which no remedy exists, unless laughter can be said to remedy anything.
Kurt Vonnegut

Remember, men need laughter sometimes more than food.
Anna Fellows Johnston

With the fearful strain that is on me night and day, if I did not laugh I should die.
Abraham Lincoln

Whoever said "laughter is the best medicine" never had gonorrhea.
Kat Likkel and John Hoberg

Seven days without laughter makes one weak.
Mort Walker

I am always thankful for laughter, except when milk comes out of my nose.
Woody Allen

Laughter is a most healthful exertion; it is one of the greatest helps to digestion with which I am acquainted; and the custom prevalent among our forefathers, of exciting it at table by jesters and buffoons, was founded on true medical principles.
Christoph Wilhelm Hufeland

We must laugh at man to avoid crying for him.
Napoleon Bonaparte

Everybody laughs the same in every language because laughter is a universal connection.
Yakov Smirnoff

LAURELS
Nothing is harder on your laurels than resting on them.
Anonymous

LAW

Laws are like cobwebs that entangle the weak, but are broken by the strong.

Solon

Laws are spider webs through which the big flies pass and the little ones get caught.

Honoré de Balzac

The reason of the law is the law.

Walter Scott

The law often allows what honour forbids.

Jacques Saurin

Law is the backbone which keeps man erect.

S.C. Yuter

The law must be stable, but it must not stand still.

Roscoe Pound

To be completely free one must be a slave to a set of laws.

Cicero

Laws, like houses, lean on one another.

Edmund Burke

The law, in its majestic equality, forbids the rich as well as the poor to sleep under bridges and to steal bread.

Anatole France

Laws were made to be broken.

Christopher North

Law is order; and good law is good order.

Aristotle

Laws grind the poor and rich men rule the law.

Oliver Goldsmith

Much as he is opposed to law-breaking, he is not bigoted about it.

Damon Runyon

The Lord Chief Justice of England recently said that the greater part of his judicial time was spent investigating collisions between propelled vehicles, each on its own side of the road, each sounding its horn and each stationary.

Philip Guedalla

It is to be regretted that the rich and powerful all too often bend the acts of government to their selfish purpose ... In the full enjoyment of the gifts of Heaven and the fruits of superior industry, economy, and virtue, every man is equally entitled to protection by law.

Andrew Jackson

The law is a sort of hocus-pocus science.

Charles Macklin

Laws can be wrong and laws can be cruel. And the people who live only by the law are both wrong and cruel.

Josef Mischel and Ardel Wray

Good people do not need laws to tell them to act responsibly, while bad people will find a way around the laws.

Plato

Probably all laws are useless; for good men do not need laws at all, and bad men are made no better by them.

Demonax the Cynic

Even when laws have been written down, they ought not always to remain unaltered.

Aristotle

Good laws have their origins in bad morals.

Ambrosius Macrobius

The law is made to protect the innocent by punishing the guilty.

Daniel Webster

How long soever it hath continued, if it be against reason, it is of no force in law.

Sir Edward Coke

Unnecessary laws are not good laws, but traps for money.

Thomas Hobbes

It is illegal to make liquor privately or water publicly.

Lord Birkett

The life of the law has not been logic: it has been experience.

Oliver Wendell Holmes

The safety of the people shall be the highest law.

Cicero

The world abounds with laws and teems with crimes.

Unknown

Ignorance of the law excuses no man.

John Selden

LAW ENFORCEMENT

Every society gets the kind of criminals it deserves. What is equally true is that every community gets the kind of law enforcement it insists on.

Robert F. Kennedy

The execution of the laws is more important than the making of them.

Thomas Jefferson

LAWSUIT

Lawsuit, *n.* A machine which you go into as a pig and come out as a sausage.

Ambrose Bierce

I never was ruined but twice – once when I lost a lawsuit, and once when I gained one.

Voltaire

LAWYERS

There is no law without lawyers.

Roscoe Pound

Whatever else their contributions may be to our society, lawyers could be an important source of protein.

The Globe and Mail

Lawyers know that truth is a kind of seeming, a subtle blend of what is demonstrable and what cannot be disproved.

John le Carré

They have no lawyers in Utopia for they consider them as a sort of people whose profession it is to disguise matters.

Sir Thomas More

A businessman who had just returned from a consultation with his attorney recounted his experience to a friend.

"But why pay all that money to a lawyer?" his friend asked. "Didn't you see all those books in his office? The answer to your problem was right there!"

"Yes," the businessman replied, "but the lawyer knows what page it's on!"

Unknown

No brilliance is needed in the law. Nothing but common sense and relatively clean fingernails.

John Mortimer

As your attorney, it is my duty to inform you that it is not important that you understand what I'm doing or why you're paying me so much money. What's important is that you continue to do so.

Hunter S. Thompson

The lawyer's first thought in the morning is how to handle the case of the ringing alarm clock.

Edward Packard, Jr

Lawyers are like rhinoceroses: thick-skinned, short-sighted, and always ready to charge.

David Mellor

Most lawyers who win a case advise their clients that "We have won," and when justice has frowned upon their cause that "You have lost."

Louis Nizer

It might be pardonable to refuse to defend some men, but to defend them negligently is nothing short of criminal.

Cicero

Everything you learn here will go for naught if you forget the fundamental rule – when it becomes apparent that somebody on your side is headed for jail, make sure it's your client.

Chauncy Depew

I don't want a lawyer to tell me what I cannot do; I hire him to tell me how to do what I want to do.

J.P. Morgan

I don't think you can make a lawyer honest by an act of legislature. You've got to work on his conscience. And his lack of conscience is what makes him a lawyer.

Will Rogers

If there were no bad people, there would be no good lawyers.

Charles Dickens

LAZINESS
Failure is not our only punishment for laziness: There is also the success of others.

Jules Renard

We make a mistake if we believe that only the violent passions like ambition and love can subdue the others. Laziness, for all her languor, is nevertheless often mistress; she permeates every aim and action in life and imperceptibly eats away and destroys passions and virtues alike.

François, duc de La Rochefoucauld

LEADER

As long as I am your leader I am going to tell you when you are wrong and I will congratulate you when you are right.

Nelson Mandela

The successful person, in any field, takes time out to confer with himself or herself … Real leaders use solitude to put the pieces of a problem together, to work out solutions, and to plan.

Dr David Schwartz

A born leader of men is somebody who is afraid to go anywhere by himself.

Clifford Hanley

Leaders are people who do the right thing: managers are people who do things right. Both roles are crucial, but they differ profoundly. I often observe people in top positions doing the wrong thing well.

Warren Bennis

O ye who lead, take heed! / Blindness we may forgive, but baseness we will smite.

William Vaughn Moody

The real leader has no need to lead – he is content to point the way.

Henry Miller

It is very comforting to believe that leaders who do terrible things are, in fact, mad. That way, all we have to do is make sure we don't put psychotics in high places and we've got the problem solved.

Tom Wolfe

It's hard to lead a cavalry charge if you think you look funny on a horse.

Adlai Stevenson

Whomsoever you follow, however great he might be, see to it that you follow the spirit of the master and not imitate him mechanically.

Mohandas Gandhi

Never follow anybody who's working less than you.

Ellis Marsalis

The first duty of a leader is to make himself be loved without courting love. To be loved without "playing up" to anyone – even to himself.

André Malraux

A good leader inspires others with confidence in him; a great leader inspires them with confidence in themselves.

Chinese proverb

Good leaders make people feel that they're at the very heart of things, not at the periphery.

Warren Bennis

Of a good leader who talks little when his work is done … [his followers] will say, "We did it ourselves."

Lao-Tse

There they go. I must hurry after them for I am their leader!

Anonymous

Those who profess to lead … are simply the fastest runners and the loudest squeakers of the herd which is rushing blindly down to its destruction.

Thomas Henry Huxley

To earn his keep a good and wise ruler shares the work of tilling the land with his people. He rules while cooking his own meals.

Hsu Hsing-liang

It is when a leader has to move from "Yes we can" to "No you can't" that he is tested.

Matthew Parris

Not all readers are leaders, but all leaders are readers.

Harry S. Truman

The secret of a leader lies in the tests he has faced over the whole course of his life and the habit of action he develops in meeting those tests.

Gail Sheehy

The final test of a leader is that he leaves behind him in other men the conviction and will to carry on.

Walter Lippmann

A good leader takes a little more than his share of the blame; a little less than his share of the credit.

Arnold Glasgow

The acts of the leader are the acts of the nation. If the leader is just,

the nation is just; if he is unjust, the nation too is unjust and is punished for the sins of the leader.

Zohar

I learned from history that a leader is a man who has the ability to make other people do what they don't want to do, and like it.

Harry S. Truman

The real leader has no need to lead – he is content to point the way.

Henry Miller

LEADERSHIP

Anyone can hold the helm when the sea is calm.

Publilius Syrus

In calm water, every ship has a good captain.

German proverb

To have his path made clear for him is the aspiration of every human being in our beclouded and tempestuous existence.

Joseph Conrad

Every leader starts by first leading himself.

Norman Bethune

Too bad all the people who know how to run the country are busy driving taxi cabs and cutting hair.

George Burns

When the eagles are silent, the parrots begin to jabber.

Winston Churchill

The art of life is the art of avoiding pain; and he is the best pilot, who steers clearest of the rocks and shoals with which it is beset.

Thomas Jefferson

Absolute identity with one's cause is the first and great condition of successful leadership.

Woodrow Wilson

Leadership is not about being nice. It's about being right and being strong.

Paul Keating

Management is doing things right; leadership is doing the right things.

Peter Drucker

Leadership and learning are indispensable to each other.

John F. Kennedy

Leadership is getting the right people to do the right thing for the right reason in the right way at the right time at the right use of resources.

Clark Crouch

No wind is favourable if we do not know in which port we are trying to sail.

Rev. Dale Turner

Perhaps the most central characteristic of authentic leadership is the relinquishing of the impulse to dominate others.

David Cooper

The shepherd always tries to persuade the sheep that their interests and his own are the same.

Stendhal

Authority is a poor substitute for leadership.

John Luther

Leadership consists not in degrees of technique but in traits of character; it requires moral rather than athletic or intellectual effort, and it imposes on both leader and follower alike the burdens of self-restraint.

Lewis Lapham

The art of leadership is saying no, not saying yes. It is very easy to say yes.

Tony Blair

Surround yourself with the best people you can find, delegate authority, and don't interfere as long as the policy you've decided upon is being carried out.

Ronald Reagan

LEARN
You live and learn. At any rate, you live.

Douglas Adams

Oh, when will they ever learn?

Pete Seeger

It is impossible for a man to begin to learn what he thinks he knows.

Epictetus

All human beings should try to learn before they die what they are running from, and to, and why.

James Thurber

The brighter you are, the more you have to learn.

Don Herold

We learn something every day, and lots of times it's that what we learned the day before was wrong.
Bill Vaughan

Those who receive with most pains and difficulty remember best; every one thing they learn being, as it were, burnt and branded on their minds.

Plutarch

Live as if you were to die tomorrow. Learn as if you were to live forever.

Mohandas Gandhi

A man who carries a cat by the tail learns something he can learn in no other way.

Mark Twain

LEARNED
A learned man is an idler who kills time with study. Beware of his false knowledge: it is more dangerous than ignorance.

George Bernard Shaw

He that lives well is learned enough.
George Herbert

LEARNING
Learning is a treasure which follows its owner everywhere.

Chinese proverb

The only things worth learning are the things you learn after you know it all.

Harry S. Truman

Learning is not child's play; we cannot learn without pain.

Aristotle

Learning is not compulsory; neither is survival.
W. Edwards Deming

Some people will never learn anything, for this reason: Because they understand everything too soon.
Alexander Pope

You have learnt something. That always feels at first as if you had lost something.
George Bernard Shaw

It is better to be able neither to read nor write than to be able to do nothing else.
William Hazlitt

Learn as much by writing as by reading.
Lord Acton

When the student is ready, the lesson appears.
Gene Oliver

Much learning does not teach understanding.
Heraclitus

Things take indeed a wondrous turn/When learned men do stoop to learn.
Bertolt Brecht

A learned man is an idler who kills time with study.
George Bernard Shaw

A little learning is a dangerous thing;/Drink deep, or taste not the Pierian Spring.
Alexander Pope

The wisest mind has something yet to learn.

George Santayana

Beware of the man who works hard to learn something, learns it, and finds himself no wiser than before.

Kurt Vonnegut

I have always had a curious nature; I enjoy learning, but I dislike being taught.

Winston Churchill

The purpose of learning is growth, and our minds, unlike our bodies, can continue growing as long as we live.

Mortimer J. Adler

It is what we think we know already that often prevents us from learning.

Claude Bernard

Anyone who stops learning is old, whether at twenty or eighty.

Henry Ford

Seeing much, suffering much, and studying much, are the three pillars of learning.

Benjamin Disraeli

LECTURES
Most people tire of a lecture in ten minutes; clever people can do it in five. Sensible people never go to lectures at all.

Stephen Leacock

LEGISLATORS
When buying and selling are controlled by legislation, the first things to be bought and sold are legislators.

P.J. O'Rourke

LEISURE
People who know how to employ themselves always find leisure moments, while those who do nothing are forever in a hurry.

Marie-Jeanne Roland

It is in the improvident use of our leisure, I suspect, that the greatest wastes of American life occur.

Robert Park

The future will belong not only to the educated man, but to the man who is educated to use his leisure wisely.

C.K. Brightbill

Your job today tells me nothing of your future – your use of your leisure today tells me just what your tomorrow will be.

Robert H. Jackson

We are closer to the ants than to the butterflies. Very few people can endure much leisure.

Gerald Brenan

If you can spend a perfectly useless afternoon in a perfectly useless manner, you have learned how to live.

Lin Yutang

Leisure is work you volunteer for.

Robert Robinson

The superficiality of the American is the result of his hustling. It needs leisure to think things out; it needs leisure to mature. People in a hurry cannot think, cannot grow.

Eric Hoffer

LEND

It is better to give than to lend, and it costs about the same.

Philip Gibbs

LESBIAN

It's so tiring, making love with women, it takes forever. I'm too lazy to be a lesbian. Let me get a little air.

Camille Paglia

LESS

Less is more.

Robert Browning

LESSONS

When you lose, do not lose the lesson.

Dalai Lama

There are who teach only the sweet lessons of peace and safety /But I teach lessons of war and death to those I love.

Walt Whitman

LET

A Zen master once asked an audience of Westerners what they thought was the most important word in the English language. After giving his listeners the chance to think about such favourite words as love, truth, failure, and so on, he said, "No, it's a three letter word; it's the word 'let.' Let it be. Let it happen."

W. Timothy Gallwey

LETTING GO

It's all right letting yourself go as long as you can let yourself back.

Mick Jagger

LIARS

The liar's punishment is not in the least that he is not believed but that he cannot believe anyone else.

George Bernard Shaw

He led a double life. Did that make him a liar? He did not feel a liar. He was a man of two truths.

Iris Murdoch

The most mischievous liars are those who keep sliding on the edge of truth.

Julius and Augustus Hare

The reason we hate a liar is not his immorality, but his gall in thinking that we'd believe him.

Charles P. Curtis

I was brought up in a clergyman's household so I am a first-class liar.

Dame Sybil Thorndike

No one is such a liar as the indignant man.

Friedrich Nietzsche

LIBERAL

We who are liberal and progressive know that the poor are our equals in every sense except that of being equal to us.

Lionel Trilling

A liberal is someone who feels a great debt to his fellow man, which debt he proposes to pay off with your money.

G. Gordon Liddy

A liberal is a conservative who has been arrested.

Tom Wolfe

A liberal is a person whose interests aren't at stake at the moment.
Willis Player

A liberal is a man too broadminded to take his own side in a quarrel.

Robert Frost

I can remember way back when a liberal was one who was generous with his own money.

Will Rogers

Liberals claim to want to give a hearing to other views, but then are shocked and offended to discover that there are other views.

William F. Buckley, Jr

LIBERTY

Liberty is a right of doing whatever the laws permit; and if a citizen could do what they forbid, he would no longer be possessed of liberty, because all of his fellow-citizens would have the same power.

Montesquieu

They that give up essential liberty to obtain a little temporary safety deserve neither liberty nor safety.

Benjamin Franklin

Liberty, too, must be limited to be possessed.

Edmund Burke

In my youth I stressed freedom, and in my old age I stress order. I have made the great discovery that liberty is a product of order.

Will Durant

Liberty too can corrupt, and absolute liberty can corrupt absolutely.

Gertrude Himmelfarb

Liberty doesn't work as well in practice as it does in speeches.

Will Rogers

I prefer liberty to chains of diamonds.

Lady Mary Wortley Montagu

The liberty of the individual must be thus far limited: he must not make himself a nuisance to other people.

John Stuart Mill

Eternal vigilance is the price of liberty.

Thomas Jefferson

Liberty is a beloved discipline.
George Caspar Homans

O Liberty! what crimes are committed in thy name.

Marie-Jeanne Roland

Liberty is being free from the things we don't like in order to be slaves of the things we do like.

Ernest Benn

If liberty means anything at all, it means the right to tell people what they do not want to hear.

George Orwell

Liberty does not consist merely of denouncing Tyranny, any more than horticulture does of deploring and abusing weeds, or even pulling them out.

Arthur Bryant

The only liberty an inferior man really cherishes is the liberty to quit work, stretch out in the sun, and scratch himself.

H.L. Mencken

Liberty means responsibility. That is why most men dread it.

George Bernard Shaw

A free spirit takes liberties even with liberty itself.

Francis Picabia

Liberty is the one thing you can't have unless you give it to others.

William Allen White

It behooves every man who values liberty of conscience for himself, to resist invasions of it in the case of others.

Thomas Jefferson

The liberties of none are safe unless the liberties of all are protected.

William O. Douglas

The spirit of liberty is the spirit which is not too sure that it is right.

Billings Learned Hand

The same liberty that protects me also protects members of the Mafia.

Barbara Amiel

LIBRARIES

A library, to modify the famous metaphor of Socrates, should be the delivery room for the birth of ideas – a place where history comes to life.

Norman Cousins

My library was dukedom large enough.

William Shakespeare

If you file your waste-paper basket for fifty years, you have a public library.

Tony Benn

Your library is your portrait.

Holbrook Jackson

When an old man dies a library burns down.

African proverb

Libraries are the collective memory of mankind

Herbert Samuel

LIES

A lie which is half a truth is ever the blackest of lies.

Alfred, Lord Tennyson

Never chase a lie. Let it alone and it will run itself to death.

Lyman Beecher

I do not mind lying, but I hate inaccuracy.

Samuel Butler

A lie has always a certain amount of weight with those who wish to believe it.

E.W. Rice

If a lie is repeated often enough all the dumb jackasses in the world not only get to believe it, they even swear by it.

Billy Boy Franklin

A lie told often enough becomes the truth.

Vladimir Lenin

If you tell a big enough lie and tell it frequently enough, it will be believed.

Adolf Hitler

Repetition does not transform a lie into truth.

Franklin D. Roosevelt

A lie can be halfway around the world before the truth has got its boots on.

James Callaghan

We lie loudest when we lie to ourselves.

Eric Hoffer

In human relations kindness and lies are worth 1,000 truths.

Graham Greene

There are three kinds of lies – lies, damned lies, and statistics.

Mark Twain

Whoever would lie usefully, should lie seldom.

Lord Hervey

The cruelest lies are often told in silence.

Robert Louis Stevenson

There is no greater lie than a truth misunderstood.

William James

Pretending that you believe a liar is also a lie.

Arthur Schnitzler

I have been tempted to make a proposal to our Republican friends; that if they stop telling lies about us, we would stop telling the truth about them.

Adlai Stevenson

Husband a lie, and trump it up in some extraordinary emergency.

Joseph Addison

One lies to oneself more than to anyone else.

Lord Byron

Truth is beautiful, without doubt; but so are lies.

Ralph Waldo Emerson

White lies are but the ushers to black ones.

Frederick Marryat

Those who think it permissible to tell a white lie soon grow colourblind.

Arthur O'Malley

A lie is an abomination unto the Lord and a very present help in trouble.

Adlai Stevenson

Half the lies they tell about me aren't true.

Yogi Berra

And after all what is a lie?/'Tis but/the truth in masquerade.

Lord Byron

LIFE

My theory is to enjoy life, but the practice is against it.

Charles Lamb

We are always complaining that our days are few, and acting as though there would be no end of them.

Seneca

Life is divided into the horrible and the miserable.

Woody Allen

Life is full of misery, loneliness, and suffering – and it's all over much too soon.

Woody Allen

Life is too short for men to take it seriously.

George Bernard Shaw

Life is like a game of cards. The hand that is dealt you represents determinism; the way you play it is free will.

Jawaharlal Nehru

Life is a tragedy full of joy.

Bernard Malamud

Life is like riding a bicycle. You don't fall off unless you stop pedalling.

Claude Pepper

Henceforth I shall accept what I am and what I am not. With my limitations and my gifts, I shall go on using life as long as I am in this world and afterwards. Not to use life – that alone is death.

George Sand

Life is too short to be little.

Benjamin Disraeli

Life is one long process of getting tired.

Samuel Butler

We do not know what to do with this short life, yet we yearn for another that will be eternal.

Anatole France

Life is strange. Every so often a good man wins.

Frank Dane

Life is a dream for the wise, a game for the fool, a comedy for the rich, a tragedy for the poor.

Sholem Aleichem

Life is like playing a violin solo in public and learning the instrument as one goes on.

Samuel Butler

One must live the way one thinks or end up thinking the way one has lived.

Paul Bourget

To die and not be lost is the real blessing of a long life.

Lao-Tse

There are two things to aim at in life: first, to get what you want; and, after that, to enjoy it. Only the wisest of mankind achieve the second.

Logan Pearsall Smith

I'm not going to starve to death just so I can live a little longer.

Irene Peter

Life is hard. After all, it kills you.
Katherine Hepburn

How long do you have to live before the odds of getting to your next birthday are worse than 50:50? The answer is encouraging – 104.
Norris McWhirter

There are two ways to slide easily through life: to believe everything or to doubt everything: both ways save us from thinking.
Alfred Korzybski

There is an ambush everywhere from the army of accidents; therefore the rider of life runs with loosened reins.
Hafiz

You have a choice of two things in life: remembering and hoping.
Paul Villeneuve

Life does not consist mainly – or even largely – of facts and happenings. It consists mainly of the storm of thoughts that is forever blowing through one's head.
Mark Twain

Life is either a daring adventure or nothing.
Helen Keller

Life is a succession of lessons enforced by immediate reward, or, oftener, by immediate chastisement.
Ernest Dimnet

We arrive at the various stages of life quite as novices.
François, duc de La Rochefoucauld

The best part of our lives we pass in counting on what is to come.
William Hazlitt

Few people make all of life's journey on a green light.
Dr Ernest A. Fitzgerald

Somehow life doesn't always pay off to those who are most insistent.
Max Lerner

Life is too short for traffic.
Dan Bellack

The world is so constructed that if you wish to enjoy its pleasures, you must also endure its pains. Whether you like it or not, you cannot have one without the other.
Brahmananda

If you look at life one way, there is always cause for alarm.
Elizabeth Bowen

Life for the European is a career; for the American, it is a hazard.
Mary McCarthy

Life is a campaign, not a battle, and has its defeats as well as its victories.
Don Platt

The art of living is more like wrestling than dancing.
Marcus Aurelius

Life is not a spectator sport.
Jackie Robinson

Life, I fancy, would very often be insupportable, but for the luxury of self-compassion.
George Gissing

I finally figured out the only reason to be alive is to enjoy it.

Rita Mae Brown

Life is change. Growth is optional. Choose wisely.

Karen Kaiser Clark

Not only is life a bitch, it has puppies.

Adrienne E. Gusoff

Life is made up of two phases. In the first you try to make a name for yourself and in the second you try to keep it.

Bits & Pieces

I think the purpose of life is to be happy, to be useful, to be responsible, to be honourable, to be compassionate. It is, above all, to matter; to count, to stand for something, to have made a difference that you lived at all.

Leo Rosten

Life is made up of constant calls to action, and we seldom have time for more than hastily contrived answers.

Billings Learned Hand

Life's under no obligation to give us what we expect.

Margaret Mitchell

Live your life so that if someone says "Be yourself," it's good advice.

Robert Orwen

If I were to begin life again, I should want it as it was. I would only open my eyes a little more.

Jules Renard

The difficulty in life is the choice.

George Moore

The great secret of life is to learn lessons, not to teach them.

Thomas Chandler Haliburton

Life is short, art long, opportunity fleeting, experience treacherous, judgment difficult.

Hippocrates

It's life, Jim … but not as we know it.

Spock

The basic fact about human existence is not that it is a tragedy, but that it is a bore. It is not so much a war as an endless standing in line.

H.L. Mencken

What a rotten writer of detective stories life is.

Nathan Leopold

Life flows on within you and without you.

George Harrison

Human life is mainly a process of filling in time until the arrival of death or Santa Claus.

Eric Berne

Life is not for everyone.

Michael O'Donoghue

Try to arrange your life in such a way that you can afford to be disinterested. It is the most expensive of all luxuries, and the one best worth having.

Dean Inge

Life may have no meaning. Or, even worse, it may have a meaning of which I disapprove.

Ashley Brilliant

If you want my final opinion on the mystery of life and all that, I can give it to you in a nutshell. The universe is like a safe to which there is a combination. But the combination is locked up in the safe.

Peter De Vries

That's the secret to life – replace one worry with another.

Charles M. Schultz

By his very success in inventing labour-saving devices, modern man has manufactured an abyss of boredom that only the privileged classes in earlier civilizations have ever fathomed.

Lewis Mumford

Life is made up of marble and mud.

Nathaniel Hawthorne

Life is a copiously branching bush, continually pruned by the grim reaper of extinction, not a ladder of predictable progress.

Stephen Jay Gould

Organic life, we are told, has developed gradually from the protozoon to the philosopher, and this development, we are assured, is indubitably an advance. Unfortunately, it is the philosopher, not the protozoon, who gives us this assurance.

Bertrand Russell

It is only knowing how little life has in store for us that we are able to look upon the bright side and avoid disappointment.

Ellen Glasgow

Life's a tough proposition, and the first hundred years are the hardest.

Wilson Mizner

Life is a great bundle of little things.

Oliver Wendell Holmes

Life is a gamble at terrible odds – if it was a bet, you wouldn't take it.

Tom Stoppard

Life after fifty: Your back goes out more than you do.

Rex Guinn

You make a living by what you get. You make a life by what you give.

Winston Churchill

Life is not a spectacle or a feast; it is a predicament.

George Santayana

We live in a rainbow of Chaos.

Paul Cézanne

The fullness of life is in the hazards of life.

Edith Hamilton

If you don't run your own life, somebody else will.

John Atkinson

It takes a lifetime to know what to do with life.

Juliette Greco

An imaginative man is apt to see, in his life, the story of his life; and is thereby led to conduct himself in his life in such a manner as to make a good story of it rather than a good life.

Sir Henry Taylor

No one achieves a house by blueprints alone, no matter how accurate or detailed. A time comes when one must take up hammer and nails. In building a house, the making of blueprints may be delegated to an architect, the construction to a carpenter. In building the house of one's life or in its remodelling, one may delegate nothing.

Allen Wheelis

Life is a long lesson in humility.

J.M. Barrie

I'd always assumed I was the central character in my own story, but now it occurred to me I might in fact be only a minor character in someone else's.

Russell Hoban

I don't want the cheese; I just want out of the trap.

Graffito

Life is not a static thing. The only people who do not change their minds are incompetents in asylums, who can't, and those in cemeteries.

Everett M. Dirksen

My grandfather always said that living is like licking honey off a thorn.

Louis Adamic

Life is very singularly made to surprise us (when it does not utterly appall us).

Rainer Maria Rilke

We live our lives, forever taking leave.

Rainer Maria Rilke

One must choose in life between boredom and torment.

Madame de Staël

In life, as in chess, one's own pawns block one's way. A man's very wealth, ease, leisure, children, books, which should help him to win, more often checkmate him.

Charles Buxton

Life depends on awkward people.

Margaret Thatcher

Life is a zoo in a jungle.

Peter De Vries

Though we seem grieved at the shortness of life in general, we are wishing every period of it at an end.

Joseph Addison

Life is uncertain. Eat dessert first.

Ernestine Ulmer

We are always getting to live, but never living.

Ralph Waldo Emerson

Life is a succession of lessons which must be lived to be understood.

Ralph Waldo Emerson

The true meaning of life is to plant trees, under whose shade you do not expect to sit.

Nelson Henderson

The tragedy of life is not that man loses but that he almost wins.
Heywood Broun

Flops are part of life's menu, and I've never been a girl to miss out on any of the courses.
Rosalind Russell

Life is something to do when you can't get to sleep.
Fran Lebowitz

The life which is unexamined is not worth living.
Plato

All that matters is love and work.
Sigmund Freud

To be able to enjoy one's past life is to live twice.
Martial

In three words I can sum up everything I've learned about life: it goes on.
Robert Frost

It's a funny old world – a man's lucky if he gets out alive.
W.C. Fields

Life would be tolerable but for its amusements.
Sir George Cornewall Lewis

I long ago came to the conclusion that all life is six to five against.
Damon Runyon

Life is made up of sobs, sniffles, and smiles, with sniffles predominating.
O. Henry

Human life begins on the other side of despair.
Jean-Paul Sartre

The goal of life is living in agreement with nature.
Zeno of Citium

The essential of life is statistical improbability on a colossal scale.
Richard Dawkins

Life is what happens to you when you're busy making other plans.
John Lennon

Life is what is happening to us while we are making other plans.
Allen Saunders

Life isn't fair. It's just fairer than death, that's all.
William Goldman

Oh, isn't life a terrible thing, thank God?
Dylan Thomas

Man is born to live, not to prepare for life.
Boris Pasternak

To beautify life is to give it an object.
Jose Marti

Life is like an onion: you peel it off one layer at a time and sometimes you weep.
Carl Sandburg

Don't take life too seriously – you will never get out of it alive.
Elbert Hubbard

Life isn't meant to be easy. It's hard to take being on the top – or on the bottom.

Richard M. Nixon

Life is what happens to us while we are making other plans.

Thomas La Mance

Everyone sees life through their job. To the doctor, the world is a hospital, to the broker it is a stock exchange, to the lawyer a vast criminal court, to the soldier a barracks and area of manoeuvre, to the farmer soil and bad weather, to truck drivers a road system, to dustmen a midden, to prostitutes a brothel, to mothers an inescapable nursery, to children a school, to film stars a looking-glass, to undertakers a morgue, and to myself as a security installation powered by the sun and only crackable by death.

Alasdair Gray

You're only here for a short visit. Don't hurry. Don't worry. And be sure to smell the flowers along the way.

Walter Hagen

Life ain't all beer and skittles, and more's the pity, but what's the odds, so long as you're happy?

George du Maurier

I can't believe it's happened to me.

John Lennon/Paul McCartney

The most important things in life you cannot see – civility, justice, courage, peace.

Unknown

Life is a moderately good play with a badly written third act.

Truman Capote

All human beings should try to learn before they die what they are running from, and to, and why.

James Thurber

Life is the art of drawing without an eraser.

John W. Gardner

Life may not be the party we hoped for, but while we're here, we should dance.

Unknown

At first we do not know how to live; and when we know how to live it is too late.

Jean-Jacques Rousseau

The world is getting to be such a dangerous place, a man is lucky to get out of it alive.

W.C. Fields

Being a sprinter may be glamorous, but life is a distance event.

Margot Silk Forrest

I am convinced, both by faith and experience, that to maintain one's self on this Earth is not a hardship, but a pastime, if we will live simply and wisely.

Henry David Thoreau

Most people get a fair amount of fun out of their lives, but on balance life is suffering, and only the very young or the very foolish imagine otherwise.

George Orwell

Life is easier to take than you'd think; all that is necessary is to accept the impossible, do without the indispensable, and bear the intolerable.

Kathleen Thompson Norris

The tragedy of life is what dies inside a man while he lives.

Albert Schweitzer

Life is like a ten-speed bicycle. Most of us have gears we never use.

Charles M. Schultz

Let your life lightly dance on the edges of Time like dew on the tip of a leaf.

Rabindranath Tagore

Let your boat of life be light, packed with only what you need – a homely home and simple pleasures.

Jerome K. Jerome

Life is hard. I don't think dying's hard, but life is a lot of work.

June Callwood

Life is either always a tightrope or a featherbed. Give me a tightrope.

Edith Wharton

You learn to hate the small and the little. Life is a pie which you cut large slices, not grudgingly, not sparingly.

Alice Foote MacDougall

We cannot tear out a single page of our life, but we can throw the whole book in the fire.

George Sand

Life is a train of moods, like a string of beads, and, as we pass through them, they prove to be many-coloured lenses which paint the world their own hue, and each shows only what lies in its focus.

Ralph Waldo Emerson

The art of life lies in a constant readjustment to our surroundings.

Okakura Kazuo

The worst-constructed play is a Bach fugue when compared to life.

Helen Hayes

As I look back upon my life, I see that every part of it was a preparation for the next.

Margaret Sanger

The longer I live, the more beautiful life becomes.

Frank Lloyd Wright

As for life, it is a battle and a sojourning in a strange land; but the fame that comes after is oblivion.

Marcus Aurelius

Life is like a sewer … what you get out of it depends on what you put into it.

Tom Lehrer

Better to live one year as a tiger than 1,000 as a sheep.

Tipu Sahib

Life is like an overlong drama through which we sit being nagged by the vague memories of having read the reviews.

John Updike

Life is the art of drawing sufficient conclusions from insufficient premises.

Samuel Butler

Life is like a foreign language; all men mispronounce it.

Christopher Morley

The greatest use of a life is to spend it for something that outlasts it.

Henry James

Let us endeavour so to live that when we come to die even the undertaker will be sorry.

Mark Twain

Life is a play! 'Tis not its length, but its performance that counts.

Seneca

Life is a game show where the people who enjoy it are the winners.

Orson Bean

After all, it is hard to master both life and work equally well. So if you are bound to fake one of them, it had better be life.

Joseph Brodsky

Life is a little bit like a message in a bottle, to be carried by the winds and the tides.

Gene Tierney

LIFE EXPECTANCY
It is astonishing to realize that the human species survived hundreds of thousands of years, more than ninety-nine per cent of its time on the planet, with a life expectancy of only eighteen years.

Leonard Hayflick

Life is a shipwreck but we must not forget to sing in the lifeboats.

Voltaire

Life hardens what is soft within us and softens what is hard.

Joseph Fort Newton

Life's a reckoning we cannot make twice over. You cannot amend a wrong subtraction by doing your addition right.

George Eliot

When people complain of life, it is almost always because they have asked impossible things of it.

Ernest Renan

Life expectancy would grow by leaps and bounds if green vegetables smelled as good as bacon.

Doug Larson

LIFE (MYSTERIES OF)
When we remember that we are all mad, the mysteries disappear and life stands explained.

Mark Twain

We must reach out and attempt to put our finger on this astonishing finesse, that the value of life cannot be assessed.

Friedrich Nietzsche

LIGHT
There are two ways of spreading light: to be/The candle or the mirror that reflects it.

Edith Wharton

There is a crack in everything, that's how the light gets in.

Leonard Cohen

If we want light, we must conquer darkness.

J.T. Fields

LIGHT BULBS

How many divorced men does it take to change a light bulb? None, because they never get the house.

How many Vietnam vets does it take to change a light bulb? You don't know, man. You weren't there.

Lenny Henry

LIGHTHOUSES

Lighthouses don't go running all over an island looking for boats to save; they just stand there shining.

Anne Lamott

LIGHTNING

It is the mountaintop that the lightning strikes.

Horace

LIKE

Some people will like me and some won't. So I might as well be myself, and then at least I'll know that the people who like me, like me.

Hugh Prather

We must love one another, yes, yes, that's all true enough, but nothing says we have to like each other.

Peter De Vries

Everything must be like something, so what is this like?

E.M. Forster

LIMITATIONS

Every man takes the limits of his own field of vision for the limits of the world.

Arthur Schopenhauer

Between the ages of twenty and forty, we are engaged in the process of discovering who we are, which involves learning the difference between accidental limitations, which it is our duty to outgrow, and the necessary limitations of our nature which we cannot trespass with impunity.

W.H. Auden

I have flying limitations, but I fly. I fly because we humans like to find ways to solve problems. It's one of the great gifts of our nature. If we can't fly, we invent airplanes. If we want to water our gardens, we invent hoses. It's what we do. … We all live around our limitations. Everybody does it. We just don't often think about it. Every cup of coffee we drink is living around the limitation that we can't hold steaming hot coffee using our bare hands as a cup. Every snowstorm we walk through wearing clothes and staying warm is living around the limitation that we don't grow fur.

Alison Bonds Shapiro

LIONS

It's better to be a lion for a day than a sheep all your life.

Sister Elizabeth Kenny

LISTEN

To listen is an effort, and just to hear is no merit. A duck hears also.
Igor Stravinsky

Give us the grace to listen well.
John Keble

He hears but half who hears one party only.
Aeschylus

No one really listens to anyone else, and if you try it for a while you'll see why.
Mignon McLaughlin

If you tell people what they want to hear, they'll listen to what you have to say.
Louis Morgante

The reason why we have two ears and only one mouth is that we may listen the more and talk the less.
Zeno of Citium

Nature has given to men one tongue, but two ears, that we may hear from others twice as much as we speak.
Epictetus

From listening comes wisdom, and from speaking, repentance.
Italian proverb

The hearing ear is always found close to the speaking tongue.
Emerson

A good listener is a silent flatterer.
Bits & Pieces

He listens well who takes notes.
Dante Alighieri

No one ever listened himself out of a job.
Calvin Coolidge

It is the disease of not listening, the malady of not marking, that I am troubled withal.
William Shakespeare

The older I grow, the more I listen to people who don't say much.
Germain Glidden

Think how much better we could all communicate if we tried to really listen to people on the other side – even if they are morons.
Faye Flam

LITERACY

The ratio of literacy to illiteracy is constant, but nowadays the illiterates can read and write.
Alberto Moravia

LITERATURE

Literature is the art of writing something that will be read twice; journalism what will be grasped at once.
Cyril Connolly

Literature is news that stays news.
Ezra Pound

If a nation's literature declines, the nation atrophies and decays.
Ezra Pound

The end of doubt is the beginning of prose.
Petrarch

Woe to that nation whose literature is cut short by intrusion of force.
Alexandr Solzhenitsyn

Nearly all literature, in one sense, is made up of guidebooks.
Herman Melville

In literature the ambition of the novice is to acquire the literary language; the struggle of the adept is to get rid of it.
George Bernard Shaw

Literature is landscape on the desk, and a landscape is literature on the earth.
Chang Chao

LITTLE
Little enemies and little wounds are not to be despised.
German proverb

Little things affect little minds.
Benjamin Disraeli

LIVE
To live means to finesse the processes to which one is subjugated.
Bertolt Brecht

Live as you would have wished to live when you are dying.
Christian Fürchtegott Gellert

One must live the way one thinks or end up thinking the way one has lived.

Paul Bourget

Live as if you expected to live a hundred years, but might die tomorrow.

Ann Lee

Only those live who do good.
Leo Tolstoy

LIVER
Your liver is the size and weight of a small chicken. It receives twenty-five per cent of the blood your heart pumps – more than two litres a minute. Without it, you'd be unable to digest a meal, and your cholesterol reading would go through the roof. And yet your liver grabs none of the recognition it deserves – until something goes wrong.
Men's Health

LIVES
Our individual lives cannot, generally, be works of art unless the social order is also.
Charles Horton Cooley

LIVING
The living are just the dead on holiday.

Maurice Maeterlinck

One can live for years sometimes without living at all, and then life comes crowding into one single hour.

Oscar Wilde

Living is like working out a long addition sum, and if you make a mistake in the first two totals, you will never find the right answer.

Cesare Pavese

This life is worth living, we can say, since it is what we make it.

William James

LOAN
I just need enough to tide me over
til I need more.
Bill Hoest

LOATHING
My loathings are simple: stupidity,
oppression, crime, cruelty, soft
music.
Vladimir Nabokov

LOGIC
Logic is like the sword – those who
appeal to it shall perish by it.
Samuel Butler

Logic is the art of making truth
prevail.
La Bruyère

No mistake is more common and
more fatuous than appealing to
logic in cases which are beyond her
jurisdiction.
Samuel Butler

If it was so, it might be; and if it
were so, it would be; but as it isn't,
it ain't. That's logic.
Lewis Carroll

Logic, too, rests on assumptions
that do not correspond to anything
in the real world.
Friedrich Nietzsche

Logic is the art of going wrong
with confidence.
Joseph Wood Krutch

Logical consequences are the scare-
crows of fools and the beacons of
wise men.
Thomas Henry Huxley

Logic: an instrument for bolstering
a prejudice.
Elbert Hubbard

LONELINESS
If you're lonely while you're alone,
you're in bad company.
Jean-Paul Sartre

Loneliness is the poverty of self;
solitude is the richness of self.
May Sarton

Why should I feel lonely: Is not our
planet in the Milky Way?
Henry David Thoreau

There is no lonelier man in death,
except the suicide, than a man who
has lived many years with a good
wife and then outlived her. If two
people love each other there can be
no happy end to it.
Ernest Hemingway

Loneliness is now so widespread it
has become, paradoxically, a
shared experience.
Alvin Toffler

Loneliness and cheeseburgers are a
dangerous mix.
Matt Groening

LOOKING BACK
Don't look back. Something may
be gaining on you.
Leroy (Satchel) Paige

LOSE
No man can lose what he never
had.
Izaak Walton

LOSER
If there was a contest to find the world's biggest loser, I'd win – unless there was a prize.

Stan Bowles

There are two kinds of losers: (1) the good loser, and (2) those who can't act.

Laurence J. Peter

He turned being a big loser into a perfect triumph.

Gore Vidal

Show me a good and gracious loser, and I'll show you a failure.

Knute Rockne

All the world loves a good loser.

Kin Hubbard

LOSING
Men hate to lose. I once beat my husband at tennis six-love six-love. I came right out and asked him, "Are we ever going to have sex again?" He said, "Yes, but not with each other."

Rita Rudner

Sometimes it is too late to win. But it's never too late to lose.

Tom Watson

The art of losing isn't hard to master.

Elizabeth Bishop

LOSS
It is better to lose the saddle than the horse.

Italian proverb

There are occasions when it is undoubtedly better to incur loss than to make gain.

Plautus

Sometimes, when one person is missing, the whole world seems depopulated.

Alphonse de Lamartine

LOST
A lost thing could I never find.

Hilaire Belloc

LOST SOULS
The real lost souls don't wear their hair long and play guitars. They have crew cuts, trained minds, sign on for research in biological warfare, and don't give their parents a moment's worry.

J.B. Priestley

LOTTERIES
There are few things in the world more reassuring than an unhappy lottery winner.

Tony Parsons

LOVABLE
To be loved, be lovable.

Ovid

LOVE
The love that dare not speak its name has become the neurosis that does not know when to shut up.

Time magazine

The art of love … is largely the art of persistence.

Dr Albert Ellis

When someone says, "It's better to have loved and lost than never to have loved at all," keep in mind you're talking to a loser. Try to find someone who's never loved at all and get their side of the story.

Rich Hall

Love: an ocean of emotions entirely surrounded by expenses.

Lord Thomas Dewar

A man when he is making up to anybody can be cordial and gallant and full of little attentions and altogether charming. But when a man is really in love he can't help looking like a sheep.

Agatha Christie

Love does not consist in gazing at each other, but in looking together in the same direction.

Antoine de Saint-Exupéry

Of course there is such a thing as love or there wouldn't be so many divorces.

Edgar Watson Howe

Civilized people cannot fully satisfy their sexual instinct without love.

Bertrand Russell

Four be things I'd been better without:/Love, curiosity, freckles, and doubt.

Dorothy Parker

There's nothing worth the wear of winning but laughter and the love of friends.

Hilaire Belloc

Love conquers all things except poverty and toothache.

Mae West

Love is the only disease that makes you feel better.

Sam Shepard

What will survive of us is love.

Philip Larkin

Love never dies of starvation, but often of indigestion.

Ninon de L'Enclos

Love is what we call the situation which occurs when two people who are sexually compatible discover that they can also tolerate each other in various other circumstances.

Marc Mailhuerd

The first duty of love is to listen.

Paul Tillich

I was taught when I was young that if people would only love one another, all would be well with the world. This seemed simple and very nice; but I found when I tried to put it in practice not only that other people were seldom lovable, but that I was not very lovable myself.

George Bernard Shaw

I believe that love produces a certain flowering of the whole personality which nothing else can achieve.

Ivan Turgenev

We are shaped and fashioned by what we love.

Johann Wolfgang von Goethe

The way to love anything is to realize that it might be lost.

> *G.K. Chesterton*

Love makes your soul crawl out from its hiding place.

> *Zora Neale Hurston*

A crowd is not company, and faces are but a gallery of pictures, and talk is but a tinkling cymbal, where there is no love.

> *Francis Bacon*

Love is what happens to a man and woman who don't know each other.

> *W. Somerset Maugham*

Love ... is the extremely difficult realization that something other than oneself is real.

> *Iris Murdoch*

Love is the triumph of imagination over intelligence.

> *H.L. Mencken*

Sometimes I wish I could fall in love. Then at least you know who your opponent is.

> *Peter Ustinov*

Love is an act of endless forgiveness, a tender look which becomes a habit.

> *Peter Ustinov*

Where they love they do not desire and where they desire they do not love.

> *Sigmund Freud*

I was in love with loving.

> *St Augustine*

Love doesn't just sit there, like a stone, it has to be made, like bread; remade all the time, made new.

> *Ursula K. Le Guin*

True love comes quietly, without banner or flashing lights.

> *Erich Segal*

Love is like any other luxury. You have no right to it unless you can afford it.

> *Anthony Trollope*

Real love is like a pilgrimage. It happens when there is no strategy, but it is very rare because most people are strategists.

> *Anita Brookner*

Love sets you going like a fat gold watch.

> *Sylvia Plath*

Love is space and time made perceptible to the heart.

> *Marcel Proust*

Falling out of love is one of the great human experiences.

> *Iris Murdoch*

Love is the noblest frailty of the mind.

> *John Dryden*

The wise man will love; all others will desire.

> *Afranius*

Do you want me to tell you something really subversive? Love is everything it's cracked up to be. That's why people are so cynical about it. ... It really is worth fighting for, being brave for, risking everything for. And the trouble is, if you don't risk anything, you risk even more.

Erica Jong

We've got this gift of love, but love is like a precious plant. You can't just accept it and leave it in the cupboard or just think it's going to get on by itself. You've got to keep watering it. You've got to really look after it and nurture it.

John Lennon

Love is not a state; it is a direction.

Simone Weil

Greater love than this hath no man that he should lay down his friends for his life.

Jeremy Thorpe

Love is what you've been through with somebody.

James Thurber

Passion may be blind; but to say that love is, is a libel and a lie. Nothing is more sharp-sighted or sensitive than true love, in discerning, as by an instinct, the feelings of another.

William H. Davis

Love and time, those are the only two things in all the world and all of life, that cannot be bought, but only spent.

Gary Jennings

Love is never defeated, and I could add, the history of Ireland proves it.

Pope John Paul II

Love is an exploding cigar we willingly smoke.

Lynda Barry

Everything terrible is something that needs our love.

Rainer Maria Rilke

Love is like the measles. The older you get it, the worse the attack.

Rainer Maria Rilke

Loving can cost a lot but not loving always costs more, and those who fear to love often find that want of love is an emptiness that robs the joy from life.

Merle Shain

Love is but the discovery of ourselves in others, and the delight in the recognition.

Alexander Smith

Love is the word used to label the sexual excitement of the young, the habituation of the middle-aged, and the mutual dependence of the old.

John Ciardi

Love keeps the cold out better than a cloak.

Henry Wadsworth Longfellow

People who are sensible about love are incapable of it.

Douglas Yates

Too much love will kill you / Just as sure as none at all.

*Brian May, Frank Musker,
and Elizabeth Lamers*

Those who love deeply never grow old.

Sir Arthur Pinero

Love is the irresistible desire to be irresistibly desired.

Robert Frost

One word frees us of all the weight and pain of life: that word is love.

Sophocles

True love stories never have endings.

Richard Bach

Love is the most subtle form of self-interest.

Holbrook Jackson

Love lives on propinquity and dies of contact.

Thomas Hardy

Love comes unseen – we only see it go.

Henry Austin Dobson

When you fish for love, bait with your heart, not your brain.

Mark Twain

Love is a snowmobile racing across the tundra and then suddenly it flips over, pinning you underneath. At night, the ice weasels come.

Matt Groening

LOVELINESS

I have a left shoulder-blade that is a miracle of loveliness. People come miles to see it.

W.S. Gilbert

LOVERS

The quarrels of lovers are like summer storms. Everything is more beautiful when they have passed.

Suzanne Necker

It is easier to keep half a dozen lovers guessing than to keep one lover after he has stopped guessing.

Helen Rowland

LOYALTY

You can buy people's time; you can buy their physical presence at a given place; you can even buy a measured number of their skilled muscular motions per hour. But you cannot buy enthusiasm ... you cannot buy loyalty ... you cannot buy the devotion of hearts, minds, or souls. You must earn these.

Clarence Francis

Fidelity bought with money can be overcome by money.

Seneca

I'll take fifty percent efficiency to get 100 percent loyalty.

Samuel Goldwyn

The children will not leave England unless I do. I shall not leave unless their father does, and the King will not leave the country in any circumstance.

Elizabeth, Queen Mother

Loyalty is a fine quality, but in excess it fills political graveyards.

Neil Kinnock

LUCK

I am a great believer in luck, and I find the harder I work, the more I have of it.

Stephen Leacock

The only sure thing about luck is that it will change.

Bret Harte

Some folk want their luck buttered.

Thomas Hardy

It is a great piece of skill to know how to guide your luck even while you're waiting for it.

Baltasar Gracian

When luck joins the game, cleverness scores double.

Yiddish proverb

The protected man doesn't need luck; therefore, it seldom visits him.

Alan Harrington

Shallow men believe in luck ... Strong men believe in cause and effect.

Ralph Waldo Emerson

Care and diligence bring luck.

Thomas Fuller, MD

Not a man alive/Has so much luck that he can play with it.

William Butler Yeats

It will generally be found that men who are constantly lamenting their ill-luck, are only reaping the consequences of their own neglect, mismanagement, and improvidence, or want of application.

Samuel Smiles

Of course I don't believe in it. But I understand that it brings you luck whether you believe in it or not.

Niels Bohr, explaining why he had hung a horseshoe on the wall

Never have anything to do with an unlucky place or an unlucky man. I have seen many clever men, very clever men, who had no shoes to their feet. I never act with them. Their advice sounds very well, but they cannot get on themselves; and if they cannot do good to themselves, how can they do good to me?

Mayer Rothschild

Luck never made a man wise.

Seneca

Some people are so fond of ill luck that they run half-way to meet it.

Douglas Jerrold

Do not reveal your thoughts to everyone, lest you drive away your good luck.

Sirach 8:19

Luck is being ready.

Brian Eno

True luck consists not in holding the best of cards at the table;/ Luckiest he who knows just when to rise and go home.

John Milton Hay

We must believe in luck. For how else can we explain the success of those we don't like?

Jean Cocteau

If there is such a thing as luck, then I must be the most unlucky fellow in the world. I've never once made a lucky strike in all my life. When I get after something that I need, I start finding everything in the world that I don't need – one damn thing after another, and then comes number one hundred, and that – at the very last – turns out to be just what I had been looking for.

Thomas Edison

Some luck lies in not getting what you thought you wanted, but getting what you have.

Garrison Keillor

Born under a bad sign I been down since I began to crawl. If it wasn't for bad luck, I wouldn't have no luck at all.

Booker T. Jones / William Bell

Once you're lucky, you don't have to work for other people. You make them work for you.

Dan Totheroth, Stephen Vincent Benet, William Dierterle

I think we consider too much the good luck of the early bird, and not enough the bad luck of the early worm.

Franklin D. Roosevelt

Luck is of little moment to the great general, for it is under the control of his intellect and his judgment.

Livy

Hard work and a proper frame of mind prepare you for the lucky breaks that finally come along – or don't.

Harrison Ford

Luck is not chance – /It's Toil –/ Fortune's expensive smile/Is earned.

Emily Dickinson

The worst cynicism: a belief in luck.

Joyce Carol Oates

People always call it luck when you've acted more sensibly than they have.

Anne Tyler

Now and then there is a person born who is so unlucky that he runs into accidents which started out to happen to somebody else.

Don Marquis

"Trusting to luck" is only another name for "trusting to laziness."

Josh Billings

Luck affects everything. Let your hook always be cast. In the stream where you least expect it, there will be fish.

Ovid

Sure, luck means a lot in football. Not having a good quarterback is bad luck.

Don Shula

You cannot expect to be a lucky dog if you spend all your time growling.

Arkansas Baptist

In bad luck hold out; in good luck, hold in.

German proverb

A pound of pluck is worth a ton of luck.

James A. Garfield

LUNATIC

I guess the definition of a lunatic is a man surrounded by them.

Ezra Pound

LUST

Anybody who repudiates the lust for life because he is caught in the lust for ideals has not advanced in the most fundamental sense.

Eugen Herrigel

LUXURIES

Give us the luxuries of life and we will dispense with the necessities.

J.L. Motley

Take care of the luxuries and the necessities will take care of themselves.

Dorothy Parker

Every luxury must be paid for, and everything is a luxury, starting with being in the world.

Cesare Pavese

Luxury either comes of riches or makes them necessary; it corrupts at once rich and poor, the rich by possession and the poor by covetousness; it seals the country to softness and vanity; and takes away from the State all its citizens, to make them slaves one to another, and one and all to public opinion.

Jean-Jacques Rousseau

The saddest thing I can imagine is to get used to luxury.

Charlie Chaplin

LYING

I do not mind lying, but I hate inaccuracy.

Samuel Butler

Any fool can tell the truth, but it requires a man of some sense to know how to lie well.

Samuel Butler

Lord, Lord, how this world is given to lying.

William Shakespeare

Lying is like trying to hide in a fog. If you move about, you are in danger of bumping your head against the truth. And as soon as the fog blows away you are gone, anyhow.

William Hazlitt

The essence of lying is in deception, not in words.

John Ruskin

Lying is like alcoholism. You are always recovering.

Steven Soderbergh

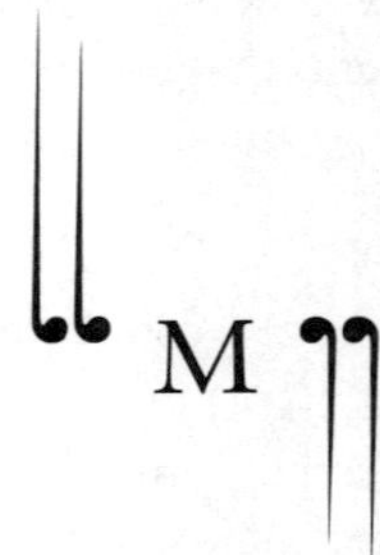

MACHINES

Man is a slow, sloppy, and brilliant thinker; the machine is fast, accurate, and stupid.

William M. Kelly

One machine can do the work of fifty ordinary men. No machine can do the work of one extraordinary man.

Elbert Hubbard

But I suppose sooner or later the machinery would have stalled without your fine Italian hand.

Kathleen Thompson Norris

The larger and more complex a machine, the more unforgiving it is when something goes wrong.

Unknown

MACHISMO

The tragedy of machismo is that a man is never quite man enough.

Germaine Greer

MAD

There is less harm to be suffered in being mad among madmen than in being sane all by oneself.

Denis Diderot

The only difference between me and a madman is that I am not mad.

Salvador Dali

We are all born mad. Some remain so.

Samuel Beckett

Most men are within a finger's breadth of being mad.

Diogenes the Cynic

Everyone is more or less mad on one point.

Rudyard Kipling

MAGAZINES

Magazines all too frequently lead to books and should be regarded by the prudent as the heavy petting of literature.

Fran Lebowitz

MAGIC

Any sufficiently advanced technology is indistinguishable from magic.

Arthur C. Clarke

Disbelief in magic can force a poor soul into believing government and business.

Tom Robbins

MAINTENANCE
Another flaw in the human character is that everybody wants to build and nobody wants to do maintenance.

Kurt Vonnegut

MAJORITY
We go by the majority vote, and if the majority are insane, the sane must go to the hospital.

Horace Mann

When you get too big a majority, you're immediately in trouble.

Sam Rayburn

Whenever you find yourself on the side of the majority, it's time to pause and reflect.

Mark Twain

The object of life is not to be on the side of the majority, but to escape finding oneself in the ranks of the insane.

Marcus Aurelius

MALES
There is, of course, no reason for the existence of the male sex except that one sometimes needs help with moving the piano.

Rebecca West

MALICE
Malice is only another name for mediocrity.

Patrick Kavanagh

MAN
Man is a social animal who dislikes his fellow men.

Eugène Delacroix

Man is a two-legged animal without feathers.

Plato

Man is the only creature that consumes without producing.

George Orwell

Men are cruel, but man is kind.

Rabindranath Tagore

But we were born of risen apes, not fallen angels, and the apes were armed killers besides ... The miracle of man is not how far he has sunk but how magnificently he has risen. We are known among the stars by our poems, not our corpses.

Robert Audrey

Mankind is not a tribe of animals to which we owe compassion. Mankind is a club to which we owe our subscription.

G.K. Chesterton

Maybe in order to understand mankind, we have to look at the word itself. Basically, it's made up of two words: "mank" and "ind." What do these words mean? It's a mystery, and that's why so is mankind.

Jack Handey

The intellect of man is forced to choose/Perfection of the life or of the work.

William Butler Yeats

The greatest nuisance to mankind is man.

Samuel Butler

The man who is master of his passions is Reason's slave.

Cyril Connolly

A man who is master of himself can end a sorrow as easily as he can invent a pleasure.

Oscar Wilde

I believe that our Heavenly Father invented man because he was disappointed in the monkey.

Mark Twain

Man is the creature made at the end of the week's work when God was tired.

Mark Twain

Man is a gaming animal. He must be always trying to get the better in something or other.

Charles Lamb

Man is an intellectual animal and, therefore, an everlasting contradiction to himself. His senses centre in himself, his ideas reach to the ends of the universe; so that he is torn in pieces between the two, without a possibility of its ever being otherwise.

William Hazlitt

To be a man is to feel that one's own stone contributes to building the edifice of the world.

Antoine de Saint-Exupéry

Man is by nature a political animal.

Aristotle

Man is the only animal that blushes. Or needs to.

Mark Twain

Man will only become better when you make him see what he is like.

Anton Chekov

The ultimate measure of a man is not where he stands in moments of comfort and convenience, but where he stands at times of challenge and controversy.

Martin Luther King, Jr

Man must be invented each day.

Jean-Paul Sartre

It's a man's world, and you men can have it.

Katherine Anne Porter

Man is the only creature who refuses to be what he is.

Albert Camus

Man is the only animal that laughs and has a state legislature.

Samuel Butler

To be sure, man is, zoologically speaking, an animal. Yet, he is a unique animal, differing from others in so many fundamental ways that a separate science for man is well-justified.

Ernst Mayr

Man in general, if reduced to himself, is too wicked to be free.

Joseph de Maistre

Man, only – rash, refined, presumptuous man, Starts from his rank, and mars creation's plan.

George Canning

What are men to rocks and mountains?

Jane Austen

There is a perfect ant, a perfect bee, but man is perpetually unfinished. He is both an unfinished animal and an unfinished man. It is this incurable unfinishedness which sets man apart from other living things. For, in the attempt to finish himself, man becomes a creator. Moreover, the incurable unfinishedness keeps man perpetually immature, perpetually capable of learning and growing.

Eric Hoffer

The tragedy of our time is that we have succeeded in splitting the atom before acquiring the wisdom to unite humanity.

Rabbi Julius Mark

MANAGEMENT

So much of what we call management consists in making it difficult for people to work.

Peter Drucker

The secret if managing is to keep the five guys who hate you away from the guys who are undecided.

Casey Stengel

You don't manage people; you manage things. You lead people.

Admiral Grace Hooper

It is possible that people need to believe that they are unmanaged if they are to be managed effectively.

John Kenneth Galbraith

The myth of management is that it exists.

Robert Heller

If you pick the right people and give them the opportunity to spread their wings – and put compensation as a carrier behind it – you almost don't have to manage them.

Jack Welch

MAÑANA

Mañana is often the busiest day of the week.

Spanish proverb

Tomorrow is often the busiest day of the year.

Spanish proverb

MANHOOD

Years ago, manhood was an opportunity for achievement, and now it is a problem to be overcome.

Garrison Keillor

MANNERS

The only substitute for good manners is fast reflexes.

Steven Wright

Good manners always mean our manners.

G.K. Chesterton

What is the test of good manners? Being able to bear patiently with bad ones.

Solomon ibn Gabirol

MANUSCRIPT

Manuscript: something submitted in haste and returned at leisure.

Oliver Herford

MARDI GRAS
Mardi Gras is a state of mind.
Ed Muniz

MARKET
There are two fools in every market: one asks too little, one asks too much.

Russian proverb

MARRIAGE
The fellow who waits to get married until he has enough money isn't really in love.

Kin Hubbard

Marriage is like a cage; one sees the birds outside desperate to get in, and the birds on the inside desperate to get out.

Michel de Montaigne

Even if we take matrimony at its lowest, even if we regard it as no more than a sort of friendship that is recognized by the police ... marriage is a step so grave and decisive that it attracts light-headed, variable men by its very awfulness.

Robert Louis Stevenson

So that is marriage, Lily thought, a man and a woman looking at a girl throwing a ball.

Virginia Woolf

Both my marriages were failures! Number one departed and number two stayed.

Gustav Mahler

As a general thing, people marry most happily with their own kind. The trouble lies in the fact that people usually marry at an age when they do not really know what their own kind is.

Robertson Davies

Marriage is a lot like the army; everyone complains, but you'd be surprised at the large number that re-enlist.

James Garner

The most happy marriage I can picture or imagine to myself would be the union of a deaf man to a blind woman.

Samuel Taylor Coleridge

I think – therefore I'm single.

Lizz Winstead

I have yet to hear a man ask for advice on how to combine marriage and a career.

Gloria Steinem

Before a man starts climbing the ladder of success he should pick the right girl to stay on the ground and hold it steady for him.

Dr O.A. Battista

I never married because there was no need. I have three pets at home which answer the same purpose as a husband. I have a dog which growls every morning, a parrot which swears all afternoon, and a cat that comes home late at night.

Marie Corelli

He tricked me into marrying him. He told me he was pregnant.

Carol Leifer

All marriages are mixed marriages.
Chantal Saperstein

There's only one way to have a happy marriage and as soon as I learn what it is I'll get married again.

Clint Eastwood

In a happy marriage, it is the wife who provides the climate, the husband the landscape.

Gerald Brennan

Instead of getting married again, I'm going to find a woman I don't like and just give her a house.

Lewis Grizzard

All the unhappy marriages come from the husband having brains.

P.G. Wodehouse

Marriage consists not in two people looking into each other's eyes, but in two people, standing shoulder to shoulder, both looking in the same direction.

Halford E. Luccock

Marriage has many pains, but celibacy has no pleasures.

Samuel Johnson

All marriages are happy. It's the living together afterward that causes all the trouble.

Raymond Hull

I married beneath me, all women do.

Nancy Astor

It is always incomprehensible to a man that a woman should refuse an offer of marriage.

Jane Austen

The critical period in matrimony is breakfast time.

A.P. Herbert

Staying married may have long-term benefits. You can elicit much more sympathy from friends over a bad marriage than you ever can from a good divorce.

P.J. O'Rourke

Marriage is a great institution, but I'm not ready for an institution yet.

Mae West

They who marry where they do not love will love where they do not marry.

Thomas Fuller, MD

Marriage is a wonderful invention; then again, so is a bicycle repair kit.

Billy Connolly

Marriage is a book of which the first chapter is written in poetry and the remaining chapters in prose.

Beverley Nichols

I think men who have a pierced ear are better prepared for marriage. They've experienced pain and bought jewelry.

Rita Rudner

The great secret of successful marriage is to treat all disasters as incidents and none of the incidents as disasters.

Harold Nicolson

Every marriage tends to consist of an aristocrat and a peasant. Of a teacher and a learner.

John Updike

Marriage is one long conversation, checkered by disputes.

Robert Louis Stevenson

Love is moral even without legal marriage, but marriage is immoral without love.

Ellen Key

Once you get married, you understand how wars start.

Fay Weldon

A woman may read her husband like a book – and still wonder about earlier editions.

Luke Neely

I have no plans to get married. Frankly, I've never even been drunk enough to get a tattoo.

Richard Jeni

You that are going to be married think things can never be done too fast, but we that are old and know what we are about must elope methodically, madam.

Oliver Goldsmith

How sensible of Mr and Mrs Carlyle to marry one another and so make two people miserable instead of four, besides being very amusing.

Samuel Butler

Marriage probably originated as a straightforward food-for-sex deal among foraging primates. Compatibility was not a big issue, nor, of course, was there any tension over who would control the remote.

Barbara Ehrenreich

It doesn't much signify whom one marries, for one is sure to find next morning that it was someone else.

Samuel Rogers

Though courtship turns frogs into princes, marriage turns them quietly back.

Marge Piercy

Marriage is like a warm bath. Once you get used to it, it's not so hot.

Joey Adams

I wish Adam had died with all his ribs in his body.

Don Boucicault

The most difficult year of marriage is the one you're in.

Franklin P. Jones

Lots of girls say they want no part of money. After they're married they still want no part of it – they want all of it.

Herb Shriner

God help the man who won't marry until he finds a perfect woman, and God help him still more if he finds her.

Ben Tillett

MARTINI
The proper union of gin and vermouth is a great and sudden glory; it is one of the happiest marriages on earth and one of the shortest-lived.

Bernard De Voto

MARTYRDOM

Martyrdom ... is the only way in which a man can become famous without ability.

George Bernard Shaw

To know how to say what other people think is what makes men poets and sages; and to dare to say what others only dare to think makes men martyrs or reformers.

Elizabeth Rundle Charles

MARTYRS

There have been quite as many martyrs for bad causes as good ones.

Martin Van Loon

Let us all be brave enough to die the death of a martyr, but let no one lust for martyrdom.

Mohandas Gandhi

It is the cause, not the death, that makes the martyr.

Napoleon Bonaparte

MARXIST

All I know is that I am not a Marxist.

Karl Marx

MASOCHISM

I had to give up masochism – I was enjoying it too much.

Mel Calman

MASSES

I can't help feeling wary when I hear anything said about the masses. First you take their faces from 'em by calling 'em the masses, and then you accuse 'em of not having any faces.

J.B. Priestley

The masses have never thirsted after truth. They turn aside from evidence that is not to their taste, preferring to deify error, if error seduce[s] them. Whoever can supply them with illusions is easily their master; whoever attempts to destroy their illusions is always their victim.

Gustave Le Bon

Leave this hypocritical prating about the masses. Masses are rude, lame, unmade, pernicious in their demands and influence, and need not be flattered but to be schooled. I wish not to concede anything to them, but to tame, drill, divide, and break them up, and draw individuals out of them.

Ralph Waldo Emerson

The quality of ideas seems to play a minor role in mass-movement leadership. What counts is the arrogant gesture, the complete disregard of the opinion of others, the single-handed defiance of the world.

Eric Hoffer

The lower sort of men must be indulged the consolation of finding fault with those above them; without that, they would be so melancholy that it would be dangerous, considering their numbers.

George Savile, Marquess of Halifax

MASTER

The man who gives me employment, which I must have or suffer, that man is my master, let me call him what I will.

Henry George

The strongest is never strong enough to be always the master, unless he transforms his strength into right, and obedience into duty.

Jean-Jacques Rousseau

MASTERY

The human race is challenged more than ever before to demonstrate our mastery – not over nature but of ourselves.

Rachel Carson

MATERIALISM

The cure for "Materialism" is to have enough for everybody and to spare. When people are sure of having what they need they cease to think about it.

Henry Ford

Materialism is the belief that if there are other things in life besides money, it takes money to buy them.

Evan Esar

He who has the most toys when he dies wins.

Anonymous

When we try in good faith to believe in materialism, in the exclusive reality of the physical, we are asking ourselves to step aside; we are disavowing the very realm where we exist and where all things precious are kept – the realm of emotion and conscience; of memory and intention and sensation.

John Updike

MATHEMATICS

Moriarty: "How are you at mathematics?" Harry Secombe: "I speak it like a native."

Spike Milligan

If a man's wit be wandering, let him study the mathematics.

Francis Bacon

I don't believe in mathematics.

Albert Einstein

All the mathematical sciences are founded on relations between physical laws and laws of numbers.

James Clerk Maxwell

Mathematics becomes very odd when you apply it to people. One plus one can add up to so many sums.

Michael Frayn

As far as the laws of mathematics refer to reality, they are not certain, and as far as they are certain, they do not refer to reality.

Albert Einstein

MATTER

What is Matter? Never mind. What is Mind? No matter.

Punch

MATURITY

Maturity is the capacity to endure uncertainty.

John Finley

Maturity is only a short break in adolescence.

Jules Feiffer

He that has seen both sides of fifty has lived to little purpose if he has no other views of the world than he had when he was young.

William Cowper

A mark of maturity seems to be the range and extent of one's feeling of self-involvement in abstract ideals.

Gordon Wallport

The immature mind hops from one thing to another; the mature mind seeks to follow through.

H.A. Overstreet

The nobler and more perfect a thing is, the later and slower it is in arriving at maturity.

Arthur Schopenhauer

If only I may grow firmer, simpler – quieter, warmer.

Dag Hammarskjold

A real test of maturity is the ability to remain equally unruffled when the elevator boy calls you "Pop" and the senior partner calls you "Sonny."

Ivern Boyett

MAXIM

It is more trouble to make a maxim than it is to do right.

Mark Twain

MEAN

To the mean, all becomes mean.

Friedrich Nietzsche

MEANS

When we deliberate it is about means and not ends.

Aristotle

Take care of the means and the end will take care of itself.

Mohandas Gandhi

Those means recommended in textbooks as the best, means perfectly appropriate for the template case, turn out to be completely unsuitable in individual cases.

Anton Chekhov

The end may justify the means as long as there is something that justifies the end.

Leon Trotsky

The line, often adopted by strong men in controversy, of justifying the means by the end.

St Jerome

MEDIA

The media's power is frail. Without the people's support, it can be shut off with the ease of turning a light switch.

Corazón Aquino

Nobody's interested in sweetness and light.

Hedda Hopper

Avoid this crowd like the plague. And if they quote you, make (darn) sure they heard you.

Barbara Bush to Hillary Clinton

MEDICINE

Formerly, when religion was strong and science weak, men mistook magic for medicine; now, when science is strong and religion weak, men mistake medicine for magic.

Thomas Szasz

I am interested in physical medicine because my father was. I am interested in medical research because I believe in it. I am interested in arthritis because I have it.

Bernard Baruch

Medicine, to produce health, has to examine disease; and music, to create harmony, must investigate discord.

Plutarch

The art of medicine consists of amusing the patient while nature cures the disease.

Voltaire

Medicine, the only profession that labours incessantly to destroy the reason for its own existence.

Lord Bryce

Medicine heals doubts as well as diseases.

Karl Marx

MEDIOCRITY
Only a mediocre person is always at his best.

Laurence J. Peter

Only the mediocre are always at their best.

Jean Giraudoux

If there were no mediocrity in the arts, there would be no masterpieces.

George F. Whitcomb

It's more than magnificent – it's mediocre.

Samuel Goldwyn

There is not much between mediocrity and talent; merely a decimal point called application.

J. Trevena

MEDITATION
Reading and conversation may furnish us with many ideas of men and things, yet it is our own meditation that must form our judgment.

Isaac Watts

My son has taken up meditation – at least it's better than sitting doing nothing.

Max Kauffman

MEEK
Pity the meek, for they shall inherit the earth.

Don Marquis

MEEKNESS
Meekness, *n.* Uncommon patience in planning a revenge that is worthwhile.

Ambrose Bierce

MELANCHOLY
He's a Fool that is not melancholy once a Day.

Thomas Fuller, MD

MEMBERS
When she saw the sign "Members Only," she thought of him.

Spike Milligan

MEMOIRS

To write one's memoirs is to speak ill of everyone except oneself.

Marshal Pétain

MEMORANDUM

A memorandum is written not to inform the reader but to protect the writer.

Dean Acheson

MEMORY

How is it that our memory is good enough to retain the least triviality that happens to us, and yet not good enough to recollect how often we have told it to the same person?

François, duc de La Rochefoucald

How feeble are Man's efforts against the unyielding forces of nature – until the struggle is recounted for the grandchildren.

Jeanette Kubin

As we grow older our memory of past events grows better and better, whether they happened or not.

Mark Twain

Memory is the thing you forget with.

Alexander Chase

We do not remember days; we remember moments.

Cesare Pavese

It's a poor sort of memory that only works backwards.

Lewis Carroll

You never know when you're making a memory.

Rickie Lee Jones

My memory is so bad that many times I forget my own name!

Miguel de Cervantes

Memory is what tells a man that his wife's birthday was yesterday.

Mario Rocco

A great memory does not make a philosopher, any more than a dictionary can be called a grammar.

John Henry Newman

Life without memory is no life at all. … our memory is our coherence, our reason, our feeling, even our action. Without it, we are nothing.

Luis Buñuel

Our memories are independent of our wills. It is not so easy to forget.

Richard Brinsley Sheridan

The palest ink is better than the best memory.

Chinese proverb

Memory feeds imagination.

Amy Tan

A good memory constitutes about seventy per cent of what commonly passes for genius.

Hesketh Pearson

Intelligence may be the pride – the towering distinction of man; emotion gives colour and force to his actions; but memory is the bastion of his being. Without memory, there is no personal identity, there is no continuity to the days of his life. Memory provides the raw material for designs both great and small. Thus governed and enriched by memory, all the enterprises of man go forward.

D. Ewen Cameron

In memory, everything seems to happen to music.

Tennessee Williams

Every man's memory is his private literature.

Aldous Huxley

Are you not the future of all the memories stored within you? The future of a past?

Paul Valéry

Memory is the primary and fundamental power, without which there could be no other intellectual operation.

Samuel Johnson

We find a little of everything in our memory; it is a sort of pharmacy, a sort of clinical laboratory, in which our groping hand may come to rest, now on a sedative drug, now on a dangerous poison.

Marcel Proust

If you can look back on your life with contentment, you have one of man's most precious gifts – a selective memory.

Jim Fiebig

Memories are the key not to the past, but to the future.

Corrie Ten Boom

What we have once enjoyed we can never lose. All that we love deeply becomes a part of us.

Helen Keller

You have to forget your last marathon before you try another. Your mind can't know what's coming.

Frank Shorter

Nothing fixes a thing so intensely in the memory as the wish to forget it.

Michel de Montaigne

Men with remarkable memories are rarely, if ever, conspicuous for original thought.

W.J. Turner

Nothing hurts a man's memory more than making good resolutions.

Franklin P. Jones

MEN
There are men I could spend eternity with. But not this life.

Kathleen Norris

Men need women. Most single men don't even live like people. They live like bears with furniture.

Rita Rudner

I know this – a man got to do what he got to do.

John Steinbeck

Some men are so selfish that they read a book or go to a concert for their own sinister pleasure, instead of doing it to improve social conditions, as the good citizen does when drinking cocktails or playing bridge.

Jacques Barzun

Men build bridges and throw railroads across deserts, and yet they contend successfully that the job of sewing on a button is beyond them. Accordingly, they don't have to sew buttons.

Heywood Broun

Thank God, men cannot as yet fly, and lay waste the sky as well as the Earth.

Henry David Thoreau

If men can rule the world, why can't they stop wearing neckties? How intelligent is it to start the day by tying a little noose around your neck?

Linda Ellerbee

Men, like nails, lose their usefulness when they lose direction and begin to bend.

Walter Savage Landor

Men are so romantic, don't you think? They look for a perfect partner when what they should be looking for is perfect love.

Fay Weldon

It's not the men in my life that count; it's the life in my men.

Mae West

If the world were a logical place, men would ride side saddle.

Rita Mae Brown

God creates men, but they choose each other.

Niccolò Machiavelli

There are three classes of men – lovers of wisdom, lovers of honour, lovers of gain.

Plato

Men are the only animals who devote themselves assiduously to making one another unhappy.

H.L. Mencken

Men have a much better time of it than women; for one thing they marry later; for another thing they die earlier.

H.L. Mencken

The male is a domestic animal which, if treated with firmness and kindness, can be trained to do most things.

Jilly Cooper

Male, *n.* A member of the unconsidered, or negligible sex. The male of the human race is commonly known (to the female) as Mere Man. The genus has two varieties: good providers and bad providers.

Ambrose Bierce

A man is like a phonograph with half-a-dozen records. You soon get tired of them all; and yet you have to sit at table whilst he reels them off to every new visitor.

George Bernard Shaw

There was, I think, never any reason to believe in any innate superiority of the male, except his superior muscle.

Bertrand Russell

I like two kinds of men: domestic and foreign.

Mae West

A man's womenfolk, whatever their outward show of respect for his merit and authority, always regard him secretly as an ass, and with something akin to pity.

> *H.L. Mencken*

Women like silent men. They think they're listening.

> *Marcel Achard*

Women speak because they wish to speak, whereas a man speaks only when driven to speech by something outside himself – like, for instance, he can't find any clean socks.

> *Jean Kerr*

Men lived like fishes; the great ones devoured the small.

> *Algernon Sidney*

I require only three things of a man. He must be handsome, ruthless, and stupid.

> *Dorothy Parker*

I refuse to consign the whole male sex to the nursery. I insist on believing that some men are my equals.

> *Brigid Brophy*

Even the wisest men make fools of themselves about women, and even the most foolish women are wise about men.

> *Theodor Reik*

Women want mediocre men, and men are working hard to be as mediocre as possible.

> *Margaret Mead*

Without thinking highly either of men or matrimony, marriage had always been her object; it was the only honourable provision for well-educated young women of small

fortune, and however uncertain of giving happiness, must be their pleasantest preservative from want.

> *Jane Austen*

Men in great places are thrice servants: servants of the sovereign or state, servants of fame, and servants of business.

> *Francis Bacon*

A man of action forced into a state of thought is unhappy until he can get out of it.

> *John Galsworthy*

Any man who goes to a psychiatrist should have his head examined.

> *Samuel Goldwyn*

A man who has not passed through the inferno of his passions has never overcome them.

> *Carl Jung*

The name of a man is a numbing blow from which he never recovers.

> *Marshall McLuhan*

Men should not care too much for good looks; neglect is becoming.

> *Ovid*

Men's men: gentle or simple, they're much of a muchness.

> *George Eliot*

I'd never seen men hold each other. I thought the only thing they were allowed to do was shake hands or fight.

> *Rita Mae Brown*

Every man is made of clay and daimon, and no woman can nourish both.

Lawrence Durrell

The last thing a woman will consent to discover in a man whom she loves, or on whom she simply depends, is want of courage.

Joseph Conrad

Nearly all our best men are dead! Carlyle, Tennyson, Browning, George Eliot! – I'm not feeling very well myself.

Punch, 1893

A belief in a supernatural source of evil is not necessary; men alone are quite capable of every wickedness.

Joseph Conrad

The first time Adam had a chance, he laid the blame on women.

Nancy Astor

Probably the only place where a man can feel really secure is in a maximum security prison, except for the imminent threat of release.

Germaine Greer

MENTAL HEALTH
Support mental health or I'll kill you.

Anonymous

MENTAL PROBLEMS
Mental health problems do not affect three or four out of every five persons, but one out of one.

William Menninger

MERCHANT
For the merchant, even honesty is a financial speculation.

Charles Baudelaire

MERCY
Nothing emboldens sin so much as mercy.

William Shakespeare

There is no more mercy in him than there is milk in a male tiger.

William Shakespeare

Fire, water, and government know nothing of mercy.

Albanian proverb

MERE
I must take issue with the term "a mere child," for it has been my invariable experience that the company of a mere child is infinitely preferable to that of a mere adult.

Fran Lebowitz

MERIT
Heaven goes by favour. If it went by merit, you would stay out and your dog would go in.

Mark Twain

Charms strike the sight, but merit wins the soul.

Alexander Pope

Merit envies success, and success takes itself for merit.

Jean Rostand

True merit is like a river, the deeper it is, the less noise it makes.

Edward F Halifax

MESSES
It's not the tragedies that kill us, it's
the messes.
Dorothy Parker

METAPHORS
Since finding out what something
is is largely a matter of discovering
what it is like, the most impressive
contribution to the growth of intel-
ligibility has been made by the
application of suggestive metaphors.
Jonathan Miller

The metaphor is probably the most
fertile power possessed by men.
José Ortega y Gasset

We need metaphors of magic and
monsters in order to understand
the human condition.
Stephen Donaldson

METAPHYSICS
Metaphysics is the finding of bad
reasons for what we believe upon
instinct; but to find these reasons is
no less an instinct.
Francis H. Bradley

METHOD
At all times it is better to have a
method.

Mark Caine

MICROSOFT
News Release 4 January, 1999
Redmond, Washington

Bill Gates, Chairman and CEO of
Microsoft Corporation, announced
today that the latest version of

their Windows operating system,
Windows 2000, would be delayed
until the second quarter of 1901.
No reason was given.
Internet, before apprehended
Y2K crisis

MIDDLE AGE
Middle age is when you're sitting
home on Saturday night and the
telephone rings and you hope it
isn't for you.
Ogden Nash

Middle age is when your age starts
to show around the middle.
Bob Hope

Middle age: the time when a man is
always thinking that in a week or
two he will feel just as good as ever.
Don Marquis

Middle age is when you stop criticizing the older generation and
start criticizing the younger one.
Laurence J. Peter

Don't worry about middle age:
you'll outgrow it.
Laurence J. Peter

Today's middle-aged man is a
bloke, a geezer, a laugh, a riot. He's
still hot. He's still sexy. He wants to
party, not sit around listening to
the radio. He is, come to think of
it, exactly like a teenager but with
less hair.
India Knight

MIDDLE-CLASS
Slums may well be breeding
grounds of crime, but middle-class

suburbs are incubators of apathy and delirium.

> *Cyril Connolly*

MILITARY

The military don't start wars. Politicians start wars.

> *William Westmoreland*

The only inexcusable offence in a commanding officer is to be surprised.

> *Matthew Ridgway*

MILK

My illness is due to my doctor's insistence that I drink milk, a whitish fluid they force down helpless babies.

> *W.C. Fields*

MILLION

I feel like a million tonight – but one at a time.

> *Mae West*

MILLIONAIRES

I'm opposed to millionaires, but it would be dangerous to offer me the position.

> *Mark Twain*

MIND

The pendulum of the mind oscillates between sense and nonsense, not between right and wrong.

> *Carl Jung*

His mind was an intricate, multigeared machine, or perhaps some little animal with skittery paws.

> *Anne Tyler*

Some open minds should be closed for repairs.

> *Toledo Blade*

Our minds are lazier than our bodies.

> *François, duc de La Rochefoucauld*

All sorts of bodily diseases are caused by half-used minds.

> *George Bernard Shaw*

The mind is not a vessel to be filled but a fire to be kindled.

> *Plutarch*

Where there is an open mind, there will always be a frontier.

> *Charles F. Kettering*

The only man who can change his mind is a man who has got one.

> *Edward Noyes Westcott*

The flesh endures the storms of the present alone; the mind, those of the past and future as well as the present.

> *Epicurus*

A closed mind saves time.

> *E.O. Phillips*

Great minds have purposes, little minds have wishes.

> *Washington Irving*

Great minds discuss ideas; average minds discuss events; small minds discuss people.

> *Eleanor Roosevelt*

I have not lost my mind – it's backed up on disk somewhere.

> *Unknown*

The eyes are not responsible when the mind does the seeing.
Publilius Syrus

The eye may see for the hand, but not for the mind.
Henry David Thoreau

I believe in an open mind, but not so open that your brains fall out.
Arthur Hays Sulzberger

I don't know very much, but what I do know I know better than anybody, and I don't want to argue about it. I know what I think about an actor or actress, and I am not interested in what anybody else thinks. My mind is not a bed to be made and re-made.
James Agate

It is not enough to have a good mind; one must use it well.
René Descartes

Your hair may be brushed, but your mind's untidy.
Ogden Nash

The mind is its own place, and in itself can make a heaven of hell, a hell of heaven.
John Milton

Minds are like parachutes, they work best when they are open.
Anonymous

It never ceases to puzzle me that, while men's and women's bodies fit jigsaw tight in an altogether miraculous way their minds remain wretchedly unaligned.
Beryl Bainbridge

Is the mind more like a fancy system of domino chains or a bathtub full of spring-loaded mousetraps? I'm betting on the latter.
Douglas Hofstadter

The primary indication ... of a well-ordered mind is a man's ability to remain in one place and linger in his own company.
Seneca

MINISTERS
I don't mind how much my ministers talk – as long as they do what I say.
Margaret Thatcher

It is even more damaging for a minister to say foolish things than to do them.
Cardinal de Retz

MINORITY
The minority is always right.
Henrik Ibsen

Minorities ... are almost always in the right.
Sydney Smith

It is always the minorities that hold the key of progress; it is always through those who are unafraid to be different that advance comes to human society.
Raymond B. Fosdick

MINUTES
It is characteristic of committee discussions and decisions that every member has a vivid recollection of them and that every member's

recollection differs violently from every other member's recollection. Consequently we accept the convention that the official decisions were those and only those which are officially recorded in the minutes and any decision officially reached was recorded in the minutes and any decision not recorded in the minutes was not officially reached even if one or more members believe that they recollect it, so in this particular case if the decision had been officially reached it would have been officially recorded by the officials in the minutes. And it isn't so it wasn't.

Yes, Prime Minister, BBC

MIRACLES

The Age of Miracles is forever here!

Thomas Carlyle

It was a miracle of rare device.
Samuel Taylor Coleridge

Miracles sometimes occur, but one has to work terribly hard for them.
Chaim Weizmann

The miracle isn't that I finished. The miracle is that I had the courage to start.

John Bingham

MIRRORS

All mirrors are magical mirrors; never can we see our faces in them.
Logan Pearsall Smith

They do it with mirrors.
Agatha Christie

MISBEHAVE

I don't say we all ought to misbehave, but we ought to look as if we could.

Orson Welles

MISCHIEF

Physicists and astronomers see their own implications in the world being round, but to me it means that only one-third of the world is asleep at any given time and the other two-thirds is up to something.

Dean Rusk

MISERS

If the prodigal quits life in debt to others, the miser quits it still deeper in debt to himself.
Charles Caleb Colton

The miser and the pig are of no use until dead.
French proverb

Water will not slip through the miser's grasp.
Malay proverb

MISERY

Extreme hopes are born of extreme misery.

Bertrand Russell

MISFORTUNE

Some people think that all the world should share their misfortunes, though they do not share in the sufferings of anyone else.
Achille Poincelot

To be brave in misfortune is to be worthy of manhood; to be wise in misfortune is to conquer fate.

Agnes Repplier

If all misfortunes were laid in one common heap whence everyone must take an equal portion, most people would be contented to take their own and depart.

Socrates

The greatest misfortune of all is not to be able to bear misfortune.

Bias of Priene

Almost all our misfortunes in life come from the wrong notions we have about the things that happen to us.

Marie-Henri Beyle

Some misfortunes we bring upon ourselves; others are completely beyond our control. But no matter what happens to us, we always have some control over what we do about it.

Suzy Szasz

People don't ever seem to realize that doing what's right's no guarantee against misfortune.

William McFee

I am convinced that we have a degree of delight, and that no small one, in the real misfortunes and pains of others.

Edmund Burke

We are easily comforted for the misfortunes of our friends, when those misfortunes give us an occasion of expressing our affection and solicitude.

François, duc de La Rochefoucauld

Little minds are tamed and subdued by misfortune; but great minds rise above it.

Washington Irving

MISGIVING
A prudent mind can see room for misgiving, lest he who prospers should one day suffer reverse.

Sophocles

MISQUOTATION
I improve on misquotation.

Cary Grant

Misquotation is, in fact, the pride and privilege of the learned. A widely read man never quotes accurately, for the rather obvious reason that he has read too widely.

Hesketh Pearson

Any fool can be accurate with a book of reference at his elbow, but it takes a scholar to know so many quotations that he makes mistakes in every one of them.

Hilaire Belloc

MISSION
Those who have found some sense of Mission have a very special joy, which no one can take from them.

Richard Bolles

MISSOURI
I am from Missouri. You have got to show me.

Willard Vandiver

MISTAKES

If you don't profit from your investment mistakes, someone else will.
Yale Hirsch

It is a capital mistake to theorize before one has data.
Sherlock Holmes

To stumble twice against the same stone is a proverbial disgrace.
Cicero

Who thinks it is just to be judged by a single error?
Beryl Markham

There is nothing wrong with making mistakes. Just don't respond with encores.
Anonymous

The greatest mistake you can make in life is to be continually fearing you will make one.
Elbert Hubbard

Don't make the wrong mistakes.
Yogi Berra

Mistakes live in the neighbourhood of truth and therefore delude us.
Rabindranath Tagore

We must learn from the mistakes of others. You can't possibly live long enough to make them all yourself.
Sam Levenson

The habitually punctual make all their mistakes right on time.
Laurence J. Peter

Don't look where you fell, but where you slipped.
African proverb

Every great mistake has a halfway moment, a split second when it can be recalled and perhaps remedied.
Pearl S. Buck

Half of our mistakes in life arise from feeling where we ought to think, and thinking where we ought to feel.
Churton Collins

When you realize you have made a mistake, take immediate steps to correct it.
Dalai Lama

I make mistakes: I'll be the second to admit it.
Jean Kerr

We never make mistakes.
Alexandr Solzhenitsyn

When I make a mistake, it's a beaut!
Fiorello H. La Guardia

The able man is one who makes mistakes according to the rules.
Paul Valéry

I never made a mistake in my life; at least, never one that I couldn't explain away afterwards.
Rudyard Kipling

A life spent in making mistakes is not only more honourable but more useful than a life spent doing nothing.
George Bernard Shaw

There is no mistake so great as the mistake of not going on.
William Blake

If we could be twice young and twice old we could correct all our mistakes.
Euripides

Recently, I was asked if I was going to fire an employee who made a mistake that cost the company $600,000. No, I replied, I just spent $600,000 training him. Why would I want somebody else to hire his experience?
Thomas Watson, Sr

It is very easy to forgive others their mistakes. It takes more grit and gumption to forgive them for having witnessed your own.
Jessamyn West

MISTRUST
Trust dies but mistrust blossoms.
Sophocles

He who mistrusts most should be trusted least.
Theognis

MIXED METAPHORS
While I write this letter, I have a pistol in one hand and a sword in the other.
Boyle Roche

All along the untrodden paths of the future, I can see the footprints of an unseen hand.
Boyle Roche

The only thing to prevent what's past is to put a stop to it before it happens.
Boyle Roche

Mr. Speaker, I smell a rat. I see him forming in the air and darkening the sky. Let us nip him in the bud.
Boyle Roche

MOAT
To the question "What shall we do to be saved in this world?" there is no other answer but this: "Look to your moat."
George Savile, Marquess of Halifax

MOB
It was the pleasantest mob I ever lost a tooth in.
Bob Hope

MODERATION
Moderation is good but boring.
Anonymous

He is almost always a slave who cannot live on little.
Horace

Moderation has been declared a virtue so as to curb the ambition of the great and console lesser folk for their lack of fortune and merit.
François, duc de La Rochefoucauld

A society so riven that the spirit of moderation is gone, no court can save.
Billings Learned Hand

Who loves the golden mean is safe from the poverty of a tenement, and is free from the envy of a palace.

Horace

MODERN

Don't bother about being modern. Unfortunately it is the one thing that, whatever you do, you cannot avoid.

Salvador Dali

MODESTY

Modesty is the only sure bait when you angle for praise.

Lord Chesterfield

Modesty is a vastly overrated virtue.

John Kenneth Galbraith

I'm very modest. I tend to hide my light under a peck.

Ken Mullen

The only worse thing than false modesty is no modesty at all.

Joseph Epstein

With people of only moderate ability, modesty is mere honesty; but with those who possess great talent, it is hypocrisy.

Arthur Schopenhauer

Whenever someone makes badly what we expected to be well-made, we say: "I could do as well as that myself." There are few expressions that betray so much modesty.

Georg Christoph Lichtenberg

Modesty is the art of drawing attention to whatever it is you are being humble about.

Unknown

A modest little person, with much to be modest about.

Winston Churchill

Modesty is to merit, what shade is to figures in a picture; it gives it strength and makes it stand out.

Jean de La Bruyère

MONARCHY

A monarchy conducted with infinite wisdom and infinite benevolence is the most perfect of all possible governments.

Ezra Stiles

MONDAY

Mondays are the potholes in the road of life.

Tom Wilson

MONEY

When a man says money can do anything, that settles it; he hasn't any.

Edgar Watson Howe

I cannot afford to waste my time making money.

Louis Agassiz

If money is your hope for independence you will never have it. The only real security that a man can have in this world is a reserve of knowledge, experience, and ability.

Henry Ford

Money is better than poverty, if only for financial reasons. Not that it can buy happiness. Take the case of the ant and the grasshopper: The grasshopper played all summer, while the ant worked and saved. When winter came, the grasshopper had nothing, but the ant complained of chest pains.

Woody Allen

Money is how people with no talent keep score.

Anonymous

Lack of money is the root of all evil.

George Bernard Shaw

We're really all of us bottomly broke. I haven't had time to work in weeks.

Jack Kerouac

Money doesn't always buy happiness. People with $10-million are no happier than people with $9-million.

Hobart Brown

If all the rich men in the world divided up their money amongst themselves, there wouldn't be enough to go around.

Jules Bertillon

Among the things that money can't buy is what it used to.

Max Kauffmann

Whoever said money doesn't buy happiness didn't know where to shop.

Anonymous

He without benefit of scruples / His fun and money soon quadruples.

Ogden Nash

Money and success don't change people; they merely amplify what is there.

Will Smith

Money, it turned out, was exactly like sex, you thought of nothing else if you didn't have it and thought of other things if you did.

James Baldwin

When it is a question of money, everybody is of the same religion.

Voltaire

If money could talk, it would say goodbye.

Elbert Hubbard

How did the fool get all that money in the first place?

Robert Byrne

Plenty of people despise money, but few know how to give it away.

François, duc de La Rochefoucauld

To be clever enough to get all that money, one must be stupid enough to want it.

G.K. Chesterton

To be clever enough to get a great deal of money, one must be stupid enough to want it.

George Bernard Shaw

With money in your pocket, you are wise and you are handsome and you sing well too.

Yiddish proverb

Do you think money grows on trees?

Dad

Money may buy the husk of many things, but not the kernel. It brings you food, but not appetite, medicine but not health, acquaintances but not friends, servants but not faithfulness, days of joy but not peace or happiness.

Henrik Ibsen

Money often costs too much.
Ralph Waldo Emerson

Money always implies the promise of magic, but the effect is much magnified when, as now, people have lost faith in everything else.
Lewis Lapham

As often as not it isn't the money itself that means anything; it is the use of money as the currency of the soul.

Lewis Lapham

The price we have to pay for money is paid in liberty.
Robert Louis Stevenson

What better way to prove that you understand a subject than to make money out of it?
Harold Rosenberg

There is no problem about money, except who has it.
Montagu Norman

What's money? A man is a success if he gets up in the morning and goes to bed at night and in between does what he wants to do.

Bob Dylan

Money doesn't talk, it swears.
Bob Dylan

It is a kind of spiritual snobbery that makes people think they can be happy without money.
Albert Camus

Money isn't everything. Usually it isn't even enough.

Anonymous

Having money is rather like being a blond. It is more fun, but not vital.

Mary Quant

The safest way to double your money is to fold it over twice and put it in your pocket.
Kin Hubbard

There are people who have money and people who are rich.
Coco Chanel

For me, affection was more visible in terms of finance than in terms of words. People can talk and not mean what they say, but with money, you know it will not let you down.

Bienvenida Sokolow

Money cannot buy you love, but it sure as hell buys you great shoes.
Katie Hopkins

Money is flat and meant to be piled.
New England saying

Make money your god and it will plague you like the devil.
Henry Fielding

It is physically impossible for a well-educated, intellectual, or brave man to make money the chief object of his thoughts.

John Ruskin

Don't marry for money. You can borrow it cheaper.

Scottish proverb

And being rich is about acting too, isn't it? A style, a pose, an interpretation that you force upon the world? Whether or not you've made the stuff yourself, you have to set about pretending that you merit it, that money chose right in choosing you, and that you'll do right by money in your turn. Money-mad or just money-smug, you have to pretend it's the natural thing.

Martin Amis

Every time you spend money, you're casting a vote for the kind of world you want.

Anna Lappé

The waste of money cures itself, for soon there is no more to waste.

M.W. Harrison

But it is pretty to see what money will do.

Samuel Pepys

Money is the root of all evil, and yet it is such a useful root that we cannot get on without it any more than we can without potatoes.

Louisa May Alcott

You pays your money and you takes your choice.

Punch

Money that is earned by blood, sweat, and tears is seldom spent like water.

Dr O.A. Battista

The civility which money will purchase, is rarely extended to those who have none.

Charles Dickens

Money never made a man happy yet, nor will it. The more a man has, the more he wants. Instead of filling a vacuum, it makes one.

Benjamin Franklin

Money is human happiness in the abstract: He, then, who is no longer capable of enjoying human happiness in the concrete, devotes his heart entirely to money.

Arthur Schopenhauer

MONKEY
Year by year, the monkey's mask reveals the monkey.

Basho

MONSTERS
He who fights with monsters might take care lest he thereby become a monster. And if you gaze long into an abyss, the abyss gazes also into you.

Friedrich Nietzsche

MONTREAL
Some say that no one ever leaves Montreal.

Leonard Cohen

MONUMENTS

Those only deserve a monument who do not heed one.

William Hazlitt

When smashing monuments, save the pedestals – they always come in handy.

Stanislaw J. Lec

MOON

Everyone is a moon, and has a dark side which he never shows to anybody.

Mark Twain

MOONING

Mooning, as if one were a rampant ape, is a gesture of contempt for others, but it is especially a gesture of contempt for oneself.

Mary Leland

MOONSHINE LIQUOR

A sudden violent jolt of it has been known to stop the victim's watch, snap his suspenders, and crack his glass eye right across.

Irvin S. Cobb

MORAL QUALITY

There are few things more disturbing than to find, in somebody we detest, a moral quality which seems to us demonstrably superior to anything we ourselves possess.

Pamela Hansford Johnson

MORALITY

Human models are more vivid and more persuasive than explicit moral commands.

Daniel Boorstin

If we are told that a man is religious, we still ask what are his morals. But if we hear that he has honest morals, we seldom think of the other question.

Earl of Shaftesbury

That was why the world he knew was poor, for it insisted morality and caution were identical.

Norman Mailer

Be not too hasty to trust or to admire the teachers of morality: They discourse like angels but they live like men.

Samuel Johnson

The most important human endeavour is the striving for morality in our actions. Our inner balance and even our existence depend on it. Only morality in our actions can give beauty and dignity to life. To make this a living force and bring it to clear consciousness is perhaps the foremost task of education.

Albert Einstein

We may pretend that we're basically moral people who make mistakes, but the whole of history proves otherwise.

Terry Hands

Morality is the custom of one's country and the current feeling of one's peers. Cannibalism is moral in a cannibal country.

Samuel Butler

There are many religions, but there is only one morality.

John Ruskin

MORALS

If your morals make you dreary, depend on it, they are wrong.

Robert Louis Stevenson

We spend much more time tending to the quality of our emotional lives than to the quality of our moral lives. Many people are prepared to shake up their lives in a mad bid for emotional happiness,' but few will disturb their moral suppositions. When was the last time you asked yourself hard questions about your values?

Joshua Halberstam

Eats first, morals after.

Bertolt Brecht

In matters of prudence, last thoughts are best; in matters of morality, first thoughts.

Robert Hall

From the point of view of morals, life seems to be divided into two periods. In the first, we indulge; in the second, we preach.

Will Durant

The higher the buildings, the lower the morals.

Noel Coward

Everything has got a moral, if only you can find it.

Lewis Carroll

One becomes moral as soon as one is unhappy.

Marcel Proust

Never let your sense of morals get in the way of doing what's right.

Isaac Asimov

What is moral is what you feel good after.

Ernest Hemingway

The art of acting morally is behaving as if everything we do matters.

Gloria Steinem

I have found that people are usually much more moved by economics than by morals.

Norah Phillips

Movie morals have changed. When I was a kid, a film was obscene if the horse wasn't wearing a saddle.

Danny Thomas

MORE

Nothing's better than more, more, more / Nothing's better than more.

Stephen Sondheim

MORNING

Never glad confident morning again!

Robert Browning

It is not time for mirth and laughter, the cold, grey dawn of the morning after.

George Ade

MORTALITY

Old and young, we are all on our last cruise.

Robert Louis Stevenson

We are all here for a spell; get all the good laughs you can.

Will Rogers

MOSQUITOES
Why didn't Noah swat those two mosquitoes?

Unknown

MOTHERS
Mother is far too clever to understand anything she does not like.

Arnold Bennett

I was on a corner [in Los Angeles] the other day when a wild-looking sort of gypsy-looking lady with a dark veil over her face grabbed me right on Ventura Boulevard and said, "Karen Haber! You're never going to find happiness and no one is ever going to marry you." I said, "Mom, leave me alone."

Karen Haber

In the eyes of its mother, every beetle is a gazelle.

Moroccan proverb

In our society, mothers take the place elsewhere occupied by the Fates, the System, Negroes, Communism, or Reactionary Imperialist Plots; mothers go on getting blamed until they're eighty, but shouldn't take it personally.

Katharine Whitehorne

Begin, baby boy, to recognize your mother with a smile.

Virgil

God could not be everywhere, and therefore he made mothers.

Rudyard Kipling

Only mothers can think of the future – because they give birth to it in their children.

Maxim Gorky

Whatever else is unsure in this stinking dunghill of a world, a mother's love is not.

James Joyce

[Motherhood] is a dead-end job. You've no sooner learned the skills than you are redundant.

Claire Rayner

A suburban mother's role is to deliver her children – obstetrically once and by car forever after.

Peter De Vries

Biology is the least of what makes someone a mother.

Oprah Winfrey

MOTION PICTURES
Pictures are for entertainment, messages should be delivered by Western Union.

Samuel Goldwyn

There is only one thing that can kill the movies, and that is education.

Will Rogers

We didn't need dialogue in those days. We had faces then!

Gloria Swanson

Movies are about people who do things. The No. 1 fantasy of the cinema is that we can do something – we are relatively impotent in our own lives so we go to movies to watch people who are in control of their lives.

Paul Schrader

MOTIVE

Never ascribe to your opponent motives meaner than your own.

J.M. Barrie

It is motive alone that gives character to the actions of men.

Jean de La Bruyère

MOURN

Nature's law,/That man was made to mourn.

Robert Burns

MOURNING

I do not believe that it will always be popular to wear mourning for our friends, unless we feel a little doubtful about where they went.

Bill Nye

MOUSE

The mouse is an animal which, killed in sufficient numbers under carefully controlled conditions, will produce a PhD thesis.

Journal of Irreproducible Results

MOUSETRAP

In baiting a mousetrap with cheese, always leave room for the mouse.

Saki

Build a better mousetrap and the world will beat a path to your door.

Ralph Waldo Emerson

MOUTH

A closed mouth gathers no feet.

American saying

MOVE

When you see a good move, wait, look for a better one.

Rudolph Spielmann

MURDER

One murder makes a villain, millions a hero. Numbers sanctify, my good fellow.

Charlie Chaplin

Other sins only speak; murder shrieks out.

Daniel Webster

MURPHY'S LAW

Murphy's Law fails only when you try to demonstrate it.

Anonymous

MUSHROOM

I got the mushroom treatment ... they keep you completely in the dark and every once in a while they come in and throw manure on you.

Gordie Howe

MUSIC

Without music life would be a mistake.

Friedrich Nietzsche

A musician must make music, an artist must paint, a poet must write, if he is to be ultimately at peace with himself.

Abraham Maslow

Too many pieces [of classical music] finish too long after the end.

Igor Stravinsky

Wagner's music is better than it sounds.

Bill Nye

There is something about music that keeps its distance even at the moment that it engulfs us. It is at the same time outside and away from us and inside and part of us.

Aaron Copland

After silence, that which comes nearest to expressing the inexpressible is music.

Aldous Huxley

In music one must think with the heart and feel with the brain.

George Sznell

I'll play it first and tell you what it is later.

Miles Davis

The flute is not an instrument which has a good moral effect. It is too exciting.

Aristotle

A good ear for music and a taste for music are two very different things which are often confounded; and so is comprehending and enjoying every object of sense and sentiment.

Lord Greville

Van Gogh became a painter because he had no ear for music.

Nikki Harris

The trouble with a lot of songs you hear nowadays is that someone forgot to put them to music.

Sammy Kahn

Music is a language by whose means messages are elaborated. That such messages can be understood by the many but sent out only by few, and that [music] alone among all the languages unites the contradictory character of being at once intelligible and untranslatable – these facts make the creator of music a being like the gods.

Claude Lévi-Strauss

Music is a means of rapid transportation.

John Cage

Music is spiritual. The music business is not.

Van Morrison

All art constantly aspires towards the condition of music.

Walter Pater

What music is more enchanting than the voices of young people, when you can't hear what they say?

Logan Pearsall Smith

Only sick music makes money today.

Friedrich Nietzsche

When you are about thirty-five years old, something terrible always happens to music.

Steve Race

One good thing about music, when it hits you feel no pain.

Bob Marley

Sometimes you have to fight with music. .

Bob Marley

I don't know anything about music. In my line you don't have to.

Elvis Presley

Music is Love in search of a word.

Sidney Lanier

Music is the shorthand of emotion.

Leo Tolstoy

All musical people seem to be happy; it is to them the engrossing pursuit, almost the only innocent and unpublished passion.

Sydney Smith

Of all noises, I think music is the least disagreeable.

Samuel Johnson

When people hear good music, it makes them homesick for something they never had, and never will have.

Edgar Watson Howe

You have Van Gogh's ear for music.

Billy Wilder

The music ain't worth nothing if you can't lay it on the public.

Louis Armstrong

You've got to know much more than just the technicalities of notes; you've got to know what goes between the notes.

Jimi Hendrix

Take a music bath once or twice a week and you will find that it is to the soul what the water bath is to the body.

Oliver Wendell Holmes

Music is the only language in which you cannot say a mean or sarcastic thing.

John Erskine

Is it not strange that sheep's guts should hale souls out of men's bodies?

William Shakespeare

It don't mean a thing if it ain't got that swing.

Duke Ellington

I don't do something because I think it will sell thirty million albums. I couldn't care less. If it sells one, it sells one.

Oscar Peterson

Music is moonlight in the gloomy night of life.

Jean-Paul Richter

Remember: Information is not knowledge; knowledge is not wisdom; wisdom is not truth; truth is not beauty; beauty is not love; love is not music; music is the best.

Frank Zappa

Music is the fourth great material want of our natures – first food, then raiment, then shelter, then music.

Christian Nestell Bovee

MUSICAL HIT

I've never heard such corny lyrics, such simpering sentimentality, such repetitious, uninspired melody. Man, we've got a hit on our hands!

Brad Anderson

The more you jump around, the bigger your hat is, the more people listen to your music. ... The only important thing is to sell, and make money. It's nothing to do with talent.

George Harrison

MUSICIAN

A musician, if he's a messenger, is like a child who hasn't been handled too many times by man.

Jimi Hendrix

Musicians don't retire; they stop when there's no more music in them.

Louis Armstrong

I've never known a musician who regretted being one. Whatever deceptions life may have in store for you, music itself is not going to let you down.

Virgil Thomson

MYSTERIOUS

The most beautiful thing we can experience is the mysterious. It is the source of all true art and all science.

Albert Einstein

MYSTERY

No object is mysterious. The mystery is in your eye.

Elizabeth Bowen

The true mystery of the world is the visible, not the invisible.

Oscar Wilde

The possession of knowledge does not kill the sense of wonder and mystery. There is always more mystery.

Anaïs Nin

MYTHS

Myths which are believed in tend to come true.

George Orwell

Are we the ones who think up myths or is it myths who think us up?

Carlo Ginzburg

It is a sure sign that a culture has reached a dead end when it is no longer intrigued by its myths.

Greil Marcus

The myths of failure touch us with the tragedy of life, but those of success only with their own incredibility.

Joseph Campbell

NAGGING

Nagging is the repetition of unpalatable truths.

Baroness Edith Summerskill

NAMES

Names are but noise and smoke,/ Obscuring heavenly light.

Johann Wolfgang von Goethe

Names are an important key to what a society values.

David S. Slawson

Tigers die and leave their skins; people die and leave their names.

Japanese proverb

NARCISSIST

A narcissist is someone better looking than you.

Gore Vidal

NATIONAL DEBT

I am one of those who do not believe that a national debt is a national blessing ... it is calculated to raise around the administration a moneyed aristocracy dangerous to the liberties of the country.

Andrew Jackson

NATIONALISM

Nationalism is an infantile disease. It is the measles of mankind.

Albert Einstein

NATIONALITY

Science and art belong to the whole world, and before them vanish the barriers of nationality.

Johann Wolfgang von Goethe

NATIONS

If people behaved the way nations do, they would all be put in straitjackets.

Tennessee Williams

A nation without the means of reform is without the means of survival.

Edmund Burke

The great nations have always acted like gangsters, and the small nations like prostitutes.

Stanley Kubrick

A nation is a society united by delusions about its ancestry.

Dean Inge

There are truths that can kill a nation.

Jean Giraudoux

A common memory and a common ideal – these, more than a common blood, make a nation.

C. Delisle Burns

NATURAL LAWS

People make the mistake of talking about natural laws. There are no natural laws. There are only temporary habits of nature.

Alfred North Whitehead

NATURAL RESOURCES

The nation behaves well if it treats the natural resources as assets which it must turn over to the next generation increased, and not impaired, in value.

Theodore Roosevelt

NATURE

Let us permit nature to have her way; she understands her business better than we do.

Michel de Montaigne

Nature is not human-hearted.

Lao-Tse

Accuse not Nature, she hath done her part; Do thou but thine.

John Milton

[In a state of nature] No arts; no letters; no society; and which is worst of all, continual fear and danger of violent death; and the life of man, solitary, poor, nasty, brutish, and short.

Thomas Hobbes

It is unfair to blame man too fiercely for being pugnacious; he learned the habit from Nature.

Christopher Morley

In the eyes of Nature, we are just another species in trouble.

Lionel Tiger and Robin Fox

Nature's laws affirm instead of prohibit. If you violate her laws you are your own prosecuting attorney, judge, jury, and hangman.

Luther Burbank

Like all compulsory legislation, that of Nature is harsh and wasteful in its operation. Ignorance is visited as sharply as willful disobedience – incapacity meets with the same punishment as crime. Nature's discipline is not even a word and a blow, and the blow first; but the blow without the word. It is left up to you to find out why your ears are boxed.

Thomas Henry Huxley

All things are artificial, for nature is the art of God.

Sir Thomas Browne

God, or in other words, Nature.

Baruch Spinoza

Nature does nothing uselessly.

Aristotle

We cannot command Nature except by obeying her.

Francis Bacon

Nature has made up her mind that what cannot defend itself shall not be defended.

Ralph Waldo Emerson

A morning glory at my window satisfies me more than the metaphysics of books.
Walt Whitman

Nature never deceives us; it is always we who deceive ourselves.
Jean-Jacques Rousseau

The more we learn about the details of natural processes, the more evident it becomes that these processes are themselves creative. Nothing transcends Nature like Nature itself.
Loyal Rue

To me nature is ... spiders and bugs, and big fish eating little fish, and plants eating plants, and animals eating ... It's like an enormous restaurant, that's the way I see it.
Woody Allen

Nature teaches more than she preaches. There are no sermons in stones.
John Burroughs

Make no mistake, the weeds will win, nature bats last.
Robert Michael Pyle

He loves nature in spite of what it did to him.
Forrest Tucker

All nature wears one universal grin.
Henry Fielding

One of the nice things about Old Mother Nature is the manner in which she blushes before disrobing.
Wes Lawrence

Till now man has been up against Nature; from now on he will be up against his own nature.
Dennis Gabor

NECESSITY
Necessity is the plea of every infringement of human freedom. It is the argument of tyrants; it is the creed of slaves.
William Pitt

Our necessities are few but our wants are endless.
Anonymous

Necessity relieves us from the embarrassment of choice.
Marquis de Vauvenargues

Where necessity speaks, it demands.
Russian proverb

Necessity is not an established fact, but an interpretation.
Friedrich Nietzsche

Are these things then necessities? / Then let us meet them like necessities.
William Shakespeare

I don't think necessity is the mother of invention. Invention, in my opinion, arises directly from idleness, possibly also from laziness. To save oneself trouble.
Agatha Christie

Necessity has the face of a dog.
Gabriel Garcia Marquez

Necessity hath no law.
Oliver Cromwell

Necessity gives the law and does not itself receive it.

Publilius Syrus

You cannot escape necessities but you can conquer them.

Seneca

NECTAR

Nectar, *n.* A drink served at banquets of the Olympian deities. The secret of its preparation is lost, but the modern Kentuckians believe that they come pretty near to the knowledge of its chief ingredient.

Ambrose Bierce

NEED

I just need enough to tide me over until I need more.

Jerry Dennis

We never understand how little we need in this world until we know the loss of it.

J.M. Barrie

One of the oldest human needs is having someone to wonder where you are when you don't come home at night.

Margaret Mead

NEGOTIATE

Let us never negotiate out of fear. But let us never fear to negotiate.

John F. Kennedy

NEIGHBOUR

Love thy neighbour as yourself, but choose your neighbourhood.

Louise Beal

Love thy neighbour, but pull not down thy hedge.

John Ray

Everybody wants to right the world; nobody wants to help his neighbour.

Henry Miller

The problem with neighbours is that they live next door.

Jon Canter

Choose your neighbours before you buy your house.

Hausa proverb

NEUROSIS

A neurosis is a secret you don't know you're keeping.

Kenneth Tynan

NEUROTICS

I prefer neurotic people. I like to hear rumblings beneath the surface.

Stephen Sondheim

A mistake which is commonly made about neurotics is to suppose that they are interesting. It is not interesting to be always unhappy, engrossed with oneself, malignant and ungrateful, and never quite in touch with reality.

Cyril Connolly

NEUTRALITY

The hottest places in Hell are reserved for those who, in time of great moral crisis, maintain their neutrality.

Dante Alighieri

NEW
What is valuable is not new, and what is new is not valuable.
Daniel Webster

There is no subject so old that something new cannot be said about it.
Fyodor Dostoyevsky

New things are made familiar, and familiar things are made new.
Samuel Johnson

There is nothing new under the sun, but there are lots of things we don't know.
Ambrose Bierce

NEW YORK
As only New Yorkers know, if you can get through the twilight, you'll live through the night.
Dorothy Parker

Traffic signals in New York are just rough guidelines.
David Letterman

New York: an attitude surrounded by an island.
Anonymous

When you leave New York, you are astonished at how clean the rest of the world is. Clean is not enough.
Fran Lebowitz

NEWS
It's not the world that's got so much worse but the news coverage that's got so much better.
G.K. Chesterton

People everywhere confuse what they read in newspapers with news.
A.J. Liebling

NEWS VALUE
To have news value is to have a tin can tied to one's tail.
T.E. Lawrence

NEWSPAPERS
Let me make the newspapers, and I care not what is preached in the pulpit or enacted in Congress.
Wendell Phillips

My brother cuts the time it takes to read a newspaper by skipping everything in the future tense; and it's amazing what he doesn't miss.
Katharine Whitehorn

Newspaper editors are men who separate the wheat from the chaff and then print the chaff.
Adlai Stevenson

The probability of learning something unusual from a newspaper is far greater than that of experiencing it.
Robert Musil

A newspaper reporter is related to a telephone as a musician is related to a piano.
James B. Stewart

If you don't read the newspaper you are uninformed; if you do read the newspaper you are misinformed.
Mark Twain

A newspaper is a device for making the ignorant more ignorant and the crazy crazier.

H.L. Mencken

Everything you read in the newspapers is absolutely true except for the rare story of which you happen to have first-hand knowledge.

Erwin Knoll

The careful reader of a few good newspapers can learn more in a year than most scholars do in their great libraries.

Benjamin Franklin

Were it left to me to decide whether we should have a government without newspapers or newspapers without government, I should not hesitate to prefer the latter.

Thomas Jefferson

Newspapers are owned by individuals or corporations, but freedom of the press belongs to the people.

Richard J. Finnegan

NICE GUYS
Nice guys finish last, but we get to sleep in.

Evan Davis

A nice man is a man of nasty ideas.

Jonathan Swift

NIGHT
Don't try to solve serious matters in the middle of the night.

Philip K. Dick

When the night surrounded me I was born again: I was the owner of my own darkness.

Pablo Neruda

NIGHTMARE
Have you noticed … there is never any third act in a nightmare? They bring you to a climax of terror and then they leave you there. They are the work of poor dramatists.

Max Beerbohm

NO
It is a great evil, as well as a misfortune, to be unable to utter a prompt and decided "No."

Charles Simmons

NOBILITY
The truth is that there is nothing noble in being superior to somebody else. The only real nobility is in being superior to your former self.

Whitney Young

The nobility of a human being is strictly independent of that of his convictions.

Jean Rostand

NOBODY
I am a nobody. Nobody is perfect, therefore I am perfect.

Internet

NOD
A nod is as good as a wink to a blind bat.

Eric Idle

NOISE
Noise proves nothing. Often a hen who has merely laid an egg cackles as if she had laid an asteroid.
Mark Twain

NONCONFORMITY
Nonconformity is an empty goal, and rebellion against prevailing opinion simply because it is prevailing should be no more praised than acquiescence to it. Indeed, it is often a mask for cowardice, and few are more pathetic than those who flaunt outer differences to expiate their inner surrender.
William Whyte

Non-conformity has become the major if not the only sin we know today.
Robert Lindner

NONSENSE
The importance of nonsense can hardly be overstated. The more clearly we experience something as "nonsense," the more clearly we are experiencing the boundaries of our own self-imposed cognitive structures. "Nonsense" is that which does not fit into the pre-arranged patterns we have superimposed on reality. ... Nonsense is nonsense only when we have not yet formed the point of view from which it makes sense.
The Dancing Wu Li Masters by Gary Zukav

To attack a man for talking nonsense is like finding your mortal enemy drowning in a swamp and jumping in after him with a knife.
Sir Karl Popper

Nonsense and beauty have close connections.
E.M. Forster

We're not blind and we're not fools. We're just plain, sensible people who refuse to be fooled by a lot of supernatural nonsense.
Eric Taylor

NORMAL
The trouble with normal is it always gets worse.
Bruce Cockburn

Nobody realizes that some people expend tremendous energy merely to be normal.
Albert Camus

The only normal people are the ones you don't know very well.
Joe Ancis

I am not strange, I am just not normal.
Salvador Dali

NORTH
The north focuses our anxieties.
Margaret Atwood

NOSE
A great nose indicates a great man – genial, courteous, intellectual, virile, courageous.
Edmond Rostand

A nose that can see is worth two that sniff.
Eugène Ionesco

NOSINESS

Enquire not what boils in another's pot.

Thomas Fuller, MD

NOSTALGIA

Nostalgia isn't what it used to be.

Peter De Vries

Nostalgia is a seductive liar.

George Ball

Nostalgia is longing for a place you wouldn't move back to.

Anonymous

A society which has made "nostalgia" a marketable commodity on the cultural exchange quickly repudiates the suggestion that life in the past was in any important way better than life today.

Christopher Lasch

Sharp nostalgia, infinite and terrible, for what I already possess.

Juan Ramon Jimenez

NOTHING

I used to believe that anything was better than nothing. Now I know that sometimes nothing is better.

Glenda Jackson

Nothing is often a good thing to do, and almost always a clever thing to say.

Will Durant

Of those who say nothing, few are silent.

Thomas Neill

When one does nothing, one believes oneself to be responsible for everything.

Jean-Paul Sartre

Nothing, like something, happens anywhere.

Philip Larkin

"You mean you can't take less," said the Hatter. "It's very easy to take more than nothing."

Lewis Carroll

NOTHINGNESS

Nothingness haunts being.

Jean-Paul Sartre

NOVEL

A novel worth reading is an education of the heart. It enlarges your sense of human possibility, of what human nature is, of what happens in the world.

Susan Sontag

One should not be too harsh on English novels; they are the only relaxation of the intellectually unemployed.

Oscar Wilde

NOVELIST

The economy of a novelist is a little like that of a careful housewife who is unwilling to throw away anything that might perhaps serve its turn.

Graham Greene

NOVELTY

Novelty has charms that our minds can hardly withstand. The most valuable things, if they have for a long while appeared among us, do not make any impression as they are good, but give us a distaste as they are old. But when the influence of this fantastical humour is over, the same men or things will come to be admired again by a happy return of our good taste.

William Makepeace Thackeray

NUMBERS

I have often admired the mystical way of Pythagoras, and the secret way of numbers.

Sir Thomas Browne

History repeats itself and numbers never lie.

John Voorhees

I'm not even thinking straight anymore. Numbers buzz in my head like wasps.

Kurt Neumann

There is no safety in numbers, or in anything else.

James Thurber

OBEDIENCE
The reluctant obedience of distant provinces generally costs more than it (the territory) is worth.

Thomas Babington Macaulay

Wicked men obey from fear; good men from love.

Aristotle

Let them obey who know not how to rule.

William Shakespeare

OBFUSCATION
Our disputants put me in mind of the skuttle fish, that when he is unable to extricate himself, blackens all the water about him, til he becomes invisible.

Joseph Addison

OBITUARIES
I have never killed a man, but I have read many obituaries with great pleasure.

Clarence Darrow

OBITUARIES (WITH A STING)
He was liked, even loved, by all his neighbours. Many of their children looked upon him as a father, not without cause.

She spent all of her time involved in the lives of others. Now she has time for herself. Praise the Lord.

A self-made millionaire through stock-market investments, much to his credit he handled the investments of others.

It was an untimely death; but his books reveal that here was a man who must surely have had much more to say.

His commitment to atheism was total. He believed that there is no heaven or hell and strove unselfishly to share this belief with everyone at every opportunity. Wherever he is now, nothing is too good for him.

In authoring his own epitaph, "The paths of glory lead but to the grave," the professor reminded us one last time of his dedication to originality.

In memory of our neighbour's dog, who faithfully fertilized our lawn every day.

His race run, he leaves a grateful world.

The departed gang boss, who died in his bed aged eighty-five, will be sadly missed by his early associates.

A lifelong participant in the country's political process, he will be remembered by those who knew him for what he was.

Farewell to Eileen Ann Stagger, whose devotion to John Barleycorn in later years caused Molson's to reach a high of $38 and whose passing will necessitate downsizing of the brewery industry in the Southwestern Ontario region.

A pillar of the community passed away suddenly last Monday. A devoted father, a faithful husband, a rare lover.

Widely respected for his innovative approach to justice, the judge will always be fondly remembered by his many friends at the Repeat Offenders association.

After a long career in banking, he developed a sudden interest in travel. His wife of thirty years remained in Canada, but he was accompanied by his new secretary, Fifi Latour, to Brazil, where he died yesterday.

With the demise of our most active stockbroker, we cannot begin to calculate the loss to our firm and clients. We know many in the investment community will share our grief.

The unorthodox teacher had a profound influence on his students, most of whom cannot praise him eloquently enough. A remedial literacy class will be established in his memory.

He was a sports celebrity viewed by many as an unqualified success. In honouring him posthumously, our only regret is that it was not possible to do so sooner.

The lobbyist was well-known to some MPs for his generosity and persuasiveness, and to many others for his ability to simultaneously practise those two virtues.

He had great plans for his success, and only his untimely demise at the age of eighty prevented him from making his mark on the world.

After a visit to Elmer's friendly barber shop on Main Street, his customers always left feeling they had been clipped.

While his willingness to run for public office was admired by those who knew him, this trait was particularly appreciated by the candidates running against him.

The Globe and Mail

OBJECTIONS
Nothing will ever be attempted if all possible objections must first be overcome.

Samuel Johnson

OBJECTIVE
You must keep your mind on the objective, not the obstacle.
William Randolph Hearst

You spend your whole life believing that you're on the right track, only to discover that you're on the wrong train.
Anonymous

OBLIGATIONS
There are inalienable obligations as well as inalienable rights.
Abraham Joshua Heschel

OBSCURITY
The obscure we see eventually; the completely apparent takes longer.
Edward R. Murrow

Obscurity is the refuge of incompetence.
Robert Heinlein

OBSERVATION
In the fields of observation, chance favours only the mind that is prepared.
Louis Pasteur

You can observe a lot just by watching.
Yogi Berra

One must always tell what one sees. Above all, which is more difficult, one must always see what one sees.
Charles Péguy

Many eyes go through the meadow, but few see the flowers in it.
Ralph Waldo Emerson

All of us are watchers – of television, of time clocks, of traffic on the freeway – but few are observers. Everyone is looking, not many are seeing.
Peter Leschak

Seeing through is rarely seeing into.
Elizabeth Bibesco

When it's dark enough, you can see the stars.
Charles Beard

To observations which ourselves we make,/We grow more partial for th' observer's sake.
Alexander Pope

Things seen are mightier than things heard.
Alfred, Lord Tennyson

He saw nearly all things as through a glass eye, darkly.
Mark Twain

One who is too wise an observer of the business of others, like one who is too curious in observing the labour of bees, will often be stung for his curiosity.
Alexander Pope

Mind not only what people say, but how they say it; and if you have any sagacity, you may discover more truth by your eyes than by your ears. People can say what they will, but they cannot look just as they will; and their looks frequently [reveal] what their words are calculated to conceal.
Lord Chesterfield

For a clever eye, one glance is enough, while a dunce may stare all day long.

Chinese proverb

OBSTACLES

Obstacles cannot crush me. Every obstacle yields to stern resolve. He who is fixed on a star does not change his mind.

Leonardo da Vinci

If there are obstacles, the shortest line between two points may be the crooked line.

Bertolt Brecht

Obstacles are what you see when you take your eyes off the objective.

Henry Ford

Little minds are tamed and subdued by misfortune; but great minds rise above them.

Washington Irving

OBSTINACY

Obstinacy's ne're so stiff/As when t'is in a wrong belief

Samuel Butler

Fools and obstinate men make rich lawyers.

Spanish proverb

No man is good for anything who has not some particle of obstinacy to use upon occasion.

Henry Ward Beecher

I regret many follies which sprang from my obstinacy; but without that trait I would not have reached my goal.

Carl Jung

An obstinate man does not hold opinions, but they hold him.

Alexander Pope

We call it firmness when we agree, obstinacy when we don't.

Herbert Samuel

OBVIOUS

Familiar things happen, and mankind does not bother about them. It requires a very unusual mind to undertake the analysis of the obvious.

Alfred North Whitehead

He can see a louse as far away as China but is unconscious of an elephant on his nose.

Malay proverb

Ours is one of those times when it is the duty of an intelligent man to repeat the obvious.

George Orwell

To see what is in front of one's nose needs a constant struggle.

George Orwell

It pays to be obvious, especially if you have a reputation for subtlety.

Isaac Asimov

To spell out the obvious is often to call it in question.

Eric Hoffer

OCCULT

Some kids do get fascinated with the occult, and some of them will pull out a Ouija board or try to hold an awkward seance at some point. But what keeps them from becoming full-fledged witches or warlocks is that they quickly find out that none of the stuff actually works.

Bill Ferguson

OCEAN

Ocean, *n.* A body of water occupying about two-thirds of a world made for man – who has no gills.

Ambrose Bierce

ODDS

And how can a man die better/ Than facing fearful odds?

Thomas Babington Macaulay

If we do what is necessary, all the odds are in our favour.

Henry Kissinger

OFFEND

Never offend people with style when you can offend them with substance.

Sam Brown

OFFICE

A man who has no office to go to – I don't care who he is – is a trial of which you can have no conception.

George Bernard Shaw

A tough day at the office is even tougher when your office contains spectator seating.

Nik Posa

OIL

Oil is like a wild animal. Whoever captures it has it.

J. Paul Getty

OLD

I love everything that's old: old friends, old times, old manners, old books, old wines.

Oliver Goldsmith

When your friends begin to flatter you on how young you look, it's a sure sign you're getting old.

Mark Twain

The older you get, the older you want to get.

Keith Richards

Our generation are the new old. I remember what someone of sixty looked like when I was a kid. They didn't look like me.

Jack Nicholson

The value of old age depends on the person who reaches it. To some men of early performance, it is useless. To others, who are late to develop, it just enables them to finish the job.

Thomas Hardy

OLD AGE

We've put more effort into helping folks reach old age than into helping them enjoy it.

Frank A. Clark

It is old age, rather than death, that is to be contrasted with life. Old age is life's parody, whereas death transforms life into a destiny.

Simone de Beauvoir

The tragedy of old age is not that one is old, but that one is young.

Oscar Wilde

Old age is the most unexpected of all the things that happen to a man.
Leon Trotsky

One's age should be tranquil, as childhood should be playful. Hard work at either extremity of life seems out of place. At mid-day the sun may burn, and men labour under it; but the morning and the evening should be alike calm and cheerful.

Thomas Arnold

Old men are dangerous; it doesn't matter to them what is going to happen to the world.
George Bernard Shaw

Age in a virtuous person of either sex carries in it an authority which makes it preferable to all the pleasures of youth.
Sir Richard Steele

Old age is an incurable disease.
Seneca

All diseases run into one, old age.
Ralph Waldo Emerson

Do not regret growing older. It is a privilege denied to many.
Unknown

OLD-FASHIONED
I want an old-fashioned house with an old-fashioned fence, And an old-fashioned millionaire.
Marve Fisher

OLYMPIC GAMES
Pythagoras used to say life resembles the Olympic Games; a few men strain their muscles to carry off a prize; others bring trinkets to sell to the crowd for a profit; and some are there who seek no further advantage than to look at the show and see how and why everything is done. They are spectators of other men's lives in order to better judge and manage their own.
Michel de Montaigne

OLYMPIC HONOUR
And I now close in recalling to you one of the old Olympic Torch games. Each contestant started in the race with a lighted torch in his hand, and the winner was the youth – not the one who arrived first at the goal – but he who first reached the goal with the torch still burning brightly.

The beauty and symmetry of this restriction as touching life I leave to every man to apply and to take to his own discerning heart. To-day, as in that far-off time, the real winner is not the man who first arrives, whom the world so shallowly regards as first in the race, in terms of wealth, station, garish honours or other false standards of success.

Many a man has thus arrived apparently triumphant, but with his torch extinguished in irredeemable gloom; the torch of health, the torch of honour, the torch of domestic bliss or of parental joy. The true winner, the real winner, is he who pressed earnestly, even passionately to the goal; who has safely guarded the sacred flame, and who has held high to the end of the torch of health, the torch of honour, the torch of true fellowship, the torch of precious friends of his hour and day, the torch of everything that enriches life, and, what an encouraging thought, that in such a race every contestant may, if he so strives, win some prize.

Address of the Chief Justice of Ontario, delivered at a dinner tendered to the Rt Hon. Sir William Mulock, KCMG, by the Ontario members of the Canadian Bar Association on the occasion of his ninetieth birthday, 12 Can. Bar Review (1934) at pp. 40–1

OPEN MIND

The trouble with having an open mind, of course, is that people will insist on coming along and trying to put things in it.

Terry Pratchett

The world is full of people who have never, since childhood, met an open doorway with an open mind.

E.B. White

OPERA

The opera is like a husband with a foreign title: expensive to support, hard to understand, and therefore a supreme social challenge.

Cleveland Amory

No good opera plot can be sensible, for people do not sing when they are feeling sensible.

W.H. Auden

OPINION

When any opinion leads to absurdity, it is certainly false; but it is not certain that an opinion is false because it is of dangerous consequence.

David Hume

I agree with no man's opinion. I have some of my own.

Ivan Turgenev

The more unpopular an opinion is, the more necessary that he who holds it be somewhat punctilious in his observance of conventionalities generally.

Samuel Butler

Too often we … enjoy the comfort of opinion without the discomfort of thought.

John F. Kennedy

When the facts change I change my opinion. What do you do?

John Maynard Keynes

With effervescing opinions, as with the not yet forgotten champagne, the quickest way to let them go flat is to let them get exposed to the air.

Oliver Wendell Holmes, Jr

If there is an opinion, facts will be found to support it.

Judy Sproles

My opinions may have changed, but not the fact that I am right.

Ashley Brilliant

There are a great many opinions in this world, and a good half of them are professed by people who have never been in trouble.

Mavis Gallant

Those who most obstinately oppose the most widely held opinions more often do so because of pride than lack of intelligence. They find the best places in the right set already taken, and they do not want back seats.

We credit scarcely any persons with good sense except those who are of our opinion.

Unless they share our opinions, we seldom find people sensible.

François, duc de La Rochefoucauld

Some men are just as sure of the truth of their opinions as are others of what they know.

Aristotle

Men get opinions as boys learn to spell,/By reiteration chiefly.

Elizabeth Barrett Browning

People are usually more firmly convinced that their opinions are precious than they are true.

George Santayana

A man can brave opinion, a woman must submit to it.

Madame de Staël

One must judge men not by their opinions but by what their opinions have made of them.

Georg Christoph Lichtenberg

Don't quote me as saying that we will or we should increase our external aid. That would be my opinion if I had an opinion, but as a member of my government, I don't have an opinion.

Paul Martin

The opinions that are held with passion are always those for which no good ground exists; indeed the passion is the measure of the holder's lack of rational conviction. Opinions in politics and religion are almost always held passionately.

Bertrand Russell

A man has a property in his opinions and the free communication of them.

James Madison

Opinion has caused more trouble on this little Earth than plagues or earthquakes.

Voltaire

No one can have a higher opinion of him than I have, and I think he's a dirty little beast.

W.S. Gilbert

I am not one of those who in expressing opinions confine themselves to facts.

Mark Twain

A great many people mistake opinions for thought.

Herbert Victor Prochnow

Where there is much desire to learn, there of necessity will be much arguing, much writing, many opinions; for opinion in good men is but knowledge in the making.

John Milton

Facts are what pedantic dull people have instead of opinions. Opinions are always interesting. Facts are only scaffolding, the trellis up which bright opinions grow.
A.A. Gill

Risk little on the opinion of a man who has little to lose.
Unknown

Opinion is ultimately determined by the feelings, and not by the intellect.
Herbert Spencer

The opinion of the strongest is always the best.
Jean de La Fontaine

Everyone is entitled to his own opinion, but not his own facts.
Daniel Patrick Moynihan

OPINIONS (NEW)
New opinions are always suspected, and usually opposed, without any other reason but because they are not already common.
John Locke

Opinions have vested interests, just as men have.
Samuel Butler

If in the last few years you haven't discarded a major opinion or acquired a new one, check your pulse – you may be dead.
Gelett Burgess

The more opinions you have, the less you see.
Wim Wenders

Express a mean opinion of yourself occasionally; it will show your friends that you know how to tell the truth.
Edgar Watson Howe

Every new opinion, at its starting, is precisely in a minority of one.
Thomas Carlyle

OPPORTUNITY
There is no security on this Earth; there is only opportunity.
Douglas MacArthur

The opportunity that God sends does not wake up him who is asleep.
Senegalese proverb

Opportunity is often missed because we are broadcasting when we should be tuning in.
Unknown

Opportunities multiply as they are seized.
Sun Tzu

Make the most of all that comes and the least of all that goes.
Sara Teasdale

There is a tide in the affairs of men,/Which, taken at the flood, leads on to fortune; ...

On such a full sea are we now afloat,/And we must take the current when it serves,/Or lose our ventures.
William Shakespeare

Opportunity is the greatest bawd.
Benjamin Franklin

For all sad words of tongue or pen, the saddest are these: "It might have been!"
John Greenleaf Whittier

A man must make his opportunity, as oft as find it.
Sir Francis Bacon

A wise man will make more opportunities than he finds.
Sir Francis Bacon

Equal opportunity is good, but special privilege is better.
Anna Chennault

Equal opportunity means everyone will have a fair chance at becoming incompetent.
Laurence J. Peter

Gather ye rosebuds while ye may.
Robert Herrick

Opportunity is missed by most people because it is dressed in overalls and looks like work.
Thomas Edison

Opportunities are usually disguised as hard work, so most people don't recognize them.
Ann Landers

I have always tried to turn every disaster into an opportunity.
John D. Rockefeller, Jr

To hell with circumstances; I create opportunities.
Bruce Lee

This home of opportunity, where every man is the equal of every other man before the law, if he isn't careful.
Finley Peter Dunne

You create your opportunities by asking for them.
Patty Hansen

We are confronted with insurmountable opportunities.
Pogo

Every obstacle presents an opportunity to improve our condition.
Unknown

Opportunity does not trouble dead men, or dead ones who flatter themselves that they are alive.
Elbert Hubbard

It is less important to redistribute wealth than it is to redistribute opportunity.
Arthur H. Vandenberg

A good opportunity is seldom presented, and is easily lost.
Publilius Syrus

OPPOSITES
Every sweet hath its sour; every evil its good.
Emerson

Every positive value has its price in negative terms. ... Einstein leads to Hiroshima.
Pablo Picasso

OPPOSITION
Men often oppose a thing merely because they have no agency in planning it, or because it may have been planned by those whom they dislike.
Alexander Hamilton

When everything seems to be going against you, remember that the airplane takes off against the wind, not with it.

Henry Ford

OPPRESSION

He who allows oppression shares the crime.

Erasmus Darwin

OPTIMISM

I am not a pessimist; to perceive evil where it exists is, in my opinion, a form of optimism.

Roberto Rossellini

I find nothing more depressing than optimism.

Paul Fussell

Optimism is a kind of heart stimulant – the digitalis of failure.

Elbert Hubbard

The place where optimism most flourishes is the lunatic asylum.

Havelock Ellis

Optimism is the madness of insisting that all is well when we are miserable.

Voltaire

Optimism assumes, or attempts to prove, that the universe exists to please us, and pessimism that it exists to displease us. Scientifically, there is no evidence that it is concerned with us either one way or the other. The belief in either pessimism or optimism is a matter of temperament, not of reason.

Bertrand Russell

Optimism, *n.* The doctrine or belief that everything is beautiful, including what is ugly.

Ambrose Bierce

OPTIMIST

An optimist is a guy that never has much experience and a pessimist is a person who has had to listen to too many optimists.

Don Marquis

The optimist proclaims that we live in the best of all possible worlds, the pessimist fears this is true.

James Branch Cabell

An optimist is a fellow who believes what's going to be, will be postponed.

Kin Hubbard

An optimist is a guy who has never had much experience.

Don Marquis

An optimist is simply a pessimist with no job experience.

Anonymous

An optimist is someone who thinks the future is uncertain.

Anonymous

An optimist may see a light where there is one, but why must the pessimist always run to blow it out?

Michel de Saint-Pierre

Stick with the optimists. It's going to be tough even if they're right.

James Reston

I'm an optimist, but an optimist who carries a raincoat.

Harold Wilson

I am a pessimist because of intelligence, but an optimist of will.

Antonio Gramsci

The latest definition of an optimist is one who fills up his crossword puzzle in ink.

Clement Shorter

An optimist is a man who thinks his wife has stopped smoking cigarettes when he finds cigar butts around the house.

Unknown

ORATORY

Oratory: the art of making deep noises from the chest sound like important messages from the brain.

H.I. Phillips

Here comes the orator! with his flood of words and his drop of reason.

Benjamin Franklin

The object of oratory alone is not truth, but persuasion.

François, duc de La Rochefoucauld

ORCHESTRA

I'm not interested in having an orchestra sound like itself. I want it to sound like the composer.

Leonard Bernstein

There are two golden rules for an orchestra: start together and finish together. The public doesn't give a damn what goes on between.

Sir Thomas Beecham

ORDER

Order is for idiots; genius can handle chaos.

Anonymous

First thing first, but not necessarily in that order.

Doctor Who

Order marches with weighty and measured strides; disorder is always in a hurry.

Napoleon Bonaparte

Order and simplification are the first steps toward the mastery of a subject.

Thomas Mann

Order is not pressure which is imposed on society from without, but an equilibrium which is set up from within.

José Ortega y Gasset

ORDERS

There's a line in the picture where he snarls, "Nobody tells me what to do." That's exactly how I've felt all my life.

Marlon Brando

ORDINARY

A man can stand anything except a succession of ordinary days.

Johann Wolfgang von Goethe

Eschew the ordinary, disdain the commonplace. If you have a single-minded need for something, let it be the unusual, the esoteric, the bizarre, the unexpected.

Chuck Jones

ORGANIZATIONS

It is the willingness of people to give of themselves over and above the demands of the job that distinguishes the great from the merely adequate organization.

Peter Drucker

I have faith that the time will eventually come when employees and employers, as well as all mankind, will realize that they serve themselves best when they serve others most.

B.C. Forbes

ORGANIZE

Don't agonize. Organize.

Florynce Kennedy

A library may be very large; but if it is in disorder, it is not so useful as one that is small but well arranged. In the same way, a man may have a great mass of knowledge, but if he has not worked it up by thinking it over for himself, it has much less value than a far smaller amount which he has thoroughly pondered.

Arthur Schopenhauer

ORGANIZED CRIME

Organized crime in America takes in more than $40 billion a year and spends very little on office supplies.

Woody Allen

ORIGINALITY

When people are free to do as they please, they usually imitate each other. Originality is deliberate and forced, and partakes of the nature of a protest.

Eric Hoffer

Originality finds the unexpected but inevitable next step.

Mason Cooley

Originality consists not only in doing things differently, but also in "doing things better."

Edward Stedman

Originality consists in thinking for yourself, and not in thinking unlike other people.

Sir James Fitzjames Stephen

People are always talking about originality; but what do they mean? As soon as we are born, the world begins to work upon us, and this goes on to the end. What can we call our own except energy, strength, and will? If I could give an account of all that I owe to great predecessors and contemporaries, there would be but a small balance in my favour.

Johann Wolfgang von Goethe

If you have an original idea use it carefully so you won't look like you've just put on a new suit.

Jean Cocteau

All good things which exist are the fruits of originality.

John Stuart Mill

Originality is undetected plagiarism.

Dean Inge

Originality is a thing we constantly clamor for, and constantly quarrel with.

Thomas Carlyle

Originality is unexplored territory. You get there by carrying a canoe. You can't take a taxi.

Alan Alda

ORTHODOXY

Whenever you accept our views, we shall be in full agreement with you.

Moshe Dayan

OVATION

Usually, the standing ovation comes at the end of the show. I guess you're not sure I'm gonna make it that far.

George Burns

OVERCONFIDENCE

Overconfidence in one's own ability is the root of much evil.

Alice Foote MacDougall

OVERWEIGHT

Overweight is one of America's major health problems; I think this is because we love our food too little, not too much. If it tastes fabulous, if every bite delights, if we really pay attention, we will end up eating less, not to deprive ourselves, but because we will be satisfied.

Barbara Kafka

OVERWORK

In the industrial age, overwork sometimes led to horrible accidents that left factory workers maimed or disfigured. In the information age, overworked employees are more likely to have their spirits mangled.

Mike Cassidy

OWE

Don't go around saying the world owes you a living. The world owes you nothing. It was here first.

Mark Twain

OWLS

Owls teach us wisdom and sagacity and not to put our hands into hollow trees.

Will Cuppy

A wise old owl sat on an oak,/The more he saw the less he spoke;/The less he spoke the more he heard;/Why aren't we like that wise old bird?

Edward H. Richards

OWNERSHIP

Our life on Earth is, and ought to be, material and carnal. But we have not yet learned to manage our materialism and carnality properly; they are still entangled with the desire for ownership.

E.M. Forster

No man can lose what he never had.

Isaak Walton

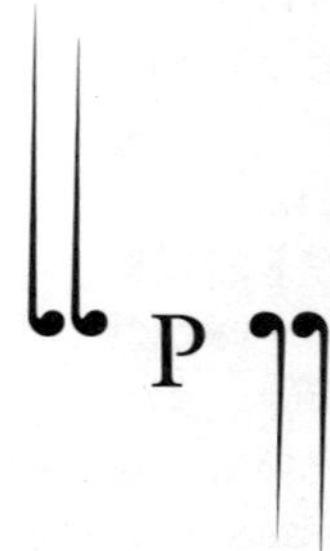

PACE (OF LIFE)

I grew up in a gentler, slower time. When Ike was president, Christmases were years apart, and now it's about five months from one to the next.

Garrison Keillor

PAIN

Those who do not feel pain seldom think that it is felt.

Samuel Johnson

An hour of pain is as long as a day of pleasure.

Proverb

How much pain have cost the evils which have never happened.

Thomas Jefferson

PAINTING

Painting is silent poetry, and poetry is painting that speaks.

Simonides

But why I cry out against Rubens is because he painted undressed people instead of naked ones.

E.M. Forster

PALACE

Even in a palace, life may be lived well.

Marcus Aurelius

PANAMA

A man, a plan, a canal – Panama.

Leigh Mercer

PANIC

We experience moments absolutely free from worry. These brief respites are called panic.

Cullen Hightower

It is very much better sometimes to have a panic feeling beforehand, and then be quite calm when things happen, than to be extremely calm beforehand and to get into a panic when things happen.

Winston Churchill

Panics in some cases have their uses; they produce as much good as hurt.

Thomas Paine

PAPERWORK

What the world really needs is more love and less paperwork.

Pearl Bailey

PARADES

Sometimes you have to pretend to join a parade in which you're not really interested in order to get where you're going.

Christopher Morley

PARADISE

The true paradises are the paradises that we have lost.

Marcel Proust

PARANOIDS

I envy paranoids; they actually feel people are paying attention to them.

Susan Sontag

I think you're the opposite of a paranoid. I think you go around with the insane delusion that people like you.

Woody Allen

Hire paranoids. Even though they have a high false alarm rate, they discover all plots.

Herman Kahn

I am a kind of paranoid in reverse. I suspect people of plotting to make me happy.

J.D. Salinger

PARENT

A suspicious parent makes an artful child.

Thomas Chandler Haliburton

Parenthood remains the single greatest preserve of the amateur.

Alvin Toffler

There are times when parenthood seems nothing but feeding the mouth that bites you.

Peter De Vries

The value to a child of poor role models is also underestimated. Parents have the idea that it is their duty to set a good example, never realizing that a bad one will do just as well, indeed better.

Jill Tweedie

It's funny the way a parent's raised eyebrow can do more damage to your psyche than, say, Chinese water torture.

Arabella Weir

PARENTING

No matter how calmly you try to referee, parenting will eventually produce bizarre behaviour, and I'm not talking about the kids. Their behaviour is always normal.

Bill Cosby

PARENTS

Ever since I lost mine, I've had my eye on other people's parents.

Ian McEwan

Parents learn a lot from their children about coping with life.

Muriel Spark

Children aren't happy without something to ignore,/And that's what parents were created for.

Ogden Nash

PARKINSON'S LAW
Work expands to fill the time available for its completion.

C. Northcote Parkinson

PARLIAMENT
Parliament is not a congress of ambassadors from different and hostile interests; which interests must each maintain, as an agent and an advocate, against other agents and advocates; but parliament is a deliberative assembly of one nation, with one interest, that of the whole.

Edmund Burke

Parliament must not be told a direct untruth, but it's quite possible to allow them to mislead themselves.

Norman Tebbit

PARTIES
Goodbye. I've barely said a word to you, but it's always like that at parties – we never really see each other, we never say the things we should like to: in fact it's the same everywhere in this life. Let's hope that when we are dead, things will be better arranged.

Marcel Proust

Never give a party if you will be the most interesting person there.

Mickey Friedman

Party is the madness of the many, for the gain of a few.

Alexander Pope

PARTING
Even more important than a friendly meeting is a friendly parting.

Chinese proverb

When two people part, it is the one who is not in love who makes the tender speeches.

Marcel Proust

PASSION
The worst sin – perhaps the only sin – passion can commit is to be joyless.

Dorothy L. Sayers

If we resist our passions, it is due more to their weakness than our own strength.

François, duc de La Rochefoucauld

The passions are the winds that fill the sails of the vessel. They sink it at times, but without them it would be impossible to make way. Many things that are dangerous here below are still necessary.

Voltaire

When the passions become masters, they are vices.

Blaise Pascal

One by one they were all becoming shades. Better pass boldly into that other world, in the full glory of some passion, than fade away and wither dismally with age.

James Joyce

Control thy passions, lest they take vengeance on thee.

Epictetus

PASSPORT
If you look like your passport photo, you're too ill to travel.
Will Kommen

PAST
When you are forty, half of you belongs to the past … And when you are seventy, nearly all of you.
Jean Anouilh

The past is not simply the past, but a prism through which the subject filters his own changing self-image.
Doris Kearns Goodwin

Not to know what has been transacted in former times is to be always a child. If no use is made of the labours of the past, the world must remain always in the infancy of knowledge.
Cicero

Living in the past has one thing in its favour – it's cheaper.
Anonymous

You can't put the toothpaste back in the tube.
Richard M. Nixon

The past is still, for us, a place that is not yet safely settled.
Michael Ondaatje

Worshippers of light ancestral make the present light a crime.
James Russell Lowell

Nothing is said that has not been said before.
Terence

Even a god cannot change the past.
Agathon

The past is the only dead thing that smells sweet.
Edward Thomas

What's past is prologue.
William Shakespeare

Those who cannot remember the past are condemned to repeat it without a sense of ironic futility.
Errol Morris

No man is rich enough to buy back his past.
Oscar Wilde

PATH
Some of necessity go astray, because for them there is no such thing as a right path.
Thomas Mann

Every path has its puddle.
English proverb

Do not follow where the path may lead. Go instead where there is no path and leave a trail.
Ralph Waldo Emerson

PATIENCE
Patience accomplishes its object, while hurry speeds to its ruin.
Sa'di

Patience and passage of time do more than strength and fury.
Jean de la Fontaine

With time and patience, the mulberry leaf becomes a silk gown.
Chinese proverb

If you wait, there will come nectar-like fair weather.
Japanese proverb

Prayer of the modern American: Dear God, I pray for patience. And I want it RIGHT NOW!
Owen Arnold

Patience is a bitter plant but it has sweet fruit.
German proverb

He who has patience may accomplish anything.
François Rabelais

The secret of patience: do something else in the meantime.
Anonymous

A handful of patience is worth more than a bushel of brains.
Dutch proverb

Patience will come to he who waits for it.
Anonymous

Our patience will achieve more than our force.
Edmund Burke

The strongest of all warriors are these two – Time and Patience.
Leo Tolstoy

Patience is passive, resignation is active.
Penelope Fitzgerald

You must first have a lot of patience to learn to have patience.
Stanislaw J. Lec

Patience and diligence, like faith, remove mountains.
William Penn

The net of the sleeper catches fish.
Greek proverb

Patience, that blending of moral courage with physical timidity.
Thomas Hardy

Nothing comes of so many things, if you have patience.
Joyce Carol Oates

Whoever has no patience has no wisdom.
Sa'di

All things come round to him who will but wait.
Henry Wadsworth Longfellow

Patience has its limits. Take it too far, and it's cowardice.
George Jackson

If you sit by the river long enough, you will see the body of your enemy float by.
Japanese proverb

Patience is sometimes considered a virtue when it is actually a case of not knowing what to do.
Sally Poplin

Patience is something you admire in the driver behind you and scorn in the one ahead.
Mac McCleary

Patience, *n.* A minor form of despair disguised as a virtue.
Ambrose Bierce

Patience is a most necessary qualification for business; many a man would rather you heard his story, than granted his request.
Lord Chesterfield

The trouble with people these days is that they want to get to the promised land without going through the wilderness.

Faith Forsythe

What I say is, patience, and shuffle the cards.

Miguel de Cervantes

PATIENTS

It is much more important to know what sort of a patient has a disease than what sort of disease a patient has.

Sir William Osler

PATRIOT

A real patriot is the fellow who gets a parking ticket and rejoices that the system works.

Bill Vaughan

PATRIOTISM

Patriotism is often an arbitrary veneration of real estate above principles.

George Jean Nathan

To strike freedom of the mind with the fist of patriotism is an old and ugly subtlety.

Adlai Stevenson

There is hopeful symbolism in the fact that flags do not wave in a vacuum.

Arthur C. Clarke

Patriotism is a kind of religion; it is the egg from which wars are hatched.

Guy de Maupassant

PAY

He who pays the piper may call the tune.

English proverb

One does not make "much of a showing" in the eyes of the large majority of people who one meets with, except by unremitting demonstration of ability to pay.

Thorstein Veblen

We're overpaying him, but he's worth it.

Samuel Goldwyn

PEACE

Peace is not made at the council table or by treaties, but in the hearts of men.

Herbert Hoover

The only good peace is a peace established by the victorious sword of a master nation.

Adolf Hitler

That they may have a little peace, even the best dogs are compelled to snarl occasionally.

William Feather

Peace, if it ever exists, will not be based on the fear of war, but on the love of peace.

Herman Wouk

If you would preserve peace, then prepare for peace.

Père Enfantin

You cannot shake hands with a clenched fist.

Indira Gandhi

Peace rules the day, where reason rules the mind.

William Collins

Peace is not merely a negative ideal, it is the condition of all positive aims.

G. Lowes Dickinson

Looking for peace is like looking for a turtle with a mustache. You won't be able to find it. But when your heart is ready, peace will come looking for you.

Ajahn Chah

Righteousness and peace have kissed each other.

Book of Common Prayer

In the arts of peace man is a bungler.

George Bernard Shaw

War makes rattling good history, but Peace is poor reading.

Thomas Hardy

You can't switch on peace like a light.

Mo Mowlam

Peace is not an absence of war, it is a virtue, a state of mind, a disposition for benevolence, confidence, justice.

Baruch Spinoza

World peace, like community peace, does not require that each man love his neighbour – it requires only that they live together with mutual tolerance, submitting their disputes to a just and peaceful settlement.

John F. Kennedy

I think that people want peace so much that one of these days governments had better get out of the way and let them have it.

Dwight D. Eisenhower

Peace is not merely a distant goal that we seek, but a means by which we arrive at that goal.

Martin Luther King, Jr

When the power of love overcomes the love of power, the world will know peace.

Jimi Hendrix

It is better to send middle-aged men abroad to bore each other than to send young men abroad to kill each other.

Robin Cook

In peace, sons bury their fathers. In war, fathers bury their sons.

Herodotus

PEACE OF MIND

Peace of mind is that mental condition in which you have accepted the worst.

Lin Yutang

PEASANTS

I prefer the company of peasants because they have not been educated enough to reason incorrectly.

Michel de Montaigne

PEDANTRY

Pedantry is the dotage of knowledge.

Holbrook Jackson

PEDESTRIANS
In parts of the world, people still pray in the streets. In this country, they're called pedestrians.

Gloria Pitzer

PEN
The pen is mightier than the sword.

Edward Bulwer-Lytton

PENILE ENLARGEMENT
I've been reading about penile enlargement and I'm saying to myself: "Do we really need larger prisons?"

Max Alexander

PEOPLE
On the whole, people are rubbish, and they deserve to be wakened to the need to change and amend themselves not by some social factor or some force of circumstance but by conversion of their soul. … All the problems of our society are caused by the false expectations of people who are led to suppose that they are entitled to these things.

Rev. Dr Edward Norman

In numerous studies [social psychologists] have documented a deep paradox of human relations – persons get along, but people don't. Encounters among individuals are generally positive, supportive, and rewarding, but those among groups are ordinarily unpleasant and confrontational. Even if people are randomly divided into groups, the groups will automatically discriminate against each other.

Atul Gawande

One of the worst things about life is not how nasty the nasty people are. You know that already. It is how nasty the nice people can be.

Anthony Powell

People can be divided into three groups: those who make things happen, those who watch things happen, and those who wonder what happened.

John Newbern

People are like birds – from a distance, beautiful; from up close, those sharp beaks, those beady little eyes.

Richard J. Needham

The people and the people alone, are the motive force in the making of world history.

Mao Zedong

The people are like water and the ruler a boat. Water can support a boat or overturn it.

William Shakespeare

PERCEPTION
We don't see things as they are. We see things as we are.

Anaïs Nin

What I hear I forget. What I see I remember. What I do I know.

Chinese proverb

We must not allow other people's limited perceptions to define us.

Virginia Satir

When you are a Bear of Very Little Brain, and you Think of Things, you find sometimes that a Thing which seemed very Thingish inside you is quite different when it gets out into the open and has other people looking at it.

A.A. Milne

What is true by lamplight is not always true by sunlight.

Joseph Joubert

A blind man who sees is better than a seeing man who is blind.

Persian proverb

There is nothing either good or bad, but thinking makes it so.

William Shakespeare

The logic of worldly success rests on a fallacy: the strange error that our perfection depends on the thoughts and opinions and applause of other men! A weird life it is, indeed, to be living always in somebody else's imagination, as if that were the only place in which one could at last become real.

Thomas Merton

Once the public decides what you are, you might as well give up trying to be anything else.

Burt Lancaster

Sometimes the heart sees what is invisible to the eye.

H. Jackson Brown, Jr

PERFECTION

Have no fear of perfection – you'll never reach it.

Salvador Dali

The greater the emphasis on perfection the further it recedes.

Haridas Chaudhuri

People who strive for excellence tend to experience satisfaction. People who strive for perfection tend not to.

Paul Hewitt

Doing a thing well is often a waste of time.

Robert Byrne

The indefatigable pursuit of an unattainable perfection … is what alone gives meaning to our life on this unavailing star.

Logan Pearsall Smith

Pictures of perfection as you know make me sick and wicked.

Jane Austen

The gem cannot be polished without friction, nor man perfected without trials.

Chinese proverb

You can't live a perfect day without doing something for someone who will never be able to repay you.

John Wooden

All men have their frailties, and whoever looks for a friend without imperfections will never find what he seeks.

Cyrus the Elder

When a man imagines, even after years if striving, that he has attained perfection, his decline begins.

Theodore Martin

Perfection does not exist; to understand it is the triumph of human intelligence; to expect to possess it is the most dangerous kind of madness.

Alfred de Musset

Perfection is achieved, not when there is nothing more to add, but when there is nothing left to take away.

Antoine de Saint-Exupéry

PERFORMANCE
There is no strong performance without a little fanaticism in the performer.

Ralph Waldo Emerson

A performance is not a contest but a love affair.

Glenn Gould

PERMANENT
Nothing is permanent in this wicked world – not even our troubles.

Charlie Chaplin

In this world of change naught which comes stays, and naught which goes is lost.

Anne Sophie Swetchine

PERMISSIVENESS
Permissiveness is the principle of treating children as if they were adults; and the tactic of making sure they never reach that stage.

Thomas Szasz

PERSECUTION
To persecute the unfortunate is like throwing stones on one fallen into a well.

Chinese proverb

PERSEVERANCE
Perseverance, *n.* A lowly virtue whereby mediocrity achieves an inglorious success.

Ambrose Bierce

The difference between perseverance and obstinacy is that one comes from a strong will and the other from a strong won't.

Henry Ward Beecher

Great works are performed not by strength but by perseverance.

Samuel Johnson

In the realm of ideas, everything depends on enthusiasm. In the real world all rests on perseverance.

Johann Wolfgang von Goethe

Perseverance is not a long race; it is many short races one after another.

Walter Elliott

The rewards for those who persevere far exceed the pain that must precede the victory.

Ted Engstrom

Stopping at third base adds no more to the score than striking out.

Unknown

Patience and perseverance have a magical effect before which difficulties disappear and obstacles vanish.

John Quincy Adams

PERSISTENCE
Nothing in this world can take the place of persistence. Talent will not; nothing is more common than

unsuccessful people with talent. Genius will not; unrewarded genius is almost a proverb. Education will not; the world is full of educated derelicts. Persistence and determination alone are omnipotent. The slogan "press on" has solved and always will solve the problems of the human race.

Calvin Coolidge

We are made to persist. That's how we find out who we are.

Tobias Wolff

The greatest oak was once a little nut who held its ground.

Unknown

Little strokes fell great oaks.

Benjamin Franklin

Fall seven times, stand up eight.

Japanese proverb

He who seeks finds, if he does not lose heart.

Alfred Thayer Mahan

All men have enough of genius in themselves to be uncomfortable in the rut of mediocrity, but only the successful few exercise enough persistence to set and maintain a course for themselves.

J. Sig Paulson

PERSONAL
Personal isn't the same as important.

Terry Pratchett

PERSONALITY
If it weren't for caffeine, I'd have no personality whatsoever.

Anonymous

If I'm too strong for some people, that's their problem.

Glenda Jackson

PERSPECTIVE
Go some distance away because the work appears much smaller and more of it can be taken in at a glance, and a lack of harmony or proportion is rapidly seen.

Leonardo da Vinci

Part of the reason for the ugliness of adults, in a child's eyes, is that the child is usually looking upwards, and few faces are at their best when seen from below.

George Orwell

The field cannot well be seen from within the field.

Ralph Waldo Emerson

Slight not what's near through aiming at what's far.

Euripides

Once the game is over, the king and the pawn go back in the same box.

Italian proverb

One man's observation is another man's closed book or flight of fancy.

Willard Van Orman Quine

There are always two people in every picture: the photographer and the viewer.

Ansel Adams

The conformation of his mind was such that whatever was little seemed to him great, and whatever was great seemed to him little.

Thomas Babington Macaulay

The crow wished that everything was black, the owl that everything was white.

William Blake

PERSUASION

Persuasion is the only true intellectual process.

Matthew Arnold

You can persuade a man to believe almost anything provided he is clever enough, but it is much more difficult to persuade someone less clever.

Tom Stoppard

His tongue dropt manna, and could make the worse appear the better reason

John Milton

The best way to persuade people is with your ears – by listening to them.

Dean Rusk

PERVERSITY

Perversity depends on reversal and substitution.

Mason Cooley

PESSIMISM

Pessimism was dear to him in its impersonation of profundity and its implication of arcane knowledge.

Candia McWilliam

Pessimism, when you get used to it, is just as agreeable as optimism. Indeed, I think it must be more agreeable, must have a more real savour, than optimism – from the way in which pessimists abandon themselves to it.

Arnold Bennett

Pessimism is depreciated will-to-live.

Albert Schweitzer

PESSIMIST

A pessimist is a man who has been compelled to live with an optimist.

Elbert Hubbard

The man who is a pessimist before forty-eight hours knows too much; if he is an optimist after it, he knows too little.

Mark Twain

There is no sadder sight than a young pessimist.

Mark Twain

A pessimist is one who builds dungeons in the air.

Walter Winchell

Things are always darkest just before they go pitch black.

Kelly Robinson

To a profound pessimist about life, being in danger is not depressing.

F. Scott Fitzgerald

A pessimist is a man who looks both ways before crossing a one-way street.

Laurence J. Peter

A pessimist is just a well-informed optimist.

Anonymous

I am not a pessimist; to perceive evil where it exists is, in my opinion, a form of optimism.

Roberto Rossellini

When men have come to the edge of a precipice, it is the lover of life who has the spirit to leap backward, and only the pessimist who continues to believe in progress.

. G.K. Chesterton

PETER PRINCIPLE
In a hierarchy each employee tends to rise to his or her level of incompetence.

Laurence J. Peter

PETTINESS
How great in number are the little-minded men.

Plautus

PHILOSOPHER
A peasant and a philosopher may be equally satisfied, but not equally happy.

Samuel Johnson

He had, he said, studied the great philosophers and had therefore come to expect very little in this life, and rather less in the next.

Alex Atkinson

You philosophers are fortunate people. You write on paper – I, poor empress, am forced to write on the ticklish skins of human beings.

Catherine the Great

PHILOSOPHY
Philosophy, *n.* A route of many roads leading from nowhere to nothing.

Ambrose Bierce

Philosophy is a battle against the bewitchment of our intelligence by means of language.

Ludwig Wittgenstein

It is easy to build a philosophy. It doesn't have to run.

Charles F. Kettering

In philosophizing we may not *terminate* a disease of thought. It must run its natural course and *slow* cure is all-important.

Ludwig Wittgenstein

The finding of arguments for a conclusion given in advance is not philosophy, but special pleading.

Bertrand Russell

Science is what you know, philosophy is what you don't know.

Bertrand Russell

On one occasion a man came to ask me to recommend some of my books, as he was interested in philosophy. I did so, but he returned the next day saying that he had been reading one of them and had found only one statement he could understand, and one that seemed to him false. I asked him what that was, and he said it was the statement that Julius Caesar is dead. When I asked him why he did not agree, he drew himself up and said: "Because I am Julius Caesar."

Bertrand Russell

Some philosophy is a very necessary companion in this world,
where, even to the most fortunate,
the chances are greatly against
happiness.

Lord Chesterfield

Greek philosophy seems to have
met with something with which a
good tragedy is not supposed to
meet, namely, a dull ending.

Karl Marx

My chief desire is to let you see
that there is that which is rational,
that which is irrational, and that
which is non-rational – and to
leave you weltering in the morass
thereafter.

Seamus Deane

Philosophy is a wonderful subject,
but it is necessarily unfinished and
unfinishable. You really can't solve
anything. At the end of my life I
want to know more than I did at
the beginning. And I couldn't get
that from philosophy.

Sir Isaiah Berlin

Philosophy: the never-ending attempt to reconcile new reason with
old intuition.

R.R. Marett

PHOBIAS

I have three phobias which, could I
mute them, would make my life
slick as a sonnet, but as dull as
ditch water: I hate to go to bed, I
hate to get up, and I hate to be
alone.

Tallulah Bankhead

PHONE CALLS

All phone calls are obscene.

Karen Elizabeth Gordon

PHOTOGRAPHS

Should you be a teenager blessed
with uncommon good looks, docu-
ment this state of affairs by the taking of photographs. It is the only
way anyone will believe you in the
years to come.

Fran Lebowitz

PHOTOGRAPHY

Most things in life are moments of
pleasure and a lifetime of embarrassment; photography is a moment
of embarrassment and a lifetime of
pleasure.

Tony Benn

PHYSICIANS

One of the first duties of the physician is to educate the masses not to
take medicine.

Sir William Osler

Commonly, physicians, like beer,
are best when they are old; and
lawyers, like bread, when they are
young and new.

Thomas Fuller, MD

PIANISTS

The notes I handle no better than
many pianists. But the pauses
between the notes – ah, that is
where the art resides!

Arthur Schnabel

PIANO

The piano is the easiest instrument to play in the beginning, and the hardest to master in the end.

Vladimir Horowitz

PICTURE

A picture is something which requires as much trickery, knavery, and deceit as the perpetration of a crime.

Edgar Degas

PIETY

Men always try to make virtues of their weaknesses. Fear of death and fear of life become piety.

H.L. Mencken

PIGS

I like pigs. Dogs look up to us. Cats look down on us. Pigs treat us as equals.

Winston Churchill

PINK

Pink isn't just a colour, it's an attitude.

Miley Cyrus

PIONEERS

There are two kinds of people in the world – those who pioneer and those who plod. The plodders always attack the pioneers. They say that the pioneers have gobbled up all the opportunity, when, as a plain matter of fact, the plodders would have nowhere to plod had the pioneers not first cleared the way.

Henry Ford

The one thing you don't hear mentioned about pioneers is that they are invariably, by their nature, messmakers.

Robert Pirsig

There has to be this pioneer, the individual who has the courage, the ambition to overcome the obstacles that always develop when one tries to do something worthwhile, especially when it is new and different.

Alfred P. Sloan

PIRATES

Why join the navy when you can be a pirate?

Steve Jobs

PITY

Then cherish pity, lest you drive an angel from your door.

William Blake

PLACEBO

The placebo cures thirty per cent of patients – no matter what they have.

David Kline

PLANNING

Measure a thousand times and cut once.

Turkish proverb

I arise in the morning torn between a desire to improve (or save) the world and a desire to enjoy (or savour) the world. This makes it hard to plan the day.

E.B. White

The time to repair the roof is when the sun is shining.

John F. Kennedy

Tis the part of a wise man to keep himself today for tomorrow, and not venture all his eggs in one basket.

Miguel de Cervantes

Planning lies with men; success lies with Heaven.

Chinese proverb

These unhappy times call for the building of plans that ... build from the bottom up ... that put their faith once more in the forgotten man at the bottom of the economic pyramid.

Franklin D. Roosevelt

The reason that everybody likes planning is that nobody has to do anything.

Jerry Brown

Meticulous planning will enable everything a man does to appear spontaneous.

Mark Caine

It does not do to leave a live dragon out of your calculations, if you live near him.

J.R.R. Tolkien

If you are planning for one year, grow rice. If you are planning for twenty years grow trees. If you are planning for centuries, grow men.

Chinese proverb

If it ain't broke, break it, then fix it. Otherwise you may be destined to address tomorrow's problems with yesterday's solutions.

Clark Crouch

If you don't know where you're going, you'll probably end up nowhere.

Clark Crouch

In preparing for battle I have always found that plans are useless, but planning is indispensable.

Dwight D. Eisenhower

When you're thirsty it's too late to think about digging a well.

Japanese proverb

It is more important to know where you are going than to get there quickly. Do not mistake activity for achievement.

Mabel Newcomer

PLANS

Our plans miscarry because they have no aim. When a man does not know what harbour he is making for, no wind is the right wind.

Seneca

Plans get you into things, but you got to work your way out.

Will Rogers

He who is not a bird should not build his nest over abysses.

Friedrich Nietzsche

It's a bad plan that can't be changed.

Publilius Syrus

Burning the candle at both ends is the worst way to make ends meet.

Anonymous

The course of true anything does not run smooth.

Samuel Butler

In every affair consider what precedes and follows, and then undertake it.

Epictetus

The more human beings proceed by plan, the more effectively they may be hit by accident.

Friedrich Dürrenmatt

Make no small plans. For they do not have the magic to stir men's souls.

Daniel H. Burnham

I'll work on a new and original plan, said I to myself, said I.

W.S. Gilbert

Make a plan and you will find she had something else in mind.

Alan Jay Lerner

Plans are nothing; planning is everything.

Dwight D. Eisenhower

When I got up, I stuck to my plan – stumbling forward and getting hit in the face.

Randall (Tex) Cobb

The man who has planned badly, if fortune is on his side, may have had a stroke of luck; but his plan was a bad one nevertheless.

Herodotus

The best plan is, as the common proverb has it, to profit by the folly of others.

Pliny the Elder

PLANTS
Plants do not wish to rule the world like us: They have higher concerns.

Ned Rorem

PLATONIC RELATIONSHIPS
Of course a platonic relationship is possible – but only between husband and wife.

Ladies Home Journal

PLATITUDE
A platitude is simply a truth repeated until people get tired of hearing it.

Stanley Baldwin

A platitude is a truth we are tired of hearing.

Godfrey Nicholson

PLAY
The true object of all human life is play. Earth is a task garden; heaven is a playground.

G.K. Chesterton

To the art of working well a civilized race would add the art of playing well.

George Santayana

Though this may be play to you, 'tis death to us.

Sir Roger L'Estrange

PLEASE

He is not yet born who can please
everybody.

Danish proverb

He is a man whom it is impossible
to please, because he is never
pleased with himself.

Johann Wolfgang von Goethe

The art of pleasing consists of
being pleased.

William Hazlitt

PLEASURE

Pleasure is very seldom found where
it is sought; our brightest blazes of
gladness are commonly kindled by
unexpected sparks.

Samuel Johnson

The test of pleasure is the memory
it leaves behind.

Jean Paul

Pleasure is a thief to business.

Daniel Defoe

I adore simple pleasures. They are
the last refuge of the complex.

Oscar Wilde

Pain has its reasons, pleasure is
totally indifferent.

Francis Picabia

Pleasure is something that you feel
you should really enjoy, which is
really virtuous, but you don't; and
sin's something that you're quite
sure you shouldn't enjoy but do.

Ralph Wightman

Most men that do thrive in the
world do forget to take pleasure
during the time that they are getting their estate, but reserve that til
they have got one and then it is too
late for them to enjoy it.

Samuel Pepys

One half of the world cannot understand the pleasures of the other.

Jane Austen

PLOTS

Plots, true or false, are necessary
things,
To raise up commonwealths, and
ruin kings.

John Dryden

Plot and counter-plot, egad!

Richard Brinsley Sheridan

POEMS

A well-rounded poem is like a
sphere. It is impossible to view it
completely.

John V. Hicks

A poem is a momentary stay
against confusion.

Robert Frost

POETRY

You will not find poetry anywhere
unless you bring some of it with
you.

Joseph Joubert

There's no money in poetry, but
then there's no poetry in money
either.

Robert Graves

I know poetry is indispensable, but
I don't know to what.

Victor Hugo

All bad poetry is sincere.
Oscar Wilde

Colloquial poetry is to the real art as the barber's wax dummy is to sculpture.
Ezra Pound

Poetry is a search for the inexplicable.
Wallace Stevens

Poetry is like fish: if it's fresh, it's good; if it's stale, it's bad: and if you're not sure, try it on the cat.
Osbert Sitwell

We make out of the quarrel with others, rhetoric, but of the quarrel with ourselves, poetry.
William Butler Yeats

There is the view that poetry should improve your life. I think people confuse it with the Salvation Army.
John Ashbery

I wish you would read a little poetry sometimes. Your ignorance cramps my conversation.
Anthony Hope

In science you want to say something nobody ever knew before, in words everyone can understand. In poetry, you are bound to say something everyone knows already in words that nobody can understand.
Paul Dirac

Poetry is the language in which man explores his own amazement.
Christopher Fry

POETS

The poet is the priest of the invisible.
Wallace Stevens

No poet or novelist wished he were the only one who ever lived, but most of them wish they were the only one alive, and quite a number fondly believe their wish has been granted.
W.H. Auden

People wish to be poets more than they wish to write poetry, and that's a mistake. One should wish to celebrate more than one wishes to be celebrated.
Lucille Clifton

Immature poets imitate; mature poets steal.
T.S. Eliot

I hate all Boets and Bainters.
George I

Poets who know no better rhapsodize about the peace of nature, but a well-populated marsh is a cacophony.
Bern Keating

I have never yet known a poet who did not think himself super-excellent.
Cicero

To know how to say what others only know how to think is what makes men poets or sages; and to dare to say what others only dare to think makes men martyrs or reformers or both.
Elizabeth Rundle Charles

In spite of all romantic poets sing,/This gold, my dearest, is an useful thing.

Mary Leapor

A tailor can adapt to any medium, be it poetry, be it criticism. As a poet, he can mend, and with the scissors of criticism he can divide.

Franz Grillparzer

A poet is someone who stands in the rain, hoping to be struck by lightning.

James Dickey

POINT OF VIEW
A point of view can be a dangerous luxury when substituted for insight and understanding.

Marshall McLuhan

It has, I believe, been often remarked that a hen is only an egg's way of making another egg.

Samuel Butler

POISE
Ah, men do not know how much strength is in poise,
That he goes the farthest who goes far enough.

James Russell Lowell

POLICE
The art of the police is to not see what is useless to see.

Napoleon Bonaparte

I'm not against the police; I'm just afraid of them.

Alfred Hitchcock

POLICE STATE
A functioning police state needs no police.

William S. Burroughs

POLISH
A whole man in himself, polished and well-rounded.

Horace

POLITENESS
A polite man is one who listens with interest to things he knows all about, when they are told him by a person who knows nothing about them.

Philippe de Mornay

Politeness is half good manners and half good lying.

Mary Wilson Little

Politeness is to goodness what words are to thought.

Joseph Joubert

Polite behaviour is performed for the sake of our relationship with other people.

Margaret Visser

POLITICAL APPOINTMENTS
We hang the petty thieves and appoint the great ones to public office.

Aesop

Now and then an innocent man is sent to the legislature.

Kin Hubbard

POLITICAL CORRECTNESS:
DEFINITIONS

Acid rain: poorly buffered precipitation

Adultery: consensual non-monogamy

Aging (the): chronologically gifted persons; the experientially enhanced

Air crash (flying into the side of a mountain or other landscape feature – per ICAO): controlled flight into terrain

Alcoholic: anti-sobriety activist

Boring speech: differently interesting address; charm-free oration

Cannibalism: intra-species dining

Cliché: previously enjoyed sound bite

Corpse: permanently static post-human mass

Corrupt: ethically different; morally challenged

Dead: actuarially mature

Drug addicts and alcoholics: the sobriety deprived; people of stupor

Education: children do not fail; they are merely "achieving a deficiency." High school dropouts are "individuals with provisionally unmet educational objectives."

Homeless: underhoused; involuntarily undomiciled

Homelessness: mortgage-free living

Hunger: nutritional shortfall; caloric insufficiency

Lie: categorical inaccuracy; counterfactual proposition; strategic misrepresentation; terminological inexactitude

Lobbyist: legislative advocate

Looters: nontraditional shoppers

Nerd: technically advantaged (*The Globe and Mail*, 19 November, 1993)

Panhandlers: unaffiliated applicants for private sector funding

Plagiarism: previously owned prose

Roadkill: vehicularly compressed maladapted life form

Sadomasochists: the differently pleasured

Shoplifter: cost-of-living adjustment specialist

Stabbing: social surgery

Toxic dumping: deep ocean storage

Vomiting: unplanned re-examination of recent food choices
Henry Beard, Christopher Cerf
International Herald Tribune,
15 July 1992
The Globe and Mail,
14 June 1993
(from The Washington Post)

POLITICAL IDEAS
What matters most about political ideas is the underlying emotions,

the music, to which the ideas are mere libretto, often of very inferior quality.

Sir Louis Naimer

There is no connection between the political ideas of our educated class and the deep places of the imagination.

Lionel Trilling

POLITICAL LANGUAGE

Political language is designed to make lies sound truthful and murder respectable, and to give an appearance of solidarity to pure wind.

George Orwell

We don't see the end of the tunnel, but I must say I don't think it is darker than it was a year ago, and in some ways lighter.

John F. Kennedy

POLITICAL PARTIES

He that espouses parties, can hardly divorce himself from their fate; and more fall with their party than rise with it.

William Penn

POLITICAL SKILLS

The President of his country was a man of stunning political gifts. He had the courage of a lion and the tactical agility of a mongoose. It was a plan that he lacked. [Narmonov] had no idea where he was going and that was his weakness.

Tom Clancy

POLITICIANS

Politicians are the same all over. They promise to build bridges, even when there are no rivers.

Nikita Khrushchev

Any party which takes credit for the rain must not be surprised if its opponents blame it for the drought.

Dwight W. Morrow

A statesman is a man who thinks he belongs to his country; a politician thinks the country belongs to him.

Die Weltwoche

Politicians make strange bedfellows, but they all share the same bunk.

Edgar A. Shoaff

Don't put it in writing if you can phone. Don't phone if you can meet. Don't speak if you can whisper. Don't whisper if you can nod. Don't nod if you can wink.

Earl Long

We are all mere petty provincial politicians at present; perhaps, by and by, some of us will rise to the level of national statesmen.

Sir John A. Macdonald

Politicians neither love nor hate. Interest, not sentiment, directs them.

Lord Chesterfield

The thing about a politician is, you have to take the smooth with the smooth.

Susan Hill

Public interest: a term used by every politician to support his ideas.

M.W. Kiplinger

Gladstone: I predict, Sir, that you will die either by hanging or of some vile disease.

Disraeli: That all depends, sir, upon whether I embrace your principles or your mistress.

Benjamin Disraeli

To become the master, the politician poses as the servant.

Charles de Gaulle

You can only realize how much you have accomplished while in office when you listen to the things your opponents oppose.

Konrad Adenauer

Election year is when a lot of politicians get free speech mixed up with cheap talk.

Dan Bennett

Politicians can forgive almost everything in the way of abuse; they can forgive subversion, being contradicted, exposed as liars, even ridiculed, but they can never forgive being ignored.

Auberon Waugh

The more you are talked about, the more you will wish to be talked about. The condemned murderer who is allowed to see the account of his trial in the press is indignant if he finds a newspaper which has reported it inadequately. ... Politicians and literary men are in the same case.

Bertrand Russell

What this country needs is more unemployed politicians.

Edward Langley

No two issues are ever so far apart that some politician can't straddle them.

Unknown

An honest politician is one who, when he is bought, will stay bought.

Simon Cameron

A man goes to Ottawa burning with zeal to inaugurate political liberation. Six months or a year produces sleeping-sickness.

Augustus Bridle

The saddest life is that of a political aspirant under democracy. His failure is ignominious and his success is disgraceful.

H.L. Mencken

Statesmen face facts; politicians distort them.

John A. Lincoln

Ninety per cent of the politicians give the other ten per cent a bad reputation.

Henry Kissinger

The politician is an acrobat. He keeps his balance by saying the opposite of what he does.

Maurice Barrès

A politician is a person who can talk in circles while standing four-square.

Unknown

An experienced politician is one who can toss his hat in the ring and still talk through it.

Mary Alkus

Having no Hollywood, our politicians are our stars. Without soap operas, Parliament has become our own pitiful drama.

Roy MacGregor

We'll jump off that bridge when we come to it.

Lester B. Pearson

He knows nothing; and he thinks he knows everything. That points clearly to a political career.

George Bernard Shaw

Old politicians, like old actors, revive in the limelight. The vacancy which afflicts them in private momentarily lifts when, once more, they feel the eyes of an audience upon them.

Malcolm Muggeridge

The safest commandment for politicians to live by is: Thou shalt not commit thyself.

D.O. Flynn

Writers and politicians are natural rivals. Both groups try to make the world in their own images; they fight for the same territory.

Salman Rushdie

To squander away the objects which made the happiness of their fellows would be to them no sacrifice at all.

Edmund Burke

To be a chemist you must study chemistry; to be a lawyer or a physician you must study law or medicine; but to be a politician you need only to study your own interests.

Max O'Rell

If the statements of opposing political candidates are true, none of them is fit to hold office.

Frances Rodman

Probably the reason many a politician stands on his record is to keep voters from examining it.

Cy N. Peace

The proper memory for a politician is one that knows what to remember and what to forget.

John Morley

The world is weary of statesmen whom democracy has degraded into politicians.

Benjamin Disraeli

POLITICS
Life somehow finds a way of transcending politics.

Norman Cousins

Ballots are the rightful and peaceful successors of bullets.

Abraham Lincoln

Politics is the science of exigencies.

Theodore Parker

To let politics become a cesspool, and then avoid it because it is a cesspool, is a double crime.
Howard Crosby

The difference between politics and statesmanship is philosophy.
Will and Ariel Durant

Assassination of rivals, a method of government hoary with age, and not ineffective, is still employed in countries which stand at the head of Western civilization.
W. Macneile Dixon

Politics is perhaps the only profession for which no preparation is thought necessary.
Robert Louis Stevenson

Three people marooned on a desert island would soon invent politics.
Mason Cooley

In politics, merit is rewarded by the possessor being raised, like a target, to a position to be fired at.
Christian Nestell Bovee

Politics is the art of the possible.
R.A. Butler

Practical politics consists in ignoring facts.
Henry Adams

Politics in Canada has always been the art of the necessary possible.
Peter C. Newman

Politics is the art of helping oneself to people.
Henry de Montherlant

Culture is the backbone of society, politics merely its entertainment.
Eleanor Koldofsky

Politics is both fraud and vision.
Donald Horne

Great men don't bother with politics.
Albert Camus

Politics makes estranged bedfellows.
Goodman Ace

Politics is the skilled use of blunt objects.
Lester B. Pearson

Politics is applesauce.
Will Rogers

A sick society must think much about politics, as a sick man must think much about his digestion.
C.S. Lewis

In politics, if you want anything said, ask a man; if you want anything done, ask a woman.
Margaret Thatcher

There can be no greater error than to expect to calculate upon real favours from nation to nation.
George Washington

Politics is made up largely of irrelevancies.
Dalton Camp

In politics the middle way is none at all.
John Adams

Just because you do not take an interest in politics does not mean politics will not take an interest in you.

Pericles

In politics, an absurdity is not a handicap.

Napoleon Bonaparte

If you want to get along, go along.

Sam Rayburn

Politics is more dangerous than war, for in war you are only killed once.

Winston Churchill

Finality is not the language of politics.

Benjamin Disraeli

What I cannot do, of course I will not do; but it may as well be understood, once and for all, that I shall not surrender this game leaving any available card unplayed.

Abraham Lincoln

Politics and the fate of mankind are formed by men without ideals and without greatness. Those who have greatness within them do not go in for politics.

Albert Camus

The word "politics" is derived from the word "poly," meaning "many," and the word "ticks," meaning "blood-sucking parasites."

Larry Hardiman

Politics has less to do with where you live than where your heart is.

Margaret Cho

Politics is the art of looking for trouble, finding it everywhere, diagnosing it incorrectly, and applying the wrong remedies.

Groucho Marx

In baseball when they say you're out, you're out. It's the same way in politics.

Gerald Ford

Politics is the gentle art of getting votes from the poor and campaign funds from the rich, by promising to protect each from the other.

Oscar Ameringer

I got fed up of all the sex and sleaze and backhanders of rock 'n' roll so I went into politics.

Tony Blair

Politics is supposed to be the second-oldest profession. I have come to realize it bears a very close resemblance to the first.

Ronald Reagan

I have climbed to the top of the greasy pole.

Benjamin Disraeli

In politics people throw themselves, as on a sickbed, from one side to the other in the belief that they will lie more comfortably.

Johann Wolfgang von Goethe

All politics are based on the indifference of the majority.

James Reston

I have never found, in a long experience of politics, that criticism is ever inhibited by ignorance.

Harold Macmillan

Politics is the diversion of trivial men who, when they succeed at it, become important in the eyes of more trivial men.
George Jean Nathan

Politics is the art of choosing between the disastrous and the unpalatable.
John Kenneth Galbraith

Politics, as a practice, whatever its professions, has always been the systematic organization of hatreds.
Henry Adams

In politics, as soon as you take a trick in diamonds, you find that hearts have become trumps.
Chris Patten

Whenever a fellow tells me he is bipartisan, I know he is going to vote against me.
Harry S. Truman

Ideas are great arrows, but there has to be a bow. And politics is the bow of idealism.
Bill Moyers

Politics, as it turned out, lent itself admirably to storytelling. Where else can you find such a mix of greed, power, lust, conspiracy, sacrifice, and secrecy?
Val Sears

Politics is the science of how who gets what, when, and why.
Sidney Hillman

The whole aim of practical politics is to keep the populace alarmed (and hence clamorous to be led to safety) by menacing it with an endless series of hobgoblins, all of them imaginary.
H.L. Mencken

Politics is the art of postponing decisions until they are no longer relevant.
Henri Queuille

In politics, as in life, we must above all things wish only for the attainable.
Heinrich Heine

Ideals in politics are never realized, but the pursuit of them determines history.
Lord Acton

An attitude of permanent indignation signifies great mental poverty. Politics compels its votaries to take that line and you can see their minds growing more and more impoverished every day, from one burst of righteous anger to the next.
Paul Valéry

One of the penalties for refusing to participate in politics is that you end up being governed by your inferiors.
Plato

The essential ingredient of politics is timing.
Pierre Elliott Trudeau

Politics is the entertainment branch of industry.
Frank Zappa

Politics is too serious a matter to be left to the politicians.
Charles de Gaulle

POLLS

One day the don't-knows will get in, and then where will we be?

Spike Milligan

The so-called science of poll-taking is not a science at all but a mere necromancy. People are unpredictable by nature, and although you can take a nation's pulse, you can't be sure that the nation hasn't just run up a flight of stairs.

E.B. White

POLLUTION

We've got to pause and ask ourselves: How much clean air do we need?

Lee Iacocca

The North alone is silent and at peace. Give man time and he will spoil that too.

Stephen Leacock

POP ART

Pop art is the inedible raised to the unspeakable.

Leonard Baskin

POPE

Anybody can be pope; the proof of this is that I have become one.

Pope John XXIII

The Pope traditionally prays for peace every Easter and the fact that it has never had any effect whatsoever in preventing or ending a war never deters him. What goes through the Pope's mind about being rejected all the time? Does God have it in for him?

Andy Rooney

POPULARITY

Anyone who is popular is bound to be disliked.

Yogi Berra

Everyone's private motto: It's better to be popular than right.

Mark Twain

Being popular is important. Otherwise, people might not like you.

Mimi Pond

The delicate balance between modesty and conceit is popularity.

Max Beerbohm

PORNOGRAPHY

What pornography is really about, ultimately, isn't sex but death.

Susan Sontag

Erotica is using a feather, pornography is using the whole chicken.

Isabel Allende

PORTRAIT

It takes two people to make a good portrait.

Arnaud Magges

Every time I paint a portrait I lose a friend.

John Singer Sargent

POSITIVE

Positive, *adj*. Mistaken at the top of one's voice.

Ambrose Bierce

A positive attitude may not solve all your problems, but it will annoy enough people to make it worth the effort.

Herm Albright

Whether you think you can or whether you think you can't, you're right!

Henry Ford

Success encourages these people; they can because they think they can.

Virgil

POSSESSIONS
The more a man possesses over and above what he uses, the more careworn he becomes.

George Bernard Shaw

You can't have everything. Where would you put it?

Steven Wright

People who get through life dependent on other people's possessions are always the first to lecture you on how little possessions count.

Ben Elton

People don't resent having nothing nearly as much as too little.

Ivy Compton-Burnett

A little in one's own pocket is better than much in another man's purse.

Miguel de Cervantes

There is something to be said for losing one's possessions, after nothing can be done about it.

Pearl S. Buck

Compare what you want with what you have, and you'll be unhappy; compare what you have with what you deserve, and you'll be happy.

Evan Esar

Before we set our hearts too much upon anything, let us examine how happy those are who already possess it.

François, duc de La Rochefoucauld

Have nothing in your houses that you do not know to be useful, or believe to be beautiful.

William Morris

I would rather be able to appreciate things I cannot have than to have things I am not able to appreciate.

Elbert Hubbard

Every increased possession loads us with new weariness.

John Ruskin

You possess only whatever will not be lost in a shipwreck.

Al-Ghazali

POSSIBILITIES
Rebellion against your handicaps gets you nowhere. Self-pity gets you nowhere. One must have the adventurous daring to accept oneself as a bundle of possibilities and undertake the most interesting game in the world – making the most of one's best.

Harry Emerson Fosdick

No. 1597. Everything is deemed possible except that which is impossible in the nature of things.

California Civil Code

POSTERITY

Posterity is as likely to be as wrong as anyone else.

Heywood Braun

Posterity weaves no garlands for imitators.

Friedrich von Schiller

When we are planning for posterity, we ought to remember that virtue is not hereditary.

Thomas Paine

We have received the world as an inheritance which not only not one of us has a right to damage but also which it is the duty of each generation to leave to posterity in an improved condition.

Joseph Joubert

POTENTIAL

Discussing the potential of a top prospect, "The guy is twenty-one right now and in ten years he has a good chance to be thirty-one."

Casey Stengel

Man is as full of potentiality as he is of impotence.

George Santayana

It's never too late to be who you might have been./You are never too old to be what you might have been.

George Eliot

For of all sad words of tongue or pen,/The saddest are these: "It might have been!"

John Greenleaf Whittier

You never know what a horse will pull until you hook him up to a heavy load.

Paul "Bear" Bryant

If you treat a man as he is, he will remain as he is; if you treat him as he ought to be and could be, he will become as he ought to be and could be.

Johann Wolfgang von Goethe

The difference between what we do and what we are capable of doing would suffice to solve most of the world's problems.

Mohandas Gandhi

It's not what you are; it's what you don't become that hurts.

Oscar Levant

I wonder what kind of a bird Humpty Dumpty would have hatched into, eh? Sadly, we'll never know.

Harry Hill

POVERTY

He is now fast rising from affluence to poverty.

Mark Twain

I've never been poor, only broke. Being poor is a frame of mind.

Mike Todd

Poverty has its compensations – nobody begs of a poor man.

The Globe and Mail

Poverty eclipses the brightest virtues, and is the very sepulchre of brave designs, depriving a man of the means to accomplish what nature has fitted him for, and stifling the noblest thoughts in their embryo. Many illustrious souls may be said to have been dead among the living, or buried alive in the obscurity of their condition, whose perfections [might] have rendered them the darlings of Providence and the companion of angels.

*Turkish Spy, pseudonym
for a writer, c. 1700*

Not he who has little, but he who wishes more, is poor.

Seneca

I come from a family where gravy is considered a beverage.

Erma Bombeck

Thousands upon thousands are yearly brought into a state of real poverty by their great anxiety not to be thought poor.

William Cobbett

Poverty is an anomaly to rich people; it is very difficult to make out why people who want dinner do not ring the bell.

Walter Bagehot

There were times when my pants were so thin I could sit on a dime and tell whether it was heads or tails.

Spencer Tracy

All the arguments which are brought to represent poverty as no evil, show it to be evidently a great evil. You never find people labouring to convince you that you may

live very happily upon a plentiful fortune.

Samuel Johnson

We have grown literally afraid to be poor. We despise anyone who elects to be poor in order to simplify and save his inner life. If he does not join the general scramble and pant with the money-making street, we deem him spiritless and lacking in ambition. We have lost the power even of imagining what the ancient idealization of poverty could have meant: the liberation from material attachments, the unbribed soul.

William James

The greatest of evils and the worst of crimes is poverty.

George Bernard Shaw

Poverty is not a shame, but being ashamed of it is.

Proverb

It is not the man who has too little but the man who craves more, that is poor.

Seneca

It is only the poor who pay cash, and that not from virtue, but because they are refused credit.

Anatole France

It's no disgrace t' be poor, but it might as well be.

Kin Hubbard

[Today's world] is like a ship in which the steerage passengers report the stern is sinking, to receive the reply from those in the first

class lounge that they'll consider helping, but first they must deal with the rise in price of fillet steak.
William Clark

The trouble with being poor is that it takes up all your time.
Willem de Kooning

If rich people could hire other people to die for them, the poor could make a wonderful living.
Yiddish proverb

The poor tread lightest upon the Earth. The higher our income, the more resources we control and the more havoc we wreak.
Paul Harrison

He found it inconvenient to be poor.
William Cowper

POWER

The only prize much cared for by the powerful is power. The prize of the general is not a bigger tent, but command.
Oliver Wendell Holmes, Jr

Power must never be trusted without a check.
John Adams

The measure of man is what he does with power.
Pittacus of Mytilene

Power can corrupt, but absolute power is absolutely delightful.
Anonymous

Power corrupts. Absolute power is kind of neat.
John Lehman

While nobody can seriously maintain that the greatest number must have the greatest wisdom, or the greatest virtue, there is no denying that, under modern social conditions, they are likely to have the most power.
Walter Lippman

Power is the ability not to have to please.
Elizabeth Janeway

The distinction that really matters is not between violence and nonviolence but between having and not having the appetite for power.
George Orwell

Power is to have others listen to your silence.
Patrick Kelly

Power never takes a back step – only in the face of more power.
Malcolm X

To play safe, I prefer to accept only one type of power: the power of art over trash, the triumph of magic over the brute.
Vladimir Nabokov

The problem of power is how to achieve its responsible use rather than its irresponsible and indulgent use – of how to get men of power to live for the public rather than live off the public.
Robert F. Kennedy

Nearly all men can stand adversity, but if you want to test a man's character, give him power.
Abraham Lincoln

Power tends to confuse itself with virtue and a great nation is peculiarly susceptible to the idea that its power is a sign of God's favor ... Once imbued with the idea of a mission, a great nation easily assumes that it has the means as well as the duty to do God's work.

J. William Fulbright

The more you are talked about, the less powerful you are.

Benjamin Disraeli

The management of a balance of power is a permanent undertaking, not an exertion that has a foreseeable end.

Henry Kissinger

Mankind is safer when men seek pleasure than when they seek the power and the glory.

Geoffrey Gorer

Power tends to corrupt and absolute power corrupts absolutely.

Lord Acton

Absence of power corrupts, absolute absence corrupts absolutely.

Pierre Elliott Trudeau

Unlimited power is apt to corrupt.

William Pitt

Power does not corrupt men: but fools, if they get into a position of power, corrupt it.

George Bernard Shaw

If someone says, that he wants to save the people, take good care to translate that to the effect that he wants power.

Jean-Paul Desbiens

Power is getting others to do one's will.

Garry Wills

A word after a word after a word is power.

Margaret Atwood

The purpose of getting power is to be able to give it away.

Aneurin Bevan

POWERFUL
The powerful are not only blind, they see things that aren't there.

Stephen Vizinczey

The man who fears nothing is as powerful as he who is feared by everybody.

Friedrich von Schiller

POWERS
This is the night of dark powers.

True Davidson

PRACTICE
If I don't practice one day, I know it; two days, the critics know it; three days, the public knows it.

Jascha Heifetz

However much thou art read in theory, if thou hast no practice thou art ignorant.

Sa'di

Men of power have no time to read; yet the men who do not read are unfit for power.

Michael Foot

Amateurs practice until they can get it right; professionals practise until they can't get it wrong.

Anonymous

Practice is the best of all instructors.

Publilius Syrus

PRAGMATISM

The great weakness of Pragmatism is that it ends up being of no use to anybody.

T.S. Eliot

PRAISE

The advantage of doing one's praise to oneself is that one can lay it on so thick and exactly in the right places.

Samuel Butler

To praise oneself is considered improper, immodest; to praise one's own sect, one's own philosophy, is considered the highest duty.

Leo Shestov

He who gladly does without the praise of the crowd will not miss the opportunity of becoming his own fan.

Karl Kraus

He who refuses praise the first time that it is offered does so because he would hear it a second time.

François, duc de La Rochefoucauld

Among the smaller duties of life, I hardly know one more important than that of not praising where praise is not due.

Sydney Smith

Praise makes good men better and bad men worse.

Proverb

I never knew any man deserve praise, who did not desire it.

Lord Chesterfield

Praise undeserved is satire in disguise.

Alexander Pope

I can stand a waste of praise.

R.S. Surtees

Praise is the best diet for us, after all.

Sydney Smith

PRAY

Pray, *v.* To ask that the laws of the universe be annulled in behalf of a single petitioner confessedly unworthy.

Ambrose Bierce

PRAYER

It's best to read the weather forecast before we pray for rain.

Mark Twain

It is folly for a man to pray to the gods for that which he has the power to obtain for himself.

Epicurus

Prayer does not change God, but it changes him who prays.

Søren Kierkegaard

I'm normally not a praying man, but if you're up there, please save me Superman.

Homer Simpson

In a dangerous world there will always be more people around whose prayers for their own safety have been answered than those whose prayers have not.
Nicholas Humphrey

Then I'll get on my knees and pray/We don't get fooled again.
Pete Townsend

No man ever prayed heartily without learning something.
Ralph Waldo Emerson

I have been driven many times to my knees by the overwhelming conviction that I had nowhere else to go. My own wisdom and that of all about me, seemed insufficient for that day.
Abraham Lincoln

The best way to pray is the way that brings the best results for you.
W.G. Sonastine

PRE-MENSTRUAL SYNDROME
Women complain about pre-menstrual syndrome, but I think of it as the only time of the month that I can be myself.
Roseanne Barr

Do you know why they call it "PMS"? Because mad cow disease was already taken.
Unknown

PREACHING
If there is no hell, a good many preachers are obtaining money under false pretenses.
Billy Sunday

Everybody should listen to a sermon occasionally. Including those who go to church.
Franklin P. Jones

PRECAUTIONS
The chief danger in life is that you may take too many precautions.
Alfred Adler

A danger foreseen is half avoided.
Proverb

PRECIPICE
It is true we may come to a perpendicular precipice, but we need not jump off, nor run our heads against it.
Henry David Thoreau

PRECISION
Everything is vague to a degree you do not realize til you have tried to make it precise.
Bertrand Russell

PRECONCEPTIONS
We want the facts to fit the preconceptions. When they don't, it's easier to ignore the facts than to change the preconceptions.
Jessamyn West

PREDICTIONS
The wisest prophet makes sure of the event first.
Horace Walpole

You can only predict things after they've happened
Eugène Ionesco

A misty morning does not signify a cloudy day.

Proverb

The best way to predict your future is to make it.

Peter Drucker

I think the team that wins Game Five will win the series. Unless we lose Game Five.

Charles Barkley

In conditions of great uncertainty people tend to predict the events they want to happen actually will happen.

Roberta Wohlstetter

The best way to suppose what may come, is to remember what is past.

George Savile, Marquess of Halifax

Never predict or forecast anything you know has not happened yet.

Boo Chanco

I was asked in Japan recently not to predict the end of the world – they were nervous it might affect the stock market.

Stephen Hawking

I confess that in 1901, I said to my brother Orville that man would not fly for fifty years. Ever since, I have distrusted myself and avoided all predictions.

Wilbur Wright

PREGNANCY

If pregnancy were a book, they would cut the last two chapters.

Nora Ephron

PREJUDICE

Prejudice is never easy unless it can pass itself off as reason.

William Hazlitt

No one who is Roman Catholic, left-handed, and red haired has anything to learn about prejudice.

Paul Johnson

Without the aid of prejudice and custom, I should not be able to find my way across the room.

William Hazlitt

Prejudices are what fools use for reason

Voltaire

Prejudice is the child of ignorance.

William Hazlitt

A great many people think they are thinking when they are merely rearranging their prejudices.

William James

He had but one eye, and the popular prejudice runs in favour of two.

Charles Dickens

She was anxious to be someone, and, no one ever having voiced a prejudice in her hearing without impressing her, had come to associate prejudice with identity. You could not be a someone without disliking things.

Elizabeth Bowen

I am free of all prejudices. I hate everyone equally.

W.C. Fields

Nobody outside of a baby carriage or a judge's chamber believes in an unprejudiced point of view.
Lillian Hellman

If we were to wake up some morning and find out that everyone was the same race, creed, and colour, we would find some other cause for prejudice by noon.
George Aiken

There is something so amiable in the prejudices of a young mind, that one is sorry to see them give way to the reception of more general opinions.
Jane Austen

Prejudice, not being founded on reason, cannot be removed by argument.
Samuel Johnson

Prejudice: the dislike for all that is unlike.
Israel Zangwill

PREPARATION
If I had eight hours to chop down a tree I would spend six sharpening my axe.
Abraham Lincoln

The best preparation for tomorrow is to do today's work superbly well.
Sir William Osler

Failing to prepare is preparing to fail.
John Wooden

He who is not ready today, will be less ready tomorrow.
Ovid

It's a funny thing: the more I practise, the luckier I get.
Arnold Palmer

No matter how deep you dig your well, it affords poor refuge in times of flood.
Chinese proverb

By failing to prepare, you are preparing to fail.
Benjamin Franklin

To be prepared is half the victory.
Miguel de Cervantes

PREPOSITIONS
Never end a sentence with a preposition unless you have nothing else to end it with.
Winston Churchill

PRESENT
The present is a rope stretched over the past. The secret to walking it is, you never look down.
Sean Stewart

There's no present. There's only the immediate future and the recent past.
George Carlin

Only in the present do things happen.
Jorge Luis Borges

PRESENTS
When thou makest presents, let them be of such things as will last long; to the end that they may be in some sort immortal and may frequently refresh the memory of the receiver.
Thomas Fuller, MD

PRESIDENT

Anyone can become president. That's one of the risks you take.

Adlai Stevenson

Being President is like running a cemetery; you've got a lot of people under you and nobody's listening.

Bill Clinton

The things that bother a press about a President will ultimately bother the country.

David Halberstam

In our brief national history, we have shot four of our presidents, worried five of them to death, impeached one and hounded another out of office. And when all else fails, we hold an election and assassinate their character.

P.J. O'Rourke

PRESS

As the free press develops, the paramount point is whether the journalist, like the scientist or scholar, puts truth in the first place or the second.

Walter Lippmann

Hastiness and superficiality are the psychic diseases of the twentieth century, and more than anywhere else this disease is reflected in the press.

Alexandr Solzhenitsyn

I'm with you on the free press. It's the newspapers I can't stand.

Tom Stoppard

Never in history has the press seized absolute power and muzzled the politicians.

David Brinkley

PRESSURE

Pressure, pushing down on me, pressing down on you.

David Bowie

PRESTIGE

Prestige is the mainspring of all authority. Neither gods, kings nor women have ever reigned without it.

Gustave Le Bon

PRETENDING

You can pretend to be serious. You can't pretend to be witty.

Sacha Guitry

We are what we pretend to be, so we must be careful about what we pretend to be.

Kurt Vonnegut, Jr

It is affectation to pretend to feel the distress of others as much as they do themselves. It is equally so, as if one should pretend to feel as much pain while a friend's leg is being cut off as he does.

Samuel Johnson

PRETTY FACE

It has been said that a pretty face is a passport. But it's not, it's a visa, and it runs out fast.

Julie Burchill

PREVENTION
You can only cure retail but you can prevent wholesale.
Brock Chisholm

It is far better to prevent than to repent.
Louis L. Mann

PRICELESS
Although human life is priceless, we always act as if something had an even greater price than life. ... But what is that something?
Antoine de Saint-Exupéry

PRIDE
Temper is what gets most of us in trouble. Pride is what keeps us there.
Unknown

Don't let your brains go to your head.
Unknown

Pride is generally censured and decried, but mainly by those who have nothing to be proud of.
Arthur Schopenhauer

Nature endowed us with pride to spare us the pain of knowing about our imperfections.
François, duc de La Rochefoucauld

If a proud man makes me keep my distance, the comfort is that he keeps his at the same time.
Jonathan Swift

Pride does not wish to owe and vanity does not wish to pay.
François, duc de La Rochefoucauld

We are rarely proud when we are alone.
Voltaire

He that is too proud to ask is too good to receive.
Proverb

One of the greatest sources of energy is pride in what we are doing.
Unknown

Small things make base men proud.
William Shakespeare

There is a paradox in pride: It makes some men ridiculous, but prevents others from becoming so.
Charles Caleb Colton

In general, pride is at the bottom of all great mistakes.
John Ruskin

PRINCIPLES
I am totally without principle – but not without interest.
Jim Lyons

It is often easier to fight for principles than live up to them.
Adlai Stevenson

He who merely knows right principles is not equal to him who loves them.
Confucius

Nature imitates herself. A grain thrown into good ground brings forth fruit; a principle thrown into a good mind brings forth fruit.

Blaise Pascal

Those who stand for nothing fall for anything.

Alex Hamilton

The time has come for all good men to rise above principle.

Huey Long

Those are my principles, and if you don't like them – well, I have others.

Groucho Marx

There is probably no direct way to get in touch with our inner selves or to seek out satisfaction and happiness. It's best to live by sound principles – honesty, courage, liberty and love – and then to await what unfolds. When, inevitably, we go astray for a time, we must return, once again, to living by the principles we cherish. The formula isn't all that difficult to understand; applying it is the work of a lifetime.

Peter Breggin

Damn your principles! Stick to your party.

Benjamin Disraeli

Whenever two good people argue over principles, they are both right.

Marie von Ebner-Eschenbach

You don't have power if you surrender all your principles – you have office.

Ron Todd

In matters of style, swim with the current; in matters of principle, stand like a rock.

Thomas Jefferson

The only way to prove that a truth or principle is practical is to practise it.

J. Sig Paulson

The most useful thing about a principle is that it can always be sacrificed to expediency.

W. Somerset Maugham

Always vote for a principle, though you vote alone, and you may cherish the sweet reflection that your vote is never lost.

John Quincy Adams

Amid the pressure of great events, a general principle gives no help.

G.W.F. Hegel

As Bismarck once blurted out, when you say that you agree to a thing in principle you mean that you have not the slightest intention of carrying it out in practice.

Henry Higgs

Rules are not necessarily sacred; principles are.

Franklin D. Roosevelt

Sir, are you so grossly ignorant of human nature, as not to know that a man may be very sincere in good principles, without having good practice?

Samuel Johnson

Any man who fights for the things he believes in must be prepared to make enemies.

Walter Reuther

Nobody ever did anything very foolish except from some strong principle.

Lord Melbourne

PRISONS

The degree of civilization in a society can be judged by entering its prisons.

Fyodor Dostoyevsky

He said to me son/They won't build no schools anymore

They won't build no hospitals/All they'll build will be prison, prison.

Lucky Dube

PRIVACY

Privacy is one of those precious modern constructions that we've dressed up as a fundamental right when it's really a frilly privilege that comes with being so affluent that we can ignore the neighbours and pretend that we don't need anyone else. In societies where folks have to live on top of one another, there's not a lot of privacy. But there is discretion. ... We've created a world of privacy without discretion, a sort of inside-out Victorianism. God save anyone who dares to ask for my Social Security number, but let's hear about my erectile dysfunction!

Mark Fisher

Privacy and security are those things you give up when you show the world what makes you extraordinary.

Margaret Cho

Where is the expectation of privacy in the commission of a crime?

Linda Tripp

PRIVILEGE

What men value in this world is not rights but privileges.

H.L. Mencken

PROBABILITY

A reasonable probability is the only certainty.

Edgar Watson Howe

The probability of someone watching you is proportional to the stupidity of your action.

A. Kindsvater

We balance probabilities and choose the most likely. It is the scientific use of the imagination.

Sherlock Holmes

PROBLEMS

Don't let us make imaginary evils, when we have so many real ones to encounter.

Oliver Goldsmith

Problems are only opportunities in working clothes.

Henry K. Kaiser

If a problem is too difficult to solve, one cannot claim that it is solved by pointing to all the efforts made to solve it.

Hannes Alfven

The real problem is what to do with the problem solvers after the problems are solved.

Gay Talese

Some people approach every problem with an open mouth.

Adlai Stevenson

Problems cannot be solved by thinking within the framework in which the problems were created.

Albert Einstein

A problem is a chance for you to do your best.

Duke Ellington

People who are only good with hammers see every problem as a nail.

Abraham Maslow

No problem can withstand the assault of sustained thinking.

Voltaire

Every problem has a gift for you in its hands.

Richard Bach

It isn't that they can't see the solution. It is that they can't see the problem.

G.K. Chesterton

Problems worthy of attack prove their worth by hitting back.

Piet Hein

Repent what's past; avoid what is to come.

William Shakespeare

We can face our problem. We can arrange our facts with order and method.

Agatha Christie

It is quite a three-pipe problem.

Arthur Conan Doyle

Intellectuals solve problems; geniuses prevent them.

Albert Einstein

If a problem has no solution, it may not be a problem, but a fact, not to be solved, but to be coped with over time.

Shimon Peres

The chief cause of problems is solutions.

Eric Sevareid

The problem is not that there are problems. The problem is expecting otherwise and thinking that having problems is a problem.

Theodore Rubin

One problem after another presents itself and in the solving of them we can find our greatest pleasure.

Karl Menninger

Every solution of a problem is a new problem.

Johann Wolfgang von Goethe

Mankind always sets itself only such problems as it can solve.

Karl Marx

PROCRASTINATION

Procrastination gives you something to look forward to.

Joan Konner

Procrastination is the art of keeping up with yesterday.

Don Marquis

Procrastination is opportunity's assassin.

Victor Kiam

If it weren't for the last minute, nothing would get done.

Anonymous

Never put off tomorrow what you can do the day after tomorrow.

Mark Twain

Every successful man I have heard of has done the best he could with conditions as he found them, and not waited until next year for better.

Edgar Watson Howe

By the street of By-and-By one arrives at the house of Never.

Miguel de Cervantes

Only put off until tomorrow what you are willing to die having left undone.

Pablo Picasso

PROCREATION

I should consent to breed under pressure, if I were convinced in any way of the reasonableness of reproducing the species.

Ezra Pound

PRODUCER

Every man is a consumer and ought to be a producer.

Ralph Waldo Emerson

PRODUCTIVITY

Productivity is being able to do things that you were never able to do before.

Franz Kafka

PROFANITY

Profanity is the effort of a feeble mind to express itself forcefully.

Unknown

PROFESSIONALS

Professionals are people who can do their job when they don't feel like it. Amateurs are people who can't do their job when they do feel like it.

Bits & Pieces

Being a professional is doing all the things you love to do on the days when you don't feel like doing them.

Julius Erving

The essence of a genuine professional man is that he cannot be bought.

H.L. Mencken

All professions are conspiracies against the laity.

George Bernard Shaw

The professions are by definition – or perhaps we should say by aspiration – autonomous, and not beholden to the mighty. Otherwise they would have no legitimacy in the public's eye: Claims to professional objectivity and neutrality cannot be made from an actual position of servility.

Barbara Ehrenreich

PROFESSORS

A professor is one who talks in someone else's sleep.

W.H. Auden

PROFITS

Nothing contributes so much to the prosperity and happiness of a country as high profits.

David Ricardo

Civilization and profits go hand in hand.

Calvin Coolidge

"Form follows profit" is the aesthetic principle of our times.

Richard Rogers

PROFUNDITY

Never try to impress people with the profundity of your thought by the obscurity of your language. Whatever has been thoroughly thought through can be stated simply.

Unknown

PROGRESS

The test of our progress is not whether we add more to the abundance of those who have much, it is whether we provide enough for those who have too little.

Franklin D. Roosevelt

Progress, therefore, is not an accident, but a necessity ... It is part of nature.

Herbert Spencer

It would take only one generation of forgetfulness to put us back intellectually several thousand years.

Dean Tollefson

Progress might have been all right once, but it's gone on too long.

Ogden Nash

Usually, terrible things that are done with the excuse that progress requires them are not really progress at all, but just terrible things.

Russell Baker

With every passing hour our solar system comes forty-three thousand miles closer to globular cluster M13 in the constellation Hercules, and still there are some misfits who continue to insist that there is no such thing as progress.

Ransom K. Ferm

What we call progress is the exchange of one nuisance for another nuisance.

Havelock Ellis

Habit creates the appearance of justice; progress has no greater enemy than habit.

Jose Marti

Those who speak most of progress measure it by quantity and not by quality.

George Santayana

We're going to turn this team around 360 degrees.
Jason Kidd

Belief in progress is a doctrine of idlers and Belgians. It is the individual relying upon his neighbours to do his work.
Charles Baudelaire

There can be no progress (real, that is, moral) except in the individual and by the individual himself.
Charles Baudelaire

A point which yesterday was invisible is its goal today, and will be its starting point tomorrow.
Thomas Babington Macaulay

Technological progress is like an axe in the hands of a pathological criminal.
Albert Einstein

Progress imposes not only new possibilities for the future, but new restrictions.
Norbert Wiener

The chief obstacle to the progress of the human race is the human race.
Don Marquis

Civilization is impossible without traditions, and progress impossible without the destruction of those traditions. The difficulty, and it is an immense difficulty, is to find a proper equilibrium between stability and variability.
Gustave Le Bon

There is only the fight to recover what has been lost and found and lost again and again.
T.S. Eliot

Everything is like a door swinging backwards and forwards.
Samuel Beckett

Without a struggle, there can be no progress.
Frederick Douglass

Now, here, you see, it takes all the running you can do, to keep in the same place.
Lewis Carroll

All progress occurs because people dare to be different.
Harry Millner

The positive news is we appear to be making progress.
Dick Cheney

I make progress by having people around me who are smarter than I am – and listening to them. And I assume that everyone is smarter about something than I am.
Henry J. Kaiser

I'm a slow walker, but I never walk back.
Abraham Lincoln

The business of life is to go forward.
Samuel Johnson

Some men a forward motion love,/ But I by backward step would move.
Henry Vaughan

For everything you have missed, you have gained something else; and for everything you gain, you lose something.

Ralph Waldo Emerson

The art of progress is to preserve order amid change, and to preserve change amid order.

Alfred North Whitehead

The European talks of progress because by the aid of a few scientific discoveries he has established a society which has mistaken comfort for civilization.

Benjamin Disraeli

Healthy discontent is the prelude to progress.

Mohandas Gandhi

Emergencies have always been necessary to progress. It was darkness which produced the lamp. It was fog that produced the compass. It was hunger that drove us to exploration. And it took a depression to show us the value of a job.

Victor Hugo

PROGRESSION

Nothing in progression can rest on its original plan. We may as well think of rocking a grown man in the cradle of an infant.

Edmund Burke

PROLETARIAT

The proletariat are far more skilled at discovering what they want than what they need; so giving them power constituted giving them power to say what they want, not giving them objectivity to see what they need.

John Fowles

PROMISE

Promise is most given when the least is said.

George Chapman

The promises of yesterday are the taxes of today.

William Lyon Mackenzie King

Better a friendly refusal than an unwitting promise.

German proverb

Better a broken promise than none at all.

Mark Twain

He who is most slow in making a promise is the most faithful in the performance of it.

Jean-Jacques Rousseau

A mind that is conscious of its integrity scorns to say more than it means to perform.

Robert Burns

PROMISED LAND

The Promised Land always lies on the other side of a Wilderness.

Havelock Ellis

PROOF

"For example" is not proof.

Jewish proverb

Scientists believe in proof without certainty: most people believe in certainty without proof.

Ashley Montagu

That which proves too much proves nothing.

French proverb

PROPAGANDA
Why is propaganda so much more successful when it stirs up hatred than when it tries to stir up friendly feeling?

Bertrand Russell

Propaganda does not deceive people; it merely helps them to deceive themselves.

Eric Hoffer

PROPERTY
Them that has china plates themselves is the most careful not to break the china plates of others.

J.M. Barrie

No man acquires property without acquiring with it a little arithmetic also.

Ralph Waldo Emerson

PROPHECY
The art of prophecy is very difficult – especially with respect to the future.

Mark Twain

Among all forms of mistake, prophecy is the most gratuitous.

George Eliot

Some people would take comfort from the end of the world, if only they had prophesied it.

Friedrich Hebbel

PROPHET
The wise man who is not heeded is counted a fool, and the fool who proclaims the general folly first and loudest passes for a prophet.

Carl Jung

The well-adjusted make poor prophets.

Eric Hoffer

The best of prophets of the future is the past.

Lord Byron

Prophets are twice stoned – first in anger; then, after their death, with a handsome slab in the graveyard.

Christopher Morley

PROPORTION
The severity of the itch is proportional to the reach.

Steven Wright

PROSPERITY
Everything in the world may be endured except continued prosperity.

Johann Wolfgang von Goethe

Such prosperity as we have known it up to the present is the consequence of rapidly spending the planet's irreplaceable capital.

Aldous Huxley

When a man arrives at great prosperity, God did it; when he falls into disaster, he did it himself.

Mark Twain

Prosperity does not exalt the wise man, nor does adversity cast him down.

Seneca

PROTEST
Protest long enough that you are right, and you will be wrong.

Yiddish proverb

PROVERBS
Solomon made a book of proverbs, but a book of proverbs never made a Solomon.

English proverb

A country can be judged by the quality of its proverbs.

German proverb

A proverb is one man's wit and all men's wisdom.

Lord John Russell

Nothing ever becomes real til it is experienced – even a proverb is not proverb to you until your life has illustrated it.

John Keats

A proverb is a short sentence based on long experience.

Miguel de Cervantes

PROVOCATION
To strike at a serpent that hisses may only cause it to spring.

Frank Moore

PRUDENCE
The eye of prudence may never shut.

Ralph Waldo Emerson

Affairs are easier of entrance than of exit, and it is but common prudence to see our way out before we venture in.

Aesop

PSYCHIATRISTS
Psychiatrists pretend not to know everything.

Bob Kaufman

Anyone who goes to a psychiatrist should have his head examined.

Samuel Goldwyn

The trouble with some psychiatrists who believe in shock treatments is they use bills instead of pills.

Dr O.A. Battista

PSYCHIC FORCES
The strongest of all psychic forces in the world is unsatisfied desire.

John Cowper Powys

PSYCHOANALYSIS
Psychoanalysis makes quite simple people feel they're complex.

S.N. Behrman

PSYCHOLOGY
The object of psychology is to give us a totally different idea of the things we know best.

Paul Valéry

Behavioural psychology is the science of pulling habits out of rats.

Douglas Busch

I don't believe in psychology. I believe in good moves.

Bobby Fischer

Psychology is as useless as directions for using poison.

Karl Kraus

PUBLIC
The public do not know enough to be experts, yet know enough to decide between them.

Unknown

The public seldom forgive twice.

Johann Kaspar Lavater

The public will believe anything, so long as it is not founded on truth.

Edith Sitwell

Most people have seen worse things in private than they pretend to be shocked at in public.

Edgar Watson Howe

PUBLIC INTEREST
Everybody thinks chiefly of his own, hardly ever of the public, interest.

Aristotle

A democracy is badly served when newspapers and television focus so intensely on the personal joys and tragedies of famous people. This kind of "news" crowds out more serious issues, and there is an important difference ... between the public interest and what interests the public.

Cass Sunstein

The things most people want to know are usually none of their business.

George Bernard Shaw

PUBLIC LIFE
Public life is the paradise of voluble windbags.

George Bernard Shaw

Public life is a situation of power and energy; he trespasses against his duty who sleeps upon his watch, as well as he who goes over to his enemy.

Edmund Burke

You will find as you grow older that courage is the rarest of all qualities to be found in public life.

Benjamin Disraeli

PUBLIC OFFICE
It is inaccurate to say I hate everything. I am strongly in favour of common sense, common honesty, and common decency. This makes me forever ineligible for any public office.

H.L. Mencken

PUBLIC OPINION
Public opinion is a compound of folly, weakness, prejudice, wrong feeling, right feeling, obstinacy, and newspaper paragraphs.

Sir Robert Peel

When the people have no tyrant, their own public opinion becomes one.

Edward Bulwer-Lytton

One should respect public opinion in so far as it is necessary to avoid starvation and keep out of prison, but anything that goes beyond this is a voluntary submission to an unnecessary tyranny.

Bertrand Russell

Your representative owes you, not his industry only, but his judgment; and he betrays instead of serving you if he sacrifices it to your opinion.

Edmund Burke

Because half-a-dozen grasshoppers under a fern make the field ring with their impudent chink, whilst thousands of great cattle, reposed beneath the shadow of the British oak, chew the cud and are silent, pray do not imagine that those who make the noise are the only inhabitants of the field; that, of course, they are many in number; or that, after all, they are other than the little, shrivelled, meager, hopping, though loud and troubled insects of the hour.

Edmund Burke

When Princes break their miserable etiquette it is always in favour of some girl or jester, and never for a man of worth. When women make themselves conspicuous, it is never for an upright man, always for a creature. In a word, when we throw off the yoke of public opinion, it is seldom for the purpose of rising above it, but nearly always to fall below.

Chamfort

Public opinion [is] a vulgar, impertinent, anonymous tyrant who deliberately makes life unpleasant for anyone who is not content to be the average man.

Dean Inge

There is ... no point in deliberately flouting public opinion; this is still to be under its domination, though in a topsy-turvy way. But to be genuinely indifferent to it is both a strength and a source of happiness.

Bertrand Russell

PUBLIC SERVICE
Why is it that when people have no capacity for private usefulness they should be so anxious to serve the public?

Sara Jeanette Duncan

The best servants of the people, like the best valets, must whisper unpleasant truths in the master's ear. It is the court fool, not the foolish courtier, whom the king can least afford to lose.

Walter Lippmann

PUBLICITY
There's no bad publicity, except an obituary notice.

Brendan Behan

The caterpillar does all the work, but the butterfly gets all the publicity.

George Carlin

PUBLISH
Publish or be damned.

Duke of Wellington

I'll publish right or wrong: Fools are my theme, let satire be my song.
Lord Byron

PUBLISHERS
One of the signs of Napoleon's greatness is the fact that he once had a publisher shot.
Siegfried Unseld

PULSE
Although you can take a nation's pulse, you can't be sure that the nation hasn't just run up a flight of stairs.
E.B. White

PUNCTUALITY
Punctuality is the virtue of the bored.
Evelyn Waugh

I have always been a quarter of an hour before my time, and it has made a man of me.
Horatio, Lord Nelson

Punctuality is the politeness of princes.
Unknown

Punctuality has been defined as the art of guessing accurately just how late the other party may be. If you can manage to reach the appointed place first … you win.
Unknown

The trouble with being punctual is that nobody's there to appreciate it.
Harold Rome

If people are early, they're anxious. If they're on time, they're obsessive. If they're late, they're angry.
Unknown

The slogan of the Procrastinators Club of America is: "We're Behind You All the Way."
Unknown

Punctuality is the art of wasting only your own time.
Franklin P. Jones

PUNDIT
A pundit is an expert on nothing but an authority on everything.
William Safire

PUNISHMENT
Beware of punishing wrongfully. Do not kill, for it will not profit you.
Merikare

The object of punishment is prevention from evil; it can never be made impulsive to good.
Horace Mann

To punish and not prevent is to labour at the pump and leave open the leak.
Thomas Fuller, MD

We are not punished for our sins, but by them.
Elbert Hubbard

PUNS
Puns are little "plays on words" that a certain breed of person loves to spring on you and then look at you in a certain self-satisfied way to indicate that he thinks that you must think that he is by far the

cleverest person on Earth now that Benjamin Franklin is dead, when in fact what you are thinking is that if this person ends up in a life-boat, the other passengers will hurl him overboard by the end of the first day even if they have plenty of food and water.

Dave Barry

PUPPET
A puppet of the gods is a tragic figure; a puppet suspended on his chromosomes is merely grotesque.

Arthur Koestler

PURE
O Lord, help me to be pure, but not yet.

St Augustine

Blessed are the pure in heart for they have so much to talk about.

Edith Wharton

I'm as pure as the driven slush.

Tallulah Bankhead

PURITAN
Art is so wonderfully irrational, exuberantly pointless, but necessary all the same. Pointless and yet necessary, that's hard for a puritan to understand.

Günter Grass

The Puritan's idea of Hell is a place where everybody has to mind his own business.

Wendell Phillips

A puritan's a person who pours righteous indignation into the wrong things.

G.K. Chesterton

The objection to Puritans is not that they try to make us think as they do, but that they try to make us do as they think.

H.L. Mencken

PURITANISM
Puritanism: the haunting fear that someone, somewhere, may be happy.

H.L. Mencken

We have long passed the Victorian era, where asterisks were followed after a certain interval by a baby.

W. Somerset Maugham

PURITY
Purity is the ability to contemplate defilement.

Simone Weil

PURPOSE
If a man hasn't discovered something he will die for, he isn't fit to live.

Martin Luther King, Jr

All that we do is done with an eye to something else.

Aristotle

If you don't know where you are going, you will probably end up somewhere else.

Laurence J. Peter

The days come and go like muffled and veiled figures sent from a distant friendly party, but they say nothing, and if we do not use the gifts they bring, they carry them as silently away.

Ralph Waldo Emerson

If you're out to beat a dog, you're sure to find a stick.

Yiddish proverb

He who has a why to live can bear almost any how.

Friedrich Nietzsche

If one does not know to which port one is sailing, no wind is favourable.

Seneca

To know your purpose, you first have to know who you are.

Idelette van Papendorp

We are not primarily put on this earth to see through one another, but to see one another through.

Peter De Vries

I think the purpose of life is to be happy, to be useful, to be responsible, to be compassionate. It is, above all, to matter; to count, to stand for something, to have made some difference that you lived at all.

Leo Rosten

Firmness of purpose is one of the most necessary sinews of character and one of the best instruments of success. Without it, genius wastes its efforts in a maze of inconsistencies.

Lord Chesterfield

A man's never wrong doing what he thinks is right.

Lorne Greene

PUZZLEMENT
The capacity to be puzzled is ... the premise of all creation, be it in art or in science.

Erich Fromm

QANTAS AIRWAYS
Complaints logged by pilots and solutions logged by maintenance engineers:

Dead bugs on windshield. Live bugs on back-order.

Evidence of leak on right main landing gear. Evidence removed.

IFF inoperative. IFF always inoperative in "off" mode.

Aircraft handles funny. Aircraft warned to straighten up, fly right, and be serious.

Target radar hums. Reprogrammed target radar with words.

QUALITY
Quality in a service or product is not what you put into it. It is what the client or customer gets out of it.
Peter Drucker

People of quality know everything without ever having been taught anything.

Molière

Quality means doing it right when no one is looking.
Henry Ford

Quality is never an accident; it is always the result of intelligent effort. ... The bitterness of poor quality lingers long after the sweetness of low price is forgotten.
John Ruskin

The good composer is slowly discovered, the bad composer is slowly found out.
Ernest Newman

It is quality rather than quantity that matters.
Seneca

QUARRELS
Quarrels would not last long if the fault was only on one side.
François, duc de La Rochefoucauld

It takes in reality only one to make a quarrel. It is useless for the sheep to pass resolutions in favour of vegetarianism while the wolf remains of a different opinion.
Dean Inge

The last sound on the worthless earth will be two human beings trying to launch a homemade space-ship and already quarrelling about where they are going next.

William Faulkner

Most quarrels amplify a misunderstanding.

André Gide

There is a sort of man who goes through the world in a succession of quarrels, always able to make out that he is in the right, although he never ceases to put other men in the wrong. The least that can be said of such a person is that he has an unhappy aptitude for eliciting whatever evil there may be in the natures with which he comes in contact; and a man who is sure to cause injuries to him wherever he goes is almost as great an evil and inconvenience as if he were himself the wrongdoer.

Sir Henry Taylor

Let's not quarrel about the skin until we kill the bear.

Sir John A. Macdonald

It takes two to make a quarrel, but only one to end it.

Spanish proverb

A bad workman quarrels with the man who calls him that.

Ambrose Bierce

The test of a man or woman's breeding is how they behave in a quarrel.

George Bernard Shaw

The quarrel is a very pretty quarrel as it stands; we should only spoil it by trying to explain it.

Richard Brinsley Sheridan

Beware of entrance to a quarrel; but, being in, bear it that the opposer may be aware of thee.

William Shakespeare

QUESTIONS

No question is ever settled until it is settled right.

Ella Wheeler Wilcox

It is better to know some of the questions than to know all of the answers.

James Thurber

A fool may ask more questions in an hour than a wise man can answer in seven years.

English proverb

He who asks questions cannot avoid the answers.

Cameroonian proverb

Judge a man by his questions rather than his answers.

Voltaire

There aren't any embarrassing questions – just embarrassing answers.

Carl Rowan

A sudden bold and unexpected question doth many times surprise a man and lay him open.

Francis Bacon

The important thing is not to stop questioning.

Albert Einstein

A prudent question is one-half of wisdom.

Francis Bacon

Don't ask *what are* questions, ask *what do* questions, don't ask *why* questions, ask *how* questions.

Sir Karl Popper

Sometimes we do a thing in order to find out the reason for it. Sometimes our actions are questions, not answers.

John Le Carré

You can tell whether a man is clever by his answers. You can tell whether a man is wise by his questions.

Naguib Mahfouz

It is not every question that deserves an answer.

Publilius Syrus

QUIET

To be simple is the best thing in the world; to be modest is the next best thing. I am not so sure about being quiet.

G.K. Chesterton

QUIT

You can never quit. Winners never quit, and quitters never win.

Ted Turner

A man is not finished when he is defeated. He is finished when he quits.

Richard M. Nixon

QUOTATIONS

On the rare occasions when I really didn't like a person, I quoted them verbatim.

Jay Scott

I hate quotations. Tell me what you know.

Ralph Waldo Emerson

It is a good thing for an uneducated man to read books of quotations.

Winston Churchill

By necessity, by proclivity – and by delight, we all quote.

Ralph Waldo Emerson

What's the use of a good quotation if you can't change it?

Doctor Who

Confound those who have said our remarks before us.

Aelius Donatus

I always have a quotation for everything – it saves original thinking.

Dorothy L. Sayers

The wisdom of the wise and the experience of the ages are perpetuated by quotations.

Benjamin Disraeli

The surest way to make a monkey of a man is to quote him.

Robert Benchley

A fine quotation is a diamond on the finger of a man of wit, and a pebble in the hand of a fool.

Joseph Roux

He wrapped himself in quotations
– as a beggar would enfold himself
in the purple of Emperors.

Rudyard Kipling

I love quotations because it is a joy
to find thoughts one might have,
beautifully expressed with much
authority by someone recognizably
wiser than oneself.

Marlene Dietrich

To be occasionally quoted is the
only fame I care for.

Alexander Smith

A quote is a personal possession
and you have no right to change it.

Ray Cave

Beware of thinkers whose minds
function only when they are fuelled
by a quotation.

E.M. Cioran

I might repeat to myself slowly and
soothingly, a list of quotations
beautiful from minds profound – if
I can remember any of the damn
things.

Dorothy Parker

Quotation is the highest compliment you can pay to an author.

Samuel Johnson

Quoting, like smoking, is a dirty
habit to which I am devoted.

Carolyn Heilbrun

RACE

The race is not to the swift, nor the battle to the strong.

Ecclesiastes 9:11

The race is to the swift;/The battle is to the strong.

John Davidson

The race is not always to the swift, nor the battle to the strong – but that's the way to bet.

Damon Runyon

For the race is won by one and one, And never by two and two.

Rudyard Kipling

The trouble with the rat race is that even if you win, you're still a rat.

Lily Tomlin

RACISM

Racism is man's gravest threat to man – the maximum of hatred for a minimum of reason.

Abraham Joshua Heschel

RADICAL

A radical man is a man with both feet firmly planted in the air.

Franklin D. Roosevelt

The radical of one century is the conservative of the next. The radical invents the views. When he has worn them out the conservative adopts them.

Mark Twain

Be as radical as reality.

Vladimir Lenin

RADIO

TV gives everyone an image, but radio gives birth to a million images in a million brains.

Peggy Noonan

RAILROAD

We do not ride on the railroad; it rides upon us.

Henry David Thoreau

RAIN

I hate all those weathermen [who] tell you that rain is bad weather. There's no such thing as bad weather, just the wrong clothing.

Billy Connolly

It is impossible to live in a country which is continually under hatches … Rain! Rain! Rain!

John Keats

RAINBOW
The way I see it, if you want the rainbow, you gotta put up with the rain.

Dolly Parton

And when it rains on your parade, look up rather than down. Without the rain, there would be no rainbow.

G.K. Chesterton

RANK
Rank is a great beautifier.

Edward Bulwer-Lytton

It is an interesting question how far men would retain their relative rank if they were divested of their clothes.

Henry David Thoreau

RANSOM
Ransom, *n.* The purchase of that which neither belongs to the seller, nor can belong to the buyer; the most unprofitable of investments.

Ambrose Bierce

RASHNESS
Rashness succeeds often, still more often fails.

Napoleon Bonaparte

You never saw a fish on the wall with its mouth shut.

Sally Berger

RAT RACE
A rat race is for rats. We're not rats. We're human beings. Reject the insidious pressures in society that would blunt your critical faculties to all that is happening around you, that would caution silence in the face of injustice lest you jeopardize your chances of promotion and self-advancement. This is how it starts and, before you know where you are, you're a fully paid-up member of the rat pack. The price is too high.

Jimmy Reid

RATIONALITY
If rationality were the criterion for things being allowed to exist, the world would be one gigantic field of soya beans.

Tom Stoppard

RATS
There must be at least 500,000,000 rats in the United States; of course, I am speaking only from memory.

Bill Nye

REACTION
It's not the situation ... It's your reaction to the situation.

Robert Conklin

What happens is not as important as how you react to what happens.

Thaddeus Golas

REACTIONARY
One is always somebody's reactionary.

Georges Clemenceau

READINESS
To be always ready, a man must be able to cut a knot, for not everything can be untied.

Henri-Frédéric Amiel

The readiness is all.
William Shakespeare

READING
Men of power have no time to read; yet men who do not read are unfit for power.
Bertrand Russell

Reading is to the mind what exercise is to the body.
Sir Richard Steele

To learn to read is to light a fire; every syllable that is spelled out is a spark.
Victor Hugo

Reading is a means of thinking with another person's mind; it forces you to stretch your own.
Charles Scribner, Jr

Reading does not make a man wise; it only makes him learned.
W. Somerset Maugham

People say that life is the thing, but I prefer reading.
Logan Pearsall Smith

Today a reader, tomorrow a leader.
W. Fusselman

REAL WORLD
The real world … is rough; it is slippery. Without the most clear-eyed adjustments, we fall and get crushed.
Clarence Day

REALIST
The pessimist complains about the wind; the optimist expects it to change; and the realist adjusts the sails.
William Arthur Ward

An idealist believes the short run doesn't count. A cynic believes the long run doesn't matter. A realist believes that what is done or left undone in the short run determines the long run.
Sydney J. Harris

REALITY
Reality is something you rise above.
Liza Minnelli

The sky is not less blue because the blind man does not see it.
Danish proverb

All the mind's activity is easy if it is not subjected to reality.
Marcel Proust

I like reality. It tastes of bread.
Jean Anouilh

Not all things are black and white. … the sooner we learn this, the sooner we reach a better understanding of reality.
Alfred Charles Kinsley

Reality is what I see, not what you see.
Anthony Burgess

The dignity of man lies in his ability to face reality in all its senselessness.
Martin Esslin

Reality's not strange, not unexpected. Reality doesn't reside in the sudden hallucination of events. Reality is uneventfulness, vacancy, flatness. Reality is that nothing happens. How many of the events of history have occurred ... for no other reason, fundamentally, than the desire to make things happen?

Graham Swift

Without our knowing it, we see reality through glasses coloured by the subconscious memory of previous experiences.

Thomas Merton

Attachment is the great fabricator of illusions; reality can be attained only by someone who is detached.

Simone Weil

Reality is that which, when you stop believing in it, doesn't go away.

Philip K. Dick

Would it not be true to say that North Americans prefer to use reality rather than to know it?

Octavio Paz

It is always better to proceed on the basis of a recognition of what is, rather than what ought to be.

Stewart Alsop

I believe in looking reality straight in the eye and denying it.

Garrison Keillor

Reality must take precedence over public relations, for nature cannot be fooled.

Richard Feynman

If the hill will not come to Mohammed, Mohammed will come to the hill.

Francis Bacon

Do not adjust your mind – the fault is in reality.

Graffito

REASON
If we live according to the guidance of reason, we shall desire for others the good we seek for ourselves.

Baruch Spinoza

Ever since Kant divorced reason from reality, his intellectual descendants have been diligently widening the breach.

Ayn Rand

We may take Fancy for a companion, but must follow Reason as our guide.

Samuel Johnson

Reason can wrestle/And overthrow terror.

Euripides

Reason respects the differences, and imagination the similitudes of things.

Percy Bysshe Shelley

Say first, of God above or man below,/What can we reason but from what we know?

Alexander Pope

Only reason can convince us of those three fundamental truths without a recognition of which there can be no effective liberty:

that what we believe is not necessarily true; that what we like is not necessarily good; and that all questions are open.

Clive Bell

If we would guide by the light of reason, we must let our minds be bold.

Louis D. Brandeis

Reason has always existed, but not always in a reasonable form.

Karl Marx

Reason commands us much more imperiously than a master. If we disobey a master we are unhappy but if we defy reason we are fools.

Blaise Pascal

So convenient a thing it is to be a reasonable creature, since it enables one to find or make a reason for everything one has a mind to do.

Benjamin Franklin

Reason only discovers the shortest way: it does not discover the destination.

George Bernard Shaw

The man who listens to Reason is lost: Reason enslaves all whose minds are not strong enough to master her.

George Bernard Shaw

I'll not listen to reason ... Reason always means what someone else has to say.

Elizabeth Gaskell

It isn't what people think that is important, but the reason they think what they think.

Eugène Ionesco

It is reason, and not passion, which must guide our deliberations, guide our debate, and guide our decision.

Barbara Jordan

Reason is the shepherd trying to corral life's vast flock of wild irrationalities.

Paul Eldridge

REASONING
Most of our so-called reasoning consists in finding arguments for going on believing as we already do.

James Harvey Robinson

Man is a reasoning rather than a reasonable animal.

Alexander Hamilton

REASONS
A man always has two reasons for doing anything – a good reason and the real reason.

J.P. Morgan

There's a mighty big difference between good, sound reasons and reasons that sound good.

Burton Hillis

REBELLION
A little rebellion now and then, is a good thing, and as necessary in the political world as storms in the physical.

Thomas Jefferson

It doesn't take a majority to make a rebellion; it takes only a few determined leaders and a sound cause.

H.L. Mencken

RECESSION

A recession is when your neighbour has to tighten his belt. A depression is when you have to tighten your belt. A panic is when you have no belt and your pants fall down.

Tommy Douglas

It is a recession when your neighbour loses his job; it's a depression when you lose yours.

Harry S. Truman

Recession is when your neighbor loses his job. Depression is when you lose yours. And recovery is when Jimmy Carter loses his.

Ronald Reagan

RECIPE

A recipe has a hidden side, like the moon.

James de Coquet

RECOLLECTION

Recollection is the only paradise from which we cannot be turned out.

Jean Paul

RECONCILIATION

Reconciliation is more beautiful than victory.

Violeta Barrios de Chamorro

REFEREE

The trouble with referees is that they know the rules, but they do not know the game.

Bill Shankly

REFLECTION

Mirrors should reflect a little before throwing back images.

Jean Cocteau

To doubt everything and to believe everything are two equally convenient solutions; both free us from the necessity of reflection.

Henri Poincaré

REFORM

Nothing so needs reforming as other people's habits.

Mark Twain

Every reform movement has a lunatic fringe.

Theodore Roosevelt

Every reform was once a private opinion.

Ralph Waldo Emerson

A reform is a correction of abuses; a revolution is a transfer of power.

Edward Bulwer-Lytton

Reform yourself. That way there will be one less rascal in the world.

Thomas Carlyle, when asked by a young man how he should go about reforming the world

But 'tis the talent of our English nation. Still to be plotting some new reformation.

John Dryden

Every time I reform in one direction I go overboard in another.
Mark Twain

Reform must come from within, not from without. You cannot legislate for virtue.
Cardinal Gibbons

The urge to save humanity is almost always only a false-face for the urge to rule it.
H.L. Mencken

The best reformers the world has ever seen are those who commence on themselves.
George Bernard Shaw

We reform others unconsciously when we walk uprightly.
Anne Sophie Swetchine

REFUSAL
When a person tells you, "I'll think it over and let you know," – you know.
Olin Miller

REGRET
Never, never waste a minute on regret. It's a waste of time.
Harry S. Truman

My one regret in life is that I am not someone else.
Woody Allen

Maybe all one can do is hope to end up with the right regrets.
Arthur Miller

I repent of my diets, the delicious dishes rejected out of vanity, as much as I lament the opportunities for making love that I let go by because of pressing tasks or puritanical virtue.
Isabel Allende

Regret for the things we did can be tempered by time; it is regret for the things we did not do that is inconsolable.
Sydney J. Harris

The follies which a man regrets most in his life are those which he didn't commit when he had the opportunity.
Helen Rowland

REINCARNATION
There's nothing wrong with you that reincarnation won't cure.
Jack E. Leonard

If I believed in reincarnation, I'd come back as a sponge.
Woody Allen

REJECTION
There's nothing like rejection to make you do an inventory of yourself.
James Lee Burke

RELATIONSHIPS
Relationships are hard. It's like a full time job and we should treat it like one. If your boyfriend or girlfriend wants to leave you, they should give you two weeks' notice. There should be severance pay and before they leave you, they should have to find you a temp.
Bob Ettinger

The most important thing in a relationship between a man and a woman is that one of them should be good at taking orders.

Linda Festa

Relationship: the civilized conversationalist uses this word in public only to describe a seafaring vessel carrying members of his family.

Fran Lebowitz

RELATIVES

The normal man's antipathy to his relatives lies in the plain fact that every man sees in his relatives, and especially in his cousins, a series of grotesque caricatures of himself. They exhibit his qualities in disconcerting augmentation or diminution; they fill him with a disquieting feeling that this, perhaps, is the way he appears to the world.

H.L. Mencken

You see this watch? This is an absolutely fantastic, very fine, elegant gold watch which speaks of breeding and was sold to me by my grandfather on his deathbed.

Woody Allen

He neither drank, smoked, nor rode a bicycle. Living frugally, saving his money, he died early surrounded by greedy relatives. It was a great lesson to me.

John Barrymore

RELATIVITY

It is impossible to travel faster than light, and certainly not desirable, as one's hat keeps blowing off.

Woody Allen

When a man sits with a pretty girl for an hour, it seems like a minute. But let him sit on a hot stove for a minute – and it's longer than any hour. That's relativity.

Albert Einstein

RELIANCE

There is no greater challenge than to have someone relying upon you; no greater satisfaction than to vindicate his expectation.

Kingman Brewster

RELIGION

I do benefits for all religions; I'd hate to blow the hereafter on a technicality.

Bob Hope

Doubt is part of all religion. All the religious thinkers were doubters.

Isaac Bashevis Singer

We must respect the other fellow's religion, but only in the sense and to the extent that we respect his theory that his wife is beautiful and that his children are smart.

H.L. Mencken

Religion is the frozen thought of men, out of which they build temples.

J. Krishnamurti

A religion without the element of mystery would not be a religion at all.

Edwin Lewis

A religion without its mysteries is a temple without a God.

Robert Hall

Religion begins with a consciousness that something is asked of us.
Abraham Joshua Heschel

Religion is born when we accept the ultimate frustration of mere human effort, and at the same time realize the strength which comes from union with superhuman reality.
John Buchan

If I had to choose a religion, the Sun as the universal giver of life would be my god.
Napoleon Bonaparte

(On going to war over religion) You're basically killing each other to see who's got the better imaginary friend.
Richard Jeni

I care not for a man's religion whose dog and cat are not the better for it.
Abraham Lincoln

Philosophy is questions that may never be answered. Religion is answers that may never be questioned.
Anonymous

As every enquiry which regards religion is of the utmost importance, there are two questions in particular which challenge our attention, to wit, that concerning its foundation in reason, and that concerning its origin in human nature.
David Hume

Religions exist primarily for people to achieve together what they cannot achieve alone.
Sloan Wilson

But what are the benefits; why do people want religion at all? They want it because religion is the only plausible source of certain rewards for which there is a general and inexhaustible demand.
Rodney Starke and Roger Finke

We have a better product than soap or automobiles. We have eternal life.
Rev. Jim Bakker

Good people will do good things, and bad people will do bad things. But for good people to do bad things – that takes religion.
Steven Weinberg

Men of sense are all of one religion. But men of sense never tell what it is.
Earl of Shaftesbury

The purpose of religion is not to satisfy the needs we feel but to create in us the need of serving ends of which we otherwise remain oblivious.
Abraham Joshua Heschel

Religion is the human response to being alive and having to die.
Forrest Church

The basic assumption of the secular society is that modernity overcomes religion.
Ulrich Beck

A little knowledge often estranges men from religion, a deeper knowledge brings them back to it.

Dean Inge

Science has made us neighbours; Religion must make us brothers.

Louis L. Mann

To know a person's religion, we need not listen to his professions of faith but must find his brand of intolerance.

Eric Hoffer

To be furious in religion is to be irreligiously religious.

William Penn

Religion is ... the calm bottom of the sea at its deepest point, which remains calm however high the waves on the surface may be.

Ludwig Wittgenstein

Religion is the idol of the mob; it adores everything it does not understand.

Frederick the Great

REMEDIES
Focus on remedies, not faults.

Jack Nicklaus

He that will not apply new remedies must expect new evils; for time is the greatest innovator.

Sir Francis Bacon

Extreme remedies are very appropriate for extreme diseases.

Hippocrates

REMEMBRANCE
I would rather be remembered by a song than by a victory.

Alexander Smith

REMINISCENCE
Reminiscences make one feel so deliciously aged and sad.

George Bernard Shaw

REMORSE
God has little patience with remorse.

Malcolm Lowry

Remorse is a violent dyspepsia of the mind.

Ogden Nash

I would far rather feel remorse than know how to define it.

Thomas à Kempis

REMUNERATION
I was underpaid for the first half of my life; I don't mind being overpaid for the second half.

Pierre Berton

RENEWAL
To be worn out is to be renewed.

Lao-Tse

REORGANIZATION
We trained hard ... but every time we were beginning to form up into teams, we would be reorganized. I was to learn later in life that we tend to meet any new situation by reorganizing ... and a wonderful

method it can be for creating the illusion of progress while producing inefficiency and demoralization.

Petronius

REPAIR
It is the neglect of timely repair that makes rebuilding necessary.

Richard Whately

REPENTANCE
The sinning is the best part of repentance.

Arab proverb

And here comes the catch. Only a bad person needs to repent: only a good person can repent perfectly. The worse you are the more you need it and the less you can do it. The only person who could do it perfectly would be a perfect person – and he would not need it.

C.S. Lewis

When I consider how my life is spent,/I hardly ever repent.

Ogden Nash

Late repentance is seldom true, but true repentance is never too late.

R. Venning

You never repent of having eaten too little.

Thomas Jefferson

REPETITION
There is repetition everywhere, and nothing is found only once in the world.

Johann Wolfgang von Goethe

If a human being is condemned and restricted to perform the same functions over and over again, he will not even be a good ant, not to mention a good human being.

Norbert Wiener

It is sometimes necessary to repeat what we know. All mapmakers should place the Mississippi in the same location, and avoid originality.

Saul Bellow

REPORTERS
If the reporter has killed our imagination with his truth, he threatens our life with his lies.

Karl Kraus

Those to whom his word was revealed were always alone in some remote place, like Moses. There wasn't anyone else around when Mohammed got the word, either. Mormon Joseph Smith and Christian Scientist Mary Baker Eddy, had exclusive audiences with God. We have to trust them as reporters – and you know how reporters are. They'll do anything for a story.

Andy Rooney

REPORTS
As we read the school reports on our children, we realize a sense of relief that can rise to delight – thank Heaven – nobody is reporting in this fashion on us.

J.B. Priestley

REPRESSION

A cat pent up becomes a lion.

Italian proverb

REPRIMAND

I never reprimand a boy in the evening – darkness and a troubled mind are a poor combination.

Frank L. Boyden

REPROACH

The sting of a reproach is the truth of it.

Thomas Fuller, MD

REPUTATION

A fellow doesn't last long on what he has done. He's got to keep delivering as he goes along.

Carl Hubbell

How many people live off the reputation of the reputation they might have made?

Oliver Wendell Holmes

I am not at all the sort of person you and I took me for.

Jane Carlyle in a letter to Thomas Carlyle

Reputation is often got without merit and lost without fault.

English proverb

Reputation is an idle and false imposition; oft got without merit, and lost without deserving.

William Shakespeare

Getting better known has its risks. Everything that's in is on its way out.

Al Ries

To get a name can happen to but a few: It is one of the few things that cannot be bought. It is the free gift of mankind, which must be deserved before it will be granted, and it is at last unwillingly bestowed.

Samuel Johnson

Reputation is a bubble which man bursts when he tries to blow it for himself.

Will Carleton

You can't build a reputation on what you are going to do.

Henry Ford

You can't build a reputation on what you intend to do.

Liz Smith

According to success do we gain a reputation for judgment.

Euripides

What people say behind your back is your standing in the community in which you live.

Edgar Watson Howe

The art of being able to make a good use of moderate abilities wins esteem, and often confers more reputation than real merit.

François, duc de La Rochefoucauld

Every tub smells of the wine it holds.

Proverb

It's not excellence which leads to celebrity, but celebrity which leads to excellence. One makes one's reputation, and one's reputation enables one to achieve the conditions in which one can do good work.

Michael Frayn

Until you lose your reputation, you never realize what a burden it was or what freedom really is.

Margaret Mitchell

The most valuable of all human possessions, next to a superior and disdainful air, is the reputation of being well-to-do.

H.L. Mencken

He lives who dies to win a lasting name.

William Drummond

By the work one knows the workman.

Jean de La Fontaine

RESEARCH

Enough research will tend to support your theory.

Murphy's Law of Research

Advertising people who ignore research are as dangerous as generals who ignore decodes of enemy signals.

David Ogilvy

As the power of endurance weakens with age, the urgency of the pursuit (in research) grows more intense. ... And research is always incomplete.

Mark Pattison

No research is ever quite complete. It is the glory of a good bit of work that it opens the way for something still better. And this repeatedly leads to its own eclipse.

Melvin Gordon

The outcome of any serious research can only be to make two questions grow where only one grew before.

Thorstein Veblen

RESERVE

Tell not all you know, believe not all you hear, do not all you are able.

Italian proverb

Most people have a furious itch to talk about themselves and are restrained only by the disinclination of others to listen. Reserve is an artificial quality that is developed in most of us but as the result of innumerable rebuffs.

W. Somerset Maugham

RESIST

It is easier to resist at the beginning than at the end.

Leonardo da Vinci

RESOLVE

We are prepared to go to the gates of hell but no further.

Pope Pius VII

Be sure you put your feet in the right place, then stand firm.

Abraham Lincoln

RESPECT

I firmly believe that if you follow a path that interests you, not to the exclusion of love, sensitivity, and cooperation with others, but with the strength of conviction that you can move others by your own efforts, and do not make success or failure the criteria by which you live, the chances are you'll be a person worthy of your own respect.

Neil Simon

Follow the three R's: Respect for self, respect for others, responsibility for all your actions.

Dalai Lama

There is a vast difference in one's respect for the man who has made himself and the man who has only made his money.

Dinah Maria Mulock

Support what is right, oppose what is wrong; what you think, speak; try to satisfy yourself, and not others; and if you are not popular, you will at least be respected; popularity lasts but a day, respect will descend as a heritage to your children.

Thomas Chandler Haliburton

The surest way of ruining a youth is to teach him to respect those who think as he does more highly than those who think differently from him.

Friedrich Nietzsche

RESPECTABILITY
The more things a man is ashamed of, the more respectable he is.

George Bernard Shaw

He must be quite respectable. One has never heard his name before in the whole course of one's life, which speaks volumes for a man, nowadays.

Oscar Wilde

RESPONSIBILITY
Somebody has to do something, and it's just incredibly pathetic that it has to be us.

Jerry Garcia

Each snowflake in an avalanche pleads not guilty.

Stanislaw J. Lec

Don't get up from the feast of life without paying for your share of it.

Dean Inge

No individual raindrop ever considers itself responsible for the flood.

Unknown

REST
Take rest; a field that has rested gives a bountiful crop.

Ovid

RESTAURANTS
The problem with allowing only a select few into a restaurant is that when the select few decide to go somewhere else – and eventually they will – the restaurant has no replacement, no core of loyal tables to fill the tables. People generally don't come to the rescue of places that have refused to let them through the door.

Alan Richman

The secret of a successful restaurant is sharp knives.

George Orwell

I wished now that I had gone to the restaurant across the street where the food had at least the merit of being tasteless.

Peter De Vries

RESULTS

Clapping with the right hand only will not produce a noise.

Malay proverb

One arrow does not bring down two birds.

Turkish proverb

Yellow cat, black cat, as long as it catches mice, it is a good cat.

Deng Xiaoping

I pass with relief from the tossing sea of Cause and Theory to the firm ground of Result and Fact.

Winston Churchill

There are many paths to the top of the mountain, but the view is always the same.

Chinese proverb

If you work very hard, and give life everything you've got, you may not quite make it.

Elwy Yost

However beautiful the strategy, you should occasionally look at the results.

Winston Churchill

RETIREMENT

We rarely find anyone who can say he has lived a happy life, and who, content with his life, can retire from the world like a satisfied guest.

Horace

retirement means twice as much husband on half as much money

Anonymous

Retirement is a wonderful dream. I mean, you can only suck in your stomach for so long.

Burt Reynolds

When a man retires and time is no longer a matter of urgent importance, his colleagues generally present him with a clock.

R.C. Sheriff

RETURN ON EQUITY

Achieving return on equity does not, as a goal, mobilize the most noble forces of our soul.

Lawrence Miller

REVENGE

Revenge is profitable, gratitude expensive.

Edward Gibbon

A man that studieth revenge keeps his wounds green, which otherwise would heal and do well.

Francis Bacon

No more tears now; I will think about revenge.

Mary, Queen of Scots

Life being what it is, one dreams of revenge.

Paul Gauguin

Live well. It is the greatest revenge.
Talmud

Don't get mad – get even.
John F. Kennedy

Living twice, maybe three times, is the best revenge.

Mordecai Richler

The longest odds in the world are those against getting even.

Unknown

The best revenge is to be unlike him who performed the injury.

Marcus Aurelius

REVERSE
The reverse side also has a reverse side.

Japanese proverb

REVIEW
I am reviewing the situation ... I think I'd better think it out again.

Lionel Bart

A bad review may spoil your breakfast but you shouldn't allow it to spoil your lunch.

Kingsley Amis

REVIEWERS
Professional reviewers read so many bad books in the course of duty that they get an unhealthy craving for arresting phrases.

Evelyn Waugh

REVISE
It is never too late – in fiction or in life – to revise.

Nancy Thayer

REVOLUTION
Inferiors revolt in order that they may be equal, and equals that they may be superior.

Aristotle

Revolution, *n.* An abrupt change in the form of misgovernment.

Ambrose Bierce

Those who make peaceful revolution impossible will make violent revolution inevitable.

John F. Kennedy

Revolutions have never succeeded unless the establishment does three-quarters of the work.

Peter Ustinov

Revolution is a trivial shift in the emphasis of suffering.

Tom Stoppard

In this revolution, no plans have been written for retreat.

Martin Luther King, Jr

Revolution is the festival of the oppressed.

Germaine Greer

REWARD
The reward of a thing well done, is to have done it.

Ralph Waldo Emerson

Only the brave deserve the fair, but only the fat, rich, cowardly merchant can afford same.

Chinese proverb

RICH

If you aren't rich, you should always look useful.

Louis-Ferdinand Céline

No man is rich enough to buy back his past.

Oscar Wilde

I've been poor and I've been rich. Rich is better.

Sophie Tucker

The only way for a rich man to be healthy is by exercise and abstinence, to live as if he were poor.

Sir William Temple

Down here (Texas) we have a saying – a man is worth twice what he owes.

Clint Murchison

People who know how much they are worth generally aren't worth too much.

Nelson Bunker Hunt

The curse of the rich is that they are not allowed to die.

S.N. Behrman

A rich man is nothing but a poor man with money.

W.C. Fields

"Rich enough" is only when you have "No, thank you" money.

Carol Matthau

The poor speak very fast, with quick movements, to attract attention. The rich move slowly and they speak slowly; they don't need to get your attention because they've already got it.

Michael Caine

To be rich nowadays merely means to possess a large number of poor objects.

Raoul Vaneigem

It is the wretchedness of being rich that you have to live with rich people.

Logan Pearsall Smith

Let me tell you about the very rich. They are different from you and me.

F. Scott Fitzgerald

There is a serious defect in the thinking of someone who wants more than anything to become rich. As long as they don't have the money, it'll seem like a worthwhile goal. Once they do, they'll understand how important other things are – and always have been.

Benjamin Jowett

RICHES

A shortcut to riches is to subtract from our desires.

Petrarch

Riches serve a wise man but command a fool.

English proverb

Riches rather enlarge than satisfy appetites.

Thomas Fuller, MD

There is nothing wrong with men possessing riches. The wrong comes when riches possess men.

Billy Graham

RIDDANCE
What belongs to a man he cannot get rid of, even though he throws it away.

Johann Wolfgang von Goethe

RIDICULE
Every nation ridicules other nations, and all are right.

Arthur Schopenhauer

Resort is had to ridicule only when reason is against us.

William James

It is commonly said, and more particularly by Lord Shaftesbury, that ridicule is the best test of truth.

Lord Chesterfield

RIDICULOUS
Look for the ridiculous in everything, and you will find it.

Jules Renard

There is only one step from the sublime to the ridiculous.

Napoleon Bonaparte

There's only one step from the sublime to the ridiculous, but there's no road leading back from the ridiculous to the sublime.

Lion Feuchtwanger

The sublime and the ridiculous are so often so nearly related that it is difficult to class them separately.

One step above the sublime makes the ridiculous, and one step above the ridiculous makes the sublime again.

Thomas Paine

RIGHT
When everyone is wrong, everyone is right.

Pierre-Claude Nivelle

Chicken Little only has to be right once.

Anonymous

Always do right. This will gratify some people and astonish the rest.

Mark Twain

Be always sure you are right – then go ahead.

Davy Crockett

People don't ever seem to realize that doing what's right's no guarantee against misfortune.

William McFee

If it is not right, do not do it; if it is not true, do not say it.

Marcus Aurelius

It is nobler to declare oneself wrong than to insist on being right – especially if one is right.

Friedrich Nietzsche

It is better to have a right destroyed than to abandon it because of fear.

Phil Mann

The one great right we all have is the right to be wrong.

Alvina Brower

RIGHTNESS
It's one thing to feel you are on the right path, but it's another to think that yours is the only path.
Paulo Coelho

RISE
Men think highly of those who rise rapidly in the world, whereas nothing rises quicker than dust, straw, and feathers.
Augustus and Julius Hare

RISK
Only those who will risk going too far can possibly find out how far one can go.
T.S. Eliot

Take into account that great love and great achievements involve great risk.
Dalai Lama

Why not go out on a limb? Isn't that where the fruit is?
Frank Scully

If you are scared to go to the brink, you are lost.
John Foster Dulles

Come to the edge. We might fall./ Come to the edge. It is too high!/ Come to the edge! And they came,/ and he pushed ... and they flew.
Christopher Logue

And the trouble is, if you don't risk anything, you risk even more.
Erica Jong

Avoiding danger is no safer in the long run than exposure.
Helen Keller

Take a big step if one is indicated: you can't cross a chasm in two steps.
David Lloyd George

Risk and reward travel side by side. Avoid one and the other will also pass you by.
Anonymous

To win without risk is to triumph without glory.
Pierre Corneille

When there is no peril in the fight, there is no glory in the triumph.
Pierre Corneille

Everything is sweetened by risk.
Alexander Smith

What is necessary is never a risk.
Cardinal de Retz

Take calculated risks. That is quite different from being rash.
General George S. Patton

Where there is no risk there can be no pride in achievement and consequently no happiness.
Ray Kroc

There are those who never stretch out the hand for fear that it will be bitten. But those who never stretch out the hand will never feel it clasped in friendship.
Michael Heseltine

The moment somebody says "this is very risky" is the moment it becomes attractive to me.
Kate Capshaw

There is no point in getting into a panic about the risks of life until you have compared the risks that worry you with the risks that do not.

Lord Rothschild

Living at risk is jumping off the cliff and building your wings on the way down.

Ray Bradbury

Which came out of the opened door – the lady or the tiger?

Frank Stockton

Why not go out on a limb? That's where the fruit is.

Will Rogers

RITUAL

I am not a religious man, but I have a ritual that I perform every day: I wash my breakfast bowl. ... Most of what we do in our lives is frivolous – watching TV, fixing the car, reading books, waiting for the bus – but the washing of dishes is important: It is necessary. Washing dishes is part of being human.

Richard Nilsen

I read somewhere of a shepherd who, when asked why he made, from within fairy rings, ritual observances to the moon to preserve his flocks, replied: "I'd be a damn fool if I didn't!"

Dylan Thomas

ROCK 'N' ROLL

Rock 'n' roll is trying to convince girls to pay money to be near you.

Richard Hell

ROCK STAR

I'm a rock star because I couldn't be a soccer star.

Rod Stewart

ROGUES

I prefer rogues to imbeciles, because they sometimes take a rest.

Alexandre Dumas, fils

See the rogues flourish, and honest folks droop.

Robert Browning

ROMANCE

Romance without finance ain't got no chance.

Charlie (Bird) Parker

Romance is a love affair in other than domestic surroundings.

Sir Walter Raleigh

ROMANTIC

My notion of a romantic evening is when my husband does the dishes. It's great foreplay.

Nora Roberts

ROPE (END OF)

When you get to the end of your rope, tie a knot and hang on.

Franklin D. Roosevelt

ROUTINE

Men fall into a routine when they are tired and slack: it has all the appearance of activity with few of its burdens.

Walter Lippmann

Routine, in an intelligent man, is a sign of ambition.

W.H. Auden

RUDENESS
Rudeness is the weak man's imitation of strength.

Eric Hoffer

Rudeness in old men is considered a sign of vitality. In fact it is quite the opposite. It springs from shrunken sympathies.

Colin Thubron

Isn't it time that being rude and thick became unfashionable?

Duncan Fallowell

RUIN
What is a ruin but time easing itself of endurance?

Djuna Barnes

The man of power is ruined by power, the man of money by money, the submissive man by subservience, the pleasure seeker by pleasure.

Hermann Hesse

RULE
No rule is so general, which admits not some exception.

Robert Burton

Learn the rules so you know how to break them properly.

Dalai Lama

Learn all the rules, every one of them, so that you will know how to break them.

Irvin S. Cobb

Any fool can make a rule, and any fool will mind it.

Henry David Thoreau

The rule is, jam tomorrow and jam yesterday – but never jam today.

Lewis Carroll

To rule is easy; to govern, difficult.

Johann Wolfgang von Goethe

M.A. Rosanoff: "Mr. Edison, please tell me what laboratory rules you want me to observe."

Edison: "Hell! There *ain't* no rules around here! We're trying to accomplish somep'n!"

Rosanoff's
"Edison in His Laboratory,"
Harper's magazine

The young break rules for fun. The old for profit.

Mason Cooley

Rules and models destroy genius and art.

William Hazlitt

When any practice has become the fixed rule of the society in which we live, it is always wise to adhere to that rule, unless it calls upon us to do something that is actually wrong.

Anthony Trollope

A rule is amended if it yields an inference we are unwilling to accept; an inference is rejected if it violates a rule we are unwilling to amend.

Nelson Goodman

Four Rules for Life: Show up. Pay attention. Tell the truth. Don't be attached to the results.

Angeles Arrien

RULERS

The worst ruler is one who cannot rule himself.

Cato the Elder

Rulers are given to employing those they can teach rather than those from whom they can learn.

Mencius

Those who rule us are like you and me. It is a frightening situation.

Brooks Atkinson

My people and I have come to an agreement which satisfies us both. They are to say what they please, and I am to do what I please.

Frederick the Great

RULERSHIP

The secret of rulership is to combine a belief in one's infallibility with the power to learn from past mistakes.

George Orwell

RUMOUR

A rumour without a leg to stand on will get around some other way.

John Tudor

The Times has published no rumours; it's only reported the facts, namely, that other, less responsible papers are publishing certain rumours.

Tom Stoppard

Rumour is a pipe blown by surmises, jealousies, conjectures, and of so easy and plain a stop, that the blunt monster with uncounted heads, the still-discordant wavering multitude, can play upon it.

William Shakespeare

RUNNING

What's the use of running when you are on the wrong road?

Proverb

RUSH HOUR

Why do they call it rush hour when nothing moves?

Robin Williams

RUSSIA

The two most powerful men in Russia were Czar Nicholas II and the last man who spoke to him.

A.J.P. Taylor

RUST

It is better to wear out than to rust out.

Bishop Richard Cumberland

RUT

You won't skid if you stay in a rut.

Kin Hubbard

SACRED COWS
Sacred cows make the best hamburger.
Mark Twain

SACRIFICE
Too long a sacrifice can make a stone of the heart.
William Butler Yeats

Upon such sacrifices, my Cordelia,/ The gods themselves throw incense.
William Shakespeare

It is a far, far better thing that I do, than I have ever done; it is a far, far better rest that I go to, than I have ever known.
Charles Dickens

Drown not thyself to save a drowning man.
Proverb

The Universe is so vast and so ageless that the life of one man can only be justified by the measure of his sacrifice.
V.A. Rosewarne

The whole point of a sacrifice is that you give up something you never really wanted in the first place.
John Osborne

Among the Nuer it is particularly auspicious to sacrifice a bull, but since bulls are particularly valuable, a cucumber will do just fine most of the time.
E. Thomas Lawson and Robert N. McCauley

SAD
This is the saddest story I have ever heard.
Ford Madox Ford

SADNESS
Sadness flies away on the wings of time.
Jean de La Fontaine

SAFETY
A ship in port is safe, but that is not what ships are built for.
Benazir Bhutto

To keep oneself safe does not mean to bury oneself.

Seneca

In skating over thin ice, our safety is in our speed.

Ralph Waldo Emerson

There is no safety in numbers, or in anything else.

James Thurber

When we walk the streets at night in safety, it does not strike us that this might be otherwise. This habit of feeling safe has become second nature.

G.W.F. Hegel

Early and provident fear is the mother of safety.

Edmund Burke

Safety doesn't happen by accident.

Unknown

SAINTS
Saints should always be judged guilty until proven innocent.

George Orwell

Many people genuinely do not wish to be saints, and it is probable that some who achieve or aspire to sainthood have never felt much temptation to be human beings.

George Orwell

SALAD
To make a good salad is to be a brilliant diplomatist – the problem is entirely the same in both cases. To know how much oil one must mix with one's vinegar.

Oscar Wilde

SALESMEN
He's a man out there in the blue, ridin' on a smile and a shoeshine ... a salesman has got to dream, boys.

Arthur Miller

SALVATION
Work out your own salvation. Do not depend on others.

Buddha

Work out your salvation with diligence.

The Pali Canon

There are two things necessary to salvation – money and gunpowder.

George Bernard Shaw

SAME
When two do the same thing, it is not the same thing after all.

Publilius Syrus

SANCTUARY
There are three classes which need sanctuary more than others – birds, wild flowers, and Prime Ministers.

Stanley Baldwin

SAND
A handful of sand is an anthology of the universe.

David McCord

SANITY
Sanity is a matter of degree.

Aldous Huxley

Sanity is madness put to good use.

George Santayana

SAPPERS
And, with a little pin, bores through his castle wall, and farewell king!
William Shakespeare

SARCASM
A sharp tongue is the only edged tool that grows keener with constant use.
Washington Irving

SATISFACTION
There is more satisfaction in being a first-rate truck driver than in being a tenth-rate executive.
B.C. Forbes

The value of life lies, not in the length of days, but in the use we make of them; a man may live long, yet live very little. Satisfaction in life depends not on the number of your years, but on your will.
Michel de Montaigne

As long as I have a want, I have a reason for living. Satisfaction is death.
George Bernard Shaw

SAVING
A penny saved is ridiculous.
Unknown

We could have saved sixpence. We could have saved fivepence. ... But at what cost?
Samuel Beckett

SAYINGS
What a good thing Adam had. When he said a good thing he knew nobody had said it before.
Mark Twain

SCANDAL
It is a public scandal that offends; to sin in secret is no sin at all.
Molière

Scandal is an importunate wasp, against which we must make no movement unless we are quite sure we can kill it; otherwise it will return to the attack more furious than ever.
Chamfort

SCARE
Anything scares me, anything scares anyone but really after all considering how dangerous everything is nothing is really very frightening.
Gertrude Stein

SCARS
Scars have the strange power to remind us that our past is real.
Cormac McCarthy

SCHOLARS
A mechanic is driven by his work all day, but it ends at night; it has an end. But the scholar's work has none.
Ralph Waldo Emerson

It is the vice of scholars to suppose that there is no knowledge in the world but that of books.
William Hazlitt

Scholars should not study so much that they have no time to think.
Unknown

SCHOLARSHIP
Pure scholarship, like pure science and art, is entirely useless. That is

why it is admirable, a demonstration that civilized man is neither an
animal nor a savage nor a peasant,
for whom nothing exists but what
is immediately useful.

Richard Aldington

SCHOOL

[School] reports always tell the
truth. The problem for parents is to
know whether it is the truth about
the pupil or the truth about the
teacher – or both.

John Rae

The school of hard knocks is an
accelerated curriculum.

Menander

Remember in elementary school,
you were told in case of fire you
have to line up quietly in a single
file line from smallest to tallest.
What is the logic in that? Do tall
people burn slower?

Warren Hutcherson

SCHOOL BOARDS

In the first place God made idiots.
This was for practice. Then he
made school boards.

Mark Twain

SCHOOLBOY

And then the whining schoolboy,
with his satchel,/And shining morning face, creeping like snail/Un-
willingly to school.

T.S. Eliot

SCHOOLDAYS

No one can look back on his
schooldays and say with truth they
were altogether unhappy.

George Orwell

SCIENCE

Science: An orderly arrangement of
what at the moment seem to be
facts.

Unknown

Do you really believe that the sciences would ever have originated
and grown if the way had not been
prepared by magicians, alchemists,
astrologers, and witches whose
promises and pretensions first had
to create a thirst, a hunger, a taste
for hidden and forbidden powers?

Friedrich Nietzsche

Though many have tried, no one
has ever yet explained away the
decisive fact that science, which
can do so much, cannot decide
what it ought to do.

Joseph Wood Krutch

Eve and the apple was the first
great step in experimental science.

James Birdie

Science is built of facts the way a
house is built of bricks; but an
accumulation of facts is no more
science than a pile of bricks is a
house.

Henri Poincaré

Science without religion is lame,
religion without science is blind.

Albert Einstein

As soon as questions of will or decision or reason or choice of action arise, human science is at a loss.

Noam Chomsky

Science is an edged tool, with which men play like children.

Sir Arthur Eddington

A science which hesitates to forget its founders is lost.

Alfred North Whitehead

There is one thing even more vital to science than intelligent methods; and that is, the sincere desire to find out the truth, whatever it may be.

Charles Sanders Peirce

To mistrust science and deny the validity of the scientific method is to resign your job as a human. You'd better go look for work as a plant or wild animal.

P.J. O'Rourke

A science is any discipline in which the fool of this generation can go beyond the point reached by the genius of the last generation.

Max Gluckman

Science is like a blabbermouth who ruins a movie by telling you how it ends.

Ned Flanders

This is what non-scientists don't know, and this is what scientists are too bashful to talk about publicly, at least until they grow old enough to become shameless. Science at its highest level is ultimately the organization of, the systematic pursuit of, and the enjoyment of wonder, awe, and mystery.

Abraham Maslow

Every great advance in science has issued from a new audacity of the imagination.

John Dewey

SCIENTISTS

Scientists are Peeping Toms at the keyhole of eternity.

Arthur Koestler

Nothing leads the scientist so astray as a premature truth.

Jean Rostand

Why then must science and scientists continue to be governed by fear – fear of public opinion, fear of social consequence, fear of religious intolerance, fear of political pressure, and, above all, fear of bigotry and prejudice – as much within as without the professional world?

William Masters and Virginia Johnson

Scientists are explorers, philosophers are tourists.

Richard Feynman

SCORE

If it doesn't matter who wins or loses, then why do they keep score?

Vince Lombardi

SCORN
Of all the griefs that harass the distressed,/Sure the most bitter is a scornful jest.

Samuel Johnson

SCRIPTURES
The Scriptures were written, not to make us astronomers, but to make us saints.

Matthew Henry

SCULPTURE
I saw the angel in the marble and carved until I set him free.

Michelangelo

SEAFOOD
Why does Sea World have a seafood restaurant? I'm halfway through my fishburger and I realize, Oh my God … I could be eating a slow learner.

Lynda Montgomery

SEARCH
Nothing's so hard but search will find it out.

Robert Herrick

It's very easy to find something you're not looking for.

Leo Rosten

SEASONS
Live each season as it passes; breathe the air, drink the drink, taste the fruit, and resign yourself to the influence of each. … Some men think that they are not well in spring, or summer, or autumn, or winter; it is only because they are not well in them.

Henry David Thoreau

To every thing there is a season, and a time to every purpose under the sun.

Ecclesiastes 3:1

SECOND THOUGHTS
Second thoughts are ever wiser.
    [In this world second thoughts, it seems, are best.]

Euripides

I have lived in this world just long enough to look carefully the second time into things that I am the most certain of the first time.

Josh Billings

SECRECY
The art of secrecy lies in being so open about most things that the few things that matter are not even suspected to exist.

B.H. Liddell Hart

There is nothing we like to communicate to others as much as the seal of secrecy – together with what lies under it.

Friedrich Nietzsche

SECRETS
Everyone old enough to have a secret is entitled to have some place to keep it.

Judith Martin

If you wish to preserve your secret, wrap it up in frankness.

Alexander Smith

Little secrets are commonly told again, but great ones generally kept.

Lord Chesterfield

None are so fond of secrets as those who do not mean to keep them. Such persons covet secrets as spendthrifts do money, for the purpose of circulation.

Charles Caleb Colton

The man who can keep a secret may be wise, but he is not half as wise as the man with no secrets to keep.

Edgar Watson Howe

The easiest way to keep a secret is without help.

Unknown

Three may keep a secret, if two of them are dead.

Benjamin Franklin

He that communicates his secret to another makes himself that other's slave.

Baltasar Gracian

I know that's a secret, for it's whispered every where.

William Congreve

There are no secrets better kept than the secrets everybody guesses.

George Bernard Shaw

The man who is inquisitive into the secret of your affairs, with which he has no concern, should be an object of your caution. Men no more desire another's secrets to conceal them, than they would another's purse for the pleasure only of carrying it.

Henry Fielding

A secret's worth depends on the people from which it must be kept.

Carlos Ruiz Zafon

He that hath a secret should not only hide it, but hide that he has it to hide.

Thomas Carlyle

SECURITY
Security does not exist in nature, nor do the children of men as a whole experience it.

Helen Keller

Security is a smile from a head-waiter.

Russell Baker

Most men love money and security more, and creation and construction less, as they get older.

John Maynard Keynes

SEDITION
The surest way to prevent seditions (if the times do bear it) is to take away the matter of them.

Francis Bacon

SEEING
I shut my eyes in order to see.

Paul Gauguin

One may have good eyes and see nothing.

Italian proverb

Sight is a faculty; seeing is an art.

Bits & Pieces

What you see, yet cannot see over, is as good as infinite.

Thomas Carlyle

SELF

I suppose everyone continues to be interested in the quest for the self, but what you feel when you're older, I think, is that … you really must make the self. It is absolutely useless to look for it, you won't find it, but it's possible in some sense to make it.

Mary McCarthy

Only you can be yourself. No one else is qualified for the job.

Anonymous

Always be a first-rate version of yourself, instead of a second-rate version of somebody else.

Judy Garland

SELF ABSORPTION

When a man is all wrapped up in himself, he makes a pretty small package.

John Ruskin

If you are all wrapped up in yourself you are overdressed.

Katherine Halvorson

We would rather speak badly of ourselves than not talk about ourselves at all.

François, duc de La Rochefoucauld

It is with narrow-souled people as with narrow-necked bottles: the less they have in them, the more noise they make in pouring it out.

Alexander Pope

Probably every poor mortal suffers from this obsession with self; but actors and actresses, and politicians, seem really plagued by it.

Beatrice Webb

SELF CONCEIT

Self-conceit may lead to self-destruction.

Aesop

SELF CONFIDENCE

Trust yourself, you know more than you think you do.

Dr Benjamin Spock

Let me listen to me, and not to them.

Gertrude Stein

Be yourself. Who else is better qualified?

Frank J. Giblin II

The privilege of a lifetime is being who you are.

Joseph Campbell

They can do all because they think they can.

Virgil

We would worry less about what others think of us if we realized how seldom they do.

Ethel Barrett

Self-confidence is at the root of most of our confidence in others.

François, duc de La Rochefoucauld

I was sorry to have my name mentioned as one of the great authors, because they have a sad habit of dying off. Chaucer is dead, Spenser is dead, so is Milton, so is Shakespeare, and I am not feeling very well myself.

Mark Twain

I have great faith in fools – my friends call it self-confidence.

Edgar Allan Poe

SELF CONTROL

He who conquers others is strong. He who conquers himself is mighty.

Lao-Tse

Not being able to govern events, I govern myself, and apply myself to them, if they will not apply themselves to me.

Michel de Montaigne

He who says what he likes shall hear what he does not like.

English proverb

Nothing ever really sets human nature free, but self-control.

Phyllis Bottome

We control circumstances only so far as we control ourselves and the greatest man in all the world is the man who is most conscious of self-dominion.

Richard Lynch

SELF CRITICISM

Self-criticism is the secret weapon of democracy.

Adlai Stevenson

SELF DECEPTION

Nothing is so difficult as not deceiving oneself.

Ludwig Wittgenstein

SELF DEFENCE

Self defence is nature's oldest law.

John Dryden

SELF DISCLOSURE

We like to read others but we do not like to be read.

François, duc de La Rochefoucauld

Everyone realizes that one can believe little of what people say about each other. But it is not so widely recognized that even less can one trust what people say about themselves.

Rebecca West

SELF ESTEEM

We do not think ourselves worse than the elephant for being smaller and shorter-lived.

George Santayana

A man cannot be comfortable without his own approval.

Mark Twain

Be grateful for yourself ... be thankful.

William Saroyan

Self-esteem is regarding yourself as a grownup.

Susan Faludi

The only thing that does make us feel good about ourselves, if this is what we are after, is doing things of which we feel proud or which we deem to be worthwhile. In other words, self-esteem is a by-product of action and can never be a goal in itself. ... Self-esteem is a red herring. It comes, it goes. It gives us a nice feeling when we have it, but no more, no less.

Virginia Ironside

The important thing is not what they think of me, it is what I think of them.

Queen Victoria

Most people do not like themselves at all. They distrust themselves, put on masks and pomposities. They quarrel and boast and pretend and are jealous because they do not like themselves. … If we could learn to like ourselves even a little, maybe our cruelties and angers might melt away. Maybe we would not have to hurt one another just to keep our ego chins above water.

John Steinbeck

Nobody will believe in you unless you believe in yourself.

Liberace

The self-esteem of the quality writer depends on his belief that those readers who care about good stuff cannot afford to buy it.

Alan Coren

Self-inspection – the best cure for self-esteem.

William Wordsworth

SELF HELP
Men are made stronger on realization that the helping hand they need is at the end of their own right arm.

Sidney J. Phillips

The gods help them that help themselves.

Aesop

If a man wants to be of the greatest possible value to his fellow creatures, let him begin the long, solitary task of perfecting himself.

Robertson Davies

The proverb warns that, "You should not bite the hand that feeds you." But maybe you should, if it prevents you from feeding yourself.

Thomas Szasz

I went to a bookstore and asked the saleswoman, "Where's the self-help section?" She said if she told me, it would defeat the purpose.

George Carlin

The spirit of self-help is the root of all genuine growth in the individual.

Samuel Smiles

SELF IMPROVEMENT
More men become good through practice than by nature.

Democritus

The most important thing to remember is this: to be ready at any moment to give up what you are for what you might become.

W.E.B. Du Bois

Try to be better than yourself.

William Faulkner

SELF INDULGENCE
A woman will always sacrifice herself if you give her the opportunity.

It is her favourite form of self-indulgence.

W. Somerset Maugham

I made up my mind long ago that life was too short to do anything for myself that I could pay others to do for me.

W. Somerset Maugham

SELF INTEREST

When tremendous dangers are involved, no one can be blamed for looking to his own interest.

Thucydides

Now is the time for all good men to come to the aid of themselves.

Felice Nelson

If we weren't all so interested in ourselves, life would be so uninteresting we couldn't endure it.

Arthur Schopenhauer

SELF KNOWLEDGE

If you know the enemy and know yourself, you need not fear the result of a hundred battles.

Sun Tzu

It is in the ability to deceive oneself that the greatest talent is shown.

Anatole France

We know what we are, but know not what we may be.

William Shakespeare

Only the shallow know themselves.

Oscar Wilde

Knowing who you are is good for one generation only.

Flannery O'Connor

Know first who you are; and then adorn yourself accordingly.

Euripides

First say to yourself what you would be; and then do what you have to do.

Epictetus

The last thing you know about yourself is your effect.

William Boyd

He who knows himself trusts no one.

Paul Eldridge

The first step to self-knowledge is self-distrust.

Proverb

"Know thyself": to what depths of vain, egocentric brooding has that dictum led!

Norman Douglas

Know thyself! A maxim as pernicious as it is ugly. Whoever observes himself arrests his own development. A caterpillar who wanted to know itself would never become a butterfly.

André Gide

SELF LOVE

Self-love so often seems unrequited.

Anthony Powell

One of the great drawbacks to self-centered passions is that they afford so little variety in life. The man who loves only himself cannot, it is true, be accused of promiscuity in his affections, but he is bound in the end to suffer intolerable boredom from the inevitable sameness of the object of his devotion.

Bertrand Russell

He who is in love with himself has at least this advantage – he won't encounter many rivals.

Georg Christoph Lichtenberg

View yourselves/In the deceiving mirror of self-love.

Philip Massinger

SELF-MADE MEN

One thing wrong with a self-made man, he tends to worship his creator.

Morris Raphael Cohen

Luck is not something you can mention in the presence of self-made men.

E.B. White

He is a self-made man and worships his creator.

John Bright

SELF MASTERY

The mastery of nature is vainly believed to be an adequate substitute for self-mastery.

Reinhold Niebuhr

If you cannot mould yourself as you would wish, how can you expect other people to be entirely to your liking?

Thomas à Kempis

You cannot master yourself unless you know yourself. There are

mirrors for the face, but none for the mind.

Baltasar Gracian

Self-conquest is the greatest of victories.

Plato

SELF OPINION

I have often wondered why everyone loves himself more than everything else, but values his own opinion of himself less than that of others.

Marcus Aurelius

SELF PITY

What poison is to food, self-pity is to life.

Oliver C. Wilson

Self-pity is easily the most destructive of the non-pharmaceutical narcotics; it is addictive, gives momentary pleasure, and separates the victim from reality.

John W. Gardner

I never saw a wild thing sorry for itself.

D.H. Lawrence

SELF PRAISE

Self-praise is no recommendation.

Proverb

It is far more impressive when others discover your good qualities without your help.

Judith Martin

SELF RELIANCE

Every tub must stand upon its own bottom.

Thomas Fuller, MD

As we are, so we do; and as we do, so it is done to us; we are the builders of our fortunes.

Ralph Waldo Emerson

What I have learned is ... there ain't no genie. I am it. If the wealth and adventure and fame are to come, I'd better get tough on the only one who can make it happen ... me!

Ty Boyd

It is seldom that we find out how great are our resources until we are thrown upon them.

Christian Nestell Bovee

SELF RESPECT

Self-respect is the fruit of discipline: the sense of dignity grows with the ability to say no to oneself.

Abraham Joshua Heschel

SELF RIGHTEOUSNESS

The greatest menace to our civilization today is the conflict between giant organized systems of self-righteousness – each system only too delighted to find that the other is wicked – each only too glad that the sins give it the pretext for still deeper hatred and animosity. The effect of the whole situation is barbarizing.

Sir Herbert Butterfield

The four most beautiful words in our common language: I told you so.

Gore Vidal

SELF UNDERSTANDING

Everything that irritates us about others can lead us to an understanding of ourselves.

Carl Jung

If you mean to know yourself, interline such of these amorphisms as affect you agreeably in reading, and set a mark to such as left a sense of uneasiness with you; and then shew your copy to whom you please.

Johann Kaspar Lavater

The delights of self-discovery are always available.

Gail Sheehy

Know thyself? If I knew myself, I'd run away.

Johann Wolfgang von Goethe

Every man contains within himself a ghost continent – a place circled as warily as Antarctica was circled 200 years ago by Captain Cook.

Loren Eiseley

In the main, it is not by introspection but by reflecting on our living in common with others that we come to know ourselves.

Bernard Lonergan

Men never think their fortune too great, nor their wit too little.

Thomas Fuller, MD

To be nobody-but-myself – in a world which is doing its best, night and day, to make you like everybody else – means to fight the hardest battle which any human being can fight, and never stop fighting.

E.E. Cummings

SELFISH

A woman means by unselfishness chiefly taking trouble for others; a man means not giving trouble to others. Thus each sex regards the other as basically selfish.

C.S. Lewis

When a man is wrapped up in himself, he makes a pretty small package.

John Ruskin

He who lives only to benefit himself confers on the world a benefit when he dies.

Tertullian

SENSE

There is nobody so irritating as somebody with less intelligence and more sense than we have.

Don Herold

When I see something that makes absolutely no sense whatever, I figure there must be a damn good reason for it.

Peter De Vries

Intellect distinguishes between the possible and the impossible; reason distinguishes between the sensible and the senseless. Even the possible can be senseless.

Max Born

SENSES

All credibility, all good conscience, all evidence of truth come only from the senses.

Friedrich Nietzsche

What can give us surer knowledge than our senses? With what else can we better distinguish the true from the false?

Lucretius

I could better eat with one who did not respect the truth or the laws, than with a sloven and unpresentable person. Moral qualities rule the world, but at short distances, the senses are despotic.

Ralph Waldo Emerson

The senses do not deceive; it is the judgment that deceives.

Johann Wolfgang von Goethe

SENTENCES

Backward ran sentences until reeled the mind.

Wolcott Gibbs

SENTIMENT

All the beautiful sentiments in the world weigh less than a single lovely action.

James Russell Lowell

The value of a sentiment is the amount of sacrifice you are prepared to make for it.

John Galsworthy

SENTIMENTALISM

Sentimentalism is a working off on yourself of feelings you haven't really got.

D.H. Lawrence

SENTIMENTALISTS

The barrenest of all mortals is the sentimentalist.

Thomas Carlyle

A sentimentalist is simply one who desires to have the luxury of an emotion without paying for it.
Oscar Wilde

The sentimentalist is always a cynic at heart. Indeed, sentimentality is merely the bank holiday of cynicism.
Oscar Wilde

SEQUENCE
The events in our lives happen in a sequence in time, but their significance to ourselves they find in their own order ... the continuous thread of revelation.
Eudora Welty

SERIOUSNESS
Seriousness is the only refuge of the shallow.
Oscar Wilde

SERMON
Americans are so tense and keyed up that it is impossible even to put them to sleep with a sermon.
Norman Vincent Peale

SERVANTS
The best servants of the people, like the best valets, must whisper unpleasant truths in the master's ear. It is the court fool, not the foolish courtier, whom the king can least afford to lose.
Walter Lippmann

SERVICE (TO OTHERS)
The service we render to others is really the rent we pay for our room on this earth.
Sir Wilfred Grenfell

Service to others is the rent you pay for your room here on Earth.
Muhammad Ali

It is our first duty to serve society, and, after we have done that, we may attend to the salvation of our own souls. A youthful passion for abstracted devotion should not be encouraged.
Samuel Johnson

The measure of a man is not the number of his servants but in the number of people whom he serves.
Paul W. Moody

SEX
Sex is the lyricism of the masses.
Charles Baudelaire

When you meet a human being, the first distinction you make is "male or female?" and you are accustomed to make the distinction with unhesitating certainty.
Sigmund Freud

Don't be so snobbish about the interest people show in [a sensational crime or trial] or so dismissive of its significance. After all, according to Genesis, when the Good Lord put us on this Earth just about the first two things that happened were a sex scandal and a murder. Great minds ever after have turned to these subjects, meditated on them, explored them.
Meg Greenfield

Women need a reason to have sex. Men just need a place.
Billy Crystal

Sex is what you can get. For some people, most people, it's the most important thing they can get without being born rich or smart or stealing.

Don DeLillo

I always thought music was more important than sex – then I thought if I don't hear a concert for a year and a half it doesn't bother me.

Jackie Mason

I know nothing about sex, because I was always married.

Zsa Zsa Gabor

I believe that sex is one of the most beautiful, natural, wholesome things that money can buy.

Steve Martin

SEX APPEAL
Sex appeal is fifty per cent what you've got and fifty per cent what people think you've got.

Sophia Loren

SEXES
I love the idea of there being two sexes, don't you?

James Thurber

There is more difference within the sexes than between them.

Ivy Compton-Burnett

SHADOW
What you are you do not see. What you see is your shadow.

Rabindranath Tagore

There is strong shadow where there is much light.

Johann Wolfgang von Goethe

SHAKESPEARE
If I had any doubts at all about my dislike for Shakespeare, that doubt vanished completely. What a crude, immoral, vulgar, and senseless work *Hamlet* is ... there is no rhyme or reason about it.

Leo Tolstoy

Alive today [Shakespeare] would undoubtedly have written and directed motion pictures, plays, and God knows what. Instead of saying "This medium is not good," he would have used it and made it good.

Raymond Chandler

The remarkable thing about Shakespeare is that he is really very good – in spite of all the people who say he is very good.

Robert Graves

I know not, sir, whether Bacon wrote the works of Shakespeare, but if he did not it seems to me that he missed the opportunity of his life.

J.M. Barrie

SHAME
One of the misfortunes of our time is that in getting rid of false shame, we have killed off so much real shame as well.

Louis Kronenberger

Shame is like everything else; live with it for long enough and it becomes part of the furniture.
Salman Rushdie

SHARING
He who shareth honey with a bear hath the least part.
Proverb

Sharing food with another human being is an intimate act that should not be indulged in lightly.
M.F.K. Fisher

Trouble shared is trouble halved.
Dorothy L. Sayers

There are some things you can't share without ending up liking each other.
J.K. Rowling

If you have knowledge, let others light their candles by it.
Thomas Fuller, MD

SHARKS
If the shark sees clearly, then it doesn't bite you, it bites the bait.
Sarah Sams

SHEPHERD
It is the part of a good shepherd to sheer his flock, not skin it.
Latin proverb

SHIPS
Being in a ship is being in a jail, with the chance of being drowned.
Samuel Johnson

SHOES
Englishwomen's shoes look as if they had been made by someone who had often heard shoes described but had never seen any.
Margaret Halsey

SHOOTING
The fascination of shooting as a sport depends almost wholly on whether you are at the right or wrong end of the gun.
P.G. Wodehouse

SHOPPING
Whole families shopping at night! Aisles full of husbands!
Allen Ginsberg

SHORT
Good things, when short, are twice as good.
Baltasar Gracian

SHORT CUT
It usually takes a long time to find a shorter way.
Anonymous

A shortcut is the longest distance between two points.
Charles Issawi

There are no shortcuts to any place worth going.
Beverly Sills

SHORT MEN
Short men have made millions, married beauties, ruled countries,

founded universities, and discovered cures for diseases. It's not exactly a handicap, okay? … I suggest you take the cards you've been dealt and figure out a better way to play your hand.

> *Cherie Bennett, to a US teenager*
> *who signed himself Dwarf Boy*

SHORTCOMINGS

It is always well to accept your shortcomings with candour but to regard those of your friends with polite incredulity.

> *Russell Lynes*

SHOW BUSINESS

To be successful in show business, all you need are fifty good breaks.

> *Walter Matthau*

SHYNESS

Shyness is just egotism out of its depth.

> *Penelope Keith*

SICK

There's nothing the matter with being sick that getting well can't fix.

> *Peg Bracken*

SICKNESS

There is something in sickness that breaks down the pride of manhood.

> *Charles Dickens*

SIDES

The reverse side also has a reverse side.

> *Japanese proverb*

SIGHS

Most of the sighs we hear have been edited.

> *Stanislaw J. Lec*

SIGHT

I can see with half an eye.

> *Miguel de Cervantes*

SIGN

Sign, sign, everywhere a sign. Blocking out the scenery, breaking my mind.

> *Les Emmerson*

SILENCE

People who make no noise are dangerous.

> *Jean de La Fontaine*

Speech may be barren; but it is ridiculous to suppose that silence is always brooding on a nestful of eggs.

> *George Eliot*

Better silent than stupid.

> *German proverb*

Silence is the best substitute for brains ever invented.

> *Henry Ashurst*

Of those who say nothing, few are silent.

> *Thomas Neill*

In human intercourse the tragedy begins, not when there is misunderstanding about words, but when silence is not understood.

> *Henry David Thoreau*

Silence is wisdom, when speaking is folly.

Thomas Fuller, MD

Silence is the virtue of fools.

Sir Francis Bacon

I have often regretted my speech, never my silence.

Publilius Syrus

When you have nothing to say, say nothing.

Charles Caleb Colton

Blessed is the man who, having nothing to say, abstains from giving in words evidence of the fact.

George Eliot

Silence is one of the hardest arguments to refute.

Josh Billings

The eternal silence of these infinite spaces terrifies me.

Blaise Pascal

Drawing on my fine command of language, I said nothing.

Robert Benchley

Silence and reserve suggest latent power. What some men think has more effect than what others say.

Lord Chesterfield

And silence sounds no worse than cheers/After death has stopped the ears.

A.E. Housman

Macaulay has occasional flashes of silence that make his conversation perfectly delightful.

Sydney Smith

Silence and tact may or may not be the same thing.

Samuel Butler

The silence of a wise man is more wrong to mankind than a slanderer's speech.

William Wycherley

Silence gives consent, or a horrible feeling that nobody's listening.

Franklin P. Jones

Silence – the most perfect expression of scorn.

George Bernard Shaw

The best way to keep one's nose clean is to keep one's mouth shut.

Dr O.A. Battista

Let your speech be better than silence, or be silent.

Dionysius the Elder

Well-timed silence hath more eloquence than speech.

Martin Farquhar Tupper

To sin by silence when they should protest makes cowards of men.

Abraham Lincoln

Silence is the true friend that never betrays.

Confucius

He who does not understand your silence will probably not understand your words.

Elbert Hubbard

SILENT

How much one has to say in order to be heard when silent.

Elias Canetti

Our lives begin to end the day we become silent about things that matter.

Martin Luther King, Jr

Sometimes you have to be silent to be heard.

Stanislaw J. Lec

SILLY
Silly things do cease to be silly if they are done by sensible people in an impudent way.

Jane Austen

The "silly question" is the first intimation of some totally new development.

Alfred North Whitehead

If people never did silly things, nothing intelligent would ever get done.

Ludwig Wittgenstein

To say silly things by chance and weakness is a common misfortune, but to say them intentionally is intolerable.

Blaise Pascal

SIMPLICITY
Simplicity is the mean between ostentation and rusticity.

Alexander Pope

Simplicity is the most deceitful mistress that ever betrayed man.

Henry Adams

Perfect simplicity is unconsciously audacious.

George Meredith

Teach us Delight in simple things,/And Mirth that has no bitter springs.

Rudyard Kipling

And all the loveliest things there be/Come simply, so, it seems to me.

Edna St Vincent Millay

Nothing is as simple as we hope it will be.

Jim Horning

Simplicity is light, carefree, neat, and loving – not a self-punishing ascetic trip.

Gary Snyder

One always begins with the simple, then comes the complex, and by superior enlightenment one often reverts in the end to the simple. Such is the course of human intelligence.

Voltaire

Simplicity is not a goal, but one arrives at simplicity in spite of oneself, as one approaches the real meaning of things.

Constantin Brancusi

Simplicity is an acquired taste. Mankind, left free, instinctively complicates life.

Katharine Fullerton Gerould

I prefer the honestly simple to the ingeniously wicked.

William Penn

SIMPLIFY

The ability to simplify means to eliminate the unnecessary so that the necessary can speak.

Hans Hoffmann

Remember me when I am dead and simplify me when I'm dead.

Keith Douglas

SIN

Sin is a dangerous toy in the hands of the virtuous. It should be left to the congenitally sinful, who know when to play with it and when to let it alone.

H.L. Mencken

There's nothing so artificial as sinning nowadays. I suppose it once was real.

D.H. Lawrence

We didn't invent sin; we are merely trying to perfect it.

Anonymous

We are not punished for our sins, but by them.

Elbert Hubbard

Some rise by sin, and some by virtue fall.

William Shakespeare

The only deadly sin I know is cynicism.

Henry Lewis Stimson

Sins become more subtle as you grow older. You commit sins of despair rather than lust.

Piers Paul Read

There is a great difference between a man who does not want to sin and a man who does not know how to.

Seneca

It may be a sin to think evil of people, but it is seldom a mistake.

H.L. Mencken

Commit the oldest sins the newest kind of ways.

William Shakespeare

The seven social sins [are] politics without principle, wealth without work, commerce without morality, pleasure without conscience, education without character, science without humanity, and worship without sacrifice.

Mohandas Gandhi

God may forgive your sins, but your nervous system won't.

Alfred Korzybski

Our sins, like our shadows when day is in its glory, scarce appear; toward evening, how great and monstrous they are!

Sir John Suckling

I am not sure how many "sins" I would recognize in the world. Some would surely be defused by changed circumstances. But I can imagine none that is more irredeemably sinful than the betrayal, the exploitation, of the young by those who should care for them.

Elizabeth Janeway

Christ died for our sins. Dare we make his martyrdom meaningless by not committing them?

Jules Feiffer

The scandal of the world is what makes the offence; it is not sinful to sin in silence.

Molière

SINCERITY
A deep, great, genuine sincerity is the first characteristic of all men in any way heroic.

Thomas Carlyle

It is dangerous to be sincere unless you are also stupid.

George Bernard Shaw

Always be sincere, even if you don't mean it.

Harry S. Truman

You can be sincere and still be stupid.

Charles F. Kettering

A little sincerity is a dangerous thing, and a great deal of it is absolutely fatal.

Oscar Wilde

SING
It is folly to sing twice to a deaf man.

English proverb

He who sings scares away his woes.
Miguel de Cervantes

SINGLE-MINDEDNESS
Single-mindedness is all very well in cows or baboons; in an animal

claiming to belong to the same species as Shakespeare it is simply disgraceful.

Aldous Huxley

SISTERS
Never praise a sister to a sister, in the hope of your compliments reaching the proper ears.

Rudyard Kipling

SIZE
She fitted into my biggest armchair as if it had been built around her by someone who knew they were wearing armchairs tight about the hips that season.

P.G. Wodehouse

SKEPTICISM
Skepticism is the first step toward truth.

Denis Diderot

She believed in nothing: only her skepticism kept her from being an atheist.

Jean-Paul Sartre

I am too much of a skeptic to deny the possibility of anything.

Thomas Henry Huxley

A wise skepticism is the first attribute of a good critic.

James Russell Lowell

SKILL
'Tis skill, not strength, that governs a ship.

Thomas Fuller, MD

He that wrestles with us strengthens our nerves and sharpens our skill. Our antagonist is our helper.

Edmund Burke

Skill and confidence are an unconquered army.

George Herbert

Politics and business can be settled by influence, cooks and doctors can only be promoted on their skill.

Penelope Fitzgerald

Better to master a small skill than to accumulate a big fortune.

Chinese proverb

SKYDIVING
If at first you don't succeed, so much for skydiving.

Unknown

SLANDER
Slander is the revenge of a coward, and dissimulation his defence.

Samuel Johnson

It takes your enemy and your friend, working together, to hurt you to the heart; the one to slander you and the other to get the news to you.

Mark Twain

SLANG
Slang is a language that rolls up its sleeves, spits on its hands, and goes to work.

Carl Sandburg

SLAVERY
That state is a state of Slavery in which a man does what he likes to do in his spare time and in his working time that which is required of him.

Eric Gill

Being favoured by your master, are you less a slave?

Blaise Pascal

They are slaves who fear to speak,/ For the fallen and the weak.

James Russell Lowell

SLEEP
The sleep of a labouring man is sweet, whether he eat little or much; but the abundance of the rich will not suffer him to sleep.

Ecclesiastes 5:12

Oh Sleep! It is a gentle thing/ Beloved from pole to pole.

Samuel Taylor Coleridge

A dying man needs to die, as a sleepy man needs to sleep, and there comes a time when it is wrong, as well as useless, to resist.

Stewart Alsop

The amount of sleep required by the average person is about five minutes more.

Max Kauffmann

SLIP
A slip of the foot you may soon recover, but a slip of the tongue you may never get over.

Benjamin Franklin

SLOWNESS
There is a slowness in affairs which ripens them, and a slowness which rots them.
Joseph Roux

SLY
He's tough, ma'am, tough, is J.B. Tough and devilish sly.
Charles Dickens

SMALL
Small is beautiful.
E.F. Schumacher

SMART
None of us is as smart as all of us.
Japanese proverb

It's not that I'm so smart, it's just that I stay with the problem longer.
Albert Einstein

SMELLS
Smells are far more evocative of the past than noises can ever be. Sounds are the clichés of memory.
Roy Hattersley

SMILE
Start every day with a smile and get it over with.
W.C. Fields

A smile is a curve that sets things straight.
Proverb

Smile and feel ten years younger; worry and get grey.
Chinese proverb

They gave each other a smile with a future in it.
Ring Lardner

The smiler with the knife under the cloak.
Geoffrey Chaucer

SMOKING
Smoking is one of the leading causes of statistics.
Fletcher Knebel

I predict that ashtrays will become as obsolete as spittoons in our lifetime.
Arthur Black

To cease smoking is the easiest thing I ever did. I ought to know because I've done it a thousand times.
Mark Twain

SNOBBERY
Snobbery is the pride of those who are not sure of their position.
Berton Braley

SNOW
Let every man shovel out his own snow and the whole city will be passable.
Ralph Waldo Emerson

There's one good thing about snow – it makes your lawn look as nice as your neighbour's.
Clyde Moore

Snow doesn't give a soft white damn whom it touches.
E.E. Cummings

If February give much snow, A fine Summer it doth foreshow.
English proverb

SNOWFLAKES
Snowflakes are one of nature's most fragile things, but look what they can do if they stick together.
Vista M. Kelly

SNOWMEN
Snowmen fall from heaven … unassembled.
Unknown

SNOWSTORM
Few things are as democratic as a snowstorm.
Bern Williams

SOAP
In Marseilles they make half the soap we consume in America, but the Marseillaise only have a vague theoretical idea of its use, which they have obtained from books of travel.
Mark Twain

SOBRIETY
There's nothing wrong with sobriety in moderation.
John Ciardi

The worst thing about some men is that when they are not drunk they are sober.
William Butler Yeats

Always do sober what you said you'd do drunk. That will teach you to keep your mouth shut.
Ernest Hemingway

SOCIAL LIFE
The nice thing about social life, as opposed to real life, is that in social life you are what you seem.
Clive James

SOCIALISM
It is a socialist idea that making profits is a vice; I consider the real vice is making losses.
Winston Churchill

Under capitalism, man exploits man; under socialism, the reverse is true.
Polish proverb

SOCIALITY
No human being – not even a hermit in the desert – can contract out of being a social creature; sociality is a built-in feature of human nature.
Arnold Toynbee

SOCIETY
Society cannot exist without law and order, and cannot advance except through vigorous innovators.
Bertrand Russell

Men would not long live in society were they not the dupes of one another.
François, duc de La Rochefoucauld

Life cannot subsist in society without reciprocal concessions.
Samuel Johnson

What is not good for the swarm is not good for the bee.

Marcus Aurelius

A civilized society is one which tolerates eccentricity to the point of doubtful sanity.

Robert Frost

Society needs to condemn a little more and understand a little less.

John Major

There is no such thing as society. There are individual men and women, and there are families.

Margaret Thatcher

We are born charming, fresh, and spontaneous and must be civilized before we are fit to participate in society.

Judith Martin

I'm against a homogenized society, because I want the cream to rise.

Robert Frost

Society is like a large piece of frozen water; and skating well is the great art of social life.

Charles Lamb

Among the cheerful robots of the mass society, not human virtue but human shortcomings, attractively packaged, lead to popularity and success.

C. Wright Mills

Human society is like an arch, kept from falling by the mutual pressure of its parts.

Seneca

When the fabric of society is so rigid that it cannot change quickly enough, adjustments are achieved by social unrest and revolutions.

John Boyd Orr

SOCKS

A man is about thirty-eight before he stockpiles enough socks to be able to get one truly matching pair.

Merrily Harpur

SOFT-HEADEDNESS

I think there is only one quality worse than hardness of heart, and that is softness of head.

Theodore Roosevelt

SOFTWARE

If we built houses the way we build software, the first woodpecker to come along would destroy civilization.

U.S. Deputy Defense Secretary John Hamre, believing that the Year 2000 problem had global implications "that we can't even comprehend."

SOLAR ENERGY

The use of solar energy has not been opened up because the oil industry does not own the sun.

Ralph Nader

SOLDIERS

Soldiers are citizens of death's grey land.

Siegfried Sassoon

When soldiers have been baptized in the fire of a battlefield, they have all one rank in my eyes.
Napoleon Bonaparte

All that a man hath will he give for his life; and while all contribute of their substance the soldier puts his life at stake, and often yields it up in his country's cause.
Abraham Lincoln

SOLITUDE
Whosoever is delighted in solitude is either a wild beast or a god.
Francis Bacon

The worst solitude is to be destitute of sincere friendship.
Francis Bacon

Man cannot long survive without air, water, and sleep. Next in importance comes food. And close on its heels, solitude.
Thomas Szasz

Solitude is the furnace of transformation.
Henri Nouwen

Solitude is dangerous to reason, without being favourable to virtue.
Samuel Johnson

SOLUTIONS
Someone once said that for every problem there is a solution that is simple, attractive … and wrong.
Arthur C. Clarke

What we're saying today is that you're either part of the solution or you're part of the problem.
Eldridge Cleaver

It is not always by plugging away at a difficulty and sticking at it that one overcomes it; but, rather, often by working on the next one to it. Certain people and certain things require to be approached at an angle.
André Gide

There is always an easy solution to every human problem – neat, plausible, and wrong.
H.L. Mencken

The chief cause of problems is solutions.
Eric Sevareid

Off-the-rack solutions, like bargain basement dresses, never fit anymore.
Françoise Giroud

Within the problem lies the solution.
Milton Katselas

SONG
Anything too stupid to be said is sung.
Voltaire

A book is a story for the mind. A song is a story for the soul.
Eric Pio

SOPHISTICATION
I have always thought of sophistication as a rather feeble substitute for decadence.
Christopher Hampton

SORROW
You cannot prevent the birds of sorrow from flying over your head,

but you can prevent them from building nests in your hair.

Chinese proverb

We should feel sorrow, but not sink under its oppression; the heart of a wise man should resemble a mirror, which reflects every object without being sullied by any.

Confucius

The lives of happy people are dense with their own doings – crowded, active, thick … But the sorrowing are nomads, on a plain with few landmarks and no boundaries; sorrow's horizons are vague and its demands are few.

Larry McMurtry

Don't let your sorrow come higher than your knees.

Swedish proverb

SOUL

In the dark night of the soul it is always 3 o'clock in the morning.

F. Scott Fitzgerald

The lie in the soul is a true lie.

Benjamin Jowett

The soul is placed in the body like a rough diamond; and must be polished, or the lustre of it will never appear.

Daniel Defoe

A good soul like a good body should be as unobtrusive as possible; insofar as it functions properly, it should not be noticed for good or for ill.

C.E.M. Joad

Yes, we have a soul; but it's made of tiny robots.

Daniel C. Dennett

SOUNDS

Not many sounds in life, and I include all urban and rural sounds, exceed in interest a knock at the door.

Charles Lamb

SOVEREIGN

The sovereign has … three rights – the right to be consulted, the right to encourage, the right to warn.

Walter Bagehot

SOVEREIGNTY

We have learned that the only policy suited to enlightened men is to be sovereign over one's own affairs and not to have the ridiculous pretensions of imposing it on others.

Charles-Maurice de Talleyrand

SOVIET UNION

The Soviet empire did not fall apart because spooks had bugged the men's room in the Kremlin or put broken glass in Mrs. Brezhnev's bath but because running a huge, closed, repressive society in the 1980s had become – economically, socially, militarily, and technologically – impossible.

John le Carré

SPACE

Space isn't remote at all. It's only an hour's drive away if your car could go straight upwards.

Fred Hoyle

It's very hard to take yourself too seriously when you look at the world from outer space.

Thomas K. Mattingly II

Nothing puzzles me more than time and space; and yet nothing troubles me less, as I never think about them.

Charles Lamb

SPEAKING

He hasn't got much to say, but at least he doesn't try to say anything else.

Robert Benchley

Veteran speakers usually gesture vigorously and walk around. A moving target is harder to hit.

Franklin P. Jones

The opposite of speaking is not listening; it is waiting.

Jan Poulsson

I take the view, that if you cannot say what you have to say in twenty minutes, you should go away and write a book about it.

Lord Brabazon

I am the most spontaneous speaker in the world because every word, every gesture, and every retort has been carefully rehearsed.

George Bernard Shaw

A speech is like a bad tooth; the longer it takes to draw it out, the more it hurts.

W.E. Suter

Spontaneous speeches are seldom worth the paper they are written on.

Leslie Henson

I do not object to people looking at their watches when I am speaking – but I strongly object when they start shaking them to make certain they are still going.

Lord Birkett

It is a sad thing when men have neither the wit to speak well nor judgment to hold their tongues.

Jean de La Bruyère

Speeches are like babies – easy to conceive but hard to deliver.

Pat O'Malley

Speeches are often like eggs. You don't need to eat the whole of an egg nor hear the whole of a speech to know that it is bad.

Walter Hines Page

After-dinner speeches should be like my second Schmelling fight and last about three seconds.

Joe Louis

Make sure you have finished speaking before your audience has finished listening.

Dorothy Sarnoff

SPEAKING OUT

Don't be ashamed to say what you are not ashamed to think.

Michel de Montaigne

Speak, demon! What is it that you wish?/I wish you'd stop beating that damn gong.

Ron Goulart

It is terrible to speak well and be wrong.

Sophocles

I will begin to speak, when I have that to say which had not better be unsaid.

Cato the Younger

SPECIAL STATUS

Groups or segments of society who always want to be recognized as "special" risk forever being on the outside of the decision making looking in.

Stewart Kronberg

SPECIALIST

A specialist is one who knows everything about something and nothing about anything else.

Ambrose Bierce

A specialist is someone who does everything else worse.

Ruggiero Ricci

The specialist learns more and more about less and less until, finally, he knows everything about nothing; whereas the generalist learns less and less about more and more until, finally, he knows nothing about everything.

Donsen's Law

The trouble with specialists is that they tend to think in grooves.

Elaine Morgan

More and more, our life has been governed by specialists who know too little of what lies outside their province to be able to know enough about what takes place within it.

Lewis Mumford

SPECULATION

There are two times in a man's life when he should not speculate: when he can't afford to, and when he can.

Mark Twain

SPEECH

It usually takes me more than three weeks to prepare a good impromptu speech.

Mark Twain

Speeches that are measured by the hour will die with the hour.

Thomas Jefferson

Speech is civilization itself. The word, even the most contradictory word, preserves contact – it is silence which isolates.

Thomas Mann

Every time I accept an invitation to speak, I really make four addresses. First is the speech I prepare in advance. That is pretty good. Second is the speech I really make. Third is the speech I make on my way home, which is the best of all; and fourth is the speech the newspapers the next morning say I made, which bears no relation to any of the others.

William Lyon Phelps

Speech is conveniently located midway between thought and action, where it often substitutes for both.

John Andrew Holmes

SPEED

I'll be with you in the squeezing of a lemon.

Oliver Goldsmith

It is impossible to travel faster than the speed of light, and certainly not desirable, as one's hat keeps blowing off.

Woody Allen

Have you ever noticed? Anybody going slower than you is an idiot, and anyone going faster is a moron?

George Carlin

Every car has a lot of speed in it. The trick is getting the speed out of it.

A.J. Foyt

SPEED READING

I took a speed reading course and read *War and Peace* in twenty minutes. It involves Russia.

Woody Allen

SPELLING

He respects Owl, because you can't help respecting anybody who can spell T-u-e-s-d-a-y, even if he doesn't spell it right; but spelling isn't everything. There are days when spelling Tuesday simply doesn't count.

A.A. Milne

SPENDTHRIFTS

Kings and ministers are themselves always, and without any exception, the greatest spendthrifts in the society.

Adam Smith

SPIRIT

In the long run the sword is always beaten by the spirit.

Napoleon Bonaparte

In the depth of winter, I finally learned that within me there lay an invincible summer.

Albert Camus

SPORTS

I hate sports as rabidly as a person who likes sport hates common sense.

H.L. Mencken

Sports do not build character. They reveal it.

Heywood Broun

Everything about sport is derived from the hunt: there is no sport in existence that does not base itself either on the chase or on aiming, the two key elements of primeval hunting.

Desmond Morris

If I died tomorrow, Don would find a way to preserve me until the season was over and he had time for a nice funeral.

Dorothy Shula

Serious sport has nothing to do with fair play. It is bound up with hatred, jealousy, boastfulness, disregard of all rules, and sadistic pleasure in witnessing violence. In other words it is war minus the shooting.

George Orwell

Auto racing, bull fighting, and mountain climbing are the only real sports ... all others are games.

Ernest Hemingway

You're a good loser if you can grip the winner's hand without wishing it was his throat.

Hal Chadwick

SPRING

In the spring a young man's fancy lightly turns to what he's been thinking about all winter.

Vina Delmar

Poor, dear, silly spring, preparing her annual surprise.

Wallace Stevens

Spring has returned. The Earth is like a child who knows poems.

Rainer Maria Rilke

STAB

True friends stab you in the front.

Oscar Wilde

STANDING STILL

Standing still is the fastest way of moving backwards in a rapidly changing world.

Unknown

Be not afraid of growing slowly, be afraid only of standing still.

Chinese proverb

There are many ways of going forward, but only one way of standing still.

Franklin D. Roosevelt

STARS

All the atoms we are made of are forged from hydrogen in stars that died and exploded before our solar system formed. So if you are romantic, you can say we are literally stardust. If you're less romantic, you can say we're the nuclear waste from the fuel that makes stars shine.

Sir Martin Rees

We emerged to see – once more – the stars.

Dante Alighieri

No one regards what is before his feet; we all gaze at the stars.

Quintus Ennius

We are a people who seek to know everything about the stars except why they were once regarded as divine.

Theodore Roszak

If you follow your star, you cannot fail to reach a glorious haven.

Dante Alighieri

START

In the dim background of our mind, we know what we ought to be doing but somehow we cannot start.

William James

STATE

The state is like the human body. Not all of its functions are dignified.

Anatole France

Nevermore let the great interests of the State depend upon the thousand chances that may sway a piece of human frailty.
Sir Thomas Talfourd

The state has no business in the bedrooms of the nation.
Pierre Elliott Trudeau

STATESMAN
A statesman is any politician it's considered safe to name a school after.
Bill Vaughan

I don't for a minute flatter myself that I am a statesman or a diplomat, but I don't think it makes too much difference if I bring to this job a high sense of responsibility.
Lord Alexander before being sworn in as Governor General

The first requirement of a statesman is that he be dull.
Dean Acheson

Men are not great statesmen merely because they happen to fill great offices.
John Bright

A politician thinks of the next election. A statesman, of the next generation.
James Freeman Clarke

STATESMANSHIP
The difference between politics and statesmanship is philosophy.
Will and Ariel Durant

STATISTICS
Facts are stubborn things, but statistics are more pliable.
Laurence J. Peter

STATURE
Out of the last war emerged their status, out of this one their stature.
Vincent Massey

STATUS QUO
Status quo. Latin for the mess we're in.
Jeve Moorman

STEALING
A man who will steal *for* me will steal *from* me.
Theodore Roosevelt, upon firing one of his cowboys who had applied the Roosevelt brand to a steer belonging to a neighbouring ranch

STIGMAS
Stigmas are the corollaries of values. If work, independence, responsibility, respectability are valued, then their converse must be devalued, seen as disreputable. The Victorians, taking their values seriously, also took seriously the need for social sanctions that would stigmatize and censure violations of those values.
Gertrude Himmelfarb

STOCK MARKET
It will fluctuate.
J.P. Morgan, when asked what the stock market would do in the future

People who always try to play the market to its lowest point always miss it.

Earl Peattie

Never sell stocks when the sap is running up the tree.

Edwin Levevre

The suckers haven't permanently deserted the stock market. They are merely waiting until the prices get too high again.

Unknown

The secret of financial success is to buy sound stock, wait until it goes up and then sell it. If it does not go up, don't buy it.

Calvin Coolidge

Don't gamble. Take all your savings and buy some good stock and hold it until it goes up, then sell it. If it don't go up, don't buy it.

Will Rogers

In the stock market, bulls make money, bears make money, but pigs just get slaughtered.

Wall Street truism

The main purpose of the stock market is to make fools of as many men as possible.

Bernard Baruch

STOMACH
A fat stomach sticks out too far. It prevents you from looking down and seeing what is going on around you.

Norman Reilly Raine

STOP
Whether on the road or in an argument, when you see red it's time to stop.

Anonymous

STRANGERS
The largest part of mankind are nowhere greater strangers than at home.

Samuel Taylor Coleridge

We were in some little time fixed in our seats, and sat with that dislike which people not too good-natured usually conceive of each other at first sight.

Sir Richard Steele

Sometimes you have to get to know someone really well to realize you're really strangers.

Mary Tyler Moore

My mother used to say that there are no strangers, only friends you haven't met yet. She's now in a maximum security twilight home in Australia.

Dame Edna Everage
(Barry Humphries)

STRATEGIC PLANNING
If I called a strategic meeting, there would be dead silence, then people would fall out of their chairs laughing.

Oprah Winfrey

Strategic planning is worthless – unless there is first a strategic vision.

John Naisbitt

The end we aim at must be known, before the way can be made.

Jean Paul

STRATEGY
When you find a good move, look for a better one.

Bobby Fischer

The true aim is not so much to seek battle as to seek a strategic situation so advantageous that if it does not of itself produce the decision, its continuation by battle is sure to achieve this.

B.H. Liddell Hart

STRENGTH
For the strength of the Pack is the Wolf,/and the strength of the Wolf is the Pack.

Rudyard Kipling

If we are strong, our strength will speak for itself. If we are weak, words will be no help.

John F. Kennedy,
from the address he was to give
November 22, 1963

We all have strength to endure the misfortunes of others.

François, duc de La
Rochefoucauld

May the strength of three be in your journey.

Irish proverb

It is the nature, and the advantage of strong people that they can bring out the crucial questions and form a clear opinion about them. The weak always have to decide between alternatives that are not their own.

Dietrich Bonhoeffer

No tree becomes rooted and sturdy unless many a wind assails it. For by its very tossing it tightens its grip and plants the roots more securely; the fragile trees are those that have grown in a sunny valley.

Seneca

On a recent trip to California, a friend took me to see the redwoods. She told me that for such large trees, they had very shallow root systems. When I asked her how they were able to stand, she said: "Simple – they grow close together and the roots interlock. That's how they get their strength." We all do.

Dan Gottlieb

Strength is the capacity to break a chocolate bar into four pieces with your bare hands – and then to eat just one of the pieces.

Judith Viorst

We acquire the strength we have overcome.

Ralph Waldo Emerson

STRIFE
From things that differ comes the fairest attunement; all things are born through strife.

Heraclitus

STRINGS
Yes, I had two strings to my bow; both golden ones, egad! and both cracked.

Henry Fielding

STRUGGLE

It is the eternal struggle between these two principles – right and wrong – throughout the world.

Abraham Lincoln

STUBBORN

Time has a way of demonstrating/ the most stubborn are the most intelligent.

Yevgeny Yevtushenko

STUDENTS

It is important that students bring a certain ragamuffin barefoot irreverence to their studies; they are not here to worship what is known, but to question it.

Jacob Bronowski

Students achieving Oneness will move on to Twoness.

Woody Allen

I don't want to send them to jail. I want to send them to school.

Adlai Stevenson

STUDIES

Studies perfect nature and are perfected by experience.

Francis Bacon

The proper study of mankind is man.

Alexander Pope

STUPIDITY

Against stupidity the gods themselves struggle in vain.

Friedrich von Schlegel

It is stupidity rather than courage to refuse to recognize danger when it is close upon you.

Sherlock Holmes to Dr Watson

Stupidity does not consist in being without ideas. Such stupidity would be the sweet, blissful stupidity of animals, molluscs, and the gods. Human stupidity consists in having lots of ideas, but stupid ones.

Henry de Montherlant

The difference between genius and stupidity is that genius has its limits.

Unknown

There is nothing worse than aggressive stupidity.

Johann Wolfgang von Goethe

It's not getting any smarter out there. You have to come to terms with stupidity and make it work for you.

Frank Zappa

Only two things are infinite – the universe and human stupidity, and I'm not so sure about the universe.

Albert Einstein

The two most abundant things in the universe are hydrogen and stupidity.

Harlan Ellison

You can be sincere and still be stupid.

Charles F. Kettering

Even those honest enough to admit being wrong a thousand times are not honest enough to admit even once to being stupid.

David Kipp

As if there were safety in stupidity alone.

Henry David Thoreau

It is physically impossible for anybody to act intelligently even one-tenth as often as to act stupidly.

Walter Pitkin

The most dangerous form of stupidity is a sharp intellect.

Hugo von Hofmannsthal

Strange as it may seem, no amount of learning can cure stupidity, and formal education positively fortifies it.

Stephen Vizinczey

The trouble with the world is that the stupid are cocksure and the intelligent are full of doubt.

Bertrand Russell

You must have taken great pains, sir; you could not naturally have been so very stupid.

Samuel Johnson

Genius may have its limitations, but stupidity is not thus handicapped.

Elbert Hubbard

Never underestimate the power of stupid people in large groups.

George Carlin

STYLE
There is no desolation so bleak that it cannot be made habitable by style. If we live inside a bad joke, it is up to us to learn, at best and worst, to tell it well.

Jonathan Raban

Know your limitations and call them your style.

Adam Scott

Fashions fade, style is eternal.

Yves Saint Laurent

STYROFOAM
After they make Styrofoam, what do they ship it in?

Steven Wright

SUBLIME
It is only a step from the sublime to the ridiculous.

Napoleon, following return from Moscow

SUBLIMITY
Sublimity is the echo of a noble mind.

Unknown

SUBMISSION
Oddly, submission to powerful, frightening, even terrible persons, like tyrants and generals, is not experienced as nearly so painful as is submission to unknown and uninteresting persons, which is what all luminaries of industry are.

Friedrich Nietzsche

SUBSERVIENT
There is nothing more subservient than an arrogant man when his

arrogance has once been broken in some particular instance.

Joseph Conrad

SUBSTANCE

In arguing of the shadows, we forgo the substance.

John Lyly

Beware lest you lose the substance by grasping at the shadows.

Aesop

It is not only fine feathers that make fine birds.

Aesop

SUBTRACTION

A man has one hundred dollars and you leave him with two dollars; that's subtraction.

Mae West

SUCCESS

Tell the truth or trump – but get the trick.

Mark Twain

In order to succeed, your desire for success should be greater than your fear of failure.

Bill Cosby

There are moments when everything goes well; don't be frightened, it won't last.

Jules Renard

I've missed more than 9,000 shots in my career. I've lost almost 300 games. Twenty-six times, I've been trusted to take the game winning shot and missed. I've failed over and over again in my life. And that is why I succeed.

Michael Jordan

Success is just a matter of luck. Ask any failure.

Earl Wilson

Success took me to her bosom like a maternal boa constrictor.

Noel Coward

The Lord gave us two ends – one to sit on and the other to think with. Success depends on which one we use the most.

Ann Landers

Nothing recedes like success.

Walter Winchell

There would be no triumph in success if there had been no hazard in failure.

John Henry Newman

If there is any great secret of success in life, it lies in the ability to put yourself in the other person's place and to see things from his point of view – as well as your own.

Henry Ford

The world continues to offer glittering prizes to those who have stout hearts and sharp swords.

F.E. Smith (Earl of Birkenhead)

The world is made up of people who never quite get into the first team and who just miss the prizes at the flower show.

Jacob Bronowski

Success is never final.
Winston Churchill

All you need in this life is ignorance and confidence; then success is sure.
Mark Twain

Success is more dangerous than failure, the ripples break over a wider coastline.
Graham Greene

I owe my success to having listened respectfully to the very best advice and then going away and doing the exact opposite.
G.K. Chesterton

The toughest thing about success is that you've got to keep on being a success.
Irving Berlin

Success is that old A-B-C – ability, breaks, and courage.
Charles Luckman

If people knew what they had to do to be successful, most people wouldn't.
Lord Thomson of Fleet

To deserve success is more important than to achieve it.
Lester B. Pearson

The secret of success is constancy to purpose.
Benjamin Disraeli

I cannot give you a formula for success, but I can give you a formula for failure; try to please everybody.
Herbert Bayard Swope

How can you say my life is not a success? Have I not for more than sixty years got enough to eat and escaped being eaten?
Logan Pearsall Smith

One need not hope in order to undertake; nor succeed in order to persevere.
William of Orange

We may stop ourselves when going up, never when coming down.
Napoleon Bonaparte

The road up and the road down are the one and the same.
Heraclitus

Success in life is never to let your ego outstrip your talent.
Don Shebib

The common thought that success spoils people by making them vain, egotistic, and self-complacent is erroneous; on the contrary it makes them, for the most part, humble, tolerant, and kind. Failure makes people bitter and cruel.
W. Somerset Maugham

By the time we've made it, we've had it.
Malcolm Forbes

Success and failure are both difficult to endure. Along with success come drugs, divorce, fornication, bullying, travel, meditation, medication, depression, neurosis, and suicide. With failure comes failure.
Joseph Heller

The only place where success comes before work is in the dictionary.

Vidal Sassoon

If at first you don't succeed, go back to bed.

Anonymous

The difference between failure and success is doing a thing nearly right and doing it exactly right.

Edward Simmons

By the time you've found the key to success, they've changed the lock.

Anonymous

Whenever an individual or business decides that success has been attained, progress stops.

Thomas Watson, Jr

It is not the going out of port, but the coming in, that determines the success of a voyage.

Henry Ward Beecher

The great secret of success is intense faith in oneself.

The Globe and Mail

Successful people are very lucky. Just ask any failure.

Michael Levine

Success is a great deodorant.

Elizabeth Taylor

This proverb flashes through his head,/The many fail, the one succeeds.

Alfred, Lord Tennyson

If I have seen further, it is standing on the shoulders of giants.

Sir Isaac Newton

The line between failure and success is so fine that we scarcely know when we pass it: so fine that we are often on the line and do not know it.

Elbert Hubbard

Success is the realization of the estimate which you place upon yourself.

Elbert Hubbard

Success makes us intolerant of failure, and failure makes us intolerant of success.

William Feather

It's lonely at the top, but you eat better.

Robert Harrison

If at first you do succeed, try not to look astonished.

Anonymous

Success isn't permanent and failure isn't fatal.

Mike Ditka

Achieving high-level success requires the support and cooperation of others. Remember this: When you take over the leadership of a group, persons in that group immediately begin to adjust themselves to the standards you set.

Dr David Schwartz

If at first you don't succeed, you're running about average.

M.H. Alderson

If *A* is a success in life, then *A* equals *X* plus *Y* plus *Z*. Work is *X*; *Y* is play; and *Z* is keeping your mouth shut.

Albert Einstein

It is often the fifth ace that makes all the difference between success and failure.

J.B. Morton

It is just as difficult to overcome success as it is to overcome failure.

Sir William Walton

Behind every successful man is a surprised woman.

Maryon Pearson

The penalty of success is to be bored by people who used to snub you.

Nancy Astor

Don't aim at success – the more you aim at it and make it a target, the more you are going to miss it. For success, like happiness, cannot be pursued; it must ensue … as the unintended side-effect of one's personal dedication to a course greater than oneself.

Viktor Frankl

People who reach the top of the tree are only those who haven't got the qualifications to detain them at the bottom.

Peter Ustinov

Eighty per cent of success is showing up.

Woody Allen

Some people reach the top of the ladder only to find it is leaning against the wrong wall.

Anonymous

The only infallible criterion of wisdom to vulgar minds – success.

Edmund Burke

Success is paralyzing only to those who have never wished for anything else.

Thornton Wilder

Success is like death. The more successful you become, the higher the houses in the hills get and the higher the fences get.

Kevin Spacey

Success is a lousy teacher. It seduces smart people into thinking they can't lose.

Bill Gates

Success has ruined many a man.

Benjamin Franklin

Success comes in a can … I can!

Wally Amos

True success is overcoming the fear of being unsuccessful.

Paul Sweeney

We are both great men, but I have succeeded better in keeping it a profound secret than he has.

Bill Nye

Success is the ability to go from one failure to another with no loss of enthusiasm.

Winston Churchill

You have reached the pinnacle of success as soon as you become uninterested in money, compliments, or publicity.

Dr O.A. Battista

Success seems to be connected with action. Successful men keep moving. They make mistakes, but they don't quit.

Conrad Hilton

Success depends on three things: who says it, what he says, and how he says it; and of these three things, what he says is the least important.

John Morley

Becoming number one is easier that remaining number one.

Senator Bill Bradley

Success is more a function of common sense than it is of genius.

An Wang

To travel hopefully is a better thing than to arrive, and the true success is to labour.

Robert Louis Stevenson

I would sooner fail than not be among the greatest.

John Keats

The measure of success is not whether you have a tough problem to deal with, but whether it's the same problem you had last year.

John Foster Dulles

Success is a consequence and must not be a goal.

Gustave Flaubert

You always pass failure on the way to success.

Mickey Rooney

Success that goes to a man's head usually pays a very short visit.

Dr O.A. Battista

A sure sign that a man is not a failure is the generosity with which he gives others credit for his success.

Dr O.A. Battista

If at first you don't succeed, try, try again. Then quit. No use being a damn fool about it.

W.C. Fields

Success is simple. Do what's right, the right way, at the right time.

Arnold Glasgow

SUDDEN
He's sudden if a thing comes in his head.

William Shakespeare

SUEZ
Ship me somewheres east of Suez, where the best is like the worst.

Rudyard Kipling

SUFFERING
If suffer we must, let's suffer on the heights.

Victor Hugo

Suffering isn't ennobling; recovery is.

Christiaan Barnard

Perhaps the worst thing about suffering is that it finally hardens the hearts of those around it.

Gloria Steinem

SUICIDE
Anybody who has listened to certain kinds of music, or read certain kinds of poetry, or heard certain kinds of performances on the concertina, will admit that even suicide has its brighter aspects.
Stephen Leacock

Suicide … is about life, being in fact the sincerest form of criticism life gets.

Wilfrid Sheed

Guns are always the best method for a private suicide. They are more stylish looking than single-edged razor blades and natural gas has gotten so expensive. Drugs are too chancy. You might mistake the dosage and just have a good time.
P.J. O'Rourke

Suicide sometimes proceeds from cowardice, but not always; for cowardice sometimes prevents it; since as many live because they are afraid to die, as die because they are afraid to live.
Charles Caleb Colton

There are many who dare not kill themselves for fear of what the neighbours will say.
Cyril Connolly

Suicide is man's way of telling God, "You can't fire me – I quit."
Bill Maher

Suicide is belated acquiescence in the opinion of one's wife's relatives.

H.L. Mencken

More than one soul dies in a suicide.

Unknown

SUN
Following the light of the sun, we left the old world.
Christopher Columbus

The sun is gone, but I have a light.
Kurt Cobain

SUNBEAMS
If sunbeams were weapons of war, we would have had solar energy long ago.
Sir George Porter

SUNDAY
For this is Sunday morning,/Fate's great bazaar.
Louis MacNeice

SUNSHINE
I cannot endure to waste anything as precious as autumn sunshine by staying in the house.
Nathaniel Hawthorne

SUPERIORITY
There is nothing noble about being superior to some other men. The true nobility is in being superior to your previous self.
Hindu proverb

If you're one in a million, there are 5,000 people just like you.
Hal Rubenstein

The superior man is firm in the right way, and not merely firm.
Confucius

The more wit you have, the more good nature you must show, to induce people to pardon your superiority, for that is no easy matter.

Lord Chesterfield

The superiority of some men is merely local. They are good because their associates are little.

Samuel Johnson

We pay a person the compliment of acknowledging his superiority whenever we lie to him.

Samuel Butler

SUPERSTITIONS

Natives who beat drums to drive off evil spirits are objects of scorn to smart Americans who blow horns to break up traffic jams.

Mary Ellen Kelly

It is the customary fate of new truths to begin as heresies and to end as superstitions.

Thomas Henry Huxley

Superstition is the poetry of life.

Johann Wolfgang von Goethe

Superstition is to religion what astrology is to astronomy; the mad daughter of a wise mother.

Voltaire

SURFACE

The world is content with setting right the surface of things.

John Henry Newman

SURGEONS

Surgeons must be very careful/ When they take their knife!/

Underneath their fine incisions/ Stirs the Culprit – Life!

Emily Dickinson

SURPRISE

I know enough of the world now, to have almost lost the capacity of being much surprised by anything.

Charles Dickens

SURRENDER

Never give in, never give in, never, never, never – in nothing, great or small, large or petty – never give in except to convictions of honour and good sense.

Winston Churchill

Surrender is essentially an operation by means of which we set about explaining instead of acting.

Charles Péguy

The Guards die, but never surrender.

Pierre Cambronne

We shall never surrender.

Winston Churchill

Surrender is a perfectly acceptable alternative in extreme circumstances.

Leigh Brackett, George Lucas, and Irvin Kershner

SURVIVAL

Oh, don't worry about Alan ... Alan will always land on somebody's feet.

Dorothy Parker about her ex-husband

On the whole, I think we shall survive. The outlook is as bad as it ever has been, but thinking people realize that – and therein lies the hope of its getting better.

Jawaharlal Nehru

Rule of survival: pack your own parachute.

T.L. Hakala

It isn't important to come out on top; what matters is to be the one who comes out alive.

Bertolt Brecht

Survival is triumph enough.

Harry Crews

Survival of the fittest implies multiplication of the fittest.

Herbert Spencer

The human race's prospects of survival were considerably better when we were defenceless against tigers than they are today when we have become defenceless against ourselves.

Arnold Toynbee

It is not the strongest of the species that survive, nor the most intelligent, but the one most responsive to change.

Charles Darwin

The history of the world, my sweet, is who gets eaten and who gets to eat.

Stephen Sondheim

SUSPENSE
There is nothing to be gained by keeping the judge in suspense.

Paul M. Perell

Even cowards can endure hardship; only the brave can endure suspense.

Mignon McLaughlin

SUSPICION
Suspicion is a thing very few people can entertain without letting the hypothesis turn, in their minds, into fact.

David Cort

Pure love and suspicion cannot dwell together: at the door where the latter enters, the former makes its exit.

Alexandre Dumas

Suspicions amongst thoughts are like bats amongst birds: they ever fly by twilight.

Francis Bacon

Most of our suspicions of others are aroused by our knowledge of ourselves.

Raymond Massey

When you buy a vase cheap, look for the flaw; when a man offers favours, look for the motive.

Japanese proverb

Suspicion is the cancer of friendship.

Petrarch

SWANS
Swans sing before they die – 'twere no bad thing/Did certain persons die before they sing.

Samuel Taylor Coleridge

SWAP

They have concluded that it is not best to swap horses while crossing the river.

Abraham Lincoln

SWEARING

Swearing was invented as a compromise between running away and fighting.

Finley Peter Dunne

The man who first abused his fellows with swear words instead of bashing their brains out with a club should be counted among those who laid the foundations of civilization.

John Cohen

Never swear, for that is a crime without excuse as there is no pleasure in it.

The Atlanta Monthly Almanac

SWEAT

Never let them see you sweat.

Deodorant advertisement

SWEATER

Sweater: a garment worn by a child when his mother feels chilly.

Alma Denny

SWIM

My Mom said she learned how to swim when someone took her out in the lake and threw her off the boat. I said, "Mom, they weren't trying to teach you how to swim."

Paula Poundstone

SWITZERLAND

In Switzerland, they had brotherly love; they had 500 years of democracy and peace and what did that produce? The cuckoo clock.

Orson Welles

SWORD

The sword is the axis of the world and its power is absolute.

Charles de Gaulle

SYLLABLES

Syllables govern the world.

Sir Edward Coke

SYMMETRY

Our notion of symmetry is derived from the human face. Hence we demand symmetry horizontally and in breadth only, not vertically nor in depth.

Blaise Pascal

SYMPATHY

All sympathy not consistent with acknowledged virtues is but disguised selfishness.

Samuel Taylor Coleridge

I can sympathize with other people's pains, but not with their pleasures. There is something curiously boring about somebody else's happiness.

Aldous Huxley

Anyone can sympathize with another's sorrow, but to sympathize with another's joy is the attribute of an angel.

Arthur Schopenhauer

Our sympathy is cold to the relation of distant misery.
Edward Gibbon

SYSTEM
Unhappy the general who comes on the field of battle with a system.
Napoleon Bonaparte

The system doesn't have to be pure, but it does have to work.
Aminu Kano

I must create a system or be enslaved by another man's.
William Blake

It is impossible to design a system so perfect that no one needs to be good.
T.S. Eliot

If you think the system is working, ask someone who isn't.
American saying

SYSTEMATIC
It is best to do things systematically, since we are only human, and disorder is our worst enemy.
Hesiod

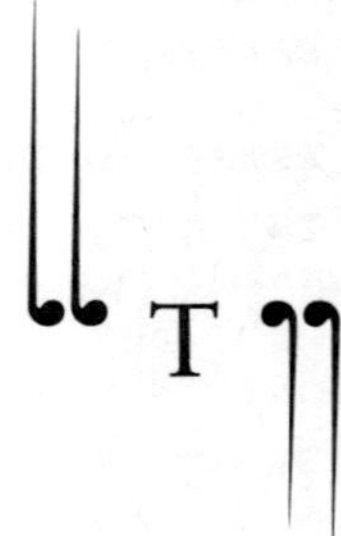
"T"

Gals Beware! Crossing Time Zones Could Get You Pregnant (*National Enquirer*)

Russian Airline Has Lost 307 Passengers ... But Not One Piece of Luggage (*Weekly World News*)

Travel by Fax Machine! Go Anywhere in the World in Minutes, Says Inventor (*Weekly World News*)

Space Aliens Sold in Pet Stores by Mistake ... Your Child's Hampster May Be a UFO Monster (*Sun*)

Dope Dealer's Baby Turns Him into Cops (*National Enquirer*)

Tall People Almost Never Get Fired (*Weekly World News*)

Steroids Turn Five-pound House Cat into a 135-pound Lion (*Weekly World News*)

Cannibal Hunger Strike! They Won't Eat Anyone Who Lives on Junk Food (*Weekly World News*)

Sixty-foot-tall Gorilla Eats 26 Villagers (*Weekly World News*)

Pampered Pooch Inherits $100 million – Now He's Set to Buy His Own Soccer Team (*Globe*)

Chimps Being Trained for Army Duty (*Sun*)

Man Trains Shark to Fetch His Mail (*Weekly World News*)

Newborn Triplets Talk in Three Different Languages (*Weekly World News*)

God Plucked Me Out of the Gutter at 66 to be a Lawyer (*Globe*)

Florida to Become Part of England; Brits Find Loophole in Ancient Treaty (*Sun*)

Space Aliens Endorse Rush Limbaugh for President (*Weekly World News*)

Californians Must Shed 300 Million Pounds of Flab ... Because Their Excess Weight Causes Earthquakes, Warns Expert (*Weekly World News*)

Killer's First Day Pass in 33 Years Ends in Murder: "A space alien made us do it!" (*Public Eye: Canada's true news and picture paper*)

Scientists Confirm ... Wing Found in Arizona Came From an Angel (*Weekly World News*)

NASA to Blow up Moon Within Months; Scientist's Plan Will Turn Earth into a Garden of Eden (*Weekly World News*)

Castro Makes Big Bucks Selling $49.95 Defection Kits to Fed-up Cubans (*Weekly World News*)

Eight Million Americans May Have Been Abducted by UFOs, Top University Researchers Reveal (*National Enquirer*)

Cities Found on Venus – But Scientists Try to Keep It a Secret (*Sun*)

Earth's Gravity is Increasing ... Making Us All Heavier and Tired, Says Scientist (*Weekly World News*)

Jesus's Lost Scrolls Found: Ancient Sermons Written in His Handwriting (*Sun*)

T-SHIRT SLOGANS

In this world it rains on the Just and the Unjust, but the Unjust have the Just's umbrella.

I'm out of estrogen and I have a gun.

The purpose of art is to hold a mirror up to life. Clearly, life needs more sleep.

The secret is to find out what people really want and then call it self-awareness.

TACT

Tact is the ability to see others as they wish to be seen.

Anonymous

Tact: Ability to tell a man he's open-minded when he has a hole in his head.

F.G. Kernan

Tact is after all a kind of mind-reading.

Sarah Orne Jewett

Being tactful in audacity is knowing how far one can go too far.

Jean Cocteau

Tact is the art of making a point without making an enemy.

Howard W. Newton

Tact is the ability to give a person a shot in the arm without letting him feel the needle.

Dr O.A. Battista

TACTICS

With foxes we must play the fox.

Thomas Fuller, MD

In making tactical dispositions, the highest pitch you can attain is to conceal them; conceal your dispositions, and you will be safe from the prying of the subtlest spies, from the machinations of the wisest brains.

Sun Tzu

TALE-BEARERS

Tale-bearers are as bad as the tale-makers.

Richard Brinsley Sheridan

TALENT

Talent is like money; you don't have to have some to talk about it.

Jules Renard

In the battle of existence, talent is the punch; tact is the clever footwork.

Wilson Mizner

There is no such thing as great talent without great willpower.

Honoré de Balzac

Everyone has talent. What is rare is the courage to follow the talent to the dark place where it leads.

Erica Jong

Everyone has talent at twenty-five. The difficulty is to have it at fifty.

Edgar Dégas

All of us do not have equal talent, but all of us should have an equal opportunity to develop our talents.

John F. Kennedy

I have no special talents. I am only passionately curious.

Albert Einstein

Talent is cheaper than table salt. What separates the talented individual from the successful is a lot of hard work.

Stephen King

Use what talents you possess: The woods would be very silent if no birds sang there except those that sang best.

Henry Van Dyke

My name is Marc, my emotional life is sensitive and my purse is empty, but they say I have talent.

Marc Chagall

Never confuse the size of your pay-cheque with the size of your talent.

Marlon Brando

TALK
Too much talk will include errors.

Burmese proverb

Talk low, talk slow, and don't talk too much.

John Wayne

Talk is cheap because supply exceeds demand.

Unknown

If you do not wish a man to do a thing, you had better get him to talk about it; for the more men talk, the more likely they are to do nothing else.

Thomas Carlyle

Considering how foolishly people act and how pleasantly they prattle, perhaps it would be better for the world if they talked more and did less.

W. Somerset Maugham

Don't talk unless you can improve the silence.

Jorge Luis Borges

To talk much and arrive nowhere is the same as climbing a tree to catch a fish.

Chinese proverb

TALKERS
The most fluent talkers or most plausible reasoners are not always the justest thinkers.

William Hazlitt

TALKING
She probably laboured under the common delusion that you made things better by talking about them.

Rose Macaulay

Talk doesn't cook rice.

Chinese proverb

If to talk to oneself when alone is folly, it must be doubly unwise to listen to oneself in the presence of others.

Baltasar Gracian

TANGENTS
All men are the same. They take no notice of the stag in the thicket because they are already chasing the hare.

Jean Giraudoux

TASKS

No task is a long one but the task on which one dare not start. It becomes a nightmare.

Charles Baudelaire

Nothing is so fatiguing as the eternal hanging on of an uncompleted task.

William James

TASTE

I hate a man who swallows [food], affecting not to know what he is eating. I suspect his taste in higher matters.

Charles Lamb

There is nothing more dreadful than imagination without taste.

Johann Wolfgang von Goethe

Taste is the feminine of genius.

Edward Fitzgerald

Taste is the enemy of creativity.

Pablo Picasso

There is no accounting for tastes, as the woman said when someone told her son was wanted by the police.

Franklin P. Adams

TAX LAWYERS

A dog who thinks he is man's best friend is a dog who has obviously never met a tax lawyer.

Fran Lebowitz

Tax avoidance means that you hire a $250,000-fee lawyer, and he changes the word "evasion" into the word "avoidance."

Franklin D. Roosevelt

TAX POLICY

Tax policies are the means of redistributing wealth among those who have the most political clout.

Jim Borden

To tax and to please, no more than to love and be wise, is not given to men.

Edmund Burke

The art of taxation consists in so plucking the goose as to procure the greatest quantity of feathers with the least possible amount of hissing.

Jean-Baptiste Colbert

TAXES

The reward of energy, enterprise, and thrift is taxes.

William Feather

The only difference between a tax man and a taxidermist is that the taxidermist leaves the skin.

Mark Twain

The politicians' promises of yesterday are the taxes of today.

William Lyon Mackenzie King

Why does a slight tax increase cost you two hundred dollars and a substantial tax cut save you thirty cents?

Peg Bracken

If Patrick Henry thought taxation without representation was bad, he should see it with representation.

Judge Earl R. Hoover

The taxes are indeed very heavy, and if those laid by the government were the only ones we had to pay, we might more easily discharge them; but we have many others, and much more grievous to some of us. We are taxed twice as much by our idleness, three times as much by our pride, and four times as much by our folly; and from these taxes the commissioners cannot ease or deliver us by allowing us an abatement.

Benjamin Franklin

Taxes are the price society pays for civilization.

Oliver Wendell Holmes

Only the little people pay taxes.

Leona Helmsley

We contend that for a nation to try to tax itself into prosperity is like a man standing in a bucket and trying to lift himself up by the handle.

Winston Churchill

Why sir, there is every possibility that you will soon be able to tax it!

Michael Faraday, responding to William Gladstone as to the usefulness of electricity

Taxes, after all, are the dues we pay for the privileges of membership in an organized society.

Franklin D. Roosevelt

It is no more immoral to directly rob citizens than to slip indirect taxes into the price of goods that they cannot do without.

Albert Camus

Our taxes reflect a continuing struggle among contending interests for the privilege of paying the least.

Louis Eisenstein

Tax legislation clearly derives from private pressures exerted for selfish ends.

Louis Eisenstein

Taxes are the changing product of earnest efforts to have others pay them.

Louis Eisenstein

The avoidance of taxes is the only pursuit that still carries any reward.

John Maynard Keynes

The wages of sin are death, but by the time taxes are taken out, it's just sort of a tired feeling.

Paula Poundstone

Collecting more taxes than is absolutely necessary is legalized robbery.

Calvin Coolidge

"Much noise and little wool," said the devil when he sheared a pig.

English proverb

TAXIS

No nice men are good at getting taxis.

Katharine Whitehorn

TEA

Love and scandal are the best sweeteners of tea.

Henry Fielding

TEACHERS

Make your friends your teachers and mingle the pleasures of conversation with the advantages of instruction.

Baltasar Gracian

A teacher is better than two books.
German proverb

That is the difference between good teachers and great teachers: good teachers make the best of a pupil's means, great teachers foresee a pupil's ends.

Maria Callas

The test of a good teacher is not how many questions he can ask his pupils that they will answer readily, but how many questions he inspires them to ask him which he finds it hard to answer.

Alice Wellington Rollins

A good teacher is someone who can understand those not very good at explaining and explain it to those not very good at understanding.

W.H. Palmer

A courage which looks easy and yet is rare; the courage of a teacher repeating day after day the same lessons – the least rewarded of all forms of courage.

Honoré de Balzac

The mediocre teacher tells. The good teacher explains. The superior teacher demonstrates. The great teacher inspires.

William Arthur Ward

Study from new books but from old teachers.

Turkish proverb

TEACHING

Spoon feeding in the long run teaches us nothing but the shape of the spoon.

E.M. Forster

There is none who cannot teach somebody something, and there is none so excellent but he is excelled.
Baltasar Gracian

Most people do not care to be taught what they do not already know; it makes them feel ignorant.
Mary McCarthy

School is an institution built on the axiom that learning is the result of teaching. And institutional wisdom continues to accept this axiom, despite overwhelming evidence to the contrary.

Ivan Illich

Is there any college that puts a premium on good teaching? Is there any university that rewards – in pay and promotion – outstanding teachers? Always and everywhere in academia, recognition, promotion, tenure depend on what a faculty member publishes. Teaching? Exciting the minds of undergraduates? Turning them on to learning? Weighing pounds of print the way butchers weigh beef, faculty fathers more often butcher those who show brilliance in lecturing or in the classroom. Publish or perish is an option. Teach well and perish is for sure.

Malcolm Forbes

Good teaching is one-quarter preparation and three-quarters theatre.
Gail Godwin

Those who are incapable of teaching young minds to reason pretend that it is impossible. The truth is, they are fonder of making their pupils talk well than think well; and much the greater number are better qualified to give praise to a ready memory than a sound judgment.

Oliver Goldsmith

We teach people how to remember, we never teach them how to grow.
Oscar Wilde

The object of teaching a child is to enable him to get along without his teacher.

Elbert Hubbard

TEAM
Team spirit is what gives so many companies an edge over their competitors.

George L. Clements

The main ingredient of stardom is the rest of the team.

John Wooden

TEARS
A tear dries quickly, especially when it is shed for the troubles of others.

Cicero

To make wail and lament for one's ill fortune, when one will win a tear from the audience, is well worthwhile.

Aeschylus

The dew of compassion is a tear.
Lord Byron

The tears of strangers are only water.

Russian proverb

TECHNICIAN
A technician is a man who knows exactly what to do the moment he has done something else.
Victor Mollo

TECHNIQUE
Technique is noticed most markedly in the case of those who have not mastered it.

Leon Trotsky

TECHNOLOGY
Technology … the knack of so arranging the world that we need not experience it.

Max Frisch

TEDIOUSNESS
The man who suspects his own tediousness is yet to be born.
Thomas Bailey Aldrich

TEENAGERS
Weird clothing is de rigeur for teenagers, but today's generation is finding it difficult to be sufficiently weird. [Those who] went through adolescence in the sixties and

seventies used up practically all the available weirdness.

> *P.J. O'Rourke*

TELEPHONE
Today the ringing of the telephone takes precedence over everything. It reaches a point of terrorism, particularly at dinnertime.

> *Niels Diffrient*

If the phone doesn't ring, it's me.

> *Jimmy Buffet*

TELEVISION
He who is created by television can be destroyed by television.

> *Theodore H. White*

Television is simply automated daydreaming.

> *Lee Loevinger*

All television is children's television.

> *Richard P. Adler*

Television has spread the habit of instant reaction and stimulated the hope of instant results.

> *Arthur M. Schlesinger, Jr*

Television is not a visual medium. It is an acoustic medium.

> *Marshall McLuhan*

Why should people go out and pay to see bad movies when they can stay home and see bad television for nothing?

> *The Observer*

Television is inextricably woven into our lives, and television has so much spare time that everybody will be on it in the end.

> *Quentin Crisp*

Television hangs on the questionable theory that whatever happens anywhere should be sensed everywhere.

> *E.B. White*

Television thrives on unreason and unreason thrives on television. It strikes at the emotions rather than the intellect.

> *Sir Robin Day*

When I got my first television set, I stopped caring so much about having close relationships.

> *Andy Warhol*

Television has raised writing to a new low.

> *Samuel Goldwyn*

There is a middlebrow snobbery in America that praises everything on public television and disdains everything on commercial television as a blight.

> *Henry Fairlie*

[A television critic] is forced to be literate about the illiterate, witty about the witless, and coherent about the incoherent.

> *John Crosby*

Television, despite its enormous presence, turns out to have added pitifully few lines to the communal memory.

> *Justin Kaplan*

The great networks are there to prove that ideas can be canned like spaghetti.

Frederic Raphael

Television is the first truly democratic culture – the first culture available to everyone and entirely governed by what people want. The most terrifying thing is what people want.

Clive Barnes

Don't be deluded into believing that the titular heads of the networks control what appears on their networks. They all have better taste.

Edward R. Murrow

The world is going mad at an accelerating rate and television is the Typhoid Mary of this madness.
Edward Robb Ellis

Television probably has become the most evocative, widely observed signpost we have.

Robert McC. Adams

The human race is faced with a cruel choice; work or daytime television.

Unknown

Television has proved that people will look at anything rather than each other.

Ann Landers

I don't watch television, I think it destroys the art of talking about oneself.

Stephen Fry

The darkest spot in human history is a small luminous screen.

Régis Debray

Because television can make so much money doing its worst, it often cannot afford to do its best.

Fred Friendly

Imitation is the sincerest form of television.

Fred Allen

There's so much comedy on television. Does that cause comedy in the streets?
Dick Cavett, on the subject of violence on television

Television is about performance. It is visual rather than verbal. It has little tolerance for argument, hypothesis, or explanation, which is why frequent TV viewers don't either. Television encourages us to judge everything by one criterion alone: Is it entertaining? Unfortunately, much of what is important in life is not entertaining.

Neil Postman

Television has brought back murder into the home – where it belongs.

Alfred Hitchcock

The television set in American homes is like the toaster. You press a button and the same thing pops out almost every time.

Alfred Hitchcock

Pure drivel tends to drive ordinary drivel off the TV screen.

Marvin Kitman

All television ever did was shrink the demand for ordinary movies. The demand for extraordinary movies increased. If any one thing is wrong with the movie industry today, it is the unrelenting effort to astonish.

Clive James

A medium so called because it is neither rare nor well done.

Ernie Kovacs

Most of us no longer watch television; we graze, zapping back and forth between channels whenever our boredom threshold is triggered. No one does any one thing at a time. A new culture has taken shape which caters to people with the attention span of a flea.

Michael Ignatieff

Television … often cannot cover the passing of the torch without fanning the flames in the process.

Martin Schram

If you read a lot of books, you're considered well-read. But if you watch a lot of TV, you're not considered well-viewed.

Lily Tomlin

Television is more interesting than people. If it were not, we should have people standing in the corners of our rooms.

Alan Coren

The vast wasteland of TV is not interested in producing a better mousetrap but in producing a worse mouse.

Laurence C. Coughlin

I find television very educating. Every time somebody turns on the set, I go into the other room and read a book.

Groucho Marx

TELEVISION ADS
Watching fifteen seconds of nasal passages unblocking sure beats watching thirty seconds.

Barbara Lippert

TEMPER
Your temper is one of your more valuable possessions. Don't lose it.

Bits & Pieces

A tart temper never mellows with age, and a sharp tongue is the only edged tool that grows keener with constant use.

Washington Irving

The worst-tempered people I've ever met were the people who knew they were wrong.

Wilson Mizner

TEMPTATION
Don't worry about temptation – as you grow older, it starts avoiding you.

Old Farmer's Almanac

"Every man has his price." This is not true. But for every man there exists a bait which he cannot resist swallowing.

Friedrich Nietzsche

Few men have virtue to withstand the highest bidder.

George Washington

The only way to get rid of a temptation is to yield to it.

Oscar Wilde

TENACITY

My strength lies solely in my tenacity.

Louis Pasteur

TENNIS

The serve was invented so that the net could play.

Bill Cosby

TENTERHOOKS

Tenterhooks are the upholstery of the anxious seat.

Robert Sherwood

TERRORISM

Fighting the war on terrorism is a big idea that requires international cooperation; invading Iraq is a small idea born of weak leadership and sustained by the credulity of the misled and the lightly informed.

William Milton

Fighting terrorism is like being a goalkeeper. You can make a hundred brilliant saves, but the only shot that people remember is the one that gets past you.

Paul Wilkinson

TEST

The test of a people is what they can do when they're tired.

Winston Churchill

TEXAS TALK

The engine's running, but ain't nobody driving.

It's so dry the trees are bribin' the dogs.

This ain't my first rodeo.

He looks like the dog's been keepin' him under the porch.

Time to paint your butt white and run with the antelope.

Don't that give you the saddle rash?

She could start a fight in an empty house.

He was so ugly his mother borrowed a baby to take to church.

Dumber than a barrel of hair.

Never sign nothin' by neon.

No matter how popular you are, the size of your funeral depends on the weather.

Denser than dog shit.

Two years older than dust.

Unknown

THEATRE

In the theatre, the audience want to be surprised – but by things they expect.

Tristan Bernard

THEORIZE

It is a capital mistake to theorize before one has data.

Arthur Conan Doyle

THEORY

Theory helps us to bear our ignorance of facts.

George Santayana

In theory, there is no difference between theory and practice. In practice, there is.

Jan van de Snepscheut

Don't confuse hypothesis and theory. The former is a possible explanation: the latter the correct one. The establishment of theory is the very purpose of science.

Martin H. Fischer

First a new theory is attacked as absurd; then it is admitted to be true, but obvious and insignificant; finally it is seen to be so important that its adversaries claim that they themselves discovered it.

William James

It is a test of true theories not only to account for but to predict phenomena.

William Whewell

Your theory is crazy, but it's not crazy enough to be true.

Bertolt Brecht

THERAPY

Many a patient, after countless sessions, has quit therapy, because he could detect no perceptible improvement in his shrink's condition.

Brendan Francis

THIEF

If you give to a thief he cannot steal from you, and he is then no longer a thief.

William Saroyan

He that first cries out stop thief, is often he that has stolen the treasure.

William Congreve

THINGS

The best things in life aren't things.

Art Buchwald

THINKING

If you make people think they're thinking, they'll love you; but if you really make them think, they'll hate you.

Don Marquis

Thinking is the hardest work there is, which is the probable reason so few engage in it.

Henry Ford

To think is to differ.

Clarence Darrow

Do not ever mistake a clear view with a short distance.

Bill Gates

Thinking is hard work. One cannot bear burdens and ideas at the same time.

Remy de Gourmont

Think wrongly if you please, but in all cases think for yourself.

Doris Lessing

The mind is everything; what you think, you become.

Buddha

As the shadow follows the body, As we think, so we become.

Buddha

Those who have read about everything are thought to understand everything, too, but it is not always so. Reading furnishes the mind only with materials of knowledge; it is thinking that makes what we read ours. We are of the ruminating kind, and it is not enough to cram ourselves with a great load of collections. We must chew them over again.

William Channing

When the mind is thinking, it is talking to itself.

Plato

Those who have finished by making all others think with them, have usually been those who began by daring to think for themselves.

Charles Caleb Colton

Thinking doesn't seem to help very much. The human brain is too high-powered to have many practical used in this particular universe.

Kurt Vonnegut

If a man sits down to think, he is immediately asked if he has a headache.

Ralph Waldo Emerson

Never be afraid to sit awhile and think.

Lorraine Hansberry

It is godlike ever to think on something beautiful and on something new.

Democritus

Beware when the great God lets loose a thinker on this planet.

Ralph Waldo Emerson

What is the hardest task in the world? To think.

Ralph Waldo Emerson

The real question is not whether machines think but whether men do.

B.F. Skinner

The shrewd guess, the fertile hypothesis, the courageous leap to a tentative conclusion – these are the most valuable coin of the thinker at work.

Jerome Bruner

Do not think what you want to think until you know what you ought to know.

John Crow

And if they think, they fasten their hands upon their hearts.

A.E. Housman

Many people would sooner die than think. In fact, they do so.

Bertrand Russell

There is no expedient to which a man will not resort to avoid the real labour of thinking.

Sir Joshua Reynolds

To most people nothing is more troublesome than the effort of thinking.

Lord Bryce

We haven't got the money, so we've got to think.

> *Ernest Rutherford*

I think, therefore I am.

> *René Descartes*

As long as you're going to be thinking anyway, think big.

> *Donald Trump*

Forbid a man to think for himself or to act for himself and you may add the joy of piracy and the zest of smuggling to his life.

> *Elbert Hubbard*

Think for yourselves and let others enjoy the privilege to do so, too.

> *Voltaire*

Man is only a reed, the weakest thing in nature; but he is a thinking reed.

> *Blaise Pascal*

Never try to discourage thinking, for you are sure to succeed.

> *Bertrand Russell*

THINKING AHEAD
It will be a shock to men when they realize that thoughts that were fast enough for today are not fast enough for tomorrow; but thinking tomorrow's thoughts today is one kind of future life.

> *Christopher Morley*

THOUGHT
The brightest flashes in the world of thought are incomplete until they have been proved to have their counterparts in the world of fact.

> *John Tyndall*

Not a hundredth part of the thoughts in my head have ever been or ever will be spoken or written as long as I keep my senses, at least.

> *Jane Carlyle*

If you jot down every silly thought that pops into your mind, you will soon find out everything you most seriously believe.

> *Mignon McLaughlin*

Many people have played themselves to death. Many people have eaten and drunk themselves to death. Nobody ever thought himself to death.

> *Gilbert Highet*

Profundity of thought belongs to youth, clarity of thought to old age.

> *Friedrich Nietzsche*

As soon as you have made a thought, laugh at it.

> *Lao-Tse*

A thought which does not result in an action is nothing much, and an action which does not proceed from a thought is nothing at all.

> *Georges Bernanos*

Every thought has been thought of before, but the problem is to think of it again.

> *Johann Wolfgang von Goethe*

From the moment of birth we are immersed in action, and can only fitfully guide it by taking thought.

> *Alfred North Whitehead*

Action and faith enslave thought, both of them in order not to be troubled or inconvenienced by reflection, criticism, and doubt.
Henri-Frédéric Amiel

The highest possible stage in moral culture is when we recognize that we ought to control our thoughts.
Charles Darwin

When a thought is too weak to be expressed simply, it should be rejected.
Marquis de Vauvenargues

I think that naught is worth a thought, and I'm a fool for thinking.
W.M. Praed

Along with thoughts which are unworthy of us, we have ones of which we are not worthy.
Edmond Rostand

Chance gives rise to thoughts, and chance removes them; no art can keep or acquire them.
Blaise Pascal

Men use thought only to justify their wrongdoings, and words only to conceal their thoughts.
Voltaire

We find it hard to believe that other people's thoughts are as silly as our own, but they probably are.
James Harvey Robinson

With too much quickness ever to be taught;/With too much thinking to have common thought.
Alexander Pope

The very minute a thought is threatened with publicity it seems to shrink toward mediocrity.
Oliver Wendell Holmes

THOUGHTLESS
The thoughtless are rarely word-less.
Howard W. Newton

THREATS
Threatened folks live longer.
Thomas Fuller, MD

THRIFT
It is thrifty to prepare today for the wants of tomorrow.
Aesop

Men are divided between those who are as thrifty as if they would live forever, and those who are as extravagant as if they were going to die the next day.
Aristotle

Though you live near a forest, do not waste firewood.
Chinese proverb

Thrift is the really romantic thing; economy is more romantic than extravagance ... thrift is poetic because it is creative; waste is unpoetic because it is waste ... if a man could undertake to use all of the things in his dustbin, he would be a broader genius than Shakespeare.
G.K. Chesterton

There are no alternatives to thrift in the absence of money.
Scottish proverb

Thrift comes too late when you find it at the bottom of your purse.
Seneca

Beware of little expenses; a small leak will sink a great ship.
Benjamin Franklin

THRONE

You can build a throne with bayonets, but you can't sit on it for long.
Boris Yeltsin

THROW

Never be afraid of throwing away what you have. If you can throw it away, it is not really yours.
R.H. Tawney

TIDE

A single breaker may recede; but the tide is eventually coming in.
Thomas Babington Macaulay

TIME

It is an undoubted truth, that the less one has to do, the less time one finds to do it in.
Lord Chesterfield

Time is the small change of eternity.

Irving Layton

Time is the friend of the wonderful company, the enemy of the mediocre.

Warren Buffett

Vladimir: "That passed the time."/Estragon: "It would have passed in any case."/Vladimir: "Yes, but not so rapidly."

Samuel Beckett

Time spent getting even is better spent getting ahead.

Anonymous

Nothing, of course, begins at the time you think it did.

Lillian Hellman

Those who make the worst use of their time are the first to complain of its brevity.

Jean de La Bruyère

If you want to kill time, why not try working it to death?

Sam Levenson

For time will teach ye soon the truth.

Henry Wadsworth Longfellow

Dost thou love life? Then do not squander time, for that's the stuff life is made of.

Benjamin Franklin

Half our life is spent trying to find something to do with the time we have rushed through life trying to save.

Will Rogers

Time's fun when you're having flies.

Kermit the Frog

Nothing really belongs to us but time, which even he has who has nothing else.

Baltasar Gracian

A stitch in time would have confused Einstein.

Frank Baer

If time be of all things most precious, wasting time must be the

greatest prodigality, since lost time is never found again; and what we call time enough always proves little enough. Let us then be up and be doing, and doing to the purpose; so by diligence we shall do more with less perplexity.
Benjamin Franklin

The butterfly counts not months but moments and has time enough.
Rabindranath Tagore

Wait for the wisest of all counselors, time.
Pericles

Be ruled by time, the wisest counselor of all.
Plutarch

Again the shadow moveth o'er the dial-plate of time.
John Greenleaf Whittier

There is never enough time, unless you are serving it.
Malcolm Forbes

The innocent and the beautiful/ Have no enemy but time.
William Butler Yeats

Time hath a taming hand.
John Henry Newman

Time flies when you're having fun; even when you're not.
Ells MacNeil

A time to get and a time to lose, a time to keep and a time to cast away.
Ecclesiastes 3:6

Remember that time is money.
Benjamin Franklin

Time shall teach thee all things.
Martin Farquhar Tupper

Ah! The clock is always slow;/It is later than you think.
Robert Service

There must be something drastically wrong when a man starts wishing time away. Time was given us like jewels to spend, and it's the ultimate sacrilege to wish it away.
Sloan Wilson

Time is of the essence.
Anonymous

Time goes, you say? Ah no! Alas, Time stays, we go.
Henry Austin Dobson

You may delay, but time will not.
Benjamin Franklin

But at my back I always hear/Time's winged chariot hurrying near.
Andrew Marvell

Every time I ask what time it is, I get a different answer.
Henny Youngman

Now is the time for all good men to come to.
Walt Kelly

The bell strikes one. We take no note of time/But from its loss.
Edward Young

Time has a wonderful way of showing us what really matters.
Margaret Peters

Time is no law of nature. It is a plan. When you look at it with awareness, or start to touch it, then it starts to disintegrate.

Peter Hoeg

Nothing great is created suddenly, any more than a bunch of grapes or a fig. If you tell me that you desire a fig, I answer you that there must be time. Let it first blossom, then bear fruit, then ripen.

Epictetus

TIMING
Observe due measure, for right timing is in all things the most important factor.

Hesiod

If you trap the moment before it's ripe,/The tears of repentance you'll certainly wipe;/But if once you let the ripe moment go,/You can never wipe off the tears of woe.

William Blake

Sometimes, when they say you're ahead of your time, it's just a polite way of saying you have a real bad sense of timing.

George McGovern

First things first, second things never.

Shirley Conran

Even a correct decision is wrong when it is taken too late.

Lee Iacocca

A great man always considers the timing before he acts.

Chinese proverb

We must beat the iron while it is hot, but we polish it at leisure.

John Dryden

A man of sense knows when he pleases or is irksome; he goes away the very minute before it might have been thought he stayed too long.

Jean de La Bruyère

Now is not the hour that requires such help, nor those defenders.

Virgil

You're leaping over the hedge before you come to the stile.

Miguel de Cervantes

The reason I beat the Austrians is, they did not know the value of five minutes.

Napoleon Bonaparte

TOBACCO
Usually we trust that nature has a master plan. But what was it she expected to do with tobacco?

Bill Vaughan

TODAY
Believe me, wise men do not say, "I shall live to do that"; tomorrow life's too late: live today.

Martial

TOGETHER
We are all in this together – by ourselves.

Lily Tomlin

TOGETHERNESS
Constant togetherness is fine – but only for Siamese twins.

Victoria Billings

TOLERANCE

If it was necessary to tolerate in other people everything that one permits oneself, life would be unbearable.

Georges Courteline

When I was very young, I was disgracefully intolerant but when I passed the thirty mark I prided myself on having learned the beautiful lesson that all things were good, and equally good. That, however, was really laziness. Now, thank goodness, I've sorted out what matters and what doesn't. And I'm beginning to be intolerant again.

G.B. Stern

Tolerance merely means putting up with people, being able to stand things.

E.M. Forster

Tolerance is a tremendous virtue, but the immediate neighbours of tolerance are apathy and weakness.

Sir James Goldsmith

Say now Shibboleth; and he said Sibboleth, for he could not frame to pronounce it right. Then they took him and slew him.

Judges 12:6

The test of courage comes when we are in the minority. The test of tolerance comes when we are in the majority.

Ralph W. Stockman

Once lead these people into a war and they will forget there ever was such a thing as tolerance.

Woodrow Wilson

What is toleration? It is the prerogative of humanity. We are all steeped in weaknesses and errors: Let us forgive one another's follies, it is the first law of nature.

Voltaire

Tolerance: another word for indifference.

W. Somerset Maugham

TOMORROW

If you wait for tomorrow, tomorrow comes. If you don't wait for tomorrow, tomorrow comes.

Malinke (West African) proverb

When I consider life, 'tis all a cheat;/ Yet, fooled with hope, men favour the deceit;/Trust on, and think tomorrow will repay./ Tomorrow's false than the former day.

John Dryden

TONGUE

Beware the tongue. It's normally wet and likely to slip.

Unknown

TOOLS

Men have become the tools of their tools.

Henry David Thoreau

Look for a tough wedge for a tough job.

Publilius Syrus

Give us the tools and we will finish the job.

Winston Churchill

TOP

There is always room at the top.

Daniel Webster

TORONTO

This is the second time I have performed in Toronto, not counting my honeymoon.

Carol Lawrence

Indeed I have always found that the only thing in regard to Toronto which far-away people know for certain is that McGill University is in it.

Stephen Leacock

TORTOISE

A tortoise on the right path will beat a racer on the wrong path.

Francis Bacon

TOUPEE

No matter how well a toupee blends in the back, in front it always looks like hell.

Leonard Louis Levinson

TRADITION

Tradition may be defined as an extension of the franchise. Tradition means giving votes to the most obscure of all classes, our ancestors. ... Democracy tells us not to neglect a good man's opinion, even if he is our groom; tradition asks us not to neglect a good man's opinion, even if he is our father.

G.K. Chesterton

Tradition is a guide and not a jailer.

W. Somerset Maugham

Tradition is entirely different from habit, even from an excellent habit, since habit is by definition an unconscious acquisition and tends to become mechanical, whereas tradition results from a conscious and deliberate acceptance ... Tradition presupposes the reality of what endures.

Igor Stravinsky

Traditions deserve to be respected only insofar as they are respectable – that is, exactly insofar as they themselves respect the fundamental rights of men and women.

Amin Maalouf

TRADITIONALISTS

Traditionalists are pessimists about the future and optimists about the past.

Lewis Mumford

TRAGEDY

The bad end unhappily, the good unluckily. That is what tragedy means.

Tom Stoppard

TRANSITION

Life is pleasant. Death is peaceful. It's the transition that's troublesome.

Isaac Asimov

TRAP

I don't want the cheese; I just want to get out of the trap.

Latin American proverb

He who digs a hole for another may fall in himself.

Russian proverb

Man needs to know but little more than a lobster to catch him in his traps.

Henry David Thoreau

Brains, your Majesty! It had none, or it would never have fallen into your trap.

Aesop

TRAVEL

Travelling is almost like talking with men of other centuries.

René Descartes

The use of travelling is to regulate imagination by reality, and, instead of thinking how things may be, to see them as they are.

Samuel Johnson

The person who finds his homeland sweet is still a tender beginning; the person to whom every soil is a native one is already strong; but he is perfect to whom every soil is as a foreign land.

Hugo of St Victor

The only aspect of our travels that is interesting to others is disaster.

Martha Gellman

Travelling through hyperspace ain't like dusting crops, boy.

George Lucas

I was born and raised in a neighborhood called Noah's Ark. If you didn't travel in pairs, you just didn't travel.

Stanley Shapiro

To travel is to discover that everyone is wrong about other countries.

Aldous Huxley

Modern travelling is not travelling at all; it is merely being sent to a place, and very little different from becoming a parcel.

John Ruskin

Yet there isn't a train I wouldn't take, No matter where it's going.

Edna St Vincent Millay

A man travels the world over in search of what he needs and returns home to find it.

George Moore

Travel makes a wise man better but a fool worse.

Thomas Fuller, MD

TRAVELLERS

The trouble with many travellers is that they take themselves along.

Joseph Prescott

TREACHERY

Treachery and violence are spears pointed at both ends; they wound those who resort to them worse than their enemies.

Emily Brontë

TREASON
Treason doth never prosper: what's the reason?/For if it prosper, none dare call it treason.
John Harrington

TREES
I like trees because they seem more resigned to the way they have to live than other things do.
Willa Cather

He that plants trees loves others beside himself.
Thomas Fuller, MD

As the poet said, "Only God can make a tree," probably because it's so hard to figure out how to get the bark on.
Woody Allen

TRIAL (FAIR)
The defendant is entitled to a fair trial before I hang him.
"Hanging" Judge Jeffreys

TRICKS
Everybody has some tricks they can do, but each has his own way of doing them.
Chinese proverb

The most ingenious men continually pretend to condemn tricking – but this is often done that they may use it more conveniently themselves, when some great occasion or interest offers itself to them.
François, duc de La Rochefoucauld

The craftiest trickery is too short and ragged a cloak to cover a bad heart.
Johann Kaspar Lavater

TRIFLES
Trifles make the sum of human things, /And half our misery from our foibles springs.
Hannah Moore

To throw away the dearest thing he owned /As 'twere a careless trifle.
William Shakespeare

TRIUMPH
Oh! Wherefore come ye forth in triumph from the north?
Thomas Babington Macaulay

If you can meet with Triumph and Disaster/And treat those two imposters just the same…
Rudyard Kipling

TROUBLE
Most of the trouble in the world is caused by people wanting to be important.
T.S. Eliot

When an elephant is in trouble, even a frog will kick him.
Hindu proverb

Troubles hurt most when they prove self-inflicted.
Sophocles

It is a painful thing/To look at your own trouble and know/That you yourself and no one else has made it.
Sophocles

Many a man's tongue broke his nose.

Seamus MacManus

There's one thing said for inviting trouble: it generally accepts.

May Maloo

People could survive their normal all right if it weren't for the trouble they make for themselves.

Ogden Nash

Half the trouble in this world comes from saying "yes" too quick, and "no" not soon enough.

American saying

Most troubles only come because we go halfway to meet them.

Duc de Lévis

If there must be trouble let it be in my day, that my child may have peace.

Thomas Paine

She would take any amount of trouble to avoid trouble.

Willa Cather

Sometimes trouble is more fun than stagnation.

Clarence Budington Kelland

TRUE
Be so true to thyself, as thou be not false to others.

Francis Bacon

This above all: to thine own self be true,/And it must follow as the night the day/Thou canst not then be false to any man.

William Shakespeare

A thing is not necessarily true because it is badly uttered, nor false because spoken magnificently.

St Augustine

TRUST
Trust thyself only, and another shall not betray thee.

Thomas Fuller, MD

It's a vice to trust all, and equally a vice to trust none.

Seneca

It is an equal failing to trust everybody and to trust nobody.

Thomas Fuller, MD

We distrust our heart too much, and our head not enough.

Joseph Roux

A man who doesn't trust himself can never really trust anyone else.

Cardinal de Retz

I wonder men dare trust themselves with men.

William Shakespeare

Put your trust in God, my boys, and keep your powder dry!

Valentine Blacker

Trust everybody, but cut the cards.

Finley Peter Dunne

After all, one never trusts anyone that one has deceived.

Jonathan Lynn and Sir Antony Jay

Before you trust a man, eat a peck of salt with him.

Anonymous

Even brothers should keep careful accounts.

Chinese proverb

The only way to make a man trustworthy is to trust him.

Henry Lewis Stimson

Never put anything on paper, my boy, and never trust a man with a small black moustache.

P.G. Wodehouse

We have to distrust each other: it is our only defence against betrayal.

Tennessee Williams

To be trusted is a greater compliment than to be loved.

George Macdonald

TRUTH
And ye shall know the truth, and the truth shall make you free.

John 8:32

Ye shall know the truth, and the truth shall make you mad.

Aldous Huxley

Truth has bounds; Error has none.

William Blake

An error cannot be believed sincerely enough to make it a truth.

Robert G. Ingersoll

Truth is mighty and will prevail. There is nothing the matter with this, except that it ain't so.

Mark Twain

One has only to think of the sinister possibilities of the radio, state-controlled education and so forth, to realize that "truth is great and will prevail" is a prayer rather than an axiom.

George Orwell

There are truths on this side of the Pyrenees, which are falsehoods on the other.

Blaise Pascal

What a word is truth. Slippery, tricky, unreliable.

Lillian Hellman

That which has always been accepted by everyone, everywhere, is almost certain to be false.

Paul Valéry

The (pure and simple) truth is rarely pure, and never simple.

Oscar Wilde

Artistic growth is, more than it is anything else, a refining of the sense of truthfulness. The stupid believe that to be truthful is easy; only the artist, the great artist, knows how difficult it is.

Willa Cather

Just as most issues are seldom black or white, so are most good solutions seldom black or white. Beware of the solution that requires one side to be totally the loser and the other side to be totally the winner. The reason there are two sides to begin with usually is because neither side has all the facts. Therefore, when the wise mediator effects a compromise, he is not acting from political motivation. Rather, he is acting from a deep sense of respect for the whole truth.

Stephen R. Schwambach

Beware of half-truths: you may have gotten the wrong half.

> *Unknown*

It has always been desirable to tell the truth, but seldom if ever necessary.

> *Arthur Balfour*

Pure truth hath no man seen nor e'er shall know.

> *Xenophanes*

I would rather offend with the truth, than please with adulation.

> *Seneca*

Truth is more a stranger than fiction.

> *Mark Twain*

Why *shouldn't* truth be stranger than fiction? Fiction, after all, has to make sense.

> *Mark Twain*

Truth is stranger than fiction, but it is because fiction is obliged to stick to possibilities: truth isn't.

> *Mark Twain*

There was things which he stretched, but mainly he told the truth.

> *Mark Twain*

Every violation of truth is not only a sort of suicide in the liar, but is a stab at the health of human society.

> *Ralph Waldo Emerson*

It is hard to believe that a man is telling you the truth when you know that you would lie if you were in his place.

> *H.L. Mencken*

The scornful nostril and the high head gather not the odors that lie on the track of truth.

> *George Eliot*

Truth is the daughter of time, not of authority.

> *Francis Bacon*

The truth is more important than the facts.

> *Frank Lloyd Wright*

Whoever is careless with the truth in small matters cannot be trusted with important matters.

> *Albert Einstein*

Men stumble over the truth from time to time, but most pick themselves up and hurry off as if nothing happened.

> *Winston Churchill*

I should think it hardly possible to state the opposite of the truth with more precision.

> *Winston Churchill*

Truth never damages a cause that is just.

> *Mohandas Gandhi*

The truth would become more popular if it were not always stating ugly facts.

> *Henry S. Haskins*

Truth exists; only falsehood has to be invented.

> *Georges Braque*

What probably distorts everything in life is that one is convinced that one is speaking the truth because one says what one thinks.

> *Sacha Guitry*

All truth is good, but not all truth is good to say.

African proverb

Opinion is a flitting thing,/But Truth outlasts the Sun/If then we cannot own them both/Possess the oldest one.

Emily Dickinson

If you always tell the truth you don't have to remember anything.

Mark Twain

Truth is the most valuable thing we have. Let us economize it.

Mark Twain

The dictum that truth always triumphs over persecution is one of those pleasant falsehoods which men repeat after one another til they pass into commonplace, but which all experience refutes.

John Stuart Mill

We have reached an uncomfortable impasse. We need belief to make life meaningful, yet we cannot allow ourselves to believe in anything. Every faith, institution, political faction, and ideal has proved at some level to be a tissue of hypocrisy. We decry our own cynicism, but recognize that, at some level, it is merely realism. Some [people] retreat into conventional orthodoxies; others free-float, aimless in an increasingly valueless society. But there is another alternative: starting from scratch to see if we may discover for ourselves something like universal truth and build the whole thing over again.

Richard Nilsen

The greatest homage to truth is to use it.

Ralph Waldo Emerson

Every truth has two sides; it is well to look at both, before we commit ourselves to either.

Aesop

Pushing any truth out very far, you are met by a counter-truth.

Henry Ward Beecher

The pursuit of truth is like picking raspberries. You miss a lot if you approach it from only one angle.

Randal Marlin

All great truths begin as blasphemies.

George Bernard Shaw

Believe those who seek the truth. Doubt those who find it.

André Gide

Nobody speaks the truth when there is something they must have.

Elizabeth Bowen

Speak the truth, but leave immediately after.

Slovenian proverb

You can't win: if you tell lies, you'll be distrusted; if you tell the truth, you'll be disliked.

Jean Anouilh

There are certain persons for whom pure truth is a poison.

André Maurois

How often have I said to you that when you have eliminated the impossible, whatever remains, however improbable, must be the truth?

Arthur Conan Doyle

In the long run, a harmful truth is better than a useful lie.

Thomas Mann

Something unpleasant is coming when men are anxious to tell the truth.

Benjamin Disraeli

No blame should attach to telling the truth. But it does, it does.

Anita Brookner

Truth is a pathless land, and you cannot approach it by any path whatsoever, by any religion, by any sect.

J. Krishnamurti

The discovery of truth is prevented more effectively, not by the false appearance things present and which mislead into error … but by preconceived opinion, by prejudice.

Arthur Schopenhauer

As a general thing, if you want to get at the truth of a particular argument, hear both sides and believe neither.

Josh Billings

The truth is too simple: one must always get there by a complicated route.

George Sand

He who does not bellow the truth when he knows the truth makes himself the accomplice of liars and forgers.

Charles Péguy

If you do not tell the truth about yourself, you cannot tell it about other people.

Virginia Woolf

It is always the best policy to tell the truth, unless, of course, you are an exceptionally good liar.

Jerome K. Jerome

'Tis strange – but true; for truth is always strange;/Stranger than fiction.

Lord Byron

Truth is always duller than fiction.

Piers Paul Read

The reason for the sadness of the modern age and the men who live in it is that it looks for the truth in everything and finds it.

Edmond and Jules de Goncourt

What I tell you three times is true.

Lewis Carroll

There are no new truths, but only truths that have not been recognized by those who have perceived them without noticing. A truth is something that everybody can be shown to know and to have known, as people say, all along.

Mary McCarthy

Everything deep is also simple and can be reproduced simply as long as its reference to the whole truth is maintained. But what matters is not what is witty but what is true.

Albert Schweitzer

What is truth? said jesting Pilate, and would not stay for an answer.

Francis Bacon

All truths are easy to understand once they are discovered; the point is to discover them.

Galileo Galilei

The great enemy of the truth is very often not the lie – deliberate, contrived and dishonest – but the myth – persistent, persuasive and unrealistic.

John F. Kennedy

The truth does not change according to our ability to stomach it.

Flannery O'Connor

The full truth of this odd matter is what the world has long been looking for, and public curiosity is sure to welcome.

Robert Louis Stevenson

Truth, like a torch, the more it's shook it shines.

Sir William Hamilton

The number of human beings who want to see the truth is extraordinarily small. What dominates mankind is fear of the truth, unless truth is useful to them.

Henri-Frédéric Amiel

It is one thing to show a man that he is in error and another to put him in possession of the truth.

John Locke

If one tells the truth, one is sure, sooner or later, to be found out.

Oscar Wilde

Fraud and falsehood only dread examination. Truth invites it.

Samuel Johnson

When honour and truth are at odds, let truth prevail.

José Raúl Bernardo

TRYING
For us, there is only the trying.

T.S. Eliot

Ever tried. Ever failed. No matter. Try again. Fail again. Fail better.

Samuel Beckett

TUNNEL
If you can see the light at the end of the tunnel, you are looking the wrong way.

Barry Commoner

TWO-FACED
If I were two-faced, would I be wearing this one?

Abraham Lincoln

TYPING
I type 101 words a minute. But it's in my own language.

Unknown

TYRANNY
Where law ends, tyranny begins.

William Pitt

If they take you in the morning, they will be coming for us that night.

James Baldwin

Tyranny is always better organized than freedom.

Charles Péguy

TYRANTS
So long as men worship the Caesars and Napoléons, Caesars and Napoléons will arise to make them miserable.

Aldous Huxley

No man can terrorize a whole nation unless we are all his accomplices.

Edward R. Murrow

Today the tyrant rules not by club or fist, but, disguised as a market researcher, he shepherds his flocks in the ways of utility and comfort.

Marshall McLuhan

In every tyrant's heart there springs in the end this poison, that he cannot trust a friend.

Aeschylus

UGLY
There are no ugly women, only lazy ones.
Helena Rubinstein

ULCERS
I don't get ulcers, I give them.
Samuel Bronfman

UMBRELLA
An umbrella is of no avail against a Scotch mist.
James Russell Lowell

UNANIMITY
You only find complete unanimity in a cemetery.
Abel Aganbegyan

UNCERTAINTY
All uncertainty is fruitful ... so long as it is accompanied by the wish to understand.
Antonio Machado

The quest for certainty blocks the search for meaning. Uncertainty is the very condition to impel man to unfold his powers.
Erich Fromm

There is nothing so uncertain as a sure thing.
Scotty Bowman

UNCONSTITUTIONAL
The illegal we can do right now; the unconstitutional will take a little longer.
Henry Kissinger

UNDERDOGS
You will never find an Englishmen among the underdogs – except in England, of course.
Evelyn Waugh

UNDERGRADUATE
There is no more vulnerable human combination than an undergraduate.
John Sloan Dickey

UNDERSTANDING
One half of the world cannot understand the pleasures of the other.
Jane Austen

Understanding is a two-way street.
Eleanor Roosevelt

This has been a most wonderful evening. Gertrude [Stein] has said things tonight it will take her ten years to understand.
Alice B. Toklas

I hear and I forget. I see and I remember. I do and I understand.
Chinese proverb

Seeing through is rarely seeing into.
Elizabeth Bibesco

Not only is there but one way of doing things rightly, but there is only one way of seeing them, and that is, seeing the whole of them.
John Ruskin

Too much light often blinds gentlemen of this sort. They cannot see the forest for the trees.
Christoph M. Wieland

It takes a long time to understand nothing.
Edward Dahlberg

To be surprised, to wonder, is to begin to understand.
José Ortega y Gasset

To be totally understanding makes one very indulgent.
Madame de Staël

How can you expect a man who's warm to understand one who's cold?
Alexandr Solzhenitsyn

No law or ordinance is mightier than understanding.
Plato

Being understood is not the most essential thing in life.
Jodie Foster

If you do not understand a man, you cannot crush him. And if you do understand him, very probably you will not.
G.K. Chesterton

UNEXPLORED
In everything there is an unexplored element because we are prone by habit to use our eyes only in combination with the memory of what others before us have thought about the thing we are looking at. The most insignificant thing contains some little unknown element. We must find it.
Guy de Maupassant

UNHAPPINESS
The most intelligent young people in Western countries tend to have that kind of unhappiness that comes of finding no adequate employment for their best talents.
Bertrand Russell

Unhappiness is not knowing what we want and killing ourselves to get it.
Don Herold

Men who are unhappy, like men who sleep badly, are always proud of the fact.
Bertrand Russell

UNIFICATION
Observe the invincible tendency of the mind to unify. It is a law of our constitution that we should not

contemplate things apart without the effort to arrange them in order with known facts and ascribe them to the same law.

Ralph Waldo Emerson

UNITED NATIONS

To succeed at the United Nations requires a combination of protocol, geritol, and alcohol.

Unknown

UNIQUENESS

Always remember that you are absolutely unique. Just like everyone else.

Margaret Mead

Nature made him and then broke the mold.

Ludovico Ariosto

UNITY

When spider webs unite, they can tie up a lion.

Ethiopian proverb

What the heck do the words matter, long as we sing the same tune.

Seth Akins

Real unity tolerates dissent and rejoices in variety of outlook and tradition, recognizes that it is man's destiny to unite and not to divide.

Northrop Frye

UNIVERSE

The universe is full of magical things, patiently waiting for our wits to grow sharper.

Eden Phillpotts

To a man of the world, the universe is a suburb.

Elizabeth Bibesco

The universe is a big place, perhaps the biggest.

Kurt Vonnegut

Suppose that I came to the outer limits of the universe. If I now thrust out a stick, what would I find?

Archytas

There is no chance and anarchy in the universe. All is system and gradation.

Ralph Waldo Emerson

If you want to make an apple pie from scratch, you must first create the universe.

Carl Sagan

Not only are we not at the centre of the universe, but we're not even made of the same stuff as most of the universe.

David Caldwell

Just because some of us can read and write and do a little math, that doesn't mean we deserve to conquer the universe.

Kurt Vonnegut

If it's true that our species is alone in the universe, then I'd have to say the universe aimed rather low and settled for very little.

George Carlin

UNIVERSITY

The university brings out all abilities, including incapability.

Anton Chekhov

The first duty of a university is to teach wisdom, not a trade; character, not technicalities. We want a lot of engineers in the modern world, but we don't want a world of engineers.

Winston Churchill

A university should be a place of light, of liberty, and of learning.

Benjamin Disraeli

The most important function of the university in an age of reason is to protect reason from itself.

Allan Bloom

University politics are vicious precisely because the stakes are so small.

Henry Kissinger

In my day, the principal concerns of university students were sex, smoking dope, rioting, and learning. Learning was something you did only when the first three weren't available.

Bill Bryson

The quality of a university is measured more by the kind of student it turns out than the kind it takes in.

Robert Kibbee

Our major universities are now stuck with an army of pedestrian, toadying careerists, Fifties types who wave around Sixties banners to conceal their record of ruthless, beaverlike tunneling to the top.

Camille Paglia

At best, most college presidents are running something that is somewhere between a faltering corporation and a hotel.

Leon Botstein

University degrees are a bit like adultery: you may not want to get involved with that sort of thing, but you don't want to be thought incapable.

Peter Imbert

Is God a Yale man?

Wilmarth Lewis

I was a modest, good-humored boy. It is Oxford that has made me insufferable.

Max Beerbohm

I often think how much easier the world would have been to manage if Herr Hitler and Signor Mussolini had been at Oxford.

Edward Wood

Four years was enough of Harvard. I still had a lot to learn, but had been given the liberating notion that now I could teach myself.

John Updike

In universities and intellectual circles, academics can guarantee themselves popularity – or, which is just as satisfying, unpopularity by being opinionated rather than by being learned.

A.N. Wilson

There is only one justification for universities. They must be centres of criticism.

Robert M. Hutchins

UNKNOWN

Whoever starts out toward the unknown must consent to venture alone.

André Gide

To the man in the street, it has always seemed miraculous that anyone should turn aside from the beaten track with its known destinations, and strike out on the steep and narrow path leading into the unknown. Hence it was always believed that such a man, if not actually crazy, was possessed by a demon or a god; for the miracle of a man being able to act otherwise than as humanity has always acted could only be explained by the gift of demonic power or divine spirit.

Carl Jung

Give me a light that I may tread safely into the unknown.

Minnie Louise Haskins

As a result of a general defect of nature, we are either more confident or more fearful of unusual and unknown things.

Julius Caesar

Penetrating so many secrets, we cease to believe in the Unknown. But there it sits, nevertheless, calmly licking its chops.

H.L. Mencken

UNPREDICTABILITY

Unpredictability, too, can become monotonous.

Eric Hoffer

There is many a slip 'twixt the cup and the lip.

Palladas

UNSEEN

Greet the unseen with a cheer!

Robert Browning

UNTHINKABLE

We must dare to think about "unthinkable things," because when things become "unthinkable," thinking stops and action becomes mindless.

J. William Fulbright

UPBRINGING

I was brought up to believe that the only thing worth doing was to add to the sum of accurate information in the world.

Margaret Mead

I think she must have been very strictly brought up, she's so desperately anxious to do the wrong thing correctly.

Saki

UPS AND DOWNS

It is a truth universally acknowledged that as soon as one part of your life starts looking up, another falls to pieces.

Helen Fielding

USELESS

To be employed in useless things is half to be idle.

Thomas Fuller, MD

USERS

Why is it drug addicts and computer aficionados are both called users?

Clifford Stoll

USURY

No man of ripe years and of sound mind, acting freely, and with his eyes open, ought to be hindered … from making such a bargain, in the way of obtaining money, as he see fit.

Jeremy Bentham

UTILITY

Utility is our national shibboleth: the saviour of the American businessman is fact and his uterine half-brother, statistics.

Edward Dahlberg

They say everything in the world is good for something.

John Dryden

UTOPIA

An acre in Middlesex is better than a principality in Utopia.

Thomas Babington Macaulay

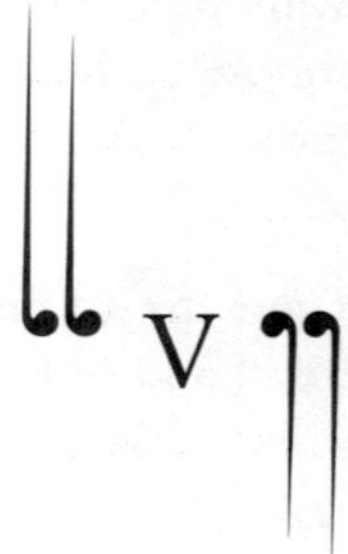

VACUUM
Living in a vacuum sucks.
Adrienne E. Gusoff

VAGUENESS
There cannot be a precise answer
to a vague question.
Samuel Johnson

If you can't be kind, at least be
vague.
Judith Martin

Even vagueness can be explicit if it
is explained well enough.
Dr Edward J. Pfeiffer

Everything is vague to a degree you
do not realize til you have tried to
make it precise.
Bertrand Russell

VALIANT
I love the valiant, but it is not
enough to wield a broadsword;
one must also know against whom.
Friedrich Nietzsche

VALUE
The only thing in the world of
value is the active soul.
Ralph Waldo Emerson

The value of a sentiment is the
amount of sacrifice you are prepared to make for it.
John Galsworthy

Everything is worth what its pur-
chaser will pay for it.
Publilius Syrus

Anything that has real and lasting
value is always a gift from within.
Franz Kafka

Try not to become a man of success, but rather try to become a
man of value.
Albert Einstein

VALUES
Our scientific power has outrun
our spiritual power. We have
guided missiles and misguided
men.
Dr Martin Luther King, Jr

Values are tapes we play on the Walkman of the mind; any tune we choose so long as it does not disturb others.

Jonathan Sacks

There are so many who can figure costs, and so few who can measure values.

Unknown

VAMPIRES

The thing about vampires, is that they provide an opportunity to make a meditation on death.

Neil Jordan

VANITY

The highest form of vanity is love of fame.

George Santayana

Vanity plays lurid tricks with our memory.

Joseph Conrad

Vanity makes men ridiculous, pride odious, and ambition terrible.

Sir Richard Steele

Vanity and pride are different things, though the words are often used synonymously. A person may be proud without being vain. Pride relates more to our opinion of ourselves; vanity to what we would have others think of us.

Jane Austen

Women are less vain than men. This has been my experience.

Yousuf Karsh

If there is a single quality that is shared by all great men, it is vanity. But I mean by "vanity" only that they appreciate their own worth. Without this kind of vanity they would not be great. And with vanity alone, of course, a man is nothing.

Yousuf Karsh

Vanity is other people's pride.

Sacha Guitry

VARIATION

Change is upsetting. Repetition is tedious. Three cheers for variation.

Mason Cooley

VARIETY

No pleasure endures unseasoned by variety.

Publilius Syrus

VEGETARIAN

I am not a vegetarian because I love animals; I am a vegetarian because I hate plants.

A. Whitney Brown

A vegetarian is a person who won't eat anything that can have children.

David Brenner

Why is it that when vegetarians come to you, you're expected to provide food for them, but if you went to their house, you'd never say, "I can't eat this muck. Would you grill me a thick steak?"

Simon Hoggart

VENICE
Venice is like eating an entire box of chocolate liqueurs in one go.
Truman Capote

VERBAL SKILLS
A study in the *Washington Post* says that women have better verbal skills than men. I just want to say to the authors of that study: Duh.
Conan O'Brien

VERBOSITY
Verbosity leads to unclear, inarticulate things.
Dan Quayle

VERDICT
The verdict of the world is conclusive.
St Augustine

VERIFICATION
The meaning of a proposition is the method of its verification.
Moritz Schlick

VICE
There will be vices as long as there are men.
Tacitus

Virtues and vices are of a strange nature; for the more we have, the fewer we think we have.
Anonymous

It is the function of vice to keep virtue within reasonable bounds.
Samuel Butler

We make a ladder of our vices if we trample them underfoot.
St Augustine

When the vices give us up we flatter ourselves that we are giving them up.
François, duc de La Rochefoucauld

How like herrings and onions our vices are in the morning after we have committed them.
Samuel Taylor Coleridge

To vice, innocence must always seem only a superior kind of chicanery.
Ouida

VICIOUS
You can't expect a boy to be vicious til he's been to a good school.
Saki

VICTIMS
I hate victims who respect their executioners.
Jean-Paul Sartre

VICTOR
The victor belongs to the spoils.
F. Scott Fitzgerald

Victor and vanquished never unite in substantial agreement.
Tacitus

VICTORY
Victory is by nature insolent and haughty.
Cicero

The war horse is a vain hope for victory.

Psalm 33:17

Victory has a hundred fathers, but defeat is an orphan.

Count Galeazzo Ciano

Once you hear the details of victory, it is hard to distinguish it from a defeat.

Jean-Paul Sartre

The moment of victory is much too short to live for that and nothing else.

Martina Navratilova

Those who know how to win are much more numerous than those who know how to make proper use of their victories.

Polybius

Victory is won not in miles but in inches. Win a little now, hold your ground, and later, win a little more.

Louis L'Amour

There is no substitute for victory.

Douglas MacArthur

Victories that are cheap are cheap. Those only are worth having which come as the result of hard fighting.

Henry Ward Beecher

Another such victory over the Romans, and we are undone.

Pyrrhus of Epirus

VIDEO GAMES

Video games are bad for you? That's what they said about rock 'n' roll.

Shigeru Miyamoto

VIEWPOINT

How strange it is to see with how much passion/People see things only in their own fashion!

Molière

VILLAGE

A man's village is his peace of mind.

Anwar Sadat

VILLAIN

One may smile, and smile, and be a villain.

William Shakespeare

VIOLENCE

Violence is the last refuge of the incompetent.

Salvor Hardin

Victory attained by violence is tantamount to a defeat, for it is momentary.

Mohandas Gandhi

Violence is not a knife in the hand. It grows like a poison tree inside other people who have not learned to value other human beings.

Frances Lawrence

If I die a violent death, as some fear and a few are plotting, I know that the violence will be in the thought and the actions of the assassins, not in my dying.

Indira Gandhi

No society that feeds its children on tales of successful violence can expect them not to believe that violence in the end is rewarded.

Margaret Mead

Violence kills what it intends to create.

Pope John Paul II

For me, violence is profoundly moral, more moral than transactions and compromises.

Benito Mussolini

Non-violence is a flop. The only bigger flop is violence.

Joan Baez

I'm a student of violence because I'm a student of the human heart.

Sam Peckinpah

Violence is not power, but the absence of power.

Ralph Waldo Emerson

VIRTUE
Virtue has never been as respectable as money.

Mark Twain

Sincerity and truth are the basis of every virtue.

Confucius

Successful and fortunate crime is called virtue.

Seneca

Virtue is not left to stand alone. He who practises it will have neighbours.

Confucius

Search others for virtues, thyself for vices.

English proverb

A large part of virtue consists in good habits.

Barbara Paley

Amusements are to. virtue, like breezes of air to the flame; gentle ones will fan it, but strong ones will put it out.

David Thomas

Fine words and an insinuating appearance are seldom associated with true virtue.

Confucius

First secure an independent income, then practise virtue.

Greek saying

To be innocent is to be not guilty; but to be virtuous is to overcome our evil inclinations.

William Penn

Virtue consists, not in abstaining from vice, but in not desiring it.

George Bernard Shaw

Virtue is bold, and goodness never fearful.

William Shakespeare

The cardinal virtue was no longer to love one's country. It was to feel compassion for one's fellow men and women.

Noel Annan

Virtue is its own punishment.

Aneurin Bevan

The most glorious exploits do not always furnish us with the clearest discoveries of virtue or vice in men.

Plutarch

He has all of the virtues I dislike and none of the vices I admire.

Winston Churchill

Who can tell the mischief which the very virtuous do?
William Makepeace Thackeray

It has been my experience that folks who have no vices have very few virtues.
Abraham Lincoln

Many wish not so much to be virtuous, as to seem to be.
Cicero

I think no virtue goes with size.
Ralph Waldo Emerson

The love of economy is the root of all virtue.
George Bernard Shaw

VIRUSES
I think computer viruses should count as life. I think it says something about human nature that the only form of life we have created so far is purely destructive. We've created life in our own image.
Stephen Hawking

VISION
Every man takes the limits of his own field of vision for the limits of the world.
Arthur Schopenhauer

No man sees far; the most see no farther than their noses.
Thomas Carlyle

Vision is the art of seeing things invisible.
Jonathan Swift

The most pathetic person in the world is someone who has sight, but has no vision.
Helen Keller

The difference between an impractical dreamer and a man of vision is usually about two generations.
Ivern Boyett

VISIONARY
Visionary people are visionary partly because of the very great many things they don't see.
Berkeley Rice

VISIT
Once in a while you have to take a break and visit yourself.
Audrey Giorgi

Santa Claus has the right idea: visit people once a year.
Victor Borge

VOCABULARY
One forgets words as one forgets names. One's vocabulary needs constant fertilization or it will die.
Evelyn Waugh

VOCATION
The test of a vocation is the love of the drudgery it involves.
Logan Pearsall Smith

VOICES
The black telephone's off at the root, the voices just can't worm through.
Sylvia Plath

VOTERS

Your every voter, as surely as your chief magistrate, exercises a public trust.

Grover Cleveland

The voters have spoken. The bastards.

Morris Udall

Fifty per cent of people won't vote, and fifty per cent don't read newspapers. I hope it's the same fifty per cent.

Gore Vidal

When people put their ballots in the boxes, they are, by that act, inoculated against the feeling that the government is not theirs. They then accept, in some measure, that its errors are their errors, its aberrations their aberrations, that any revolt will be against themselves. It's a remarkably shrewd and rather conservative arrangement when one thinks of it.

John Kenneth Galbraith

Hell, I never vote for anybody, I always vote against.

W.C. Fields

This is a frightening statistic. More people vote in American Idol than in any US election.

Rush Limbaugh

VOTES

A straw vote only shows which way the hot air blows.

O. Henry

Voting is simply a way of determining which side is the stronger without putting it to the test of fighting.

H.L. Mencken

The vote means nothing to women. We should be armed.

Edna O'Brien

Vote, *n.* The instrument and symbol of a free man's power to make a fool of himself and a wreck of his country.

Ambrose Bierce

As long as I count the votes, what are you going to do about it?

William (Boss) Tweed

If God wanted us to vote, he would have given us candidates.

Jay Leno

If voting changed anything, they'd make it illegal.

Emma Goldman

VULGARITY

Vulgarity is the garlic in the salad of life.

Cyril Connolly

Very notable was his distinction between coarseness and vulgarity (coarseness, revealing something; vulgarity, concealing something).

E.M. Forster

Many think that vulgarity is the opposite of snobbery; but snobbery is only a form of the vulgar. The real opposite of vulgarity is dignity.

Robert Hughes

Vulgarity is, in reality, nothing but a modern, chic, pert descendant of the goddess Dullness.

Edith Sitwell

Vulgarity has its uses. Vulgarity often cuts ice which refinement scrapes at vainly.

Max Beerbohm

WAGES

If you pay peanuts, you get monkeys.

Sir James Goldsmith

It is not the employer who pays the
wages. He only handles the money.
It is the product that pays the
wages.

Henry Ford

WAITING

Keeping another person waiting is
a basic tactic for defining him as
inferior and oneself as superior.

Thomas Szasz

All things come too late for those
who wait.

Elbert Hubbard

There are two kinds of people in
one's life: people whom one keeps
waiting and the people for whom
one waits.

S.N. Behrman

People count up the faults of those
who keep them waiting.

French saying

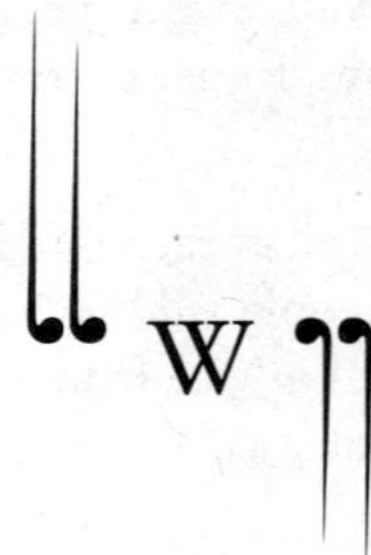

WALK

A vigorous five-mile walk will do
more good for an unhappy but
otherwise healthy adult than all
the medicine and psychology in the
world.

Paul Dudley White

Just walk. The road knows where
you are going.

Arne Nyman

It is impossible to walk rapidly and
be unhappy.

Dr Howard Murphy

The sum of the whole is this: Walk
and be happy; walk and be healthy.
The best way to lengthen out our
days is to walk steadily and with
a purpose. The wandering man
knows of certain ancients, far gone
in years, who have staved off infir-
mities and dissolution by earnest
walking – hale fellows, close upon
ninety, but brisk as boys.

Charles Dickens

WALL STREET
Wall Street people learn nothing and forget everything.

Benjamin Graham

Wall Street is the only place that people ride to in a Rolls-Royce to get advice from those who take the subway.

Warren Buffett

WALLS
Before I built a wall I'd ask to know/What I was walling in or walling out.

Robert Frost

WANDER
Not all those who wander are lost.

J.R.R. Tolkien

WANTS
How few are our real wants! and how easy it is to satisfy them! Our imaginary ones are boundless and insatiable.

Julius and Augustus Hare

No man can have all he wants, but a man can refrain from wanting what he has not, and cheerfully make the best of the bird in the hand.

Seneca

Our necessities are few but our wants are endless.

Josh Billings

We are designed to want: with nothing to want, we are like windmills in a world without wind.

John Fowles

WAR
When the war of giants is over, the wars of the pygmies will begin.

Winston Churchill

War is like love, it always finds a way.

Bertolt Brecht

War doesn't determine who's right. War determines who's left.

Anonymous

There never was a good war or a bad peace.

Benjamin Franklin

Older men declare war, but it is youth that must fight and die.

Herbert Hoover

The quickest way of ending a war is to lose it.

George Orwell

The tragedy of war is that it uses man's best to do man's worst.

Harry Emerson Fosdick

War would end if the dead could return.

Stanley Baldwin

Sometime they'll give a war and nobody will come.

Carl Sandburg

Throughout history, the world has been laid waste to ensure the triumph of conceptions that are now as dead as the men that died for them.

Henry de Montherlant

The first casualty of war is truth.

Hiram Johnson

Blue is the smoke of war, white the bones of men.

Tu Fu

Mankind must put an end to war or war will put an end to mankind.

John F. Kennedy

Sometimes I think that war is God's way of teaching us geography.

Paul Rodriguez

War is a series of catastrophes that results in a victory.

Georges Clemenceau

After each war there is a little less democracy to save.

Brooks Atkinson

See that little stream – we could walk to it in two minutes. It took the British a month to walk to it – a whole empire walking very slowly, dying in the front and pushing forward behind. And another empire walked very slowly backward a few inches a day, leaving dead like a million bloody rugs.

F. Scott Fitzgerald

Against the beautiful and the clever and the successful, one can wage a pitiless war, but not against the unattractive.

Graham Greene

The lamps are going out all over Europe.

Lord Grey of Fallodon

I hate war as only a soldier who has lived it can, only one who has seen its brutality, its futility, and its stupidity.

Dwight D. Eisenhower

The truth about the war comes out twenty years after you died in it.

Richard J. Needham

C'est magnifique, mais ce n'est pas la guerre.

French general, observing the charge of the Light Brigade

It is well that war is so terrible. We should grow too fond of it.

Robert E. Lee

Among the calamaties of war, may be justly the diminution of the love of truth, by the falsehoods which interest dictates, and credulity encourages.

Samuel Johnson

War is the province of chance. In no other sphere of human activity must such a margin be left for this intruder. It increases the uncertainty of every circumstance and deranges the course of events.

Karl von Clausewitz

War: first, one hopes to win; then one expects the enemy to lose; then, one is satisfied that he too is suffering; in the end, one is surprised that everyone has lost.

Karl Kraus

The possession of battle ready troops, a well-filled state treasury and a lively disposition, these were the real reasons which moved me to war.

Frederick the Great

Wars teach us not to love our enemies, but to hate our allies.

W.L. George

Everyone, when there's war in the air, learns to live with a new element: falsehood.

Jean Giraudoux

No poor bastard ever won a war by dying for his country. He won it by making other bastards die for their country.

General George S. Patton

The belief in the possibility of a short decisive war appears to be one of the most ancient and dangerous of human illusions.

Robert Wilson Lynd

You can no more win a war than you can win an earthquake.

Jeanette Rankin

How good bad music and bad reasons sound when we march against an enemy.

Friedrich Nietzsche

Everything in war is very simple, but the simplest thing is difficult.

Karl von Clausewitz

In war there is only one winner: war itself.

Edmund Blunden

War is only a cowardly escape from the problems of peace.

Thomas Mann

I don't know whether war is an interlude during peace or peace an interlude during war.

Georges Clemenceau

More than an end to war, we want an end to the beginnings of all wars.

Franklin D. Roosevelt

All wars are popular for the first thirty days.

Arthur M. Schlesinger, Jr

History is littered with wars which everybody knew would never happen.

Enoch Powell

As long as war is regarded as wicked, it will always have its fascination. When it is looked upon as vulgar it will cease to be popular.

Oscar Wilde

War has been, and still is, the school of collectivism, the warrant of tyranny.

Charles William Eliot

Wars to end all wars are an illusion. Wars, more than any other form of human activity, create the conditions which breed more war.

John Foster Dulles

Never think that war, no matter how necessary, nor how justified, is not a crime.

Ernest Hemingway

WARLIKE
There are no warlike peoples – just warlike leaders.

Ralph Bunche

WARNING
Take warning by the mischance of others, that others may not take warning of thine.

Sa'di

WARTIME
Nothing is more dangerous in wartime than to live in the temperamental atmosphere of a Gallup Poll, always feeling one's pulse and taking one's temperature.
Winston Churchill

WASHINGTON
Washington is a city of southern efficiency and northern charm.
John F. Kennedy

I love to go to Washington – if only to be near my money.
Bob Hope

Washington is the only place where sound travels faster than light.
C.V.R. Thompson

When I first went to Washington, I thought, what is l'il ole me doing with these ninety-nine great people? Now I ask myself, what am I doing with these ninety-nine jerks?
Senator S.I. Hayakawa

WASTE
And willful waste, depend upon't,/ Brings, almost always, woeful want!
Ann Taylor

We must realize that we can no longer throw our wastes away because there is no "away."
William Cahill

It is vain to do with more what can be done with less.
William of Occam

Wanting to be someone else is a waste of the person you are.
Kurt Cobain

WASTING TIME
Much may be done in those little shreds and patches of time, which every day produces, and which most men throw away, but which nevertheless will make at the end of it no small deduction from the life of man.
Charles Caleb Colton

He has spent his whole life in letting down empty buckets into empty wells; and he is frittering away his age in trying to draw them up again.
Sydney Smith

WATCHING
She watches him, as a cat would watch a mouse.
Jonathan Swift

WATER
We never know the worth of water til the well is dry.
Thomas Fuller, MD

Thousands have lived without love, not one without water.
W.H. Auden

Filthy water cannot be washed.
West African proverb

WEAK
In the process of tearing loose from nature, it was the weak who took the first steps. Chased out of the forest by the strong, they first

essayed to walk erect, and in the intensity of their soul first uttered words, and first grabbed a stick to use as a weapon and tool. The weak's singular capacity for evolving substitutes for that which they lack suggests that they played a chief role in the evolvement of technology.

Eric Hoffer

WEAK MEN
Like all weak men he laid an exaggerated stress on not changing one's mind.

W. Somerset Maugham

WEAKNESS
The highest point to which a weak but experienced mind can rise is detecting the weaknesses of better men.

Georg Christoph Lichtenberg

Flee an enemy who knows your weakness.

Pierre Corneille

Strong people have strong weaknesses.

Peter Drucker

WEALTH
I wish to become rich, so that I can instruct the people and glorify honest poverty a little, like those kind-hearted, fat, benevolent people do.

Mark Twain

With luck and resolution and good guidance ... the human mind can survive not only poverty, but even wealth.

Gilbert Highet

Nobody who has wealth to distribute ever omits himself.

Leon Trotsky

I am richer than [financier A.E.] Harriman. I have all the money I want and he doesn't.

John Muir

Wealth is not without its advantages, and the case to the contrary, although it has often been made, has never proved widely persuasive.

John Kenneth Galbraith

Never in the history of the world have so many people been so rich; never in the history of the world have so many of those same people felt themselves poor.

Lewis Lapham

In every well-governed state, wealth is a sacred thing; in democracies it is the only sacred thing.

Anatole France

There is no wealth but life.

John Ruskin

One of the penalties of wealth, Sergeant, is that the older you grow, the more people there are in the world who would rather have you dead than alive.

C.H.B. Kitchin

Those who condemn wealth are those who have none and see no chance of getting it.

William Penn Patrick

Surplus wealth is a sacred trust which its possessor is bound to

administer in his lifetime for the good of the community.
Andrew Carnegie

WEATHER
A change in the weather is sufficient to recreate the world and ourselves.
Marcel Proust

The weather is like the government, always in the wrong.
Jerome K. Jerome

Some are weather-wise, some are otherwise.
Benjamin Franklin

Don't knock the weather; nine-tenths of the people couldn't start a conversation if it didn't change once in a while.
Kin Hubbard

The weather belongs to us all.
Margaret (Ma) Murray

If the thermometer had been an inch longer we'd all have frozen to death.
Mark Twain

Wherever you go, the weather is, without exception, exceptional.
Kingsley Martin

Whenever people talk to me about the weather, I always feel quite certain that they mean something else.
Oscar Wilde

There's no such thing as bad weather, only unsuitable clothing.
Alfred Wainwright

WEEKEND
There aren't enough days in the weekend.
Steven Wright

Weekends don't pay as well as weekdays, but at least there's football.
S.A. Sachs

WEIRD
The weirder you are going to behave, the more normal you should look. It works in reverse, too. When I see a kid with three or four rings in his nose, I know there is absolutely nothing extraordinary about that person.
P.J. O'Rourke

WEST
Comrade, look not on the west. It will have the heart out of your breast.
A.E. Housman

WHITE HOUSE
There can be no whitewash in the White House.
Richard M. Nixon

WHOLE
The whole is always worth less than the sum of its parts.
David Russell

WICKED
The weak sometimes want to be thought wicked, but the wicked want to pass for good.
Marquis de Vauvenargues

It's so easy to be wicked without knowing it, isn't it?

Lucy Maud Montgomery

WICKEDNESS

Wickedness is always easier than virtue; for it takes the short cut to everything.

Samuel Johnson

WIDOWHOOD

The comfortable estate of widowhood is the only hope that keeps up a wife's spirits.

John Gay

WIFE

My first wife was a philosophy major. She would infuriate me by proving I didn't exist.

Woody Allen

Basically, my wife was immature. I'd be at home in the bath and she'd come in and sink my boats.

Woody Allen

I tended to place my wife under a pedestal.

Woody Allen

It is a truth universally acknowledged, that a single man in possession of a good fortune, must be in want of a wife.

Jane Austen

Many a man owes his success to his first wife and his second wife to his success.

Jim Backus

WILD

Serve the dinner backward, do anything – but for goodness sake, do something wild.

Elsa Maxwell

WILD OATS

In the rotation of crops there was a recognized season for wild oats, but they were not sown more than once.

Edith Wharton

WILL

People do not lack strength; they lack will.

Victor Hugo

Great souls have wills; feeble ones have only wishes.

Chinese proverb

WIN

Anybody can win, unless there happens to be a second entry.

George Ade

You're never as good as everyone tells you when you win, and you're never as bad as they say when you lose.

Lou Holtz

Winning is like shaving – you do it every day or you wind up looking like a bum.

Jack Kemp

Winning isn't everything, but it beats anything that comes in second.

Paul "Bear" Bryant

Winning may not be everything, but losing has little to recommend it.

Dianne Feinstein

WIND

The older you get the stronger the wind gets – and it's always in your face.

Jack Nicklaus

A great wind is blowing, and that gives you either imagination or a headache.

Catherine the Great

WINE

This wine is too good for toast-drinking, my dear. You don't want to mix emotions up with a wine like that. You lose the taste.

Ernest Hemingway

The dipsomaniac and the abstainer both make the same mistake: They both regard wine as a drug and not a drink.

G.K. Chesterton

Let us have wine and women, mirth and laughter,/Sermons and soda-water the day after.

Lord Byron

One of the disadvantages of wine is that it makes a man mistake words for thoughts.

Samuel Johnson

What I like to drink most is wine that belongs to others.

Diogenes the Cynic

Nothing makes the future look so rosy as to contemplate it through a glass of Chambertin.

Napoleon Bonaparte

Quickly, bring me a beaker of wine, so that I may wet my mind and say something clever.

Aristophanes

One not only drinks wine, one smells it, observes it, tastes it, sips it, and – one talks about it.

King Edward VII

I've drunk wine for seventy-five years, and I never drink water. I have a constitution of iron, and water rusts iron.

André L. Simon

It's a Naïve Domestic Burgundy, Without Any Breeding, But I think you'll be Amused by its Presumption.

James Thurber

A good general rule is to state that the bouquet is better than the taste, and vice versa.

Stephen Potter

The Germans are exceedingly fond of Rhine wines; they are put up in tall, slender bottles, and are considered a pleasant beverage. One tells them from vinegar by the label.

Mark Twain

Men are like wine – some turn to vinegar, but the best improve with age.

Pope John XXIII

WINNER

A winner [is] somebody you don't mess with only if you don't mind getting your block knocked off.

Russell Baker

WINNING

Winning isn't everything – it's the only thing.

Vince Lombardi

If winning isn't everything, then why do they keep score?

Vince Lombardi

I would be a winner because I was a loser! That's right, I dream of failure every night of my life, and that's my secret.

Donald Freed

Lose as if you like it; win as if you were used to it.

Tommy Hitchcock

Whoever is winning at the moment will always seem to be invincible.

George Orwell

WINTER

Winter is reality, summer is illusion.

Toivo Pekkanen

Winter makes us know new negatives: white darkness.

Douglas Barber

To shorten winter, borrow some money due in the spring.

W.J. Vogel

I like these cold, grey winter days. Days like these let you savour a bad mood.

Bill Watterson

WISDOM

The art of being wise is knowing what to overlook.

William James

The Chinese tell a story based on three or four thousand years of civilized wisdom. Two merchants were arguing heatedly in the midst of a crowd. A stranger, noting the depth of their anger, expressed surprise that no blows were being struck. His friend explained, "The man who strikes first admits that his ideas have given out."

Clever men are impressed in their differences from their fellows. Wise men are conscious of their resemblance to them.

R.H. Tawney

Life is a festival only to the wise.

Ralph Waldo Emerson

He who knows others is learned; he who knows himself is wise.

Chinese proverb

Wise men appreciate all men, for they see the good in each and know how hard it is to make anything good.

Baltasar Gracian

A wise man gets more use from his enemies than a fool from his friends.

Baltasar Gracian

The philosophies of one age have become the absurdities of the next, and the foolishness of yesterday has become the wisdom of tomorrow.

Sir William Osler

To question a wise man is the beginning of wisdom.

German proverb

The beginning of wisdom is the definition of terms.

Socrates

A word to the wise ain't necessary – it's the stupid ones who need the advice.

Bill Cosby

The most exquisite folly is made of wisdom spun too fine.

Benjamin Franklin

Wise men say nothing in dangerous times.

John Selden

A wise man hears one word and understands two.

Yiddish proverb

A silent man is easily reputed wise. The unknown is always wonderful.

Frederick William Robertson

Wisdom and beauty form a very rare combination.

Petronius

What is strength without a double share of wisdom?

John Milton

Knowledge is a process of piling up facts; wisdom lies in their simplification.

Martin H. Fischer

Penny wise, pound foolish.

Robert Burton

Wisdom is knowing when you can't be wise.

Paul Engle

Knowledge is awareness of the fact that fire will burn; wisdom is remembrance of the blister.

Robert Quillen

The wisest mind has something yet to learn.

George Santayana

'Tis not knowing much, but what is useful, that makes a wise man.

Thomas Fuller, MD

The wise man doesn't give the right answers, he poses the right question.

Claude Lévi-Strauss

Any man can ride a train. Only a wise man knows when to get off.

Eric Hoffer

A wise man does not venture all his eggs in one basket.

Miguel de Cervantes

Wisdom denotes the pursuing of the best ends by the best means.

Francis Hutcheson

It is better to speak wisdom foolishly like the saints than to speak folly wisely like the deans.

G.K. Chesterton

Science is organized knowledge. Wisdom is organized life.

Immanuel Kant

Be wiser than other people if you can, but do not tell them so.

Lord Chesterfield

Common sense suits itself to the ways of the world. Wisdom tries to conform to the ways of Heaven.

Joseph Joubert

It is easier to be wise for others than for ourselves.

François, duc de La Rochefoucauld

We are made wise not by the recollection of our past, but by the responsibility for our future.

George Bernard Shaw

Knowledge without wisdom is a load of books on the back of an ass.

Japanese proverb

Be wise with speed:/A fool at forty is a fool indeed.

Edward Young

Knowledge cuts up the world. Wisdom makes it whole.

Brazilian proverb

We were wise indeed, could we discern truly the signs of our own time.

Thomas Carlyle

Knowledge can be communicated but not wisdom.

Hermann Hesse

Pain makes you think. Thought makes you wise. Wisdom makes life endurable.

John Patrick

To whom hath the root of wisdom been revealed?

Ecclesiasticus 1:6

Knowledge comes by taking things apart. But wisdom comes by putting things together.

John A. Morrison

Wisdom has never really proved to be much help to anyone (nobody ever said: "I can't open this jar of marmalade – you do it – you're wiser than me") and yet as we all get older, we would like to think we are acquiring wisdom. But why? Is it really wise to be wise? When the revolution comes, isn't it always the wise who get to chop firs? Perhaps it's more sensible to be unwise.

Miles Kington

It is bad taste to be wise all the time, like being at a perpetual funeral.

D.H. Lawrence

He is a wise man who does not grieve for the things which he has not, but rejoices for those which he has.

Epictetus

It's so simple to be wise. Just think of something stupid to say, and then don't say it.

Sam Levenson

It is in the half fool and the half wise that the danger lies.

Johann Wolfgang von Goethe

Many ideas no more make a wise man than many soldiers make a great general.

Chamfort

Ninety per cent of all human wisdom is the ability to mind your own business.

Robert Heinlein

To acquire knowledge, one must study; but to acquire wisdom, one must observe.

Marilyn vos Savant

All human wisdom is summed up in two words – wait and hope.

Alexandre Dumas, père

We learn wisdom from failure much more than from success. We often discover what will do, by finding out what will not do; and probably he who never made a mistake never made a discovery.

Samuel Smiles

WISH
A wish is a desire without an attempt.

Frank Baur

We would often be sorry if our wishes were gratified.

Aesop

We are never further from our wishes than when we imagine that we possess what we have desired.

Johann Wolfgang von Goethe

Be careful what you wish for. You might get it.

Proverb

It is not good for all our wishes to be filled; through sickness we recognize the value of health; through evil, the value of good; through hunger, the value of food; through exertion, the value of rest.

Heraclitus

WIT
Wit is the only wall between us and the dark.

Mark Van Doren

Your wit's too hot, it speeds too fast, 'twill tire.

William Shakespeare

Wit is educated insolence.

Aristotle

Look, he's winding up the watch of his wit; by and by it will strike.

William Shakespeare

WITTY
A witty saying proves nothing.

Voltaire

There's many witty men whose brains can't fill their bellies.

Benjamin Franklin

I fear nothing so much as a man who is witty all day long.

Madame de Sévigné

WOLVES
Wolves are hunters; they are adaptable with eyes that absorb their landscape. Be like the wolf. Fascinating and alive with curiosity.

Michael Duncan

WOMEN
Give women the vote, and in five years there will be a crushing tax on bachelors.

George Bernard Shaw

It occurred to me when I was thirteen and wearing white gloves and Mary Janes and going to dancing school that no one should have to dance backwards all their lives.

Jill Ruckelshaus

Ginger Rogers did everything Fred Astaire did. She just did it backwards and in high heels.

Bob Thaves

Do you know why God withheld the sense of humour from women? That we may love you instead of laughing at you.

Mrs Patrick Campbell

Women should try to increase their size rather than decrease it, because I believe the bigger we are, the more space we'll take up, and the more we'll have to be reckoned with. I think every woman should be fat like me.

Roseanne Barr

Take my word for it, the silliest woman can manage a clever man; but it needs a very clever woman to manage a fool.

Rudyard Kipling

A woman's guess is much more accurate than a man's certainty.

Rudyard Kipling

Some women are not beautiful – they only look as though they are.

Karl Kraus

Equal rights for the sexes will be achieved when mediocre women occupy high positions.

Françoise Giroud

You don't know a woman until you have had a letter from her.

Ada Leverson

You don't know anything about a woman until you meet her in court.

Norman Mailer

The majority of women (happily for them) are not very much troubled with sexual feelings of any kind. No nervous or feeble young man need, therefore, be deterred from marriage by an exaggerated notion of the duties required from him.

Dr William Acton

A woman's always younger than a man of equal years.

Elizabeth Barrett Browning

That is the worst thing about being a middle-class woman … you have more knowledge of yourself and the world: you are equipped to make choices, but there are none left to make.

Alison Lurie

Women sometimes forgive a man who forces the opportunity, but never a man who misses one.

Charles-Maurice de Talleyrand

No woman ever falls in love with a man unless she has a better opinion of him than he deserves.

Edgar Watson Howe

If a woman has to choose between catching a fly ball and saving an infant's life, she will choose to save the infant's life without even considering if there are men on base.

Dave Barry

When women are depressed they either eat or go shopping. Men invade another country.
Elayne Boosler

You see a lot of smart guys with dumb women, but you hardly ever see a smart woman with a dumb guy.
Erica Jong

Women often do not understand opinions but seldom mistake acts.
Damon Runyon

Plain women know more about men than beautiful ones do.
Katharine Hepburn

Woman's virtue is man's greatest invention.
Cornella Otis Skinner

The one certain way for a woman to hold a man is to leave him for religion.
Muriel Spark

Why are the needle and the pen thought incompatible by men?
Esther Lewis

A woman has to be twice as good as a man to go half as far.
Fannie Hurst

No person should be denied equal rights because of the shape of her skin.
Pat Paulsen

Men will often admit that other women are oppressed but not you.
Sheila Rowbotham

A woman watches her body uneasily, as though it were an unreliable ally in the battle for love.
Leonard Cohen

When people say women can't be trusted because they cycle every month, my response is that men cycle every day, so they should only be allowed to negotiate peace treaties in the evening.
Jean Reinisch

I didn't fight to get women out from behind the vacuum cleaner to get them onto the board of Hoover.
Germaine Greer

Sometimes I think that the biggest difference between men and women is that more men need to seek out some terrible lurking thing in existence and hurl themselves upon it … Women know where it lives but they can let it alone.
Russell Hoban

A dead woman bites not.
Lord Patrick Gray, arguing for the execution of Mary, Queen of Scots

From birth to age eighteen, a girl needs good parents. From eighteen to thirty-five, she needs good looks. From thirty-five to fifty-five, a woman needs personality. And from fifty-five on, the old lady needs cash.
Kathleen Thompson Norris

Women don't look for handsome men. They look for men with beautiful women.
Milan Kundera

Women tell men things that men are not likely to find out for themselves.

Robertson Davies

Where women love each other, men learn to smother their mutual dislike.

George Eliot

Being a woman is a terribly difficult trade, since it consists principally of dealing with men.

Joseph Conrad

To be a woman is something so strange, so confusing and so complicated that only a woman could put up with it.

Søren Kierkegaard

In point of morals, the average woman is, even for business, too crooked.

Stephen Leacock

When women kiss, it always reminds one of prize fighters shaking hands.

H.L. Mencken

On one issue at least, men and women agree; they both distrust women.

H.L. Mencken

The years that a woman subtracts from her age are not lost; they are added to the ages of other women.

Diane de Poitiers

Women have been trained to speak softly and carry a lipstick. Those days are over.

Bella Abzug

WONDER
Wonder is the basis of worship.

Thomas Carlyle

Wonder rather than doubt is the root of all knowledge.

Abraham Joshua Herschel

Anything looked at closely becomes wonderful.

A.R. Ammons

Find something that isn't a miracle; you'll have cause to wonder then.

Laurence Housman

WORD (PRINTED)
The day of the printed word is far from ended. Swift as is the delivery of the radio bulletin, graphic as is television's eyewitness picture, the task of adding meaning and clarity remains urgent. People cannot and need not absorb meaning at the speed of light.

Erwin Canham

WORD (RIGHT)
The difference between the right word and almost the right word is the difference between lightning and the lightning bug.

Mark Twain

WORDS
Use no word that under stress of emotion you could not actually say.

Ezra Pound

Man does not live by words alone, despite the fact that sometimes he has to eat them.

Adlai Stevenson

Words are all we have.
Samuel Beckett

Handle them carefully, for words have more power than atom bombs.
Pearl Strachan

Thanks to words, we have been able to rise above the brutes; and thanks to words, we have often sunk to the level of the demons.
Aldous Huxley

The words! I collected them in all shapes and sizes and hung them like bangles in my mind.
Hortense Calisher

A mean word like an arrow cannot be taken back.
Anonymous

Words that do not match deeds are not important.
Che Guevara

Words are, of course, the most powerful drug used by mankind.
Rudyard Kipling

Never use a big word when a diminutive phrase can be utilized.
Frank L. Visco

As long as a word remains unspoken, you are its master; once you utter it, you are its slave.
Solomon ibn Gabirol

Check to see if you any words out.
Graffito

There is always time to add a word, never to withdraw one.
Baltasar Gracian

Words are wise men's counters, they do but reckon with them; but they are the money of fools.
Thomas Hobbes

When ideas fail, words come in very handy.
Johann Wolfgang von Goethe

It is exactly where a thought is lacking/That just in time, a word shows up instead.
Johann Wolfgang von Goethe

And once sent out, a word takes wing beyond recall.
Horace

If the advocate cannot justify the presence of a word, then that word should be deleted from his or her prose.
Paul M. Perell

A multitude of words is no proof of a prudent mind.
Thales

Words ought to be a little wild for they are the assault of thoughts on the unthinking.
John Maynard Keynes

Do not accustom yourself to use big words for little matters.
Samuel Johnson

Words form the thread on which we string our experiences.
Aldous Huxley

Words are like leaves; and where they most abound,/Much fruit of sense beneath is rarely found.
Alexander Pope

The trouble with words is that you never know whose mouths they've been in.

Dennis Potter

Do not the most moving moments of our lives find us all without words?

Marcel Marceau

One kind word can warm three winter months.

Japanese proverb

The question in every case is whether the words used are used in such circumstances and are of such a nature as to create a clear and present danger.

Oliver Wendell Holmes

Cold words freeze people, and hot words scorch them, and bitter words make them bitter, and wrathful words make them wrathful. Kind words also produce their own image on men's souls; and a beautiful image it is. They soothe, and quiet, and comfort the hearer.

Blaise Pascal

For words, like Nature, half reveal/ And half conceal the Soul within.

Alfred, Lord Tennyson

A word is not a crystal, transparent and unchanged; it is the skin of a living thought and may vary greatly in colour and content according to the . circumstances and time in which it is used.

Oliver Wendell Holmes, Jr

A word to the wise is enough, and many words won't fill a bushel.

Benjamin Franklin

Amongst my most prized possessions are the words that I have never spoken.

Orson Rega Card

He can compress the most words into the smallest idea of any man I know.

Abraham Lincoln

Strong and bitter words indicate a weak cause.

Victor Hugo

If you would be pungent, be brief; for it is with words as with sunbeams. The more they are condensed, the deeper they burn.

Robert Southey

WORK

It is an article of faith in my creed to pick the man who does not take himself seriously, but does take his work seriously.

Michael C. Cahill

Work is much more fun than fun.

Noel Coward

The more I want to get something done, the less I call it work.

Richard Bach

All that is great in man comes through work, and civilization is its product.

Samuel Smiles

My grandfather once told me that there are two kinds of people: those who do the work and those who take the credit. He told me to try to be in the first group; there was less competition there.

Indira Gandhi

By working faithfully eight hours a day you may eventually get to be a boss and work twelve hours a day.
Robert Frost

The biggest mistake you can ever make is to believe that you are working for someone else.
Earl Nightingale

For one person who dreams of making 50,000 pounds, a hundred people dream of being left 50,000 pounds.
A.A. Milne

Anybody can become a success in America if he's willing to work while nearly everybody else is killing time.
Dr O.A. Battista

Choose a job you love, and you will never have to work a day in your life.
Confucius

Most people like hard work, particularly when they're paying for it.
Franklin P. Jones

The one important thing I have learned over the years is the difference between taking one's work seriously and taking one's self seriously. The first is imperative, the second disastrous.
Margot Fonteyn

Thunder is good, thunder is impressive, but it is the lightning that does the work.
Mark Twain

Roasted pigeons will not fly into one's mouth.
Pennsylvania Dutch proverb

Chop your own wood and it will warm you twice.
Proverb

Every man is the son of his own works.
Miguel de Cervantes

It is the privilege of any human work which is well done to invest the doer with a certain haughtiness. He can well afford not to conciliate, whose faithful work will answer for him.
Ralph Waldo Emerson

If there is no wind, row.
Latin proverb

The bitter and the sweet come from the outside, the hard from within, from one's own efforts.
Albert Einstein

Work is a fine thing if it doesn't take too much of your spare time.
Anonymous

I've met a few people in my time who were enthusiastic about hard work. And it was just my luck that all of them happened to be men I was working for at the time.
Bill Gold

Work to become, not to acquire.
Elbert Hubbard

When your work speaks for itself, don't interrupt.
Henry J. Kaiser

One beats the bush; another catches the bird.

German proverb

Nothing you can't spell will ever work.

Will Rogers

Blessed is he who has found his work; let him ask no other blessedness.

Thomas Carlyle

If people really liked to work, we'd still be plowing the ground with sticks and transporting goods on our backs.

William Feather

When work is a pleasure, life is a joy. When work is a duty, life is slavery.

Maxim Gorky

I have long been of the opinion that if work were such a splendid thing, the rich would have kept more of it for themselves.

Bruce Grocott

Any man can do any amount of work, provided it isn't the work he's supposed to be doing.

Robert Benchley

Work is delegated down to the level at which it cannot be competently be carried out.

Christopher Bradshaw

Every morning I get up and look through the Forbes list of the richest people in America. If I'm not there, I go to work.

Robert Orben

How many years of fatigue and punishment it takes to learn the simple truth that work, that disagreeable thing, is the only way of not suffering in life, or at all events, of suffering less.

Charles Baudelaire

The world is mine; I am as free as air;/ Let others work that I may eat.

José de Espronceda

While none of the work we do is important, it is important that we do a great deal of it.

Joseph Heller

When I work, I relax. Doing nothing makes me tired.

Pablo Picasso

Work is not man's punishment. It is his reward and his strength and his pleasure.

George Sand

It is necessary to work, if not from inclination, at least from despair. In the end, work is less boring than amusing oneself.

Charles Baudelaire

Work is the curse of the drinking class.

Oscar Wilde

The greatest analgesic, soporific, stimulant, tranquillizer, narcotic, and, to some extent, even antibiotic – in short, the closest thing to a genuine panacea – known to medical science is work.

Thomas Szasz

It has been my experience that one cannot, in any shape or form, depend on human relations for lasting reward. It is only work that truly satisfies.

Bette Davis

This new attitude towards effort and work as an aim in itself may be assumed to be the most important psychological change which has happened to man since the end of the Middle Ages ... the development of a frantic activity and a striving to do something.

Erich Fromm

If you don't want to work you have to work to earn enough money so that you don't have to work.

Ogden Nash

What is called a sincere work is one that is endowed with enough strength to give reality to an illusion.

Max Jacob

It's not work if you love what you're doing.

Steve Sears

The great thing with work is to be on top of it, not constantly chasing after it.

Dorothy Thompson

Work is an extension of personality. It is achievement. It is one of the ways in which a person defines himself, measures his worth, and his humanity.

Peter Drucker

One way to make sure everyone gets to work on time would be to have ninety-five parking spaces for every one hundred employees.

Michael Iapoce

Which of us ... is to do the hard and dirty work for the rest – and for what pay? Who is to do the pleasant and clean work, and for what pay?

John Ruskin

WORKING CLASSES
Imagine ... the universal outcry that would occur if every year several corporate headquarters routinely collapsed like mines, crushing sixty or seventy executives. ... Try to imagine the horror ... if thousands of university professors were deafened every year or lost fingers, hands, sometimes eyes, while on their jobs.

Andrew Levison

The worst fault of the working classes is telling their children they're not going to succeed, saying "There is life, but it's not for you."

John Mortimer

WORKPLACES
Appealing workplaces are to be avoided. One wants a room with no view, so imagination can meet memory in the dark.

Annie Dillard

WORKSHOP
If there's one word that sums up everything that's gone wrong since the War, it's Workshop.
Kingsley Amis

WORLD
The world is extremely interesting to a joyful soul.
Alexandra Stoddard

The world belongs to the enthusiast who keeps his cool.
William McFee

It's a small world but I wouldn't want to paint it.
Steven Wright

As for the just and noble idea that nations, as well as individuals, are parts of one wondrous whole, it has hardly passed the lips or pen of any but religious men and poets.
Harriet Martineau

The world is my lobster.
Henry J. Tillman

All the world's a cage.
Jeanne Philips

The most incomprehensible thing about the world is that it is comprehensible.
Albert Einstein

The world is a force, not a presence.
Wallace Stevens

The world does not require so much to be informed as to be reminded.
Hannah More

We live in a Newtonian world of Einsteinian physics ruled by Frankenstein logic.
David Russell

The world is a tragedy to those who feel, but a comedy to those who think.
Horace Walpole

WORRY
Worry is the interest paid on trouble before it falls due.
Dean Inge

If there be no remedy, why worry?
Spanish proverb

Worrying helps you some. It seems as if you are doing something when you are worrying.
Lucy Maud Montgomery

The reason worry kills more people than work is that more people worry than work.
Robert Frost

Worry is a darkroom where negatives develop.
Anonymous

That the birds of worry and care fly over your head, this you cannot change, but that they build nests in your hair, this you can prevent.
Chinese proverb

People should worry about each other. Because worry is just love in its worst form. But it's still love.
Simon Gray

When you worry, you go over the same ground endlessly and come out the same place you started. Thinking makes progress from one place to another; worry remains static. The problem of life is to change worry into thinking and anxiety into creative action.

Harold R. Walker

Worrying is the most natural and spontaneous of all human functions. It is time to acknowledge this, perhaps even learn to do it better.

Lewis Thomas

Worry is to life and progress what sand is to the bearings of perfect engines.

Roger W. Babson

Worry is today's mice nibbling on tomorrow's cheese.

Unknown

WORTH
You can never know too little of what is not worth knowing at all.

Anonymous

WRATH
Men often make up in wrath what they want in reason.

William Alger

WRINKLES
Wrinkles should merely indicate where smiles have been.

Mark Twain

WRITERS
For a writer only one form of patriotism exists; his attitude toward language.

Joseph Brodsky

Writers really live in the mind and in the hotels of the soul.

Edna O'Brien

The creations of a great writer are little more than the moods and passions of his own heart, given surnames, and Christian names, and sent to walk the earth.

William Butler Yeats

My idea is always to reach my generation. The wise writer ... writes for the youth of his own generation, the critics of the next, and the schoolmasters of ever afterward.

F. Scott Fitzgerald

For a country to have a great writer is like having a second government. That is why no regime has ever loved great writers, only minor ones.

Alexandr Solzhenitsyn

A writer who takes political, social, or literary positions must act only with the means that are his. These means are the written words.

Jean-Paul Sartre

The shelf life of the modern hardback writer is somewhere between the milk and the yogurt.

John Mortimer

Life can't ever defeat a writer who is in love with writing, for life itself is a writer's lover until death.

Edna Ferber

A writer is, after all, only half his book. The other half is the reader and from the reader the writer learns.

P.L. Travers

It takes more than a mastery of words to be an excellent writer. First, good writers thoroughly understand the point they are trying to make, or the impression they are trying to convey. Then they get to it quickly. When it is accomplished, they get off the page. They never hang around wasting time and taking bows.

John L. Beckley

Writers, like teeth, are divided into incisors and grinders.

Walter Bagehot

A publisher offers you $30,000 to write a 350-page guidebook. Thirty thousand dollars! Congratulations! Guess what? You're about to go broke.

Tom Brosnahan

It would be dangerous for a writer instantly to think of a global audience because he may be robbing himself of his own voice.

Pico Iyer

Why do writers write? Because it isn't there.

Thomas Berger

The most essential gift for a good writer is a built-in shock-proof shit-detector.

Ernest Hemingway

If writers were good businessmen, they'd have too much sense to be writers.

Irvin S. Cobb

The profession of letters is, after all, the only one in which one can make no money without being ridiculous.

Jules Renard

Great writers are not those who tell us we shouldn't play with fire but those who make our fingers burn.

Stephen Vizinczey

Writers don't need tricks or gimmicks or even necessarily need to be the smartest fellows on the block. At the risk of appearing foolish, a writer sometimes needs to be able to just stand and gape at this or that thing – a sunset or an old shoe – in absolute and simple amazement.

Raymond Carver

It is the glory and merit of some men to write well, and of others not to write at all.

Jean de La Bruyère

Some writers take to drink, others take to audiences.

Gore Vidal

Until you understand a writer's ignorance, presume yourself ignorant of his understanding.

Samuel Taylor Coleridge

In America only the successful writer is important, in France all writers are important, in England no writer is important, in Australia you have to explain what a writer is.

Geoffrey Cotterell

Some day I hope to write a book where the royalties will pay for the copies I give away.

Clarence Darrow

No author is a man of genius to his publisher.

Heinrich Heine

They're fancy talkers about themselves, writers. If I had to give young writers advice, I would say don't listen to writers talk about writing or themselves.

Lillian Hellman

Some American writers who have known each other for years, have never met in the daytime or when both were sober.

James Thurber

Talent alone cannot make a writer. There must be a man behind the book.

Ralph Waldo Emerson

A man who uses a great many words to express his meaning is like a bad marksman who instead of aiming a single stone at an object takes up a handful and throws it in hopes he may hit.

Samuel Johnson

It took me fifteen years to find out that I wasn't a writer, but by that time I was so successful that I couldn't afford to give it up.

Robert Benchley

I am always interested in why young people become writers, and from talking with many I have concluded that most do not want to be writers working eight and ten hours a day and accomplishing little; they want to have been writers, garnering the rewards of having completed a bestseller. They aspire to the rewards of writing but not to the travail.

James A. Michener

WRITING
The art of writing requires a constant plunging back into the shadow of the past where time hovers ghost-like.

Ralph Ellison

All good writing is swimming under water and holding your breath.

F. Scott Fitzgerald

An old tutor of a college said to one of his pupils: Read over your compositions, and whenever you meet with a passage which you think is particularly fine, strike it out.

Samuel Johnson

If Thomas Wolfe sold, I'd write like Thomas Wolfe.

Mickey Spillane

I have learned in my thirty-odd years of serious writing only one sure lesson: Stories, like whiskey, must be allowed to mature in the cask.

Sean O'Faolain

A playwright must be his own audience. A novelist may lose his readers for a few pages; a playwright never dares lose his audience for a minute.

Terence Rattigan

Sometimes I think [my writing] sounds like I walked out of the room and left the typewriter running.

Gene Fowler

Nothing matters but the writing. There has been nothing else worthwhile ... a stain upon the silence.

Samuel Beckett

It's none of their business that you have to learn how to write. Let them think you were born that way.

Ernest Hemingway

No tears in the writer, no tears in the reader.

Robert Frost

It is a sobering thought that each of us gives his hearers and his readers a chance to look into the inner working of his mind when he speaks or writes.

J.M. Barker

My writing goes well when there is something out there that amazes me or fascinates me – and it is a big damn world.

Tim Cahill

You must write for children the same way as you write for adults, only better.

Maxim Gorky

The secret of popular writing is never to put more on a given page than the common reader can lap off it with no strain whatsoever on his habitually slack attention.

Ezra Pound

To write simply is as difficult as to be good.

W. Somerset Maugham

Against the disease of writing one must take special precautions, since it is a dangerous and contagious disease.

Peter Abelard

Writing is not an activity, but a condition.

Robert Musil

Writing is like getting married. One should never commit oneself until one is amazed at one's luck.

Iris Murdoch

In my writing I am acting as a map maker, an explorer of psychic areas ... a cosmonaut of inner space.

William S. Burroughs

I do most of my work sitting down; that's where I shine.

Robert Benchley

Contrary to what many of you might imagine, a career in letters is not without its drawbacks – chief among them is the unpleasant fact that one is frequently called upon to sit down and write.

Fran Lebowitz

Writing a book is an adventure: it begins as an amusement, then it becomes a mistress, then a master, and finally a tyrant.

Winston Churchill

That's not writing – that's typing.

Truman Capote
(about Jack Kerouac)

The profession of book-writing makes horse racing seem like a solid, stable business.

John Steinbeck

Writing is the only profession where no one considers you ridiculous if you earn no money.

Jules Renard

… the dullest speeches I ever heard. The Agee woman told us for three quarters of an hour how she came to write her beastly book, when a simple apology was all that was required.

P.G. Wodehouse

I write when I am inspired, and I see to it that I'm inspired at nine o'clock every morning.

Peter De Vries

Cut out all those exclamation marks. An exclamation mark is like laughing at your own joke.

F. Scott Fitzgerald

There are three rules for writing the novel. Unfortunately no one knows what they are.

W. Somerset Maugham

I was working on the proof of one of my poems all the morning, and took out a comma. In the afternoon I put it back again.

Oscar Wilde

What is written without effort is in general read without pleasure.

Samuel Johnson

Think much, speak little, write less.

Proverb

WRITING ON THE WALL
Most of us can read the writing on the wall; we just assume it's addressed to someone else.

Ivern Ball

WRONG
The wrong way always seems the more reasonable.

George Moore

(There is) no right way for doing wrong.

Kevin Mitchell

It is better to suffer wrong than to do it, and happier to be sometimes cheated than not to trust.

Samuel Johnson

Wrong cannot afford defeat but right can.

Rabindranath Tagore

Sometimes I lie awake at night, and I ask, "Where have I gone wrong?" Then a voice says to me, "This is going to take more than one night."

Charles M. Schultz

WRONG NUMBER
Well, if I called the wrong number, why did you answer the phone?

James Thurber

WRONGDOING
A sense of wrongdoing is an enhancement of pleasure.

Oliver Wendell Holmes, Jr

WRONGS
Two wrongs don't make a right, but they make a good excuse.

Thomas Szasz

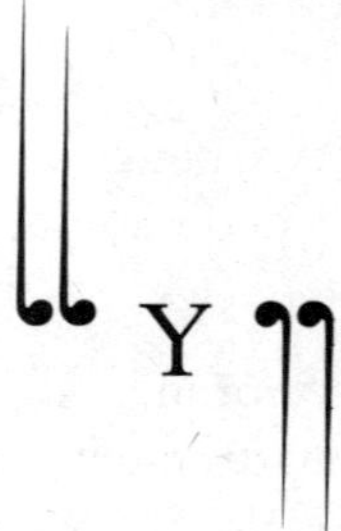

YEARS
And in the end, it's not the years in your life that count. It's the life in your years.

Abraham Lincoln

YEARNING
A little yearning is a dangerous thing.

Graffito

"YES MEN"
I don't want any yes-men in this firm. I want people who speak their minds, even if it does cost them their jobs.

Samuel Goldwyn

YOUNG
He says he's young at heart – but slightly older in other places.

Anonymous

YOUNG PEOPLE
The last people with any ideas are young people. The age in which we live, this non-stop distraction, is making it impossible for the young generation to ever have the curiosity or the discipline … because you need to be alone to find out anything.

Vivienne Westwood

A young person is a person with nothing to learn,/One who already knows that ice does not chill and fire does not burn.

Ogden Nash

YOUTH
You are only young once, but you can stay immature indefinitely.

Ogden Nash

We must view young people not as empty bottles to be filled, but as candles to be lit.

Robert H. Shaffer

Young men are apt to think themselves wise enough, as drunken men are apt to think themselves sober enough.

Lord Chesterfield

Don't laugh at a youth for his affectations; he is only trying on one face after another til he finds his own.

Logan Pearsall Smith

It is better to waste one's youth than do nothing with it at all.

Georges Courteline

As for me, except for an occasional heart attack – I feel as young as I ever did.

Robert Benchley

Youth is a malady of which one becomes cured a little every day.

Benito Mussolini

Blessed are the young, for they shall inherit the national debt.

Herbert Hoover

I am not young enough to know everything.

J.M. Barrie

It is fitting that we should hold the young in awe. … Only when a man reaches the age of forty or fifty without distinguishing himself in any way can one say, I suppose, that he does not deserve to be held in awe.

Confucius

Youth is glorious, but it isn't a career.

Unknown

There is a strong disposition in youth, from which some individuals never escape, to suppose that everyone else is having a much more enjoyable time than we are ourselves.

Anthony Powell

If men and women are to understand each other, to enter into each other's nature with mutual sympathy, and to become capable of genuine comradeship, the foundation must be laid in youth.

Havelock Ellis

Youth would be an ideal state if it came a little later in life.

Herbert Henry Asquith

Youth is wholly experimental.

Robert Louis Stevenson

No wise man ever wished to be younger.

Jonathan Swift

You remain young as long as you can still learn, can accept new conventions, and can stand contradictions.

Marie von Ebner-Eschenbach

Young men exaggerate; old men pretend.

Robin Skelton

If youth knew; if age could.

Henri Estienne

I think I don't regret a single "excess" of my responsive youth – I only regret, in my chilled age, certain occasions and possibilities I didn't embrace.

Henry James

You're only as young as the last time you changed your mind.

Timothy Leary

If youth is the season of hope, it is often only in the sense that our elders are hopeful about us.

George Eliot

Youth had been a habit of hers for so long that she could not part with it.

Rudyard Kipling

Being young is not having any money; being young is not minding not having any money.

Katharine Whitehorn

Young people don't know what age is, and old people forget what youth was.

Irish proverb

Almost everything that is great has been done by youth.

Benjamin Disraeli

There's nothing worse than being an aging young person.

Richard Pryor

Denunciation of the young is a necessary part of the hygiene of older people and greatly assists in the circulation of their blood.

Logan Pearsall Smith

The youth of the present day are quite monstrous. They have absolutely no respect for dyed hair.

Oscar Wilde

If youth be a defect, it is one that we outgrow only too soon.

James Russell Lowell

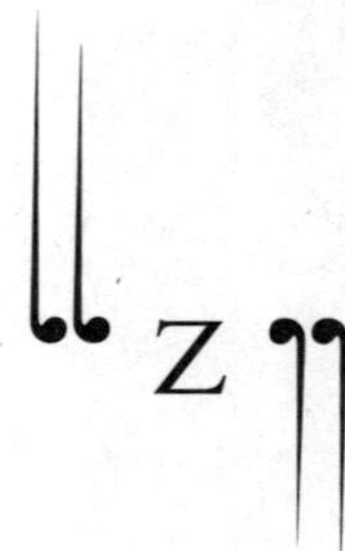

ZEN
The bigger the front, the bigger the
back.

Zen saying

ZERO SUM
The single biggest misunderstanding built into the mentality of the
popular culture is that one person's
gain is another person's loss.

James Heckman

Index